ISBN 978-1-330-25381-6
PIBN 10002485

1 MONTH OF
FREE
READING

at

www.ForgottenBooks.com

By purchasing this book you are eligible for one month membership to ForgottenBooks.com, giving you unlimited access to our entire collection of over 700,000 titles via our web site and mobile apps.

To claim your free month visit: www.forgottenbooks.com/free2485

Similar Books Are Available from
www.forgottenbooks.com

Advertising Outdoors

A magazine devoted to the interests of the Outdoor Advertiser

VOL. 2, No. 1

CONTENTS for JANUARY 1931

Harold L. Eves
Editor

Ralph B. Patch, *Associate Editor*
James P. Dobyns, *Advertising Manager*

Eastern Advertising Representatives:
Walworth and Wormser,
420 Lexington Ave., New York City.

ADVERTISING OUTDOORS is published on the 1st of every month by the Outdoor Advertising Association of America, Inc., 165 W. Wacker Drive, Chicago, Ill. Telephone Randolph 1692. Harold L. Eves, Editor and Manager.
Subscriptions for the United States, Cuba, Porto Rico, Hawaii and the Philippines, $3.00 a year in advance; Mexico and Canada, $3.25; for all other countries, $3.50. Thirty cents the copy. Make all checks, money orders, etc., payable to Outdoor Advertising Association of America, Inc.
Entered as second-class matter, March 21st, 1930, at the Post Office at Chicago, Ill., under the act of March 3, 1879, by Outdoor Advertising Association of America, Inc. Printed in U. S. A.

"WE ARE AN OUTDOOR PEOPLE IN CANADA"

CHARLES BAKER
LIMITED
TORONTO

Official Solicitors
Poster Advertising
Association
of Canada.

Ap. 22 32

Bound
Periodical

Page 2

SPENDING TENDENCIES
v.s. BUYING POWER

THE present business depression has brought out the new and interesting factor in the forecasting of territorial sales. It has been graphically shown that it is the spending tendency rather than the latent buying power that determines the success or failure of merchandising effort.

For years business forecasters and statisticians have furnished figures on which to base sales quotas that were developed through a buying *power* index. These figures were arrived at through various methods, among them being such items as bank clearings, savings accounts totals and income represented by wages and corporation profits.

Now we have learned that buying power may be present but latent. A New Englander with $1,000 in cash may not spend the same proportion as a Montana man with that same amount. Power to buy doesn't necessarily mean willingness to spend.

Modern merchandising as it has developed in the past few years has thrown another disturbing factor into business forecasts under the buying *power* method. Automotive, radio and furniture merchandising has put credit or installment selling into an important place in American business. Today a large portion of luxury items are sold with the aid of this system. The masses now spending money that is not even included in their buying power.

Because Advertising Outdoors believes that the development of a reliable spending *tendency* index is important in the forecasting of sales we have started a department called "Spending Tendencies" which will in months to come attempt to evolve an index and apply it to different communities through actual interviews with business leaders.

THE FARMER
and National Prosperity

by Senator Arthur Capper

● Nothing will do so much to restore normal business conditions in the United States today as to increase the farmers' buying power. When the business interests of the country fully appreciate, as they should, that it is to their own interests to right the farmers' ills as speedily as possible, overproduction will become less of a specter. It is not a question of over-production as much as it is a problem of poor distribution. By equalizing things, the exchange of goods and services of the farmer for the goods and services of industry is facilitated. This is the basis of all business and is the only real way for prosperity.

In his message to Congress in 1929, President Hoover declared:

"There is no fundamental conflict between the interests of the farmer and the worker. Lowering of the standards of either, tends to destroy the other. The prosperity of one depends upon the well being of the other."

● Employers and employees are cooperating today to an extent undreamed of a few years ago. The merchant has an entirely different attitude toward his customer that he had a few years ago.

The old industrialist believed in cheap labor, cheap raw material and the highest selling price the market would bear. He wanted a large profit on each article manufactured; the cheaper he could produce it and the higher he could sell, the better.

SENATOR ARTHUR CAPPER

Modern industrialist believes in purchasing power, in mass production; in selling oftener at a small margin of profit each article produced.

The merchant of today follows the same line of thought and action. Quick turnovers, mass sales at small profit-margins, satisfied customers will come back for more. He has learned his lesson.

Big business has learned that high wages and leisure time gives larger numbers of people greatly increased purchasing power, enlarge the market for their products and make for better business. The more money the working man makes, the more he will spend. The more leisure time he has the more different luxuries will become necessities.

The industrial world today regards unemployment with dread and horror to a greater extent than ever before. The unemployed not only threaten to become a public charge, worse than that, they have no purchasing power. People with money will buy things. The more people with money, the more they will buy,—so the ideal of the industrialist today is to have everyone have plenty of money and enough time to spend his money freely.

● I would like to be able to say that industry and big business learn this of their own free will and accord. But candor compels the admission that to a great extent organized labor had to teach it to them.

Organized labor, by forcing (Continued on page 28)

Outdoor Advertising Merchandises
FARM PRODUCTS

by Ralph B. Patch

● Out in Kansas the hogs are feasting on wheat that was raised for the nourishment of human beings. Their owner has found that he will receive more money through selling his corn and oats at prevailing prices and feeding what once was the aristocrat of grains to his livestock. The Federal Farm Board through the Grain Stabilization Corporation is the dismayed possessor of more than 100,000,000 bushels of wheat and is holding it for the long-awaited increase in price. American agriculture is demanding that some steps be taken to insure the farmer an adequate return for his investment and his labor and the spectre of Farm Relief is causing many a sleepless night in Washington. The price of farm products is, in many cases, below the cost of production.

● That the present situation has seriously affected the buying power of the farmer is obvious—but it is not only the farmer who has suffered. Communities all through the agricultural sections of the United States have found the farmers inability to buy immediately reflected in their own purchases. The grocer finds that the farm trade has curtailed its buying to necessities and his next orders are correspondingly smaller. The physician finds that he is just as busy but that his receipts are considerably reduced; consequently, his own purchases are cut down. The sales volume of almost every class of commodity is lessened all through rural America. The urban manufacturer's sales are reduced

The first posting of the Farmers' Prosperity campaign in Indianapolis. In the picture, left to right, R. A. Roblee, Walter Sheater, John Leerkamp, Clarence Henry, Lewis Taylor, James R. Moore (with large brush), Walter Ristow, W. Rex Bell, Harry S. Rogers, H. S. Musselman, R. E. Verins and R. W. Wishard.

and some of his laborers are laid off. Overhead in one plant has been cut but the national overhead—society's unproductive and non-purchas- (Continued on page 29)

BUY MORE FARM PRODUCTS *and*
SPEED INDUSTRIAL EMPLOYMENT

Your Bread and Butter is the Farmer's Prosperity

THE RADIO INDUSTRY
and Its Problems

by Duane Wanamaker

Vice-President in Charge of Advertising
GRIGSBY-GRUNOW COMPANY

● Radio, in common with all other industries, has felt the hardening or softening influence (as you please) of the new day economic era which probably dated from the market crash of November a year ago and it is a tribute to this great industry, which has grown from Liliputian size to an industrial giant in a period of seven short years, that even in times of so-called depression, people have bought and continue to buy radio sets in mighty volume. Surely it has been amazing to contemplate the hold that radio has taken on the American public as evidenced by the fact that a radio set today is not considered a luxury, but a necessity in every home which can afford one.

When an industry grows so big in so short a time, many make-shift methods of exploitation and distribution naturally come into being. Many blind pathways are followed to be abandoned later when settling down processes are arrived at and when the industry in question is fully stabilized.

Radio, being the glamorous thing that it is, invited a great deal of malpractice in merchandising, but much of it was being abandoned even before economic conditions, bringing with them the necessity for more sober and matter-of-fact sales methods, had forced the change.
● There is every indication that the radio industry is ready to take its place as one of the stable, solid busi-

DUANE WANAMAKER

nesses of America and it faces 1931 with courage and with every sincere belief that this New Year will see considerable progress made. This means not only greater public interest through improved radio sets and through increased need of radio, but through improved merchandising methods. Like all new industries, the radio industry, once it got "hot" as a business, invited every type of manufacturer from the man who had

Airplane view of some of the units of the Majestic Radio Cabinet works and the cabinet plants of the Majestic Household Utilities Corporation.

lots of money and squandered it just for fun in hope of being a radio magnate, to the man who had a hammer and a saw and waste space in the barn hoped to start making three sets a day and later make 3,000 of them. This naturally jumbled up values, raised havoc with distribution and merchandising and encouraged illegitimate practices of all kinds which acted as a mill stone about the neck of progressive merchandising.

● Along the same line, from a retail angle, thousands of dealers sprang up over night having no intention of staying in the business and building up a responsible name and a respect for radio values, but rather with the hope of making a few quick dollars while the making was good and then taking it, as the underworld familiarly calls it, "on the lam."

With the beginning of 1931, the industry looks about itself and finds it is in the hands of a comparatively small number of legitimate, sincere manufacturers who have the serious purpose in view of building greater respect for radio values in the public mind, building honest merchandise at a legitimate profit and doing business in a sane, stabilized manner. Furthermore, the number of real radio dealers has decreased from some thirty-five or forty thousand to a possible eighteen or twenty thousand real dealers who hope to do business in a businesslike manner and make money at it. Not until such a state was reached could radio as an industry and radio merchandising hope to arrive at a stabilized basis of operation. There are, of course, many problems yet to be solved in the radio industry and in radio merchandising, the same as in the merchandising of any other product, but they are being ironed out rapidly. There are always problems in every industry.

● Probably never before has an industry witnessed such an orgy of advertising as characterized the radio industry during the past seven years. Much of it was wasted, yet the business was in such a shape that manufacturers who wished to be (Continued on page 34)

The Business Romance
of WILLIAM WRIGLEY, JR.

by James P. Dobyns

● There are no closed doors in the Chicago executive offices of Wm. Wrigley, Jr. Nor are there any doors marked "private."

Thus the visitor entering these offices begins to get his first insight into the character of the man who has built up one of the greatest business enterprises of all time. From this first glimpse of his offices—with every door open—you know he hates red tape, hates the high and mighty attitude of bureaucracy.

Now Wrigley's business is a one-man policy. Every major move that is made is colored by the swift decisive personality of this man. It might be said that his business is run autocratically, but it is a benevolent autocracy, with the advantage that once one of the lightning-like decisions of this one man is made, there is no delay—action follows immediately.

● That these decisions almost invariably work out right is due to his vast accumulation of experience. In these days of "specialists" it seems strange to find a man that is a specialist in all phases of a business. But then we recall that Wrigley has been all through the *making* of this gigantic business. In the early days when this giant was but an infant, he necessarily *had* to know economics, manufacturing processes, merchandising, marketing and distribution.

Today the biggest executives in his employ often go into his office to learn from his vast experience the probable outcome of some proposed line of action. Wrigley is a good guesser. He doesn't claim to always guess right, but he tells his executives, "If you can guess right nine times out of ten, you're a mighty good guesser—forget the tenth time."

● His attitude towards his employees is to give them a job to do; a definite job. He doesn't interfere after the job has been assigned; if the man can't do it, someone who can will be obtained. For Wrigley hates failure—won't admit failure. This goes a long way in explaining why his executives are men of action; men of initiative. The constant reports he gets on the activities of his various departments keep the picture of the entire organization before him, and when conditions call for an abrupt change in policy he knows what to do about it.

During all the years that the business was developing, Wrigley didn't forget that the product he was selling sold for only a penny a stick, and that it took plenty of sticks to make any money. And so he kept his overhead low. His dislike of sham and show has been carried over from the early days of his success.

● When he first came to Chicago, he lived in a room with only one gas jet, which served for cooking as well as lighting purposes. Of course he could have afforded

Avalon Bay, Catalina Island. The gorgeous two million dollar Casino, with its twenty thousand square feet of dance floor is on the point to the right.

Wm. Wrigley, Jr. builder of one of the world's largest business enterprises. Photo courtesy Chambers, Chicago.

better quarters but he wanted to make that business of his grow. He followed the policy of "saving" by throwing his savings back into the business, rather than putting them into a bank.

● "You can't make a success of that!" How many times has he heard that phrase! And how many times has he gone ahead and made a success of it! That has been his greatest satisfaction in life—doing the thing "that couldn't be done." Money means nothing to him; only the joy of accomplishing something.

"I can only ride in one automobile at a time" he says. "I can only wear one suit at a time. Those things mean nothing. It is the satisfaction of seeing a well-thought-out plan succeed that keeps a man young and enthusiastic."

"Nothing great was ever achieved without enthusiasm" says a framed legend that has hung on the wall of his office for many many years. Always that has been one of the basic qualities of the man—enthusiasm. What he undertakes he undertakes enthusiastically, always looking ahead of the black period.

And a look at his photograph shows the keen human enthusiasm there. There is nothing of boredom about this man. Business—working to accomplish something —enthusiasm—has kept Wm. Wrigley, Jr., looking a great deal younger than his years.

● His is the gift of doing the right thing at the right time. Unerringly he picks the timely moment to do the right thing with his advertising, as in all things.

In 1919, when prices were soaring skyward, when

people were paying any price for anything, when it seemed as if there never would be a letup in rising wages and salaries, when luxuries came to be considered necessities, Wrigley abruptly changed an entire advertising schedule already planned, with a terse wire to his office: "Copy in all advertising to read 'Wrigley's—five cents before the war, five cents during the war, five cents now."

● "Let's keep our feet on the ground," he told his executives. "This thing is going to lead to trouble, and we're going to keep this business on a sound basis."

Thus was his fundamental knowledge of economics proved. For in 1920 things did collapse, but Wrigley's gum continued to sell, continued to be a source of satisfaction to its founder, continued to be a monument to Wrigley's business ability.

Again his fundamental knowledge of advertising was shown when he steadfastly refused to allow art work to predominate over the advertising message. He believes that advertising's main object is to carry a sales message, and the wisdom of this belief has been proved again and again in the immense success of his business.

"Ninety-five per cent of a market can be acquired easily," he teaches his men. "But that other five per cent can't be obtained for an additional five per cent expenditure. In other words you cannot dominate a market one hundred per cent unless you have a mo-

nopoly." And so he plans his advertising campaigns to get that ninety-five per cent and doesn't waste his efforts on the remainder.

● "You can't make a success of that!" Again that old cry was heard when Wrigley decided to market his Spearmint flavored gum. "You've got to sell the people what they want," he was advised.

Wrigley was certain that the public wanted the Spearmint flavor. It simply hadn't been called to people's attention. "If you have a good product in the first place and something people want, it's just like rowing down

The simple, effective design of this poster shows why Wrigley's Gum is known throughout the world. This is a straight selling message with just enough "art work" to attract the eye.

stream. But be sure you know which way the stream is flowing," he smiled at his critics.

● Because of his immense expenditures in advertising some people have called "W. W.," as he is known to his intimates, a gambler. But if he is a gambler he is a uniformly successful one. Often his advertising expenditures in a market far exceed his returns for years. But: "Advertising is pretty (Continued on page 36)

DRINK A BITE TO EAT

By Julian Capers, Jr.

● One of the most interesting stories of merchandising development current in the Southwest, the amazing progress of which during the past decade has attracted nation-wide attention, is that of the Dr. Pepper Company of Dallas, Texas.

The Dr. Pepper Company manufactures a five-cent soft drink, "Dr. Pepper." The company was organized about 30 years ago as a small local business in Waco, Texas, being built around the formula which a local pharmacist there had developed for a beverage of remarkable flavor, food value and thirst-quenching properties. It developed a large local market, and during the varying fortunes of the original company, at times extended its distribution into other sections of the Southwest.

The World War period, however, almost put an end to the business, because of the difficulty of obtaining sugar and other ingredients of the product, many of which had to be imported from tropical countries.

● Following a reorganization, in 1925, the company was moved to Dallas, under the general managership of J. B. O'Hara—a man who believed in modern, progressive merchandising and advertising methods. With the aid of his agency, Tracy-Locke-Dawson, Inc., of Dallas, Mr. O'Hara worked out a comprehensive advertising campaign for Dr. Pepper, which was tried out the first year in a small territory which included three large Texas cities. The plan, which included liberal use of newspapers and outdoor display throughout the year, to exploit the merits of Dr. Pepper, not only as a taste-

ful and pleasing beverage, but also—due to its invert sugar content—as a supplier of energy at the mid-meal fatigue hours, proved very successful during the first year in the limited territory then served.

Without radical change in plan, but with constant revision to keep Dr. Pepper advertising in tune with the spirit of progress and modernity, the market for this beverage has been extended, and the advertising effort intensified, until this year finds Dr. Pepper soundly established in 15 Southern and Southwestern states, and plans under way for a continuation of the expansion process until the entire nation ultimately is served.

● The Dr. Pepper Company concentrates upon its slogan, "Drink A Bite To Eat At 10, 2 and 4 o'clock." It constantly reminds its public of the merits of the beverage as a supplier of concentrated energy necessary to overcome fatigue at these "low point" hours in the worker's day. Not only has it succeeded in extending its sales territory as outlined above, but it has also achieved definite progress in the matter of leveling off the seasonal slump which all soft drink manufacturers encounter during the winter months. Through its advertising, which is continued throughout the year, it has influenced the beverage (Continued on page 23)

While the "Drink a Bite to Eat" slogan started off the Dr. Pepper campaign, the "10, 2 and 4" copy with which the previous phrase was joined is used in most of the posters.

Who pays the ADVERTISING DOLLAR?

by Gilbert T. Hodges

First of a series of Talks on the A. F. A. Program

● Not long ago the Federation received a letter from the dean of an important school. He wrote:

"I can never understand the magic by which a million can be spent for advertising without throwing the burden upon someone."

Like many other uninformed critics, he thinks there must be some magic at work when millions of dollars can be spent for advertising which results in larger profits for the advertiser and smaller prices for the consumer.

It does sound like a paradox, but is it?

This is a question that cannot be side-stepped. It cannot be answered with glittering generalities. It will not do to answer the question dogmatically. We must have the facts.

The Bureau of Research and Education of the Advertising Federation of America has brought to light some information which seems to prove the advertising bill is not really paid by the consumer at all, even though the advertiser does not pay it out of his profits.

● Advertising is not a thing separate and distinct from business. It is an integral part of the distribution machinery which brings the product to the consumer.

It is like a high speed motor truck which a manufacturer uses, instead of an army of messenger boys, to deliver goods to his customers. Just as a labor saving machine speeds up production, so does advertising speed up distribution.

Advertising is but one of the items making up the total cost of distribution to the ultimate consumer. Other items are personal selling, warehousing, and transportation, and all of these are naturally included in the price. Advertising is as logically and economically a part of the price of an article as is the cost of the locomotive which hauls it to market, or the cost of the machine which makes it, or the labor of the mechanic who runs the machine.

● A detailed research of 35 national advertisers places their advertising expense at 3 per cent of total sales.

A study of 266 department stores shows an average advertising cost of 2 per cent.

The record of 1000 retail stores of all kinds reveals an advertising charge of 1.6 per cent.

Now let us glance at the total figures on advertising and sales from a national standpoint.

For the sake of comparison let us overstate rather than understate our annual advertising bill. I am sure that you will agree that it is not more than two billion dollars.

1916

GROSS SALES

2.14%

ADVERTISING

750 MILLIONS   35 BILLIONS

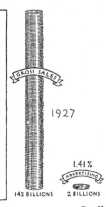

GROSS SALES

1927

1.41%

ADVERTISING

142 BILLIONS   2 BILLIONS

The latest government figures place the annual gross sales of all corporations at 142 billion dollars. Our 2 billion dollar advertising bill is therefore less than one and a half per cent of our total sales. It is 1.4 per cent to be exact.

Now what does this mean in terms of dollars and cents to you and to me when we go into the market to buy something?

How much do we actually pay for the service which advertising renders?

● On the average, it means that for every dollar's worth of sales, we pay one and one half cents for the advertising. It means, that for every ten dollar's worth of sales, we pay fifteen cents for advertising. It means that for every one hundred dollar's worth of sales, we pay one dollar and fifty cents for the advertising.

Now compare this advertising cost of one and one half cents in each dollar with these other costs;—production, traveling salesmen, jobbers, retailers, warehouses and transportation, not to mention the cost of delivery from the store to our homes, which item alone makes the advertising cost look insignificant.

The enormous increase in the volume of advertising in recent years has created the impression in many minds that it has placed an additional burden upon the shoulders of the buying public.

They would be surprised to learn that the exact opposite is more nearly the truth. It is quite true that advertising has increased tremendously. In 1916 our total advertising bill was about $750,000,000 (750 million dollars). By 1927 it had mounted to the huge sum of about two billion dollars.

These estimates are probably too high, but we have preferred to leave them high so that no one could say that we favored the side of advertising by understating the annual expenditure.

Now the people who have entertained wrong impressions about the cost of advertising have left out of their calculations a most important item. And that is, that while the total advertising expense has been increasing by nearly 200 per cent, the gross sales receipts have shown an increase of over 300 per cent.

Our figures showing this increase in sales receipts are based upon the gross sales of all corporations combined, as compiled from Federal income tax returns.

The earliest record is for 1916 when the combined sales of all corporations were something over 35 billion dollars. This amount increased rapidly with many fluctuations until the enormous amount of 142 billion dollars was reached in 1926. In 1927 it was without doubt much larger, but the figures are not yet available.

● Now let's do a little mental arithmetic. Going back to 1916 and comparing the advertising bill of 750 million dollars with the gross sales of 35 billion dollars, we find that the advertising expense was 2.14 per cent of the total sales.

Now, making the same comparison for 1927, we find that the 2 billion dollar advertising bill is only 1.41 per cent of the gross sales of 142 billion dollars.

In other words, our figures seem to indicate that the

GILBERT T. HODGES

advertising expense per sales unit has not increased at all, but on the contrary, has actually decreased from 2.14 per cent in 1916 to 1.41 per cent in 1927, or a percentage decrease in the past eleven years of about 33-1/3 per cent.

It seems conclusively proven that the more the advertising has increased the lower the percentage of expense has become.

Now, how do the prices of advertised commodities compare with the prices of unadvertised merchandise?

● The Federation's Bureau has made a study of this question and the data used were obtained from the United States Bureau of Labor Statistics. The advertised groups included, in addition to the well-known advertised brands, entire classes of advertised commodities.

The study resulted in the discovery that the average price of these groups of commodities affected by advertising has increased by 10 per cent from 1913 to 1930.

During the same period all commodities combined, including both advertised and unadvertised goods, have gone up in price by 20 per cent.

Thus it appears that, during the past 17 years, all commodities combined have advanced just twice as much in price as have those groups of commodities affected by advertising.

In addition to this, it showed that the advertised commodities have maintained a more constant price level, with much less fluctuation, than have all commodities combined.

We must not conclude from this that advertising actually causes prices to be lowered, for advertising is only one of the many factors which influence price.

But as we ardently desire to get at the truth about advertising, and just now, specifically, about the truth of who pays for the advertising, I have thought it well to mention a few instances of (Continued on page 30)

MEN'S SPECIALTY SHOP
puts its okay on outdoor advertising
by Augusta Leinard

● Vaughn-At-Sather-Gate is the unusual name for an unusual specialty shop for men. Vaughn stands for J. R. Vaughn, the owner, and Sather Gate is known far beyond the confines of California as the impressive steel archway which constitutes the main entrance to the University of California in Berkeley. This name, therefore, instantly establishes in the minds of those who read it the location of Mr. Vaughn's shop, which is perhaps the largest of its kind west of Chicago.

Scarcely three years ago Mr. Vaughn after finishing four years inside of Sather Gate, launched into business directly outside of it. As a university student he had run a little men's wear shop and had become convinced that a men's specialty shop near the university would be a big success if the policy of selling a one-model type of college clothing was strictly adhered to. Numerous small stores on Telegraph Avenue, which begins at Sather Gate and is the shopping thoroughfare of Berkeley, dealt in college men's furnishings but in nowhere's near the extensive and individual way covered by this college student's dream.

● Everybody advised him against the venture, saying it would be a failure, but, being an independent thinker whose mind works along Be-sure-you're-right-then-go-ahead processes, this young man in his early twenties thought the matter through and started with one room where he stressed the fact that this was to be strictly a specialty shop for men.

He established his desired atmosphere of combined English impeccability and collegiate "snap" first of all by store appearance. Outside, a foundation of red brick laid criss-cross with an upper portion of black pine as a setting for "well-groomed" window displays. Inside, black, hand-tooled pine, inexpensive yet distinctive, with black composition flooring in tile effects. Red velvet hangings on wrought iron rods cleverly offset any sombreness and served as a foil for the folded men's wear stocked on shelf upon shelf built into the walls.

● Mr. Vaughn did not go in for the bizarre or extreme collegiate styles. What he did was to select one practical and attractive model—which from his own knowledge he was capable of doing—and have this model made up in all sizes and fabrics. A one-model shop in every line of college men's wear was what he opened to the public.

The store was a success from the first. In three years it has tripled its floor space and proportionately increased its patronage. The stock is the largest carried by anybody in that line and the personnel now consists of five salesmen, five workroom employees, two office employees, and a continual addition of part-time help called in from the campus.

An unusual poster to advertise an unusual Men's specialty shop. The woodcut treatment and the figure dressed in a style popular back in 1840 give distinction to this design.

Vaughn-At-Sather-Gate does not draw its business from the university alone. The clientele includes former students—who invariably go back to fill their needs—young business men, and men who want to look young. A man who wants a Vaughn model will make the trip to Berkeley in preference to toiling through a number of stores where many models are carried.

In becoming an outdoor advertiser the young merchant followed his usual Be-sure-you're-right tactics with his usual success. Many times the outdoor advertising salesman had called on him, but while Mr. Vaughn was a courteous listener he said little and gave no encouragement. The salesman hardly considered him a prospect and when he dropped in after a lapse of many months simply because he happened to be in the neighborhood he was surprised to be greeted thus:
● "I've been waiting for you to come in. I'm ready now to go ahead with that outdoor advertising."

As Mr. Vaughn talked it became evident to the salesman that he had thoroughly considered every angle and, after deciding that the outdoor medium was a good one for him, he had gone ahead and planned his campaign, even to the style of poster he intended using. That style, by the way, is one of the chief reasons for the success of his designs. He had chosen a wood-lock English technique, to be carried out in crisp black and white. As a result the Vaughn-At-Sather-Gate posters stand out smartly against their vivid-hued neighbors. They look like Old English wood-cuts and, as Mr. Vaughn explained, he chose the style for two reasons:

First: because England and correctness in men's clothing are as closely linked in the minds of well-groomed men as are Paris and women's attire in the feminine mind.

Second: because it would harmonize with the atmosphere and merchandise he carries and with all the placards, price cards, and printed matter used, which follow the same technique.

● Vaughn-At-Sather-Gate started in April, 1930, with a half showing of posters to be changed every thirty days. This was later increased to a full showing, or 20 posters, used exclusively in Berkeley, a town of about 82,000. The first poster advertised a college clothing sale; then came one announcing a sport clothes event. There was one on tuxedos and one featuring the store's line of shoes—a British make imported from Northampton, England.

The November poster was followed by remarkable results. Mr. Vaughn, wishing to move certain goods to make room for new winter stock, put on a half-price sale, which was to be shown in a poster for thirty days. After two weeks he requested that the poster be covered because the half-price merchandise had been completely sold out.

Berkeley is the home of many commuters who work in San Francisco and who would be difficult to reach in any other way. As Mr. Vaughn expressed it, "The outdoor medium is the most effective way to cover all of Berkeley."

● He is gradually adding painted bulletins to his poster showing, having already contracted for two. One of these is on College Avenue, a direct artery to a residential neighborhood that could not be covered by any other one medium. The present intention is to change the painted design six times a year instead of the customary three.

"My purpose is to establish through a series of posters the different departments such as tuxedos, sports wear, British shoes, and to advertise special events," Mr. Vaughn said. "I am pleased with the outdoor medium because it does bring results. We have many sales which we can actually trace to our posters, where people tell us that they drove out to the store because they noticed our board. This is the first time that customers have commented on our advertising. Another thing, outdoor advertising carries prestige; it makes the public realize that you are not running a hand-to-mouth business."

The Economic Law of
"MARGINAL CONSUMPTION"

by Charles B. Brown
FOSTER & KLEISER COMPANY

● The law of "Marginal Consumption" has such a direct bearing on copy and advertising appeal that it presented itself as a logical theme for discussion.

In order to make full use of the productive power of an advertisement it is necessary that its appeal be directed at that market in which rests the greatest sales potential.

In all products used by the masses such as foods and clothing, other than imported or expensive items, the appeal must be particularly directed to what is termed "the marginal consumer class."

There are roughly, three classes of consumers; rich, middle-class and poor. The rich care little if the price of bread rises, the middle-class will perhaps be a little more economical in its use while the poor will be forced to cut their consumption of bread to a minimum. In this case the poor are the marginal consumers. It should not, however, be construed that the poor are the only marginal consumers on all products, as in the case of an automobile costing $1500, marginal consumers would consist of those who could not invest more than $1000 to $1200 in an automobile. When the cost soars beyond this price this group ceases to represent prospects for this particular car and either a lower priced car must be built to fit their purses or competition offering such a vehicle will secure the business.

The pricing and advertising of merchandise must always be based on these factors if the market is to be properly and thoroughly cultivated.

● Joseph French Johnson, Dean, New York University of Commerce, defines the marginal consumer as "the consumer who is least anxious to buy and consume, whether because his want is the least intense or because his purchasing power is small, is called the marginal consumer. An advance of the price drives him out of the market; he gives up the article altogether and looks for a substitute which will be cheaper. His place as marginal consumer has been taken by another, by one who is barely willing and able to pay the higher price. On the other hand, if the price is lowered another type of marginal consumer may come into the market, one whose desire for the good is less intense or whose means are less ample even than those of the first. Thus any change in the price of an article affects the quality and rank of the marginal consumer who buys it.

"When we take into account the fact that society is virtually divided into many different classes of consumers, different because of their tastes and incomes, we can see clearly why it is that a change in the market price of a commodity brings about a change in the effective demand for it, why a rise in its price causes one class of consumers to hold off and so to reduce its consumption, and why a lowering of the price brings into the market a new class of consumers causing increased sales.

"In any industry the marginal consumer class is of great importance. That class and the one just below it are the ones to which the appeals of the advertiser must be especially directed. In fact, from this point of view we might define the essential aim of advertising as being able to hold the marginal consumer and gradually to lower the margin of consumption, so that people who are now indifferent to an article because of its price or lack of desire for it shall be persuaded to buy it. To some people the telephone is almost a necessity. They will have it in their offices and in their homes almost regardless of the price. To others it seems a luxury which they can hardly afford. Among these latter are found the marginal consumers and those who are almost persuaded. It is to these that the advertisements of the telephone company should be addressed."

● The problems of many of our clients could well be studied from the standpoint of the marginal consumption factor. Suppose for instance it were a Cleaner and Dyer with a given price range with a minimum of $1.75 for cleaning and pressing a man's suit, say the marginal consumer could not afford much more than one dollar and a quarter; he therefore has his garments cleaned and pressed less often or if possible, patronizes a competitor who maintains a lower price range. Sometimes a monthly service consisting of so many suits at a given rate is offered, the rate bringing down the cost per suit, and thus a portion of the marginal market is held.

The laundry industry long ago faced this problem and developed a wide range of services with which to combat the market resistance. Thus we may have our laundry wet-wash, rough-dry or completely serviced. Once we recognize the factor of marginal consumption in our sales work, we immediately understand the peculiar price scales of various services and readily grasp the problems which these prices were designed to meet.

If an advertising campaign is not pulling as it should, the element of marginal consumption may well prove the key to the problem.

This is naturally a very brief outline of this subject. Its importance to our selling activities should be recognized and consideration given its relative position in every advertising problem.

Advertising for
PROSPERITY

by Harold L. Eves

● There may be some argument as to what caused the present business depression but no one will argue about its existence. Almost everyone you meet has his idea of what caused the depression, along with a pet theory as to how business can entice prosperity back.

Business men as a whole took it for granted that the depression was inevitable and would undoubtedly last for a long while. Many of them reacted to the start of the depression much as a hibernating bear does to the first days of fall. By instinct they felt that lean months were ahead and, therefore, the proper thing to do was "crawl in their hole and stay there until spring." This act was caused by too quick a reaction to conditions and too little study of the facts. They believed that a

business depression was due and, therefore, assisted in creating one.

The fact is that the depression we are now in is a *mental* depression rather than a *financial* depression.

You might almost say that the real reason for the present hard times is an excess of thrift on the part of individuals and corporations. Savings can be as destructive to our modern business structure as lavish spendings. Thrift as preached even up to the time of Benjamin Franklin, was created by fear and inherited from a time when the world was never quite free from the dread of famine and when winter was an unproductive time between crops, through which one could live comfortably only by storing food or wealth. A crop failure in that age meant a year of depression. More than one year of failure was pretty apt to mean a panic.

● But today transportation has made the world smaller and the community larger. We are no longer dependent upon the immediate territory in which we live. Diversified crops and diversified industries have helped to even out the valleys and peaks of business.

The real problem that is facing American business today is neither production nor finance but rather the state of mind in which we find the consumers who are still able to buy normally.

The belief that we were in a financial depression spread like a plague. The thought in the mind of an executive that he might have to curtail production because of an anticipated loss in sales was soon picked up by everyone in his organization. His fear was transmitted to them, he feared loss of volume they feared loss of jobs. Automatically buying slackened—one doesn't buy more than necessities when he is afraid of losing his position. So fear in the minds of the consumers actually brought on the condition that the executive so feared.

● Loss in sales means the necessity for restriction of production which is apt to cause unemployment and unemployed people have no power to buy.

But the unemployment situation is not as serious as we are apt to think. Figures vary, but we could almost concede two, three or four million to anybody's figures and still have a market worth selling, except in some particularly stricken area.

Who buys things in America? About 2% of our population is rich and they receive some 20% of our national income. Their money is tied up in stocks and bonds. For the first six months of 1930 the profits of 250 of America's leading corporations was off about 30% as compared with 1929.

But these same corporations were still earning at the rate of 9.2% on their capital and surplus.

Granted that this class of people might have suffered a loss of 30%, they still had ample funds to buy luxuries. Under ordinary circumstances they devoted only 11% of their income to living expenses, the balance according to Ralph Borsudi was either saved or reinvested. It is only this latter portion that suffers in depressions like this.

● Another 15% receive approximately 27% of the national income, this group in normal years saves about 10%. Students of the business situation assure us that this particular middle group has been practically unaffected, most of them being professional people, executives and general wage earners.

The remaining 83% present somewhat of a mixed picture. While it is from this group that we must subtract the large part of our unemployed we find that on a whole they have not suffered any substantial reduction of buying power.

If we were to express this group's wealth by its power to buy rather than its income in dollars we would find that they are in a condition almost equal to 1929 and certainly equal to 1927 and 1928. Commodity prices have tumbled faster than incomes this last year.

Thus we find 2% just as able to buy luxuries as ever; we find 15% not only with their income the same but with income *purchasing* wealth increased from 15% to 20% and then we find 83% with an almost normal *purchasing* wealth despite the fact that a few million of them are unemployed.

● The urge to buy must be directed at all classes "mass advertising will cure depression" says Roger Babson, "that is the trouble; money is held instead of circulated. The basic cause which the jobless should seek is that not too few mills are running but that too few advertising campaigns are running. Mass production of goods requires mass production of customers and that is possible only through advertising."

The mental state into which the American public has worked itself has made them afraid to buy; fear has caused depression. Only by strong optimistic measures will we be able to remove this mental barrier and revive buying. As soon as we overcome the buying reluctancy of the masses business will be on the high road to prosperity for tomorrow.

In his book "The Crowd" Gustave Lehon said, "An idea once started among the mass soon becomes a conviction unless conflicting ideas of equal force appear * * * When the crowd is convinced its action is emotional to the extreme."

The masses, or as Lebon calls them, the crowds, have become convinced of depression more by propaganda than by personal experience.

According to Dr. Walter Dill Scott, President of Northwestern University, the average person seldom performs an act of reason. Most of their acts are as a result of imitation or suggestions just as the present masses have built their own propaganda upon the false basic idea that depression was with us.

● There is a tremendous latent buying power existing in America today. The banks collected during this past year in their Christmas Savings Fund over $675,000,000 as compared with the $590,000,000 collected during 1929. This money was put in the hands of the people December first. A large portion of it went for Christmas spending. The very act of spending these millions for merchandise has created one of the conflicting ideas that Lebon says is necessary to overcome the conviction of depression. Merchandisers who build strong campaigns in the first part of 1931 will offer additional conflicting ideas that will help the masses return to normal buying.

According to the Federal Reserve there are in savings accounts in the United States $50,641,000,000 this year compared to $50,853,000,000 of last year. A tremendous latent purchasing power.

Certainly a mass that has proved itself capable of raising billions of dollars for war loans, Red Cross, charity, etc., should have little difficulty in accelerating the return of prosperity by a concentrated drive upon the stores and retail markets of the country.

America must be sold on the idea of buying. It must be sold on the doctrine of spending. The old idea that wealth was the result of saving is only half a truth and a very dangerous one at that.

Over 80% of the people have the ability to spend and if convinced of that fact through constructive merchandising can and will restore business prosperity. Production, employment, wages and buying are all closely meshed together and need only the driving force of constructive advertising to throw business back into "high."

The Unemployment Problem

● The Governor-elect Phil La Follette Employment campaign which was originated and executed by the officers of the Outdoor Advertising Association of Wisconsin went into action on January second. The space used is a representative showing in every city and town with more than 1,000 population. The campaign opened just three days before Mr. La Follette's inaugural on January fifth.

The lithography and paper was furnished by the Edwards and Deutsch Lithograph Company of Milwaukee at a small charge for plates. The space on the panels was donated by Wisconsin plant owners and all minor expenses were paid by the Outdoor Advertising Association of Wisconsin.

Ice Industry *leaps ahead ten years*
THRU MODERN
MERCHANDISING

An interview with J. F. Nickerson, Editor, ICE AND REFRIGERATION

● In August, 1917, when an entire nation hummed and throbbed at the business of making war, the constant cry was, "FOOD—MORE FOOD!" Thousands and hundreds of thousands of soldiers must be fed. The ordinary routine of life was upset. A large portion of the food-producing populace was now concerned with other tasks, but it still consumed food. And one item played a most important part in supplying food to the thousands of men concentrated at the various camps throughout the United States. This item was ICE.

In order that every form of cooperation could be offered the government facing this problem, the National Association of Ice Industries was formed.

● Out of this Association, formed for patriotic purposes, has come the salvation of the Ice Industry itself. Few people could visualize the immense stimulus to things mechanical that the frenzied activity of war-time was to bring about. Yet to the Ice Industry this mechanical age brought a new competitor in the mechanical refrigerator for the home.

Unlike many present-day industries, the Ice Industry had not been constantly pressed with outside competition. Consequently, merchandising of the advantages

J. F. Nickerson, editor, Ice and Refrigeration, formerly Chairman of The Committee on National Publicity, National Association of Ice Industries.

of ice had been slow in developing. As the population of the country increased, and the standard of living raised, the growth of the use of ice had been steady and satisfactory.

● The average increase in urban families was 340,000 yearly. Taking $25.00 a year as the average annual gross bill per family for ice, the total new business which could be expected from increased population was

The design of this poster leaves no room for doubt as to what is being sold and the sales message itself is direct and to the point.

The variety of colors and arrangement of the designs in the series is illustrated by this poster. The same simple theme is carried throughout, yet individuality is achieved.

$8,500,000 annually. This seemed to be a satisfactory growth in volume which assured the continued prosperity of the business for many years.

● In 1921, at the time the Committee on National Publicity recommended an adequate advertising campaign, few engaged in the ice business felt that the household machine could make an inroad on their business, because the machines were imperfect, poorly financed, and excessively priced. At that time it was estimated that there were about 55,000 of these machines in operation.

But in 1925, it was estimated that there were some 200,000 machines of thirty different makes in use, and an eminent authority estimated that in 1925 there would be more machines sold than in the entire previous time they had been on the market.

It was pointed out that while the total tonnage of ice affected was relatively small, it was a classification profitable to the ice manufacturer, and a portion of their business which should not be allowed to slip away from them without a struggle.

The producers of domestic ice machines were doing a very thorough advertising and selling job. Every conceivable form of advertising was used, and powerful forces were getting behind the promotion of the machines.

● The power companies were interested in the fact that a widespread use of this equipment would:

"Provide 100% increase in revenue

Be 85% non-peak load

Require no additional investment in transmission equipment

Require no additional meters

Require no new consumers."

Here, then, was a really attractive proposition for the power companies. Every wired home was a potential market for mechanical refrigerators, and potentially an additional load for the power companies. And since the growth in the number of homes wired had jumped from 8,000,000 in 1920 to

17,000,000 in 1925, this represented a really serious condition.

The average man in the ice business found little outside understanding of what he had to contend with. Practically every well-established concern in the business is rendering a vital service to the community in which it is located. It is supplying that community with one of the basic necessities of modern, civilized life. The men engaged in the ice business knew this, but the rest of the world didn't. About the only time the average man thought of the ice manufacturer at all was when something went wrong with his day's delivery.

With millions invested in ice-making equipment, it became obvious that something must be done to insure the continued growth of the industry. New uses for ice could be suggested, the advantages of ice could be stressed, new and better ice refrigerators could be designed, the use of ice over a greater portion of the year could be encouraged, and the use of ice in homes where it had never been used could be promoted.

This was possible under article one of the Association's Purposes, which reads: "To study the relation of the ice industries to the economic necessities of the day and through education and publicity make known wherein these industries can be of service."

● Study of the results secured by other Associations convinced the committee that money spent on advertising under the direction of capable and experienced people would produce profitable results for the ice industry. It was felt that the broadest benefits that would be derived would be institutional benefits—the feeling of confidence that the men engaged in the ice business would do what they said they would do, and that they would serve their customers faithfully.

These benefits would be closely tied in with the commercial benefits—public acceptance of fair prices, an increased use of ice, and the stabilization of consumption to more evenly distribute (Continued on page 32)

Once more the selling message is forceful and clear. Action is introduced into the design by the hand without confusing the prospect as to the product.

Drink a Bite to Eat

(Continued from page 12) drinking public to regard its product as something more than a mere thirst-quencher, something pleasant to drink in the heat of summer days, and to drink for its energy-supplying properties, regardless of the atmospheric temperature.

In doing this important job for Dr. Pepper, outdoor advertising has been accorded a major share of the sales work. The company has consistently utilized the services of the most able American poster artists. It intensified the advertising appeal and greatly increased its effectiveness. Examples of the Dr. Pepper poster campaign for 1930-1 are reproduced herewith.

● Dr. Pepper posters feature short, terse copy with a distinctly human interest appeal. They reflect the ideas of modern youth, frequently capitalizing the vivid colloquial campus expression which is vogue at the moment. Another strong idea frequently used in Dr. Pepper poster designs is the "children's appeal," this being directly capitalized upon through the absolute purity and wholesomeness of the product, which makes it healthful for children's use.

■ ■ ■

Associated Industries Bulletin Boosts Outdoor Medium

● Says a weekly bulletin of the Associated Industries of Kentucky, dated December 11, "Every State in the Union has scenery perhaps second in quantity only to atmosphere. Because an occasional owner of a little dab of it is willing for some advertiser to make colorful use of his landscape, so-called Nature admirers and others have protested in recent years that billboards are everything from undesirable to a downright nuisance.

● "That the lowly billboard has done its bit in reminding people about Liberty Loan drives, Red Cross campaigns, Christmas seal attacks on tuberculosis and the like may or may not be forgotten by the groups.

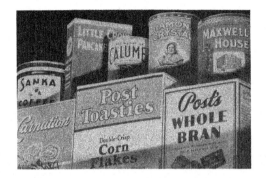

We know our groceries

FOODS are our dish. When it's a job of whetting appetites

on the hone of outdoor advertising, there may be something

in our uncommonly wide experience to give our clients just

an "edge." Photographed above are some of the products

that high-spot the standing of this alert organization in

the field of food. . . . If you want outdoor SERVICE—

OUTDOOR

A NATIONAL OUTDOOR ADVERTISING ᵀORGANIZATION

SERVICE

INCORPORATED

230 NORTH MICHIGAN AVE., CHICAGO

BUY NORMALLY

by W. T. Stokes

● What is the matter with business? Opinions are many. Be as it may there are certain basic causes.

Economists tell us that the economic structure of the world is out of line. Over-production, due to bringing back to productive peacetime pursuits a great number of persons formerly engaged in war activities and the aftermath.

Moreover, machinery is steadily taking the place of manual labor, both skilled and unskilled. Now, 10 men with modern agricultural machinery can produce a larger crop of wheat than 200 men produced in the same time in former years.

The condition applies not only to agriculture, but industry and commerce in general. Competition for the markets of the world is becoming keener.

While these conditions exist to a certain extent, publicity has magnified them. A gradual readjustment of economic measures will meet the situation.

The leadership of America has helped the old world in many ways and America again will lead her sister nations out of the gloom into the light of sound business progress.

● What brought about this "Unemployment Situation?" —an expression on the tips of the tongue of far too many—heard and discussed everywhere. Is it as bad as the great mass of people are prone to think?

It is stated that less than 20% of the people in this country are unemployed. Therefore, if 80% of the people are enjoying normal incomes, it is evident that the demon FEAR has penetrated their minds, which accounts for locking money tills and tightening of purse strings.

Enormous publicity has been devoted to news of the stock market crash, which was only natural, for "All that goes up must come down," particularly so when ascending to abnormal heights without foundation to sustain. Over financing, inflation, false values of securities, then the toppling and the falling.

● The little fish found themselves in a maelstrom of cross currents and eddies which they could not withstand. Paper profits melted like the dew before an August sun, and those who had been so unwise as to risk surplus or borrow for stock gambling purposes paid the penalty.

Stories of losses of individuals spread like a prairie fire; friends and neighbors sympathized ⌐ ⌐ ⌐ ⌐ Fear entered and a policy of cutting dow⌐ in buying followed and spread like a c⌐ ease. Consumers stopped buying, which ⌐ to retailers, wholesalers and (Continued

The "Buy Normally" poster which is aiding the ca⌐ paign to induce the steady buying that will haste the return of prosperity. It is another example of the assistance which organized Outdoor Advertising is willing to lend to a worthy cause.

BUY NORMALLY "STEADY BUYING STEADIES BUSINESS"

Space used here for Advertisers imprint

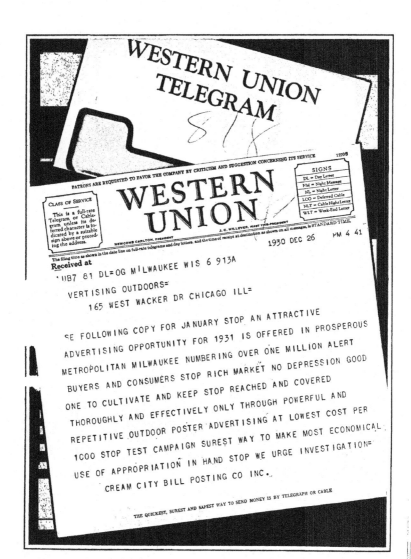

WESTERN UNION
TELEGRAM

PATRONS ARE REQUESTED TO FAVOR THE COMPANY BY CRITICISM AND SUGGESTION CONCERNING ITS SERVICE   1220B

WESTERN UNION

CLASS OF SERVICE

This is a full-rate Telegram, or Cablegram unless its deferred character is indicated by a suitable sign above or preceding the address.

NEWCOMB CARLTON, PRESIDENT   J. C. WILLEVER, FIRST VICE-PRESIDENT

SIGNS
DL = Day Letter
NM = Night Message
NL = Night Letter
LCO = Deferred Cable
NLT = Cable Night Letter
WLT = Week-End Letter

The filing time as shown in the date line on full-rate telegrams and day letters, and the time of receipt at destination as shown on all messages, is STANDARD TIME.

1930 DEC 26   PM 4 41

Received at

11B7 81 DL=OG MILWAUKEE WIS 6 913A

VERTISING OUTDOORS=
165 WEST WACKER DR CHICAGO ILL=

SE FOLLOWING COPY FOR JANUARY STOP AN ATTRACTIVE
ADVERTISING OPPORTUNITY FOR 1931 IS OFFERED IN PROSPEROUS
METROPOLITAN MILWAUKEE NUMBERING OVER ONE MILLION ALERT
BUYERS AND CONSUMERS STOP RICH MARKET NO DEPRESSION GOOD
ONE TO CULTIVATE AND KEEP STOP REACHED AND COVERED
THOROUGHLY AND EFFECTIVELY ONLY THROUGH POWERFUL AND
REPETITIVE OUTDOOR POSTER ADVERTISING AT LOWEST COST PER
1000 STOP TEST CAMPAIGN SUREST WAY TO MAKE MOST ECONOMICAL
USE OF APPROPRIATION IN HAND STOP WE URGE INVESTIGATION=
CREAM CITY BILL POSTING CO INC=

THE QUICKEST, SUREST AND SAFEST WAY TO SEND MONEY IS BY TELEGRAPH OR CABLE

This design is notable for its simplicity. The product, the result of its use and an easily understood copy line makes this a poster that is sure to put over its message.

In this poster, the radio itself has remained the important unit while the copy theme and the illustration have been subordinated to the product and name.

The elimination of any unnecessary elements and the picturesqueness of the presentation forms an attractive and effective design. This campaign is also being posted without charge.

Another of Outdoor Advertising's contributions to this veteran's organization. The Veterans of Foreign Wars have expressed themselves as highly pleased with the results.

This picture, its technique marking it as one of the Maxwell House series even when seen without a name, is a very colorful and decorative painting.

The portrait of the man whose name is featured, the name itself and the name of the paper are the three simple units that make a good design.

THIS MONTH

A design that is similar in treatment to previous posters. Distinctive technique and a careful simplicity makes this poster easy to understand and to remember.

Here again the radio and the name are given prominence, with the crowd and the copy line subordinated.

Here is an effective seasonal poster. There are many units in this design yet, due to the careful placing, there is not the crowded appearance that might easily have resulted.

Another motor oil poster with much the same theme. Note how the action of the figure leads the eye to the Champlin trade mark and on down into the name.

This effective bulletin puts over the Dodge message simply yet powerfully while the illustration ties in very well with the "New Beauty" copy line.

The Farmer and National Prosperity

(Continued from page 4) higher wages and shorter working hours has had a great share in bringing industrial prosperity to the United States. The credit does not all go to machinery and the mass production it made possible.

Industry has been forced to realize that cheap labor does not pay. But industry still is sure that *cheap raw materials* are necessary in prosperous industry.

Included in raw materials, they figure food commodities. Industry and big business still figure cheap food as essential. And that belief, which is also due to be exploded, is responsible for much of the trouble between the farmer and industry.

● The understanding and cooperation between employer and employee in industry, must be broadened to include understanding and cooperation between industry and agriculture.

There are some 6,000,000 farms in this country. Roughly the farm population is a little under 30,000,000. Their gross income is some 12 billion dollars per year or a little more than one-tenth of the national income. Until ten years ago, they regularly got one-fifth of the National income. Increase their individual income by $100 and you will have increased their purchasing power three thousand million dollars.

And they will spend it all.

Industry would have that much more of a domestic market, three thousand million dollars more of a market. It would call for that much more production of manufactured articles, which would call for more labor, bring more dividend, and keep the wheels of industry turning more hours—thus restoring our national prosperity.

The farmer is a liberal spender when he has the money. Practically every cent more that he gets will be spent for manufactured products in the long run. And that will be passed on and on thru the retailer—the wholesaler—the manufacturer—with labor getting a slice all the way.

● We are in a period of over-production in this country —in agriculture as well as industry. This can be remedied only by good will—better understanding—and by team work all along the line from the raw to the finished product. And it is in the interest of fair-play only that I speak for the great food producing area of the United States.

Agriculture is the basis of our wealth. Business and industry cannot hope to be prosperous until agriculture is prosperous. Nothing will do so much to restore normal business conditions in the United States today as to increase the farmers buying power. When the business interest of the country fully appreciate, as they should, that it is to their own interest to write the farmers' ills as speedily as possible, over-production will cease to worry big business.

Outdoor Advertising Merchandises
FARM PRODUCTS

(Continued from page 5) ing elements have been increased. The vicious circle of unemployment reducing buying power and leading to more unemployment has begun.

● Naturally it cannot be claimed that the present economic situation is solely the result of the prevailing prices of farm products. There can be no doubt, however, that the present situation of the farmer is having a great influence upon national prosperity.

The farmer has placed upon the market a quantity of products that is far in excess of the demand for those products. There may have been many contributing factors to this situation—bumper crops, increased acreage, reduced foreign market—but the fact remains that there are more farm products in existence than the demand justifies.

Two remedies are obvious, to curtail production or to increase consumption. Unfortunately the curtailment of production is practically impossible. The farmer is an individualist and therefore, in most cases, selfish. The knowledge that the acreage of some particular crop was to be cut would be the cue for many an agriculturist to increase his planting of that crop in order that he might cash in on the increased price. The result would be the defeat of the whole program. The farmer is also a creature of habit. In some sections wheat is almost the only crop; in others corn is the habitual planting. The farmer must have some substitute which he knows will pay him as well or better than what he has been raising and he is going to be a hard customer to convince.

Commodity prices abroad are as low or lower than in America; moreover many countries are erecting tariff walls which will effectually bar wheat from the United States. Increased consumption in this country is the solution that is most obvious and most practical.

A manufacturer confronted with a similar problem of selling would call upon an advertising program to increase the acceptance of his product. The farmer and the agencies that are operating to assist him have no means of doing this very necessary job. Advertising interests can, however, cooperate with farm organizations and the work of the government in an advertising program. This the Outdoor Advertising Association is doing.

● Conferences between representatives of the Outdoor Advertising industry and government officials showed the need for an advertising campaign designed to increase consumption of farm products. At the National Convention of the Outdoor Advertising Association in Milwaukee last October Mr. Ivan B. Nordhem, of Nordhem Service, Inc., introduced a resolution to the effect that the organized Outdoor Advertising industry give space on their panels for a four months' Outdoor Advertising campaign to aid the farmer. The resolution was passed unanimously and preparations were immediately begun for the opening of the campaign in December.

The keynote of the situation was struck by Mr. George W. Kleiser, President of the Outdoor Advertising Association of America, in a letter to members of the Association. Mr. Kleiser said, "the biggest job with which our country is confronted today is to restore prosperity. It is the principal concern of the Federal Administration at Washington. A call for volunteers has been issued, because obviously some of the business development forces of the country can help more than others. Our organization has ever answered the call of our country in any national emergency."

"The cornerstone of national prosperity is normal conditions on the farm. When wheat and other products of the soil are not consumed in normal amounts, the reaction is felt in every city and hamlet in the United States and, in fact, the whole world."

The baking and allied industries, when informed of the proposed advertising campaign, at once shouldered the cost of the posters, amounting to some $200,000. An Art and Copy Committee, comprising some of the best known advertising men in the country worked out the theme of the campaign and between thirty and forty thousand posters of the first design, "Your Child's Bread and Butter Can Solve the Wheat Problem" were posted in December.

● The response from the farm leaders was immediate and enthusiastic. "* * * I am in receipt of a full size poster. This is excellently done and the message is well set out and driven home," said a letter from Arthur M. Hyde, Secretary of Agriculture to Mr. Nordhem. "I want to thank you and your organization," continued Mr. Hyde's letter, "for their cooperation which, I feel, will be very valuable in attracting the attention of the country to some of the problems of the farmer."

George S. Milnor, president of the Grain Stabilization Corporation and Alexander Legge, Chairman of the Federal Farm Board are among the other officials who have expressed their appreciation and enthusiasm.

The first posting of the December poster was attended with considerable ceremony in Indianapolis. Among the Indiana farm leaders present were John Leerkamp, President of the Indianapolis Vegetable Association; Lewis Taylor, President of the Indiana Farm Bureau Federation; James R. Moore, editor of the Hoosier Farmer; Clarence Henry, County Agent; and Walter Ristow, President of the Indianapolis Greenhouse Association.

A similar program was put on in Louisville, Kentucky where Kentucky agriculture was represented by A. B. Sawyer, President of the Kentucky Farm Bureau Federation; C. C. Keeley, Secretary of the Associated Industries of Kentucky; Adolph Moser, President of the Jefferson County Farm Bureau and S. W. Anderson, County Agent.

In Minneapolis the first posting was attended by B. B. Sheffield of the Minneapolis Civic and Commerce Association; Mayor Kunze of Minneapolis and John Brandt, President of the Land O' Lakes Creameries.

● The unselfish move of the Outdoor Advertising Association is lending its resources to the cause of Farm Relief is probably as valuable and as timely a program as could have been undertaken. Many comments have been received by individual plant operators as well as by the Association which indicate that business leaders generally are appreciative of the service that is being rendered. Newspaper publicity has compared the present campaign with the Rotary Prosperity Campaign of 1921 and 1922—which Mr. Nordhem also suggested—and with the efforts that won the gratitude of the nation during the war. The same medium that aided the sword is now enlisted in behalf of the plowshare.

Trade magazines in the baking and milling industries and advertising publications have devoted a great deal of space to discussion of the Outdoor Advertising Association's program. Baker's Weekly, in the course of a page story, said,

"Bakers all over the country will no doubt be surprised to see the 24-sheet posters, as depicted on this page, springing up in their communities from Maine to California, and will naturally wonder who is behind this effective display; in fact, how a campaign of this sort came to be started at this time.

"For the information and enlightenment of the industry, we wish to say that we are at the beginning of a Farmers' Prosperity Campaign, which started on December 1st and is to continue through the next four months. Of course, everybody knows that the lot of the farmer, and especially the wheat grower, has not been a happy one during recent months, and everybody is also aware of the fact that so long as the farmer is not happy and prosperous the rest of the country cannot enjoy happiness and prosperity. Everybody in the land is trying his level best to correct market conditions as they affect the wheat farmer, and the present campaign has been devised as an effective way to increase the consumption of wheat products and thus directly bring more business, and perhaps better prices for the wheat grower's products.

● "The Farmers' Prosperity Campaign, which is under the supervision of the Grain Stabilization Corporation, has been made possible through the generosity of the Outdoor Advertising Association of America, Inc., who unanimously and enthusiastically, at their Milwaukee convention adopted an idea presented to them by Ivan B. Nordhem to donate sufficient panels to carry the message of the need for greater wheat consumption all over the country. The owners of these outdoor panels promptly contributed space to the value of $2,000,000, and thus it will be possible to display between 40,000 and 45,000 of these 24-sheet posters in 18,000 communities.

Since the bakers are the greatest customers of the wheat farmer, it is but natural that the campaign should incidentally carry the message of the baking industry, and much thought and time have been spent to devise copy for these posters that will have the desired effect. The selection of the right appeal was no easy matter, and it is said that several sessions of men representing

a million dollars worth of gray matter and including well known experts, such as Bruno Barton, George Gottfried and M. Lee Marshall of the Continental Baking Company and Henry Stude, president of the American Bakers Association, devoted much time and thought to the problem before them and as the first poster that has now made its appearance will show, they have succeeded splendidly in presenting a message that should have the desired result and be ultimately beneficial to the wheat grower.

"At the November meeting of the Bakers Club, New York, when the campaign was outlined in detail by Mr. Nordhem, such men as Lee Marshall, George Gottfried, Fred Frazier, Howard Ward, Earl Cox, and others unanimously endorsed the undertaking and promised to do everything in their power, so far as the baking industry was concerned, to make it a success.

"At the suggestion of Howard Ward, the different posters will be copyrighted to prevent their use for individual purposes, since the whole idea behind the campaign is, of course, the desire to help the farmers of the country."

● Similar articles have appeared in many other publications and it is the opinion of practically all who have expressed themselves in regard to the campaign that the Outdoor Advertising Association is making a valuable contribution to the cause of the farmer. Advertising has sold billions of dollars worth of goods for America's manufacturers. The same power that it has shown when applied to farm products will aid in increasing consumption—the object of the present campaign and will thereby reduce the present surplus, increase the farmer's purchasing power and hasten the return of normal conditions. The Outdoor Advertising Association, in sponsoring the Farmers' Prosperity Campaign, is not only helping the farmer but it is doing its share in bringing increased volume to every one of the nation's industries.

Who pays the Advertising Dollar?

(Continued from page 14) American business concerns whose success is intimately related to advertising, and especially to see what happened to the prices of their products while they were building up volume through advertising.

Shall we stop once more to ask: Who pays for advertising?

But who actually does pay the bill still remains in doubt.

The advertiser apparently does not pay it out of his profits, and it doesn't seem to come out of the pocket of the consumer.

The correct answer appears to be: That advertising pays its own bill—by stimulating consumption and speeding up production, and thereby creating enough additional wealth to pay the bill many times over.

MAIN STREET

is now

FARM CONSCIOUS

* Colorful twenty four sheet posters pictorially featuring the products of the farm ready for human use are being displayed on poster panels located on Main Street, U. S. A. at 30,000 places in 17,000 cities and towns.

* This display is seen repeatedly—daily—by a resident population of over 80 millions of the American Public and frequently by more than 20 million more of the residents of sparsely settled districts en route to and from market and home.

° This tremendous force of impression will continue for one hundred and twenty days through the cooperation of the Grain Stabilization Corporation of the Federal Farm Board of the Department of Agriculture, and the members of the Outdoor Advertising Association of America.

"The health and wealth of the nation is cradled in the soil"

Buy Normally

(Continued from page 24) the source of production. Consequently, savings banks deposits have increased enormously. The excessive hoarding of money never did anyone any good.

● Publicity, to a large degree, was responsible for creating this condition and publicity should be applied as a remedy. Publicity must perform the vitally important task of bringing back NORMAL BUYING and STEADY BUSINESS and stop the unwise hoarding of money. If the 80% of people now enjoying normal incomes would buy normally and with optimism, activity in business would soon gain momentum and the unemployment situation would be on the way to complete recovery.

The gears of the machines of industry and commerce dropped from high to neutral and have coasted in the procession of the mourners long enough. All interests, in Chicago, sponsored by the Chicago Association of Commerce, have started putting the pep and power of publicity into business for the purpose of a consistent, steady pull over the mountain of Fear, the first in the range of depression. This is being done by the "BUY NORMALLY" Campaign, as illustrated in the poster.

To encourage steady buying, a campaign of Metropolitan scope started Dec. 15th, arranged for a 90 day display of 24 sheet posters carrying the "STEADY BUYING STEADIES BUSINESS" message. Several prominent advertisers are participating in this cooperative campaign. Space is left for imprint in the lower right hand corner.

Contracts for more than 300 posters per month, for a period of three months, were placed with the Chicago Office of the General Outdoor Advertising Company prior to Dec. 15th, the first posting date.

Car cards, an exact reproduction of the poster, have been placed with the Chicago Surface Lines, the Chicago Elevated Lines, suburban trains and motor busses. Department Stores and newspaper advertisers are being urged to use mats carrying the message: "STEADY BUYING STEADIES BUSINESS" in all or in part, in their daily copy.

● Chicago newspapers have enlisted their aid in backing the "STEADY BUYING" movement in their editorial and advertising columns. Several leading radio stations and radio advertisers are sending the "BUY NORMALLY" message, to support this movement, in their program. Some merchants of Chicago have stated that buying has increased steadily within three days after the "BUY NORMALLY" campaign started. One merchant stated that this increase was not the normal holiday buying, but the buying of staple merchandise other than for gift purposes.

NOW, the Outdoor Advertising industry, true to tradition, may perform its part in accelerating the return to normal business in participating in the "STEADY BUYING STEADIES BUSINESS" program.

Ice Industry *Leaps Ahead*

(Continued from page 22) the load throughout the year.

Efforts were first directed at the preparation of material that could be used locally by the members, and numerous bulletins were prepared and distributed to schools by the Household Refrigeration Bureau, containing educational features on the care of refrigerators, where to place food in refrigerators, the care of children's food in the home, and similar items.

● Each year the Committee continued to recommend an advertising campaign national in scope until in 1927, a large campaign was undertaken, using magazines, weeklies, major newspapers and outdoor advertising.

The success and value of this effort is attested by the fact that the 1930 output of ice of approximately sixty million tons equals the output originally estimated for 1940, while the average load factor for the plants was increased from 150 days a year to 180 days.

Each year the use of outdoor advertising has become more widespread in the Association's plans, until the plans for 1931 include a most ambitious outdoor campaign. Eight posters have been designed, providing a long campaign. These posters, displayed by a large number of companies throughout the country will have a truly "national" effect.

Commenting on the use of outdoor advertising in a bulletin issued by the Trade Development Bureau of the Association, the Committee states: "We believe that ICE needs outdoor poster advertising because, among other reasons:

1. Outdoor Advertising reaches the mass market at low cost.
2. Outdoor advertising works twenty-four hours a day, seven days a week.
3. By Color and Size, Outdoor Advertising drives messages home, quickly and surely.

"In selling ICE, outdoor advertising has proved increasingly effective. Your Trade Development Bureau for four years has prepared poster campaigns, and each year each campaign has proved more successful than its predecessor and more members have shared in its success.

"Your Committee esteems outdoor advertising so highly that it has made the poster campaign the basis of the 1931 Trade Development program. Each poster will be duplicated in full color on truck banners, movie slides, perhaps blotters, and in black and white newspaper mats. Thus we may tie in all forms of advertising, greatly strengthening each advertising medium we use by repeating the same message at the same time in different places."

● The posters which form the basis of the 1931 campaign are of colorful, striking design. Crisp, short wording makes the message easy to read and understand, with the result that the ideas stand out in the shortest possible written form. There is no mistaking the import of the messages of these posters—they advertise ICE as the best refrigerant.

POSTERS in CANADA

WE have built the most extensive business in Canada and maintain the confidence of the most successful advertisers in the Dominion.

THE results achieved for our various clients suggest that we might be of service to you. Real sales-producing service.

WE attend to every detail of campaigns and give you the benefit of wide experience and technical skill.

WRITE for sketches, prices and information.

if you have your own ideas, let us carry them out.

if you desire ideas, we have trained talent for the purpose.

We handle every detail of Poster Advertising

The Canadian Poster Company

4530 St. Lawrence Blvd.,   Montreal, Canada

The Radio Industry and its Problems

(Continued from page 7) heard at all, regardless of their intrinsic merit, had to yell from the house tops whereas a manufacturer in a more stabilized industry could have been content to yell from the front or back door. There will be plenty of advertising on radio during the coming year, but it will be of a more sane and orderly kind. The radio industry believes in advertising and as indicated, has done more than its share to date.

● What the industry needs more than anything else at the present time, in my humble opinion, is for the public to be made to realize that there is a set of standards to be upheld and that there is a difference between two sets that look alike and are in the same size box, notwithstanding the fact that one is priced at $49.50 complete with tubes and the other $149.50 less tubes. The thought must be gotten over that probably the $149.50 set is the better buy. Buyers of automobiles have learned long ago that the size of a car has not a whole lot to do with the price of it and that you get just what you pay for. Buyers of radio must learn the same thing and until manufacturers and dealers get together and put over this thought, the industry will not be stabilized. I do believe, however, that they are going to do it.

One of the greatest problems now facing the industry is to help the dealer now in business—I am speaking of the radio dealer who really has a right to be called that—to find out his overhead and operating expenses and to stick to legitimate, sane methods of merchandising. Wild cat competition, wild claims and exaggerated promises have caused many dealers to run about like flies on a hot griddle trying to keep ahead of competition and not knowing how to do it. Dealers unfortunately have become accustomed to think that no line is absolutely stable and that by merely changing lines, because the latest salesman to arrive has a few extra green dots in his tie and says his set has a triple-x gadget, they will automatically draw all the prospects to their store like a magnet. Dealers must be taught that unless they pick a good line or two lines, give them 100% loyalty, have faith in the manufacturers, learn all there is to learn about these sets and stick with them through thick and thin, they are not going to be a permanent factor. Changing lines means changing advertising and merchandising methods. It means lost motion in every respect, it means telling one story today and having to learn a new one tomorrow:

● Getting the whole thing down to brass tacks, it is up to manufacturers from now on to spend some time educating their dealers, helping them in every way to realize that they should not be swayed by sudden moves which often mean nothing and that to succeed permanently, they must live with one line and follow it through for better or worse, unless of course it turns out to be permanently worse.

Dealers must be taught to understand that they cannot build up respect for themselves or the products they sell in the public mind when they will take on new and practically unknown lines just because they can be sold cheaper, when they lose sight of later service troubles and costs. How all this is going to be done is in itself a problem. It is not easy to reconstruct thought and national merchandising methods over night. Nevertheless, it does not push aside the facts in the case and the facts, as generaly recognized, are that radio manufacturers have perhaps spent too much time shouting to the public, trying to put on some new stunt, add some new quirk to their radio receivers, rather than to educate their dealers in the paths of loyalty and, what is more practical, in the paths of proper merchandising.

Prices of radio receivers will, generally speaking, be lower for 1931. And why not? Manufacturing methods have improved, production costs have been lowered and it was only natural that with a new merchandising era to face, radio would come up smiling to face it with other industries. Yet price alone—low price alone—will not sell radio sets. In the past, there has been too much of a tendency to rely on price alone. With severe competition obtaining, most manufacturers bent their energies toward seeing if they could make a price lower than the other fellow and still exist and dealers were quick to follow suit, thereby encouraging the public to lose sight of the advantages of radio, what it ought to offer, etc. and concentrate on the one big factor of "How much will it cost?" From now on price will be a big factor, yes, just as it is a factor in automobiles and everything else, but the manufacturer who wants to continue to exist and have public respect and confidence must spend some time stressing other things than price and so must the dealer.

● I am constantly being asked by people in other industries, "What is the future of radio as regards improvements and public demand?" Nobody knows the real future of radio. It is a wonderful industry in my opinion and is just beginning. Television right now seems distantly removed, but it will be consummated undoubtedly. And before television,—I mean real, perfected television for everybody—reaches us, we may find many more startling things about radio which could easily start an entirely new merchandising era in this amazing industry. Sets are as near perfection today as we can hope to have them for some time. Of course, there will be minor improvements, some of them of an important nature, but generally speaking, no one should hesitate to buy a radio set hoping that tomorrow, a month or three months from now he will have vindicated his smartness by having saved his money to purchase a set totally different from what he could have secured three months previous.

As I have said, radio has everything in its favor today for facing the New Year with hope and confidence and I, for one, look for 1931 to see a host of improved conditions in the manufacturing, distributing and retail branches of the industry. I, for one, look for 1931 to be one of radio's greatest years.

The Business Romance of
WILLIAM WRIGLEY, Jr.

(Continued from page 11) much like running a furnace," he explains. "You've got to keep on shoveling coal. Once you stop stoking, the fire goes out." By and large, throughout the years, he has probably received a dollar and a half for every dollar spent in advertising.

Wrigley believes in the shoemaker sticking to his last. He has never given out piffle to boost the stock of his company—has never gambled on the market. He has stuck to the business of making chewing gum, and today his five plants—in Chicago, Toronto, Canada, Sydney, Australia, London, England and Frankfort Germany, produce more chewing gum than all other chewing gum manufacturers combined.

In the early days when credit information on his company was requested, the answer was always, "We pay all our bills promptly, and we ask for no credit." One of Wrigley's business fundamentals is the belief that the overwhelming majority of people are instinctively honest. He has always dealt fairly with everyone and expects others to deal fairly with him.

● Notably enough, this man still works at his business. He admires work for the purpose of it. He has no objection to sports that build up the body nor the mental relaxation that freshens a man for the next day's work, but he believes man is on earth to better the world, and each man can accomplish that purpose in his own way in his own work.

II

And what of the life of the man that has built up this character?

We must picture Wm. Wrigley—selling newspapers on the streets of New York; sleeping on the ventilator of the old New York Tribune Building; sleeping under wagons in dingy side streets; carrying bundles; peeling potatoes; cutting the rigging out of ancient sailing-vessels! To the average person strolling up Michigan Avenue in Chicago, that picture of Wm. Wrigley is hard to visualize, as the white bulk of the building that bears his name strikes the eye.

Yet always behind these monuments marking an astounding success there is a man—a man with something outstanding in his character—a man such as the Wrigley we have already seen. And to those who have looked behind the visible evidence of immense achievement, it seems that there is nearly always found something of that cheerful acceptance of the meaner jobs of life, that willingness to perform the little tasks first.

Always Wrigley's has been the spirit that does and dares. The amazing regularity with which he was dismissed from school was but an evidence of the boundless health and energy that have seen him through a life of thrilling successes and temporary reverses.

● The summer he was eleven years old he ran away from home—bound for New York, fame and fortune. On his own in America's largest city at an age when most boys are still playing the games of childhood!

After a characteristically decisive look at the possibilities, young Wrigley invested the few pennies he had in copies of the metropolitan dailies and joined the hard little band of newsies along Park Row.

● The rush and hurry of the big city offered a thousand thrills a day to the boundless enthusiasm and interest of the boy. Everything he saw whetted his hunger for knowledge of the great game of living.

When the job of selling newspapers palled, he tackled odd jobs without number—learning, always learning in the stiff school of experience. Occasional postcards home, saying that he was well and in New York City was the only word his family had from him during that long summer.

His final expulsion from school came that fall when he returned home. After life in the city, the quiet ways of school seemed rather tame, and when his boyish prank of plastering a spoiled pie over an old fashioned brownstone name plate on a building did not meet with the approval of the school authorities, his formal schooling was ended. His father, out of patience at last, refused to attempt to get him back into school, but set him to work in his scouring-soap factory instead.

Here young Wrigley was given one of the hardest manual tasks the factory afforded—stirring the thick soap in the boiling pot with a wooden paddle. Doubtless this heartbreaking toil did much to lay the foundation for the physical vigor that makes him today look like a man of 45.

There aren't many thirteen year old salesmen today, but at that early age Wm. Wrigley, Jr. convinced his father that he could make more money for him by selling than he could by stirring soap for him. The persistence that marks the true salesman landed his first order for him. He literally wore out the dealer he was trying to sell.

● "Well, sonny," the dealer said at last. "I see that I will have to buy some of your soap if I expect to do any business today."

But soon he was sending orders back daily, and this early training did much to give him his keen understanding of humans and their reasons for buying.

The natural gift for advertising that is his asserted itself when he drove through the high-grass towns of Pennsylvania behind a four-horse team with jingling bells on the harness. To put it conservatively, he created a sensation. Everyone came to know the "boy salesman" and his sales mounted steadily. For many years after he was an outstanding figure in the business world a picture of those four horses hung on the wall of his office, reminding him of his first venture into advertising.

These were the years during which the traits of character that have placed him where he is today were being formed. His endless quest for knowledge and experience drew him westward when he was about nineteen years old. The tales of cities sprung up over night, of gold and silver mines, of high adventure, called him strongly.

● But Fortune, in the form of an ill-considered wind that blew his hat through an open window of the train —and with it his ticket— decreed that Kansas City was as far west as he was to get. Once more he was in a strange city with but sixty-five cents in his pocket. After a short period during which he waited table in a cheap restaurant, his knowledge of selling again came to his rescue, and once again he was able to return home well clad and loaded with presents for his family. A few weeks later he was again back on the road selling scouring soap for his father.

The spring of 1891 marked a great turning point in the career of young Bill Wrigley. He was twenty-nine now, and he still was far from accomplishing the things he dreamed of doing. He believed that if he opened a Chicago office, he would have a central place to which the scouring soap could be shipped. Thus he made the first step in improving the distribution of the product he was selling—a step which has been followed by many other long strides which have made him a world wide authority on distribution.

At this time he made another sudden and startling step. With competition growing keener in the soap business, his soap, which retailed for five cents a cake was not taking well with the dealers. The margin of profit was so slender they preferred to carry other higher priced lines. Wrigley met the situation readily enough. He raised the price of the five cent cake to a dime and offered the dealer an umbrella as a premium with every box. From this simple beginning Wrigley developed the premium idea until he was the largest distributor of premiums in the world.

● The umbrella premium produced business in volume, but it was still far short of Wrigley's ambitions. He added a baking powder to his line, and in the face of advice that the idea worked out, he decided to compile a 150 page book and offer it free with a 50 cent can of baking powder. Before long he was distributing the books at the rate of 50,000 a week, and his baking powder sales were so large that he dropped the soap altogether.

A disastrous experience in the premium-offering game followed when a manufacturer with whom he had contracted for a silver-plated filigree cologne bottle, in his haste to turn out large orders, put such a thin coating of silver on the bottles that they were tarnished by the time they were delivered. Wrigley had to make good on practically the entire contract and saw all his accumulated profits swept away.

His next venture proved more successful. He made a deal with a chewing gum company to use the gum as a premium. After a time the gum proved more popular than the baking powder, and he decided to make the gum the recipient of his merchandising efforts. Gum could be shipped cheaply all over the country; all over the world, in fact. For Wrigley was already thinking in terms of world markets.

The premium idea continued to make good. Wrigley decided to make his offers so attractive that the dealers would take the gum to get the premium, if for no other

reason. There followed a steady stream of articles that the dealers used every day—scales, coffee grinders, show cases, cheese cutters, cash registers, desks, scoops, ladders, trucks and nail-pullers. Contracting with the manufacturers for his premiums in huge quantities to get rock-bottom prices, he took tremendous chances on guessing rightly what the dealers would want, but most of the time he *was* right. And in all his offers to the dealers he figured that in addition to the free premium the dealer would make a goodly cash profit from the sale of the gum.

Wrigley learned early that he must figure the dealer's profit, first. Though his own profit might be much smaller than his dealer's, the *many* dealers, each adding a little to his profit, made possible the constant expansion of his operations.

● Wrigley was sales-minded. When other gum companies advertised their gum as an aid to digestion, he arranged to have his gum placed in restaurants next to the cash register, so that patrons paying their checks would have the open boxes before their eyes.

During all this time he was feeling his way toward the great advertising campaigns in which he was later to spend millions upon millions of dollars. In 1897 he tried his first campaign of Outdoor Advertising in a southern locality. Gradually, as his resources increased, he branched into other fields of advertising.

In these early days, he did not attempt to enter the larger markets, but waited until he felt he had sufficient capital to really tackle a big city. In 1902 he made a characteristic plunge; throwing his accumulated earnings of one hundred thousand dollars into a campaign in New York City.

"I didn't even make a ripple on the surface," he admitted afterwards.

He smiled at the failure of a like attempt when he had accumulated another hundred thousand, and determined that the next time he assailed New York that city would know he had been there.

In northern New York there was a territory including the cities of Buffalo, Rochester, and Syracuse where sales were far from satisfactory. His next big campaign was turned loose on this sales desert. He purchased every square foot of available poster advertising space, every vacant space in the street cars of the three cities and contracted for spreads in all the important newspapers. The campaign unloosed a flood of sales that more than paid for it.

"Now I shall tackle New York City, again" he declared. "I'm going back to pick up that two hundred thousand dollars I dropped in the big town."

● And despite the protests of his friends and business associates a quarter of a million dollars' worth of advertising rained about the head and shoulders of New York's citizens. This time New York responded; his former losses were salvaged, and a handsome profit resulted.

The current talk of depression, and the sage advice to advertisers to put forth their efforts during a depression recalls the vision and sheer courage with which Wrigley plunged into the panic of 1907. When other national advertisers were seeking ways of retrenching, Wrigley slipped into New York and in three days bought up a million and a half dollars' worth of advertising space. He followed this up by distributing coupons entitling dealers to a free box of gum when presented to their jobber. For a few weeks nothing happened. Then as dealers found that there was no "catch" to it, they resurrected the coupons out of pigeonholes in their desks, follow-up sales trailed the free distribution, the factory began to hum, and business doubled and trebled.

Wrigley has an unqualified belief in the power of advertising. The millions he has spent attest it; the tremendous business he has built up approves it. But he learned early that the same type of advertising appeal cannot be made to people in widely differing parts of the world.

● He once staged a Chicago campaign in London and it nearly proved disastrous. His posters were seventy-two times the size of the English posters then in use. His spreads in the newspapers rather shocked them, and the offer of giving a box of gum free simply wasn't believed. He had to tone down his advertising and modify his distribution offer so that the dealer could get one box free if he bought one box.

The constant drive to accomplish something led him to purchase Catalina Island, with its five hundred thousand dollar hotel. Not because he wanted something more to glorify himself, but because he wanted to accomplish something—make Catalina a pleasure resort that would be known throughout the country. The island cost him three million dollars, and he purchased the transportation company that connects the island with the mainland. Today hundreds of thousands of tourists and natives of California visit the island every year. In adding to the human happiness of the millions who have visited the island, Wrigley has made money out of the deal, but that has been an incidental to him. His main object—of accomplishing something—making a going concern out of the island—concerned him most.

● When he took over the Cubs baseball team it was hopelessly in the hole. His friends shook their heads sadly, and groaned at the thought of sinking money into that bottomless pit. Yet today the Cubs are known throughout the country. Their games attract immense crowds, and they are paying their owner dividends. For years the team didn't pay, but here again it was because Wrigley knew how to save by putting everything back into the business that brought the team out on top. He had the patience to wait for the fruit to ripen before he attempted to eat it. "Fruit that is not ripe is apt to give the one who eats it a stomach-ache," he shrewdly comments.

His ideas on the rearing of a son are very definite. To Wm. Wrigley, Jr., the greatest school is the school of experience, and although he gave his son, P. K. Wrigley, an excellent formal education, he still kept in close touch with the direction the boy's education was taking him, with the result that today, "P. K." for whom the famous small packages of sugar-coated gum were named, is president of the company, and carrying on the business in a manner that is a source of pride to his father.

● Wm. Wrigley, Jr. still carries out the fundamental, basic ideas that have made his life a happy, successful one. He does not claim to be the sole instigator of the ideas that have made his ventures go. He shifts the wheat from the chaff—again thanks to his wide experience—and unerringly selects the things that are good. He is still full of the joy of doing things, still interested in every human being from elevator boy to millionaire. That interest in humans and the ability to see things from the other fellow's view point has made Wm. Wrigley, Jr. the man he is today.

DAVID ALLEN'S OWN PANELS ARE SEEN BY 10,000,000 people IN THE BRITISH ISLES EVERY DAY

BRITISH OUTDOOR ADVERTISING is best handled by

DAVID ALLEN'S

We offer to American advertisers the largest, most modern outdoor advertising service in Great Britain. Our studios rank among the finest in the British Isles, and we have secured for our clients the work of Ludwig Hohlwein and Septimus Scott. R.O.I.

Only the most efficient machinery and workmen are employed in our printing factories in London and Liverpool. We can claim the most intimate knowledge of British markets, a knowledge founded on half a century's experience in handling National contracts. Our panels in 250 of the principal towns in Great Britain are seen daily by 10 million people.

You can increase your market in the British Isles. We are well equipped to help you.

DAVID ALLEN & SONS, BILLPOSTING LTD
INCORPORATED IN NORTHERN IRELAND
ALLEN HOUSE, BUCKINGHAM GATE, LONDON, S.W.1
ENGLAND
CABLES - ADVANCEMENT LONDON

SPENDING TENDENCIES

● To determine in which sections of the country people are spending money and to advise upon the best merchandising approach to secure a portion of that money is a big responsibility.

Perhaps it is even a bigger responsibility for a magazine to assume the burden of developing a new index for America's merchandising efforts.

Big as this burden and responsibility is, ADVERTISING OUTDOORS feels that with the help of the twelve hundred members of the Outdoor Advertising Association of America who will, within the next few months interview thousands of business men throughout the United States as to merchandising conditions and spending tendency factors, it will be able to do the job.

Readers will be interested in both watching and helping to develop this new merchandising index. If it is being developed to aid the reader in his merchandising efforts, he should be willing to contribute his advice and check the figures with his experience in the various territories. Therefore, everyone is invited to comment both upon the method of deduction and the conclusions reached.

For this issue we are presenting as a result of some three or four hundred interviews a survey of the business conditions in certain localities, together with the

spending tendency reflected through motion picture attendance and habits reflected through sport participation and attendance.

The reason motion pictures have been selected as a spending tendency factor is that practically the same pictures are presented throughout the country. Therefore, with the exception of the very few communities that object to motion pictures, like the few that have no Sunday movies, it is believed that motion picture attendance, being practically a luxury, should reflect the luxury spending tendency of each community.

1   BOSTON, MASS.
December 23rd

GENERAL BUSINESS CONDITIONS: Due to the number of businesses that are maintaining their levels of last year and the large number of new industries that are coming into existence, conditions in Boston while slightly under 1929, are on a level with 1928.

SPORT ATTENDANCE: Using sport attendance as a spending tendency factor we find that Harvard this year had an attendance of 356,000 which while under the 1929 attendance of 410,000 is above the 1928 attendance of 351,000. Hockey attendance in Boston this season seems to indicate the spending tendency of the present season. Boston is supporting in addition to the college teams, several professional teams, chief among which are the Bruins and the Tigers, each playing to packed houses in the new Boston Gardens which has a seating capacity of 20,000.

MOVING PICTURE ATTENDANCE: Moving picture attendance in downtown Boston is approximately 25% less than last year, while in metropolitan Boston which is the real Boston, the attendance is down 10%.

2   MANCHESTER, N. H.
December 17th

GENERAL BUSINESS CONDITIONS: As compared with last year, business is slightly less in volume. Sales are about the same in number, the difference being the class of merchandise being bought. This is the point of view of the fourteen merchants interviewed.

SPORT ATTENDANCE: The attendance at local football games has been the same as in previous years. The only important games are played by the Central High School and inasmuch as they have been the winning team for several years, they have a large following.

MOVING PICTURE ATTENDANCE: It was impossible to get comparative figures but it is acknowledged and stated by the theatrical groups in this city that business is better than they expected.

3   NEW YORK, N. Y.

GENERAL BUSINESS CONDITIONS: Business at present is a little behind last year's volume due to the general nation-wide depression. Because of the diversity of business in New York, the general recession has not been so drastic as in most large cities. New York always enjoys a brisk business during the winter. A large number of wealthy people move into the city from their suburban homes in the winter. Buyers from all over the country come to the city in the winter. Many business representatives attend the numerous conventions—automobile shows—motor boat shows and so forth and of course all these people spend generously while in the metropolis.

4   JERSEY CITY, N. J.

GENERAL BUSINESS CONDITIONS: Interview with Mr. Hirsh Schpoont, President Jersey City Businessmen's Association.

"The merchants of Newark Avenue, Jersey City, have not suffered any considerable loss of business due to the so called general depression, but have found it rather the opposite. That is to say, that people are not buying toys or gifts of a luxurious nature, but rather buy more substantial articles of merchandise.

Interview with Mr. Harry F. O'Mealia, President Bergen Trust Company. "From a banking standpoint I earnestly believe that there is much activity in the shopping districts of our city. This is indicated principally by the fact that immediately following the mailing of checks in payment of our recent Christmas Club, we had a return of deposits in savings accounts of some thirty odd per cent, clearly indicating that this percentage were comfortably situated to the extent that they could afford to lay aside this Christmas saving in a savings account. The other sixty odd per cent that went into general distribution was used for the purchase of substantial articles of merchandise, such as clothing and necessities for the home as was indicated by the endorsements upon the checks received.

Interview with Mr. Edwin B. Lord, Executive Vice President and General Manager, Jersey City Chamber of Commerce.

"From our relations and contact with the merchants and manufacturers of Jersey City, I am firmly of the opinion that business conditions in our city have shown a decided improvement within the last few months, principally during the so called holiday season.

MOVING PICTURE ATTENDANCE: Interview, Manager of State Theatre (Capacity 2400). "We have enjoyed a better year than any time since the opening of the theatre."

Interview, Manager of Loew's Jersey City (capacity 3000). "Business is substantially as good this year as any other year, particularly because we have upheld our high grade of entertainment at attractive prices."

Interview, Manager Stanley Theatre (capacity 5000). "Have not noticed any marked decrease in business of theatre attendance due to the so called business depression, rather proved just the opposite. Some of our individual months in the past year have exceeded capacity by far."

5   BUFFALO, N. Y.
December 18th

GENERAL BUSINESS CONDITIONS: According to a compilation of the local Chamber of Commerce, business shows a decline in practically every line of business except one—flour milling.

SPORT ATTENDANCE: The attendance at local football games showed a loss of 18.2%.

MOVING PICTURE ATTENDANCE: Figures taken from Shea's Buffalo and Shea's Hippodrome, the two largest and best theatres show that the moving picture business in Buffalo has not suffered as badly as in some other cities. This is attributed to the great number of diversified industries. During the first ten months in 1930, there was a decline of 3%. November and December however, show a falling off of 18 to 20%.

6   WILLIAMSPORT, PENNA.
December 15th

GENERAL BUSINESS CONDITIONS: Employment in industry is approximately 10% less in 1930 than for the same period in 1929. The majority of the retail merchants report less volume. A few individual merchants report a slight gain.

MOVING PICTURE ATTENDANCE: According to the best information, the combined attendance at the Rialto and Capitol theatres has been practically equal to the same period in 1929. The attendance at other theatres is off about 5%.

JOHNSTOWN, PENNA.
December 15th

GENERAL BUSINESS CONDITIONS: Department store sales for 1930 are approximately 8% less than in 1929. The same condition prevails for the wholesale trade as far as the survey discloses. Inventories are considerable, but no estimate can be secured until after January 1st.

The soft coal business is recovering again, and the volume for the year may equal that of 1929. Approximately $2,500,000 worth of improvements to the Cambria plant of the Bethlehem Steel Company at Johnstown were completed during 1930. The Bethlehem Steel Company normally employs 13,000 men. On December 15th, their payroll numbered only 5,500 men. Production is only 40% as against 85% at the same time in 1929 which was the highest in several years previous.

Freight receipts are 30% less in 1930 than they were in the same period, 1929.

SPORT ATTENDANCE—Football during the Fall months attracted 25% more people than in 1929. This was partly due to the introduction of night football.

MOVING PICTURE ATTENDANCE: The moving picture theatres reported an increase in attendance of 6 to 8% in 1930 as compared with 1929.

8   HARRISBURG, PENNA.
December 23rd

GENERAL BUSINESS CONDITIONS: Business conditions in this district have improved in the last thirty days so that business men claim at the present time that it is almost normal with the exception of radio which has fallen down considerably below that of 1929.

SPORT ATTENDANCE: Attendance at the football games during 1930 was off approximately 8% from that of 1929.

MOVING PICTURE ATTENDANCE: During the past two months, moving picture attendance has been very good and will compare favorably with that of 1929.

9   WILMINGTON, DELAWARE
December 17th

GENERAL BUSINESS CONDITIONS: Interviews with several leading merchants.

Miller Bros., largest furniture dealers. "We are making money and have no complaint to make. We have had, of course, our share of customers out of work and on short time who could not meet their obligations as fast as they would like, but upon figuring this, we find

that such delinquent accounts amount to only a fraction of 1%, so that the financial depression has not affected us to any considerable extent.

Finkel's Credit Clothing Store. "This constant talk about the lack of employment has done more harm than the lack of employment itself.

C. L. Pierce & Co., largest plumbers in Wilmington. "We have had a very good year. At present we are employing sixty men and are keeping them busy. We do not expect to lay off any, and are very well satisfied with the year 1930."

Farmers' Mutual Fire Insurance Company. "We have no complaint to make regarding the business done by our company in 1930. On account of our inspection and fire prevention service, our company is in stronger and healthier condition than at any time in its history. We look forward to the coming year with confidence."

George W. McCaulley & Sons Co., electric fixtures and tile setters. "Business leaders tell us that we should not compare the year 1930 with that of 1929 as 1929 was exceptional and should not be used as a criterion.

Diamond State Window Shade Company. "Business has been exceptionally good with us. We have done more work this year than ever before. Not only has it been good, but it continues to be good. We have taken on extra men this week, and will have to put on more next week. We have sufficient work to keep us busy from now till next April."

Harry Braunstein, ladies' apparel store. "Business at our establishment is going ahead of last year. The outlook for the future is favorable."

Delaware Power & Light Company. "Our merchandise sales for 1929, eleven months, was $299,447.19, merchandise sales for eleven months, 1930, $386,682.69 or an increase of 29%.

MOVING PICTURE ATTENDANCE: Warner Brothers who control most of the moving picture theatres in Wilmington state that attendance is now equal to last year's figures. During the summer it fell off to the extent of about 5%.

10   CUMBERLAND, MD.
December 17th

GENERAL BUSINESS CONDITIONS: The artificial silk industry in our locality is operating on a basis estimated to be greater than last year by 25%, due to the placing in operation of additional working units. Automobile tire and rubber manufacturing is at present operating on approximately a 70% capacity. Railroad car loadings in line with the general average, are estimated to be off 15%.

SPORT ATTENDANCE: Football attendance for 1930 is estimated to be double that 1929. This is due to the local awakening interest in high school football.

MOVING PICTURE ATTENDANCE: The various managers of the theatres on being interviewed stated that the attendance for 1930 has suffered an approximate loss of 20% from the total attendance of 1929.

11   LYNCHBURG, VA.
December 16th

GENERAL BUSINESS CONDITIONS: The manufacturing business in the locality has fallen off somewhat but most of the dealers and merchants report that business is about the same as for the same period last year.

Automobile registrations are more and consequently gasoline consumption is considerably greater than last year.

MOVING PICTURE ATTENDANCE: The average daily attendance at local theatres is approximately three thousand which makes the attendance off about 15% as compared with the same period in 1929.

12   WINSTON-SALEM, N. C.
December 16th

GENERAL BUSINESS CONDITIONS: Tobacco of which this city is the world's largest producer of the manufactured product is being produced in a greater volume than last year. This commodity represents over 65% of the community's industrial wealth. National and seasonal depressions have affected the furniture, underwear and hosiery industries, whose products are also produced in large amounts in this city. Blankets, another major industry, are being produced in a greater volume than last year.

SPORT ATTENDANCE: College football is not represented. The attendance at games between the local high schools and nearby institutions has been quite a good deal in excess of last year.

MOVING PICTURE ATTENDANCE: The attendance at moving pictures has been about the same for 1930 as compared with 1929.

13   CHARLESTON, S. C.
December 22nd

GENERAL BUSINESS CONDITIONS: Business conditions in 1930 as compared with 1929 in and around the trading area are about the same. This is due to the fact that this section is largely engaged in truck farming. It is also a point of export for cotton and tobacco which due to the large crop this year has been somewhat above normal. Wholesalers, distributing groceries, drugs and various commodities, report practically normal local business.

SPORT ATTENDANCE: Attendance at football games held during the Fall season has been practically up to the 1929 average.

MOVING PICTURE ATTENDANCE: Attendance at moving picture shows has recently increased in Charleston.

14   SAVANNAH, GA.
December 15th

GENERAL BUSINESS CONDITIONS: Comparing 1930 with 1929 in the Savannah trading area, business both wholesale and retail shows about a 10% increase for 1930. This figure was obtained by a survey made by the Chamber of Commerce.

SPORT ATTENDANCE: Attendance at football games shows a 33.5% increase in 1930.

MOVING PICTURE ATTENDANCE: Moving picture attendance in line with the general good conditions shown above, shows an increase of 10% for the chain theatres and 25% for the one individual theatre.

15   ATLANTA, GA.
December 20th

GENERAL BUSINESS CONDITIONS: According to B. S. Barker, Secretary of the Chamber of Commerce, more than twelve local firms have reported to him that their 1930 business exceeds their 1929 volume. Mr. Eugene R. Black, Governor of the Federal Reserve Bank in Atlanta, says, "Our industries are on a sound basis and their products yield a cash return twice as large as our agricultural products.

Mr. W. J. Weinman, Thompson, Weinman & Page Mining Companies, said that the outlook for their firm is much better than it was in November of 1929.

SPORT ATTENDANCE: Attendance at football games during the Fall was approximately 25% off comparing 1930 with 1929.

MOVING PICTURE ATTENDANCE: While no accurate figures were gathered, it is reported to be off from 25 to 30%.

16   SELMA, ALA.
December 17th

GENERAL BUSINESS CONDITIONS: Seven wholesale concerns were visited and one of them reported a gain in 1930 over 1929 of 5%; another reported a volume about the same; one reported a loss of 5%; another reported a loss of 25% and the two remaining ones estimated their loss at approximately 35%.

MOVING PICTURE ATTENDANCE: Moving picture attendance at the two local theatres shows a loss of about 30% as compared with 1929.

17   COLUMBUS, OHIO
December 15th

GENERAL BUSINESS CONDITIONS: At the present time, business is about 10% off when compared to the same period in 1929.

SPORT ATTENDANCE: Attendance at football games has been approximately 20% off. Locally this was attributed to the fact that Ohio State got off to a bad start in football instead of poor business.

MOVING PICTURE ATTENDANCE: At the time of this report, it was estimated by the various theatre managers that attendance in 1930 as compared with 1929 is off from 12 to 15%.

18   MARION, INDIANA

GENERAL BUSINESS CONDITIONS: Business is reported to be about 10% higher in 1930 as in 1929. Employment is 86% normal. This figure is based on full time employment, and not on any part time methods to meet the emergency.

MOVING PICTURE ATTENDANCE: Attendance at moving picture theatres is reported to be 90% normal.

19   KALAMAZOO, MICHIGAN
December 12th

GENERAL BUSINESS CONDITIONS: According to Chamber of Commerce officials and the president of the Retail Dealers Ass'n, conditions look promising for an increase in business over the previous year.

SPORT ATTENDANCE: Attendance at local football games during 1930 indicates an increase. The Western State Teachers College which has a very large athletic field, reports an increase of 35%. Kalamazoo reports an increase of 20%. The two high schools report increases of 50% and 35%.

MOVING PICTURE ATTENDANCE: Theatre business is reported to have increased 2% for the last part of 1930 as compared with the last part of 1929.

20   MILWAUKEE, WIS.
December 12th

GENERAL BUSINESS CONDITIONS: It is reported that the retail business in general has held up quite well as far as necessity and stable goods are concerned. However, the sale of luxury goods such as jewelry, furs and so forth has dropped off considerably in 1930 as compared with 1929.

SPORT ATTENDANCE: Local statistics show that local attendance at football games has been almost double that of 1929. This is partly due to the charity games played.

MOVING PICTURE ATTENDANCE: The attendance at local theatres has fallen off at the outlying theatres but has held up quite well in the downtown first-run houses.

21   PEORIA, ILLINOIS
December 16th

GENERAL BUSINESS CONDITIONS: Business interviewed as follows: Electrical, 5% less than in 1929; department stores (largest) 10% less, (second largest) 5% less; plumbing, normal; largest hotel, 10% less, second largest, just a small per cent off; leading dairy products firm, 10% off.

SPORT ATTENDANCE: Attendance at local football games is 25% more than in 1929.

MOVING PICTURE ATTENDANCE: Moving picture theatres report the poorest year for some time. Two theatres have closed since 1929.

22   BURLINGTON, IOWA
December 12th

GENERAL BUSINESS CONDITIONS: Burlington and the surrounding trade territory for the last months of 1930 is reported as being slightly under that of 1929. However, Burlington is in a portion of the country that has been very little hurt by the general business depression, and most merchants feel that 1931 will bring them back to at least 1928 sales volume.

SPORT ATTENDANCE: Football attendance during the fall months of 1930 was almost double that of the same period in 1929. This was mainly brought about by the introduction of night football.

MOVING PICTURE ATTENDANCE: Reports show that Burlington theatres are having an increased attendance.

23   DAVENPORT, IOWA
December 18th

GENERAL BUSINESS CONDITIONS: After contacting sixty people the following comparison was arrived at:

    Advertising Specialties & Direct Mail—20% less
    Hotels—10% less
    Radio—No change
    Jewelry—Slight Increase
    Department Stores—10% less
    Men's Clothing—30% less
    Automotive—10% less
    Cafeterias—No change
    Cafes—30% less.

SPORT ATTENDANCE: According to figures compiled, there is a slight decrease.

MOVING PICTURE ATTENDANCE: Moving picture theatres report a decrease of 10% in attendance in 1930 as compared with 1929.

24   LA CROSSE, WIS.
December 17th

GENERAL BUSINESS CONDITIONS: Business is not nearly as good for the year 1930 as it was in the same period in 1929. The wholesale grocery business is the nearest to normal, reporting a decrease of 7%. A wholesale distributor of smoked and canned fish, mayonnaise and bottle product shows a slight increase in distribution of commodities but a lessened money volume on account of decrease in prices. Retail shoe dealer advises his business is off 18% as compared with 1929; a Chevrolet dealer's business is off 25%; a wholesale candy and cookie distributor advises, candy shows a decrease of 30% and cookies, 8%; retail furniture has a decrease of 25%; radios, musical instruments, 20%.

SPORT ATTENDANCE: The La Crosse Teachers College football attendance was off 40%.

MOVING PICTURE ATTENDANCE: Attendance at all local moving picture theatres has dropped off considerably; however, no accurate figures were available.

25 DULUTH, MINN.
December 20th

GENERAL BUSINESS CONDITIONS: According to Mr. Ray L. Secard of the Duluth Chamber of Commerce the following gives a picture of the conditions of that city. "Grouping the most important lines of endeavor, which may be considered as retail, wholesale and jobbing, manufacturing, mining, transportation, banking and public utilities, it is believed that the average of all these businesses is between eighty to eighty-five per cent normal. The recent trend is showing a slight improvement.

"A prominent industrialist at the Head of Lake Superior says that the larger manufacturing industries in Duluth are moving slightly above normal, with the smaller industries from seventy to eighty per cent normal. In the jobbing business, the food concerns are doing a normal business or slightly above."

26 MASON CITY, IOWA
December 16th

GENERAL BUSINESS CONDITIONS: Following are reports from various manufacturers and business houses. "Jacob E. Deckers & Sons (packers) enjoyed a good year and are putting on extra help. The American Beet Sugar Company will have the longest run this season in their history. Our brick and tile plants recently changed hands and are now controlled by The United Light and Power Corporation.
MOVING PICTURE ATTENDANCE: There is about a ten per cent increase in moving picture attendance.

27 DES MOINES, IOWA
December 18th

GENERAL BUSINESS CONDITIONS: The average retail sales covering all commodities and lines has to date this year averaged 7% less than the same period to date in 1929. The month of November was 8% less than November of 1929 and statistics to date show that December is about 7% less than it was at the same time in 1929. Christmas shopping could probably be credited to increase the percentage for December so that 1929 and 1930 would be about equal.
SPORT ATTENDANCE: The business office of Drake University stated that the total average attendance at local football games in 1930 was about equal that of the 1929 season.
MOVING PICTURE ATTENDANCE: Theatre attendance during the month preceding the report exceeded the attendance of 1929 by a fair margin.

28 OMAHA, NEBRASKA
January 3rd

GENERAL BUSINESS CONDITIONS: There is an increase in the receipts of grain and livestock but this increase does not signify added income because of lower prices. The wholesale and manufacturing interests report about the same volume of business but because of reduced prices of articles, there has been a decrease in income. The retail trade reports a volume of sales far above normal and the cash income within 4% of 1929.
SPORT ATTENDANCE: There was a decrease in attendance at Creighton University football games.

29 LINCOLN, NEBRASKA
December 13th

GENERAL BUSINESS CONDITIONS: It is estimated that business in general is off about 10%. Some merchants report just as large a volume but because of a decrease in prices, their money volume will not be as large as in 1929.
SPORT ATTENDANCE: No figures were available but the attendance at football games at the University of Nebraska was much below that of 1929.
MOVING PICTURE ATTENDANCE: Five moving picture theatres have been closed since 1929. However, the remaining ones seem to have about the same volume of business as they had in 1929.

30 ABERDEEN, S. DAK.
December 15th

GENERAL BUSINESS CONDITIONS: Business in this territory is not as good in 1930 as it was in 1929. It is thought that business could be better than in 1929 if it were not for the credit situation which has tightened up very much during the past year. There is practically no problem of unemployment.
SPORT ATTENDANCE: Football games locally were about four times as well attended in 1930 as in 1929 which was due solely to changing to night football.
MOVING PICTURE ATTENDANCE: Moving picture attendance has fallen off about 50%.

31 ST. JOSEPH, MO.
December 19th

GENERAL BUSINESS CONDITIONS: Conferences with Chamber of Commerce officials both in St. Joseph and surrounding towns brought out the fact that for the early part of 1930 and up to about the 1st of November, business conditions were at a rather low ebb, both wholesale and retail.
SPORT ATTENDANCE: Attendance at football games held during the Fall of 1930 is reported to be approximately the same as for those in 1929.
MOVING PICTURE ATTENDANCE: Investigation among the managers of the leading theatres indicates

that there has been some falling off in the attendance at local theatres. It was impossible to secure a figure as to the exact percentage.

32   JOPLIN, MO.
December 15th

GENERAL BUSINESS CONDITIONS: Business as a whole is off in 1930 as compared to 1929. In ladies' ready-to-wear business, the higher and cheaper priced merchandise is off while the medium priced merchandise is ahead of last year's business. The volume in furs is much greater this year because of the low prices. Men's clothing is off about 20% and foodstuffs are holding their own.

SPORT ATTENDANCE: There was a small decrease in the attendance at local football games but the cause could probably be attributed to a losing team rather than the depression.

MOVING PICTURE ATTENDANCE: The better moving picture theatres are off in attendance about 20%, and the others are holding their own.

33   SPRINGFIELD, MO.
December 17th

GENERAL BUSINESS CONDITIONS: Business prospects look much more favorable for 1931 than they did for 1930 at the same time in 1929.

SPORT ATTENDANCE: Attendance at football games at the two colleges and high schools averaged 12% better attendance in 1930 than in 1929.

34   HUTCHINSON, KANSAS
December 17th

GENERAL BUSINESS CONDITIONS: Hutchinson and its trade territory have not experienced a depression to any great extent. An automobile company reports that for the month of November and up to the time of this report, their business was 50% better than in 1929. A bottling company reports that volume at the time of the report was not quite up to a year ago, but that they will show an increase of 20% for the entire year. The Hutchinson Chamber of Commerce reports the following: "Retail sales for the first eleven months of 1929 show a loss of from eight to ten per cent in value which, in many lines, is more than offset by the reduction in price. Sales by wholesale establishments for the eleven months ending December 1, 1930 as compared with the first eleven months in 1929 show a decrease of from twelve and a half to seventeen per cent, or an average of approximately fifteen per cent in value.

SPORT ATTENDANCE: Attendance at football games in 1930 is 35 to 50% greater than in 1929.

MOVING PICTURE ATTENDANCE: Attendance at moving picture theatres is on a par with last year.

35   SHREVEPORT, LA.
December 17th

GENERAL BUSINESS CONDITIONS: While no figures of comparison were sent in, yet it seems that business in 1930 would be equal to that in 1928 and would fall short about 15% of that in 1929.

SPORT ATTENDANCE: Centenary College reports a decrease of 20% in 1930 as compared with the same football season in 1929.

MOVING PICTURE ATTENDANCE: There has been a decrease of about 25% in moving picture attendance as compared with 1929.

37   CORPUS CHRISTI, TEXAS
December 17th

GENERAL BUSINESS CONDITIONS: There was a gain in cotton production over 1929. Bank statements show more than $1,000,000 increase in deposits in 1930 as compared with 1929. There has been twice as many boats and twice as many tons of freight handled in 1930 as compared with 1929. It is estimated that 5,000 cars of vegetables will be shipped between November 15th and January 30th.

MOVING PICTURE ATTENDANCE: Attendance in 1930 is on a par with that in 1929.

38   SAN ANTONIO, TEXAS
December 16th

GENERAL BUSINESS CONDITIONS: Business in 1930 has been on a par with 1929. The outlook for 1931 seems to be better than it was for 1930.

SPORT ATTENDANCE: The attendance at football games in 1930 as compared with 1929 has been larger.

MOVING PICTURE ATTENDANCE: Comparing attendance in 1930 with that in 1929, we find there is a 20% decrease.

39   AUSTIN, TEXAS
December 26th

GENERAL BUSINESS CONDITIONS: Business is reported to be off about 9%.

40   WACO, TEXAS
December 17th

GENERAL BUSINESS CONDITIONS: There has been a decrease in the volume in 1930 as compared with 1929.

41   BROWNWOOD, TEXAS
December 15th

GENERAL BUSINESS CONDITIONS: Business in 1930 as compared with business at the same time in 1929 is 10% lower among the better class of business houses and about 17% lower among the lower class of business houses. This condition exists fairly close within a radius of 50 miles of Brownwood. Business, when this report was made, was about 10% ahead of the same period in 1929.

SPORT ATTENDANCE: Attendance at local football games was 17.5% greater in 1930 than it was for 1929. This was in part attributed to good weather conditions and better highways.

MOVING PICTURE ATTENDANCE: Attendance at moving picture theatres increased 5% over that for 1929.

42   AMARILLO, TEXAS
December 18th

GENERAL BUSINESS CONDITIONS: After interviewing merchants in the towns around Amarillo, and in Amarillo itself, business was found to be about equal to that of 1929, with a small percentage of increase in unpaid accounts.

SPORT ATTENDANCE: In comparing the attendance at local football games, the following were obtained: 1929, 31,000; 1930, 41,000.

MOVING PICTURE ATTENDANCE: Five moving picture theatres reported a decrease of 10% in attendance in 1930 as compared with 1929.

43   EL PASO, TEXAS
December 15th

GENERAL BUSINESS CONDITIONS: Business, generally, in retail lines is off about 15% as compared with 1929. Department stores are only off about 6%. The building permits for 1930 are $1,000,000 less than in 1929.

SPORT ATTENDANCE: Attendance at local football games is on a par with that of 1929.

MOVING PICTURE ATTENDANCE: The attendance at moving picture theatres is 22% higher than in 1929.

44   CASPER, WYOMING
December 19th

GENERAL BUSINESS CONDITIONS: Interviews with merchants, wholesalers, jobbers, etc., reveal that for the first ten months of 1930, each month has had an increase in business of not less than 5% and in some cases as high as 50% with the exception of the automobile dealers, lumber yards and clothing stores.

SPORT ATTENDANCE: Comparing football attendance in 1930 with that in 1929, there was an increase of 20%.

MOVING PICTURE ATTENDANCE: There has been a decrease of 15% in attendance at moving picture theatres in 1930 as compared with 1929. This in part might be due to the remodeling and refinishing of several theatres.

45   BILLINGS, MONTANA
December 13th

GENERAL BUSINESS CONDITIONS: Interviews with the different merchants give the following information: Mr. Corbett, manager of Bowen's Clothing Store, the largest men's and boys' furnishing store, advises us that business is very, very good. Mr. Koppe of the Koppe Jewelry Company says that the actual sales are the same as last year. Mr. Albin of the Hart-Albin Company (the largest department store in the state) advises their sales figure the same as last year so far for December, but that actually more units have been sold than in 1929. He stated that November showed a slight decrease but that October was an increase of 10%.

An interview with three of the wholesale grocery concerns here, indicates that business conditions are very good.

SPORT ATTENDANCE: Attendance at local high-school football games has been double that of 1929. This might be due in part to the expenditure of $15,000 in two years for a football field.

MOVING PICTURE ATTENDANCE: Mr. O'Keefe, owner of the three theatres advises that business is about the same as last year up to this time.

46   HAVRE, MONTANA
December 14th

GENERAL BUSINESS CONDITIONS: Business is reported to be 20% less in 1930 than in 1929.

SPORT ATTENDANCE: Attendance at local football was approximately the same in 1930 as in 1929 according to figures of the local Chamber of Commerce.

MOVING PICTURE ATTENDANCE: Attendance at moving picture theatres is approximately 5% less in 1930 than in 1929.

47   HELENA, MONTANA
December 21st

GENERAL BUSINESS CONDITIONS: Interviews with representative business men give the conditions as follows: Addison K. Lusk, Gen. Mgr. of the Mont. Record-Herald. "Speaking for Helena and its trading territory, we say without doubt that prospects are good for 1931 and base that statement on the following facts.

Increase in local advertising in this newspaper for November over the same period in 1929; no shrinkage in bank deposits, savings or demand; pay-roll increases for state and federal employees; construction program for 1931 and gold mining activities.

E. J. Murphy of the Murphy Wholesale Grocery Co. "We feel that we are in a position to state facts regarding the wholesale grocery business of Helena and that part of Montana which we consider the Helena territory.

In brief statistics show that food stuffs have declined from 15 to 18% below a year ago (throughout the country) whereas the wholesale business in this immediate territory is running equal or but slightly less than a year ago.

E. C. Smith, Sec'y of Smith Motor Co. (Chrysler Dealers): "Our experience for the past five months is that our business has been much better than in the same period for 1929 and in some respects better than any previous year for the past five.

A. T. Hibbard, Cashier, Union Bank & Trust Co. (Associated with the Northwest Bancorporation) "Money is not 'tight' in this territory. There is a surplus available for loans to any legitimate enterprise."

A. T. Hibbard, Sec'y and Mgr. of the Montana Livestock Loan Company says of that industry: "While there has been a more severe price deflation (in live stock) than in 1920-21, every grower is operating on a more economic basis than in a great many years.

According to W. C. Whipps, Sec'y of the Montana State Highway Commission, there will be a material increase in highway construction and contract expenditure this coming year, and this territory will receive its proportion. This will bring direct added revenue as well as indirect revenue due to increased travel.

MOVING PICTURE ATTENDANCE: Mr. C. W. Eckhardt, Mgr. of the Marlow Theatre says, "No complaint to make. Business is better than ever."

48   POCATELLO, IDAHO
December 13th

GENERAL BUSINESS CONDITIONS: Business is about 8 to 10% less in 1930 than in 1929. Conditions were better for buying and there was not the corresponding decrease in selling and this means that the margin of profit is slightly above that of 1929.

SPORT ATTENDANCE: Attendance at football games was just a little less in 1930 than in 1929.

MOVING PICTURE CONDITIONS: There was an increase in the attendance at moving picture theatres of 10 to 12% in 1930 as compared with 1929.

49 ᵀ   SEATTLE, WASHINGTON
December 17th

GENERAL BUSINESS CONDITIONS: From contacts with the retail trade, business is about 93% normal in 1930 as compared with 1929.

SPORT ATTENDANCE: At the University of Washington, there was an increase of 25% in the attendance at 1930 football games as compared with 1929. The high schools and semi-pro games showed similar increases.

MOVING PICTURE ATTENDANCE: Seattle supports 57 theatres with a total attendance each week of 125,000 people. Business is reported to be on a level with last year.

GALVESTON, TEXAS
December 24th

GENERAL BUSINESS CONDITIONS: Business conditions in 1930 as compared with 1929 are off from 5 to 15%.

SPORT ATTENDANCE: Attendance at local football games shows an increase of 20%.

MOVING PICTURE ATTENDANCE: There is a decrease of 19% in moving picture attendance in 1930 as compared with 1929.

COLUMBUS, GA.
December 16th

GENERAL BUSINESS CONDITIONS: According to J. Ralston Cargill, Secretary and Treasurer of the Columbus Chamber of Commerce, conditions in 1930 are not quite up to the volume of business in 1929. This is financially. However, the number of articles sold is about the same. The change has been in the price grade.

SPORT ATTENDANCE: Football attendance in Columbus is a little off as compared with 1929. This is due to a lesser number of games rather than attendance at individual games.

MOVING PICTURE ATTENDANCE: Theatre owners in Columbus advise that attendance is better than in the same period in 1929.

NASHVILLE, TENN.
December 18th

GENERAL BUSINESS CONDITIONS: Despite general economic depression and local conditions aggravated by the failure of a large bond house and several banks as well as the forced merger of other banks, business in Nashville and the surrounding territory does not compare badly with that of 1929.

Business men and business men's associations in Nashville are looking forward to 1931 with an optimism that seems well grounded. Retail trade in Nashville according to the reports of the sixth Federal Reserve District up to November shows only 4% less in sales than during the first ten months of 1929.

Unemployment is less in Nashville than in any other city in the United States for a city with a population of 100,000 or greater.

SPORT ATTENDANCE: Attendance at university football games fell off approximately 20%. This is partially due to a weak schedule.

MOVING PICTURE ATTENDANCE: Moving picture theatre managers estimate the loss in attendance in 1930 as compared with 1929 to be approximately 15 or 20%.

ACTUAL FUTURE BUSINESS: The Southern Borden Company has announced a 20% expansion of its investment for 1931. The building trades have announced a big program for the next few months.

Outdoor Advertising of 1300 B. C.

An Egyptian wall painting from the Necroplis of Thebes,
XIXth dynasty of Pharaoh Mienptah - Hotephimat.

THE THRILL
OF
ACCOMPLISHMENT

is the reward when dreams take shape. And we feel that
we are doing something different in the trade magazine
field, when we make Advertising Outdoors the kind of
magazine it is. Each month there will be further improvements and refinements; more interesting articles;
more of value to you as one of our readers. To make
sure that you won't miss a single copy, send your three
dollars today for a year's subscription.

ADVERTISING OUTDOORS
165 W. WACKER DRIVE
CHICAGO

Naturally, we are not entirely
impartial nor disinterested in our
viewpoint of Outdoor Advertising
and Foster and Kleiser service.

But many advertising agencies
and advertisers have found our
representatives genuinely helpful
because of specialized knowledge
of Outdoor Advertising, and its
place in their advertising plans.

AT LOWEST COST PER THOUSAND CIRCULATION

Foster and Kleiser
COMPANY
GENERAL OFFICES: SAN FRANCISCO
Operating plants in CALIFORNIA
WASHINGTON, OREGON *and* ARIZONA
Offices in NEW YORK *and* CHICAGO

NATIONWIDE OUTDOOR ADVERTISING

UTDOOR
ADVERTISING

People Are Markets!
Where People Are—There Is
Your Market.

To the genius of inventors and the progress of science goes the credit for releasing today's mothers, fathers, daughters and sons from former home-tied toils.

To Outdoor Advertising, however, is due the credit of a vision equal to the progress of things . . . a vision that has kept this potential advertising force in step with the need for constant, mass appeal in order that mass demand shall keep alive the rivet-gun tempo of today's commerce.

Today, the masses are out-of-doors . . most of the time!

WALKER & CO.

Advertising Outdoors

A magazine devoted to the interests of the Outdoor Advertiser

VOL. 2, No. 2

CONTENTS for FEBRUARY 1931

Harold L. Eves
Editor

Ralph B. Patch, *Associate Editor*
James P. Dobyns, *Advertising Manager*

Eastern Advertising Representatives:
Walworth and Wormser,
420 Lexington Ave., New York City.

Western Advertising Representatives:
Dwight Early,
100 N. La Salle St., Chicago

ADVERTISING OUTDOORS is published on the 1st of every month by the Outdoor Advertising Association of America, Inc., 165 W. Wacker Drive, Chicago, Ill. Telephone Randolph 1692. Harold L. Eves, Editor and Manager.

Subscriptions for the United States, Cuba, Porto Rico, Hawaii and the Philippines, $3.00 a year in advance; Mexico and Canada, $3.25; for all other countries, $3.50. Thirty cents the copy. Make all checks, money orders, etc., payable to Outdoor Advertising Association of America, Inc.

Entered as second-class matter, March 31st, 1930, at the Post Office at Chicago, Ill., under the act of March 3, 1879, by Outdoor Advertising Association of America, Inc. Printed in U. S. A.

TELLING A MESSAGE —
not JUST FILLING SPACE

LONG ago sales managers learned that their salesmen could not produce large volumes of orders by just calling and saying "Do you want to buy something today?" About that time they made a difference between the term solicitor and salesman. A solicitor asked for orders—a salesman sold goods.

It's about time that the advertising profession developed a word to substitute for the word advertising when applied to messages that only say "John Brown is in the plumbing business; his address is such and such."

Too much of our advertising copy might be classified under the head "space fillers" instead of "advertising messages." Too often an advertisement, regardless of whether it be outdoor, newspaper or magazine copy, is prepared by two or three men sitting around a table, thinking more of design and layout than of the actual message. One will state what he thinks is a merchandising fact. If he talks loud enough and long enough the advertisement will probably be based upon his assumption—and likely as not, his assumption, if not wrong, is at least far fetched.

A doctor doesn't give medicine simply to keep the druggist busy. Neither should an advertiser use "space" just so that some advertising medium can exist and so that he can have the pride of seeing his name. The doctor carefully analyzes the patient's troubles—and then determines just how the medicine should be prepared to best remedy the patient's ailments.

The only difference is that we do have a few healthy people without ailments—but very few businesses without merchandising problems. Most of our businesses do need medicine of some kind. The poster panel or the magazine or newspaper page is only the bottle into which the advertising manager pours his "medicine" for "transportation."

But in preparing our "medicine" or our message we should first carefully consider just what problem or "ailment" our patient is suffering from and then plan some sort of message that will actually cure him.

COOPERATIVE ADVERTISING
Industry's Battle Line
by Fred Millis
President, Millis Advertising Company

● Co-operative advertising is a significant new development of modern merchandising. In 1915, four trade
associations spent a total of $40,000 in this type of cam-
paign; by 1929, close to one hundred such groups were
investing over $25,000,000 annually in co-operative mag-
azine, newspaper, radio and outdoor advertising. This
tremendous growth came about normally and without
any outside pressure—in other words, the industry
members themselves initiated these various campaigns
because of a keen realization of the need for industry
selling.

● The "big" men in every industry are the men who
are backing these co-operative programs. They have
the future well-being of their own particular industry
at heart, for they appreciate that an individual concern
cannot prosper unless its industry prospers. Thus we
find firms like Kroehler, Simmons, Karpen, Armstrong,
Showers and Heywood-Wakefield backing the National
Home Furnishings Program; firms like Procter & Gamble and American Laundry Machine Company backing
the Laundryowners' campaign; Eastman Kodak the
moving spirit in the Photographers' campaign; firms
like Mueller, Pillsbury, Foulds and Quaker Oats sup-

*Fred Millis, President,
Millis Advertising
Company,
Indianapolis, Indiana.*

porting the National Macaroni campaign. When concerns of this calibre support a movement of this kind
and give liberally of their money to its success, there is
evidence of the basic soundness of the co-operative idea.

● Briefly, co-operative advertising recognizes that in
these days of over-production and under-consumption,
no man has enough money to satisfy all his wants. He
must decide, then, which he will satisfy and which he
will neglect. With seventy cents of the average income

*This attractive poster uses warm colors to convey the
impression of ease and comfort. Few local advertisers could afford to use design of this quality individually.*

The Modern Mother *knows*

THE LAUNDRY
is her most
valuable helper

dollar requisitioned for the necessities of life, obviously the surplus will be spent on those things which the individual *wants most*. And we know that he is very apt to want most the things which have been *sold best*.

Advertising by a single manufacturer, distributor or retailer rarely attempts to sell the *idea* behind a product or service. It is more likely to urge the buyer: "When you are in the market for this class of merchandise, buy mine," and then cite reasons for the superiority of that particular brand.

The co-operative campaign, on the other hand, does not assume that Mr. or Mrs. or Miss Consumer is in the market for the product or service of that industry. Instead, it *sells* the potential buyer on the fundamental need for what the industry has to offer. Thus it creates new customers, new volume, for those in the industry, in place of merely intensifying the competition for the already existing buyers.

● As Merle Thorpe, editor of Nation's Business, has so ably pointed out, the fight is no longer the Smith Furniture Store against the Jones Furniture Store, or the Blank Davenport against the Blink. The issue in the family buying conference is not, "Which kind of new davenport shall we buy, and where shall we buy it?" but rather, "Shall we buy a new davenport *at all*, or shall we make the old one do and get a new fur coat for Daughter?" That is the kind of thing that is coming up constantly in every home—that is what has brought about the modern competition, *between industries*.

Sensing the growing importance of this kind of advertising, our organization some six years ago gave up all other accounts to specialize exclusively in the co-operative field. We have invested for clients some $30,000,000 in various media and tie-ups, all along the lines of selling an industry idea rather than the product of any single firm within that industry. In each case, the co-operative campaigns we have handled or are now handling originated spontaneously among the leaders of the respective industries, and this agency entered the picture only at the specific request of those who

One of the posters used by the Laundryowners' National Association. The use of the figures in close-up makes them much more effective than if a more distant view had been used.

were fathering the contemplated group program. I mention this fact merely to show that this type of advertising is no flash in the pan, fostered by forced, high-pressure methods, but a healthy development that is destined for an even more important place in the merchandising plans of the future.

● Outdoor advertising has formed an essential element in our plans for a number of the co-operative campaigns we have handled, notably the "Say It With Flowers" campaign of the Society of American Florists; the National Home Furnishings Program; and the campaign of the Laundryowners National Association. In each of these cases, the purpose of the outdoor displays has been to provide a strong local tie-up for the subscribing retailer with the national advertising effort.

Each of the three accounts I have mentioned is of the joint-sponsorship type, supported by retailers as well as producers—or, in the case of the Laundry campaign, by the machinery and supply allies. Thus the retailer who subscribes to such a campaign must identify himself with the national magazine advertising in order to direct the local results toward himself. A general campaign selling the idea of buying flowers, for example, will benefit all florists; the subscribing retailer must localize the message, and tie it in with his own place of business, if he is to make his investment pay maximum dividends.

We have found outdoor advertising one of the most effective methods of providing this local tie-up. By repeating the message embodied in the magazine copy, and at the same time giving a prominent display to the local dealer's name, the poster impresses upon the minds of prospects where they can go in their own town to get the thing they have seen advertised in the magazines.

● The link between the nation-wide co-operative campaign and the local dealer is the campaign emblem. In the case of the Home Furnishings Industry this is a shield-shaped device carrying the slogan, "First furnish your home—it tells what you are." The Society of American Florists uses the slogan, "Say It With Flowers" with a distinctive emblem which is placed on the subscribing florist's show-window. The Laundryowners National Association employs the phrase, "Let the Laundry Do It." Since this phrase, slogan or emblem as the case may be is always prominently featured in the magazine advertising, the local subscriber thus secures a positive identity through his posters—in addition to their effect upon those who may not have seen the publication campaign.

● The poster ideas for each of our clients using this tie-up are created in the agency by the same men who develop the magazine advertising. This gives us a consistency and continuity of appeal. Occasionally it is possible to use the same art work in both media, but as a rule we prefer to use special paintings for the twenty-four sheets. An effective poster display demands a technique quite different from that ordinarily found in magazine illustrations. This applies not only to delineation of detail, but also to treatment of backgrounds and particularly to color.

Nor are we able, as a regular thing, to lift copy ideas bodily from our publication displays and transplant them to poster panels. A good magazine headline may not be good poster copy. The magazine headline is like the bait on the end of a hook, which is attached to a line. If the bait looks attractive, the prospect will nibble—and then it is up to the text matter to land him. But the poster copy corresponds to a bullet—if it misses its mark, the chance is gone!

● So while we adhere to the same general theme in both our magazine and our outdoor displays, we adopt a different method of approach. Thus the current publication series for the Laundryowners National Association is a photographically illustrated "continued story" that takes the reader behind the scenes in a present-day laundry. Month by month the reader learns the successive steps that safeguard fabrics and colors, assure the hygienic cleanliness and the gentle handling of the

family washing. This idea did not lend itself to vivid poster treatment. But in the magazine copy we had the underlying theme of leisure plus safety—a basic thought which could be dramatically picturized.

Accordingly we planned our poster series as a succession of statements by typical, citizens of the community, each citing a characteristic reason for patronizing the laundry. One headline reads: "The Club Woman says: 'Let the Laundry do it—it gives time for culture.'" Another one, "The Merchant's Wife knows Laundry Service saves Time—Money—Clothes."

On some of the designs it was possible to secure a close tie-up with the magazine insertions. The March, 1931, poster for example reads, "The Home Manager says: 'Laundry Washed Blankets are Luxuriously Soft.'" This fits in nicely with our magazine advertisement for the month, headlined "Why laundry-washed blankets are luxuriously soft." Another magazine headline which made good poster copy was "Men want MATES—Not Martyrs!"

The Laundry poster series is illustrated with large, lifelike heads typifying the speaker. In all but one, a woman is used; the single exception is that of a doctor to accompany the text, "The Doctor advises: 'Conserve your ENERGY—Let the Laundry do it!'"

● Additional tie-ups with the Laundryowners' series are furnished by blotters, reproducing the poster designs in full colors, and two sizes of truck cards which may be used on delivery trucks or as window displays.

The poster campaign for the National Home Furnishings Program is a combination of merchandising and idea-selling displays, each design being identified with the extensive magazine campaign by means of the featured shield-shaped emblem. During 1931, the poster every other month will carry the phrase, "First Furnish Your Home" followed by a subhead such as, "—— for the Children's sake and yours," "Your Most Vital Obligation," or "It's here that memories are made." These are thoughts developed (Continued on page 31)

The Society of American Florists have used a series of colorful designs similar to this with excellent results.

The ROMANCE of BUSINESS

By Leonard Dreyfuss

President United Advertising Corporation

● When a man tells me that business has become very monotonous he definitely stamps himself a monotonous man.

It is true, though, that today business must be fast on its feet. No longer is anything permanent in this country except *change*. Fifteen years ago the strategy of business was taking raw material and turning it into a manufactured product, so that it may be turned out for less than your competitors. Today the strategy of business is not manufacturing, but merchandising.

In every industry the business that is on top is the one that has best organized its selling. Manufacturing has come to the place where, for instance, the consumer may walk to the street where fifteen different makes of automobiles are lined up. With his eyes closed he could walk to almost any automobile and know that he is buying a product that is made with precision and worth the price asked for it. So the problem that remains with all the manufacturers of those fifteen automobiles is one of distribution. H_{ow} can he find sufficient sales for his product? Therein lies a great deal of the romance of business.

● As an illustration of how fascinating the romance back of a business can be, let me cite one or two cases:

Eleven years ago, in Newark, New Jersey, there was a Scotch delicatessen keeper. His hobby in life was making mayonnaise. People came from blocks around to buy it. Then he bought a horse and wagon to deliver it and then one, two, five automobiles. Then on and on until, in a short space of eleven years, just six months ago, he sold his business to the Kraft·Phenix Cheese

It is a dull man, indeed, who can see nothing but monotony in business today.

LEONARD DREYFUSS

Corporation for considerably more than two million dollars.

● Down in New Brunswick, also in New Jersey, some seventeen years ago there was a little hosiery business that got into difficulties and went into bankruptcy. The business was purchased by a man in New Brunswick, who believed in it. I understand his purchase price was something like $5,000. Today that business—Interwoven Socks—is the largest manufacturer of hosiery in the world, with sales considerably over twenty million dollars per year.

I could go on and on (but space in these pages will not permit) with these fascinating romances of the up-building of important businesses. Business today is ever changing. Yesterday coal was in the ascendency. Today the burning of oil (Continued on page 32)

WHO BENEFITS
Most From Advertising?

The second of a series of talks on advertising prepared by the A. F. A.

● Everybody knows that several classes of people are immediately and directly benefited by advertising. The advertiser makes no secret of the fact that he is, and we know or assume that there is profit in advertising for the publisher, the radio broadcaster, the outdoor advertising concern, the advertising agent and the other media that get advertising before the public. But where else do the benefits fall?

Advertising is essentially educational. It lifts men's minds out of ruts. It creates a desire for fine things. It spurs ambition and generates energy. It has walked hand in hand with progress, in our time, and even a step ahead. Ex-President Calvin Coolidge had that thought recently in one of his syndicated articles.

"When I was a boy in the hills of Vermont, twelve miles from the railroad," Mr. Coolidge wrote, "the only merchandise I saw was in the country store. But my horizon was widened by certain publications containing pictures and descriptions of things that appealed to youth. I read and I bought . . . . It is essential, in the first instance, to produce good merchandise. It is just as essential to create a desire for it. That is advertising. The person or association of persons who can produce that combination of excellence and demand is performing a real public service. They enlarge the mental horizon and provide new forms of beauty and utility. The material benefits pass over into spiritual benefits. Culture and charity are the by-products."

● That is the way that one of the keenest and most practical intelligences of our time regards advertising; and indeed there is a volume in those few lines he puts so laconically and forcefully. How many country boys besides Calvin Coolidge have been inspired to climb out of the rut by "the pictures and descriptions of things that appealed to youth?"

● Our rapid progress as we know it today, appears to be largely dependent on three important factors: transportation facilities, means of communication and advertising. Invention would have but little practical value without them. Transportation and communications could not perform their vital service in stimulating our swift advancement were it not for the informative and educational vitalizing force of advertising. The progress of material civilization was incredibly slow when advertising was lacking to educate and to stir the masses to desire, demand and labor for better things. Inventions have been quickly accepted only when advertising had itself been invented and stood ready to open up new roads. One of the most curious examples of this truth I know of is to be found in the history of plumbing. The ancient Romans had a pretty good system of plumbing, as you would see if you stood today in several of the houses preserved in the Roman Forum. In these houses are lead pipes from one to twenty-seven inches in diameter, which distributed through the households water brought over immense aqueducts from the hills fifty miles distant. Some of these leaden pipes were made in England, and bore a British trademark, for Britain was a Roman Colony in the days of the Cæsars.

● Rome fell before the onrush of barbarians who had little use for bathtubs or plumbing, and the whole science fell back into the limbo of forgotten things, lost to the world. Rome did not advertise her plumbing, you see, nor did the manufacturer in ancient Britain who made so many of the lead pipes that are as good today as when Julius Cæsar passed along the Appian Way between the lanes of cheering hero worshippers. Early in the 17th century London's water mains were hollowed logs, tree trunks. It was not until 1850 that a bathtub was installed in the White House, and in 1880 the average American home had neither a bathtub nor running water,—two thousand years after a very complete and efficient plumbing system was in use in Imperial Rome.

At about this time, two of the pioneer manufacturers of plumbing fixtures began to advertise, very timidly at first. They had much to overcome in their educational campaign. People did not know what bathrooms were for and didn't want them. There was actual prejudice against the use of bathtubs. But the acceptance of bathrooms and plumbing in houses began to spread as soon as advertising got busy. Within a comparatively few years, due in large measure to advertising, good plumbing became a common necessity for decent American life. Advertising has now accomplished the biggest part of its job in educating us to the use of plumbing and bathtubs, and has proceeded to the next step, teaching us that a bathroom can be ornamental as well as useful. We now desire beautiful, tinted porcelain fixtures with tiling, curtains, soap and towels to match.

We demand not only sanitation but beauty and art in our bathrooms. Advertising brought about within a few decades what the whole sweep of 2,000 years could not bring about without advertising.

After the hot air furnace was invented it required sixty years to get any distribution for the invention. It was not until advertising was used to sell furnaces and began to tell people everywhere what useful, convenient, labor saving, comfortable devices they were that they began to sell widely.

● Until advertising began to wave a magic wand over men's minds invention was tremendously handicapped by prejudice. The steamboat is an example of this. A Frenchman named Papin built the first one in 1707. He was almost persecuted for it and his invention got nowhere. Others followed along with practical models but it was not until Robert Fulton's fussy little Clermont stirred up the water of the Hudson that there was any beginning of steam navigation. And the beginning was slow and struggling. People hated to accept new ideas. The new steamboats had to show themselves physically in every port to gain any acceptance, and it took 50 years more to educate the masses as to what steamboats meant—what they would accomplish for human comfort and pleasure. If advertising had existed in the early days of steamboating the people would

have had a thorough understanding and belief in steamboats almost by the time that Fulton launched the Clermont. Contrast all this with what advertising in modern times has done to familiarize the masses with oceangoing steamships, to encourage steamship travel, and thus to acquaint everyone with the safety, pleasure and relative cheapness of blue water voyaging.

● Manufacturers know enough nowadays to make an immediate appeal to the masses through advertising. An example of this modern attitude is found in the electric and gas refrigerator. As soon as these were in production they were widely advertised, and the result was immediate national distribution. Almost overnight, householders, with perfect confidence in the truth of advertising, equipped their homes with these up-to-date conveniences.

Thirty years ago almost everything for the table was bought in bulk. Food was scooped out of open boxes and barrels, where it had been exposed to flies and dirt. Any woman who cooked for a family in those days knows that it was a real job to convert this loose, bulky food supply into meals. Often it took a whole day to prepare a dish which can now be purchased practically ready for the table. Women have been emancipated from the drudgery of the kitchen. Modern food comes in dirt proof tins and packages. All of this is the immediate result of national advertising. Quality has been improved from the standpoint of cleanliness, freshness and convenience. Attention has been drawn through advertising's educational campaigns to balanced diets and proper nourishment for children and adults.

The educational and stimulating effects of advertising are especially noticeable in the field of electric lighting and electrical appliances generally. We knew 120 years ago that electricity could be used for making light, and an arc lamp was installed in an English lighthouse in 1862. Edison came along with his incandescent light in 1879. But there again progress was slow, because advertising wasn't on hand to take up the new invention and trumpet its merits to the world at large. Although electric lighting was introduced rather generally about 1900, the most striking advancement has been since 1914, when the advertising of new improvements such as the tungsten lamp became more intensive. Due to advertising largely, households generally have taken advantage of a great variety of labor-saving electrical appliances. Moreover advertising has been so useful in explaining to the farmer the safety and convenience of electric installations that there are now 627,000 farms connected to electric power lines and more than 1,000,000 farms equipped with their own individual lighting plants.

● The development of the automobile is a romantic chapter in the history of industry and one of the major triumphs of advertising. In this country the horseless wagon made its appearance in 1895 when four were registered. In 1897 there were 500 registered, but nearly all were of foreign make. The next year Alexander Winton placed a one-inch advertisement in the Scientific American announcing that he had "gasoline buggies" for sale, and in that year he sold 20 or more. In 1899 Oldsmobile, Studebaker, Locomobile and other cars were put on the market, and every manufacturer began to advertise the minute he was ready to accept orders. In 1890, 8,000 cars were registered in the United States. Then the momentum of sales picked up as the volume of advertising swiftly grew. In 1929 there were 5,358,000 cars produced in this country with a total value of four billion dollars, and the advertising expenditure was approximately $60,000,000, or only one-and-a-half per cent of the total sales. In the whole field of industry it is not possible to find a more impressive instance of the benefits of advertising to a single product.

● Radio, more fascinating than a Hans Christian Andersen fairy tale, is advertising's own child. From its very birth it was nourished and developed by the best that advertising could create and devise. From the first the public was intensely interested in this marvel of the ages and advertising, comprehending the tremendous public absorption, dramatized radio as no other invention had ever been dramatized. Starting with 1920, the use of radio became almost a national obsession in the United States, and this last year the Census Bureau reported 13,600,000 receiving sets in use. Is it necessary to mention the joy that radio has given to the crippled and the sick in hospitals; to traveler, explorer and exile, as well as to the millions that lead healthful, normal lives? Radio is second only to the automobile in bringing the city to the farm. Rural isolation hardly exists nowadays. By means of radio, the farmer may have the best of entertainment in his own home and is given instantaneously the latest news of weather, crops, and current events. Advertising may fairly claim the lion's share of the credit for developing this newest of industries.

● Advertising has performed the double function of stimulating the desire to own radios and of providing the entertainment itself. Broadcasting stations could never afford to furnish their excellent programs without revenue from advertising.

Perhaps the greatest benefit of all that has come to the people through advertising is the development of the great stores of the country into emporiums of daily service. Through them are distributed in large volume and economically the manifold products created by the power of advertising. Through them comes the close educational contact with the uses of these products. Through them comes the direct demand of the people expressing their desires. Through them comes the universal distribution of the products of the world that raise the artistic and living standards of the nation.

The whole health standard of the country is being raised by the most thoughtful kind of advertising. Certain of our great insurance companies counsel the public almost daily as to the care of their health and advise frequent and thorough physical examinations to anticipate the encroachments of disease. Through advertising we are learning how to combat and defeat one of mankind's worst enemies, the common cold and a myriad other ailments and diseases. Better health is often the direct and immediate object of advertising. At other times health improvement is promoted along with the sale of certain goods or services.

● Advertising gives us friendly counsel about taking care of our teeth and regularly consulting the dentist; about conserving our eyesight and not neglecting the optometrist. Advertising warns us to keep an eye on the scales and to watch our weight as a simple index of physical condition. And advertising in the form of publicity has done a great deal, directly and indirectly, toward making us a nation devoted to sports and to the outdoor life. It is because of the attractively publicized benefits and pleasures of various sports that we have 3,000,000 golfers in the land, 2,000,000 baseball players, 1,500,000 tennis players and 3,000,000 basketball players, not to mention a host of football, polo, and hockey players and a multitude of swimmers. Clever, forceful publicity has created such keen, widespread interest in sports that Bobby Jones, Helen Wills Moody, John Doeg, and Babe Ruth are national heroes.

The cultural influence of advertising, direct and indirect, is far-reaching and powerful. Some of our finest artists are now engaged in the pictorial side of advertising, and the notion that an artist must not demean himself by labor of any useful sort is decidedly out-worn. The great artists of the Renaissance, Michael Angelo, Raphael and their contemporaries, were, after all, commercial artists, working on commissions, doing interior decorations for Popes and (Continued on page 31)

Outdoor advertising, through its scientifically placed locations makes it possible for the advertiser to cover an entire trading area. The poster, through its complete coverage of the community reaches every prospect every day. Painted display, with its individual locations, enables the advertiser to present his message to any section of that community. The remarkable circulation, low cost and flexibility of outdoor advertising are some of the factors that have given the medium its present place in American merchandising.

Photo of city copyrighted by Chicago Aerial Survey

OUTDOOR is an Economic

Winning Arguments of Radio Debate Held by Station WPAP

ARGUMENTS PRESENTED BY CHARLES O. BRIDWELL

By way of explanation I wish to state that the kind of Outdoor Advertising I am going to talk about is the standard structure as recognized today in advertising circles, namely, the standard 24-sheet poster panel, and the standard painted display panels. These are all carefully built everywhere in this country according to the same specifications and under the same regulations of efficient maintenance.

Today everyone is vitally interested in the cost of running the home. The modern dollar, because of to-day's conditions, is more difficult to earn and it must work a great deal more efficiently than it did a few years ago.

Not only do the American people want food, shelter and heat, but they want much more than that. They want an up-to-date radio, a good motor car and finer clothing. When the month is ended they want some money left over to buy these and other things which contribute to the comfort and happiness of life.

Therefore, it is well to know the facts and most people are very anxious to know them, so that they will be conscious of what is in back of the prices they must pay for goods. Anything which contributes to make things cost less and which tends to lower the cost of living is a part of the information needed for one to fulfill his responsibility toward himself and his family. Interesting and welcome is the news of anything which

makes a dollar go farther, which gives a better article for the money.

Let us picture the kitchen in a home in order to study these facts. For purpose of illustration, let us take just one thing that you eat. A package of breakfast food. What is it that determines the price of this package of cereal? Why did you pay 10c or 15c—as the cost may be? There are three factors which determine its price (1) the cost of the raw material—corn, oats, wheat or rice as it comes from the farm to the manufacturer, (2) the cost of manufacturing the cereal and placing it in a package. It is now ready to be placed on the shelves of the grocers. (3) the cost of getting the breakfast food on the grocer's shelf, unless the manufacturer is able to inform you about it and persuade you to try it and to continue to use it.

Now there are two ways by which the manufacturer might inform you of the qualities of his breakfast food. First, he could send a salesman to call at your house and he might possibly call on 25 housewives a day. Suppose that the manufacturer paid the salesman $5.00 a day, which is a cost of 20c per call. This would mean $200. cost to tell 1,000 housewives about the breakfast food. Of course this method is very costly and in fact almost out of the question. But keep this figure in your minds for a few moments. The second method is by advertising, because advertising is simply the modern method of selling goods to vast numbers of people, creating the large sales required by our great factories.

Although to many people advertising may seem complicated, it is after all a very simple economic force. The best advertising is that method by which the manufacturer can inform the most people at the lowest cost to himself. This is the point that interests the family

ADVERTISING
Benefit to the American People

person, because the cost of informing people is included in the price paid for the package, just the same as the cost of manufacturing and delivery is a part of the price. Consequently it means money in the pocket of the family when the cost of telling people is reduced to its lowest point.

If a manufacturer uses extravagant or wasteful methods in getting the package into the home, you are bound to pay an increased price by just so much. On the other hand, you have a perfect right to expect that manufacturers who sell you their products shall use the most efficient and economical distribution methods available, thereby making the price paid for the package as light as possible. The question of economical advertising strikes not only at the kitchen but every room in the house and it enters into the cost of practically everything that is bought.

There are many forms of advertising, but the subject under discussion is the economic value of outdoor advertising, one of the major vehicles available to American manufacturers. Outdoor Advertising is the oldest form of publicity. Even in the days of Egypt, Rome and Pompeii, we find evidences of authentic outdoor signs used to inform the people about the various stores and services and this was hundreds and hundreds of years before printing was invented. Outdoor Advertising is not only the oldest, but in a true sense one of the most modern forms of advertising, developed in durable structures fitted to the modern conditions under which we live.

In the United States today there are 25,000,000 motor cars, whereas 10 years ago there were only 7,500,000. The entire nation is on the move and out of doors as often and for as many hours as possible. We all know that outdoor sports are more popular than ever—golf, tennis, football, baseball, large sporting events, enormous crowds, gigantic stadiums all over the country, the moving pictures, buses, touring all the highways—all of these crowds of people are out of doors. It is well said that one room of the American home is now on wheels, and so outdoor advertising is in tune with the times because it reaches the people where they are, on the streets and highways.

There are many other mediums of advertising provided to gain the attention of the people when they are in the home and it would be fair to refer to them as indoor advertising. So that a manufacturer has the

opportunity to gain the attention of the public while they are indoors, but were he not to gain their attention while they were outdoors, he would suffer the loss of a large opportunity.

Let us go back for a minute to the salesman who called from door to door. We estimated that 1,000 buyers reached would cost $200. by that personal word of mouth method. Long ago the enlarged activity of people in their daily habits took them further from a given store or factory and so offered a problem in the marketing and distribution of goods, because obviously if the life of the people expanded beyond the area covered, it would not do merely to rely on personal sales activity at one point. It became necessary to add to the productiveness of mouth to mouth selling by publicity, today recognized under the name of advertising. Instead of reaching 1,000 buyers for a cost of $200. through a salesman going from door to door, the manufacturer using outdoor advertising places himself in the opportunity of reaching 1,000 people for a cost of from 5 to 10c. This is what we have meant by stating that the cost of the marketing goes right back into the price paid for commodities. You know from this that the merchants who use outdoor advertising are using a modern, efficient and economical method of getting the goods into the homes.

In addition to the very large number of national advertisers who use outdoor advertising and the many thousands of local merchants in every conceivable line of business using it, we find in almost every condition of community crisis or national movements, that immediately outdoor advertising is called upon to do a large job in the situation. It is an old story, but during the war well remembered how vital a part posters played in arousing the energies of the American people in every phase of complete preparation. Pictures and a few words were vital in arousing the emotions.

In every country in Europe, in the Far East and in South America, outdoor advertising is one of the oldest established kinds of advertising used by governments in their appeals to their people. Existing in the older countries for so many hundreds of years, it has an established place in economic life, just as in this country outdoor advertising has had a steady growth and recognition as an important advertising method. Even today in Russia, we read frequently of the consistent use of posters by that government to enthuse its people, to inform them, to educate them, to conform them to one train of thought.

Outdoor Advertising is of great economic benefit to the American people. It is enabling retailers and manufacturers to conduct their business at a lower distributing cost and its very continued use over all of these years is rather conclusive proof. Our government officials from time to time have stated that distribution is one of the most difficult problems in our times today and that lowering the cost of distribution is of tremendous national importance.

Right at this minute outdoor advertising on standard, well kept structures is telling the message of American business in 17,500 towns and you will be surprised to know that in point of effectiveness it is reaching all of the urban population and a great portion of the rural population to a circulation degree not enjoyed by other advertising mediums. It gets so close to the streets of a town that it is a vital daily influence, understandable to all, because of its color and picture, and economic because of its close position to the retail outlets where the goods advertised can be purchased.

There are very few services in the United States comparable to Outdoor Advertising. The Post Office Department, of course, has the largest of outlets and next to the telegraph and telephone industry, outdoor advertising is distributed in the greatest number of units in this country. The purpose of the medium is to economically serve those who have to sell their goods and patriotically to serve the communities in any community effort. As it is refined and improved, the result will be that the dollar of the public will go farther and outdoor advertising will help continue to reduce the cost of things, thereby making it easier to have money left over for finer things in life.

ARGUMENTS PRESENTED BY
SAMUEL N. HOLLIDAY

Mr. Bridwell has discussed this subject largely from the point of view of the housewife or consumer. Let us look at it now from the viewpoint of the average American Business Man.

In the past year we have all come to realize more than ever the importance of *business* to this country, and by that I mean the buying and selling of goods or services. This country is primarily a commercial nation. Our progress as a nation has been founded upon the progress of our commerce, our business. Other things are important, but surely we will all agree that if business is not good it affects adversely our entire population of over 120 million people. When business is bad it causes suffering, unhappiness and actual want. And of course our American ideal as a nation is that there must be the greatest happiness for the greatest possible number of people. So business is vital in our scheme of things, and *good business* a thing much to be desired.

We have a definite and established business system. In Russia the Soviet government does not think very

much of it, but as Americans we like it, believe in it, and are convinced that it suits us because it allows perfect freedom and opportunity to the individual. The corner stone of this system is competition, and this applies to every line of business endeavor. For example, whether you run a tea room, a restaurant, a hotel, or a chain of hotels, you are in competition. Where there is no competition in your own business it comes from other industries, all after the consumer's dollar. You are engaged in a business struggle and it is your responsibility to attract people to your place of business. You can only do this by telling them of the merits of your goods or your service. President Coolidge once said, "Advertising is the life of trade." And this is absolutely true.

In this competitive age, advertising is the method which enables the merchant or the business man to survive and prosper by selling his product to more people at a profit. It would be very difficult to find a modern business man who did not agree that advertising was a vital and tremendously important help to practically every line of business in this country engaged in selling something to the people.

I would like to give you a few examples. Let us start at the top. Suppose you were the president of a 50 million dollar concern engaged in manufacturing a food product, put up in a package and selling for 10 cents. You have spent years perfecting your product—in other words, you are turning out a splendid food, one of rare quality and high nutrition value, and you are selling it to the American people for 10 cents a package. If any individual wanted to start in business and make a similar product of his own on a limited scale, he would probably have to charge 30 or 40 cents a package for the same article. But you have attained vast quantity production at a minimum cost per unit. You turn out millions of these packages every day. You buy your raw material in enormous quantities at low prices. The success of your company, however, is dependent for its continuance upon the universal distribution and sales of this product. You know that both must be maintained on an even basis. To do this there has to be a practically automatic *acceptance* and purchase of your food product by the population from coast to coast, and this automatic sale must be secured constantly and inexpensively. Advertising is the answer, and it is the only answer.

You and your board of directors sit around the table and look over your advertising budget. Every dollar counts and every dollar must work to sell your product. Outdoor Advertising is in that budget because it serves a particular purpose. It sells the great masses of people at very low cost, and bear this in mind—*the exact function of Outdoor Advertising in selling is not duplicated by any other form of advertising.* For your food company, Outdoor Advertising has become through years virtually a matter of necessity. You cannot do without it—you cannot find anything to take its place. It is included in your appropriation because you realize first, the necessity of *maintaining* your great quantity production and your vast sales; and second, you realize the urgent necessity to reduce the cost of your distribution and to eliminate *waste* in distribution.

● Largely because of the increased use of the automobile, popularity of sports and the general tendency of all the people to spend more time in the open, organized Outdoor Advertising is one of the most efficient and economical forces that can be utilized by large-scale production concerns in their mass selling. As a matter of fact, there are 285 large national advertisers using this medium today. It is constantly depended upon by them to reach the great bulk of their respective customers with pleasing and persuasive suggestions, continually repeated month after month, which build permanent belief in the goods advertised and thus secure steady consumer demand and sales in volume sufficient to maintain production on the established scale.

Manufacturers of products having general distribution and sale use Outdoor Advertising for

1. Its universal appeal, achieved through size, color, picture and proper location.
2. Its low cost per thousand of circulation.
3. Its continuity and repetition value—in brief, its "high frequency."

● Again, let us suppose that you are the president of a bank in the Bronx. As president you know where you can get your new business. Logically, you can expect new depositors only from certain clearly defined neighborhoods in the Bronx. You don't care anything about Manhattan or Brooklyn. You are only interested in those sections of the community where your *logical prospects* live.

Seeing ahead..

PROPHECY isn't our line. We don't know when "this de-

pression" is going to fill up. But we do see a good year

ahead for vigorously handled outdoor advertising. We're

putting in extra-vigorous licks on accounts like Maxwell

House, American Chicle, Sanka, Calumet — and lots more.

We'll do it for YOU. . . . If you want outdoor SERVICE—

OUTDOOR

A NATIONAL OUTDOOR ADVERTISING ORGANIZATION

Posters Bring the Crowds
to MISSION STREET

By Augusta Leinard

● Can community advertising materially benefit an uptown shopping center? That such advertising, if wisely selected and alive with the co-operative spirit, can work wonders in keeping old business and winning new, is proved by the experience of the Mission Street Merchants Association of San Francisco. The Association has been using outdoor posters almost exclusively for years and its members will tell you that the advertising "has made Mission Street."

To those who don't know San Francisco—Mission Street is a thriving uptown business section that got its start immediately after the earthquake and fire of 1906. This part of town then consisted of a few houses and stores, and as it remained unharmed it soon became the devastated city's hub of shopping activity.

● But in 1909, when business started going back downtown, the Mission Street merchants realized that something had to be done if they wanted to stay in business. An organization was formed which was called the Mission Street Merchants Association. Its expressed purpose was, "to make an active and united bid for business," and its present purpose is to keep Mission Street before the purchasing public as a convenient shopping center. Committees were appointed for handling the

One of the effective designs used by Mission Street in its cooperative campaign. All the posters used are excellently laid out and have good continuity.

different branches of activity and among these was an advertising committee.

● The first advertising effort was a shopping news. This contained bargains for the week and was distributed to the tune of about 20,000 copies. Results were not pleasing; in fact, there weren't any. Outdoor advertising was then given a trial and proved more successful. It was used, off and on, from 1911 until 1917, since which time it has been a permanent and practically the only form of advertising used by the Association.

This came about when Gus Lachman, president of a gigantic house-furnishing store located in the heart of the Mission District, was made president of the Mission Street Merchants Association, in which he had been active from its beginning. Having long been an outdoor advertiser and a strong advocate of the medium, he proposed that an aggressive and uninterrupted poster campaign be launched. This was to last for six months and during that period the sum of $750.00 was collected each month and put into the outdoor program. Since that time the amount has fluctuated and today the association is spending around $950.00 a month on outdoor posters.

● "Outdoor advertising and the Coupon Company have made Mission Street," said J. C. Marshall, one of the charter members of the association, who has served as its president and has held the office of secretary since 1917.

The Coupon Company, he explained, sells coupon books to the merchants. The idea is similar to the trading stamp project that was in vogue years ago. Nearly all the Mission Street merchants give coupons redeemable in merchandise or premiums and the idea is very successful. The coupon company sets aside 10 per cent of its receipts to be placed in the advertising fund of the association. This and the association dues provide the money for the community advertising.

● The dues for membership in the association, which contains about 200 members, has been admirably worked out. In the beginning the members made voluntary contributions. Some gave $5.00, some $10.00, whatever they felt was right. Property owners also contributed, as did

the banks and others interested in the upbuilding of Mission Street. But as the association developed a systematic method of regulating finances had to be devised.

● Association dues today are figured according to the number of feet and the location of a merchant's business. The minimum is $2.00 and dues range as high as $25.00 a month. The cost is so much a foot according to the block. The west side, being the choice side of the street, pays more than the east side, and the best block in the shopping district brings the highest dues from members. When a new member comes in he is told what his minimum dues will amount to and receives a printed schedule showing how it is figured.

The design is submitted by the outdoor advertising company and approved by the chairman of the association. The merchants have been requested to watch the boards and notify the association secretary of any criticism.

● One event that has become a notable success largely through outdoor advertising is Dollar Day. This is held twice a year, in February and August, and draws thousands of people to Mission Street. The merchants cooperate by having signs in their windows and streamers throughout the stores as nearly as possible similar in style and coloring to the poster on display. The streets are decorated and all participating members are expected to have as many Dollar Day specials as possible. It has been pointed out at association meetings that these must be legitimate values, otherwise the sale would injure rather than benefit Mission Street.

Six Greater Mission Day Sales are also held throughout the year all advertised through outdoor posters, and the Christmas holidays are also played up.

One of the outstanding benefits derived from the outdoor advertising has been the popularizing of the slogan of the Mission Street Merchants Association—*Buy For Less In The Mission.* As

one member puts it: "By being persistently displayed, this slogan has become as well known as some of the national advertising trade-marks and subconsciously means to the purchasing public: a lower price for the same quality."

When the tremendous value of the slogan was realized it was copyrighted and it is now used in innumerable ways: stickers in wrapping parcels, placards, and individual company advertising all play it up. In the outdoor posters the slogan is always given important space.

● The history of this progressive association is preserved in printed bulletins recording the monthly doings prepared by the secretary, Mr. Marshall, who is in the printing business. He has bound the bulletins into volumes and the successive years tell a graphic story of the association's helpful activities.

A 1919 bulletin speaks of the first Dollar Day as follows:

Results exceeded the most sanguine expectations. Doubtful subscribers have become enthusiastic boosters and it was proved that community advertising was much cheaper and had five times the buying power of individual advertising.

In July of the same year the advertising committee of the association went on record with this statement:

It is absolutely necessary for a district to advertise in order to get ahead.

● Such comments are found throughout the series of bulletins and they are backed up by statements of results from the advertising that indicate that the speakers know whereof they speak.

In this poster the emphasis of the month gives added interest. Here again careful composition has avoided monotony.

Outdoor Industry COOPERATES
for Roadside Beauty

By George W. Kleiser

President, Outdoor Advertising Association
of America, Inc.

● On January 8 a Conference on roadside business and rural beauty was held at the Chamber of Commerce of the United States, Washington, D. C. At this time the representatives of those industries and groups interested in the regulation, recognition and preservation of the natural scenic beauties of America were gathered together. I attended this Conference as one of the representatives of the Outdoor Advertising Association of America.

Our Association is desirous of taking an active part in this laudable movement which is of such vital interest to every good citizen and to those who come to America to view its beauties and charm. It is gratifying to note that the Conference was attended by such a large number of representative organizations and groups, national in scope, exhibiting a deep interest in this most important subject.

Such Conferences, in the opinion of our Association, offer an opportunity which has not heretofore been presented for a thorough study and genuine consideration of the problems involved in the harmonizing of commerce and beauty throughout the rural areas of America.

Most interests affected were represented at the first conference. It is but natural that there exist varying opinions and views with respect to the manner in which the purpose of the Conference can be accomplished. In order that results may be accomplished, no doubt each of us may be called upon to yield in some degree in our varying opinions and perhaps make personal sacrifices in a business way in order that we may reach a common ground for effective action.

We are living in an age where mere utility is not enough. Beauty enters into the every-day life of practically every citizen of our country. The American business man and the manufacturer has learned that to be successful he must give due regard to beauty in the manufacture and sale of his products. Modern factory buildings as well as modern office buildings, the schoolhouse and the residence, all seek some expression of beauty in their design and construction, not at the expense of usefulness, but as an additional attribute.

● The modern factory with its spacious grounds, lawns and flowers, provides a pleasing setting for the day's

GEO. W. KLEISER

work. The American public has learned to expect and appreciate the expression of beauty in business.

● This desire for beauty on the part of the public is recognized by the advertiser and finds its expression in the artistic character of the present-day advertisements. Every advertising medium, to be successful, must recognize this growing demand. Realizing this, organized outdoor advertising has made much progress in the development of more attractive advertising structures and advertising copy.

With the advent of more and better highways and with the tremendous increase in the use of the automobile for both business and pleasure, there has developed a demand for advertising along the favorite routes of travel.

The members of the Outdoor Advertising Association of America, mindful of the importance of the natural beauties existing in this country both to its citizens and its visitors, have officially at their annual convention committed themselves to a policy of recognition and protection of the natural scenic beauties of the landscape, and the active cooperation of the state government departments, civic and (Continued on page 30)

Cooperative Advertising
aids COAL DEALERS

● The modern way of meeting competition is by advertising of some sort or other—and that it's a successful way has been proved again. This time it's the coal dealers in the San Francisco-East Bay marketing area who, awakening to the fact that serious competition was treading on their industrial toes, launched an outdoor advertising campaign as effective as it is unusual. WARMTH WITHOUT MONEY is the slogan being put over in this advertising, which might be termed semi-co-operative because common copy is being used and yet each dealer has individual control over his own locations.

A nice easy-going business the coal business used to be. Competition was confined chiefly to the ranks of the dealers themselves, and even they considerately kept within definite marketing grooves, letting their brother dealer look after the trade within his own community.

But how things have changed! Outside competition is making deep inroads into the coal dealers' domain. Gas and oil, electric heaters and generating plants, all are offered to the public with heavy advertising to back them up. No longer can Mr. Coal Merchant periodically look after his year-in-and-year-out business and then depart on a summer's fishing trip to recuperate from the winter's strenuous and profitable activities. Today he must make an earnest effort not alone to retain his steady customers but to get his share of the additional business that should be his by right of increasing population.

● Fighting competition with advertising is the modern way, as has been stated; yet the coal industry was making little use of that weapon. Brief campaigns, spasmodic and sporadic, were put on only to flicker out after a short period.

For several years a large San Francisco outdoor advertising plant saw the coal dealers' need and made efforts to get them to put on a definite and dynamic campaign. Finally, the advertising company's Special Paint Department Manager, whom we shall call Mr. A, presented a plan to the California Retail Fuel Merchants Association in an attempt to get the industry to work collectively. His plan was voted excellent but no action was taken. Pursuing the matter further, Mr. A approached the dealers individually with the same plan slightly modified to fit the new situation.

● The terms of the proposed agreement called for painted walls or bulletins. Each dealer would have to sign up for not less than three years and use common copy. No advertiser could change the design in any detail, but he was to have his own imprint used on his locations. He could take as many or as few walls as he felt his business warranted and the smallest advertiser was as great a factor as the largest in the co-operative movement.

It was pointed out that this plan would give the small dealer the chance to use high-grade publicity which he could get in no other way because the producing of the design alone would cost two or three times the net profit made in a year on an order for, say two walls, when taking into consideration the creating of the design, blueprinting, making of paunces, and all the etceteras attendant upon getting out a de luxe painted bulletin. But with the dealers working together a sufficient number of contracts was assured to make the advertising possible for all. (Continued on page 37)

The cool colors which predominate in the original of this design emphasize the warm hues of the windows of the house.

Bakery Advertising Features
APPETITE APPEAL
by A. W. Roe

● Baking companies, both wholesale and retail, give outdoor advertising high rating among the advertising media that they use to carry their messages to the consuming public.

They find that outdoor advertising can be employed to advantage in securing more than one happy result. Where the community is relying to an appreciable degree upon home baking or upon nondescript products put out by small neighborhood bakeshops, outdoor posters and painted boards, used over an extended period of time, prove effective educational forces, centering the attention of individuals upon the bakery products so advertised. Thus company prestige is built up, and the goodwill engendered naturally blossoms into active demand for the company's products.

Outdoor advertising tends to pull consumers away from brands that are not well advertised, and to cause them to become constant users of bakery products that they have learned to like through the tutorage of the outdoor advertising medium. Outdoor copy has been so used in more than one case by aggressive baking concerns in opening plants in new locations or in enlarging the customer demand of plants already in operation.

Preeminent services are offered by outdoor advertising in establishing the brand name in the consciousness of consumers. Such advertising can be employed successfully as merchandising agencies in somewhat the same fashion as is newspaper display copy in calling attention to products when they are especially seasonal or in giving publicity to new products that the bakery may be introducing.

While it is not the writer's intention to enter exhaustively into the relative merits of newspaper copy and outdoor advertising as far as bakeries are concerned, it might be noted in passing that the outdoor medium has certain advantages over newspaper copy.

● First of all, it can avail itself of the compelling forces of color. Newspaper copy may be illustrated with attractive cuts of the company's breads and cakes, but such copy layouts will lack the appeal inherent in a carefully designed poster or painted board. This is because outdoor displays carry conviction straight to the emotional centers of the brain through portraying the product in its natural colors. At the same time such use of auxiliary colors can be made as to attract the attention of the pedestrian or motorist in the street much more effectively than a mere black and white-faced advertisement can do.

A very well laid out poster that carries a strong appetite appeal—a necessity in bakery advertising.

● Color captures the fancy of the observer and stimulates not only the imagination but reacts upon the nerves of taste as well, thus producing an agreeable emotional response. It is natural for us to think of strawberries as being red, chocolate cake as being of a rich dark brown and the crusts of bread as being of a golden straw color. Several years ago strawberry growers learned that a berry of pale color could not stand up in the market in competition with rich red varieties. The berry might be just as sweet, but it failed to make an emotional appeal; in other words, it could not "make the potential customer's mouth water."

Outdoor display copy, realistically designed and carefully executed, puts the natural color in a display in such a manner as to "make the mouth water" when the observer sees breads and cakes so pictured and advertised.

Outdoor advertising occupies a key position in the advertising arch of the Fehr Baking Companies of Texas in the matter of introducing plants in new territories and in popularizing products made and distributed by the bakeries.

Fair-Maid Bread and Cake first made their appearance in Texas a little more than three years ago when a new plant was opened in San Antonio in July of 1927. Since then other plants, bearing the name of Fehr Baking Company, have been established in Houston and Corpus·Christi. Although controlled by separate organizations, the products, made and distributed by each of these plants, are identical. The brand names are the same, and the advertising and merchandising policies are much the same. In each locality, served by the three bakeries, outdoor advertising has played· and is still playing a conspicuous part in making new friends for and consumers of Fair-Maid products.

For the last fifteen years before coming to San Antonio, Charles J. Fehr, president of the companies that bear his name, had been production manager for one of the large baking chains, and in such capacity, he had had splendid opportunities of observing the way advertising functions in popularizing bakery products.

Since the establishment of the first of the Fehr bakeries in San Antonio, it has been Mr. Fehr's policy to try out practically all forms of advertising. He has been a consistent user of both newspaper and outdoor space. Motion pictures, showing actual bakery operations and the many pleasing ways bakery products may be used, are used repeatedly. Radio programs also bear the Fair-Maid message, a comic sketch, "Frank and Herman," being sponsored each Wednesday night by the bakeries. 27,000 people filed through the San Antonio plant in July when it was first opened, and plant visiting has been fostered steadily since then. More than 14,000 school children of San Antonio were transported to and from the bakery during a recent school year.

● The foregoing statements as to the kind of advertising, specified and used by Mr. Fehr, show that he has tried out about all media known to the advertising profession. And during the three-year period the organizations of the different Fehr companies have been consistent and liberal buyers of outdoor advertising.

Six, large painted bulletins in addition to other outdoor advertising were used by Mr. Fehr three years ago when he was presenting his new plant and products to San Antonio for the first time. It is significant of the regard he has for the outdoor medium to record that this number has been increased from six to fourteen painted bulletins, all within the city limits of San Antonio. Posters and painted bulletins in even greater proportion are maintained in Houston, in Corpus Christi, and in and around both Waco and Harlingen, Texas, in both of which cities are bakeries in which Mr. Fehr is interested.

Motor delivery is a good indicator of the growth of a concern. When the San Antonio plant was opened a twenty-two truck delivery fleet took care of city consumption very nicely for a time, but since then increas-ing demand has made the addition of new units imperative from time to time until the motor fleet now numbers thirty-one, almost a third more than when the first Fair-Maid truck began its maiden delivery journey to the homes of San Antonio grocers.

● The growth just recorded was made possible by the company's first having standardized, quality products, and second letting the public know about them through well directed advertising, a generous part of which is outdoor display of the kinds now under description.

A pleasing color scheme is a marked characteristic of all Fair-Maid posters and painted bulletins. Color is used not only to portray breads and cakes in their natural color blends but also as a background and in the lettering so as to make the board an attention-compelling composite. Nearly all outdoor copy is illustrated. Breads and cakes are shown both in packages and with the paper wrappers pulled back to reveal the tasty contents.

Messages carried by posters and boards are always brief, and they emphasize quality and service. Expressed in slogan fashion, they are easy to read and easy to remember. "Fair-Maid Bread & Cake" always appear in big letters and in the same type of lettering used in newspaper advertisements, on company trucks, on bread and cake wrappers, and on any other form of advertising, signs, counter cards, and whatnot that are used in advertising. "Always Fresh" is another slogan-like phrase, stressing quality. "At Your Grocer" is another phrase that ties the products in with their retail outlets. Lately, another phrase, "Made from the Finest Ingredients," has come to occupy a prominent position on painted boards.

Effort is made to have the boards tie in with the seasons. Products that are especially seasonal are played up on the posters and bulletins when the particular season rolls round. For instance, Fair-Maid Rainbo Bread, "Made especially for picnics," as the sub-line informs us, is given special outdoor space during the summer months.

● The company has only one trade name for all its breads and cakes. This is "Fair-Maid", and all advertising energy is bent towards making this a household word in the communities where Fair-Maid products are sold. (Continued on next page)

● Lately the San Antonio bakery has placed particular stress on merchandising products of its cake department. Five cake delivery trucks, lettered to convey the fact that they are used for cake delivery only, can now be seen daily on the city streets. Simultaneously, the company has installed in a strategic position overlooking San Pedro Park an attractive painted bulletin that is devoted exclusively to advertising Fair-Maid cake.

Fair-Maid cake is also being advertised in an ingenious way on another painted bulletin.

The picture of the cake on the board under description has been painted in a frame so that at the end of the month it can be easily changed from rich, yellow, plain loaf cake to Christmas fruit cake without disturbing the other portions of the copy.

Such an advertising campaign as the one of the Fehr Baking Companies, herewith described, not only builds consumer demand for the products so advertised, but does much towards influencing grocers and other retail outlets to boost the products concerned. Grocers are usually very willing to put in special window displays, make counter displays and whatnot, when they know that the products that they are thus advertising are also advertised in newspapers and through other such effective agencies as outdoor posters and painted bulletins.

OUTDOOR ADVERTISING
is of Economic Benefit
to the American People

(Continued from page 17) A friend of mine has a beautiful resort hotel. It is situated off the main highway, and yet his business must come from tourists. He told me not long ago that he could not exist, he could not stay in business, without the help of a beautifully painted bulletin which we have placed for him on the main highway not far from his hotel. On this bulletin we show a picture of the hotel, in a few words we describe the wonderful home-cooking, and then we tell the tourist how to get there.

You see that Outdoor Advertising fills a distinct economic need. In thousands of small towns there is no other form of localized intensive publicity. In such towns Outdoor Advertising is plainly a helpful selling force, not only for the local merchant but also for the big national advertiser.

● Fifteen thousand local merchants in business of the widest possible range are users of this form of advertising. In fact, in our own company alone in the months of September and October of this year, business was placed by 4800 different contracts for the use of Outdoor Advertising for the year 1931. This cross-section of American business indicates the value of the medium to them in the development of their business, and it proves their conviction as to its economic place in planning next year's activities.

In organized Outdoor Advertising every structure that is built is placed on ground leased from property holders.

But that is not all. In the majority of cases this utilization of property for advertising structures is a source of income that would not be available at all, except for this purpose, because such properties are awaiting future development.

Outdoor Advertising is one of the foremost examples of self-regulation in business, and this has been accomplished through our national association—the Outdoor Advertising Association of America. Fixed standards have been adopted, not only for locations, structures and service, but for all matters affecting the public interest.

The work of improvement and further refinement continues from coast to coast, and this association, sponsors a very definite program of constructive development, the objective being to bring Outdoor Advertising to the highest possible point of scientific efficiency without waste, so that the American manufacturer and local merchant may find it an increasingly effective aid in solving future problems of distribution and sale.

●Speaking for the organized industry, Kerwin H. Fulton, Chairman of the Board of Directors of the Association, and President of the General Outdoor Advertising Company, spoke as follows of the plans: "We have now come to another definite and important period of refinement in Outdoor Advertising . . . In every step we have taken, the public interest has been carefully considered, and it is worth noting here that this *public* interest coincides absolutely with the desires and best interests of the *advertiser*. We realize that our medium is peculiarly a public medium, and it is our responsibility to see that it pleases the people. The enforcement of these new standards will, no doubt, be burdensome to the industry, but the final result will be worth all it may cost."

The end and purpose of all that is being done by the members of our association is to give the advertiser an effective, economic and convenient method of selling his merchandise at a low cost, and to give the public a real, sound, cost-lowering system of national distribution of the products they buy.

I should like to quote Calvin Coolidge who, when president, received the announcement of the annual convention of the Outdoor Advertising Association of America, wrote:

"It is a reminder of the fine service which this organization and its members have rendered to the national interest at more than one period during the trying years through which the country has lately been passing. That service contributing so much as it did to the establishment and maintenance of the national morale, is the fullest guarantee that in the future the organization will be very helpful to the nation."

CLEVELAND TRUST'S
Electrical Advertising
Based on Careful Study

by I. I. Sperling
Asst. Vice - Pres., The Cleveland Trust Co.

"Well, in *our* country," said Alice, still panting a little, "you'd generally get to somewhere else—if you ran very fast for a long time as we've been doing."

"A slow sort of country!" said the Queen. "Now, here, you see it takes all the running *you* can do, to keep in the same place. If you want to get somewhere else, you must run at least twice as fast as that!"

—Alice in Wonderland.

● Not even the mighty financial giant, the bank with millions of deposits and hundreds of thousands of depositors may become complacent about its size in these parlous times.

Even the smallest bank if it is to survive, realizes that aggressive merchandising and advertising of its services is essential. The old criticism that the banker waited in his lobby for customers to come in is no longer current although it was justified at one time.

● These days the spirit of service pervades the modern bank and bankers actually compete with one another for new ways to serve the customer.

● Even one of the nation's largest banks, like the Cleveland Trust Company, which was one of the pioneers in advertising some 25 years ago, continues to plan and search for new ways of merchandising its services, creating new services and customers out of old ones and striving constantly to keep itself before its public. And this in spite of the fact that with its 58 branch banks in a metropolitan district with a population of 1,250,000, it has already won more than 530,000 accounts or about one for every two people in the district.

Printed advertising is good. It has always been the bulwark of the banker's advertising appropriation because it not only established the name and kept it in a prominent place in people's minds, but it gave them a clear and complete picture of just what the bank could do for them.

● However, the alert bank has been quick to make use of every conceivable advertising medium and particularly those media which have been tried and found productive in the much older field of retail selling.

Naturally, as a pioneer in financial advertising, this bank long ago made use of electrical advertising. At

The roof display, because of its brilliance, motion and flowing lines of light is attention compelling.

Circulation area of displays at start of program.　　Circulation area of displays under present program.　　Estimated circulation area of additional recommended real displays.
All branches to have "sidewalk" identification by means of projection or focus signs.

first without any particular plan but later as its branches grew, it used electric signs of various sorts to "trade-mark" the locations of its offices.

● These branch markers were of particular value in re-minding those who work or live in the vicinity that "here is the bank." Such markers also contribute in some degree, to general impression-building, in that they are seen by those who ride and if they are repeatedly seen in all parts of the city, people get a new and better idea of the size and scope of the organization and its service.

In addition, a branch bank or a main office of the bank for that matter, is a living, pulsating factor in the business life of the community up to 3 o'clock each day. After that, unless some device is substituted, its doors, closed for the day, reduce it to an inanimate, lifeless thing. Electrical advertising revitalizes the bank therefore, between the hours of dusk and midnight and makes it a living advertisement of financial service.

● There was a time too, when the bank had the only outstanding building in town; when everybody knew its location and was quick to point to it with pride. At night as well as by day, it impressed the public with its dignity and sometimes its austerity; its size symbolized its influence in the community.

Times change however, and unless the bank keeps pace with modern progress in architecture and advertising, its efforts become feeble and inadequate, These days the building of the telephone company or the theatre probably is outstanding—at night the theatre certainly is—and a host of new industries clamor for attention in the night sky. The bankers find that they have real competition.

● So realizing that competition is a constantly progressive force, we began to study our electrical advertising equipment more closely.

Through the medium of a flow map, both the advertiser and manufacturer can best visualize the necessary steps in a well-rounded program. The circles of effectiveness clearly indicate the degree of legibility of each display.

● We found that some displays were good while others were simply blurs of light. In some instances, the size of letters was inadequate for the potential visibility; some window displays were effective, and others were not. The competition of growing communities with their blazing theatrical lights and improved retail store lighting, created competition which some of our anti-quated equipment was unable to meet.

Apparently in this sign business there was an even greater need for technical service and advice than in the matter of typography. So we went to Nela Park, the Cleveland laboratories of the General Electric Company, recognized authorities on illumination, for this lighting advice.

Together we analyzed the various aspects of our problem and as a result Nela Park engineers made a detailed survey of all of our branches and gave us recommendations on all phases of a complete electrical advertising program. The investigation and compiling of the report required a considerable amount of time, yet the program is flexible enough to cover our needs for years to come. For example, in rapidly growing locations, electric service lines and wiring were provided so that if competition required it, we could "step up" our illumination.

● Our bank with its 58 branches distributed throughout a metropolitan area, was in an ideal position to carry out a most carefully-planned program, including clear, definite marking of all branches, effective to pedestrians and autoists alike, as well as a number of commanding displays on branches located on principal traffic arteries, or where no suitable branch location was available, on carefully-selected leased locations.

● In order to derive the greatest advantage from such a city-wide coverage, the display must have recognition value. People should recognize the Cleveland Trust almost without reading. Since many of our banks are located in leased quarters or were acquired by merger, there was a lack of similarity in their architecture which the branch markers had to remedy. We have long used a characteristic lettering which we now placed in an inverted triangle with rounded corners. The lettering is a modified old English text with the thinner parts thickened up for maximum legibility.

In some places of course, the triangle shape was impractical so we used the distinctive lettering in a rectangular sign placed flat against the building. The triangle signs, it should be understood, are double-faced and the same arrangement of a triangular border of lights surrounding the lettering is used on large roof signs. Similarly, painted wall signs were done in this trade-mark fashion.

● On a map of the city of Cleveland we spotted the branches having existing displays and those which offered good possibilities for a display, from the standpoint of traffic, good showing, etc. By referring to this map, if for example, we desired to erect only one roof display, we could pick out the most advantageous location, and should we desire to continue the program, we could pick out the best possible locations for future signs.

Then we studied costs. We knew what it cost to reach a given group through any printed medium. So we analyzed the electrical advertising part of our program on the same basis. Statistics were readily available regarding the amount of automotive traffic which passed various branches that were particularly recommended as locations for electrical display advertising. On the other hand, pedestrians, street car and bus traffic figures were not so readily available. We reduced the actual automotive traffic figures to allow for people who might not see the display because of distraction or obstruction; even then the total potential circulation from this one source alone was 105,000,000 people per year. We found that our electrical advertising cost would be less than 19 cents per thousand and this, not even counting pedestrian and street car and bus traffic.

● Twenty months have elapsed since the complete electrical advertising analysis was made. In this period we have completed the following installations:

37 branch marker signs
10 large roof displays
32 show window lighting installations
2 floodlighting installations, one at our Main Office

Each of these installations represents the most modern lighting practice, and is outstanding in character. From

the advertising standpoint we feel that the displays are excellent examples of well-applied effort to obtain the maximum of advertising value.

ELECTRICAL ADVERTISING
Conference Meets in New York

● An Electrical Advertising Conference under National Electric Light Association sponsorship will be held at the Westinghouse Lighting Institute, in New York, February 25th, 26th and 27th. Mr. E. A. Mills, The New York Edison Company, has been appointed general chairman and Mr. W. T. Blackwell, Public Service Electric and Gas Company of New Jersey, vice chairman.

A program of unusual excellence will be presented. Subjects definitely scheduled include: Why Everybody Profits from Electrical Advertising; An Historical Outline of Outdoor Advertising; Electrical Advertising Practice—Construction and Installation; Design; Color and Its Uses in Outdoor Advertising; Architectural Provisions for the Use of Electrical Advertising; New Developments in Electrical Advertising; The Use of Photoelectric Cells in the Control of Electrical Advertising; Legislative and Electrical Code Considerations; Power Factor Corrections in Electrical Advertising; Maintenance; Blazing New Electrical Advertising Trails; Central Station Electrical Advertising Field Experiences; Where Electrical Advertising Fits into the Advertising Picture, and Electrical Advertising in Dealer Identification.

Canada

Include Canada in your advertising and selling plans. Here you will find a prosperous market of ten million people, best reached by Poster Advertising.

Any of the following Poster Advertising Agencies will be pleased to give you the facts and figures about Canada:

The Canadian Poster Company, Limited, Montreal, Que.
The Gould-Baird Poster Company, Limited, Brantford, Montreal, Toronto, London, Vancouver.
H. E. Dickinson Advertising Co., Limited, Toronto, Ont.

E. L. Ruddy Co., Limited, Toronto, Hamilton, Winnipeg, St. John, Vancouver.
Lindsay-Walker Co., Limited, Winnipeg.
Ruddy-Duker, Limited, Vancouver.
Charles Baker, Ltd., Toronto, Ont.

Poster Advertising Association

Bank of Hamilton Bldg.   **of Canada**   **Toronto**

A NEW Market
for an Old Product

by Lorenzo Benedict
President, Worcester Salt Company

● New uses can be developed even for a product as old as salt. This fact has been proven by the new demand we have successfully built up for our own product—"Worcester Salt", through advertising it for use in the bath.

During 1929, we began featuring this new use of Worcester Salt in our advertising and a favorable response was apparent almost immediately. One incident in particular that happened shortly after we started this advertising still sticks in my mind. I'll tell you about it, because it proved to me the ability of Outdoor Advertising to help us in developing our market.

It happened last winter in Paterson, N. J. Our salesman covering that territory reported that a grocer, who is one of his regular customers, when placing his customary order for Worcester Salt increased it by a dozen packages over the usual amount and, in doing so, remarked that his supply was just about run out. This prompted the salesman to ask him if his business were increasing. But no, that wasn't it. The druggist across the street had been calling on him for Worcester Salt during the past two or three weeks. This new source of demand, the grocer explained, was the reason for his ordering the extra packages.

● Here was a new one for our salesman. He had never heard of a drug store selling salt. The grocer, however, insisted that the druggist sold it. So the salesman de-

LORENZO BENEDICT

cided to investigate and ascertain for himself just what was causing this unusual demand for salt at the drug store. He called on the druggist, told him that his friend the grocer had mentioned the fact that he had been supplying him with Worcester Salt for his customers. It was unusual for people to (Continued on page 33)

One of the bulletins which introduced Worcester Salt to a new market.

Outdoor Industry COOPERATES for Roadside Beauty

(Continued from page 20) other public-spirited groups for the accomplishment of this purpose. The members of this Association, therefore, are most hopeful and desirous that some practical plan and method of procedure may be evolved at this Conference for the accomplishment of this object, in which event all interests represented here could immediately become active in making the plan effective in every state in the Union, and in bringing about immediate and permanent results.

● It is evident that an objective so comprehensive as this in scope and so far-reaching in effect cannot be successfully accomplished by any individual interest, but requires the united efforts of all of us and the full cooperation of every interested and affected party. It is very apparent that we all agree upon the result to be accomplished, that we are sincere and wholeheartedly interested in the subject, and it only remains for us to arrive at the proper solution.

As previously stated, the solution of this problem requires cooperative effort and a spirit of give and take. This spirit has been expressed in the orderly development of cities and towns through zoning. Why is it not then logical to assume that the orderly development of counties and states could best be accomplished through the adoption of a similar method? Any zoning plan necessarily involves some restrictions as to the use of property. However, if the necessity or demand be sufficient and the restriction be reasonable and not discriminatory, the cooperation of affected parties can be secured. Therefore, it is our view that in the consideration of this subject due regard must be given to the property rights of affected parties. Indeed, it is upon this principle and in this spirit that the courts have sustained the regulations by zoning.

● It is the hope of the Association which I have the honor to represent that as a result of the Conference on roadside business and rural beauty some plan may be unanimously agreed upon by those present, through study of all of the phases that present themselves, and a free discussion and a careful analysis should lead us to a practical solution. Once a unanimous decision as to the proper plan to be adopted, rapid and lasting results can obtain.

– – –

After Electric Signs—What?

La Revue Francaise, Paris, publishes an article by M. Jacques Maret under the title, "Placards and Windows," in which he maintains that illuminated signs are becoming so popular that they will finish by becoming commonplace and it will soon be necessary to invent a new form of advertisement in order to attract the increasingly rapid passer-by.

COOPERATIVE ADVERTISING
Industry's Battle Line

(Continued from page 8) in the magazine copy. Alternate months will emphasize the need of furnishings room by room, taking up successively the living room, bedroom, dining room, kitchen, and a separate poster for floor coverings.

In the January 1931, magazine copy retail subscribers to the National Home Furnishings Program offered for free distribution an unusually helpful portfolio of home arrangement ideas called "The Home Furnishings Planbook." Interested people could obtain a copy without charge from any dealer displaying the Program emblem, or the Planbook would be mailed for one dollar. This afforded an opportunity for a direct tie-in between the magazine and poster series, and the January poster accordingly was devoted to the Planbook offer. Results clearly indicate the responsiveness of poster readers to an appeal of this nature.

● The poster designs for the Society of American Florists are issued for seven months of the year, to coincide with the major selling events—the Fall chrysanthemum season, Thanksgiving, Christmas, St. Valentine's Day, Easter, Mothers Day and the June Bride and Anniversary season. Flowers and pretty girls form the winning team for the florists, whose appeal is primarily to men. "Say it with Flowers," the tremendously valuable slogan of the organization, is of course prominently featured throughout the year.

● All three of the associations mentioned here use the same arrangement for poster campaigns. The poster paper is furnished without cost to the individual subscribers in any amount required. The expense of art work and lithography is charged against the general campaign fund. All costs for posting are borne by the subscribers themselves. This plan enables a dealer or laundryowner to determine the extent to which he will use outdoor displays locally, since he is a better judge of his needs than any centralized committee, placing his order for service through the authorized agents, the Donaldson Poster Service, Newport, Ky.

Total figures as to the annual volume of posting space employed by these three associations are decidedly interesting. The Laundryowners National Association, through various subscribers scattered throughout the country, invests nearly three quarters of a million dollars a year in this medium. Retail subscribers to the National Home Furnishings Program contract for about $700,000 annually in poster space. The Society of American Florists, through individual members, takes space to the extent of $500,000 yearly.

WHO BENEFITS MOST
from Advertising?

(Continued from page 12) Grand Dukes. Possibly business today is beginning to furnish to artists the stimulant offered by the patronage of the church in olden times.

Advertising claims more than a little credit for the improvement of taste in the furnishing and decoration of our American homes. Some of the best literature of the day appears in the form of advertising copy, a statement which may startle some people but which I believe to be true. Brevity and simplicity, force and conciseness; warmth, sympathy, cheerfulness, are all necessaries of good advertising writing, just as they are raw materials of literature. When an advertiser spends many thousands of dollars for a single message to the public, a message which must be concise and yet tremendously appealing, he is going to call upon the best talent available.

● When we take into account all of the contacts of advertising—its educational side, its cultural influence, its part in raising the standard of living, its distribution of comforts, conveniences and luxuries, its emphasis upon health protection and the joy and value of athletics and outdoor sports, its insistence upon truth and honesty—its whole service to society without cost to the people—then, I think, we may conclude that the individual citizen, the consumer, of all the persons and groups touched and influenced by advertising, is the most benefited. He is the great gainer.

● Did you ever pause to think that advertising, in this year of our Lord 1931, has placed the common man, the man of the people, the ordinary man working for a weekly salary or wage, upon a basis of comfort, and luxury as well, that only the rich and high-placed know and could afford only a little while ago. Of all the achievements and triumphs of advertising that is the most striking, the most dramatic; to make the poor man peer of the prince; to put within the means of the hard-worked and the humble the art, literature, the entertainment, the standard of living and other material things that were, only a few decades ago, reserved solely for the aristocrat and the plutocrat. It has been the magician of the masses—a magician which has produced high wages, which has made onetime luxuries the necessaries of life; which has furnished the automobile to emancipate the working man from the imprisonment of four walls; which has given us the benefits of education and in old age and adversity the helping hand of insurance; which has sweetened our souls with culture, and broadened our lives through the opportunities of recreation and travel.

Advertising has been, in short, the right hand of democracy and the companion of progress. Some day the achievements and triumphs of advertising will be written in golden letters upon the walls of the temple of history.

THE ROMANCE of Business

(Continued from page 9) has taken the important place in fuel consumption. Already the shadow of natural gas is over-hanging the oil industry—natural gas being piped two thousand miles from Texas across the country. Only a few years ago knitted ties were worn by everyone. They are gone. Just a few years ago the hair net industry was an enormous one. Even in the advertising business we have an illustration—Ten years ago the best slogan in the business was "Rock of Gibraltar." It stood for impregnability. In this day and age of aerial warfare, the "Rock of Gibraltar" is merely a symbol. It no longer counts as a strategic fortification. In all, this spirit of change in American industry advertising plays the most important part, because advertising is the mass salesman. It takes the hard facts of business and puts them before the vast buying public attractively and creates a buying urge.

● These are days of tremendous competition for attention. The radio in nearly every home, the automobile, super movies, etc., are taking people's attention from the printed word. We have become a nation of *headline* readers. So it is important to consider this fact: Advertising has two main divisions—the explanatory, as represented by the newspaper, magazine, direct-by-mail; and the exclamatory, of which the best examples are outdoor advertising, radio, and window display. If a manufacturer is to make and hold his market, he must first explain his product and then everlastingly exclaim it, or he cannot prevail.

Outdoor advertising is the strongest of the exclamatory media. It greets the buying public on every highway and byway. It dominates because of its large size and the ability to use color. It gives the consumer the "feel of the merchandise." Because of its forcefulness outdoor advertising is very completely in the public eye.

Like every other, our industry has its enemies and, unfortunately, the newspapers give wide publicity to any agitation against our business. Those who agitate against outdoor advertising, I find hold their opinions mostly because of ignorance of the subject. They are on the small side of the megaphone. Here are the facts that are out of the large end:

The outdoor advertising industry directly employs 30,000 people. It would be impossible to estimate the number of people who are kept employed by outdoor advertising thru its allied industries—lumber, lithography, paper, paint, steel, and a hundred others.

● There is spent annually for outdoor advertising by manufacturers and merchants in the United States a hundred million dollars. The average expenditure for national advertising is not over 10% of the selling price and, therefore, it can be authoritatively stated that outdoor advertising markets yearly a billion dollars' worth of fine American goods. This statement cannot be questioned because the same national advertisers year after year return to a greater use of outdoor advertising. They would not do this were it not highly profitable.

Then, too, the outdoor advertising industry is paying millions of dollars each year to over 200,000 property owners. Stupendous figures, these!

On the other hand, unquestionably, there is an occasional sign placed out in the country with a scenic background. Undoubtedly this sign should not be there, but was there anything in this world letter-perfect?

The Outdoor Advertising Association of America has taken a very definite stand for the protection of the scenic beauty of the country. As an industry, we are definitely opposed to any outdoor advertising that violates scenic beauty. As yet this self imposed program of betterment is very young but thousands of structures have been removed or relocated. We ask you men to consider both sides of outdoor advertising. Here is a trade facility that is very necessary to our country's marketing structure. Here is an industry that employs many thousands of men and helps pay taxes to several hundred thousand property owners. Certainly you would want to give intelligent consideration to the commercial aspect of this important industry.

In conclusion, let me repeat that nothing in America is permanent except change; that business today must be fast on its feet if it would prevail; that the merchant or manufacturer who will have the most fun out of his business and reach the top in his particular field is the man who is keenly alive to the romance of his business; and that the business man who will head the list a year hence, is the one who will take his coat off now and prepare for the battle of his life throughout this difficult year.

— — —

Electrolux joins A. N. A.

According to a recent announcement, Electrolux Refrigerator Sales, Inc., New York, have been admitted into membership in the Association of National Advertisers, Inc.

William Reynolds, Advertising Manager, will be representative of Electrolux in the Association.

■ ■ ■

McCandlish organizes Cleveland Department

The McCandlish Lithograph Corporation, Philadelphia, announces the organization of a Cleveland sales and service department.

L. M. Middlemas, for a number of years in a managerial capacity with Morgan Lithograph Company, is in charge of the new McCandlish office.

R. O. (Bill) Bailey, long identified with creative art in connection with the lithograph industry, is at the head of the Cleveland art service department.

■ ■ ■

No Foreign Language Allowed

All electric signs over business premises in Prague must in the future be in Czech, no foreign language being allowed.

A NEW MARKET
for an Old Product

(Continued from page 29) ask for salt at drug stores. Hence, as representative of the Worcester Salt Company, he was naturally interested in learning more about how such a demand originated.

● "Why, my customers ask for it," was the simple explanation from the druggist. "They say they want it for use in their baths—that a big sign at the Five Corners says that Worcester Salt in the bath helps prevent colds." Here was the explanation in a nutshell.

Our salesman had known of the advertisement, but it had not occurred to him to connect it with the demand for our salt at the drug store. Of course, as soon as the druggist mentioned the display at the Five Corners, which is one of the points of greatest circulation in Paterson, the salesman told me that he could readily understand how the big illuminated bulletin, 12 ft. high by 40 ft. long, which showed a package of Worcester Salt, in full colors, with the word copy "Worcester Iodized Salt—In Your Bath—Helps Prevent Colds" would attract the public's attention. People who passed daily could not escape seeing it, and the constant repetition of its message would cause them to think of Worcester Salt as the one outstanding salt on the market. The terse message which called attention to the use of Worcester Salt in the bath could be read at a glance. Hence it was only natural that people being reminded daily that "Worcester Salt in the Bath helps prevent colds" would wish to try it, and it was also natural for them to ask for it at the drug store, where they were accustomed to getting other articles for use in the bath.

● We were pleased to see how well the advertising was working, but we realized that the demand must not be allowed to just grow without definite direction. This meant that people must be directed to the grocery store to buy Worcester Salt, because the grocer is the one who stocks our product and, of course, the one that our advertising is aimed to support. Therefore, we had the line "At your Grocers" added to the copy on the display in order that new users would know the proper place to get Worcester Salt.

Just as care was required in directing the new demand to the grocery store, care was also required to avoid any possibility of the public getting the impression that Worcester Salt contained any compounds that might be associated with toilet preparations. Any such impression would tend to lessen its acceptance for general table use. Hence, the copy which followed the design featuring Worcester Salt for the bath, in turn featured it for table use so as to let the public know that it was just the same table salt used in a new way.

It has been very gratifying to us that the public has accepted this view and consequently we are enjoying a splendid increase in sales this year over what we consider our normal increase. This additional increase we attribute largely to the demand for Worcester Salt for the bath.

● To be successful in developing a new use for our salt, it was essential that it possess a utility for the new use. In this respect, salt in the bath is a logical use for it. Salt has a certain medicinal background. It has an invigorating and refreshing effect on the skin. It stimulates the surface circulation and gives a pleasant tingling feeling of freshness. Athletic clubs all over the country use salt in their baths. Such well-known athletes as Jack Dempsey, Gene Tunney, and Joie Ray have used salt in the bath while training for championship events. This use of salt in the bath for physical training indicates that its beneficial effects had already been recognized, but it was through advertising that the new use was extended to the public in general.

In all our advertising, the name Worcester Salt stands out prominently. Our message is given in a few simple words which are instantly grasped and which the public remembers; so that when the time of purchase comes for this everyday necessity in the American household, it is natural to ask for "A Package of Worcester Salt."

Photo Courtesy General Outdoor Advertising Co.

Old Gold goes toward the modern in design in this interesting poster. Plenty of white space has been left around the lettering without giving a scattered and spotty impression.

Photo Courtesy Erie Lithographing and Printing Co.

This poster shows a very carefully thought out and effective composition. The figure is very attractive and the other elements are tied together to make the poster carry its message as one unit.

Photo Courtesy Outdoor Service

This design marks a radical departure from the previous posters used by this company. It is, however, more direct an approach and its difference will result in increased attention value.

Photo Courtesy Continental Lithograph Corp.

This poster keeps to the general style set in this campaign. The head is well done. One feels that a little less crowded feeling at the bottom would have made this a more effective design.

Photo Courtesy Edwards and Deutsch

This poster has everything that goes to make good design; action, color, simplicity and exceptionally good composition. This should be one of the outstanding designs on the panels.

Photo Courtesy Erie Lithographing and Printing Co.

Conoco uses an interesting tie-up between blended tea and a blended gasoline. The design is well arranged and competently executed.

THIS MONTH

CONSIDER GENERAL MOTORS VALUES

Photo Courtesy Edwards and Deutsch

General Motors keep the continuity of their campaign with this dignified carefully considered poster.

Photo Courtesy Edwards and Deutsch

Chevrolet continues its poster campaign with this simple, characteristic design.

Photo Courtesy Edwards and Deutsch

Here is a design that could hardly be excelled for appropriateness. The rectangular background emphasize the idea of "Phalanx" while the figures are so treated that they do not receive attention to the exclusion of the product.

Photo Courtesy Erie Lithographing and Printing Co.

A difficult subject has been well handled in this case. The product is shown in giant size and is also given special appeal by the use of the figure. In black and white the background seems to interfere with the lettering but the color probably eliminated this difficulty in the original.

Photo Courtesy Erie Lithographing and Printing Co.

The health appeal of Sunkist is put over in an inviting and colorful manner in this poster. The copy is short, forceful and well-placed in the design.

Photo Courtesy Continental Lithograph Corp.

Here is a simple, selling design that tells its story effectively and briefly. Every unessential has been eliminated and the careful layout makes this a very good poster.

FROM THE EDITOR'S NOTE BOOK

Electric Refrigeration Rapidly Developing

Any business that can make the strides that the electric refrigeration industry has made during the past ten years warrants a close study.

Despite the depression of 1930 this industry has shown an increase of approximately 11%. During 1930 approximately 1,000,000 refrigeration units were placed in operation; of this number 770,000 were placed in homes. This sale of household units is especially significant when it is considered that while there was an 11% gain in the industry there was a 38% gain in the sale of electric refrigeration for homes.

The merchandising activity of the large electric refrigeration companies have been the vital point in making it virtually a household necessity. The effect of this activity has been so widespread that it has even helped sell more refrigeration and consequently has been of value to the ice business itself. How the ice business solved its problem was graphically described in the January issue of ADVERTISING OUTDOORS.

In selling refrigeration to the public both in the case of electric refrigeration concerns and the ice industry, outdoor advertising has played a very important part. This year it is practically the backbone of the campaign of the National Association of Ice Industries and is very important in most electric refrigeration campaigns.

Hardwood Lumber to Advertise

The decision of the hardwood lumber interests, announced this month, to put on a cooperative account comes almost as proof of the statement made by Mr. Millis in his story which starts on page six of this issue. In his story on cooperative advertising by industries Mr. Millis brings out the ever increasing number of prominent industries who realize that their competition is more between industries than between members of each industry.

The hardwood lumber men want to eradicate the false idea that there is not an adequate supply of hardwood lumber to meet needs. These men are beginning to realize that because of their silence they are losing their markets to the manufacturers of substitutes for wood. It is their intention to tell the public of the various kinds of hardwood, where the trees grow and what particular uses each type of lumber will best serve.

Lumber as lumber, perhaps is sold more to the contractor than it is to the general public but certainly in the decision as to whether or not a substitute for lumber will be used must be made by the home builder himself. Therefore, hardwood lumber men would do well to carefully read Mr. Millis' article and profit by the experiences of these other industries who, in the past few years have invested $30,000,000 in creating good will for their particular industries. They will do well to note that the industries referred to, while making use of national mediums have capitalized on poster advertising to localize their message.

— ∎

Automotive Industry Speeds Up Production

According to the report at this time, February production in the automobile industry will exceed the January figure by quite a wide margin. This increase is credited in automotive circles to the recent automobile shows and to the lack of buying during the past year.

Most automotive executives and many bankers interpret the present automotive buying tendency to indicate a return of prosperity.

∎ · ∎

There is Truth in This One

The Chicago Journal of Commerce has recently run several editorials cautioning newspapers against starting fires that might spread and damage their own property. Recently a bill was introduced in New York whose intent was to tax the newspaper business.

The Chicago Journal of Commerce on January 16 comments editorially as follows:

"It has been remarked in these columns now and then that it is impossible for the newspaper business to remain forever safe from the griefs it is causing to be imposed on other businesses. The New York Bill is a portent. So was the recent bill of Governor Long of Louisiana for a heavy tax on newspaper advertising. There is as much justification for regulating and taxing the subscription and advertising rates of newspapers as for dealing with other businesses in a parallel fashion. The newspapers deserve a dose of their own medicine, and unless they alter their ways they are going to get it."

COOPERATIVE ADVERTISING
aids Coal Dealers

(Continued from page 21) Mr. A's method was to first get his plan approved by the California Retail Coal Dealers Association. He could then go to the retailers with the sanction of that body, and be sure of a hearing at least.

● At first the dealers couldn't see the necessity for this widespread campaign, declaring that they were doing as much business as they had done ten years ago. "Ah, but you should be doing twice as much because the population has doubled," was Mr. A's comeback. "And, besides, although the older generation is familiar with the merits of coal as a fuel, remember there is outside competition that was not even dreamed of by your old customers and there's a new generation springing up that has to be educated to the merits of coal and constantly reminded if you want to hold on to your old business and get your new."

An illustrative analogy cited was the grocery business. The chain store organization can go ahead and buy to advantage through the number of stores it controls. The independent stores therefore found it necessary to band together in buying goods to enable them to compete with the chains. That was what the proposed paint campaign was calculated to do. Through presenting a united front the coal dealers were to buy the best advertising at the lowest rate.

Gradually the dealers began to see the feasibility of the proposition and came into line with the result that the campaign, which started in September, 1930, gained momentum so fast that in three months approximately 26 dealers and 100 walls were included, with the number increasing daily. The territorial radius at this writing stretches from Oakland to San Jose and as far north as Vallejo, but the interest displayed by the dealers warrants the expectation that the whole Pacific Coast will eventually participate. Those few advertisers who were already using the outdoor medium were persuaded to change their design and join in the co-operative paint campaign, which they willingly did. Many dealers have also had the design painted upon the walls of their building, improving its appearance.

The design, according to present intentions, will be changed annually, but repaint contracts are being accepted from individual dealers to keep their bulletins looking new and fresh at all times.

● A design of universal appeal has been worked out, one that has brought dealers many compliments from their trade. It depicts a night scene. A star-spangled background is of a cold blue strongly suggesting wintry weather, with the following text in lighter blue:

WARMTH WITHOUT WORRY
Your Home is Safe
When you use
C O A L

the word coal being a warm red. Against a black mass that symbolizes the blackness of the night is a gray stucco bungalow with a green roof. Its lighted windows,

together with the smoke rising from the red brick chimney, cleverly accentuate cozy indoor comfort. It is difficult to indicate in the accompanying illustration the potency of that message of genial warmth given out by the colorful design, and doubly effective are the bulletins across the highway from some of the coal companies in the East Bay District that maintain architecturally beautiful office buildings and landscaped grounds.

Surprisingly few were the problems encountered in developing this unique campaign that has all the advantages of a co-operative movement with the added benefit of individual representation. The question of overlapping came up, but this was met by a careful grouping of locations. For instance, Mr. A opens a map plotted out according to contracts already closed and asks a prospect: "Where do you draw your trade from?" He replies, "From here and here and there." He is then shown what locations are open to him. If there is a dealer nearby, Mr. A says, "You don't want to get too close to this street because so-and-so has a wall there. But we can give you this and that." And the dealer is perfectly willing to co-operate because he realizes that each wall with its common copy becomes a contributing factor in a hundred walls all pulling for him through their cumulative value no matter where they may be located. One of the outstanding advantages accruing to the dealer from this campaign is that he need commit himself only to such financial outlay as he can afford and yet he shares equally with the biggest advertisers in the benefits. Another advantage is that the coal industry can now follow the program of competitive fuels by advertising all summer as well as in the winter.

● "Like many other industries the coal business has found it necessary to consider the adage 'United we stand—divided we fall,'" said Paul M. Jones, one of the largest and most enthusiastic advertisers. Mr. Jones is the president of the East Bay Coal Company and also of the California Retail Fuel Merchants Association. "The value of a united front cannot be too emphatically stressed in a situation such as ours. Besides raising the morale of the coal merchants it is materially helping us meet competition and I am hoping coal merchants in other localities will follow the plan. I should like to see such advertising made national in our field with the slogan, WARMTH WITHOUT WORRY, carrying its message to the public and helping the coal merchant retain his prestige in spite of new fuels and expensive publicity introduced by his competitors."

McCandlish Opens Pittsburgh Offices

The McCandlish Lithograph Corporation, Philadelphia, has opened Pittsburgh offices in the Bessemer Building, in charge of W. E. Kusen who has, for a number of years, been identified with lithographic sales in the western Pennsylvania metropolis.

OUTDOOR ADVERTISING ABROAD

Outdoor Convention to be held in Holland

A sub-committee of the Genootschap voor Reclame (the Dutch Advertising Association which has recently enrolled its 800th member) has been for some time considering the proposal put forward by some outdoor advertising firm to hold a convention and exhibition of outdoor advertising in Amsterdam, according to Advertiser's Weekly.

This would be an international event and some German interests have already intimated that Amsterdam would be a satisfactory city as far as they are concerned. This, however, is not official so far and negotiations are going forward.

Should the International Outdoor Advertising Convention not be held in Amsterdam, it is urged that the local interest in the matter is so great that an exhibition should be held, nevertheless. The rough plans of this are already in hand and there is little doubt that the exhibition will be held.

At a recent meeting of the sub-committee the exhibition plan was unanimously agreed to and it now awaits the acceptance of the idea by the Genootschap's General Committee.

English Agency uses Posters

One of the foremost apostles of newspaper advertising in Great Britain, Sir Charles Higham, has given the most practical testimony to the value of poster publicity by placing three big poster campaigns which will be seen shortly, according to Advertiser's Weekly. This is a new departure for Sir Charles's agency but it is understood that the agency will work in conjunction with an outdoor advertising company.

Australian Paper Protests "Outdoor" Legislation

A quotation from the Sydney (Australia) Morning Herald which is given in "Outdoor Advertising," a folder published by the City and Suburban Bill-posting Company, of Perth, Australia, says: "the art of the hoarding has made great strides in recent years and its progress is perceptible even in Australia. To argue in favour of its prohibition on the ground that public taste is offended by the defiling of the countryside generally is simply to ignore the fact that the public habitually defiles picnic spots with picnic litter in a fashion which suggests very little taste to be offended. A mayor's prejudice against 'odd effects' and a local council's aesthetic judgment in this matter are likely to be too arbitrary at times to carry public endorsement. Yet there are attempts to dogmatize on those very lines, for a local government ordinance is expected which will vest 'in municipal bodies the power not only of controlling hoardings but of pulling down those that are deemed offensive to aesthetic tastes.' Whose aesthetic tastes? Can such a taste be decided by a majority vote of a council?"

British Association Boosts Branded Products

The British Poster Advertising Association has issued an attractive booklet, pocket size in stiff orange covers, entitled "Protection," the theme being that "the known name, the asked-for brand, is equivalent to a tariff" and that posters are the best advertising for branded goods.

British Outdoor Advertising Takes Upward Turn

In regard to the 1931 prospects for outdoor advertising in England, J. H. Wingrave, managing director of Willing and Company, Limited, says in Advertiser's Weekly, "There appear at the moment indications that poster advertising this year will show an appreciable improvement over the 1930 conditions.

"The larger national advertisers obviously provide the foundation of the turnover and these are extending rather than reducing their allocations. It is an open secret that one of the largest users of posters in the past is returning to the hoardings. In view of one or two recent and notable successes, this return to a policy which established the business in question is hardly surprising.

"The destruction of outdoor advertising by legislation, which is neither more nor less than the result intended by a small minority of the advocates for 'the amenities,' will no doubt continue to be advanced under other pleas in Parliament as in past years, but one can hardly imagine that the more rabid opponents of the trade can have failed to have outworn any welcome they may have had in the Houses of Parliament, since one Bill has scarcely become law before another is introduced."

DAVID ALLEN'S OWN PANELS ARE SEEN BY 10,000,000 people IN THE BRITISH ISLES EVERY DAY

BRITISH OUTDOOR ADVERTISING is *best handled by*

DAVID ALLEN'S

We offer to American advertisers the largest, most modern outdoor advertising service in Great Britain. Our studios rank among the finest in the British Isles, and we have secured for our clients the work of Ludwig Hohlwein and Septimus Scott. R.O.I.

Only the most efficient machinery and workmen are employed in our printing factories in London and Liverpool. We can claim the most intimate knowledge of British markets, a knowledge founded on half a century's experience in handling National contracts. Our panels in 250 of the principal towns in Great Britain are seen daily by 10 million people.

You can increase your market in the British Isles. We are well equipped to help you.

DAVID ALLEN & SONS, BILLPOSTING L™

INCORPORATED IN NORTHERN IRELAND

ALLEN HOUSE, BUCKINGHAM GATE, LONDON, S.W.1
ENGLAND

CABLES -ADVANCEMENT LONDON

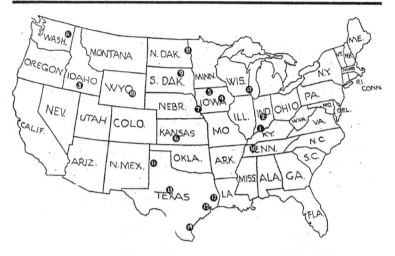

SPENDING TENDENCIES

I

EVANSVILLE, INDIANA
February 20, 1931

GENERAL BUSINESS CONDITIONS: When Mr. A. P. Eberling, Secretary of the Evansville Chamber of Commerce was interviewed on business conditions in Evansville, he stated that at the worst time of the depression employment was at least 30% of normal. At the present time it has improved so that it stands about 86% normal. Mr. Eberling predicts that by April or May employment figures will show about a normal average.

This small decrease in employment figures is due to the diversification of industries in Evansville. The prediction that April or May will see normal and healthy business conditions is based not only on the increased production of the local manufacturing plants but is also due to the widespread public improvements, including the building of the bridge across the Ohio River which will complete a direct route from Chicago to Florida.

Several merchants were also interviewed for this section. One of the largest department stores reported that their December business for 1930 was slightly smaller than the volume in 1929; their January 1931 volume compared favorably with the January 1930 volume and the first two weeks of February 1931 showed a slight increase over February 1930. Another large department store manager reported that their business also showed approximately a 5% decrease in volume as compared to 1930.

One of the leading jewelers of Evansville stated that in comparing his January 1930 and January 1931 volume he found them within $85 of the same figure. A shoe dealer selling only high grade shoes for both men and women reported that his business was off approximately 12%. The leading ladies' ready to wear store reported a 5% decrease in 1931 volume. A local music store reported business about the same as last year; a leading men's wear store reported their business as about the same.

MOTION PICTURE ATTENDANCE: When interviewed the managers of the three leading motion picture houses in the city made the following report. The two largest experienced a decrease of approximately 10%. Comparing January this year with January 1930 the third house reported a decrease of 30%. Considering the total attendance it is estimated that amusement attendance is off about 15% this year.

AUTOMOTIVE: The State oil inspector for the first district of Indiana, in which Evansville is located, reported that in January 1930, Vanderburg County (Evansville) showed a consumption of 1,340,000 gallons of gasoline against 1,194,500 gallons for the same period in 1931.

2
INDIANAPOLIS, INDIANA
February 20, 1931

GENERAL BUSINESS CONDITIONS: According to the Fletcher American National Bank the department store sales are showing a nice gain over the same period last year. Total bank debits for the year were 13:5% under 1929, while bank clearings for 1930 were 15.1% under 1929. Volume of advertising is reported to be approximately 15% under that of 1929.

Several lines of trade and industry responded to seasonal influence and registered gains during the last part of 1930, but a survey of general business discloses very little change in conditions as exceeding during the last part of 1930. General business is estimated at about 23% below normal.

3
TWIN FALLS, IDAHO
February 3, 1931

GENERAL BUSINESS CONDITIONS: The volume of wholesale and retail business was approximately the same through 1930 as in 1929 although profits on all lines were less. Bank clearings for 1930 equaled approximately those for 1929. There was an increase in building permits, telephone, water and electrical services increased during 1930.

MOVING PICTURE ATTENDANCE: One moving picture house reported a 12% increase during 1930 as compared with 1929. The second house reported a decrease.

4
CEDAR RAPIDS, IOWA
February 20, 1931

GENERAL BUSINESS CONDITIONS: In a report made especially for this section of Advertising Outdoors Mr. Charles D. Manson, Executive Secretary of the Cedar Rapids Chamber of Commerce, says that retail enterprises of Cedar Rapids report from 1 to 2% increase in volume for January 1931 over the corresponding period of 1930. He also says that industry conditions are good, several plants working two shifts.

MOTION PICTURE ATTENDANCE: In this same report, motion picture and entertainment enterprises are credited with a slightly increased patronage in Cedar Rapids and vicinity.

AUTOMOTIVE: Mr. Manson also reports that gasoline sales in and around Cedar Rapids are on a par with those of 1930. Various oil companies report that they consider the prospects for the coming season as very good.

5
MASON·CITY, IOWA
February 13, 1931

GENERAL BUSINESS CONDITIONS: General business conditions reports show an improvement of January 1931 over January 1930.

One furniture dealer reports a 20% increase and one department store reports a 15% increase. Wholesale firms report a slight increase and with the open winter also report less delivering expenses.

The Decker Packing concern reached its peak in January with 1,300 employees. The American Sugar Corporation report the largest run in history.

MOTION PICTURE ATTENDANCE: Mr. Tom Arthur, manager of Cecil Theatre, reported a 10% increase in attendance in January 1931 as compared with January 1930. Mr. Heffner of the Palace Theatre reports a 1% decrease.

AUTOMOTIVE: Mr. Gillmore of Mid-Continent Corporation reports an increase of 5% in January 1931 as compared with January 1930. Mr. Kornbaum of Champlin Refining Company reports a 15% increase partly due to an open winter and brighter outlook for 1931.

6
HUTCHINSON, KANSAS
February 7, 1931

GENERAL BUSINESS CONDITIONS: R. H. Goldberg, President of the leading merchants clothing store, says: "We have just closed our semi-annual clearance sale and are very happy to report that we had a larger volume of business than in 1928 or 1929. Business conditions in general are very good with us and at the present time are on a par with this same period in 1930. We are offering greater values in popular merchandise and are keeping up our stock anticipating a good volume of business this year. Greater values will have a tendency to increase volume. The Jones O'Neal Shoe Company, a store handling high grade shoes, have closed a year of very satisfactory business." Don Ennis reports: "Our sales in Hutchinson for 1930 were slightly under 1931. January sales were far ahead of expectation. We are planning on 1931 equaling last year's volume, as the demand for high grade shoes is holding up. Hutchinson, like most cities, has its share of shoe stores but we fully expect to push ahead."

Mr. B. H. Salyers, President of the Gibson-Salyers Motor Company, Chevrolet dealers, reports that they are enjoying a very brisk business. "Our entire organization is working 100% and are producing results of which we are very proud," quotes Mr. Salyers. "Sales for January were approximately 20% better than a year ago. Our used car sale shows an enormous increase. New car sales lead last year's volume for this period. We have every reason to expect a continuance of good business."

MOTION PICTURE ATTENDANCE: Hutchinson's motion picture attendance for this January was 20% better than in January 1930. "We are disregarding this talk of depression," said Mr. Ed. Hass, city manager of the local Fox Theatres. "Our plans and appropriations are made on the basis of good times. The steady increase and attendance attests to the fact that we have taken the right procedure. We have under construction a $500,000 deluxe Fox Theatre, which we are rushing through at the quickest time humanly possible. Do you think we are giving consideration to this pessimism so prevalent—quite to the contrary."

AUTOMOTIVE: Reports obtained from some of the large gasoline companies show that the gasoline consumption for January 1931 equaled that of January 1930. Some report a slight increase in volume.

7
OMAHA, NEBRASKA
February 20, 1931

GENERAL BUSINESS CONDITIONS: It is reported that there are 5,000 more men employed by the Union Pacific this year than at the same period of 1930. It is also reported by the Metropolitan Insurance Company that Omaha's employment situation is one of the most favorable in the United States; this statement was made following a survey made by Metropolitan in 46 selected cities. Recently Commissioner G. B. Eastburn made a tour of western Nebraska and comments like the following were made to him: "Better business than in 10 years"—"More money and less indebtedness"—"Soundest financial condition since the war"—"Not hit by the depression," and many others like them. It is also interesting to note that there were fewer business failures during 1930 in Omaha than there were in 1929, this is especially interesting due to the fact that for the United States as a whole there was an increase of 15%.

8
GRAND FORKS, N. DAK.
February 3, 1931

GENERAL BUSINESS CONDITIONS: Unemployment is slightly greater than the usual seasonal level because of the railroads laying off so many men. The largest firms representing the dairy, packing and milling businesses are all employing large forces. The city has given employment to many idle men on street cleaning, laying of new water mains and sewer repair jobs.

The three combination wholesale fruit houses report tonnage for January comparable with that for the last five year period for this month; prices however on some commodities are lower than before in history. The general average of commodity prices 15-20% less than a year ago. Prospects for 1931: optimistic, conservative and "hand-to-mouth" buying by small town and neighborhood merchants; no excessive stocks anywhere. There was a 10% cut in all wholesale fruit house salaries made in December.

Grand Forks is in the most favorable of all North Dakota cities this winter.

MOVING PICTURE ATTENDANCE: The business for December 1930 and January 1931 compare favorably with the corresponding months of 1929 and 1930. The managers report attendance 75% normal.

9
ABERDEEN, S. DAK.
February 4, 1931

GENERAL BUSINESS CONDITIONS: Business in general is picking up very fast in this trade area. December and January showed a marked increase in retail sales over the previous year.

The amount of cash buying in local retail outlets is surprising. This indicates that there is money in this section, even in the farm community where it had been generally supposed that the farmer was hard pressed for cash.

Dealers are buying now very slowly from wholesalers, depending on a rapid turnover for their profits. As a result, wholesale sales are not at this time as large in proportion to retail sales as in 1929, but considerably larger than a year ago.

MOTION PICTURE ATTENDANCE: The motion picture business for January picked up also. It is still under a year ago in patronage. This is probably due to two reasons. Cash buying instead of credit in the retail trade takes much cash out of circulation that would in normal times go to amusements. There is also the fact that the ownership of the theatres has changed.

10
NASHVILLE, TENN.

GENERAL BUSINESS CONDITIONS: . The following interviews give a good idea of general business conditions.

Paul Davis, President of the American Banks: "Business in January, 1931 does not appear quite as good as in January 1930, but it is really better. In my opinion, business in 1931 will be better than in 1930."

Jeff Yarbrough, Manager of the Neuhoff Packing Co.: "Business in January, 1931 was about the same as in 1930. There are indications of improvement."

Wm. Wemyss, Vice President, Jarman Shoe Co.: "Our business was 31% better in January 1931, than in January 1930. Advertising has helped bring this about. We shall increase our advertising this year. Mail orders are improving, which is a good sign. I have traveled in forty states recently and find business brightening up."

J. W. N. Lee, President, Rock City Construction Co.: "There was more construction in January 1930 than in January 1931. However, much of that was made up of older contracts, still incomplete. There is not so much construction going on now, but there is more encouragement for the future than there was last year; there is lots of planning going on. So, in the building trades, I should say that while conditions are not as good as a year ago, the atmosphere is better."

Manager of a large department store: "Per unit, we are 10% ahead of January 1930. Mild weather has helped. There is less demand for heavy goods. There is good activity."

MOVING PICTURE ATTENDANCE: Motion picture attendance for January 1931 as compared with January 1930 is slightly under.

AUTOMOTIVE: One large gas and oil company reports that sales for January 1931 were approximately equal to those of January 1930. Another reports a slight gain over the previous year.

11

AMARILLO, TEXAS
February 14, 1931

GENERAL BUSINESS CONDITIONS: The general business conditions are best seen from the personal interviews made.

Mr. R. D. Kirk, manager of Amarillo's oldest general dry goods firm, White & Kirk, says, "The sales volume for the first six weeks in 1931 is practically the same as in 1930. Unquestionably 1931 will be a better year than 1930. Business conditions generally sound in Amarillo, and in the trade territory."

Mr. M. Sherman, manager The Marizon, Amarillo's leading ladies ready to wear store, said, "January sales this year, show a nice increase over January of 1930. I expect 1931 to be a somewhat better year than 1930 on account of Amarillo's many assets—wheat, jobbing, railways, air center, cattle interests and oil and gas."

Mr. H. E. Hertner, owner Hertner & Son Plumbing Co., said, "The volume of business so far this year is about equal to 1930. This should be a better year than 1931. There is a reason for Amarillo being in the 'white' on the American Business Map in Nation's Business and Babson's for 27 consecutive months."

Mr. Walter Blackburn, manager of Blackburn Bros.—men's leading clothing store said, "We have had a splendid increase in volume of sales for the first six weeks this year over the same period in 1930. We have been in business in Amarillo for 23 years, and confidently expect 1931 to be the best year we have ever had."

MOTION PICTURE ATTENDANCE: Attendance for January 1931 is about the same as that for January 1930.

AUTOMOTIVE: The following actual figures gives you a very definite comparison between 1930 and 1931.

Simms Oil Company	Gulf Refining Company
1930—22,615 gallons	1930—70,714 gallons
1931—39,630 gallons	1931—94,712 gallons
Plains Lubricating Company	Continental Oil Company
1930—41,539 gallons	1930—23,700 gallons
1931—24,586 gallons	1931—46,000 gallons
Gibson Oil Corporation	Magnolia Petroleum Company
1930—not in business then	1930—51,488 gallons
1931—72,000 gallons	1931—97,816 gallons
Texas Oil Company	Texas-Pacific Coal and Oil Company
1930—105,000 gallons	1930—not in business
1931—135,000 gallons	1931—30,000 gallons

12

BEAUMONT, TEXAS
February 13, 1931

GENERAL BUSINESS CONDITIONS: Definite, although slight, improvement is reported to us from practically every line of business. The recent opening of the oil field in East Texas is bringing a stimulation of business to an important part of the city's trade territory.

MOTION PICTURE ATTENDANCE: Motion picture attendance for January 1931 as compared with that of January 1930 is 20% below.

AUTOMOTIVE: The oil refineries of the district, the largest grouping in the world, while not putting on any new employees, are assuring continuous employment to those already engaged and there is some improvement in oil export.

13

BROWNWOOD, TEXAS
February 13, 1931

GENERAL BUSINESS CONDITIONS: General conditions are not bad and even much better than expected four months ago. Mr. Renfro, owner of Renfro Drug Chain in Brownwood states that he believes we would really be having a boom in this section if conditions were normal, there being a' highway and irrigation project in the process of being built. This means employment for more than seven hundred men and is costing nearly five million dollars. Mr. Fain, manager of the Hemphill-Fain Company, Brownwood's largest department store, states that their annual January sale of 1931 ran fully as high as in January 1930 even though prices were lower. No commercial failures were reported during January and most of the progressive firms state they will increase their efforts for business with the coming of early spring with greater advertising expenditures. Enough moisture has fallen to insure spring crops.

MOTION PICTURE ATTENDANCE: Motion picture attendance fell 7½% in January 1931 as compared with January 1930.

AUTOMOTIVE: Gasoline sales are reported off by some companies and others report practically the same volume as in 1930. Automobile sales are gaining but most of the gain is being made in the lower price range.

14
CORPUS CHRISTI, TEXAS
February 14, 1931

MOTION PICTURE ATTENDANCE: The attendance at motion picture theatres shows a slight decline.

AUTOMOTIVE: The four major gasoline companies show a gain from 25% to 40%.

15
HOUSTON, TEXAS
February 7, 1931

GENERAL BUSINESS CONDITIONS: Heavy winter clothing off 15% to 20%; general clothing line up 6%; furniture, household furnishings, office supplies, etc., average from 4 to 10% up this January as compared to January of last year.

MOTION PICTURE ATTENDANCE: Motion picture attendance for January 1931 as compared to January 1930 varied from 97% to 101.6%. In regard to the Motion Picture attendance we find that the theater managers have experienced only a variation in attendance dependent upon the class of pictures shown during a particular time. It so happens that pictures with the same amount of pulling power were run in January 1931 as were run in January 1930.

AUTOMOTIVE: Gasoline consumption average about 4% off. New car automobile sales off 45%.

16
SPOKANE, WASHINGTON
February 13, 1931

GENERAL BUSINESS CONDITIONS: According to the Secretary of the Chamber of Commerce, three banks' and several leading merchants' business for January 1931 showed a slight increase over January 1930. This upward swing in local conditions is indicative of a return to modified prosperity and the general feeling throughout the city is more optimistic.

MOVING PICTURE ATTENDANCE: Several moving picture theatres reported attendance as large as that

during January 1930 and one of the principal houses reported a slight increase.

AUTOMOTIVE: Gasoline consumption for January 1931 as compared with January, 1930 showed a decrease of 10%.

17
MILWAUKEE, WIS.
February 4

GENERAL BUSINESS CONDITIONS: Leading Milwaukee business men report a definite trend toward business recovery in various lines of endeavor. There is a noticeable lessening of pessimism and industry as a whole is looking forward to definite recovery although the process will not be rapid.

MOTION PICTURE ATTENDANCE: Motion picture attendance for January 1931 is somewhat spotty. A good business, however, is being enjoyed by outstanding theatres who advertise and exploit their attractions in a forceful manner.

AUTOMOTIVE: Gasoline consumption is holding up fairly well, being off about 5%.

18
CASPER, WYOMING
February 20, 1931

GENERAL BUSINESS CONDITIONS: Interviews were made in Casper with the three largest banks. Mr. P. C. Nicolaysen, President of the Casper National Bank, reported that Christmas savings accounts have increased 11% over last year while savings accounts have decreased approximately 8%. This decrease in the savings accounts is principally due to the fact that sheep men are drawing out their savings for the purpose of feeding their stock. Mr. Carl W. Schumaker, Vice President and Cashier of the Wyoming National Bank, reported an increase of approximately 10% in savings accounts and 15% in Christmas savings. Mr. R. C. Cather, Vice President of the Wyoming Trust Company, reports that savings accounts have increased between 10 and 15% over January of last year and that Christmas savings had increased a great deal more than this.

MOTION PICTURE ATTENDANCE: The manager of the three local theatres in Casper reports that there has been a decrease of about 8% in the attendance this year as compared with 1930.

AUTOMOTIVE: Station owners in this territory when interviewed reported that there had been a very noticeable increase in the sale of gasoline and oil consumption during the first part of this year as compared with last year. While some of this increase is due to the open winter it does, however, show a decided spending tendency in this territory.

PRACTICAL "FARM RELIEF"

ADVERTISING has sold billions of dollars worth of goods for America's manufacturers. That same power is being applied to farm products today in the campaign of twenty-four sheet posters now displayed on panels in 17,500 cities and towns in 30,000 locations.

Seen repeatedly every day by a resident population of over eighty millions of the American Public and frequently by more than twenty million more of the residents of the sparsely settled districts, this tremendous force of impression is presenting the products of the farm ready for human use in a manner that will reduce the present surplus, increase the farmer's purchasing ability and hasten the return to normal conditions.

This appliance of the power of advertising to the marketing problems of the American Farmer has been made possible through the cooperation of the Grain Stabilization Corporation of the Federal Farm Board of the Department of Agriculture and the Outdoor Advertising Association of America.

Educational Division
OUTDOOR ADVERTISING ASSOCIATION OF AMERICA, INC.
165 West Wacker Drive   Chicago, Ill.

Outdoor Advertising of Today

Everywhere that people move, whether in the great cities or the small towns, outdoor advertising is driving home the advertiser's message.

The Receptive Moment!
It Has Changed From
Fireside to Outside. Outdoors!

Four hundred and six thousand passenger automobiles in Detroit . . . more passenger cars than there are families!

Don't you think that has made a change in the Receptive Moment for advertising?

Two hundred theatres luring hundreds of thousands of persons nightly from fireside fiction.

Don't you think this also has influenced a change in the Receptive Moment for Advertising?

The ceaseless repetition of unavoidable Outdoor Advertising transmits its powerful influence in close step with today's most logical Receptive Moment and in today's most acceptable terse way.

DETROIT

GRAND RAPIDS   SAGINAW   FLINT

OUTDOOR ADVERTISING

at lowest cost per thousand circulation

During 1930 a veteran advertiser increased his appropriation, used 46% of it in Outdoor Advertising, and surpassed his 1929 profits by more than a million dollars.

Many advertising agencies and advertisers find the representatives of Foster and Kleiser Company genuinely helpful because of their *factual* knowledge of Outdoor Advertising and its place in advertising plans.

Foster and Kleiser

C O M P A N Y

GENERAL OFFICES: SAN FRANCISCO
Operating plants in California
Washington, Oregon and Arizona
Offices in New York and Chicago

NATIONWIDE OUTDOOR ADVERTISING

Advertising Outdoors

A magazine devoted to the interests of the Outdoor Advertiser

Vol. 2, No. 3

CONTENTS for MARCH 1931

Harold L. Eves
Editor

Ralph B. Patch, *Associate Editor*
James P. Dobyns, *Advertising Manager*

Eastern *Advertising Representatives*:
Walworth and Wormser,
420 Lexington Ave., New York City.
Western *Advertising Representatives*:
Dwight Early,
100 N. La Salle St., Chicago

ADVERTISING OUTDOORS is published on the 1st of every month by the Outdoor Advertising Association of America, Inc., 165 W. Wacker Drive, Chicago, Ill. Telephone Randolph 1692. Harold L. Eves, Editor and Manager.

Subscriptions for the United States, Cuba, Porto Rico, Hawaii and the Philippines, $3.00 a year in advance; Mexico and Canada, $3.25; for all other countries, $3.50. Thirty cents the copy. Make all checks, money orders, etc., payable to Outdoor Advertising Association of America, Inc.

Entered as second-class matter, March 21st, 1930, at the Post Office at Chicago, Ill., under the act of March 3, 1879, by Outdoor Advertising Association of America, Inc. Printed in U. S. A.

TOMORROW — What!

MANY of the successful businesses of today were built on foundations laid during depressions. Business men who were quick on their feet capitalized almost as much in times like these as from times of prosperity.

Following each depression, there has been a boom period in which great institutions were built or expanded to take care of the demands created by the competitors who fell by the wayside during the hard times.

The institutions that will come to the front in the next few years will expand on *new ideas, new merchandising methods*, rather than in building back to a quantity production of yesterday's merchandising.

The next few years will see new corporations as industry's leaders and new men at executives' desks. New factories will be turning out new products. Products that were modern yesterday will be obsolete tomorrow. Names that were household words yesterday will be forgotten tomorrow.

Prosperity will follow this period of depression just as surely as it has followed previous depressions. Reputations are going to have to be made over. Old reputations will have to compete with new, vigorous and ambitious institutions. The new institutions through the force of merchandising and advertising are going to sell to people who are again prosperous the idea of linking new name with quality products.

Now—and tomorrow—the business institution that wishes to continue and to regain its position, must develop a reputation through service—and advertising.

POSTERS BRING CUSTOMERS
to Unique Cafe

By Augusta Leinard

● One of the most unique store-fronts in America was recently shown in exact coloring in a beautiful outdoor poster. This was used in a "flash" campaign, one-quarter showing, or 32 panels in the metropolitan area of San Francisco, for 30 days, the objective being to familiarize the public with the new exterior of Bernstein's Fish Grotto at 123 Powell Street.

Started in 1906 Bernstein's is known the world over for its seafood dishes—the restaurant where fish caught at 5:00 a. m. are served the same day. You couldn't get a steak there at any price but the seafood and fresh fish are the finest the market affords.

The new exterior is built like the prow of a ship closely following the lines of the *Nina*, flagship of Christopher Columbus's fleet and it juts out to the sidewalk, which is of rubber blocks made to look like weather-beaten wood.

The main entrance, leading through two sets of brass paneled swinging doors, opens on a spacious dining salon with galleries on three sides. Here the atmosphere of the sea is ingeniously carried out by rough timber pilings with wrought iron rails and stanchions and woven rope.

● Maurice Bernstein resolved a quarter of a century ago to capitalize on the rich variety of fish that the San Francisco location made possible. From the humble beginning of a retail oyster stall he built up the vast enterprise that has made him an acknowledged leader in his line. Today he has hatcheries of his own and also journeys abroad to keep informed on the best liked recipes of chefs in Paris, Berlin, and other continental centers. Some of these recipes are duplicated at Bernstein's and others form a basis for seafood dishes which can be secured no other place in the world.

● "In addition to featuring our store front in the poster," Mr. Bernstein said, "we also wanted to advertise our $1.10 dinner which had just become a nightly event. That direct results followed the advertising was evidenced by the prompt increase in our dinner and Sunday evening trade and we knew this came through the poster because no other form of advertising was being used at the time. The increase was particularly gratifying because the restaurant business was anything but good at that time. In fact, we have been so pleased that we are running a poster campaign during the summer months in Stockton, Sacramento and all through San Joaquin Valley.

"One striking feature of our design was the background of rippling waves in marine blues and greens and we are putting the same background on the painted bulletin maintained continuously above Bernstein's Fish Grotto at 6 Sacramento Street in San Francisco and will also use it in advertising done at our Los Angeles grotto."

Here is the poster that put over the message of quality food in distinctive surroundings so well that the program has been enlarged to include other cities.

THE MARKETING PROBLEMS
of
AMERICAN BUSINESS

Number One of The Series

Colonel Randolph says: . . . .
"All lines of industry have diversified problems in putting
their products or services in the hands of the ultimate
user. Nevertheless, many of the problems which have
been met and overcome by one line of industry are constantly making their appearance in another line . . . and
if the leaders of American Business will make their vast
fund of knowledge of the problems of lowering selling
costs available, a vastly improved state of efficiency will
be noted."

■ In this first of an important series on the marketing
and distribution problems of American Business, Colonel
Robert Isham Randolph, President of The Chicago Association of Commerce, vividly pictures Business making
every effort to reduce production costs, and paying all
too little attention to the inefficient marketing systems
now existent. Other articles in the series will represent
Business' answer to Colonel Randolph's plea for study
in this field.

another. What one industry learned about the mysterious processes of marketing has not been passed on to other industries. The sum total of the knowledge on this important problem could very probably answer the needs of individual producers in every respect.

● The difficulty is that the sum total of this knowledge is not available to industry as a whole, as is the engineering knowledge of manufacturing problems. Moreover Colleges and Universities turn out engineers by the thousands every year. But they don't graduate men at least equally trained in this even more serious business problem. It is doubtful if there is a University in the country that gives courses in marketing, distribution, merchandising, and advertising which offer young men a background of training comparable to the engineering training that is available in hundreds of schools throughout the country.

Until such courses are made available, this problem is apparently going to be a responsibility of American Business. Industry as a whole will have to be the great laboratory—the great University for training of men in this field. The best brains of business have been turned to the problem of reducing manufacturing costs. In the future we may expect to see them turned to the intriguing problem of reducing marketing costs.

● The teachers in this educational effort will have to be the leaders of Business themselves—the merchandising geniuses of our great industries.

These men really owe it to the business structure to

pass on the lessons they have learned. The small business of today is the large corporation of tomorrow. It is equally certain that every failure in business hurts the giant industries as well as the small concern that fails. Each failure means an actual loss in the purchasing power of the personnel of that failed business, and when the thousands of failures every year are added together this means a very substantial loss not alone in the purchasing power of the personnel of these organizations, but it offers a dampening effect on the confidence of people in general. (Continued on page 32)

ADVERTISED GOODS
Bring Profits to Local Merchant
by James P. Dobyns

The merchant who is on his toes today is more than ever before apt to reap the benefits of his wisdom. Most of the merchandise that is sold in the United States is advertised widely. If it is something that is sold in several stores in a community, presumably each merchant in town gets an equal share of the advertising appropriation set aside to influence that community. Actually, however, there may be four merchants supposed to benefit from the manufacturer's efforts—but because three of them are asleep—not pushing the manufacturer's goods, and one of them is awake, actively promoting the sales of this particular product, the one live merchant really assures himself of by far the greater portion of the advertising and merchandising effort put behind the product.

● The live merchant ties in with the advertising the manufacturer is doing. He dresses up his show windows; he arranges counter-displays; he displays the product attractively; he has his clerks suggest the purchase of the product to every customer that comes into the store . . . . and he gets tremendous value out of the manufacturer's advertising.

To illustrate this: The housewife, out for the daily round of shopping, sees an advertisement; say on a poster panel. She receives a definite impression from that advertisement, even though this impression may be subconscious.

Arriving at the store where she does her shopping

The advertised product has a prestige which the intelligent merchant recognizes as a valuable asset.

she receives a second advertising impression—is reminded of the first advertisement by a window display which closely ties in with it. This second reminder, coming at the point of purchase—*as she goes into the store*—actively paves the way for a sale.

● Inside the store a counter-display carries her mind once more to the product. And there, in plain sight, where she can examine it while the clerk is filling out her orders, is the product itself. When the clerk suggests the purchase of this article, a sale is almost certain to result, for the prospect's thoughts have been directed into the proper channels.

Now suppose the housewife has been sufficiently impressed by the advertisement she has seen to go to her regular store and ask to buy the product. The merchant doesn't have it. She leaves the store—perhaps with the definite purpose of going some place else, or perhaps with no intention of searching further for it. But in walking down the street she passes the window of a competitor, who is featuring the very product she had set out to buy. She goes into that store and *buys* that particular brand of coffee, shoes, flatiron, or whatever the case may be.

More important still. . . . She has made this purchase at a time when she is displeased with the store where she has regularly made purchases in the past. The competitor is thus offered a golden opportunity to secure a customer for other goods—a customer who will regularly come to *his* store, rather than go to the one where she had shopped previously.

● Many merchants have been led astray in featuring and pushing products not so (Continued on page 28)

NEWS OF THE OUTDOOR INDUSTRY

Kent-Dickinson Changes Name

E. H. Dickinson Advertising Company, Ltd., is the name by which the firm, formerly operating as Kent-Dickinson, Ltd., will hereafter be known. This Company is one of the official solicitors of the Poster Advertising Association of Canada, and specialize in outdoor advertising. E. H. Dickinson, President and Manager of the Company, and H. W. Fleckney, Secretary-Treasurer, have been actively engaged in the advertising business in Canada for over twenty years.

G. O. A. Elects Directors

At the annual meeting of stockholders of General Outdoor Advertising Company, B. L. Robbins and Russell L. Fay were elected directors to succeed H. E. Fisk and William S. Yerkes.

Name Jury for Exhibit of Outdoor Advertising Art

A jury has been named in anticipation of the Second Annual Advertising Art Exhibit to be held by the Chicago Advertising Council next October.

The members are Dewey Bertke, art director, Lord & Thomas and Logan; Oscar Bryn, art director, Erwin, Wasey & Co.; Donald Douglas, vice-president, Quaker Oats Co.; G. R. Schaeffer, advertising manager, Marshall Field & Co.; Mark Seelen, art director, General Outdoor Advertising Co., and Hadden Sundblom, Stevens, Sundblom & Stults.

Old Gold Sales Boost Profits

The P. Lorillard Company profit of over 500 per cent, registered during the depression year, is largely due, according to Lorillard officials, to greatly increased sales of their leading brand, Old Gold cigarettes. The company reports that Old Gold sales showed an increase each successive month, throughout 1930.

While the tobacco industry fared better than others last year, the Lorillard gain represents the largest percentage of increase in net nearnings among the major tobacco companies; and this gain was accompanied by a three million dollar increase in surplus, and six million in cash on hand. Inventories were reduced by four million, and there was a million and a quarter reduction in bonded indebtedness.

K. H. Fulton Nominated Director U. S. Chamber of Commerce

Kerwin H. Fulton, President of General Outdoor Advertising Company and Chairman of the Board of the Outdoor Advertising Association of America has consented to become a candidate for Director of the Chamber of Commerce of the United States.

Mr. Fulton, if elected, will be one of the two Directors representing the Department of Domestic Distribution. Inasmuch as his life work has been devoted to the solving of the distribution problems of national advertisers, Mr. Fulton is admirably fitted for this position.

It is felt that Mr. Fulton can bring to the Department of Domestic Distribution a wealth of knowledge, experience and ability concerning the problems of distribution and its related subjects for which that department is responsible.

That this opinion is concurred in widely, is indicated by the fact that his nomination is being sponsored by all of the following organizations:

Outdoor Advertising Association of America, Inc., Chicago.

United States Trade Mark Association.

Tea Association of the United States of America.

Merchants & Manufacturers Association, Washington, D. C.

Colorado Manufacturers & Merchants Association, Denver, Colo.

National Manufacturers of Soda Water Flavor, Brooklyn, N. Y.

Northeastern Retail Lumbermens Association, Milwaukee, Wis.

National Engine & Belt Manufacturers Association, New York, N. Y.

Furniture Manufacturers Association of New York.

Northwestern Retail Lumbermens Association, Rochester, N. Y.

Wire Cloth Manufacturers Association, Washington, D. C.

Macaroni Manufacturers Association, New York, N. Y.

Dried Fruit Association of California, San Francisco, Calif.

National Association of Dyers and Cleaners of the United States and Canada, Washington, D. C.

City National Bank & Trust Company of Evanston, Illinois. (Continued on page 31)

CHIEF HEALTHWATER
blends Art with Atmosphere

● When a tie-up between art-work and atmosphere is so strong that it gives the onlooker precisely the reaction needed to put over the message, precedent shows that that outdoor advertising is a success. *Rancho Malibou de la Costa*, kept to Early Spanish California in its pictorials and is now the playground for the elite of the motion picture stars, many of whom maintain seashore homes there. Also, in the experience of the Rio Grande Oil Company, which picturizes the traditions of the Southwest so realistically that motorists in the territory are getting to think oil whenever they see the name Rio Grande.

Another outstanding example of this achievement of a tie-up is an Indian used by Richardson Springs, a famous California health resort which abounds in mineral springs of curative value. This Indian, when created by Emil Grebs of the Foster and Kleiser San Francisco Art Department, was to be a joint design for Richardson Springs and the Sacramento Northern Railway, but it created such a sensation that Lee Richardson, manager of the Richardson Springs resort, adopted it as a trade figure. It is now being used on advertising material of every description. Very impressive is a huge cut-out of the Indian, devoid of advertising copy, stretched out high up on a cliff in the mountains forming the background for the 200-room hotel conducted at the resort.

● Richardson Springs is in the foothills of the Sierra Nevada Mountains in Butte County, California, twelve miles from Chico, and the appropriateness of this trade symbol may be appreciated when it is stated that there are indisputable proofs that for years, and perhaps centuries, the locale was the Indians' stamping ground. The early Redskins made pilgrimages there to drink the waters of the springs. It was a gathering place for the tribes, the site of their council feasts, the scene of their quaint ceremonials, and the common ground upon which they met and formulated their treaties. The rugged grandeur of the scenery typifies the primitive Indian, which may be one reason why the picture about to be described was more successful, from an advertising standpoint, than the proverbial "thousand words."

● A young Indian, lean, lithe, muscles rippling under his bronzed skin, is stretched out drinking the health-giving waters of the spring. He wears a blue G string (loin cloth), and a coral colored hair-band confines his jet black hair. Simplicity, vigor, perfect health are the qualities he radiates that arouse the stimulating response in the minds of those who see the de luxe painted bulletins dominated by this figure. In the latest bulletin he was given the name Chief Healthwater and it is interesting to note that this addition seems to have increased his prestige and individuality. Twenty-four panels are being used in locations extending from Grants Pass, Oregon, to Stockton, California; and in Marin County, California, from San Rafael to Sausalito.

"We are absolutely sold on our outdoor advertising," said Lee Richardson. "We have a health and pleasure resort that is open the year round and in checking on our advertising we find that the bulletins are unquestionably producing results. In our experience it is the best medium through which to reach the tourist and traveling public as well as (Continued on page 21)

Chief Healthwater, the symbolic figure which Richardson Springs is using so successfully

N. E. L. A. Conference
Studies Electrical Advertising

● For the third time in as many years, the "fatted calf" of electrical advertising was taken apart and put together again. The operation was performed at the Westinghouse Lighting Institute, New York City, under the auspices of the N. E. L. A., and required three days, February 25, 26, and 27.

More than 300 representatives of public utilities, manufacturers, maintenance companies, and sales organizations gathered to hear and take part in not only the customary educational talks on the history, construction, installation, operation, and design of electrical signs, brought up-to-date from past years, but also to hear an impressive array of inspiring and instructive talks covering the more non-technical phases of electrical advertising. Gilbert T. Hodges, President, Advertising Federation of America, New York, left the pungent thought that if the available potential field were fully developed, it would yield annually at least 300 million dollars of electrical advertising income.

● Getting off to a prompt start under the chairmanship of E. A. Mills, the conference was opened with the talk, "Why Everybody Profits from Electrical Advertising,"

From a social standpoint, the high spot of the Conference program was the dinner and entertainment arranged at Leonards on Thursday evening, February 26th.

by Clarence L. Law, General Commercial Manager of The New York Edison Company. His contribution to the sales aspect of electrical advertising was:—

"Whatever the circumstances of the merchant's business, the fact remains that the electric sign is part and parcel of the user's scheme for sales promotion and shares his budget with other forms of advertising and other sales efforts . . . . . . Commercially the electric sign business in New York means an estimated annual revenue to the utilities of approximately 6½ million dollars. Nearly half of this is derived from Manhattan Island alone, which of course includes the famous 'Great White Way.' "

● Relative to the difficulties frequently encountered in municipal ordinances which restrict unfairly the erection of electrical signs, R. V. Sommerville, Claude Neon Lights, Inc., New York, speaking on installation in electrical advertising practice, concisely concentrated all existing objections of this nature when he said:—

"How an electric sign may be installed, where it may be hung, and who shall do it is controlled by the municipality. The sign ordinance or code, unfortunately, in the majority of cities came into being because of an outstanding accident that caused death or a great amount of property damage. It was, therefore, initiated as a regulatory civic measure (Continued on page 25)

Dreyfuss Addresses Association of Advertising Men

Leonard Dreyfuss, President of the United Advertising Corporation, in an address delivered before the Association of Advertising Men at Grand Central Palace, offered a solution to present day merchandising problems.

Taking as his theme "What is America going to do about the present day situation of production having run away with selling?" Mr. Dreyfuss spoke of the necessity of knowing one's markets and the opportunities presented for intelligent and intensified selling. "In all of the states of the union there are 3,068 counties. In 12 of these counties are 30% of the retail outlets and 33-1/3% of the nation's business; in 66 counties, 55% of the nation's trade; and in 225 counties, 75% of our national business is contracted. Bearing out these figures, we have in the United States, 336,880 grocery stores, 98,770 of which are located within the confines of 12 counties. If a manufacturer starts out to do a first-class national selling job he must first conduct an intensive sales campaign in 66 counties of the United States."

Mr. Dreyfuss closed his address by calling to task the average agency executive for his small knowledge of one of the most important modern trade facilities, namely, outdoor advertising.

"The successful advertiser, when introducing a new product to any market no matter how large or small, must first *explain* it in newspapers, magazines, trade papers, etc., and, second, if he intends to hold this market he must everlastingly *explain* it through outdoor advertising.

Highway Commission Removes Tack Signs

The Highway Commission of Kentucky recently removed hundreds of tack signs and highway markers from the Bardstown Road out of Louisville, Kentucky.

Advertising Combats
ANTI-CHAIN PROPAGANDA

By Delphine Schmitt

Advertising Manager, Denver Division
Piggly Wiggly and MacMarr Stores

● In many districts of the United States the chain store has taken the place of the trusts and the railroads as the symbol of "Big Business" in the worst meaning of the term. The chains are represented as huge octopi, sucking the money that is the life blood of the small community to the chain headquarters in Wall Street where they crouch, snarling, over their ill-gotten gains. The name "Wall Street," in many parts of the country, is sufficient to reduce radio announcers to frenzy and, when combined with "Chain Store" provides an issue that many unscrupulous politicians have seized upon with glee.

The chains have, for the most part, declined to reply to the attacks made upon them and have trusted to the service rendered to defend them. About a year ago, however, the anti-chain campaign seemed to reach its height with attacks of every kind being carried on through both newspapers and radio with the radio giving vent to the "hottest" and more unjustified propaganda.

● Denver was far from exempt from this type of persecution, the worst tirades against us being conducted over two local radio stations. A very large proportion of the charges brought against the chains were without any foundation in fact, at least as far as the Piggly Wiggly and MacMarr Stores were concerned.

The copy space in price advertisements similar to this was devoted for a month to an explanation of what the chain store does for the community.

● We determined to tell our customers the truth concerning the points upon which we were being attacked. We were already using a weekly price advertisement in newspapers and a part of this was devoted to an editorial and illustration designed to build good-will for our organization. We decided that this space would be used for a month to tell the truth about the Piggly Wiggly and MacMarr Stores in Denver and vicinity. In addition to this, an outdoor (Continued on page 32)

Colorado products are featured on all bulletins used by the Piggly Wiggly-MacMarr stores.

Outdoor Advertising
ADVERTISES OTHER MEDIA

By Frank T. Carroll

Telephone Directory Manager
Northwestern Bell Telephone Co.

● The first job of advertising—whatever its ultimate purpose may be—is to place a message before a large number of people. There are scores of ways in which this first job may be performed. Which one or ones of these scores of means are used by an advertiser depends on the particular thing he wants to accomplish. One means may be ideally suited to his particular problem, and yet be entirely unsuited to solving the problems of another advertiser.

The failure to recognize that different businesses face different problems in merchandising their products or services is largely responsible for the feeling among laymen or beginners in advertising that the different media are competitive. It may be said that practically all forms of advertising supplement other forms.

When a conscious effort is made to actively make one form of advertising effort merchandise or advertise the other forms being used, when the copy theme is the same throughout the media being used, and when the sum total of the effort focuses on the thing being sought —all at the same time—a real merchandising job is being performed.

● An interesting example of this type of coordinated effort is found in the campaign being conducted by the Carbon Coal Company of Des Moines, Iowa; one of the largest coal dealers in Iowa.

It was recognized that the problem was largely one of having the telephone number of this company so well known that when coal was needed their number or where it could easily be found at once, would come to mind. It was also felt that the majority of people order their coal over the telephone, rather than making a personal call at the company office. These two factors would immediately suggest the telephone directory as a medium. The name, repeated every day of the year in the directory offered the necessary institutional advertising advantages, and would be the first place the potential customer would look when ready to order coal. And since the majority of orders come over the 'phone, this was a logical place to advertise.

● With the purpose of merchandising this key-advertising effort, it was decided to use direct mail and outdoor advertising to call potential customers' attention to the directory advertising.

Government postal cards announcing the fact that the inside front cover of the new directory would carry *the* telephone number to call when fuel was needed, were mailed to all telephone users. This was followed up with a letter to 25,000 potential coal buyers.

Just prior to the issue of the new directory twenty painted bulletins were placed at strategic locations, covering the main highways leading in and out of Des Moines, and on well traveled streets adjacent to the business district. Each of these bulletins bore the caption "Turn the front cover" and pictured the new directory in a manner that made it immediately recognizable as a telephone directory. (Continued on page 21)

The Carbon Coal Company has used this design with the characteristic figure to call attention to their advertising in the telephone directory.

What's Wrong with
POSTER DESIGN

By Oscar Bryn

Art Director, Erwin, Wasey and Co., Ltd.

● It is, unfortunately, obvious that the general level of poster advertising in America is distinctly below that of the work appearing in the magazines of today. In "Modern Publicity," a survey of present-day advertising published by Commercial Art magazine, Earnest Elmo Calkins said:

"The highest pitch of excellence in advertising art is reached in the magazine pages. We do not have in the United States any such poster work as is common in Europe for several reasons. The first is the shape and size of our billboards. Instead of the smaller and better proportioned sheet that is used in Europe, we have a large oblong sheet which doesn't lend itself to good designing. More than that, for some reason, there is not the same freedom of expression, the same daring and originality used in poster designing that is manifest in the advertising pages of the magazines. So our best work is not found on the billboards as it is in Europe, but in the color pages which adorn the magazines and successfully compete in interest and attractiveness with the editorial features of the book."

Although Mr. Calkins' statement as to the relative merits of magazine and Outdoor Advertising cannot be seriously disputed, the reasons which he gives as the cause of the difference are open to question.

That the large size and the oblong shape of the twenty-four sheet poster is a direct cause of inferior design is a statement that would seem difficult to substantiate. The proportion is practically the same as that of the European posters which are so successfully designed—except that the American poster is turned on the horizontal.

● This horizontal proportion is not arbitrarily designated but is essential in present day America. Life moves more swiftly in this country than in Europe. America is on wheels moving rapidly—horizontally. Just as the modern skyscraper has developed from the tendency to concentrate business into small areas so the modern poster has developed from the speed at which America is moving. The poster must be turned on the horizontal or go unread. The time allowed for an impression is seldom more than five seconds and if the poster were vertical, this impression time would be

Traffic hides the lower part of this panel from the circulation across the street. The upper part of the design is, therefore, important for messages, designs and color. This is a problem in urban areas only.

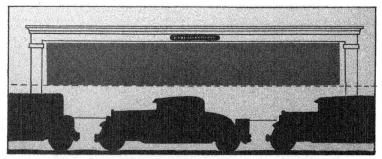

appreciably diminished with a resultant loss of value. For the same reason, the large size of the standard poster springs from necessity. It must be large or lose much of its effectiveness.

● This oblong proportion is not particularly difficult to work with. A well-designed painting is still as good design, though perhaps not as intelligible, when viewed on its side or even upside down as when it is seen right side up. In other words, the arrangement of the masses and the colors must be pleasing in themselves. It is not necessary from a design standpoint to identify the various elements such as girl, automobile or package. The shape of the standard twenty-four sheet poster is a part of the problem of the artist. It is up to him to attain good design with the materials that he has. (Mr. Calkins' statement is more a criticism of the ingenuity of poster artists rather than a criticism of the poster itself.) Good posters have been produced. There is no insuperable obstacle to increasing their number.

"For some reason," says Mr. Calkins, "There is not the same freedom of expression, the same daring and originality used in poster designing that is manifest in the advertising pages of magazines."

This reason is not difficult to find. Any task which is approached in a patronizing manner, as something to get done so that the worker can go on to something more interesting, is almost certain to be turned out in a slipshod manner; and this patronizing manner is precisely the attitude of most advertising men and artists toward outdoor advertising.

Nor is the cause of this feeling hard to find. Outdoor advertising, while the oldest of advertising media, is also, paradoxically enough, one of the youngest. Strictly speaking, there was no outdoor advertising thirty years ago. True, the fences and barns of America were covered with bills and with crudely painted signs—and these signs brought results to the advertiser. But the methods were still the methods of the circus billposter, the majority of the men who were serving the outdoor advertiser of that day having begun as circus billposters and continued to use circus methods.

● There was, naturally, criticism of the shoddy structures, the unsightly fences and the carelessly posted bills that constituted the outdoor medium. Improvement was essential and it came rapidly. Poster sizes and poster structures were standardized until today the twenty-four sheet and the three-sheet panels are the only sizes recognized by organized outdoor advertising. Construction methods were improved, each poster being placed on an individual structure, posted more carefully and surrounded with an area of white blanking paper which set it apart from its neighbors even more. In 1925 the present type of construction was adopted with its lattice at the bottom and the sides to individualize the poster still more and make certain that each design is so separated from its neighbors as to make the unit impression so necessary to advertising effectiveness.

Traffic is travelling from right to left in this illustration while the copy is read from left to right. This cuts down the reading time and makes short copy essential. This is true of both city and country.

● In the early "billsticking" days, the posters were hung dry with the result that the wet paste caused them to expand and wrinkle. Little care was taken to remove the excess paste on the surface of the poster and this dried in unsightly white blotches which considerably detracted from the appearance of the design. Today, however, non-wrinkle posting is the order of the day in almost every outdoor advertising plant in the United States. The poster is dampened before being placed on the panel and contracts as it dries, smoothing out all wrinkles. The surface is carefully washed to remove paste. The result is a smooth panel which brings out all the colors of the original design. Some plants now go to the extent of varnishing the surface of the poster, the varnish bringing out the colors with even greater brilliancy.

"The evil that men do lives after them," and the nondescript methods of the old billposters have left a legacy of opposition to the present outdoor advertising industry. Snipe and tack signs, with which organized outdoor advertising is in no way concerned and for which it is not responsible, persist and lend weight to attacks which are leveled at the organized industry as the only tangible target. Criticism which approaches virulence is the penalty suffered by the responsible plant operator for the offenses of the irresponsible sniper. That some standard structures are so placed as to interfere with a scenic view is hardly to be questioned, but these structures are so few as to be negligible when compared with the hosts of small, uncared for and unsightly signs and, if they are wrongly located, a protest will bring action.

Intelligent zoning regulations offer a logical solution to the situation but concessions must be made by both sides. Outdoor advertising must concede some of its locations—and has made clear its willingness to do so while a change must be made in the attitude of many of its opponents that whatever nature has created is beautiful. The African warthog is one of nature's products but his most enthusiastic admirers will hardly claim that he is beautiful. The addition of a few out-

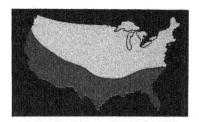

door advertising structures to the "warthog" type of scenic view will not be a serious menace to rural amenities.

● At present, outdoor advertising because of the criticism to which it has been subjected, is regarded as a sort of step-child of advertising. That the medium has even survived to the present day is a tribute to its intrinsic worth. One of the greatest stumbling blocks in the path of its further development is this attitude of unwarranted criticism that is taken toward it by the public and even by other media and the careless neglect of the study that it requires from the men who are engaged in the creative branch of the industry.

The poster presents to the artist a problem quite different from that of the magazine advertisement. In the first place, the magazine artist is not, in all probability, also the layout man. The various elements of the advertisement, headline, copy, illustration and logotype are placed by a layout specialist. The illustration's purpose is either decorative or informative or both, illustrating the copy and adding to the interest of the layout. The artist, while he should know something of advertising, is not necessarily an advertising man. He is shown the layout, given an idea as to the character of the illustration desired and is then free, in most cases, to work out the problem as he wishes. He uses a technique that he believes is suitable for the product, he knows that the picture will always be viewed against one standard background and he is able to use tone harmonies to express a mood, trusting to the layout of the entire advertisement to attract attention and to the copy to sell the product.

The poster presents an entirely different sort of problem and requires a far different handling. Since design principles are constant the artist who understands composition and color, who is a good draughtsman and who knows something of advertising has all the tools that are necessary for good poster design. But, unless he has had experience the poster he produces is very likely to be a bad one.

He must, in the first place, work with a proportion that is unfamiliar to him. He must create in that proportion a design that is artistically competent yet which will force the attention of the passer and impress its message in a few seconds. He must consider the colors of the design in relation to all possible backgrounds. His poster must shout but it must shout harmoniously.
● Outdoor advertising must shout for attention because of the nature of the medium. Its competitors are buildings which dwarf it in size, moving vehicles of every description—and the attention value of motion is no small item of competition—and the noises of the typical street. Despite these distracting elements the poster must attract the attention of busy people and impress its message upon them. Obviously the poster panel is no place for a modest and self-effacing design.

The poster has dropped one of the elements which make up the magazine advertisement. There is no copy as the magazine man understands it. Strictly speaking there is no illustration since heading, illustration and logotype are welded into one single unit by the artist who must think of the entire poster as a picture he is painting and must so arrange the elements of his picture that the greatest possible advertising value is attained without the sacrifice of pleasing design. The artist without experience in the designing of posters is very likely to underestimate the difficulties that he faces.
● The green moulding and lattice of the standard structure must be taken into consideration when painting the poster. If allowance is not made for this color frame a design that is successful when considered alone may become a disastrous failure when placed upon the standard structure.

Since the poster is displayed out of doors the effectiveness of the colors is to a great extent dependent upon the seasons. Here is another problem which is not faced by the artist who is working upon magazine advertising. The magazine is almost certain to be read indoors. The page is always—except in the special cases that prove the rule—white. Even the position in the magazine is often specified.

The background for the poster is the entire United States with its sectional differences in climate, in opinion and in color. In winter the predominant tone is dull and cold and grey and warm, brilliant hues provide the most effective contrast. In summer the situation is reversed. Yellows and yellow greens make up the background and cool colors will attract more attention. Sectional considerations are an additional problem in this connection. On the Pacific coast, for example, the colors of posters which have adequate brilliance and carrying power in other parts of the country are dulled and made ineffective because of the more highly keyed background hues of the landscape.

The tendency of nature is to reduce all colors to one monotone—therefore, strongly complimentary colors furnish the most powerful contrast with nature with a resulting gain in attention value. The artist in the magazine, having no such competition as the poster artist knows that his design will have, is free to use tone harmonies that attract attention in a more subtle manner than the poster can use successfully. No color rule can be formulated for the use of the poster artist but it can be said that, unless analogous colors are used remarkably well, they will not produce as good a poster as will the use of complimentaries. The artist must never forget that the function of the poster is first, last and always to *sell*.

The artist who gains his effects through the use of an individual technique is likely to find himself lost when he approaches the problem presented by the poster. It is not the way the illustration is done, the rendering, that particularly matters. The man who is primarily a technician finds that his technique is more a hindrance than a help. It makes no difference whether he presents the message of the advertiser in his own peculiar way or not. The question is, has he presented the message so that it is effective? And the effectiveness depends more upon the layout of the entire poster than upon the interesting handling of one part. The time that the poster is seen does not permit of admiration for deft handling. Good draughtsmanship and sound handling is always essential, but the tricky methods that demand attention in themselves do not make for good poster design.

In the same way, much of the daring and originality that appears in magazine pages would be out of place upon the poster panels. Magazines, appealing to a class circulation, can get results from such advertisements but outdoor advertising is a mass medium, and the mass of the people are not educated to an appreciation of cleverness. Once again, the time that the poster has for impression enters into the situation. A clever presentation that increases the effectiveness of the advertiser's message is highly desirable but a cleverness that adds to the complexity of the poster is most emphatically out of place.

It is possible that in Europe clever, modernistic designs have a greater chance of success than in this country. The spirit of modernism, especially on the continent, is in the air; it crops up spontaneously. In America this same spirit is forced, is more synthetic and for that reason is not convincing.

Without doubt the layout of our present posters, with a few notable exceptions, could be much improved. A solution may be in the preparation of a layout for the guidance of the artist, the layout to be prepared by a man who understands the problems presented by outdoor advertising more thoroughly than the majority of artists know these problems. In some cases, of course, the artist may be trusted with the creation of the entire poster. The men who do the work for national accounts are usually competent to handle the complete job. In the sectional field, however, there is a great need for improvement. It is possible that the advertiser

must be educated to understand that inferior design is directly reflected in the returns that he receives from his advertising. Certainly the difference between the price of good art and poor art when compared with the cost of an entire campaign, should convince the advertiser that good art more than pays its way.

Every good advertising man should be, to some extent, poster minded; for, poster is advertising reduced to its essentials. Layout, copy, illustration and logotype all combine to put over one unified message. The qualities that are absolutely required to make a good poster are the same qualities that make other advertising good but, in other media, weakness is not so instantly apparent. When art directors and artists and advertisers are educated to understand the special needs of poster design which spring from the necessity of eliminating the unessential and from the special conditions under which outdoor advertising is displayed, an improvement, not only in outdoor but in all advertising, will automatically follow.

■   ■   ■

CHIEF HEALTHWATER
Blends Art with Atmosphere
(Continued from page 13)

local residents.

"Outdoor advertising, if of the high quality represented by our Indian, is in no way objectionable. Many people have told us that if all advertisers would keep their boards in such attractive colors and design, the 'Oust the Billboard Club' would find little to complain about. This Indian with his splendid physique is a happy symbol of what Richardson Springs stands for and it has been proved to us that it reaches the mind of the public with exactly the message we want to convey."

■   ■   ■

Outdoor Advertising
ADVERTISES OTHER MEDIA
(Continued from page 17)

The Carbon Chunk Man, which has long been used in all the Carbon Coal Company's advertising, was placed at one side, pointing to the directory, and the telephone number was placed in a prominent position in the center.

This coordination of three advertising media, two of which advertise another medium being used, is the type of modern merchandising which assures results to an advertiser. Each telephone subscriber had the fact that the number was in a prominent position in the telephone directory called to his personal attention through the direct mail effort, everyone moving about out outdoors was certain to pass one or more of the bulletins, and the directory itself was always in the possession of the 42,500 subscribers in the city.

It can readily be seen that in this instance there is no competition between the means used, but the closest sort of coordination, which should always be the case when a campaign has been carefully planned.

Advertising as a
BUSINESS STABILIZER

The third of a series of talks on advertising prepared by the A. F. A.

● Our first message, *"Who Pays America's Two Billion Dollar Advertising Bill?"*, must have been a revelation to critics of advertising when they learned that instead of being a burden on the consumer, advertising was actually a benefit because it helped to raise the quality of the product and to reduce its price.

Such critics must have been further surprised when, in our second message, entitled *"Who Profits Most from Advertising?"* it was found that society, civilization, the public at large, was the principal beneficiary; that advertising was largely responsible for raising our standards of living, and for promoting educational and cultural advancement; that it was likewise at least partly responsible for distributing among the workers of the country the comforts, luxuries and recreational privileges formerly enjoyed only by the rich.

And now we come to another function of advertising which has not received the attention its importance demands, and that is the influence advertising exerts in stabilizing business, in softening and shortening periods of economic depression, and in hastening the return of prosperity.

Our third message, therefore, raises the question: "Does Advertising Help to Stabilize Business?" May we bring this subject before you by stating a few propositions which seem to be fundamentally sound?

It is generally concluded that our present standard of living and prosperity would have been impossible without the force of advertising. This standard of living is the admiration of the rest of the world. This high level of prosperity has been the envy of all other nations.

Is it not reasonable to assume that if they are to be preserved at their high level, advertising must likewise be kept up to *its* high level?

In our second message we described the foundation of our business structure and our present civilization as a three-legged stool.

The first leg is *advertising*, which stimulates demand and creates, as has been said, "a divine discontent." The second leg is *production*, which creates the product. The third leg is *consumption*, which satisfies the demand and relieves the discontent.

● Is it not essential to the full strength of this economic stool that it be kept in balance? Is it not important that all of the three legs be maintained in equal strength and length?

If the advertising leg be shortened will not the stool itself become lopsided? Is it not true that the more this leg is shortened the more the other legs must be cut down? And is it not obvious that if the advertising leg were to be removed entirely the stool itself would fall to the ground?

Do we hear a gentle murmur of protest? Do we hear a critical voice saying, "Here's the shoemaker sticking to his last. Here comes the old bromide that bad times are the best times to advertise most?"

Well, we are going to stick to our last, for it's a good last. It's tried and true.

But we certainly are not going to claim that advertising is a panacea for all the ills of business. Neither shall we claim that there would have been no depression if advertising had been kept up to the high level of a year or so ago.

● We are not going to argue that the depression is *entirely* psychological and that the buying power of the country has scarcely been affected by losses in the market and by unemployment. We would have a hard time convincing the man who is out of a job and whose family is suffering from actual want. We are not going to harp on the theme that our *only* handicap today is fear, the fear of spending, the fear of taking a chance. No matter how much truth there may be in such statements it is futile to advance them at present. There have been too many Pollyannas, and too many prophets. Most of the prophets, you may have noticed, have taken to the tall timber.

No we are going to stick to our last. No matter what the situation is today, or what its causes were, it is pertinent and profitable to raise the question of the value of advertising as a cushion for such blows.

Advertising cannot change economic laws any more than it can suspend the law of gravity. Innumerable individuals and business concerns have been caught in the grip of circumstances beyond their control.

In many cases advertising has had to be cut down or cancelled because of heavy losses of capital or impairment of credit. In many cases it became utterly impossible to maintain a liberal and forthright advertising policy even when the value of such a policy was perfectly understood.

We have no quarrel with advertisers who have been forced by special circumstances to reduce their advertising. We have no criticism to make of them. To understand their plight and their problem and sympathize with it.

All of us know it is one thing to chart the functions and values of advertising in normal and prosperous times and quite another thing to maintain the chart when things go wrong and when calamity or the fear of calamity paralyzes the buying power of the country.

Probably the most glaring example of the misuse of advertising was the lamentable over-advertisement of this very depression by some of our business leaders.

Conferences were called. Rigid economy, lower overhead, less expansion, lower inventories were decreed. All this was poured into the ears of executives, salesmen, office people and workmen. These people all went home in fright and advertised the coming big storm to their wives.

No wonder fear was bred and spread to every stratum of our social and business structure. No wonder the well-springs of buying ran almost dry. No wonder we were plunged into a buying strike more formidable than any strike of workingmen we ever experienced.

● No wonder we were changed over night from a people who gladly spent their high wages to enjoy a fuller and happier life to a people who were waiting with apprehension for the storm to break!

The depression has, however, brought us some valuable lessons—one of the most important is that the people cannot quit buying for any reason whatsoever without destroying the markets so vital to industry and to their own jobs.

How then, can the lessons of recent experience be utilized for our future tranquility and safety? Are there authentic records of business which indicate that advertising has helped to keep a safe balance between what we produce and what we buy? Is there evidence that in past difficulties advertising has indicated its power to help stabilize business?

With one eye on past experience and one eye directed to the future, let us see if we can demonstrate the influence of advertising on general business. Let us examine the whole period of 240 months from 1910 to 1930.

There were 159 months when the volume of business was above normal. During these months advertising was four percent above average.
There were 81 months when the volume of business was below normal. During these months the advertising was nine percent below average.

● In other words, when advertising was high, business was high. When advertising was low, business was low. The significance of this will become apparent when taken in connection with my next statement.

Here is a record of great importance. The upturns and declines in advertising volume *have invariably come slightly earlier than corresponding movements in general business*. Either advertisers are mighty good guessers or else business *does* expand or contract with the increase or decrease of advertising.

In those twenty years there were fourteen important business movements, seven upward movements and seven periods of decline. The expansions totalled 131 months and the declines 102. Advertising was 9 percent heavier during times of expansion than in the periods of decline.

These figures appear to show, that *advertising has a definite relation to the trend of business up or down*. They seem to show that when advertising is fearless and liberal business expands, and that when it is fear-smitten and contracted business withers.

Most of you drive a car and you know this, that when your car is running beautifully on the level the momentum carries it along with a normal amount of gasoline. And you know that when your car strikes rough roads, steep hills and tough going you have to give it more gasoline.

Is it not a thought worth dwelling on that advertising is to business what gasoline is to the motor car?

● When business encounters hills of resistance and the deep ruts of depression more advertising is needed to keep up the momentum. When our automobile be-

Our standard of living is the envy of almost every foreign nation.

Experience has shown that the firm which continues its advertising through a period of depression is very substantially rewarded for its courage.

gins to labor up hill we certainly don't get out and punch a hole in the gasoline tank. When business begins to labor, why deprive it of advertising, which is its motive power?

● We don't pretend to assert that more advertising would have kept business running at 1929 speed all through 1930. Undoubtedly we would have been forced to go into a lower gear.

But don't you believe that if business had been given the gasoline, the motive power it so urgently required when obstacles were encountered—it would have made the grade much more quickly, with less labor?

Let's see if we can't find some historical instances of what took place when the gas was turned on, and when it was turned off. The statistics of upturns and declines show certain things.

In three out of seven business declines in the last twenty years advertising was drastically reduced. The ensuing declines in business were deep and long.

In the four other instances there was only moderate reductions in advertising. The following declines did not last so long or go so deep.

Doesn't this look very much like the operation of our old friend, the law of cause and effect?

Our whole study of the hard facts of the business depressions of the past two decades seems to indicate to the open mind that one potent method of accelerating recovery is through the appeal of advertising; that advertising will lessen the evils of depressions; shorten their tenure, and quicken the return of prosperity.

Let us see if there is a lesson in the figures of even more recent experience. The records for 1930 are still incomplete, naturally, but the Advertising Federation of America found available the experience of 77 national advertisers for that year.

Twelve of these concerns reduced their advertising from 15 to 100 percent. Thirteen companies decreased their advertising by less than 15 percent, and fifty-two companies actually increased their advertising.

● Keep in mind, please, the analogy of your automobile and its gasoline supply. Of course the average profits of each group declined from the heights of 1929.

But the group which cut its advertising by more than 15 percent showed a decline in its net profits of 41.2 percent.

The group which reduced advertising by less than 15 percent had a decline in profits of 13.2 percent.

And the group of concerns which were able to increase their advertising—which stepped on the gas when the road got steep and hard—showed the smallest decline in profits, only 9.6 percent.

Perhaps there were important differences in policies. Some of you may say the concerns whose profits were

the least affected had better management than the others.

● But isn't it equally believable that it was the good judgment of the better-managed concerns which enabled them to see that it was good business to increase their advertising in times of stress?

We can go way back to the severe depression of 1921 —a period worse in many fundamental ways than the present depression—for still other examples of the apparent working of cause and effect in the relation of sustained advertising to sustained business.

We have the record of 125 national advertisers. 58 of them increased their advertising in that trying year of 1921, and 67 decreased it.

Those that increased had a decline in sales of only 12 percent while those that decreased their advertising were faced with a sales decline of 26 percent.

And when we follow those two groups for three years through to 1924, it is very interesting to note that:

The sales of the companies that increased their advertising in the pinch were 31 percent greater than in 1920, while the sales of the companies that decreased were only 5 percent greater.

The percentage of gain in business was more than six times as great for those concerns that increased their advertising as for those that decreased their advertising in 1921.

Here is credible, convincing evidence that advertising not only stimulates the volume of immediate business; but sows good seed for future business.

We believe that premise is demonstrable from the experience of a group of concerns which increased their advertising in the two minor business depressions of 1924 and 1927. (Continued on page 29)

N. E. L. A. Conference
Studies Electrical Advertising

(Continued from page 14) to correct what was believed to be a hazard, if not a real menace to the safety of the persons or prosperity of the community. This idea is still dominant in the minds of a great number of people. And yet it is extremely rare now for an accident to happen because of the falling of a sign. When one does occur, it is usually traceable to conditions beyond the sign itself or those who installed it. I refer to such instances as where a sign falls carrying with it parts of its anchorage. That the electric sign, despite this prejudice, has won general recognition and acceptance is a genuine testimonial to its value and use to the business world."

One of the more clever speaker arrangements of this advertising conference included representatives of the associations of both 5th Avenue, with its dearth of electric signs, and Broadway, with its world-famous electrical array. On the opening day of the conference, Capt. Wm. J. Pedrick, of the 5th Avenue Association, told the history and present aims of his organization. He said:—

"'Quality' was the adjective most frequently attached to a Fifth Avenue store and its merchandise. 'Exclusiveness for the masses' was a slogan appealing to democratic America. 'Dignity' marked every activity in connection with this street, and with these key words and ideals to guide him—the merchant and investor in the Avenue sought ways for perfecting and improving what he already had.

● "A multiplicity of signs, these merchants believed defeated the very purpose for which the sign was created, and hence all signs were turned flat against the building or woven into the material of the building itself, and today the visitor to Fifth Avenue is frequently puzzled as to what it is that makes Fifth Avenue 'different'—only to realize, perhaps weeks later, that this difference, or at least a part of it comes from the clear view he obtained of all the Avenue, its buildings, and stores, whether he was on the sidewalk, in his car or on a bus . . . . . .

"How is the Fifth Avenue Merchant going to place his particular piece of merchandise before his audience? If he knows his Fifth Avenue, he will know that efforts which succeed elsewhere are not applicable here—the display which resorts to mechanical devices to arrest the attention of the passing crowds may intrigue for the moment, but it is too frequently the device itself and the mechanics of it that brings the crowd to block his windows—and not his goods on display. The same holds true of live models, bizarre decorations, spectacular display methods, signs, pasters, 'window stickers,' and other forced 'attention-callers' to his window. What then is left to him to do? To my mind, the merchant who uses all of these methods and then asks that question has overlooked the most powerful, the most compelling, the most dramatic aid that could be given him

to call attention to his piece of merchandise, and that is—LIGHT.

"Light can do what every other method attempts to do, and yet never intrudes itself in such a way that it detracts the article displayed. On the contrary it will when properly, carefully, and artistically applied and controlled, bring out every desirable quality in the article on display and show those qualities to their best advantage. And that, I assure you, is the ultimate in the desire of Fifth Avenue Merchants."

● W. E. Beehan of the General Outdoor Advertising Company, New York, who spoke on the subject, "Legislative and Electrical Code Considerations," told how various state governments had passed laws making taxable outdoor signs, particularly the sign-board type. He said that such action was a result of unfair propaganda by various clubs not aware of the true conditions. All such activity, according to Mr. Beehan, indicated a false fear that signboards would eventually hide all natural scenery. He appealed to the men interested in electrical advertising to fight this growing menace to their business.

Light on the saturation point of signboards in this country was disclosed in the talk of Pierson A. Skelton, of the National Outdoor Advertising Bureau of New York. He said:—

"For many reasons which are obvious to us, including the building congestion in the larger centers of population, and the agitation against Outdoor Advertising structures in the strictly rural sections, I believe there will be no marked increase over the present number of displays, and it is possible that there may be no increase at all. Therefore, any real progress that is to be made in the better development of outdoor Advertising must be made in the improvement of location of the present number of displays and also an improvement in the advertising value of those improved displays. This, naturally leads to the consideration of illumination for the Special Poster location, Illuminated Painted Bulletins and other Electrical Displays. These, principally because of the large circulation they enjoy, which is largely responsible for high lease costs, are the highest priced outdoor displays and, after we allow for high lease costs, high selling costs, high labor costs and illumination, many of the painted and electrical displays are almost prohibitive in price to the National Advertiser who wants to buy coverage in a city as well as large circulation."

● The talk, "Dealer Identification," by L. K. Austin, Chevrolet Motor Company; proved to be one of the most enlightening talks of the entire conference because it contained the experiences and viewpoints of an actual user of signs. Startling facts to both the sign man and public utility representative were evolved from information imparted in this talk. Mr. Austin said:

"Totalling the number of signs in use by Chevrolet dealers and computing the kilowatt hours, Chevrolet Motor Company, through its dealers, is supplying you with a current demand of 31,740,000 kilowatt hours per year. Putting it another way, if every electric sign in use by Chevrolet dealers was discontinued tonight, your current load would be reduced to 105,800 kilowatt hours per night. *The figures I have given* do not include our large electric spectaculars scattered throughout the country, such as the one at Times Square, or the hundreds of illuminated bulletins we use, nor the current consumed by Chevrolet and its dealers for illumination and power. Maybe Chevrolet deserves a place on your sales payroll. However, whether or no, we are going to keep on enlarging our sign program.

● "Why does the National Advertiser, Chevrolet especially, take so much interest and give so much study to dealer identification signs? The answer is 'if our dealers are equipped with the same general types of signs, the public will look upon each Chevrolet dealer as part of a National Institution. In other words, if you are a prospect for an automobile and are impressed that the service, trade-in policies, guarantees and financing, offered by our dealer, are handled by the factory under a general policy in effect for all of our dealers, you are going to have a feeling of confidence in our car that you do not have in the one offered by the competitive dealer who is running his business entirely on his own initiative. Our standard signs then typify standard policies, consequently we *know* that they have real value."

John Gratke, Secretary Broadway Association, in contrast to the point of view of the 5th Avenue Association, said that his group of merchants advocated more light —not less—simply because light is Broadway's life. Mr. Gratke said the importance of this thought was firmly fixed in his mind when he once witnessed the great White Way of Broadway one early morning when all the signs were extinguished. Light is Broadway's life, and more electrical signs add, not detract, from the gayety.

In his talk, "Psychological Factors in Electrical Advertising," Dr. E. E. Free named the four aims of advertising as:

1—To impart information.
2—To attract attention.
3—To create the desire to buy.
4—To arouse curiosity.

Tying in these facts with electrical advertising, he said:

● "Electrical advertising has obvious and important uses in all of these classifications but there are two tasks in which the chief kind of electrical advertising, that is electric signs, is especially effective. One of these is in attracting attention, like a flashing traffic signal at a dangerous street corner. The other way is in arousing curiosity and getting itself talked about, like each novelty, introduced amid the luminous panorama of the Great White Way.

"The vast majority of electric signs, to consider first that one phase of electric advertising, have for their chief object, whether or not this fact is recognized by the advertiser, to attract attention of the inattentive passerby. If the eye is portal to the brain it is a duty of this kind of advertising to unlock the door. One thing that the sign maker needs to know is, quite obviously, what keys unlock this optic door most easily. From what the opticians, physiologists and psychologists can tell us about the nature of this portal to the brain, two keys seem the most important. One of them is contrast, as where a single brilliant sign stands out against a featureless background. The other is motion. It is, I realize, a somewhat heterodox conclusion but motion seems to me the more important, and this for reasons which go back a good many millions of years in the history of the human sense of vision."

No one was better qualified to express the newspaper and magazine opinion of electrical advertising than Gilbert T. Hodges, Advertising Federation of America. His words pertinent to electrical advertising were:

"You gentlemen whose minds are trained in both advertising and electricity are indeed fortunate to be able to combine two such extremely potent forces.

"Happily, there is no conflict between electrical and other forms of advertising. Electrical advertising forcefully supplements the printed advertisement whether national or local in character.

"Because of its flexibility, animation and color, it is unquestionably modern, and a publicity medium of forcefulness. It has the distinct advantage of willingly working for twenty-four hours a day, if necessary.

● "It effectively and tersely re-creates printed advertising thought in trademark displays or by slogans, identifies and establishes locations, permits of variety and is adaptable to most users.

"I am reliably informed that approximately 70 million dollars are spent annually for electrical advertising of which the utilities receive about 40 million dollars for electricity. The same source of information discloses that if the available potential field were fully developed, it would yield at least 300 million dollars annually of electrical advertising income of which perhaps two million would represent the sale of electricity by the utilities.

"If this is so, certainly no job for special commendation has been effected. The surface hasn't even been scratched."

"Pointblank, Earl E. Whitehorne, McGraw-Hill Publications, New York, asked the members of the conference what they intended to do with all the information obtained in the past three days, as he closed the conference with his talk, "Vindicating Your Conviction on the Value of Electrical Advertising."

The New York conference on Electrical Advertising inaugurates a series to be held in leading cities throughout the United States under the auspices of the National Electric Light Association.

OUTDOOR ADVERTISING ABROAD

Posters Pay in South Africa

H. C. Lindsell, in "South African Railways and Harbors Magazine," says of outdoor advertising:

"In a country like South Africa, where the towns are so far apart and the population so scattered, the poster is undoubtedly one of the most successful methods of advertising.

"The use of the poster has not been exploited fully in South Africa. If one excepts theatre proprietors, and the makers of cigarettes, soaps and one or two other commodities, few firms make extensive use of poster advertising. Retail firms, particularly mail order houses, would find that, as an aid to sales, the poster is of inestimable value; and the display of posters in native dialects, in districts largely populated by natives, offers an excellent means of opening up new markets.

"The peculiar conditions in South Africa render the railway stations, and also railway vehicles, invaluable as media for the display of posters or bills.

"The inauguration of road motor services, opening up the more isolated parts of the country, has forged a link between town and country which the advertiser should not neglect. The distribution of his goods being considerably easier and the demand having naturally increased, it follows that advertising in these more remote areas has become a necessity; the demand is there and competition is keen.

"In many parts of the country a trip to the railway station is an event, and suitable poster displays in such venues are eminently worthwhile.

"Naturally enough, the display of posters should be governed by the numerical strength and character of the population, the large towns demanding more concentration than the smaller towns. In the very small villages, with a community of twenty to thirty families, the few posters that may be exhibited are bound to receive attention, and when the demand for a certain article arises, those advertised would be immediately brought to mind.

"A drawback to poster advertising in South Africa is the devastating effect of the sun. Some posters, rich in coloring on arrival from the printers, are not long on the hoardings before they are faded beyond recognition. This necessitates constant renewals or, if the expense can be borne, a double printing of the fugitive colors would help to prevent fading."

Daily Mail uses Outdoor

The Daily Mail, prominent London Newspaper, has been using outdoor advertising extensively to advertise a new film contest.

French Outdoor Advertising Methods Differ from American

Jean Giraudy, Managing Director of L'Affichage Giraudy, Paris, gives some timely information as to outdoor advertising's value in France in an article in a recent issue of Advertiser's Weekly.

"In recent years," says M. Giraudy, "the outdoor advertising industry in France has developed in consequence of a demand and of the certainty of return and also because of the progress that has been made in adapting the panels to the growing needs of well-conducted business.

"It is not possible today to ensure the launching of a product, nor to increase sales without the use of the outdoor advertising.

"Suggestion every day, every moment, from a poster on a good site inevitably ends by working on the mind and the will of the passer-by, without him even being aware of it.

"A few weeks ago I carried out, for one of our leading advertisers, a posting scheme intended to stimulate a demand for samples. We put up ten hand-painted posters, about fifty feet square, in different parts of Paris. They were only exhibited for ten days.

"They pulled 800 replies. No other publicity of any sort was put out at the same time for this product. Thus there can be no doubt that these ten posters did the work.

"This example, from among many others, will serve to show that posting is indispensable, provided always that it is carried out according to certain rules regarding sites and display.

"Education in the use of outdoor advertising (over a long period of years, it is true) has taught our advertisers that the size of the poster has nothing to do with the space occupied and paid for. Thus, on a panel twelve feet by fifteen, it has become usual to place a poster ten feet by twelve. That is to say, the advertiser pays (sometimes at a high rate) for 180 square feet to show a poster of 120 square feet, because he has learned that when a poster is well framed, with plenty of air, it gives a result that is not to be compared with that which may be obtained from a poster occupying exactly its own space.

"On this point I would like to mention that in France, and particularly in Paris, very large size panels are used. It is not unusual to find a product or a big store or a famous brand using for outdoor publicity panels of 150, 300, 600 or 900 square feet.

"Here arises the question of the proper choice of display for each client, indeed, I would say for each poster and each site.

"The days are long past when bill-posting consisted solely of sticking bills on walls for a minute payment which allowed little or no profit.

"Today the outdoor publicity firm which wants to satisfy its clients must have the collaboration of well-known poster-artists. Their skill makes possible a display of the posters which will form a harmonious and attractive color scheme.

"Then comes the question of display. Take a hoarding of 180 square feet, for example. It can carry four posters of thirty square feet each. It can be laid out in superposed rectangles or in steps or on the slant, according to the nature of the product or the article advertised.

"Outdoor publicity has become a real industry which calls not only for sound financing, for the cost of sites is high, but also for a cultivated artistic sense, which is of a higher standard every day. If one can say of advertising that it is the soul of business, the posters are the charm and the decoration.

"I would warmly invite all advertisers who want to launch their product in France to make use of the professional knowledge and skill of the various outdoor publicity firms in Paris. There they will find all the organization necessary to reach every center in France, whether provincial or rural.

"May I detail a few figures, though it is a little difficult, since for certain products certain areas are unsuitable. A moderate posting campaign, however, should be divided thus:

"Paris: At least eighty posters, each one thirty square feet (2,400 square feet in all). These must be posted in the best positions. This will cost, including tax (which is 1.30 francs for a poster 48 inches by 64, and 0.90 francs per square foot thereafter) about 80,000 francs (say $3,200). These figures apply to a good display. For an intensive campaign, when launching a product, for example, these figures only supply a basis, and may easily be doubled or trebled.

"To cover France outside Paris, a campaign including all the towns with more than 100,000 population, which means about 335 localities, there will be needed 20,000 posters (48 by 64 size), which means a space of about 120,000 square feet and costs something like 220,000 francs (say $8,800).

"It is necessary to add that these figures only apply

to 'quality' posting, with sites well chosen in advance, and consequently producing definite results.

"I cannot better close this article than by quoting one of our most famous and charming artists, the delightful painter Wilette.

"'Of all the advertising that canvasses me, I only remember one form, for my eye takes it in. It is the Poster.'"

■ ■ ■

French Organizations Move to Ban Sniping

Organizations which represent poster advertising interests in France are getting together to regularize the conditions of their industry.

These bodies have held a joint meeting, and an inter-association committee is at work on the drafting of a report which will be satisfactory to all parties. The chief improvement will be, it is understood, to condemn flyposting, and the report is also expected to deal with the rebuilding of boardings and rural sites. It is not proposed to standardise sizes.

■ ■ ■

ADVERTISED GOODS
Bring Profits to Local Merchants

(Continued from page 11) well known, upon which they can make a larger margin of profit. The salesman for the unadvertised product points out that the customer is paying for a name in the advertised product; that the advertising effort put forth on the well known product makes it necessary for advertised goods to sell at a higher price; that the merchant doesn't have the margin of profit on the advertised product that he has on the other.

But American economics doesn't work that way. The advertised product is in demand. People want to buy it, because advertising has made them want it. Americans buy what they want—and they want those things they know about—the things made by manufacturers who advertise their products.

This results in a much more rapid turnover in these goods. Five sales with a three cent profit make more money for the merchant than two sales with a five cent profit.

On the other hand, this same advertising effort has been the means of making it possible for the manufacturer to dispose of his product—sell it in a hurry—and continue the quantity production schedule that makes it possible for him to sell his goods at prices impossible under any other conditions.

Thus the merchant who ties in with the advertising and merchandising efforts of advertised goods receives a four-fold advantage: He actually gets more than his share of the advertising appropriation affecting his community, he pleases and holds his customers by being able to supply their demands, he gets new customers from among those who have been sufficiently impressed to come into the store and ask for the advertised product, and *he makes more money.*

Advertising as a
Business STABILIZER

(Continued from page 24)

The sales of this group were 5 percent larger in 1924 than in 1923. Another group in the same line of business curtailed advertising appropriations and lost 5 percent of their sales volume.

Both groups suffered about the same reduction in net profits for *that* year. But—and this seems especially interesting—the first group seems to have placed itself in a better position for *future* years.

Its sales continued to maintain their lead over the sales of the second group. Its profits went far ahead. In the three years after 1924 it made a 34 *percent better showing in profits* than was made by the group which could not, or at least did not, keep up its advertising appeal.

There is one thing history proves and experience guarantees, and that is that courage pays, courage when the outlook seems darkest. That is how mankind has forged ahead through all these thousands of years in the never-ending fight against Nature, disease, poverty, ignorance. Always within him has been that spark of courage which fired his will and drove him on to better things.

● Can any of us ever forget that dauntless message that Marshal Foch sent to Marshal Joffre when the German armies were sweeping toward Paris in September, 1914 and were within eyeshot of their goal:

"My right is crushed. My left is in retreat. I am attacking with my center."

Well we might almost say of business during the past year that its "right" was crushed and its "left" was in retreat. Is this not the time to emulate the great French commander and attack with the "center." Let us say that the "right" stands for production and the "left" for consumption. Then let advertising represent the "center" and attack with that!

I like to recall, too, the heartening words of our own American General Omar Bundy, at the worst of the Battle of Chatteau Thierry. You may remember that the French, discouraged and dismayed, advised Bundy to retreat with his American soldiers. What answer did he give?

"American soldiers don't know how to retreat! We are going to counter-attack and give 'em hell!"

That's the stuff out of which victories are made—counter attacks. It exemplifies the kind of courage and resolution which are by no means the exclusive qualities of the military, but which we like to think of as American. They used to say of U. S. Grant that the trouble with him was that he never knew when he was licked. Maybe just now business needs a little of that old Grant spirit.

The signs on all sides seem to point to this year 1931 as a year of opportunity.

It won't be the easiest year to master—there are still readjustments to be made and recovery will not be nearly as rapid as the decline—but there is unmistakable evidence that conditions are ripening into a most lucrative market for the aggressive and progressive business men to capture.

● Let us measure this market comprising 120,000,000 people educated to the enjoyment of all the good things of our high standard of living and with a grim determination to fight any movement to lower that standard, to the bitter end. Let us compare the market today with that of 1930.

Last year we were all on the defense, grimly working to protect ourselves by saving and self denial. Millions of us, completely obsessed with fear, gave up our intention of buying new things and decided to make the old ones do. Everywhere the forward march of buying was halted.

For almost a year and a half we have been wearing our old duds, driving our old cars, listening to the friendly squawking of our old radio set, getting better acquainted with our old furniture, rugs and drapes.

Instead of buying new things, we have been liquidating our obligations and putting the surplus in the savings bank.

At last we come to the heart of the whole situation, now that our installments are paid, as they are—now that our savings accounts are built up to $23,000,000,000, the largest in our history—now that most of our people still have their jobs (40,000,000 with practically no diminution of their income) now that we realize that we are getting a bit shabby; that almost everything we have is getting out of date and showing signs of wear and tear—what is the dominant desire of the day?

Don't we sense it? Don't we hear it stirring?

It is the awakening, once more, of "divine discontent;" of the desire for new and better things; for the latest styles and fashions; for the best that science, invention and production have to offer.

Never was the buying power of our 40,000,000 income earners in a better position to respond to the impulse—free from debt, money in the bank and with steady jobs and incomes.

The desire, the need and the ability to buy are all present. Nothing more is needed but the urge to buy and the greatest of all urges to buy is advertising. Does it not suggest that the opportunity is here for advertising to put new life into business, to give added impetus to the buying spirit which is reawakening?

● It will, of course, require resources, vision and courage to take advantage of the opportunity which past experience and present conditions seem to forecast as being ideal for perfect demonstration of the power of advertising to serve business and the people.

So let us step on the gas and clear the road for business. Our people will joyously climb aboard and travel with us.

FROM THE EDITOR'S NOTE BOOK

Insull Forecasts Return of Prosperity

The other day Mr. Samuel Insull addressed stockholder meetings of three of his organizations. He told the assembled stockholders that people *as a whole* seemed to show a return of confidence in values. Because of this expression of confidence on the part of the people, Mr. Insull indicated that he and other leaders of basic industries thought that prosperity is coming back.

Beyond a doubt Mr. Insull is right. Beyond a doubt the expression of confidence on the part of the buyer or the man in the streets is important but the return of confidence to men of Mr. Insull's type indicates a more important factor to us.

When the leaders faltered a year or so ago, the man in the streets—the consumer—certainly could not be expected to do anything else but follow. Our leaders must lead. Plans being made by many of the leaders of our basic industries show that with the return of confidence they are again attacking their merchandising problems. With such an attack will come accelerated buying—and prosperity.

Appleton Urges Millwork Industry to Advertise

An interesting viewpoint on over-production was brought out recently by O. L. Appleton, Secretary of the Mill Work Cost Bureau. "We often hear that over-production is a principal difficulty," said Mr. Appleton, "but there should be no complaint of over-production until as much time and money has been expended in trying to sell and develop the market that is wasted through the slip-shod and unbusinesslike practices so common within industries.

"Our industry (sash, door and interior finish manufacturing) is sick and has been for a long time. My prescription is that which has been so effectively used by the modern textile industry. It has saved that industry from what seemed certain ruin and its ailment was similar to ours. We should manufacture a quality product, trade mark and *advertise* it intelligently."

Mr. Appleton then went on to state that while many manufactured a quality product, few knew it. He said, "Advertising has advanced many industries. To

advertise is to place the proper valuation on public opinion on our industrial progress. It takes money for industry advertising and lots of it. But if only 5% of the industry's loss last year was in a general fund, there would now be available over a million dollars for real, worthwhile industry advertising program."

■ ■ ■

America's Payroll Shows Increase

According to a report of the United States Service and the Bureau of Labor Statistics of the Department of Labor, America's payroll was much better in February than it was in January. While the advance in employment is only .1 of 1%, the advance of the payroll was 4.7%. This estimate was based on reports from 42,383 establishments in fifteen major industrial groups.

From the facts brought out in this report, there is an indication that there are thousands of workers that were previously on a part time basis and have been given more work. An interesting fact also brought out is the increase in manufacturing industries which showed an employment increase of 25% and a payroll increase of 7.5%.

After all men working—and earning are the only ones to whom we can sell goods. Do all the figuring you want to but employment means prosperity.

Foreign Posters Widely Used in Holland

Advertiser's Weekly, commenting upon Outdoor Advertising conditions in Holland, says,

"By far the greatest number of large-size posters are of foreign make. They are used by importers of foreign goods, carrying in most cases a strip giving a translation of the letterpress.

The extensive use made of foreign posters is perhaps the chief reason why haphazard posting has been so long prevalent—and still is, to a certain degree. Posting concerns have to deal with American, British, German and French sizes, making the effective use of such boardings as there are rather difficult.

The result is the hasty sticking of poorly joined sheets on rough boards.

For the rest the condition of outdoor advertising is very satisfactory.

K. H. FULTON NOMINATED
Director
U. S. Chamber of Commerce

(Continued from page 12)

Helena Commercial Club, Helena, Montana.
Cycle Trade of America, Inc., New York, N. Y.
Chamber of Commerce of the Boro of Queens, Jamaica, N. Y.
Chamber of Commerce, Clinton, Iowa.
Chamber of Commerce, Atlanta, Georgia.
Chamber of Commerce of Flatbush, Brooklyn, N.Y.
Chamber of Commerce, Kokomo, Indiana.
Chamber of Commerce, Geneva, N. Y.
Chamber of Commerce, Youngstown, Ohio.
Chamber of Commerce, Atlantic City, N. J.
Chamber of Commerce, Logansport, Indiana.
Chamber of Commerce, Oakland, California.
Chamber of Commerce, Rock Island, Illinois.
Chamber of Commerce, El Paso, Texas.
Arvada Chamber of Commerce, Arvada, Colo.
Baltimore Chamber of Commerce, Baltimore, Md.

Mr. Fulton organized the Poster Advertising Company in 1916, an agency for the sale of national poster advertising. He re-organized the O. J. Gude Company, New York, in 1919, in the interest of developing the national painted display medium of advertising. In 1925 he brought about the formation of the General Outdoor Advertising Company. This company is a substantial factor in the development of national outdoor advertising, and also operates outdoor advertising facilities in 62 of the principal markets of the United States. Mr. Fulton's activities in these organizations has brought him in direct contact with a great number of national advertisers, and consequently a multiplicity of the problems of distribution. The experience which these contacts has given him will be of unusual value to the Department of Domestic Distribution.

During the past few years he has served as Committeeman on the National Business Survey Conference; the Central Committee on Market Analysis, United States Department of Commerce; the National Distribution Conference held under the auspices of the Chamber of Commerce of the United States, and is a Past Governor of the Advertising Federation of America.

In addition to being President and Director of the General Outdoor Advertising Company, Mr. Fulton is Trustee of the King's County Trust Company, Brooklyn, New York, and member of the Advisory Board of the Chemical National Bank of New York City. He is serving on a Committee of the Regional Plan Association of New York City, and is at present Chairman of the Board of the Outdoor Advertising Association of America, Inc.

Mr. Fulton is 46 years of age; his life's work has been providing American business with a scientific and efficient medium of economical distribution. He is energetic and a builder.

American Business Needs MERCHANDISING INFORMATION

(Continued from page 10)

● The business that lives into the future is going to be operated by a management that looks not alone at one phase of administration, but one that is governed much as an engineer looks at the problem of erecting a building. An engineer assembles the combined knowledge of the architect, the steel manufacturers, the brick manufacturers, the concrete makers, the electrical industry, the interior decorator, and every other element that goes into a building.

In business the knowledge of production men must be combined with the findings of groups of marketing experts, distribution experts, merchandising experts, advertising experts, and sales experts. Only in this way can the efficiency of business be raised to the point where it goes ahead with the smooth dovetailing of all operations that marks the erection of a building.

The fact that the average business man looks at his business not so much from the standpoint of making more money for himself as he looks at it as a machine which must be constantly improved in efficiency—the fact that he looks on his enterprise as a game which must be played with constantly increasing skill—and his fascination with this great game—makes it certain that this exchange of knowledge will be forthcoming.

All lines of Industry have diversified problems in putting their products or services in the hands of the ultimate consumer. Nevertheless, many of the problems which have been met and overcome by one line of industry are constantly making their appearance in other lines. If the leaders of American Business will make their vast fund of knowledge of the lowering of selling costs available, a vastly improved state of efficiency in the general structure will be noted. If the present standard of living is to be maintained; if Business is to continue to stride forward—not content to remain stationary—these men will have to step forward and help train thousands of other men in this important function.

A merchandising expert once told a young man: "My boy, if you want to assure yourself of a handsome living, learn merchandising. Every time you come in contact with an advertising manager, try to learn something from him of the ways he goes about appealing to people to buy. Every time you meet a sales manager, find out what he does to help his salesmen produce more sales. When you meet an executive of a successful firm, find out how his firm goes about entering a new market; to what extent they use specialty salesmen, house-to-house canvassing; how they select their jobbers and dealers. Every time you are in a city make it a point to learn something about the wholesale and retail distribution facilities of that city. In time you will possess a fund of knowledge on the marketing of various kinds of products that will make you a very valuable man to any business organization. There are only a few men equipped with this type of knowledge in the entire country."

● That was sound advice. The picture of our industries bending every effort towards scientific mass-production and at the same time being apparently satisfied to muddle along with our haphazard, antiquated distribution system is an absurdity which surely will not continue.

We cannot expect startling advances in production efficiency such as we have witnessed in the past. We can, however, expect rapid and dramatic increases in the efficiency of the machinery of marketing.

Advertising Combats ANTI-CHAIN PROPAGANDA

(Continued from page 16) advertising campaign was decided upon as it was felt that painted bulletins, covering the entire city of Denver for a year, would create a friendly feeling among the people and would prove to them that our stores were one of the largest purchasers and distributers of Colorado-produced foods.

The display of three of these bulletins was immediately followed by much favorable comment, not only in Denver, but throughout the state and secured for us the good-will of the producers as well as that of the consumers of Colorado-grown foods.

All the designs have been headed with the slogan, "Colorado's Growth is Dependable." The first panel referred to the sugar-beet industry, one of the state's greatest assets. "Sugar Beets," said the copy, "Add $45,000,000 Annually to Colorado's Wealth. Piggly Wiggly-MacMarr Stores, Colorado's Largest Retailers of Beet Sugar."

The second bulletin, which went up during the early fall, concerned the live stock industry. The lettering was, "Livestock—A Major Colorado Industry" and "Piggly Wiggly-MacMarr Stores favor and recommend Colorado fed meats."

The design which is now displayed features Colorado canned goods. It reads, "Colorado Produces Over 75,-000,000 Cans Annually. Piggly Wiggly-MacMarr Stores Boosters for Colorado Canned Goods."

The newspaper copy was designed along the same lines.

We have been very well pleased with the results that the campaign has gained and believe that our painted bulletins have presented Piggly Wiggly-MacMarr stores to Colorado people in the right way. We are planning on continuing our use of these bulletins throughout the coming year.

PART II

On the Panels

Photo courtesy Edwards and Deutsch

A very well executed poster. There is no crowding of elements and the simple treatment of figure and plane adds considerably to the value of the design. The line of the propeller leads through the figure of the pilot to the name.

Photo courtesy Edwards and Deutsch

An excellent tie-up between copy and illustration. The eye is led through the copy to the woman's head, along the arm to the beginning of the name, "Champlin." The cutting of the trademarks into the illustration connects the picture and the name.

Photo courtesy Erie Lithographing and Printing Co.

The figure in this poster and the copy both express admirably the vim and vigor that is found in Dr. Pepper. The trademark and the "at 10—2 and 4 o'clock" slogan are made integral parts of the design.

Photo courtesy General Outdoor Advertising Company

A poster which adapts itself very well to the product featured. A unique problem in poster design, since religious significance rarely enters into the advertising of a food product.

Photo courtesy Continental Lithograph Corp.

A human interest poster that puts over the message of the product. The figure of the old lady is very attractively painted and the composition is simple and carefully handled.

Photo courtesy Erie Lithographing and Printing Co.

Salada Tea achieves the unusual in this simple, well-balanced panel. The package is played up with the simple phrase "Tea fresh from the gardens," while the elephant's head and the geometrical design lend an oriental atmosphere.

THIS MONTH

Photo courtesy Illinois Lithographing Company

This design features appetite appeal, shows the product in use and the package and adds a timely Lenten message. Note how the exclamation mark stops the movement of the package off the poster and carries the eye to the name.

Photo courtesy Continental Lithograph Corp.

A simple and well-organized poster that combines the universal appeal of childhood with the package and with the clean clothes that are the result of using the product.

Photo courtesy General Outdoor Advertising Company

Old Gold carries its continuity forward with this attractive and well designed poster. The freedom with which the head is handled adds greatly to the effectiveness of the panel.

Photo courtesy Continental Lithograph Corp.

A modern design which features the name of the company, the three-year guarantee and the refrigerator itself. The problem of putting over the message of the guarantee has been handled very successfully.

Photo courtesy Continental Lithograph Corp.

The Cleveland Plain Dealer makes use of a very effective poster in this "Start the Day Right" design. The scene shown is familiar to everyone and it is this familiarity which makes for a selling design.

Photo courtesy Edwards and Deutsch

The concentric circles which form the background of this poster give emphasis to the "Completely Balanced" copy line. The refrigerator is attractively presented and tied with the trademark.

WHO'S WHO IN THIS ISSUE

COL. ROBERT ISHAM RANDOLPH is one of the new school of engineers who have come to the fore in national business circles during recent years. A noted proponent of inland waterways, a soldier who started as a private on the Mexican border in 1916 to rise step by step until in 1918 he was commanding a regiment of engineers in France. Col. Randolph is the first engineer ever elected president of the Chicago Association of Commerce. A graduate of Virginia Military Institute and Cornell University, Col. Randolph now is vice president of the Randolph-Perkins Co., consulting engineers.

OSCAR BRYN started his career in the art department of the San Francisco Chronicle. He has since been on the staff of the San Francisco Call, the Los Angeles Examiner and the New York American. He began free lancing in 1913 in Los Angeles. He came to Chicago in 1915 and worked as a free lance for two years. Among his accounts at that time was the Santa Fe, the Canadian Pacific, Marshall Field and Company and Erwin, Wasey and Company. He has been Art Director of Erwin, Wasey and Company since 1917.

FRANK T. CARROLL was born in 1893 at Stockton, Illinois. After working his way through university by selling books during the summer he was employed for a year in a department store at Waterloo, Iowa. He has been with the Northwestern Bell Telephone Company in various capacities for thirteen years and is at present Directory Advertising Manager at Des Moines, Iowa. He served on the Board of Governors of the Des Moines Advertising Club for two years and is at this time president of the club.

■ ■ ■

DELPHINE SCHMITT was graduated from Colorado College with the class of 1914. She studied advertising at the Denver University School of Commerce and attended a summer session at Oxford University, Oxford, England. She is at present Advertising Manager of the Rocky Mountain Division of MacMarr Stores, Inc.

■ ■ ■

MAURICE BERNSTEIN is a well-known San Francisco character. He has built his present enterprise from a beginning in a retail oyster stall. He is famous for his generosity and, last Thanksgiving, closed his restaurant to the public and fed many of the unfortunates of the city.

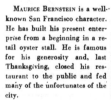

SPENDING TENDENCIES

1

DES MOINES, IOWA

GENERAL BUSINESS CONDITIONS: The larger retail stores report an increase up to three per cent in sales in February 1931 as compared with February 1930. This of course represents a larger business in view of the decline in prices.

Building permits and postal receipts for the first two months of 1931 are in excess of the first two months of 1930.

AUTOMOTIVE: Gasoline consumption, for the first two months of this year has increased over nine per cent for the same period in 1930.

During the first two months of this year, a total of 4,975 automobiles were sold. Of these, 638 were new cars and 4,317 used cars. During the first two months of 1930 there was a total of 4,269 cars sold—with a larger number of new cars and a smaller number of used cars. The new cars for the first two months of 1930 totaled 882 and the used cars 3,387. These figures are for the entire county.

During the Dollar Day held in February under the auspices of the Retail Merchants Bureau of the Chamber of Commerce, a check was made on automobiles coming into Des Moines. It was found that 800 more cars came on Dollar Day than on any peak day in June in 1930. The Chamber of Commerce makes a check of cars coming into Des Moines during the month of June, which is one of the heaviest months for traffic.

2

MASON CITY, IOWA

GENERAL BUSINESS CONDITIONS: Mr. Millington, Secretary of the Chamber of Commerce reports over a half million for new buildings in sight, about $300,000 for a new Post Office, $100,000 addition to Decker's Packing Plant, $30,000 addition to Park Hospital, $25,000 remodeling for a new Bus Depot and over $300,000 in new machinery and improvements at the Mason City Brick and Tile Company.

MOVING PICTURE ATTENDANCE: Mr. Heffner of the Palace Theater reports a slight decrease caused by the class of pictures for February as a larger percentage was of a better class in February 1930.

AUTOMOTIVE: Gasoline consumption is practically the same because of a war on prices. This means much less profit.

3
ABERDEEN, S. DAK.

GENERAL BUSINESS CONDITIONS: General Business conditions in and about Aberdeen continue to improve. This might follow the fact that the spring is the best time of the year for an agricultural state.

Bank deposits and clearings are off about 5% as compared with February 1930. General merchandise is moving the same as a year ago. Groceries show an increase in tonnage, but a loss of about 2% in net profits due to cheaper foods. Because of close buying, some firms are actually doing a net business of greater amount than in 1930 due to decreased overheads.

MOVING PICTURE ATTENDANCE: Moving picture attendance is off about 20% as compared with a year ago. Local conditions in the theatre business account for most of this.

AUTOMOTIVE: Gasoline consumption for February 1931 is 30% greater than in February 1930.

4
WILMINGTON, DELA.

GENERAL BUSINESS CONDITIONS: Business conditions as a whole were better during the month of February 1931 than they were in February 1930.

Department stores and general merchandise stores admit that they have gone ahead of last year's January and February figures.

MOTION PICTURE ATTENDANCE: Moving picture attendance was slightly increased in February 1931 as compared with February 1930.

AUTOMOTIVE: There was a gain in gallonage during January and February 1931 as compared with the same period in 1930, according to figures compiled by some of the larger companies.

5
SHREVEPORT, LA.

MOTION PICTURE ATTENDANCE: Two Publix Theatres report that their attendance is about 20% lower for February 1931 than it was for February 1930.

AUTOMOTIVE: Mr. O'Neal of Howard Motor Company reports that January 1931 was about 60% below that of January 1930, but market is now getting stronger.

Mr. Phillips of the Wray-Dickinson Company report that they are holding their own.

Mr. Overdyke of the Calcote-Shaw Gas and Oil Distribution Company reports that gas sales for January 1931 as compared with 1930 were about the same but oil was off 40%. The average decrease per station in volume was about 35%. A larger number of stations may be responsible for part of the latter figure.

6
KEENE, N. H.

GENERAL BUSINESS CONDITIONS: From a business survey published on March 3, compiled by R. G. Dun and Company, it was shown that the business depression of recent months has left and in its stead an era of mild prosperity has arrived.

"Keene and its surrounding trade territory is enjoying a prosperity far ahead of any city or district in New Hampshire. Its diversified industries are acting as a stabilizer.

"Out of a possible 2,661 positions available at local factories which were included in the survey, 2,256 men and women are now employed on nearly full time schedule. This survey was among the 29 largest manufacturing plants of Keene, and is a true cross-section. Included in the different classifications of industry are woolen manufacturing, toy manufacturing, shoe and shoe accessory manufacturing, printing, silver polish and soap makers, fieldspar and mica mining, overalls, wearing apparel, silk fibre, chair makers.

"Electric power, a barometer of industrial conditions is, of course consumed to a larger extent when factories are opened than when closed. It is significant that more power has been furnished Keene plants during the past month than during a corresponding period for many years.

"Three of the largest merchants have reported a gain in sales and net profits. Local contractors report an encouraging outlook in both residential construction and store and building remodeling.

MOVING PICTURE ATTENDANCE: Moving picture attendance is below that of last year.

AUTOMOTIVE: Gasoline consumption is about 20% more for the month of January 1931 than for the same month in 1930.

7
BOSTON, MASS.

GENERAL BUSINESS CONDITIONS: In general, conditions are much better in this period in 1931 than they were in 1930. Because of the diversity of industries, no single one accounting for more than 10% of the total output, resumption of activities in any of them means an immediate bettering of general conditions.

Retail trade is showing an increase.

AUTOMOTIVE: The automotive business has taken a definite upward swing. Comparison of sales in February 1930 with February 1931 show that sales in many places were 100% in excess this year. There was an increase in the auto registration in 1931 as compared with 1930. Over 36,000 miles of New England highways were kept open all winter. Gasoline consumption in January was two million gallons above January 1930, and six million gallons over 1929.

8

GENEVA, N. Y.

GENERAL BUSINESS CONDITIONS: Business conditions during the first part of the winter were somewhat normal but during the month of January there was a marked decline in some of the local manufacturing plants. Building operations compare favorably, and have kept the tradesmen in general occupied on an average of a five day week. There should be an improvement in conditions beginning with March due to the fact that this city is in an agricultural area, and has an extensive nursery business.

MOVING PICTURE ATTENDANCE: Mr. C. E. Dodson of the Schine Theatres reports that business is off quite a lot from the same period in 1930.

9

AMARILLO, TEXAS

GENERAL BUSINESS CONDITIONS: Amarillo has occupied the center of the "white spot" on Babson's Business Map which is a feature every month in NATION'S BUSINESS, the official organ of the U. S. Chamber of Commerce, for a period of 27 consecutive months. This indicates that Amarillo and its surrounding trade area has consistently been in the best business condition as compared with all other parts of the United States. Crop diversifications and extensive railroad building, as well as large production in the gas and oil industry have all contributed to this trade territory's prosperity in the time of nation-wide depression.

10

HOUSTON, TEXAS

GENERAL BUSINESS CONDITIONS: City building permits for January and February 1931 total $2,381,550; for the same period in 1930 the total was $2,343,304, which shows a light increase of 1.6%.

Real estate is showing signs of increased activity and most firms are decidedly optimistic.

Lower commodity prices have offset increase item sales so that general retail conditions are only slightly better than 1930.

MOTION PICTURE ATTENDANCE: Motion picture attendance was within plus or minus 2% for the larger theatres in 1931 as compared with 1930.

AUTOMOTIVE: Gasoline consumption is reported as being slightly greater in 1931 as compared with 1930.

11

COLUMBUS, OHIO

GENERAL BUSINESS CONDITIONS: Conditions seem to be above the average in other cities. Columbus is a city of diversified industries and although none of them are running at peak, yet some of them are doing an average amount of production. The retail stores are doing an average business and there is a small per cent of unemployment.

They are now building a new State office building which will cost upward to five million dollars. Building conditions are practically normal. As an evidence of this fact there was hauled into Columbus day before yesterday the biggest train load of lumber that ever was hauled on any railroad. It consisted of sixty-two full car loads of lumber. This would indicate that the lumber men and contractors anticipate business for the spring and summer.

AUTOMOTIVE: The gasoline sales in January 1930 consisted of 814,855 gallons and in January 1931, 1,164,357 gallons.

12

SPOKANE, WASH.

GENERAL BUSINESS CONDITIONS: Numerous merchants report a gain in volume for February, 1931 as compared with February, 1930 and one leading retailer reported an increase of 50%. This, however, does not accurately portray real conditions as it is the consensus of opinion that the month of February throughout the Spokane area is but slightly better than that of last year.

MOVING PICTURE ATTENDANCE: A slump has occurred in this industry, the moving picture operators reporting a decrease of 10% over last year.

AUTOMOTIVE: Gasoline consumption for February 1931 as compared with February 1930 shows a decrease of 10%.

13

OMAHA, NEBRASKA

GENERAL BUSINESS CONDITIONS: In giving facts pertaining the general business conditions, a five year period was used as a basis for comparison. In February 1931, bank clearings were 16% below the five-year average, bank debits were 13.6% below and postal receipts 2.9% under. All other indicators are favorable. Building operations increased 521%, grain receipts 28.2%, grain shipments 32.2%, livestock receipts 11.7%, and packing house output 6.4%.

During February, Omaha gained a new department store, a new hospital and a new federal building. One of our factories, the Red Arrow Burner Company purchased a Minneapolis competitor and moved the factory department here. One of the wholesale furniture houses, the Don Lee Company, outgrew its old quarters and leased one of the largest buildings in our jobbing district. All three of our radio stations completed and announced expansion programs. One of the stations revealed plans for an entirely new station.

Omaha has climbed from twenty-second place to eighteenth place among American cities in bank clearings.

In tabulating the advertising lineage of twenty-nine leading cities, the only city showing a gain was Omaha.

14

SAN DIEGO, CALIF.

GENERAL BUSINESS CONDITIONS: General business conditions during the month of February remained at the average of the preceding six months, allowing for normal increase due to holiday business. It is the consensus of opinion of retailers that there will be no definite upward trend until the early Fall months. During the past six months, the first week of each month has been above normal in retail sales, which leads to the conclusion that it is a hand-to-mouth market, the public purchasing at the time they receive their monthly incomes. The succeeding three weeks of each month have fallen off in sales.

MOVING PICTURE ATTENDANCE: Moving picture attendance during the month of February was 5% below normal.

AUTOMOTIVE: Gasoline consumption during the month of February increased about 7%.

15

PORTLAND, OREGON

GENERAL BUSINESS CONDITIONS: Business in general as regards trade is slightly on the up grade. In some lines decreases are shown in comparison with this month in 1930 and in others substantial increases.

In many wholesale lines, business is increased. Firms with national output, such as the Jantzen Knitting Mills, Columbia Knitting Mills, Pendleton Woolen Mills and the Iron Fireman Manufacturing Company report business brisk.

The combined spring opening held the middle of the month in which some two hundred retailers participated reported a considerable spurt in trade on the day following the opening.

The Portland Gas and Coke Company in less than eight days sold a million dollar stock issue to Portland residents.

A two million dollar bond issue to be voted upon in April at a special election to take care of the surplus unemployment.

MOVING PICTURE ATTENDANCE: Figures furnished by R. K. O. show a 20% better attendance than for the same time last year.

EFFECTIVE COPY

Outdoor displays are selling the products of advertisers this very minute. They insinuate the message into the public mind with ease, repeating it ceaselessly day after day.

To put the utmost into outdoor design requires experience, ability and technique, such as we offer to advertisers and their advertising agents.

*Advertising Offices
in Sixty Cities*

General Outdoor Advertising Co.

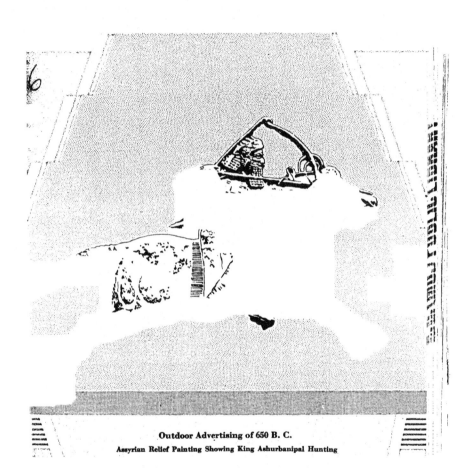

Outdoor Advertising of 650 B. C.

Assyrian Relief Painting Showing King Ashurbanipal Hunting

Canada

Include Canada in your advertising and selling plans. Here you will find a prosperous market of ten million people, best reached by Poster Advertising.

Any of the following Poster Advertising Agencies will be pleased to give you the facts and figures about Canada:

The Canadian Poster Company, Limited, Montreal, Que.
The Gould-Baird Poster Company, Limited, Brant-ford, Montreal, Toronto, London, Vancouver.
H. E. Dickinson Advertising Co., Limited, Toronto, Ont.

E. L. Ruddy Co., Limited, Toronto, Hamilton, Win-nipeg, St. John, Vancouver.
Lindsay-Walker Co., Limited, Winnipeg.
Ruddy-Duker, Limited, Vancouver.
Charles Baker, Ltd., Toronto, Ont.

Poster Advertising Association

Bank of Hamilton Bldg.   **of Canada**   Toronto

**at lowest cost per
thousand circulation**

Our organization

is continuously studying case-histories of Outdoor Advertising.

You are invited

to make full use of what we have learned about the application

of Outdoor Advertising in modern sales campaigns.

Foster and Kleiser

· C O M P A N Y ·

GENERAL OFFICE: SAN FRANCISCO
Operating plants in California
Washington, Oregon and Arizona
Offices in New York and Chicago

N A T I O N W I D E   O U T D O O R   A D V E R T I S I N G

The Receptive Moment!
It Has Changed From
Fireside to Outside. Outdoors!

Four hundred and six thousand passenger automobiles in Detroit . . . more passenger cars than there are families!

Don't you think that has made a change in the Receptive Moment for advertising?

Two hundred theatres luring hundreds of thousands of persons nightly from fireside fiction.

Don't you think this also has influenced a change in the Receptive Moment for Advertising?

The ceaseless repetition of unavoidable Outdoor Advertising transmits its powerful influence in close step with today's most logical Receptive Moment and in today's most acceptable terse way.

DETROIT

GRAND RAPIDS   SAGINAW   FLINT

Advertising Outdoors

A magazine devoted to the interests of the Outdoor Advertiser

VOL. 2, No. 4

CONTENTS for APRIL 1931

Harold L. Eves
Editor

Ralph B. Patch, *Associate Editor*
James P. Dobyns, *Advertising Manager*

Eastern Advertising Representatives:
Walworth and Wormser,
420 Lexington Ave., New York City.
Western Advertising Representatives:
Dwight Early,
100 N. La Salle St., Chicago

ADVERTISING OUTDOORS is published on the 1st of every month by the Outdoor Advertising Association of America, Inc., 165 W. Wacker Drive, Chicago, Ill. Telephone Randolph 1092. Harold L. Eves, Editor and Manager.
Subscriptions for the United States, Cuba, Porto Rico, Hawaii and the Philippines, $3.00 a year in advance; Mexico and Canada, $3.25; for all other countries, $3.50. Thirty cents the copy. Make all checks, money orders, etc., payable to Outdoor Advertising Association of America, Inc.
Entered as second-class matter, March 21st, 1930, at the Post Office of Chicago, Ill., under the act of March 3, 1879, by Outdoor Advertising Association of America, Inc. Printed in U. S. A.

Why Can't
Advertising Sales Methods
Be Changed?

IF we as advertising men had the opportunity Midas had of making one wish and having it come true, we would not ask that all the prospects we talked to would believe us, or that all the copy we wrote be perfect. We would ask that every salesman selling an advertising medium would be forced by some strange magic to confine himself to the sales features of his own proposition and refrain from slinging mud at all other media.

Perhaps it is not a charge against the various media, but rather a charge against enthusiastic salesmanship, coupled with the salesman's inability to convince his prospects by media merit alone.

If we were prospects, we know that the minute a man berated any other media, the minute he referred to all other forms of advertising as "trick" or "stunt" advertising, we would begin to question the value of the proposition he was selling.

Such a man might be an *advertising salesman* but when he becomes an *advertising man*, he begins to realize that every media has its own particular merits and its own particular place in the picture. Nothing can replace the newspaper in its own field, yet we would not use a newspaper in some large city if we wanted to reach a small group. We might use a class publication or again direct-by-mail. Neither would we use newspaper copy on a poster panel or a painted display bulletin. No one would stop to read our message. By the same token as before, we would not use poster advertising with a coverage of the entire city to reach that same small select group. Yet we might use a painted display unit strategically located where the type of people we wanted to talk to passed.

Too often salesmanship concerns itself with getting a large share of the appropriation rather than a solution of the advertiser's problem.

When Midas made his wish that everything he touched turn to gold, he considered only himself and therefore suffered. Profiting by his experience, we would wish for a type of salesmanship that would produce better advertising—better profits for the advertiser. What we touched might not turn to gold, but friendly competitors and satisfied customers would make our life easier, happier and more filled with *useful* coin of the realm.

WHY TAX ADVERTISING?

By Lee H. Bristol

President of the Association of National Advertisers, Inc.

There are several reasons why thoughtful men in the advertising business are concerned about taxes on advertising right now. During the past year at least one attempt has been made to place a general tax on newspaper advertising. I refer to the proposal introduced in Louisiana last June by Governor Huey P. Long, of corn pone and pot-likker fame, to collect a tax of 15 per cent on newspaper advertising revenue. Our Association and other organized advertising groups immediately protested vigorously enough to force its withdrawal.

● During the past month a bill was introduced in the Missouri legislature to place newspapers, magazines and periodicals carrying paid advertising matter under the jurisdiction of the Public Service Commission. In effect it was proposed to make advertising a public utility. Aside from the question of whether advertising should be subjected to this form of regulation, it is well to remember that public utilities are among the most heavily taxed of all industries. Any proposal to place advertising and public utilities under the same classification would in all probability imply that the two were fit subjects for the same taxes. Incidentally, a similar provision is attached to the State Federation of Labor bill now before the New York legislature.

Shortly after the Missouri bill made its appearance, an act was introduced in the North Carolina legislature to impose a two per cent tax on the gross income of all newspapers. The money so raised would be used to finance public schools. In advocating the measure, Representative Junius Johnson, who sponsored it said, "that newspapers have not reduced their subscription or advertising rates while prices of commodities have declined." In addition, and most important of all, he stated it as his opinion that newspapers are not adequately taxed.

● Almost half of the states in the country (22 to be exact) have proposed taxes on outdoor advertising this year. Although there is little chance that any of these bills, save one in New Mexico, will pass; nevertheless, they are a constantly increasing source of irritation. Last year, chiefly, I am told, because of an unusual political situation, New Jersey adopted a tax of three cents per square foot on outdoor advertising. The passage of that measure has acted as a spur to those who seek a similar law in other states. Almost all of the outdoor tax bills introduced this year were identical with the New Jersey law. They represent a growing sentiment to regulate outdoor signs by taxation. To the minds of many of us it seems likely that such a means of regulation might very easily be extended. Those people who object to direct mail may be the next to sponsor a tax. If the precedent be established there are others who may wish to attack certain radio advertising with the same weapon. Finally, and most dangerous of all, legislators may lose sight of the reasons behind these measures and propose a tax on newspapers and magazines, not to regulate them, but as a source of revenue. Here lies the risk in any taxation for regulation.

● This phase of the problem looms even larger just now, because most of our state legislatures and even our national Congress, on account of the depression, are faced with declining incomes from present tax laws and must create new levies for self support. I have no doubt that they would welcome a chance to tax advertising if they were given the opening. Those of you with good memories will recall the agitation for a general tax on advertising during and following the war. The national

A tax upon advertising would mean the handicapping of one of the greatest factors in distribution.

hunt for funds finally gave birth to the now historic measure introduced in Congress by Representative Thompson of Ohio "to increase the revenue of the United States and to conserve the supply of print and other paper by imposing a tax on advertising." With the money thus obtained, estimated at $50,000,000 a year, Mr. Thompson proposed to help pay a soldier's bonus. It may or may not be analogous that the Congress just adjourned voted a soldier's loan measure, amounting to a bonus, without providing for an increase in revenue to pay it. Moreover, this same Congress appropriated $300,000,000 more than the recommended budget although federal revenues will be at least $400,000,000 less than that amount. No one yet knows just where the extra seven hundred million will come from. I quote these figures simply to show you that I am not raising the red flag for a non-existent danger.

● At the same time I hope that you will not take it that this is the opening gun in a great crusade against taxing advertising. There is no need for such a crusade. The present state legislative year is rapidly coming to a close. Our national Congress adjourned some weeks ago. There is no immediate danger that some one of our law-making bodies will rise up with an unexpected and far reaching tax law. I merely wish to take this opportunity to call your attention to this problem which has long existed, which is now fairly well in hand but which may become very troublesome if we lose sight of it. I believe that I can best do that by reviewing briefly certain principles of taxation which to my mind do not permit a tax on advertising. I have taken some pains to study them during the past few months. They are to the best of my knowledge principles which have been established as just, as workable, and as practical, by students of good government.

One of the first principles of taxation which we can all agree upon, has to do with its economy. In other words, the economic and social effects of the tax must be considered. The value of any tax from the standpoint of revenue is doubtful if it tends to discourage production or check the accumulation of wealth. All taxation is burdensome and, of course, I do not believe that any can be contrived that will send people down to the Internal Revenue Office in triumphal processions rejoicing in the prosperity it brings them. However, the economic effects of a tax on advertising are worthy of every consideration. They appear insignificant insofar as some minor proposal to tax outdoor advertising is concerned, but they would undoubtedly loom large if a general levy were proposed.

● Intelligent advertising is essential to economic progress. For proof of that statement we need only to return to the period just after the war when many man-

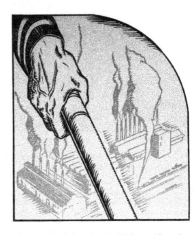

ufacturers found themselves loaded down with production facilities that had been devoted to war-time creations. They were driven to finding some means of utilizing those facilities and advertising afforded the solution. The war, I believe, gave advertising its greatest impetus, many firms which had never advertised before became advertisers because they saw just what it had done for the Red Cross, for the Liberty Loan and for our other war-time activities. In addition government officials urged manufacturers and others to buy advertising as insurance for their future business and to create good will. In so doing they hoped to, and as we now know they did, intrench their products against foreign competition. Then, as now, advertising was recognized as a creative force producing benefits out of all proportion to its own cost.

● At the present time many manufacturers are in a position not unlike that existing ten years ago. They are in possession of tremendous production facilities that advertising alone can revive to normal activity. Let us not retard their progress with a tax on their only salvation.

To tax any single medium of advertising, or to tax all advertising, is to place a burden upon a factor which makes American life cheaper and more comfortable. It is equivalent to increasing the cost of distribution and thereby increasing the cost of goods to consumers. Such a tax must inevitably be passed on to the consuming public in the form of higher prices for the necessities and comforts of life. At the same time it would be detrimental to our business, which is to get our products to the public with the help of advertising at the lowest possible price. I am sure that you will agree with me.

● A second principle of taxation (and this one too, I believe, we can agree upon) is that the proposed levy shall be equitable. Although this is a very obvious concept, it is all too often ignored. Instead, legislators as a rule tend to tax those groups or classes who squawk the least. This tendency became very apparent during the war when many advocated a tax on advertising for no particular reason except that advertisers seemed to have so much money to spend for advertising. The idea prevailing as it did in the mind of the public, made advertisers fit targets for taxation. The idea exists today among many. They believe, in the words of Congressman Thompson, whom I have already mentioned, that "advertising as now conducted in America is wasteful and extravagant and an indirect loss to the government from several angles." This last phrase referred to a charge widely circulated immediately after the war to the effect that advertisers were spending funds which otherwise would have gone to the government in the form of excess profits taxes.

To my own mind a tax on advertising, unless it is to be levied on all sales agencies, including salesmen themselves, cannot be equitable. However, I must admit that my point of view is almost wholly dependent on my belief that advertising, properly conducted, can and does operate to reduce other costs of distribution out of all proportion to its own cost. All of you here have seen the truth of that statement demonstrated. On the other hand, many of our lawmakers have not had the same opportunity and they do not recognize the full usefulness of advertising. It has been my experience that when they do learn that every well-directed advertisement is for all practical purposes nothing more or less than a very efficient salesman, they immediately see the inequalities of taxing it.

● You and I know that a tax on advertising would be a tax on a form of selling which has demonstrated its efficiency over other forms. In fact not a few of the most widely sold articles in America are sold wholly by advertising, without salesmen of any kind. Gen-

The tax burden should be equitably distributed and no one industry singled out for more than its share of the burden.

erally speaking, on any article successfully advertised, the combined selling costs of personal salesmanship and advertising are lower than the same results would cost were advertising not employed. To tax advertising would be to offer an incentive to the backward manufacturer to cling to less efficient and more costly methods. It would be putting a premium on inefficiency.

When our legislative representatives come to realize that without large scale selling, which advertising is, we cannot hope to reattain and consistently maintain our normal level of production, no one will be more hesitant to tax advertising than they. The inequalities of any such proposal will at once become apparent to them.

● As for any proposed tax on a single advertising medium as separate from other mediums. I do not believe that any can be framed that is not discriminatory. Just now the majority of advertising tax legislation is directed at outdoor advertising. There is grave danger that the adoption of any of these measures will lead to an unfair monopoly in favor of other media. There would of course be no justice in such an arrangement. Each media has its own particular place in the advertising business.

In this country any tax that discriminates between persons or things in the same classification has never been tolerated. During the last year or two, particularly, our state legislators have been busily at work trying to tax chain stores. Our courts have been just as busy declaring these proposals unconstitutional. None of them will stand the test of equality. The same thing I am sure will be true in the long run of attempts to tax a part of the advertising business. The idea clearly discriminates in favor of one medium and against the other. (Continued on page 36)

CAPITALIZING
ON STYLE

By Howard Willoughby
Sales Promotion Manager
Foster and Kleiser Company

The ultimate end of every business is to make money. The balance sheet at the end of the fiscal year is the sole index of whether store management and store policy is a success or failure; it is the one proof of competency in buying and selling merchandise.

In the interval between yearly periods of reckoning there occurs in regular sequence in the merchandising of various items of clothing, the season style cycles—spring, summer, fall and winter. And with each of these periods come fads and fancies; radical outgrowths of a fundamental style trend, which flare up like a meteor, only to disappear with a change in season. It is important to ride the crest of these so called "crazes" because they are usually on specialty items that carry a nice margin of profit.

● But far more important for the retail merchant is the necessity for deep study and thought on the style movement from which spring these immediate fads. These movements are more than seasonal; more than yearly in duration, for they represent a definite state of mind of the buying public. Dr. Paul H. Nystrom, in his recently published book, "The Economics of Fashion," concisely covers this thought when he says: "Business succeeds when it goes with fashion; fails when it goes against it."

Fashion or Style is the interpretation of the current mode of living and habits of thought expressed through design, line, mass and color. As such it is equally applicable to sky-scrapers and skye-terriers, stoves and wedding rings, shoes and Ford automobiles, toothbrushes and typewriters, as well as the cut of the cloth in men's wear.

● The modern style movement, the keynote of which is beauty, had its start with two somewhat correlated movements—symbolism in art, as contrasted with realism,—and color. The color phase is the dominant note. Where or why or how it started is beside the question. Color is here—not as a fad, fancy or craze—but it has permanently established itself in all merchandise. Utilitarianism has given way to eye-pleasure; beauty has been woven into the warp and woof of merchandise as an integral part of sales appeal. Roger Babson recently wrote, "Almost every concern is now beginning to realize that the time has passed when an ugly thing will sell. Every product which goes to the consumer should be made as attractive as possible. There is a definite value to beauty; it is not only desirable but absolutely essential today. Furthermore, beauty expressed by means of color, must be carried into one's advertising. When an attractive article is for sale, it must be set off attractively to the public."

● Commercial art has realized the selling value of color; it has found expression through the pages of the magazines, through direct mail, window displays, in a limited way in the newspapers, but in no medium in a like degree to outdoor advertising. From its very physical set up, its size and locations, outdoor advertis-

Golf surprised stylists by uncovering a latent and unsuspected desire for color in men's garments.

*The male is becoming
more and more style
conscious.*

ing has been the means whereby the artist can best interpret selling messages of merchandise, through symbolizing the emotions, in the broad flat tones called for by this new angle of sales approach. A moment's thought will substantiate the claim that through outdoor advertising, merchandise can be presented to the public in a manner to take the fullest advantages of color and symbolism, both of which are basic in the modern sales appeal.

● In the first place, the men's department does a very large volume of the total business of a community. The recent Census of Distribution organized and taken by the Department of Commerce in eleven typical cities in the United States, disclosed some interesting figures. In men's and boys' clothing for example, it showed that department stores did 18.2% of the business as against 49.5% in the men's specialty stores and 24.4% by custom tailors. In men's furnishings, the percentage increases to 31.2% for the department store as against 57.9% in the men's specialty establishments. Certainly, then here is a volume of potential business for the men's department well worth going after. However, some interesting promotional problems have come to light in the effort made to draw men into a department store for their clothing needs.

After reviewing this problem as a whole, it would seem logical, as many have done, to turn to outdoor advertising as a means of solving the question. Certainly a complete individuality for the advertising message can be accomplished through using this medium. By this we mean that there would be no physical association with other store copy. This advertising would tend to establish the men's department as a Specialty Store in itself and would offer a means of directly competing with other individual Men's stores catering to the same trade. At the same time the women members of the family would be reached and when the style and color possibilities of the medium are added, the appeal to both sexes is naturally considerably strengthened. Many department stores have and are today using the medium as the best means of overcoming men's prejudices against department store shopping.

● The male, being a conservative individual, does not react to new things or style changes with the same whole-heartedness as his counterpart. However, he is changing gradually. A picture of the "Gay Nineties" reveals the all prevailing black shoes, hats, necktie and "Sunday Suit." Later decades brought more color and finally golf surprised stylists by uncovering a latent and unsuspected desire for color in men's garments. Some of the reactions being new were violent, but at the same time they were indicative of how men felt toward color in their raiment.

This desire for that "something different" in dress has in a sense reflected adversely on the sale of men's clothing. The male clings to his sport clothes. He golfs, dines and dances in them; perhaps in his conceit he feels that he looks just a little better clothed in this informal fashion. The full dress in consequence appears infrequently; the dinner coat is worn with reluctance. One or two pairs of shoes are sufficient for all needs; a soft shirt "gets by," and the younger generation goes without hats and garters. Man has been made sporting clothes-conscious but not style conscious.

● With the money he is saving on apparel, he is spending on automobiles, radios, modern furniture, travel and the more pleasurable things of life. He spends more for gasoline than he does on his appearance.

Advertising has undoubtedly had a great deal to do with present conditions in the men's wear field. The appeal of the automobile, radio, etc., is kept before the buyer's mind attractively and continually. He is urged to buy this or to buy that; things that he actually wants to buy. The average man has never been attracted through advertising to the point where he wants to buy clothing or furnishings. He buys them because the condition of his wardrobe demands it of him. He has never been sold to the pleasure and the self-satisfaction that comes through a knowledge that he is properly dressed.

In the store-against-store competition, this big broad selling obstacle has been overlooked by the individual retailer. As Louis Blumenstock, writing in Women's Wear says, "Retail advertising is too busy claiming everything. 'A' says—'Our biggest competitors charge $10.00 to $15.00 more for identical suits. 'B' says— 'Our overhead is 12% less than any other store.' 'C' says—'You positively save $10.00 on your suits here.' That is the 'A,' 'B,' 'C' of clothing advertising." This type of advertising is not going to make men want to buy more and better clothes; it is not going to make them clothes-conscious, nor is it educating them in any way to the pride in personal appearance that will bring a pleasure to them equal to the possession of new things in other lines.

● It is evident that style and color must be sold to men as it has been sold to women. Where is the merchant to turn to advertise style and color? Certainly to the medium that can express these basic appeals to their highest degree—outdoor advertising. The price appeal is anybody's and everybody's—the store or department that will attain an individuality for itself is the store that will step out and establish itself as the style center; the store that will "go modern" and attune itself to the latest trend in fashion and thought.

The amount of money the clothing merchant can spend on local advertising depends upon the market he is attempting to reach. Based on investigations of the Harvard School of Business Administration, System, Richey Data Service, and other sources, the margin of 3.16% of gross volume can be safely allowed. This is an average figure for the United States. Owing to the rapid growth of certain states by tourists, the figure would probably reach 5%. However, there are no hard and fast rules for establishing an advertising budget or appropriation. The individual store's problem is the only determining factor.

With the percentage for advertising expense fairly well established, the merchant should study his trading area or territory to satisfy himself as to what his market is and whether he is getting the share of the business he is entitled to, and if not, where extra pressure should be brought to bear to get a larger volume. Owing to the absence of authentic figures on the subject, it has been somewhat difficult to arrive at the exact figure of how much men and boys over fifteen years of age spend annually for their clothing and general apparel. Mr. Allen Sinsheimer, Editor of "The National Retail Clothier," from sources which he has deemed authentic, has arrived at a figure of $115.25 per person per annum. With this figure as a basis, a merchant knowing the number of men and boys to whom he can logically sell, is able to broadly estimate his potential market. This market is his sales goal, and while it is not possible to get 100% of the total expenditure, a certain definite percentage based upon his position in the field should be set and striven for. Advertising is the means for obtaining increased business, and outdoor advertising due to its availability, its color, its placement in various districts of the city, is a logical force for consideration.

● The painted display branch of the medium is very well suited for advertising this classification of business. Painted bulletins serve as a quality background and also concentrate a specific message in certain districts where buying power and type of consumer indicate a most logical and profitable market for the line carried in the particular store. The painted bulletin is the medium of selective circulation.

Outdoor advertising has already proven itself an effective medium for the sale of men's wear in many sections of the United States. In this connection, we quote from Mr. Sinsheimer's book "Retail Advertising of Men's and Boys' Wear." He says, "Outdoor Advertising has a place in an advertising campaign as a reinforcement to newspaper publicity, as an advance agent for direct mail activity, and sometimes, when conditions justify, as a campaign in itself tests have revealed that a large percentage of people passing outdoor advertising daily see them, read them and remember them, particularly when they are attractively and frequently changed.

Mr. H. H. Shively of the Bureau of Business Research of Ohio State University made a survey of retail clothing advertising in Ohio. In discussing outdoor advertising, he makes the following comments: "Outdoor advertising as reported by Ohio merchants, is fairly consistent. The average per cent of their budget for merchants who use this form of media in towns under 20,000 is 15.8% and in towns over 20,000, 12.5%. The percentage of outdoor advertising are a surprise by their size and consistency. Nothing in the reports received indicate that their use is seasonal, though there are certain seasons (the Christmas season, for example) when newspaper pages are crowded with advertisements and when outdoor advertising is apparently used by retailers at even less cost for results obtained than any other medium."

● To sum up, we must remember that the buying public, and by this we mean men and boys, are becoming more insistent that color be used in the garments and apparel that they wear. Manufacturers, merchandising men, marketing men and advertising men are sensing this trend and are striving to give these customers what they want. Symbolism as a means of expressing style, has come rapidly to the fore and has been generally accepted by the public. The medium that lends itself to symbolism and color is outdoor advertising. The medium that can individualize the Men's Department and make it acceptable to men is outdoor advertising. Certainly then, outdoor advertising with its universality should find a logical place in the promotional plans of the men's store.

, ■

Announce Cigar Campaign

John P. Sweeney, Vice President of Otto Eisenlohr & Bros., Philadelphia cigar manufacturers, announces the release of a sweeping campaign effective immediately in Pennsylvania, New Jersey and Delaware on Cinco cigars. Sales for the first quarter have shown a decided increase over 1930 due to a very aggressive advertising and selling program.

THE MAGIC SENTENCE

● Ages ago, long before the advent of rapid transportation or even of rapid communication, the leaders of men and of nations faced problems as weighty as those faced by the leaders of today. True, the complexity of the problems of those past decades could not be compared with the situation of today. The facilities, however, for disposing of the various matters demanding the attention of those leaders were most inadequate. Months were required to move materials; and in case of warfare, troops could not be so quickly mobilized. News of value concerning a situation could not be known within the hour and thus serve as an aid in the rendering of decisions.

One mighty monarch, wearied by the constant procession of pleas, advice and complaints to which he was compelled to listen and pass judgment, summoned to his palace the wisest men of the kingdom. The sages gathered from the furthest corners of the realm and assembled before the king in the great audience chamber.

"I command you" said the king, "to devise for me a sentence which will serve as an answer in any situation. I grant you a year and a day for your search. Should you fail your beards shall be cut off and you shall be exiled from the kingdom. But, if you succeed, great shall be your reward."

● Great and diligent was the search which the wise men made for the magic sentence which the king demanded. Musty tomes were brought up from half-forgotten vaults and studied with minute care. The alchemists pored over their volumes of the Black Art and wove strange spells and conjured up demons, demanding that these beings reveal the secret.

And the oldest and wisest of the scholars led his fellows before their lord on the appointed day.

"Have ye brought me my sentence?" demanded the king.

"We have, your majesty."

"And what is it?"

"And this too shall pass away" replied the old scholar.

Time has clearly shown the wisdom of the selection. Today we are coming out of a situation in this country which might have been more successfully dealt with if the same words had been sold during the past year and a half to every American citizen, and particularly, to manufacturers and merchandisers.

● 1931 will unquestionably go down in the records as "Recovery Year." It will prove more than that for alert merchandisers. Sound advertising in properly selected media, continuously working and backed up by aggressive merchandising effort will produce profits for 1931 advertisers, and further, will increase their profits in 1932 and 1933 over and above those of their competitors who fail to lay the same foundations as they in 1931.

Outdoor Advertising will prove a valuable tool in the plans of these merchandisers. It is an unusually exclusive medium offering certain exclusive features not possible in other media.

Seldom does a "flash in the pan" campaign appear on this medium. *Practically every client using Outdoor Advertising Service represents an established highly rated and well respected institution.* The company one keeps on the outdoor medium may indeed seldom, if ever, be questioned.

It is a mass medium for class advertisers.

The oldest and wisest of the scholars led his fellows before their lord.

ADVERTISING
the Builder of Good Will

The fourth of a series of talks on advertising prepared by the A. F. A.

● The Advertising Federation of America is offering to all the people of the United States a series of messages designed to present the truth about advertising—its estimable importance to all of us, buyers and sellers; its educational and cultural values as well as its economic force.

The whole subject is a fascinating one, for advertising is both an art and a science; something which touches human nature very closely; something which presents almost as many facets of interest as a well cut diamond.

In recent weeks, various distinguished speakers who have presented the messages of the Federation have dealt with three of these facets, three of these contacts which advertising continually makes with the activities of the average person. They have essayed to prove to you that advertising, by a marvelous economic paradox, pays its own bill of two billions a year; that the general public is the greatest beneficiary from advertising; and that advertising has demonstrated its power to act as a stabilizer in our present day business and social structure.

● All of these preceding messages have been high-lights of the subject, but the present message stands out as the most important and inspiring of all: for this fourth message from the Federation concerns good will values in advertising. Another way to state the theme would be: "How Advertising Builds Good Will in Business Dealings." The meaning is the same. The point is as clear as crystal. This message and subject introduces into our general discussion of the importance of advertising to civilization certain equations of the human heart and spirit. We get away, a little, from the cash register and the counting house. We come to consider for a moment the tremendous imponderables of business life—those assets and influences which have no fixed market quotation but which are so invaluable and indispensable that business would perish utterly without them. We mean, of course, the imponderables and intangibles called faith and liking and friendship—those warm qualities of the heart rather than of the mind; those qualities which, after all, are the very foundation stones of prestige.

Mutual respect and mutual liking, based on a reasonable experience of fair play and general satisfaction, are what really constitute good will in business deal-

Good will values often far outweigh the more material assets of a business institution.

ings, that good will which so often outweighs and outvalues the sum total of the material assets, that good will which is to be secured mainly through the art of advertising. Advertising is, or should be, the repetition and reiteration of truth, a fact or facts stated and restated over a considerable period, so appealingly and emphatically as to create in the minds of the readers of advertising a definite picture, a picture which tends to become more and more definite, more and more colorful, more and more interesting, more and more personal, until, after a time, that picture becomes the personal property of the reader of advertising; as if he had designed it and painted it and owned it. That, is how good will is created by and through advertising.

● Perhaps you have never thought of the matter in quite the same light, but one of the greatest advertising men that ever lived was Paul the Apostle. In the days of primitive Christianity, when a new faith was struggling for a foothold in a world of paganism, the advertising genius, Paul, sent out message after message of such flaming interest as to gain converts throughout the known world. And in preparing his remarkable messages he used certain thoughts which are as fresh and valuable today as they were nineteen centuries ago. If you stop to think you must know that the Bible is rich with advertising material in the sense of appeals to duty and to truth, forcefully and richly phrased.

● It was Paul who wrote to the Galatians, "Whatsoever a man soweth that shall he also reap," and who said on another occasion: "He which soweth sparingly shall reap also sparingly; and he which soweth bountifully shall reap also bountifully." It is interesting to note that this advice from one of the shrewdest men of his times was given to a trading people, a people who delighted in barter and sale, and if that is not the original definition of what good will in business should be, then I am entirely lacking in logic and imagination. "Whatsoever a man soweth, that shall he also reap!" As a man soweth, so does he live his life in business and society.

If a manufacturer or a distributor sows confidence, square dealing and toleration there is no doubt in the world that he will reap richly in the good will of his customers. The mission of advertising, as we know, is to stand between the producer on the one hand, and the customer on the other; to carry the messages of the one to the other; to create in the mind of the customer what might be called the habit of accepting a certain article or product, without so much as taking the trouble even to think of a substitute.

Advertising Adds Prestige to Product

● Many people have discussed the factor called "good will," and often they have made of it a very complicated, involved sort of thing. It is not complicated and not involved. It is as simple as daylight. It is the built-

up accretion of friendship and confidence and fair dealing in trading relationships. Successful business is done only between friends. In the end every purchase must be based on faith in the merit of the merchandise and in the honesty of the seller; faith that the article purchased is not only intrinsically good but is held in high esteem by other purchasers. This is a most important element in the factor of good will, the element of prestige.

An instance occurred only a short while ago when an ambitious young salesman approached a merchant to interest him in a household convenience which had just come upon the market. There was no question about the merit and value of the new article. It was first-class all around. But the merchant wouldn't give it a moment's notice. He turned to the young salesman with the remark: "Young man, I think you've got your nerve with you, asking me to stock up with this contraption of yours when I have been selling Blank's for ten years. Don't you know that everybody knows Blank's machine and what it stands for? Why should I bother with you?"

● After all, why should he? Had he not the right to ask the new machine to go out and get a reputation for itself as Blank's had gotten over a ten years or so, through a long record of performance and money spent for advertising? This factor of prestige which is so important in the item of good will may make it hard for new business and new products to get launched, but that is the way the world is made. Success must be won on merit, and by hard exertion, as a rule. Prestige, like geometry, has no royal road, but when it is attained it is a Golconda of riches.

Good Will Is Worth Real Money

Here is an illustration of exactly what is meant by the astonishing value of "imponderables" and "intangibles" in any inventory of the assets of a business. In 1928 the Post Products Company handed a check for $45,000,000 to the Cheek-Neal Company, manufacturers of the nationally popular and tremendously advertised Maxwell House coffee and thereby purchased the business of the Cheek-Neal concern. But what was the most

"Whatsoever a man soweth that shall he also reap" is as true in modern times as in the days of St. Paul.

valuable thing they bought? It wasn't the plants and the physical properties in which the Cheek-Neal people had roasted and prepared their product. The whole physical layout was not worth much more than $10,-000,000. What they paid the big money for, about $35,000,000, was the trade name "Maxwell House Coffee," a trade name which had been fixed in the public mind by persistent and intelligent and honest advertising over a period of years as the name of an excellent coffee. That is good will!

I scarcely need to pause here to detail the steps in creating that $35,000,000 worth of intangible good will, an asset that you couldn't see, hear, feel, taste or smell but which was just as real as all of the buildings and machines of the company. Suffice it to say that the Cheek-Neal Company had consistently turned out an excellent product and that advertising had impressed that fact so strongly upon the public mind that the people came in time to feel almost as if they had a proprietary interest in Maxwell House Coffee. That is the way human nature works. Once we give our loyalty to a thing we are apt to feel that it belongs to us.

● It cannot be claimed that advertising creates good will in the sense that it initiates it, for that is hardly true. But what advertising does do is to build good will after it has originally been created by the manufacturer or producer. Advertising takes the little germ of liking and confidence which the manufacturer or producer has inspired by means of the merit in his product, and it nurses and nourishes that germ until it becomes a giant. It reminds the public day after day that the Blank Company's article is good, and after a time the public's confidence becomes firmly established.

What do you suppose may be the value of the good will asset of Ivory Soap, the good will which was created in the first instance by the exceptional merit of the product and built up by a continuous and intelligent advertising campaign? Nobody can say, but if Messrs. Procter & Gamble were required to set a monetary value on the name of Ivory Soap, they would undoubtedly put it at 50 per cent of the total inventory of everything they own. If they valued all of their assets at say $100,000,000 they would certainly be justified in valuing the good will at $50,000,000 at least.

● As a builder of good will, advertising stimulates instant and immediate interest in a product and builds up its reputation until the name of the product is almost a catchword. Through advertising, the public is directly and indirectly persuaded that such and such an article is peerless in its kind and class, and that it is really a distinction to be seen using the article. An illustration of this point is afforded by the instance of the automobile salesman who with great difficulty tried to interest customers in a car just placed upon the market. It was a $5,000 beauty, as handsome and competent a piece of work as the engineers and designers could turn out. But the customers shied off. The name—call it Smith-Jones—meant absolutely nothing. Fine as the new car might be, purchasers would have felt apologetic and embarrassed when admitting to their friends that they had bought a Smith-Jones car. It would always be necessary to explain to acquaintances that the Smith-Jones is a good automobile, and it cost so-and-so much. There would never be any thrill in telling about the purchase, such as would be enjoyed if they had bought a Packard, Lincoln, Cadillac, or Pierce-Arrow. It was actually a distinction, they felt rather vaguely, to be seen in one of those cars of prestige—prestige created by the twin factors of quality and advertising.

Some very interesting examples can be given of the cash value of good will as built up by advertising, the good will that creates prestige and distinction. The Gold Dust Corporation in 1925 paid the Dailey Company $8,300,000 for the Shinola, Bixby and Two-in-One businesses. The value of the plants, merchandise and accounts receivable in this transaction was just $4,300,-000. The remaining $4,000,000 represented good will value, the prestige which had been built up through the advertising of these nationally known products.

Mr. George Hill, president of the American Tobacco Company, contracted in 1925 to pay $2,250,000 a year for 99 years to the Tobacco Products Company for the right to use such cigarette trade names as "Melachrino," "Natural," "Ramesee" and "Herbert Tareyton."

● When Lehn & Fink merged with the A. S. Hinds Company in 1925 to form the Lehn & Fink Products

Company the sum of $6,214,421 was paid for the Pebeco and Hinds trade names and good will. All those millions were paid for intangibles, but intangibles which were worth far more than machinery or buildings.

What's in a Name?

I could recite a volume of such instances. The American Safety Razor Company paid $4,000,000 in cash for the assets of the Gem Safety Razor Company. Of that sum exactly $3,600,000 was paid for the use of the little three-letter word "Gem." The same concern paid $4,560,000 for the trade name "Every-Ready." It paid $278,000 for the assets of the Star Razor Corporation, and all except $28,000 was paid for the trade name "Star."

The Postum Company paid the Calumet Baking Powder. Company $32,000,000 for its assets, and we know that the Calumet's plants and material assets could be duplicated many times for $32,000,000. What Postum really bought in that transaction was the prestige of the Calumet name. In other words, it paid the better part of $32,000,000 for good will.

When Chrysler bought out the Dodge Brothers in 1926, $146,000,000 changed hands in the gigantic deal. The good will of the Dodge name and fame was set down in black and white at $79,341,318.22. How they arrived at the twenty-two cents is a mystery but there is no secret whatever as to how they arrived at the seventy-nine million. All the material assets were valued at less than $70,000,000. The prestige, the good will consistently built up by advertising, was worth more money than all the physical assets combined.

Illustrations on this theme are innumerable. When Mr. Gillette bought out the Autostrop Safety Razor Company in 1930 he paid $30,000,000 for what he got, but the actual tangible assets of the Autostrop Company were valued at only $6,385,322. In other words, this shrewd business man paid nearly $24,000,000 for the prestige value, the good will value, of a name—a name built up in the public mind by the genius of advertising.

Without firing any more statistics it might be worth while to speculate on what the good will value of some of our well known American concerns may be. What do you suppose the good will value of Heinz's 57 varieties might amount to? Or Campbell's Soups? What is the prestige valuation of Packard automobiles or Pepsodent toothpaste? What would have to be paid in hard cash for the good will intangibles of Royal Baking Powder, Hart Schaffner & Marx clothing, or Del Monte canned fruits? Scores of such examples could be offered, all appealing to the imagination and all emphasizing the point that there is no factor more important to producer and consumer alike than good will in their trade relations.

Ambassadors of Good Will

● Traveling about South America today is a young man whom we might quite accurately call "The Prince of Sales," though he bears another title in Buckingham Palace. His mission for years has been to create good will for the British empire, particularly for British business, and that is what he is doing down below the Equator today. Great Britain is giving a gigantic exhibition of her manufactures and products in Buenos Aires and the Prince of Wales with his brother, Prince George, has actually been sent as the advance agent of the exhibition—to create good will in advance. Personally he won't sell a dollar's worth of goods, but because of the liking entertained for him he will be the cause of the sale of millions of dollars' worth.

There is nothing foolishly sentimental about all this. It is good business, hard headed business, just as it was good business for both the United States and Mexico to have Col. Lindbergh make his marvelous flight to Mexico City; just as it was good business for both countries to have, as the American Ambassador in Mexico City, a man of such superb common sense, charm and tact as Dwight W. Morrow. Business comes from the heart as well as from the head. The heart must be right if the head-work is to be effective.

Every market consists of human beings, each of whom exercises his own free will, basing his buying decision on his individual judgment, prejudice and whims. Because this is true, selling is not a mechanical operation, but a study in human nature, and any selling effort must build up at least temporary good will or the customer will refuse to buy. Temporary good will is important, but the kind of good will we are most concerned with is the lasting kind, the continued friendly feeling and loyalty of purchasers toward the man whose goods have pleased them, and who has continued to talk to them through the medium of advertising. This good will is an asset which has a direct value to the consumer aside from any strictly economic aspect, as I have shown in numerous examples.

The Consumer is King

● The consumer absolutely controls the value of this good will to the manufacturer, for the consumer can withdraw his favor at any moment. For that reason—and this is most important to consider—the manufacturer who has built up a fund of good will must maintain it under penalty of substantial financial loss. It is a thing which cannot be neglected. It can be fully maintained only with the aid of advertising. And in the long run the consumer is the greatest gainer because the manufacturer, having invested his money to obtain the consumer's good will, must keep faith with the consumer or lose all his investment.

As a final thought:

"Good Will"—the minute I abuse it, I lose it.

"Good Will"—I cannot catch it, or hold it, or tie it up, and yet it is the most valuable asset to my business.

"Good Will"—it is less tangible than a summer zephyr, or the scent of a rose, and yet it exercises more power than any other element in my business.

"Good Will"—it has neither height, nor length, nor breadth, nor width, and yet it is the one indispensable element in the foundation of any business, the one all-powerful force in lifting any business from obscurity to success.

McCarthy to Direct Sylvania Tube Sales

E. H. McCarthy has been appointed general sales manager of the Sylvania Products Company, Emporium, Pa., Sylvania radio tubes. He was formerly head of the Royal Line Sales Corporation, wholesale distributors of phonographs, radios and accessories in New England.

STATEMENT OF THE OWNERSHIP, MANAGEMENT, CIRCULATION, ETC., REQUIRED BY THE ACT OF CONGRESS OF AUGUST 24, 1912, Of ADVERTISING OUTDOORS published monthly at Chicago, for April 1, 1931.

State of Illinois (ss.
County of Cook (

Before me, a Notary Public in and for the State and county aforesaid, personally appeared Harold L. Eves, who, having been duly sworn according to law, deposes and says that he is the editor and business manager of the ADVERTISING OUTDOORS and that the following is, to the best of his knowledge and belief, a true statement of the ownership, management (and if a daily paper, the circulation), etc., of the aforesaid publication for the date shown in the above caption, required by the Act of August 24, 1912, embodied in section 411, Postal Laws and Regulations, printed on the reverse of this form, to wit:

1. That the names and addresses of the publisher, editor, managing editor, and business managers are: Publisher, Outdoor Adv. Ass'n of America, Inc., 165 W. Wacker Dr., Chicago, Ill.; Editor, Harold L. Eves, 165 W. Wacker Dr., Chicago, Ill.; Managing Editor, Harold L. Eves, 165 W. Wacker Dr., Chicago, Ill.; Business Manager, Harold L. Eves, 165 W. Wacker Dr., Chicago, Ill.

2. That the owner is: (If owned by a corporation, its name and address must be stated and also immediately thereunder the names and addresses of stockholders owning or holding one per cent or more of total amount of stock. If not owned by a corporation, the names and addresses of the individual owners must be given. If owned by a firm, company, or other unincorporated concern, its name and address, as well as those of each individual member, must be given.) Outdoor Adv. Ass'n of America, Inc., a New York corporation not for profit. Geo. W. Kleiser, 1675 Eddy Street, San Francisco, Calif., President; O. S. Hathaway, 2 James Street, Middletown, N. Y., Treasurer; Joseph Harris, 165 W. Wacker Drive, Chicago, Ill., Secretary.

3. That the known bondholders, mortgagees, and other security holders owning or holding 1 per cent or more of total amount of bonds, mortgages, or other securities are: (If there are none, so state.) None.

4. That the two paragraphs next above, giving the names of the owners, stockholders, and security holders, if any, contain not only the list of stockholders and security holders as they appear upon the books of the company but also, in cases where the stockholder or security holder appears upon the books of the company as trustee or in any other fiduciary relation, the name of the person or corporation for whom such trustee is acting, is given; also that the said two paragraphs contain statements embracing affiant's full knowledge and belief as to the circumstances and conditions under which stockholders and security holders who do not appear upon the books of the company as trustees, hold stock and securities in a capacity other than that of a bona fide owner; and this affiant has no reason to believe that any other person, association, or corporation has any interest direct or indirect in the said stock, bonds, or other securities than as so stated by him.

5. That the average number of copies of each issue of this publication sold or distributed, through the mails or otherwise, to paid subscribers during the six months preceding the date shown above is................ (This information is required from daily publications only.)

HAROLD L. EVES,
Editor, Mng. Ed., and Bus. Mgr.

Sworn to and subscribed before me this 23rd day of March, 1931.

[SEAL]   ESTHER O. BRECHEISEN,
Notary

(My commission expires January 20, 1934.)

Electrical Display
in GERMANY

By Dr. A. Salmony
Berlin

● Electrical advertising, appealing to the broadest masses of the public, is at present one of the most important methods of advertising. Through technical improvement and increased consumption it has become possible to furnish electrical advertising at reasonable cost. In the course of time the style of this advertising has been subject to a good many changes. To be attractive and effective it must adapt itself harmoniously to the architecture of the buildings and streets and for that reason cooperation between the architect and the electrical engineer has been found imperative.

Electrical advertising must be applied in different ways since its effect will be undesirable unless it harmonizes with its surroundings. Electric lighting systems may be classed in three different groups. To the first group belong the incandescent lamps, commonly called bulbs, which are used for letters, for lighting transparents, for lighting of sheet signs and the so called Atrax cubes. To the second group belong the tubes, among them the Neon and Helium tubes, the Moore light and the tubes filled with nitrogen or carbon and, finally, the Wolfram tubes which are somewhat similar to elongated stage lamps. In the third group there should be mentioned the lighting of buildings with reflectors and electrical advertising with spot lights.

● The oldest and simplest method is that in which the bulbs are directly attached to the letter plate. However with this method the sign sometimes has a blinding effect which should be eliminated whenever possible. Owing to this short-coming signs of this type sometimes become undecipherable at a comparatively short distance. In day time these signs are quite frequently an eye sore, especially since letters and letter plates become dirty very easily. When the letters are fastened in a channel which is painted white inside the effect is more unified, because the channel acts as a reflector and creates a greater light compactness which prevents blinding.

The best results for day and night time are obtained where the source of light is invisible. The first form of this kind is represented by letters whose lighting channel is partly covered by sheet metal. In this case the bulbs must be arranged in such a way as to render them invisible, because otherwise no compact line of light will result.

● A very quiet, dignified, yet effective display is offered by transparent signs where the light shines through glass, cellon or marble. When the lamps are immediately behind a glass pane, opal glass must be used. It does not matter whether legend or picture are made of transparent or solid material; quite often they are etched out by a caustic solution. For the effect of these transparents it is of great importance that they be evenly lighted.

Throwing of light on advertising signs is done by reflectors. This can be done by single reflectors or by a row of reflectors arranged like stage lamps. If this arrangement is chosen the rows must be painted white inside or covered with white enamel. Compared to single reflectors they have the advantage in that they

---

The light display of the power plant "Klingenberg" is especially interesting, since here the previously made invention is made use of because the chimney must not be overstrained. The entire sign extends over 1000 square meters, and the necessary light is furnished by about 1500 lamps. The construction of the sign consists of two tubes, 20 meters apart and connected by copper wire mesh. The small weight of the construction makes mounting and demounting easy. Within a few hours the whole display can be pulled up and taken down. The net can be taken apart into strips and rolled up.

The Karstadt House was erected in 1929 in Berlin—Neukoelln. Its characteristics are the lighted pinnacles of the two towers. They are 12½ Meters high and 3 Meters wide. They are surrounded with tubes for blue Neon light. The name Karstadt is formed by transparent intensely shining letters 1¼ Meter high. 45 reflectors throw a wave of light against the two double towers. Narrow stripes of milk glass transparents run from the first to the seventh floor. The entire building is 57 Meters high.

can be placed where they are not too conspicuous and do not spoil the architectural effect of the walls. While this arrangement is preferred for signs single reflectors are more suited for lighting of more extended surfaces, such as walls, etc. Above all it is essential that the lighting strength is evenly distributed over the entire wall.

● Less popular as a medium of advertising is the use of light signals, as employed for sea and air travel. However a signal of this kind has great attention value and produces a strong and thoroughly dignified advertising effect. It is used by certain manufacturers, theatres and department stores. There are two principal types, those with one and those with three rays of light. The spot lights are just normal spot lights with incandescent lamps incased in a box that is reasonably protected against water and is suitable for outdoor use.

If, a few years ago, an architect or an engineer had been questioned regarding a material which could be used simultaneously for building lighting and decorative purposes, one would have received the answer that such a material was ideal but unavailable. Recently this ideal has been accomplished. A lighting form has

been found that is also a source and a carrier of light and thus an automatically active lighting unit has been created. This is the Atrax cube which is a lighted hollow body, fundamentally of cubic form consisting exclusively of opal glass with crystal coating without metal edging.

● On the side which is not seen the bulbs are inserted and attached. For that reason the Atrax cube appears completely shadowless and is free of all blinding effects. It has an intense lighting strength and creates the impression of materialized light. It is very much adaptable as building material, as a light brick for a good many purposes. It may be used for outside and inside walls for technical and artistic decorative effects. Besides cubic form, this light brick is made in prismatic triangle, hexagon and numerous other forms. Pictures and letters may be applied to these lighting bodies, either hand painted or etched in, in black or in color.

Besides the incandescent lamp there is another source of light for advertising purposes. Its lighting effect is produced by various gases which produce colors when the electric current flows through them. These signs are essentially different from those made of incandescent lamps in so far as the light is not produced by high temperature and the color of the light only depends on the kind of gas used for filling the tube. For that reason this light is sometimes called "cold light." In this category belong the light tubes which play a very important part in electric advertising, the color of the light being determined by the gas

The display of the Telefunken company represents a typical instance of light architecture combined with advertising. The display is mounted on a tower, 40 Meters high. It consists of a great number of blue and red Neon tubes arranged in such a way as to produce the plastic effect of brackets. These brackets form two frames in the center in which the name "Telefunken" appears twice in letters of 2 Meters height. The display is 17 Meters high and 10 Meters wide.

This moving picture theatre offers a classical example of modern light architecture. The tower consists of 36 horizontal transparents, six of which connect the two corners and are 5 Meters long and 40 cm wide. The light is furnished by 4000 lamps of 25 Watts each. The two words "Titania Palast" on two sides of the corner building are formed by blue Neon tubes. The two plastic inscriptions are illuminated by reflectors arranged like stage lamps.

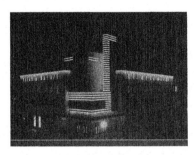

filling. Neon tubes furnish the well known intensely red light. By adding a drop of quick silver the red turns into blue; it becomes green when the Neon-quick-silver tubes are made of brown glass. A filling of Helium results in a soft pink light. In addition to these tubes filled with precious gases there are those filled with nitrogen or carbon. They give a golden yellow light, similar to natural day light. With these tubes the gas filling must continuously be renewed.

Wolfram tubes, which in their form resemble the tubes above described, are more closely related to the incandescent lamps: for in these tubes there is a wire made of Wolfram which, if electrically heated, produces light. These tubes are made in the form of letters and figures for advertising purposes but are also used for lighting of walls.

One more word about the increased color effect of electric advertising, by combining the light effect in

An interesting display of the restaurant Engelhardt, Berlin. It shows how by means of modern light architecture very good effects can be obtained by comparatively simple methods.

the dark with a favorable impression in day time. It must not be overlooked that advertising is much more valuable if it produces a strong advertising effect not only in the night but also during the daytime. For the latter effect it is very essential that the words and pictures stand out in bold contrast from their background. The harmony and the attention focusing effect of colors in daylight are important. In fact, so many elements contribute to the general effect that an ideal electric light sign suitable for night and daytime has still to be developed. It must be considered whether or not the sign is exposed to very strong light during daytime, how big the sign and the letters or figures are, and what effect the background (Continued on page 31)

Bulletin Starts Swing
to U. S. Tires

by Augusta Leinard

An outdoor painted panel with a huge revolving tire as part of its make-up has been stopping the crowds at Post and Presidio Streets in San Francisco. It has been *bringing* the crowds, in fact, for men have driven out solely to look at what has been declared by advertising authorities to be one of the most novel outdoor advertisements ever conceived and carried through to success.

● In addition to being new the bulletin is artistically executed and startlingly original. The advertiser is Jay Hirsch Co., Ltd., local United States Tire distributors, who took over this line in September and wanted to "tell the world" about it.

The tire is an exact replica of the U. S. Royal mounted on a Chrysler Eight wire wheel. Tire and wheel are built entirely of wood with the hub cap of Chromium plate. Although greatly enlarged in size the tire has exactly the same number of tread moulds as the U. S. Royal and the identical number of spokes as the wire wheel from which it was copied. The tire weighs 800 pounds, there are 48 spokes to the wheel, and the tire and wheel measure 8 feet in diameter, the tread being 22½ inches across.

The wheel is backed by a circular piece of steel which in turn is welded to the end of an automobile differential. The differential is turned, through a series of reduction gears, by a small electric motor, and the wheel revolves at the rate of 7 R.P.M. for 16 hours a day.

This illustration shows the size of the tire on the bulletin when compared with the figure of the girl and the ordinary tire below.

Jay Hirsch Co. Ltd. has perhaps the most complete line of U. S. Tires on the Pacific Coast, the president of the organization, Jay Hirsch, having been engaged in the tire business for many years in San Francisco.

● "In taking over the line I wanted to advertise U. S. tires in a way that was strikingly different," Mr. Hirsch told the writer. "When outdoor advertising was proposed to me I was not favorable toward it because I felt that an advertisement of a tire was more or less stereotyped and could not be made vitally interesting. 'I might consider it if I can get something different,' I said. Harry Bercovich, Jr., (Continued on page 41)

This is the bulletin with the unique revolving tire which has been drawing crowds in San Francisco.

Mr. Eaton Says: . . . .

. . . "The switch on the customer's premises is the real heart control of the electricity-producing industry. Throwing the switch, on the part of thousands of customers, determines the degree of efficiency at which the system can be operated. The costs of the power company are established by the customer's acts; by the amount of electricity he elects to use, by the time and place at which he chooses to use it, and by the duration of his use.

'None of the efforts to reduce generating and distributing costs can affect rates as greatly as they are affected by the nature of the consumption—its volume, its distribution over the hours of the day, and the density of the market.

■ "Thus it becomes a responsibility of the power company, not only to encourage the growth of current-consumption, but to so guide the customer's demand into a high and well distributed consumption that he can be adequately compensated for this diversity of demand by the lowered rates possible with increased efficiency. The power company is called upon for a high degree of leadership in creating a demand so distributed as to react properly on the cost of providing service."

Distributing the
ELECTRICAL LOAD

By C. J. Eaton

Vice-President in charge of Merchandise and Service Sales
Middle West Utilities Company

In the March issue of Advertising Outdoors Colonel Robert Isham Randolph said, "In marketing methods there has been little passing on of information from one industry to another. The sum total of the knowledge on the important problem of marketing could very probably answer the needs of individual producers in every respect. Industry as a whole will have to be the great laboratory—the great university—for training of men in this field. The teachers must be the leaders of business themselves."

In this article, the first to appear in response to Colonel Randolph's appeal, Mr. Eaton tells of the problem that is faced by the power company in distributing the electrical load—in the avoidance of conditions which necessitate a large overhead to take care of only one period of peak load. How the power companies found what consumers are the best prospects for increased service during off-peak hours and how they are selling increased service to these prospects makes an interesting and valuable contribution to this series.

Editor's Note.

● The switch on the customer's premises is the real heart control of the electricity-producing industry. Throwing the switch, on the part of thousands of customers, determines the degree of efficiency at which the system can be operated. The costs of the power company are established by the customer's acts; by the amount of electricity he elects to use, by the time and place at which he chooses to use it, and by the duration of his use.

The switch on the customer's premises is the real heart control of the electricity-producing industry.

None of the efforts to reduce generating and distributing costs can affect rates as greatly as they are affected by the nature of the consumption—its volume, its distribution over the hours of the day, and the density of the market.

● The company engaged in the supplying of electric current is faced with a tremendous overhead—in equipment, billing operations, meter-reading, and similar items—whether the service is used widely or not. The generating equipment must be of such capacity and design as will supply the maximum or greatest demand upon the system during any portion of a 24 hour period. Obviously, if the equipment is run at maximum output at only one peak period of the twenty-four hours, and runs at one-fifth or one-tenth load-capacity for the remainder of the day, the investment is not being utilized economically, and this inefficiency of the system is reflected in the rates which can be offered.

An example of the effect of overhead and load-factor might be illustrated by two persons in the restaurant business. Each restaurant serves 5000 customers daily. The first is called upon to serve his customers between 11 A. M. and 2 P. M. Overhead, including floor space, equipment, chefs and waitresses, is obviously out of proportion—requiring a higher charge for food. On the other hand, the second restaurant serves the same number of people during a 14 hour period with 80% less overhead, since less help and equipment is required, and his prices are far lower than the first restaurant.

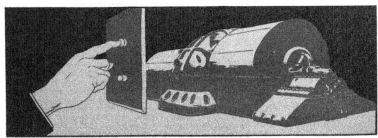

The possibilities of extending the use of, and furnishing electric service more cheaply therefor resides principally where it is used—not where it is produced. The equipment on the customer's premises is an integral part of the electric system. His investment in electric wiring and equipment for using the service, in fact, exceeds that of the electric industry in the facilities for producing it.

● Selling the broad use of electricity is thus inseparable from operation, for in this industry, mere quantity use of electric service without any consideration of the time taken to use a given quantity might result in the necessity for the company to increase its facilities with lowered operating load-factor efficiency. An increase in demand at the wrong times might conceivably jeopardize the investment.

Distribution facilities—their capacity and diversity of use—offer the opportunity of keeping the generating facilities busy the maximum number of hours out of the twenty-four.

The power company is faced with not only the ordinary sales-situation, but one in which two factors not ordinarily encountered enter into the problem—time and duration of use. The customer who will use electricity at the right time, and use it for the greatest number of hours, is then, the most desirable one to cultivate. Furthermore, the benefits which come to this customer are measured in comfort, convenience and labor-saving and resultant lower rates per unit of energy beyond the lesser user.

Thus it becomes a responsibility of the power company, not only to encourage the growth of current-consumption but to so guide the customer's demand into a high and well distributed consumption that he

can be adequately compensated for this diversity of demand by the lowered rates possible with increased efficiency. The power company is called upon for a high degree of leadership in creating a demand so distributed as to react properly on the cost of providing service.

● The merchandising problem facing the electricity-producing industry is therefor largely one of evening out the humps and valleys of the load on the production facilities. Usually dusk to nine o'clock in the evening marks the period of heaviest load, while the lightest demand on the production facilities is from ten o'clock in the evening until very early morning, when street lights constitute about the only load at present. Industrial equipment, such as motors in factories, and mines, booster pumps on pipe-lines, and similar industrial motors constitute a fairly even load in the day time, but this does not approach the peak-load of the early evening hours.

Where then, is the power company to find the load which will be drawn during the present lightly loaded hours? We must once more consider another factor—the nature of electricity itself.

Electricity is a divisible, distributable power which is uniquely fitted for both large and small jobs. The small town and rural household is enabled by electric power to carry on those cooking, sewing, laundry and similar tasks which in the larger cities have so frequently been surrendered to outside agencies. For many reasons the small town home can put electric service to greater use than the typical metropolitan domestic establishment.

Thus the small town home is to be the principal scene of additional business, followed closely by homes wherever they are located. At the same time it costs the industry relatively more in investment to put facilities into the non-metropolitan areas so that the load-factor becomes of even greater importance.

At the present time the greater portion of current for domestic use is consumed in lighting. The only appliance in general use is the electric iron, with about 94 per cent saturation. Vacuum sweepers, washing machines, refrigerators, ranges and water heaters are all load-building appliances which consume current principally during the periods of low load during the day time.

● Water heaters are now being developed which will charge a tank with sufficient hot water to last throughout the day, but which draw current only between the hours of ten P. M. and five or six A. M. The present rate structures of the power companies are being so designed that the customer is charged at an "off-peak" rate for this service.

The power company must take the lead in popularizing the use of electricity in the home. The interest of the companies is basically to get labor-saving and comfort-giving appliances in service. Toward this end they not only maintain departments for pioneering the sale of appliances, but they also invite the cooperation of other dealers in these appliances towards aggressive sales-endeavor.

● The companies are not interested in the profit derived from the sale of appliances so much as they are in the benefits received by the customer and the preservation of and increased efficiency of their investment in production equipment. The merchandising department has the expenses incurred in the merchandising of appliances charged to accounts separate from the public-utility function accounts, except in cases where in the pioneering of appliances which have not yet met with sufficient public acceptance throughout the country to be merchandise items in the stocks of local progressive dealers, they are charged proportionately to the promotion accounts of the companies.

Since the efforts of the power companies form the only continuous means of promoting the sale of electrical appliances, the best interests of the manufacturer, dealer and consumer require the continuance of these merchandising activities.

Especially is this true in 4500 small communities with an aggregate population of 6,000,000, averaging 1300 persons per community served by one group of progressive companies. The people of these communities, and the adjoining farm people as well, depend primarily upon the power companies for leadership in developing and selling new uses for service. This is largely due to the fact that the dealers in towns of this size cannot economically carry a large and varied stock of electrical appliances.

Close cooperation between the power companies' merchandising departments and local dealers is found throughout the country or is rapidly developing in that direction. Prices on equipment offered by the power companies carry an adequate margin which can be met with profit by the local dealers in the same equipment. No terms are offered that are not alike available to small merchants nor are premiums offered, which is contrary to ethical merchandising practice.

The merchants of the small towns are invited to participate in the advertising and sales efforts of the power companies when a campaign is instituted for some particular item. This may partake of the form of window cards distributed to the dealers, or items in the general advertising encouraging people to purchase from "your dealer."

● A few examples will show how strikingly domestic consumption can be increased on a system of this character with properly directed merchandising. If an additional 35 per cent saturation of range business can be developed, the average domestic consumption would be increased sixty-five per cent. An additional fifty per cent would raise consumption to 232 per cent of its present status.

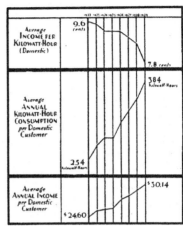

This chart shows how increased consumption has been followed by a decrease in rates and an increase in the average annual income per customer.

● An additional twenty-five per cent saturation of refrigeration business and an additional twenty-five per cent saturation of range business on existing lines would more than double the present domestic consumption.

Estimates indicate that with approximately 20,000,000 wired homes in the United States, thirty per cent of the population still lives in unwired homes.

That thirty per cent represents a substantial future market, but the immediate market—the one which presents tremendous opportunities—without additional investment in transmission equipment, without additional meters, without new consumers, and at the same time be principally non-peak-load is the domestic market of homes already wired.

The effect that an increase in consumption of this nature would have on the rates to consumers is hinted at in the chart showing how increased consumption of electricity supplied by one company has made possible lower cost service to their customers.

Development of improved load-factor, or the broadest use of service possible, spread over the greatest period of the twenty-four hour day, in order that the company's investment is paying the best return possible, is a duty the power companies owe to their customers. This is not a one man job—on the contrary, the combined brains and effort of the power company's staff together with that of the local dealers is essential to insure a continued higher standard of living at less and less cost for electric service rendered.

A SQUARE DEAL
for All Business

By John D. Ames
Publisher of the Chicago Journal of Commerce

Newspapers are neither more nor less selfish than other business enterprises. Appealing as most of them do to the general public, they frequently pass severe judgment on other forms of business while manifesting extreme leniency toward their own. From time to time The Chicago Journal of Commerce has discussed this characteristic. Governor Long's bill in Louisiana for an onerous tax on newspaper advertising was excoriated by newspapers all over the country. They were much less tender when other businesses were jeopardized. Not long ago a New York newspaper declared with tears in its eyes that the milk business should be adjudged a public utility, subject to regulation of its rates. Soon afterward a bill was introduced in the New York State legislature to make press associations and newspaper syndicates a public utility. This was poetic justice.

The Chicago Journal of Commerce has occasionally expressed its idea that the ultimate welfare of the newspaper business is interlaced with that of all business. If the heavy governmental heel goes down, the newspaper business will get its due share of the bruises. There was lately a news item about legislative proposals that would hurt the outdoor advertising industry; and The Chicago Journal of Commerce, in keeping with its usual attitude toward business-baiting legislation, remarked in its issue of March 30:

"Thirty bills to levy punitive taxes on poster panels and other outdoor advertising structures are pending in eighteen states. Any legislation of this kind is sure to receive the cordial and unselfish applause of newspapers. It is a great thing to be public-spirited.

"At certain places there are valid objections to outdoor advertising. Whenever it dangerously obstructs the view of motorists it should be removed. It should never be allowed to interfere with safety; but there should be equal diligence in attacking any other phenomenon that interferes with safety.

"Again, outdoor advertising may be objectionable for aesthetic reasons; a noble landscape may be spoiled by an advertisement of somebody's socks. But let it be observed that not all landscapes are noble, and that sometimes an advertisement of somebody's socks may be easy on the eyes. This is a fact often overlooked by people who are aesthetically illiterate; being themselves incapable of forming an aesthetic judgment they accept the cast-iron doctrine that nature is wonderful and all outdoor advertising is vulgar. And even when outdoor advertising actually impairs a scene, it may well be asked whether the government (Continued on page 35)

Zoning Plan Presented
at Roadside Beauty Conference

At the Chamber of Commerce of the United States in Washington, a second meeting of the Conference on Roadside Business and Rural Beauty was held on April 10th. After an all day informal session, sixteen representatives of organizations concerned with highways, roadside business and rural beauty, agreed to report favorably to their groups a proposed bill which is a step in the direction of zoning highways to preserve their natural beauty spots. The proposed bill was drafted by Herbert U. Nelson of the National Association of Real Estate Boards, Chicago.

George Wharton Pepper, former Senator of Pennsylvania, presided and at the conclusion of the conference the original continuation committee was enlarged. It is the duty of the continuation committee to receive reports from organizations interested and to carry on the work in connection with the conference until another is called, probably within ninety days.

The morning session was devoted to the presentation of the bill by Mr. Nelson, with discussion of a general nature concerning the objects of the conference, preserving rural beauty and at the same time making a definite place for the conduct of roadside business.

Mr. Nelson struck the keynote of the second Washington conference when he said that outdoor advertising had been made the exclusive discussion of the conference, and that a broader aspect is required than making the work of the conference a discussion of outdoor advertising.

Mr. Pepper told the representatives of a meeting of the continuation committee, which met in New York on March 9th, at which Mr. Nelson brought forward a proposal for the creation of stretches of highways that would preserve natural beauty spots.

At this meeting, in addition to Senator Pepper, Chairman, and Mr. Nelson, were Arthur N. Pack of the American Nature Association, Albert S. Bard of the National Council for Protection of Roadside Beauty, George W. Kleiser of the Outdoor Advertising Association of America, Inc., and others.

Concerning this meeting, Chairman Pepper said that Mr. Pack and Mr. Bard had been unable to agree with the continuation committee in the discharge of any of its functions, and they could not bring themselves to the point of view of having outdoor advertising on the rural highways anywhere. Mr. Pack and Mr. Bard stated that they lacked sympathy with the proposed Nelson legislation, because they could not subscribe to any system of rural zoning, and that there was no need

for a further proposal and so they withdrew from the conference.

"In other words," said Senator Pepper, "they may be said to have brought in a minority report and for the purpose of the record, I will read excerpts from a pamphlet they have published which is entitled, The Washington Conference with the Outdoor Advertising Industry and Why It Failed."

After reading various excerpts from their twelve-page pamphlet, the Senator remarked, "Regardless of their ill-advised withdrawal, let us strive together to see if we can not find a solution of the problem of roadside business and rural beauty."

The proposed legislation suggested by Mr. Nelson is that the Highway Departments of the various states shall make a plan of the rural highways and designate the highways which should be a part of a state-wide scenic system.

The bill provides that whenever a petition is filed with the State Highway Department, county, town or township, as the case may be, that governmental department may acquire by gift, purchase, or the exercise of eminent domain, an unobstructed and unmarred view of the rural scenery and landscape from the highway, and may prevent the use of a strip of land 300 feet wide or of such width as may be necessary on each side of the stretch of rural highway not less than one-half mile nor more than ten miles in length, for some or any commercial uses, with this exception:

"The view and rights acquired under this act shall not prevent any owner from using any part of his land as a site for a dwelling, farm building, or for an inn or hotel, or from advertising thereon the land or improvements, for sale or for rent, or any business conducted or any products manufactured, produced, or raised by him thereon, nor the marketing by him at the roadside in temporary quarters of produce raised or goods manufactured or produced thereon."

Such advertising or marketing will be carried on upon obtaining a permit for that purpose from the Highway Department or the proper road authorities.

The term "commercial uses," includes stations for the sale of gasoline, oil, and automobile accessories, stores, garages, eating places, refreshment stands, outdoor advertising, and places of recreation and entertainment.

● A section provides that whenever the owners of at least three-fourths of such a stretch of rural highway, to include at least three-fourths of the owners of such strip, desire that such view (Continued on page 31)

OUTDOOR ADVERTISING ABROAD

Australian Firm Donates Posters

An interesting group of civic officials and business men of Fremantle, Australia, assembled recently to inspect one of three posters which had been donated to the Fremantle Business Men's Association by the City & Suburban Billposting Co.

These posters, designed to stimulate trade in Fremantle, caused very favorable comment. Mr. Thomson, President of the Business Men's Association, was impressed and spoke appreciatively of the generosity of the firm, who, at their own cost, had designed, produced and posted the three posters.

Suggestions were made by Mr. C. J. Wroblewski, Principal of City and Suburban Billposting Co., that the Business Men of Fremantle should reinforce this poster campaign and indicated methods. Mr. Leo Holt, Secretary of the Association, immediately approved of the idea and window stickers with the same wording that appear on the posters were pasted on practically every window in the Fremantle Business district.

The Mayor (Mr. F. E. Gibson) in company with Dr. J. S. Battye considered the poster was excellent and commended the idea. Dr. Battye, in fact, went further and suggested the poster should be illuminated during the evening.

Describing the reason for the donation of the posters by his firm, Mr. Wroblewski explained that this was merely a gesture of good-will and if the people of Fremantle benefited by increased trade they would be amply rewarded for their effort. Community advertising of this character was new to Western Australia and he was hopeful that such a use of outdoor advertising would extend. In other countries consistent campaigns on similar lines had been effectively used.

— — ■

Blanketing Scotland with Posters

An interesting article on outdoor advertising in Scotland appeared in a recent issue of Advertiser's Weekly. The author, S. Nicoll, manager of the General Billposting Company, Ltd., says:

"For many years past, poster campaigns for various commodities have been launched in England but have not extended across the border, the probable reason for this being that little· or no demand for the goods was found in Scotland, owing to the different habits of the Northern buyer.

"Since the war many things have changed and not the least of these are the traveling habits of the Scots. Before the war, the majority of Scotsmen spent their holidays in Scotland, but the advent of poster advertising for such towns as Blackpool, Scarborough, Harrogate and Continental resorts has created in them a desire to travel and see something new. This has been effected to such an extent that Scotland herself is concentrating on an advertising campaign on her own behalf in England and elsewhere.

"In considering the various articles for which unlimited marketing opportunities exist in Scotland, there are two lines which are uppermost in my mind. These are foodstuffs and toilet requisites.

"The present-day Scot does not possess the hearty appreciation of 'porridge' which used to exist through the length and breadth of the land. Thus is laid open a vast market for easily cooked breakfast foods, fruits, custards, sauces and similar commodities. This market, although already tapped by enterprising manufacturers, is by no means exhausted and can yet be profitably exploited.

"This is borne out by the experience of a firm of custard powder manufacturers. A few years ago this firm adopted the boardings and launched a poster campaign in Scotland. Since that first venture their posters have appeared without a break for six months each year.

"The result, stated to the writer, has been that sales have increased each year beyond what they ever dared to expect and, moreover, are still increasing.

"Although not many years ago custard was used in Scotland only by the wealthier classes, advertising, and more particularly poster advertising, has found it a place in practically every home.

"Similar opportunities there are for canned fruits, vegetables and meats,· packet oats, biscuits and table jellies and other delicacies, and for palatable foods for the lunch and dinner table.

"Four years ago William Adams, a sausage manufacturer of Dalkeith, tried a little experiment in poster advertising. At that time his weekly output of sausages was one and half tons. In his first campaign, Mr. Adams covered Edinburgh and the surrounding districts as well as a number of Border towns. An eight-sheet poster was used and about $400 was spent in exhibiting 115 of these for a period of three months. Last year the area was extended to include Fifeshire and Stirlingshire, and the number (Continued on page 34)

Electrical Display in Germany

(Continued from page 21) has in day and night time. If electrical advertising is intended to be seen from a very great distance, a combination of day and night effect cannot as a rule be accomplished. With other kinds of electric advertising the difficulty is less. Owing to the intense lighting power of the tubes the letters or figures on which they are mounted may be so dark that they stand out effectively against a light background or against the sky. The lighted box letters offer a greater problem. If the color of the glass is so dark that in daytime even from a considerable distance an effective contrast is obtained, then in the night time the full effect will not be gained.

● Electrical advertising, particularly in connection with industrial and commercial buildings, has been developed in a good many ways depending for the effect essentially upon form and color. But only recently this form of advertising has reached imposing proportions. The most popular instance of magnificent light display for advertising purposes in Europe is to be found in Paris. There the name "Citroen" shines forth from the Eiffel tower in letters of 30 meters height, arranged one above the other.

Recently a German inventor, Haase, has developed a system of electrical advertising which means a substantial progress and for the first time actually furnishes a means toward development of electric advertising on an enormous scale. In Haase's patent the problem of placing electric signs in any height desired has been solved in principle. Electric signs 50 or 100 meters in height offer no more difficulty than smaller ones, either constructively, in regard to technical operation or even financially. The technical requirement is that the sign can be easily operated. Furthermore the initial cost of the display and the cost of the construction on which the display is mounted must be reasonable. These three requirements are fully met by the new German system. Above all the construction may be applied everywhere, on a mountain side, a tower, a chimney or any other locality. The construction consists of a few very thin wires of 1.5 mm. and therefore the weight is extremely small and the resulting wind resistance negligible. If bulbs have burned out and must be replaced the entire lamp system may be let down by means of a windlass, and then all repairs can be easily made. The height of the sign up to 100 meters does not have to be considered at all. This is of the utmost importance since otherwise this kind of electric display would be practically impossible.

● The first electric sign on a scale so far unknown constructed after this system was erected by the Rhenisch-Westfalien Electric Company, Essen, Germany. For this display iron towers of 125 meters height were erected. To this towers the three letters R W E are attached one above the other, each of them 16 meters in height. The lower line of the lowest letter is 30 meters above the ground, the upper line of the highest letter is 90 meters above the ground. The construction offered no difficulty.

Zoning Plan Presented at Roadside Beauty Conference

(Continued from page 29) be acquired, and for this purpose that specified commercial uses be prevented, and are willing to give to the state, county, town or township such rights in such strip of land, they may sign a petition to that effect and file it with the state highway department, county, town or township, as the case may be.

In the petition, such property owners shall specify what uses are to be prevented and they shall agree, in consideration of the scenic development of the highway, to convey by appropriate instrument such view and rights to the state, town, county or township. On this scenic highway, to further preserve the view, appropriate plantings are to be made and enhancing in other ways the beauty of the highway itself.

This act shall be so construed and applied as to permit between such stretches of highway, together with the abutting property so restricted, commercial intervals of such size and frequency as to serve the requirements of commercial and industrial activities and the convenience and necessities of the public.

The proceeding for the condemnation and restrictions provide for the assessment of damages for the property rights so acquired, to be taken in the same manner now provided for condemning land for road purposes. The benefits accruing by reason of such condemnation shall also be assessed, any special benefits accruing to the owner of any property shall be credited against, and deducted from, any damages sustained by him.

● The state highway department, or the proper authorities of any county, town, or township, shall preserve and protect the view so acquired and make available the funds necessary for carrying out the provisions of this act.

It was the view of the representatives of the conference that is was more effectve to iron out difficulties in a conference such as this one, rather than in legislative halls. Where there are conflicting views, it is necessary to iron out difficulties and a meeting of minds of aesthetic and commercial groups results in presenting to legislatures the best thoughts of those who have given their consideration to the problem of the commercial and non-commercial use of the highways.

Chairman Pepper said that he felt that the representatives in the conference were engaged in a public service that is groping around for a solution, seeking a line along which legislation may result, which will not be regarded by the courts as unconstitutional.

The Continuation Committee has been added to by the appointment of Fred Brenckman representing The National Grange, and Roger J. Bounds, representing the Chamber of Commerce of the United States. The Continuation Committee, at an appropriate time, will call another meeting of the Conference on Roadside Business and Rural Beauty.

NEWS OF THE OUTDOOR INDUSTRY

C. E. Marley Drowned on South American Tour

Cabled dispatches from Rio de Janeiro, Brazil, March 27th, told of the tragic drowning of Mr. C. E. Marley, president of the Poster Advertising Association of Canada, and The C. E. Marley Limited, outdoor advertising plant operating in 27 towns in western Ontario.

● Mr. Marley and several other persons members of the Canadian good will and trade mission to South America had been bathing in the surf near the Copacabana Hotel. Swept out to sea by a strong current, the group of bathers was picked up by a patrol and brought back to shore, but Mr. Marley died within a short time due to the shock and exertion he had undergone.

Mr. Marley was one of the most energetic and popular of London, Ontario, business men. His greatest interest was of course in the business that bears his name, but he was also very active in civic and fraternal affairs.

"Ed" Marley, as he was widely known to most Londoners, was born in that city, in 1886. In 1906 he started in the sign business, under the name of Jenkins & Marley. The company name was later changed to Marley & Weeks, and in 1913 was incorporated as The Signry Limited. This latter company had a remarkable growth under Mr. Marley's direction, and acquired the London Bill Posting Company and the Brown Advertising Service of Windsor, Ontario, in 1923. Since that time the company has grown until it is today one of the most widely known Canadian plants.

Mr. Marley was a great traveler, and with Mrs. Marley, had been practically all over the world. On his beautiful 55 acre estate just outside London, he kept several fine horses, and rode every morning when at home. He was also an enthusiastic hockey fan.

His interest in the Masonic orders may be judged from the list of Masonic organizations to which he belonged:

Union Lodge 380, A. F. & A. M.; St. Johns Chapter No. 3, Royal Arch Masons; Richard Couer de Lion Preceptory No. 4, Knights Templar; Member Divan Mocha Temple A. A. O. N. M. S.; London Lodge of Perfection and the Rose Croix; Ancient and Accepted Order of Scottish Rite; Moore Consistory of Hamilton.

He was also a member of the Kiwanis Club, London Club, London Hunt and Country Club, and the Highland Golf Club.

● Mr. Marley was married in 1911 to Norah Leone Pulford, who was with him on the South American tour.

Interment was made at Woodland Cemetery, London, Tuesday, April 14th.

Batten, Barton, Durstine and Osborn to Handle Hart Schaffner and Marx

Hart Schaffner & Marx, Chicago, manufacturers of men's clothing, have appointed the Batten, Barton, Durstine & Osborn Corporation, of that city, to direct their advertising account.

■ ■ ■

National Dry Goods Ass'n Represented at A. F. A. Meet

The Sales Promotion Division of the National Retail Dry Goods Association is the latest of the several national advertising groups to join the forces of the Advertising Federation of America meeting in convention at the Hotel Pennsylvania, New York, June 14-18.

In an announcement just issued by Kenneth Collins, Chairman of the Division, and Vice-president of R. H. Macy & Company, New York, Mr. Collins says:

"The directors of the Sales Promotion Division have voted in favor of holding our annual meeting in conjunction with the Advertising Federation of America convention in June. This is a particularly happy union. Undoubtedly there is much to learn from contact with men representing all phases of advertising in this general convention. There is a real advantage also in having national advertisers learn more about our specific problems.

● "Discussions of mutual problems of both fields will without question disclose a deeper significance and bring about a wider knowledge of all elements of distribution—which will be of great value in our own work. Then, too, aside from these general sessions, the Sales Promotion Division will have three or four laboratory sessions of its own—in which concrete and tangible promotional ideas and procedures will be discussed. At these sessions, the retail advertiser can rest assured that there will be a dearth of subjects dealing in generalities. Program plans are now in preparation, with one underlying idea of presenting to our members valuable and practical information on subjects of widest interest."

Gilbert T. Hodges, President of the Federation and a Member of the Executive Board of The Sun, New York, in a statement issued from Federation headquarters in New York, says:

"We are pleased to have the Sales Promotion Division hold their summer convention (Continued on page 41)

The New
ADVERTISING OUTDOORS

● This issue of Advertising Outdoors is the fourth that has appeared in new typographical dress and with a broadened editorial content. We have endeavored to publish a magazine which will reflect credit upon the industry with which it is specifically concerned and which will perform a real service not only in behalf of that industry but of all advertising.

We believe that the changed physical appearance of the magazine is deserving of comment. The typographic layout is by Don McCray, who is well-known as a layout man and was formerly associated with Frank Young, a recognized authority in this field. The style is modern without any suggestion of the more radical departures from all style which masquerade under modernism's banner. The type, Ultra-Bodoni for the heads and Bodoni medium for the body, was selected for its modern appearance and its qualities of color and legibility.

Perhaps no feature has called forth as much comment as the two papers that are being used in the body of the magazine, the one a heavy enamel which brings out every detail of the half-tone illustrations and the other a specially manufactured sheet which has the texture and appearance of a hand-laid paper. The Jahn and Ollier Engraving Company, one of the largest and best-equipped plants in the country, is at present experimenting with a special screen which can be used both on the enamel and text papers to give a distinctive effect.

The art work, in our opinion, compares favorably with that used in any modern business or trade magazine. The artist who creates most of the drawings is an instructor in a nationally known art school and has been represented by paintings in shows at the Art Institute of Chicago and several Chicago galleries.

Upon the contents page of this issue are the names of men prominent in advertising, in publishing and in industry. Each has something to say that is of value to almost every reader of Advertising Outdoors. Writers of similar caliber will be represented in succeeding issues.

Here are some of the comments which have convinced us that the showing the magazine has made has more than justified the additional labor and expense involved in the change:

● "Just a word to compliment you on the splendid appearance and general make up of Advertising Outdoors.

"For a number of years we sent some forty or fifty copies of the poster magazine to our various clients, but discontinued same upon expiration of our last order due to the fact we thought the publication had become rather cheesy.

"We thought it might make you feel good to let you know that this last issue has made such a decided impression on us that we are again going to place our order for fifty copies of Advertising Outdoors.

"Keep up the good work."

ROBINSON ADV. CO.
R. F. Robinson

"I have the January Issue of Advertising Outdoors before me; and I can't help but take this opportunity of sending "flowers" to the living, so to speak. Without any question of a doubt, it is one of the finest issues I have seen. The magazine seems to get better and better.

"I trust that you will accept my humblest, but sincerest compliments and congratulations."

HOUSTON POSTER ADVERTISING CO.
P. L. Michael

● "A great dress! It looks entirely like a new magazine. You and Fortune are now in a class by yourselves. I just received the January issue today. Congratulations."

FINANCIAL ADVERTISERS ASSOCIATION
Preston E. Reed, Executive Secretary

"The latest edition of Advertising Outdoors looks okay to me. We will do what we can to build up the circulation."

JOHN DONNELLY & SONS
E. B. O'Keefe

"We have just found opportunity to go through the March number of Advertising Outdoors.

"May we not offer a word of acknowledgment for the improvement in this publication? Its appearance will compare favorably with any magazine of its type and the writer feels that it does credit to the outdoor advertising industry and presents its message in most attractive form."

ERIE LITHOGRAPHING & PRINTING COMPANY
E. H. Russell

We are grateful for these and the many other similar expressions of appreciation that we have received. We do not, however, regard our task as complete. We shall strive to make each issue an improvement upon the last and to make Advertising Outdoors a more interesting and more valuable magazine to its readers.

Lovell to Direct United's
Public Relations Program

Interest is developing in plans for the preservation of the natural beauties of the American country-side as evidenced by the recent conference held at the Chamber of Commerce of the United States at Washington in the interests of roadside business.

● A New Jersey organization, however, is to be among the first to take definite steps toward a complete and exhaustive survey of the roadside situation.

The United Advertising Corporation announced from their offices yesterday a plan that embraces a survey of the roads and points of scenic beauty of Northern New Jersey. They also announced that they have engaged Clarence B. Lovell to be in charge of their Public Relations Department. This organization has, for many years, had a definite policy to preserve all spots of scenic beauty and has sacrificed many profitable locations for this cause.

Mr. Lovell is well equipped for this important work. As Promotion Manager of the former O. J. Gude Co., N. Y.—and later as the Advertising Manager of the General Outdoor Advertising Co., Inc., he had wide opportunity to study outdoor advertising conditions as they exist in this and surrounding states. During this connection with these organizations he was sent abroad and there made a study of the roadside conditions in England and France. On his return he was elected Secretary and General Manager of the Outdoor Advertising Association of America, Inc., with headquarters in Chicago.

In his four years with that Association he had opportunity to meet with all of the organizations, at one time or another, interested either on the affirmative or negative side of the controversy. He has appeared in practically every city in this country as guest of business organizations and many of his addresses have been published for nation-wide distribution. It will be in his jurisdiction to attend to those affairs which can fairly be classed as pertinent to Public Relations.

Active in such organizations as the Chamber of Commerce, the Advertising Federation of America, Inc., Poster Art Alliance, Business Secretaries Forum, Advertising Club of New York, Chicago Art Institute and others, he has, despite his many affiliations, contributed many articles on merchandising and marketing to the publications in the business field, in addition to acting as one of the Advertising Counselors to Northwestern University.

● At a meeting held in the offices of the Newark Branch of the United Advertising Corporation, plans were discussed by President Leonard Dreyfuss and the Executive Board relative to the conduct of this survey. It is hoped that out of Mr. Lovell's study will come some solution of a difficult problem. What is hoped for is genuine cooperation between the advertiser and the public.

Wrigley Account to
J. Walter Thompson

The Wm. Wrigley, Jr., Company, Chicago, Wrigley's chewing gums, has appointed the J. Walter Thompson Company, Inc., as its advertising agency.

Blanketing Scotland with Posters

of posters increased to 150. The approximate cost of exhibiting these was $950, the period being increased to six months.

"In an interview last month, Mr. Adams stated to a poster advertising man that his output had increased to more than three tons per week—an increase of about 100 per cent., which he attributed directly to his posters.

"Mr. Adams added that it was his intention to use 16-sheet posters and to increase his field of coverage for his next campaign.

"For toilet requisites for both men and women similar markets are available. Before the war face powders and creams, perfumes and fancy soaps were seldom, if ever, used by Scotswomen, but advertisement has caused the habit to increase to an enormous extent. And yet the field is by no means covered; in fact, the opportunities are so many and so wide that I could almost guarantee an immediate and insistent demand for the wares of any manufacturer of cosmetics who has the courage to cover Scotland by poster.

● "These remarks are also applicable to articles of toilet for men, such as hair creams, shaving soaps, razors and tooth pastes.

"In a review of the facilities afforded by the hoardings in the various towns, Glasgow, as the commercial capital of Scotland, can be given priority. Its boardings are, with very few exceptions, panelled and painted in duotone, each poster being displayed in a separate frame.

"The population of Glasgow, which covers an area of 100 square miles, is well in excess of 1,500,000. The tramway and omnibus system is claimed to be the finest in the world and carries approximately 540,000,000 passengers a year. There are 253,000 dwelling-houses, and the registered motor vehicles number 22,899. Goods can be supplied in Glasgow cheaper than in any other town in Great Britain, not excluding London.

"Edinburgh, the capital, covers 88 square miles and has a population of 425,000. Its tramways carry 138,-500,000 passengers annually; there are 105,791 dwelling-houses and 17,450 registered motor vehicles.

"Dundee extends to 25 square miles and its population is in the region of 170,000. 32,000,000 passengers are carried annually by trams and 'buses, and there are 46,756 dwelling-houses and 4,906 motor vehicles.

"Aberdeen has a population of 159,000, covers an area of 18 square miles and has 38,536 dwelling-houses within its boundaries. There are 5,544 motor vehicles registered in the city and the annual number of tramway passengers exceeds 60,000,000.

A Square Deal
for All Business

(Continued from page 28) ought to interfere. There are numberless other things which are repugnant to civilized people; the majority of our buildings would have to be demolished if aesthetics were given a free hand.

"Life would be decidedly interesting for a while if Mr. Frank Lloyd Wright, who is probably the greatest architect in the world, were granted absolute authority to do what he would with existent types of architecture. But in fact neither the people of the United States as a whole nor those of any state are particularly aesthetic; even the members of women's clubs are deficient in this respect—otherwise they could not endure the horrible papers they placidly hear read at their meetings. Many of these papers are indictments of outdoor advertising; for the notion has been sedulously cultivated that outdoor advertising is not quite nice. Perhaps the constant harangues of the newspapers have something to do with the current attitude of women's clubs.

● "In general it is best to let the individual apply his own standard of beauty, and if he finds a panel or a building or a woman that does not suit him, let him shut his eyes. Panels erected on private property should enjoy the same legal status as other structures. If they are limited or totally forbidden let it be through application of the same standards that have given us our zoning laws—the object of which, by the way, is to protect property rights, not destroy them. And in any case the desirability of panels should be judged without reference to the fact that if somebody's socks were not advertised on a panel they might be more extensively advertised in the newspapers. While the newspapers ought to make a lot of money, it should be done by some other means than the use of their power so as to destroy a competitor.

● "Indeed, newspapers will benefit in the long run if they make a general practice of defending property rights. A bill introduced in the New York legislature, with the support of the New York State Federation of Labor, would impose drastic public regulation on newspapers and news associations. Watch the wind and mark whither it bloweth. Are some forms of outdoor advertising offensive to a refined taste? Well, newspapers are not altogether a delight. The newspapers should beware of setting a precedent for a subsequent injury to themselves. Let newspapers play square with their competitors and all business. And if a newspaper is not good enough to get a reasonable amount of advertising, let it go on the junk-pile! Such is life."

I am informed that this editorial has pleased the outdoor advertising industry. Be it so. The editorial was not written as part of a "campaign" in defense of outdoor advertising. There will be no such "campaign" in The Chicago Journal of Commerce. The editorial is merely an organic part of a general policy—to wit, that all business deserves a square deal.

In mere selfishness I hope that the newspaper business prospers much more than the outdoor advertising industry. But as I publish a newspaper which specializes in business news, the welfare of all business is necessarily my concern. And I cannot perceive how the publisher of any newspaper can hope to win an ultimate benefit for his own business by setting the dogs of legislation on the milk business "as a public utility," on the outdoor advertising industry as a menace to aesthetics, on the farm middlemen as robbers of the horny-handed rustic—etcetera, etcetera, etcetera. Governor Long's proposed tax on newspaper advertising may bob up again—and stay up. Public sentiment may approve the tax. It is wonderful what a change a few years may make in public sentiment. To play safe the newspapers should give all business a square deal.

California Road Laws
Held Adequate

A joint legislative committee created by the 1929 Legislature to investigate the matter of scenic preservation of State highways has made its report to the present session. It holds that "intelligent enforcement" of present laws, "together with a true love of our State and a resultant pride in its beauties and glories, are sufficient to remedy all the difficulties that have arisen and are likely to continue to arise.

"Existing laws," the report says, "prohibit the use of public property or highway right of way for commercial purposes; consequently, all of such structures visible to the highways are situated upon private property. The constitutional rights to use private property for commercial purposes, so long as such use does not endanger the safety, health, or morals of the public, can not be disputed.

"The invasion of the right of a merchant to display, upon property owned or controlled by him, the goods which he has for sale would certainly be unwarranted and unconstitutional. Thus the right to maintain signs upon private property adjacent to the highways clearly exists.

● "More than half of all of the signs showing to the highways are owned and maintained by those operating enterprises situated along the highways or in the interests of real estate projects adjacent to the highways. It was interesting to learn that about 6 per cent of all of the signs are owned and maintained by outdoor advertising companies. The remainder are signs placed by local merchants of adjacent towns or national concerns."

WHY TAX ADVERTISING?

(Continued from page 8) A third principle of sound taxation is this: most economists and others well acquainted with public finance agree that every tax law should produce revenue and that it should have no other function. That is, they do not believe that a tax should be used for regulation. I call this principle to your attention particularly because those agencies who seek to regulate advertising, especially those who oppose outdoor signs, often deny its existence. They base their case on precedent and unfortunately it is true that many taxes for regulation do exist. For example, our custom duties. Notwithstanding these measures, I cannot believe that the American public is ready to adopt a system of indirect regulation. If a nuisance faces us, I feel that it should be prohibited by direct legislation. In this view, I am supported by the majority of political economists.

Here then are three principles of taxation that to my way of thinking stand in the way of any tax on advertising that has yet been proposed. The first prohibits such a tax because it would not be economical. It would tend to stifle one of the driving forces of our business machine. The second prohibits a tax on advertising on the grounds that it would not be equitable. It would discriminate between advertising and other selling effort. The third prohibits a tax on advertising, particularly those measures already proposed, because ordinarily taxation should be used for the sole purpose of increasing our government revenue and not for regulation. That is to say that undesirable conditions should be prohibited by direct legislation.

● There are others that I might mention. One such, to be applied to any tax for revenue, is its fiscal adequacy? That is, will it produce enough revenue to justify its existence? I seriously doubt whether any of the taxes so far proposed on outdoor advertising would stand this test. The New Jersey tax, they tell me, is expected to produce less than $200,000 this year—an infinitesimal sum so far as that commonwealth's budget is concerned.

A somewhat analogous example is the graduated sales tax in Kentucky, directed at chain stores, which, it is estimated, will lose money for the state on a turnover of approximately $100,000 annually. A general tax on advertising would, of course, be another matter.

Although, when passing in review, all of these rules seem definite and clear cut enough, it will not do simply to recite them publicly and let it go at that. There will be too many disagreeing voices. Taxation, outside of the economists' textbooks, is not yet an exact science. On the contrary, it is largely a matter of give and take, of trial and error, in legislative lobbies and committee rooms. Our law-makers are primarily politicians and they must, for their livelihood, listen to that group of voters whose cries are most insistent. When they do begin to listen, fundamental principles go overboard in favor of the majority sentiments. From one point of view this is not altogether wrong. It is the business of legislators to reflect public opinion. On the other hand, the public at large may not always know what is best for its economic good. If that be treason, make the most of it.

● Those of us who are in the business have, of course, never made it a point to educate the public to the usefulness and the effectiveness of advertising. The great masses of people remain, so to speak, economic illiterates. In the average social gathering merely the mention of the fact that a page in a magazine costs eight or ten thousand dollars or that Maurice Chevalier receives $5,000 for singing three songs a week, arouses a round of amazement. It is impossible for most people to conceive how any single agency could be worth these sums. At the same time we in the business have come to recognize them as cheap at the price when properly used—as an economy in the selling function. I am not advocating a program to give the public a short course in the usefulness of advertising although such a program was seriously considered by the Association of National Advertisers. Some of you may remember the Advertising Promotion Bureau proposed in 1917. It is my own opinion that the task of educating the public would be an unnecessary expense. After all the situation is not troublesome unless it crops up among our legislators.

I hold no brief against legislative assemblies as a group. I believe that the majority of them are composed of able, conscientious representatives. But they are faced with the necessity of raising revenue and in a day of diminishing sources the billion dollars and more spent for advertising every year cannot go unnoticed. It is only human for them to cast a covetous eye in that direction. We must simply acquaint them with the harmful results of any such proposal.

What I wish to emphasize most is that this is no time for one medium of advertising to stand aside unaroused because it is not involved in current legislation. It is a short sighted man who can view with satisfaction or indifference, the taxation of a competitor. A legislator who is willing to advocate a tax on advertising in one form or another will not be slow to adopt a similar levy at some future time with more far reaching effects. No more dangerous precedent could be established. If one tax is adopted none of us can know which medium will come in for its share of attention next. We are all involved because our business depends on the efficiency of advertising. We are all concerned because we cannot let the precedent be established that advertising is fair game for taxation.

● I believe, speaking for the Association of National Advertisers, that we can count on your cooperation. I believe through such cooperation we will have little difficulty in solving this problem. Moreover, I believe that through such cooperation we will learn to know each other better, to understand each others' problems better, and thus lay a firm and sure foundation for the solution of our mutual problems to come.

"In MILWAUKEE
concentrate your
advertising where
it will do the
most good—
OUTDOORS"

The Milwaukee market is Wisconsin's market

On the Panels

Photo courtesy Buick Motor Company

This design is singularly effective—and is unique in that it advertises a motor car without showing the car. The two figures are very well painted and the entire design is full of human interest. A remarkable design with an excellent idea behind it.

Photo courtesy Edwards and Deutsch

This attractive, modernistic poster continues the Herald and Examiner's plan of cooperating with its advertisers outdoors as well as in the other services of its advertising department.

Photo courtesy General Outdoor Advertising Co.

The use of the newspaper page as a background against which the solid block with the lettering stands out in reverse is a particularly happy idea. The copy is short and each of the elements is logically connected with the others.

Photo courtesy Continental Lithograph Corp.

Philgas uses a very striking and effective still life to put over its message. It is difficult to imagine how a figure could add more interest to this panel. The utensils have been kept very large and the copy short and to the point.

Photo courtesy Edwards and Deutsch

This poster is particularly interesting because of its use of photography. The models are well posed and lighting and composition are well worked out. The angle at which the car is shown helps very materially to make the design as effective as it is.

Photo courtesy the Erie Lithographing and Printing Co.

The simplicity and unified message of this Sunkist poster make it an excellent design. The appeal of children, when intelligently used, is one of the most forceful that can be devised. In this instance, the handling is very appropriate and the whole poster extremely effective.

THIS MONTH

Once again Dr. Pepper uses a poster that is simple, full of human interest and well-designed. This Dr. Pepper series bids fair to prove to be one of the best campaigns of the year. It is interesting to note with what an economy of means the artist has put over the message.

Maxwell House makes an emphatic change from the style of figures that have been used for so long. In place of the atmosphere of the old South we have a modern young couple posed in what is evidently an extremely modern restaurant. The figures and the lettering have been carefully and effectively placed.

Rio Grande uses this interesting picture of an old prospector to carry on the theme of the campaign of Western scenes which they have been using.

Konjola continues its "Picture of Health" campaign with this portrait of a vigorous, healthy and peppy middle-aged individual. The continuity which marks this series is exceptional.

This Northern Tissue poster is very attractive and well designed. The comparison between the softness of the silk and the texture of the product is well brought out and the product is carefully tied in with the name. Note how the line of the head and arm leads to the name.

"There is style in Howard Clothes" and also in this poster. This is a competent design, answering the purpose very well. The clothes are so carefully drawn out, however, that there is a slight feeling of fussiness—of too-carefully-done work.

WHO'S WHO IN THIS ISSUE

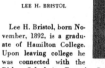

LEE H. BRISTOL

Lee H. Bristol, born November, 1892, is a graduate of Hamilton College. Upon leaving college he was connected with the Bishop Calculating Recorder Company which later became Bristol-Smith, Inc., of New York City.

In 1924 he became associated with Bristol-Myers Company as Secretary and Advertising Manager. In May, 1928, he was elected Vice-President and a director of the company and continues in charge of advertising.

Mr. Bristol was president of the Window Display Advertising Association for two years and was a Vice-President and director of the Association of National Advertisers until November, 1930, when he was elected president of that association.

C. J. EATON

C. J. Eaton was born in Detroit, Michigan, but was raised and educated in Chicago. He has always been connected with public Utilities—starting with the Commonwealth Edison Company in 1897. In 1910 he went with the Union Electric Company in Dubuque, Iowa, as Assistant to the Electrical Engineer in charge of sales. He has since been connected with various subsidiaries of the Middle-west Utilities Company as Commercial Manager. In 1919 he was transferred to the Chicago office of that company, and he was made Vice-President in 1928. He has been very active in the activities of the National Electric Light Association.

JAY HIRSCH

Jay Hirsch has had a varied career with things automotive. In the days of long long ago—he won't say when—he was a bicycle rider . . . . later he entered the automobile business and was Pacific Coast manager for Chalmers . . . . Ten years ago he invaded the tire field as Pacific Coast Manager for Century Tires. Six months ago he became San Francisco Distributor for the U. S. line . . . . and now he has gone "outdoor" in a big way.

He's a member of the Concordia Club, lives in a modernistic suite at the Mark Hopkins Hotel, belongs to Merced Golf and Country Club with golf as his hobby . . . and in slangology he's a "big shot" in the civic life of San Francisco.

JOHN D. AMES

John D. Ames is a newspaper publisher who believes that what most newspapers need most is a better sense of proportion. On leaving Princeton he entered the business office of the Chicago Journal of Commerce, where he soon became convinced that a newspaper which looks at itself from the viewpoint of its readers and advertisers, does its best to satisfy them, and refrains from boring its readers by continually boasting of its achievements, will not need to worry about its more self-centered competitors. Mr. Ames is now the publisher of the Chicago Journal of Commerce but occasionally takes the time to win a cup in a golf tournament. He was captain of the Princeton team.

Bulletin Starts Swing
to U. S. Tires

(Continued from page 22) who handles our advertising, suggested a car under glass, but I did not care for this. The Foster and Kleiser San Francisco Sales Manager offered another idea along the same line, but this did not register either. The revolving tire was really a development of our three minds working on the problem. The minute I saw the rough sketch I knew we had found what I was looking for. To say that results have doubled my expectations is not exaggerating. The panel was a winner from the first and it is drawing a tremendous amount of attention. There isn't a day that we don't get comments about it. I know of people who take their friends out to show them that display.

"I can say without hesitation that it is the best piece of advertising this company has ever done. We have added something like 140 new accounts to our sales from February 25, 1931, to March 20. As the increase closely followed the appearance of the board which was erected about the middle of January I am pretty sure it was responsible for the increased business. In fact I am so firmly convinced of it that if I had to discontinue all my advertising that outdoor panel would be the last I would dispense with. I have taken a three year lease on it and will probably duplicate the idea in other locations. We are also preparing to put replicas of the bulletin on our delivery trucks, having found that the revolving tire can be used by using a motor."

● Certainly an outdoor advertisement with such a powerful "punch" merits a detailed description. Well balanced in color and lettering, the entire composition was planned with the purpose of playing up the revolving tire. It is a spectacular type of city bulletin, the design being painted in a decorative frame of white. The upper strip is a rich red with the words "JAY HIRSCH, 1123 Post Street" in white, this text and an arrow over the tire being lighted in red Neons at night. The arrow is a clever touch, for the panel location is Post Street and the arrow points in the direction of the Post Street plant of the company advertised. Below this strip the text "The Big Swing Is to U. S. Tires" in yellow and "Safe At Any Speed" in white are on a black background. To the right the revolving tire occupies about 1/3 of the surface area. The black tire with the white rim is set off by a series of diagonal lines converging at the bottom in variegated shades of green verging from dark green to lime color. The tire, which gives the illusion of having plunged right through the steel background, is set at an angle of approximately 45 degrees. This impression of "driving through" is deepened by having the steel curled in jagged pieces on either side of the tire, the reverse side of these pieces being painted brown and henna. All the colors are blended with the utmost artistry and around the entire advertisement is a golden brown border 2 inches wide, beyond which a putty colored background extends to the white framework. Around the portion where the revolving tire is placed, a white railing has been constructed to prevent children from tampering or getting too close.

● Mr. Hirsch declares that his enthusiasm has extended way back to the eastern coast.

"Shortly after the bulletin was completed the general manager of the United States Rubber Company saw it," he said: "He was so enthusiastic that he wired L. M. Simpson, General Sales Manager of the Tire Division of the United States Rubber Company in Detroit. When Mr. Simpson arrived here on a tour he went out to see the board. His reaction may be judged from this incident. Mr. Simpson wired the Detroit office and on the strength of his comments three of these panels were immediately started there and indications are that this idea, originated in San Francisco, will be carried out by the rubber company in all parts of the country. Because of the tremendous interest displayed, the outdoor advertising company has taken out a patent on the idea."

The Jay Hirsch Co. Ltd. recently bought out another concern that had been handling the U. S. Tire and in remodelling the building they are having placed on the roof one of these painted panels with the revolving tire.

National Dry Goods Ass'n
Represented at A. F. A. Meet

(Continued from page 32) coincident with ours.

"For years we have had departmental sessions at our annual conventions for the retail advertising managers. It has been pointed out to us by Mr. Collins and his associates that many of those who have participated in our retail departmental sessions have been recruited from the ranks of the Sales Promotion Division of the National Retail Dry Goods Association. Many of the members of this Division and of our affiliated Advertising Clubs have been in the habit of attending both conventions. Others have attended either one or the other of the two conventions."

● Other of the groups that are meeting with the Federation at that time are the following: The International Trade Conference, Magazine Representatives, Newspaper Representatives, Newspaper Advertising Executives Association, Public Utilities Advertising Association, Association of Newspaper Classified Advertising Managers, Broadcast Advertisers, Direct Mail Advertising Conference, Advertising Typographers of America, Envelope Manufacturers Association of America, Manufacturers Merchandise Advertising Association, National Association of Teachers of Marketing and Advertising, Religious Press Department and the Agricultural Publishers Association.

SPENDING TENDENCIES

1

SELMA, ALA.

GENERAL BUSINESS CONDITIONS: For wholesale groceries and related lines, Stewart, King & McKenzie, largest firm of jobbers and wholesalers in this section, report a gain of 5% in volume for the month of March 1931 over February 1931 and the same ratio of gain over March 1930.

One new building is under construction, the cost of which will exceed $40,000. Bids are to be received and contract to be let within two weeks by S. H. Kress & Co. for new building, estimated to cost approximately $60,000. There are a few new residences under construction and new paved roads being built.

MOVING PICTURE ATTENDANCE: Moving picture attendance showed a decrease of 25% in March 1931 as compared with March 1930.

AUTOMOTIVE: Mr. J. L. Finklea of Finklea Motor Company, Chevrolet dealers, reports a gain in sales of 80% for the month of March 1931 as compared with the month of February 1931, and a gain of 90% over March 1930. Sales for the month of April 1931 so far show the same ration of gain over the same month last

year as was registered for the month of March. There was no decided improvement in sales shown by other auto agencies, although none show a loss in volume when compared to the same period during the year 1930.

Gasoline sales for Selma during the month of February 1931 total 156,417 gallons. For February 1930, 159,057 gallons.

2

SAN FRANCISCO, CALIF.

GENERAL BUSINESS CONDITIONS: Statistics for February are given in place of those for March as they were not available quite yet.

Bank debits, building permits, general power sales and retail sales showed a gain of 11% from the average for February during the ten preceding years but was 4% below the same month in 1930.

Business during February in several fields showed considerable improvement over February a year ago. The bright spots were in residential and municipal construction fields, real estate sales, industrial expansions, new business and utilities field. Liabilities of commercial failures were the lowest in 15 months with the exception of November. Employment conditions in the manufacturing industries showed some improvement for several groups in February compared with the preceding month.

Building permits issued during February totaled 501. The total value of $1,712,571 showed a gain of 50% over the same month in 1930 and 38% for the first two months of this year over the same period in 1930. Building permits for March totaled $2,090,129, which is a 22% gain over the building permit figures for February. February residential building permits value of $1,017,037, numbering 160 and providing accommodations for 241 families, exceeded any month during the last two years with a gain of 40% over January and 24% over the same month a year ago. Residential permits showed a gain of 229% over the same month a year ago and a gain of 196% for the year to date. Additions, alterations and repairs also installations showed gains during February over the same month a year ago and for the year to date. Municipal contracts during the month were twelve times the amount of February, 1930, and nearly five times the amount for the year to date over a similar period in 1930.

Real estate sales valued at $6,851,025 for the month of February represented a 31% gain over January and a 6% gain over February, 1930. Mortgages and deeds of trust of $12,600,389 against San Francisco real estate showed a gain of 17% over January and 28% over the same month a year ago and a 14% gain for the year to date. The releases effected during February exceeded the same month last year by close to one million dollars, representing an 11% gain with an equal gain for the year thus far.

New businesses established in San Francisco during February, numbering 310, represented a gain of 3% over January; of the total number, 34% came under the foodstuffs group; 8% in wearing apparel group; 6% in the auto group and 4% in the hardware group. New business offices, numbering 53, were reported opened during the month.

One new industry and two industrial expansions reported brought the total industries established during the first two months to ten and industrial expansions to 8. The number of industrial expansions this year to date gained 33% over the same period a year ago.

Retail Trade Index of Department Store Sales at 86 for February is 10% below February, 1930, which is approximately equal to the difference in price levels since a year ago. The index for February was equal to the average index for the ten preceding years. Retail trade measured by Department Store sales in northern California showed a gain of 2.3% over the same month in 1930.

Wholesale trade during February improved over January in Electrical Supplies and Furniture lines, but compared to February a year ago decreased in all lines.

As in retail trade commodity price downward trend has affected the dollar volume of business.

Utilities represented by industrial and commercial gas sales, water consumers, and telephone connections showed substantial improvement during February 1931 over the same month a year ago and also for the first two months of this year over a similar period. General power sales of 23.9 million kilowatt hours showed a 4% decrease over February, 1930; the total for the year to date compared to the same period in 1930 was off 2%. Industrial and commercial gas sales for February, amounting to 356.4 million cu. ft., gained 49% over February last year and was 54% ahead for the year to date. Water consumers showed a gain of 313% over January; 20% over February 1930, and 90% for the year to date.

Postal receipts of $631,769 decreased 7% over February 1930. March postal receipts, however, reached the figure of $756,200, which is nearly a 20% gain over February, the month preceding.

The weekly average for February for total loans and investments amounting to $1,939,792, reported by member banks of the 12th Federal Reserve District, increased slightly over the preceding month and the same month a year ago. The weekly average gained for investments was a 5% gain over January; 17% over February 1930, and 14% for the year to date.

Interest rates on prime commercial loans decreased from 5.03% to 4.85% in February; demand security loans from 5.24% to 5.11%. Federal Reserve Bank Discount rate remained steady at 3% compared to 4½% a year ago.

Shipping arrivals registered tonnage of 1,405,034 in San Francisco Bay during February gained 1% over February of last year and 3% for the year to date. Departures of 1,386,464 tons decreased 3%, compared to a year ago, but for the year to date was practically equal to the same period in 1930.

Carload freight movements decreased 8% from January; 18% from February 1930, and 14% for the year to date. Fruit and vegetable receipts totaling 1,340 carloads during February gained 1% over January and 3% over February 1930. Receipts of 2,671 carloads this year to date were 7% ahead of the same period a year ago. Dairy products receipts dropped off during February slightly more than seasonal compared to 1930.

The manufacturing industries in San Francisco during February reported a slight decrease from January, amounting to 0.4% in number of employees; 0.6% in weekly payroll. Average weekly earnings gained 1%. MOVING PICTURE ATTENDANCE: Figures show that attendance is about the same as in 1930.

AUTOMOTIVE: New car sales totaled 1,196 for the month of February. Automobile registration: passenger cars, 146,182; trucks, 9,706; motorcycles, 1,025.

3
ALBANY, GEORGIA

GENERAL BUSINESS CONDITIONS: Business as a whole is about the same as 1930. Business conditions in Albany are a reflection of the entire trading center for a radius of fifty miles. Extensive paved roads make the city accessible, which in turn makes business on a level with last year.

MOVING PICTURE ATTENDANCE: Theatre attendance is practically the same as in 1930.

AUTOMOTIVE: For the three months in 1931, January, February and March, gasoline consumption was 10% higher than for the same period in 1930.

4
ATLANTA, GEORGIA

GENERAL BUSINESS CONDITIONS: Three new buildings amounting to $300,000 for the Atlanta Telephone Company are to be built during 1931.

Bank clearings and bank debits for the month of January 1931 showed a decrease as compared with January 1930. Building permits and the number of telephones in use also showed a decrease. However, there was an increase in post office receipts and electric meters.

AUTOMOTIVE: Figures are given for 1929 and 1930 and show that there was a slight decrease in the number of gallons used in 1930.

There was also a decrease in the registrations in 1930 as compared with 1929.

No figures were given for the first three months of 1931.

5
SAVANNAH, GA.

GENERAL BUSINESS CONDITIONS: Retail purchases for wearing apparel during the pre-Easter season were well ahead of the same period in 1930.

Sidney Levy of B. N. Levy, Bro. & Co., reported a considerable advance in the purchase of women's wear and men's clothing. This did not apply only to dresses and suits but to accessories. This was an indication that the public was buying more steadily in 1931 than they were at the same time in 1930. A better class of merchandise is also being stocked this year.

Lester Harris of the Hub Clothing Company said that business was decidedly better now than at this time last year. Despite unfavorable weather conditions, there was also an increase during the month of March over previous months in 1931.

Washington Falk, Jr. of Falk's Clothing Company said that this is a time of values to the buyers. Better workmanship and materials is insuring real value to the purchaser.

Terrell T. Tuten, of Thomas A. Jones Company reported that the merchant can now purchase newer goods and better goods for his retail trade at a price which allows him to offer excellent values to his customers. This year there is no distressed merchandise on the market as there was a year ago, and consequently the goods sold are newer and better. Business in the clothing line is firmer now than it has been in many months.

6
DANVILLE, ILL.

GENERAL BUSINESS CONDITIONS: Several merchants reported an increase in sales for the first three months of 1931, over the corresponding period of a year ago. Few building projects are under way at the present time, but we have several in the offing, including a half-million dollar addition to the local government hospital for disabled veterans. Postal receipts show a nice increase. Bank clearings and debits show a decrease. There is some tendency toward the re-establishment of gas and electric light meters, that were cut off during the first and most serious part of the current slack in business. This shows that many who were formerly laid off are being put back to work. Several factories are gradually increasing their forces, and the Illinois Department of Labor which maintains a free employment agency in Danville, reports a smaller number of men applying for each 100 available jobs.

From January 1 to April 1, 99 new families moved to Danville from other cities.

MOVING PICTURE ATTENDANCE: Moving picture attendance shows a slight gain over the first three months of last year.

AUTOMOTIVE: New car registrations have been slightly off for the first three months of this year. However, at this time, the lower-priced car dealers are enjoying a splendid volume. Gasoline consumption is slightly below 1930.

7
SPRINGFIELD, ILLINOIS

GENERAL BUSINESS CONDITIONS: Springfield does not depend on factories for its business as there are a lot of insurance companies besides the Capitol and the legislature. Conditions are better on the whole. The manufacturers' payrolls are increasing, which would indicate that the depression is lifting.

MOVING PICTURE ATTENDANCE: There is improvement in the attendance this lent over last year during the same period.

AUTOMOTIVE: In statistics for both Springfield and Bloomington, the following automobile registrations are given: Springfield, pleasure cars, 17,342, and trucks, 2,583. In Sangamon County, pleasure cars, 23,280, and trucks, 3,522. For Bloomington we find that there are 8,054 pleasure cars and 1,107 trucks. McLean County, 13,312 pleasure cars and trucks, 2,792. These statistics compared with last year indicate that there was approximately a 2% increase.

8

INDIANAPOLIS, IND.

GENERAL BUSINESS CONDITIONS: During the first three months of 1931 there have been 92 conventions with a registered attendance of 18,352 delegates. This does not include the number attending the State Championship Basket Ball Tournament. All of this means that there was a great deal of money spent.

AUTOMOTIVE: The collections for the state gasoline tax for the month of March 1931 were $1,189,960. This is an increase of $133,360 over March 1930.

A recent survey made among the Chevrolet dealers showed that January, February and March of this year were the best three months that they ever experienced before in the like period. Chevrolet sales are ahead of a year ago. The used car market is in very good condition. There have been 5,806 used cars sold since the first of January.

9

CEDAR RAPIDS, IOWA

GENERAL BUSINESS CONDITIONS: There is a decided improvement here over the last sixty to ninety days in regard to business conditions, although the percentage is not so high.

The hotels report a good increase.

Building material companies advise there are a great many inquiries in regard to quotations.

MOVING PICTURE ATTENDANCE: There is a slight increase in attendance for March 1931 as compared with March 1930.

AUTOMOTIVE: Oil companies report a good increase in gasoline consumption, with the Cities Service Company advising that their increase is considerably larger than they had anticipated.

10

DES MOINES, IOWA

GENERAL BUSINESS CONDITIONS: Building permits during the first quarter of the year totals nearly a half million dollars.

Postal receipts for the first quarter of 1931 totaled $925,353, which is higher than a five-year average for the first quarter of the year.

The total kilowatt electrical consumption in Des Moines for the first three months of this year was 15,-126,594, as compared to 12,998,936 for a five-year average of the first quarter of the year.

AUTOMOTIVE: The total gasoline tax in Iowa for the first three months of 1931 was $2,426,605, as compared to $2,157,366 last year during the same period.

A total of 1,335 new cars was sold during the first three months of the year which was approximately equal to the five-year average.

11

MASON CITY, IOWA

GENERAL BUSINESS CONDITIONS: Mr. Lester Millingtou, Secretary of the Chamber of Commerce reports retail trade for March 1931 a slight decrease over March 1930, although a larger Easter trade than the previous two years.

Mr. Wilson Abel of Abel and Sons Clothiers reported January and February the largest in their history with a slight decrease for March and a fine Easter business.

Mr. Morgan J. McEnamey is erecting a fine new building for retailing Farm implements.

Currie Van Ness Hardware Company are erecting a new two story building for a new bottling company.

Northern Oil Company will be in their new building in about thirty days.

Three high-grade filling stations are under construction for White Eagle.

The Northwestern State Portland Cement Company have placed their men back after the usual shut down for repairs.

The contract for the new $300,000 Post Office is being let in April.

MOVING PICTURE ATTENDANCE: Mr. Heffner of the Palace Theatre reports that business is off about ten per cent for March 1931 as compared with March 1930.

12

BOSTON, MASS.

GENERAL BUSINESS CONDITIONS: Increased manufacturing activity reflected in improved employment and payrolls. Massachusetts manufacturing establishments in February showed a gain of 2.5% in wage earners and 4.1% in payrolls as compared with January. This is also the largest increase since September 1929.

The Boston Federal Reserve member banks report an increase of $8,000,000 in loans during the week ending March 11th as compared with the previous week. The country as a whole reported a drop of $65,000,000 in the same week.

Food and commodity prices have dropped as much as 15% in some lines since 1929.

Airplane travel between Boston and New York in March exceeded 1,900 passengers, an increase of 50% over the previous record.

Twenty-one conventions of national and international character, and hundreds of New England conventions are scheduled for Boston in the first six months of 1931.

MOVING PICTURE ATTENDANCE: Moving picture attendance has shown a remarkable pickup over January and February and the corresponding period of last year. Business was 20% better during Lent 1931 than during Lent 1930.

AUTOMOTIVE: The tax for January 1931 was $725,-000, which was an increase of 20% over January 1930.

13
SPRINGFIELD, MASS.

GENERAL BUSINESS CONDITIONS: Retail stores report large increases over February, particularly clothing. Pleasant weather resulted in a volume of Easter business exceeding expectations.

MOVING PICTURE ATTENDANCE: The attendance in March 1931 is holding practically even with March 1930. This is due in part of new and aggressive advertising policies being employed by theatres.

AUTOMOTIVE: New registrations on April 1st totaled the largest number in the history of the Motor Vehicle Department. Registrations for the first three months of the year were less than normal. New car dealers report great interest in new models but actual sales are lagging somewhat.

14
LINCOLN, NEBR.

GENERAL BUSINESS CONDITIONS: Figures compiled by the Federal Reserve Bank at Kansas City indicate that Lincoln in the month of February 1931 was 13.1% below those of February 1930 in payments by check.

Building permits were increased 63% in February 1931 as compared with February 1930.

Retail trade sales in two reporting department stores in Lincoln were 3.5% below those of February 1930.

15
OMAHA, NEBR.

GENERAL BUSINESS CONDITIONS: There has been a large increase in the number of building permits taken out for the construction of family dwellings in Omaha. During March there were 28 permits, valued at $126,000 which is double the permits of March 1930. This large increase in the building of homes is due partly to the favorable weather, low building costs and the scarcity of homes as revealed by the less than three per cent vacancies shown by the Omaha Real Estate Board.

The Union Pacific Railroad has been doing some consolidation for the sake of efficiency and recent rearrangements in the account departments brought one hundred men to Omaha. This railroad has the largest payroll in Omaha.

The bank call made March 25th revealed deposits of $114,300,000 which is an increase of over $2,000,000 in deposits since January 1, 1931, and an increase of over $1,000,000 in deposits over March 27, 1930.

Live stock receipts for March 1931, 2.7% above the five year average for March, and the packers of Omaha slaughtered about 1% more during March than the five year average.

Grain receipts were 28.5% above the five year average for March while bank clearings and post office receipts

showed a decrease. These same comparisons also held for March 1930 and March 1931.

Real estate is reported to be moving. One well known concern, Rasp Brothers, report that they sold fifteen properties during the month of March 1931, which was twice as many as they sold in March 1930.

16
NEW YORK, N. Y.

GENERAL BUSINESS CONDITIONS: Easter trade was very brisk and it was reported to be especially so in Men's Clothing. Many retail stores were cleaned out as a result of it,

Houses dealing in outdoor goods have reported there are many inquiries for this type of goods. This is indicative of a good buying season.

17
PORTLAND, ORE.

GENERAL BUSINESS CONDITIONS: Retail business has been increased by the Veterans' bonus checks.

Building operations are normal and unemployment has been taken care of by increased building and construction activity.

The woolen and knitting business has been working to capacity to take care of late spring and early summer orders.

MOVING PICTURE ATTENDANCE: The R. K. O. Orpheum reports an increase in attendance of 25.3% in March 1931 as compared with March 1930.

AUTOMOTIVE: There are no figures available as yet showing gasoline consumption for March, but in February 1930 there were 9,421,019 gallons consumed as compared with 10,608,074 gallons in February 1931.

18
ABERDEEN, SO. DAK.

GENERAL BUSINESS CONDITIONS: General business is still slow. Clothing and groceries show the most gain and are really on a par with 1930. Other lines do not respond as well as had been hoped earlier in the year. The average is about 10% lower than a corresponding period in 1930. Merchandise is still bought on a quick turnover basis, and credit is limited to the consumer. Much business is done on a cash basis.

MOVING PICTURE ATTENDANCE: Moving picture attendance is picking up rapidly. March records compare very favorably with March 1930. Inasmuch as this winter has been hard on the motion picture industry in this section, it is thought that this encouragement is a good indication of confidence.

AUTOMOTIVE: Gasoline consumption continues to be far ahead of 1930. An open winter and cheaper prices help this.

Auto registration is still slow. Chevrolet has passed Ford every month this year. The tendency is entirely towards lighter cars.

19
NASHVILLE, TENN.

GENERAL BUSINESS CONDITIONS: There was a drop in the employment index for March of .68% below January 1931. One group of industries showed an increase while a large number of smaller ones showed a decrease which makes the average quoted above.

There is an increase in the use of electric power during February 1931 as compared with February 1930 and in carlot shipments for the same time.

There was a decrease in bank clearings, building permits, postal receipts and in department store sales for February 1931 as compared with February 1930.

20
AMARILLO, TEXAS

GENERAL BUSINESS CONDITIONS: The April issue of "The Nation's Business" shows Amarillo and its immediate trade territory still in the "White," which makes the 28th consecutive month. Amarillo ranks third in Texas in 1931 building permits, which total to date is slightly in excess of one million dollars.

March sales in the three leading Women's Ready-to-Wear Stores show an increase over February of this year and that sales are approximately equal to March 1930. Two men's stores report March sales to be slightly lower in March 1931 as compared with March 1930.

Due to several large building projects, including a large new courthouse, and a Publix theatre costing $450,000, and two large subway projects, there is practically no unemployment in Amarillo.

MOVING PICTURE ATTENDANCE: Three theatres report approximately a 5% decrease in total admissions during March 1931 as compared with March 1930. During the latter half of March a seasonal upturn in attendance was observed.

AUTOMOTIVE: Following are actual comparative figures secured from the four largest local distributors of gasoline.

| | 1930 | | 1931 | |
	Feb.	March	Feb.	March
Texas Co.	127,518	151,940	104,000	108,000
Gulf Prod. Co.	103,465	102,790	84,482	80,786
Continental	24,000	25,000	52,000	57,000
Magnolia	49,100	59,850	77,207	84,367
Totals	304,083	339,580	317,689	330,153

Auto registration figures:

1930 total registration of passenger cars in Amarillo 13,546
" total registration of trucks in Amarillo 2,259
1931 registrations to date of passenger cars 12,254
" registrations to date of trucks...... 1,455

21
CORPUS CHRISTI, TEXAS

GENERAL BUSINESS CONDITIONS: The lumber men report that there is about a 30% decrease in the March 1931 sales as compared with the March 1930 sales.

Department store sales report no decrease, with sales holding their own.

In the grocery business the volume of sales shows a decline of about 10%. The lower commodity prices would be responsible for this decline.

Clearings at the port show an increase of 25% in number of vessels but more than 50% in tonnage. Boats are taking out heavier cargoes.

Tourist patronage has not shown any decline in numbers. In fact there has been more actual tourist business the last six months than for the same period last year. However, there has been a decrease in actual business accounted for as follows. Last year the tourist stayed two weeks to two months and spent freely. This year, they have stayed a week to three weeks and have not spent so freely.

MOVING PICTURE ATTENDANCE: The attendance for March 1931 is about the same as for March 1930, only there are four theatres this year instead of three.

22
HOUSTON, TEXAS

GENERAL BUSINESS CONDITIONS: General business in Houston, both wholesale and retail, is very slowly but surely improving. Merchants say that February was discouraging to some extent but that March, even with due allowance for the usual spring and Easter pick-up, is showing an unmistakable turn for the better. Buyers are displaying less resistance and are giving promise of new activity soon.

Unemployment is easing up in Houston with men going back to work in several lines that have previously been quiet.

MOVING PICTURE ATTENDANCE: There is an increase of 6% in moving picture attendance in March 1931 as compared with March 1930.

AUTOMOTIVE: New car registrations are off 15½% in 1931 as compared with 1930. Gasoline consumption is reported to be off between 5% and 10%.

23
WACO, TEXAS

GENERAL BUSINESS CONDITIONS: There is a $500,000 city improvement program going into action which will include considerable paving and a viaduct to alleviate traffic difficulties.

Waco was selected by the U. S. Government as the site for the new veterans' hospital. This will serve the southwest. Waco was selected because of its accessibility as a railroad center to all points from which veterans would come. This will mean prosperity for the city as a large number of men will be brought in, and also employment for the city.

Since 1899, the industrial payroll has increased 82%, and indications are for at least a normal, if not a more than normal business this year.

24
LA CROSSE, WISCONSIN

GENERAL BUSINESS CONDITIONS: The mild winter and unseasonable weather has disturbed normal business by speeding up some lines and materially slowing down others. Commodity sales are greater in March 1931 than in 1930, but in dollars and cents are greatly below 1930 due to the lowering of commodity prices.

Northern States Power Company reports gross sales for light and power 20% below the same period in 1930.

Bank clearings in 1931 to date are below the usual seasonal normal but are showing a steady increase every week. Savings accounts are on the increase. The unemployment situation is well in hand, authentic sources report less than one thousand wage earners unable, or unwilling, to find work.

MOVING PICTURE ATTENDANCE: Motion picture attendance is reported to be 20 to 25% below normal.

AUTOMOTIVE: Gasoline consumption has increased 15 to 20% in 1931 as compared with the same period in 1930.

25
MILWAUKEE, WIS.

GENERAL BUSINESS CONDITIONS: Retail business is somewhat slow, but few business failures are being reported.

The Association of Commerce officials report car loadings off about 25%. Part of this condition is of course due to the fact that short haul shipment by truck is becoming more popularized. Railroads have been quite successful in stimulating passenger traffic through excursion rates. The extremely attractive travel rates offered to the public by the various roads servicing Milwaukee have proved that the public responds quite readily to price appeal.

The banks report heavy deposits with relatively small loan applications.

MOVING PICTURE ATTENDANCE: Motion picture attendance is spotty, with good business enjoyed by such houses as are able to procure good pictures. The lack of good first-run pictures has affected attendance at small independently owned theatres to some extent, but the big first-run houses are enjoying a good business when they are able to book first-class attractions.

AUTOMOTIVE: The first quarter of 1931 as compared with 1930 shows a small increase in new car sales among the widely advertised and better known makes of cars,

with a small decrease among the lesser known makes of cars.

Statistics show that there are considerably less used cars on the open market in this territory than a year ago.

■   ■   ■
DULUTH, MINN.

GENERAL BUSINESS CONDITIONS: General business is about the same for March 1931 as it was for March 1930. General Electric Refrigerator distributor reports a 50% increase over the first three months of 1930.

MOVING PICTURE ATTENDANCE: Attendance for March 1931 is down 10% as compared with March 1930.

AUTOMOTIVE: Gasoline consumption shows an increase of 10% and auto registrations show a 3% increase.

■   ■   ■
BROWNWOOD, TEXAS

GENERAL BUSINESS CONDITIONS: General business conditions have been on an upward trend since January 1st in comparison with the same period in 1930. Larger business houses in Brownwood report a small increase in business for January and February over the same months in 1930 and a larger increase for the month of March.

Unemployment has gradually grown less and the general belief among business leaders is that by May 1st the unemployment situation will practically have solved itself.

MOVING PICTURE ATTENDANCE: Moving picture attendance increased 11% in March 1931 as compared with March 1930.

AUTOMOTIVE: Gasoline consumption increased more than 10% in March 1931 as compared with March 1930. Automobile sales in the cheaper class of cars gained about 3% but there was a decided upturn this March over March 1930 in the sale of second hand cars. Higher priced car sales were practically the same as in March 1930 with the exception of Buick sales which reported more than a 50% gain.

■   ■   ■
SPOKANE, WASH.

GENERAL BUSINESS CONDITIONS: An upward trend is now apparent. There is a general feeling of optimism.

MOVING PICTURE ATTENDANCE: Paid admissions for March 1931 are greatly ahead of March 1930 which might be attributed that prices throughout the city have been lowered. From a cash income standpoint this leaves the theatres with less volume than that of 1930 for the corresponding month. The feeling is, however, that the industry is in a very healthy state.

AUTOMOTIVE: Gasoline consumption for March 1931 is on an even keel with March 1930, showing a decided improvement over February.

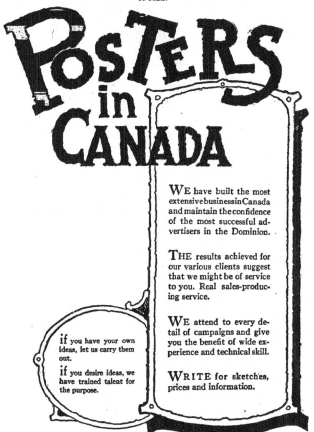

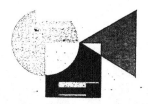

ARTISTRY

The most important phase of advertising in all mediums is the advertisement itself exposed to the public view.

Ability to gain and hold attention lies, not so much in dominating in volume of space, but rather in skill in the use of it.

To put the most into an outdoor design requires training, ability, technique and experience.

Advertising Offices in Sixty Cities

General Outdoor Advertising Co

OUTDOOR ADVERTISING
states its case

Outdoor advertising yearly markets a billion dollars' worth of American goods . . . It pays millions in rentals to over 200,000 property owners each year...The industry directly employs 30,000 people. Indirectly it furnishes livelihood to an inestimable number in such industries as lumber, steel, paint, lithography, paper, automotive and a hundred others . . . The Outdoor Advertising Industry endorses the movement to preserve the scenic highways of America and is working to that end as rapidly as possible . . . It asks all civic bodies to work with it patiently for the preservation of roadside beauty, with due regard for the commercial value of outdoor advertising in distributing American products.

Habits Have Changed!
So Have Advertising Values!

Advertising value still depends upon readers and to insure reading is still a function of good advertising.

Subscribers once meant . . . not only readers of fiction and news but ardent readers of advertisements.

That was back in the days of the big Bustle and Hatpin magnates, when the Harness Maker knew everybody in town and reading two hundred words a minute exhausted the daily paper before the cuckoo clock struck nine.

But today the old evening "ain't" what it used to be.

20,000,000 motor cars HAVE MADE A DIFFERENCE! 15,000,000 theatre attendance each week has cut in on the home time, somewhere!

Yes, it looks like there have been some real important CHANGES in HABITS.

Analyze it and you'll realize OUTDOOR ADVERTISING'S power has been dramatically enhanced by these Changes in the Habits of your prospects.

Outdoor Advertising is UNESCAPABLE advertising. Every one of your prospects reads it, constantly!

WALKER & CO.

88 Custer Ave. Detroit

In outdoor advertising, more than in any other medium, art is an integral part of every advertisement. The poster is an accurate reproduction of the work of nationally famous artists. The painted bulletin and the painted wall, demanding that the design be painted directly, is the work of men who are as skilled in their own field as the creator of the poster design is in his. In this illustration, the artist is reproducing, on a painted bulletin, the work of a famous illustrator. With only a small reproduction as his guide, he is achieving an accurate rendering of artist's work, even to retaining the distinctive technique. Outdoor advertising, through its wide use of the work of America's leading artists, may well lay claim to being the "Art Gallery of the People."

Advertising Outdoors

The PROFESSION
of BUSINESS

BEING a business man has become a profession in itself.
A man may be the executive head of a large bakery or a public
utility concern, but he need not be a baker or an electrician.
His is the job of solving business problems; of keeping the balance between production and distribution.

His life work is more than an occupation; it is a profession.
A profession in which he must give all of his waking hours—
all of his knowledge. One in which he must put years of experience. No school can properly train him in the mechanics of
his profession. Experience is the only teacher he has.

Fortunately, the business executive can, like the doctor, profit
from the experiences of others in his profession. Just as when
a doctor performs some delicate operation in an attempt to save
a life, the knowledge he gains passed on to others of his profession may save the lives of thousands. Just so the business
man faced with a problem, the proper solution of which means
the life of his organization, can if his solution is the right one,
pass on his experience to others of his profession so that their
organizations may also prosper.

When an occupation becomes a profession, ethics and a spirit
for general advancement take root. True, business of the 19th
Century had few ethics. It was an individual fight and every
man had to develop as he was able. Today, however, business
leaders realize that an exchange of merchandising knowledge
costs them little but benefits them greatly.

It is on this basis that the editorial policy of the magazine,
ADVERTISING OUTDOORS is founded. It is because of this that
such men as Fred Millis, C. J. Eaton, John Ames, E. J. Poag and
Lee Bristol and scores of others, all leaders of American business, have contributed their knowledge and their experiences.
Who would not be willing to sit down for a half hour to talk
with these men, to get the benefit of the experiences that have
cost them thousands of dollars?

[signature]

Advertising

Outdoors

A magazine devoted to the interests of the Outdoor Advertiser

VOL. 2, No. 5

CONTENTS for MAY 1931

Harold L. Eves
Editor

Ralph B. Patch, *Associate Editor*
James P. Dobyns, *Advertising Manager*

Eastern Advertising Representatives:
Walworth and Wormser,
420 Lexington Ave., New York City.

Western Advertising Representatives:
Dwight Early,
100 N. La Salle St., Chicago

ADVERTISING OUTDOORS is published on the 1st of every month by the Outdoor Advertising Association of America, Inc., 165 W. Wacker Drive, Chicago, Ill. Telephone Randolph 1692. Harold L. Eves, Editor and Manager.

Subscriptions for the United States, Cuba, Porto Rico, Hawaii and the Philippines, $3.00 a year in advance; Mexico and Canada, $3.25; for all other countries, $3.50. Thirty cents the copy. Make all checks, money orders, etc. payable to Outdoor Advertising Association of America, Inc.

Entered as second-class matter, March 21st, 1930, at the Post Office at Chicago, Ill., under the act of March 3, 1879, by Outdoor Advertising Association of America, Inc. Printed in U. S. A.

WHY BUICK
uses POSTERS

By E. J. Poag
Assistant Sales Manager in Charge of Advertising
Buick Motor Company

The Buick Motor Company has always been one of the outstanding advertisers in the business world. Buick is ever alert to new media which Buick believes will help to impart its story, and so last summer when Buick announced its new eight, the first piece of advertising to impart the story to the world was the 24 sheet poster. And this poster was built around the engine—"Buick Builds An Eight That's A Radio Wave On Wheels."

● The reader must remember that other straight eights had been on the market for years, that Buick was switching from six cylinder cars to eight cylinder cars alone. Now of course, Buick had been experimenting with eights for many years and had developed its eight to the point where Buick knew positively that it had an outstanding product. Notwithstanding this, Buick could not afford to leave undone a single thing that would help to build for confidence. And so several weeks prior to the announcement of the new eight, this great poster on the engine appeared imparting Buick's engine story to the world. Over 12,000 posters everywhere carried the same message. Day after day before

announcement, America read: "Buick Builds An Eight That's A Radio Wave on Wheels!"

● Along with this, the Buick Motor Company told its engine story through newspaper advertising, through the magazines, and through direct-by-mail, and when announcement day arrived, all the world knew that Buick had a great eight, and America was ready to accept this great eight because America knows how very well Buick manufactures.

The entire retail selling organization and the dealers were absolutely in step with Buick's message to the world in regard to the eight. There was complete unity in each move. And so the eight as Buick builds it was accepted by the American people, and Buick, within the first month, led the entire field of eights. In fact, Buick with its new eight has been outselling all other eights in its price range since the very beginning!

● The Buick Motor Company is cognizant of the fact that there are 25 million motor cars on the roads today, that millions of people literally live on wheels; therefore, Buick is sufficiently shrewd to place the story of its product on the highways and byways as well so that wherever people may drive, there they will read a message pertaining to Buick.

Buick believes, too, that in order to do this job, it must build outstanding posters. The series which has

This poster, which appeared in April, is one of the outstanding poster designs that have been on the panels this year.

The "Buick Builds an '8'" design was the first of the posters advertising the new car.

appeared, in the opinion of Buick, has been outstanding. The second poster entitled, "What An Eight" introduced a new note in American automobile advertising. Two young people, charming, all aglow because of the brilliance of their new Buick eight. Through the subtle law of suggestion, millions read the story of this eight. Millions felt the thrill which these young people did, slipping over the road like a shadow. And thousands got the story and acted, because the eight as Buick builds it was accepted almost instantaneously.

● And then immediately following, a third poster entitled, "Take The Wheel and Marvel" appeared. And that is exactly what Buick wanted the world to do—take the wheel and marvel. Through the poster advertising, through the magazines, through direct-by-mail, sales literature, all focused attention on the theme—"Take The Wheel And Marvel." Notwithstanding, the poster, because of its attractiveness, because of the message, perhaps registered most profoundly this thought, more quickly, than any other known means. Place a message on the boards for thirty days and repeat that message, "Take The Wheel And Marvel" one day right after another, and the results are almost certain.

We think it is true that 80 per cent of the people act on suggestion rather than argument, and the poster gears minutely and perfectly into the law of suggestion.

The fourth poster was entitled, "Imagine . . . $1025—Buick VIII." Now at this time Buick was very desirous of impressing the people definitely and unmistakably with the fact that Buick had a car at $1025, and this poster did that job and did it well because the sale of the Series 50 car, which is the car that lists at $1025 at the factory, began to go up simultaneously with the appearance of the poster. We do not think that the poster alone did the job; we do think the poster helped in a very material and definite way.

● Day after day for thirty days the same story "Imag-ine . . . $1025—Buick VIII" appeared. This was the last poster which Buick had during the fall of 1930.

Now beginning the new year 1931, in March, appeared the poster entitled, "Syncro-Mesh—$1025—Buick VIII." And here again this poster doubtless helped more than any other single thing to make the world conscious of the fact that the Buick car which lists at $1025 also had syncro-mesh. Let us state here that syncro-mesh was introduced in this car on January 1, 1931, that the balance of the Buick line had syncro-mesh from the beginning, or August 1, 1930. And so this spring we were very eager to impart to the world this story that the low priced car in the Buick line likewise is equipped with the Buick syncro-mesh transmission. And how could one more clearly impart the story of syncro-mesh than the way it was done—namely, just a slight touch of the finger tips on the gear shift lever? And so the story "Syncro-Mesh—$1025—Buick VIII" has helped Buick in a profound way.

● The last poster which was on the panels in April, was, in our opinion, the finest poster any one has had in a long time. It was entitled, "Boy . . . That's Travelin'." Now in that poster, Buick was very desirous of imparting a speed message to the world just as it did last summer when it built the poster, "What An Eight." In our opinion it was a great poster because it left something to the imagination. The car had traveled so fast that it didn't even appear in the picture!

This, therefore, is the story of the poster campaign back of Buick to date. What may transpire in the future is a matter of conjecture, but the Buick Motor Company has been very pleased with the results obtained so far.

This year's posting started off with this simple, easily understood "Syncro-mesh" design.

ELECTRIC CLOCKS
mark S & W Time

By Augusta Leinard

Here's a case where the outdoor display doesn't seek the public but the public seeks the outdoor display! An enviable situation but it's the actual experience of Sussman, Wormser and Company of San Francisco with their dominant outdoor panels—de luxe in every sense of the word and enlivened by accurate electric clocks.

Great results were predicted when the clock was first adopted in 1928, but every expectation has been exceeded. As W. Vincent Leahy, Director of Advertising, puts it: "The sales index at the end of a given period is a pretty good measuring stick as to the success or failure of promotional plans.

● "Recently we compared figures on our coffee. In 1929 we sold twice as much on the Pacific Coast as we did in 1928. In view of the fact that we had not intensified our efforts outside of Northern California this did not mean so much in volume as compared with other Pacific Coast roasters. However, in 1930, in a wider territory we sold three times as much as in 1929 and six times as much as in 1928.

"Our publicity, as you know, has been largely confined to outdoor advertising and radio. The big painted bulletins with the S & W clock have done their work

The electric clock on this bulletin performs a service for the public and increases the attention value of the panel.

well. Both the public and the trade have gone out of their way to speak of them. Even before we extended our advertising to the Pacific Northwest, retailers in that section commented on our California outdoor display, which they had seen while traveling."

● At the beginning of this year Sussman, Wormser and Company "crashed" new territory, adding Washington, Oregon, and Idaho. As is occasionally this company's practice, they used 24-sheet posters in addition to the paint units as the ideal way of getting a wider range of publicity. Salesmen visited the territory coincident with the posting of bulletins and posters. To aid them several hundred copies of a costly portfolio were gotten out. These contained glossy proofs of outdoor, radio, and newspaper advertising, the latter being used mainly to advertise radio programs.

It is the function of the salesmen to dramatize to dealers what the company's stupendous advertising campaign does for them. The advertising is really yours, it is pointed out, and your stores are the gainers. Window displays showing cans with a good-sized replica of the current clock design, are a tie-in on the outdoor showing. The company's trucks also carry a panel, changed each time the design is changed.

● Radio programs also help the medium by including comments like the following: "Your attention is called to the public service bulletins on the highways and by-

ways, and in the cities, from the Canadian Line to the Mexican border. Each bulletin contains an electric clock which gives you the correct time 24 hours a day—and it is now exactly ——— Pacific Time. S & W Time Is ALL THE TIME."

● "S & W Time Is All The Time" and the word "Mellow'd" constitute the chief copy on every coffee bulletin and they are hammered at in all the company's advertising.

The clock idea was born in an interesting way. Some years back Mr. Leahy found himself looking for a certain clock every day on his way to work. It occurred to him that millions of other people do the same thing. Why wouldn't a clock be a great thing in connection with outdoor advertising? he thought. Inquiry developed the fact that the Western Union was the only one feasible and that was too small, electric clocks not being what they are today. Later the Telechron came and Mr. Leahy took from his file the clock "dream" that had been gathering dust for two years. In working with Foster and Kleiser it was found that the clock was now a possibility and gradually the nebulous idea became a definite project.

The only doubt was whether the clocks would "stand up," for it was realized that an unreliable clock was worse than none at all. But the clocks have behaved wonderfully well. According to Mr. Leahy they are 99 per cent correct.

"Occasionally one stops or develops trouble and it's astonishing the number of people who let us know about it. We have had prominent men who, sitting back in their limousines, noticed in passing a certain clock that it had stopped. They would phone us about it and some have even taken the trouble to write."

● The company's principle is advertising that also gives public service and this is being admirably adhered to in the clock bulletins. They appear in highway locations, small towns, and metropolitan areas, and Chamber of Commerce and other community officials, as well as private citizens, write in thanking the company for installing the clock.

Speaking of locations, the advertising director said that these are selected for major circulation. "We aim to get into the very heart of circulation both for day and night use, preferring fewer boards with greater individual circulation. For example, one panel in Los Angeles at Wilshire and Western costs us $12,000 a year but we feel that this is more valuable to us than 12 locations at $1,000 each, for more traffic is supposed to pass that way than at any location in the United States.

"Designs are selected with two primary considerations: 24-hour illumination and day and night visibility. We prefer light backgrounds as these have been found to give better visibility. Our design is changed every four months and in selecting it we receive sketches from numerous artists. These are looked over in conference with the names of the artists withheld so that no one will be unconsciously prejudiced by knowing whose work he is considering.

● All clock bulletins have the words S & W TIME IS ALL THE TIME in red Neon lights and to several there has been added a pendulum, also in red Neons, which is suspended from the clock and swings back and forth across the panel, which has added to the attention-compelling value.

This year the company has not only branched out into new territory but into new advertising objectives. Heretofore only the coffee was advertised on the painted panels but now some of them will be used to feature the 222 food products put out by S & W. The first in this series is now in use and it shows a line of marching cooks bearing food on salvers with the text reading: 222 Fine Food Products. Consistently The Best.

The allowance for outdoor advertising for 1931 is 50 per cent greater than that for 1930, comprising about one-third of the company's entire advertising appropriation. Figures speak louder than words but Mr. Leahy's concluding remarks might be quoted as additional evidence. "Our outdoor advertising gives our products a reputation by the very dignity of the appeal. It gives you a consumer acceptance that no other medium could give so quickly."

TRUTH IN ADVERTISING—
Does It Pay?

The fifth of a series of talks on advertising prepared by the A. F. A.

It was Rudyard Kipling who said that truth was a naked lady and lived at the bottom of a well. That is doubtless the reason it took her so long to get acquainted with advertising—to get on really friendly terms with it.

And it was Montaigne, the great French philosopher, who put into one snappy, pungent phrase the whole history of this shy, timid courtship of advertising by the lady called Truth. Listen to what he said:

"I speak truth, not so much as I would, but as much as I dare; and I dare a little more as I grow older."

● The whole idea could not be put more neatly. Probably most of you have a reading knowledge of the falsehoods and misrepresentations with which advertising was tainted a century or two ago. And many know how slow and difficult a task it was to weed out—to tear out by the tough old roots—the lies and the dishonesty that had grown for years, like noxious weeds, in the garden of advertising. And surely all of us here will agree that there has been a decided change for the better.

Let us go back through the years and see how this ethical transformation was wrought in the great field of advertising—how advertisers and publishers came to see the dollars and cents value of truth in advertising, how they came to see the special application to advertising of the famous old precept: "Honesty is the best policy."

As a sample of the kind of advertising which existed in the seventeenth century, let me quote an amusing advertisement published May 26, 1657. This is said to be representative of the first food product advertising in England.

"In Bartholomew Lane, on the back side of the Old Exchange, the drink called coffee, which is a very wholesome and physical drink, have many excellent vertues, closes the orifice of the stomach, fortifies the heat within, helpeth digestion, quickeneth the spirits, maketh the heart lightsom, is good against eye-sores, coughs or colds, thumes, consumptions, headache, dropsie, gout, scurvy, King's evil, and many others; is to be sold both in the morning and at three of the clock in the afternoon."

● That was tall talk, you will admit. Evidently, misleading and untruthful advertising had a very early start. During the next two-hundred years, the progress

The extravagant claims of the old-time patent medicine salesman were reflected in the advertising of his period.

towards truth, I am sorry to say, could hardly be called startling.

● In the middle of the nineteenth century, advertising was not expected to be a statement of truth. Barnum, the circus man, did more acrobatic stunts with flaming, misleading adjectives than ever his own performers accomplished on the swinging trapeze.

The old time patent medicine had cures for everything from a common cold to cancer and blatantly asserted their infallibility. Particularly after the Civil War did the patent medicine industry expand tremendously, and it was this class of advertising, with its hold and impudent claims, that had a good deal to do with bringing disrepute upon all advertising.

The whole period of the 70's and the 80's was a period of loose and shady business practices; a period of great

commercial scandals, of Wall Street piracies, railroad-wrecking, political plundering, widespread corruption, low business standards.

● Advertising, very naturally, took on something of the color of the times. Extravagance in advertising phrases was the rule of the day. Advertisers found it necessary to claim a little more—lie a little more—than their rivals. It was the sort of competition in which the biggest liar or the craziest buffoon received the plaudits of the crowd.

Even in the Dark Ages of American business one great merchant proved that truth in advertising paid. In plain fact it was the honesty of his advertising and his general dealings that made him the greatest merchant of his time. His renowned successor, who followed in his footsteps with even greater success, said in his newspaper advertising in 1861:

"Nothing will be sold that is not all wool, and the quality of the goods will be guaranteed."

A little later he fairly startled the business world by advertising that any article sold in his store which did not fit well, or was not the proper color or quality, or did not please the folks at home or was unsatisfactory for any other reason, should be returned, and if returned within ten days money would be refunded.

People predicted that this rash gentleman would go broke in record time. Well, he didn't fail. And the business today is one of the largest retail establishments of the world.

The sorry state of advertising ethics in the old days was not due to any inherent fault in the principle of advertising itself. It was simply an unfortunate accident that crooks were the first to discover the power of advertising to sell goods.

While advertising columns were filled with dishonest claims, honest business men refused to endanger their reputations by mingling with the crooks. In fact, it was impossible for them to make straightforward advertising pay because they had to compete with the unscrupulous tactics of rival advertisers.

● It was still true, as Samuel Johnson had said much earlier, "Advertisements are now so numerous that . . . it is become necessary to gain attention by magnifi-

Today scientist and copy writer work together to establish the truth of the claims made for the product.

cence of promises, sometimes sublime and sometimes pathetic."

The profitable use of honest advertising had to await thorough housecleaning and it was the business men themselves who started the movement. It was necessary to clean house in order that legitimate business might make use of this great force in merchandising goods and expanding industry.

By 1900, the potentialities of advertising as a vocation were beginning to impress young men entering business, and there arose a demand for education in the functions and use of advertising. At the same time, advertising pioneers began to sense the need for regulatory agencies to eliminate fraudulent, misleading and objectionable advertising.

● To fulfill these requirements, local advertising clubs were organized, which led to the formation in 1905 of the Advertising Federation of America, then known as the Associated Advertising Clubs of America.

This was really the beginning of the renaissance in advertising. As higher standards of practice and ethics were adopted, advertising grew in prestige in leaps and bounds; grew in dignity, in honor, in usefulness; in the character of the men who engaged in the work—until at last today advertising takes its rightful rank among the professions most helpful to mankind. Although the child of the twentieth century, it is already one of the most honest parts of business.

Credit for this swift progress must be given to organized advertising, of which the Advertising Federation of America has been the militant leader. It was this same Federation, now 26 years old, which adopted the slogan "Truth in Advertising," which established the vigilance committees, and became the enemy of all false and misleading advertising.

It was this same Federation that organized and financed the Better Business Bureaus and nurtured them until they reached their maturity. It sponsored legislation, making it a criminal offense to publish deceptive and fraudulent advertising. It encouraged the establishment of the Audit Bureau of Circulations, and the organization of the many associations of publishers, agencies, advertisers and others, all for the betterment and advancement of advertising.

● At the beginning of, this talk, I read you the first English food advertisement of which we have any knowledge—a coffee advertisement of the seventeenth century vintage.

In 1930, the vice-president of one of the largest advertisers of food products made this statement in a public address:

"Our interests are too large to permit us to risk the reaction of public ill-will against undue claims for our products. Our business judgment would not permit us to run the risk even if we were conceivably dishonest enough to wish to do so.

"We have long followed an established policy of adhering strictly to the task of telling the truth. We have so sedulously sought to determine in advance of publication the strict accuracy of every claim made for our food products, that those who prepare our advertising copy sometimes feel our rigidly fixed list of do's and don'ts leaves them with little to say to intrigue the public interest.

"We have found that this policy pays."

The president of a pharmaceutical company, speaking of his company's advertising policy, recently made this statement:

"Our testing experience has made it clear that it takes more than reminder copy to make our advertising productive. In the background of views we put out, every statement must be true. More than that, it must be plausibly true. An experienced bacteriologist and a laboratory staff test each statement relative to our product to make certain that it is true.

"How successful our employment of advertising on laboratory principles has been is demonstrated by the fact that in 1920 we spent practically nothing in advertising and earned $115,000; while in 1930 we spent approximately $5,000,000 and earned more than $7,000,000 net after taxes.

"In each of the ten years the advertising expenditure has been larger than the preceding year."

We don't claim that advertising is perfect, and while we can point with enormous pride to the advance made from the old sinful days whem Lydia Pinkham was signing letters to women in trouble, although she had been in her grave for years, and the credulous public was being ruthlessly exploited, nevertheless, there is still room for improvement. There are still practices which must be repressed, practices which tend to weaken public confidence in advertising. I shall mention a few.

● There is exaggeration. There is too much of it. Some of it partakes of the dangerous "half truth" of which Tennyson wrote in these lines:

"That a lie which is half a truth is ever the blackest of lies;

That a lie which is all a lie may be met and fought outright;

But a lie which is part a truth is a harder matter to fight."

There is a kind of boastfulness which crops up now and then, and which should be toned down or eliminated if we want to keep the confidence of the public.

There are occasional misleading implications—not downright misstatements, but rather subtle misrepresentations by implication. This is done by picturing a beautiful thing, whatever it may be, and then mentioning some article or product alongside the picture—as if the two had a direct connection.

There are abuses in testimonial advertising which are casting suspicion upon the trustworthiness of advertising in general.

But, after all, these are minor defects compared to the evils that have been stamped out. The biggest thing today in all advertising is truth. It is bigger than all the tricks of the copywriter—stronger than all his knack for forceful language. It is truth which holds the confidence of the people and makes them buy. It is truth that counts in a big dollars and cents way.

Truth makes advertising a more effective tool in the hands of business. As advertising becomes a more effective tool it pays bigger dividends. The advertiser is, therefore, the direct and immediate beneficiary from his policy of truth in advertising.

● The publisher of a newspaper or magazine, the owner, indeed, of any advertising medium, is a gainer from truth in advertising. For instance, when people see that the advertising columns of a newspaper or magazine are to be relied upon the prestige of that publication increases. This even goes so far as to lend more authority to the editorial pages. It goes so far, indeed, as to increase the profits of the publication.

You ask me what is the consumer's interest in truth in advertising. Well, that's simple, too. When the consumer rightly reposes his confidence in the truthfulness of advertising, he helps to make this selling force more effective. Thereby he makes it possible for manufacturer and merchant to lower distribution costs. When distribution costs are lowered the eventual selling price tends to be lowered also, for competition serves to bring this about.

It is thus apparent that truth in advertising has an absolute dollars and cents value for the advertiser, publisher and the consumer.

When my mind goes back over the whole hard-fought campaign of the past thirty years I cannot help but think of what Whittier said of the strife of truth with falsehood—"a strife that never really ends; that never really can end as long as we human creatures have the will and the courage to seek to benefit ourselves; to rise to higher, better things."

And I think, too, of what Daniel Webster said of truth:

"There is nothing so powerful as truth—and often nothing so strange."

ADVERTISING—
the Builder of Employment

Prosperity, employment, production, distribution and the final sale of goods are so closely linked together that when the unemployment situation became acute in New York State, Frances Perkins, Industrial Commissioner of the State of New York, immediately turned the eyes of New York industries toward advertising as a means of getting industry back on a sound basis.

● "When unemployment first became acute in this state," said Frances Perkins, "I sent a letter to all the large employers, urging them to advertise so that the stocks in the retailers' hands would become exhausted as soon as possible.

"This is the best way to get people employed. When these stocks are depleted, the retailers send in orders for more, and the manufacturers take on help to fill the orders. These employees then have spending money, and buy the new stocks, and the situation has been cleared up.

"America's main concern, now, is to make a living.

"I suppose this will always be the main concern of everyone everywhere. Give people a decent income by stimulating industry as much as possible, and they will take care of their own aesthetic well-being."

Miss Perkins then went on to explain some of the phases of unemployment.

"Unemployment, due to seasonal variation, has become chronic in some industries," she said. "Not only millinery, clothing and the canning industries, but some others have a wide seasonal fluctuation in normal times. Some industries regard this as of no importance, and yet it is the root of a great deal of our depression.

"This constantly recurring seasonal unemployment is always just about all the community can absorb and stand; and when there is added to it a general wave of unemployment through non-seasonal trades, the curve goes down with a sudden drop.

"There is also technological unemployment, which is the replacement of men by machines. While it is true that the machinist who is replaced by a machine doing the work of fifty men, will eventually find work because new luxury trades will spring up, this is only a generality, and does not always apply to individuals. Glass blowers, harness makers, and others who have grown old in their work do not get back into industry. Time must solve this problem."

● "The Hills Brothers Company, who pack Dromedary dates, have extended the holiday demand for their product over the whole year by advertising. The Sherwin-Williams Company has conducted campaigns to

It is the task of industry to replace the peaks and valleys of the present movement of business with one level line of production.

stimulate fall and winter painting. Coca-Cola has been made a year-round drink by constant advertising.

● "Small businesses cannot by themselves effect changes in the habits of consumers, but joint effort through trade associations secures good results. The 'say it with flowers' campaign is a good example of this.

"The committee's report said:

"It may be objected that such efforts merely transfer purchasing power and thus stabilize one industry at the cost of disorganizing others. But this overlooks the fact (1) that building up seasonal valleys means at the same time reducing seasonal peaks. This is clear in the case of price discounts and is probably generally true even in off-season advertising. If more painting is done in the fall, it is likely in the long run that less will be done in the spring. (2) Even when the total business of a company or industry is increased and the sales of other firms diminished, these (Continued on page 25)

(Continued on page 25)

MERCHANDISING PROGRAM
Increases Sales 150%

● A merchandising and advertising program which more than doubled sales in six months and which is showing no signs of losing momentum resulted from the Keystone Coffee Company's effective coordination of merchandising efforts. Retail outlets have been increased, consumer and dealer acceptance won to a far greater extent than ever before.

In July, 1930, the Keystone Coffee Company was roasting from 3,000 to 10,000 pounds of coffee a month. In January, 1931, production had mounted to 25,000 pounds a month with the sales record still on the upward curve.

The Keystone Coffee Company is the outgrowth of Hunt and Hunkins, dealers in coffee and spices, a concern dating back over fifty-five years in the history of San Jose. Fifteen years ago it became the Keystone Company and two years ago the coffee division was bought out by the present owners and named Keystone Coffee Company.

● The only advertising that had been done up to the opening of the program which had shown such remarkable results was in the form of premiums offered free with each purchase. This practice was far from satisfactory, however, because, in order to meet competition, the cost of premiums had risen from 1½ cents to almost 5 cents a pound, a premium cost representing far too high a percentage of the gross sales volume for profitable business. The Keystone Coffee Company was rapidly becoming an industrious distributor of premiums while its coffee distribution was left to take care of itself. The executives realized that something would have to be done to attain wider recognition for the product.

● It was decided that outdoor advertising would firmly establish the brand name in the public consciousness and give publicity to the coffee itself rather than to the premium merchandise. The company at that time was selling four grades of coffee under as many trade names with the result that not one was outstanding in sales volume or recognition.

The company determined to feature only one brand, Keystone Coffee, and plans were laid accordingly. It is noteworthy that these plans were outlined before copy, design, style of package or advertising appropriation were even considered. The appropriation was figured on the percentage of gross sales and anticipated volume for six months.

The feature of the campaign was the interlocking of merchandising and advertising activities, all bent toward the same objectives; winning consumer acceptance and building up volume. (Continued on page 27)

This poster, the first design used by the Keystone Coffee Company, featured the premium offered with the coffee.

■ In the first of this series of articles by leaders of American business, Colonel Robert Isham Randolph called attention to the necessity for an exchange of merchandising information between various industries. Mr. C. J. Eaton in the April issue, responded with a discussion of the problem faced by the electrical industry in distributing the electrical load and the methods that are being used to solve the problem. In this issue, Lee H. Bristol tells of the new type of executive, the distribution director.

■ Few men are better qualified than Mr. Bristol to outline the need of business for a director of distribution and to list the qualifications which such a director must have. President of the Association of National Advertisers and Vice-president and director of the Bristol-Meyers Company, he has long been prominent in advertising and merchandising.

■ As conceived by Mr. Bristol in this article adapted from a talk before the Advertising Council of the Chicago Association of Commerce, the distribution director is more than a salesman, more than an advertising man and more than a financier. He must be all these and have, in

Why Business Needs
A DISTRIBUTION DIRECTOR

By Lee H. Bristol

President, Association of National Advertisers, Inc.

On October 14, 1929' it was my privilege to speak before the Association of National Advertisers on the subject of "the distribution director, a new job in American business." About a fortnight later came that eventful October day with which, I have no doubt, you are all familiar since it began an era from which we are just now emerging and the memory of which is painful, to say the least.

● But the events which have transpired since that time, the business depression we have been through has but emphasized and brought to a head what I said in my first address.

The main lesson which we have so arduously learned from the business depression is, I think, that we have been too short-sighted. We have not looked far enough ahead. Most of us were woefully unprepared. Our weaknesses were there but we did not see them. Now is the time to see where we are and whither we are tending. Prosperity will return and when it does there will be a tendency to forget the hard times we have just been through. It will be easy, with business on the upgrade, to slump back into the old habits, into a narrow but easier outlook. A little serious thinking now, a little rearrangement of management will save a great deal of soreness in the years to come.

Let us see what distribution really means. When I spoke, back in 1929, of a distribution director I had in mind a man who would coordinate sales and advertising. Since then I have come to believe that the concept is considerably broader. Production ends when the finished product is laid down at our factory door, packed and ready for shipment. From then on it is all distribution. We cannot even separate finance from it, since there is the financing of production and the financing of distribution. The man whom I have called the distribution director, although he might well be called any other title you choose, is the one who takes the product from the factory door and turns it into profits, for, after all, what we are after is profits, otherwise we have no place in business.

● For a great many years business has been studying, experimenting, researching, on production. Machinery has been scrapped because it became out of date and new inventions have been quickly absorbed. And this, after all, is but a natural thing. It has been but a few years since our distribution functions were the old jobber-to-wholesaler-to-retailer type. We did not pay

The distribution director must coordinate all the elements of distribution.

much attention to them. We did not need to. Then came the twentieth century developments—chain stores, voluntary chains, selling direct to retailers, etc. Still we did not do much about it until we woke up in 1930 and found we had no anchors to windward.

● Production is way ahead of us—and I am not so sure but what we are lucky at that. Surely it gives you and me a better chance to pull ourselves up in business.

What then, are the specific jobs this distribution director must do? First, we know the general policy of the company. He should have a hand in shaping that policy. Where is the company going? How far has it already gone? What direction is it taking and is this the direction it *should* take? These questions are not mysteries. The answer to each can be found. The distribution director must know the method of getting the answers.

Ill-advised national distribution may easily prove to be disastrous.

● When he has a clear picture of his own company he must then examine the industry as a whole and here is where he runs into that most interesting subject—trends. The study of trends is fascinating. It comprises not only the question where is *my* industry going but where is *all* industry going. What is the population trend? What is the trend of public fancy? Looking ahead, that's it. Projecting your thinking not for the next day or the next fortnight or the next year but for the next three or four years, planning, finding out what your goal is to be. The proof that it can be done is that it *is* being done. But I shall not stop to give you examples.

One of the most useful implements at the command of the distribution director should be his research department. I daresay if there had been as much distribution research as there has been production research, much of the enormous waste in present day distribution would never have happened. It is up to the distribution director to cut down this waste, for profits earned through the elimination of waste are quite as important as profits earned in any other way.

● One of the greatest forces in the world today is market research. Many companies are paying too little attention to market research. A close study of markets, of possible outlets, is in too many cases totally absent. For example, national distribution is a fine thing. It sounds great. But I can quite conceive of many cases in which companies would be foolish to attempt to gain nation-wide distribution. Their profits—note I do not say sales—are concentrated at their own doorsteps. They are highly successful companies from the standpoint of stockholders' dividends and that, after all, is the way we measure success in business. To every company, no matter how successful, there comes the ambition to broaden. It may have done business only along the Atlantic seaboard or in some other limited area.

The company executives say "If we can do it there why can't we do it further in? We will go into the midwest territory" and they go on and on; they strain their way into new and illogical outlets and then wake up some day and find that the cost of their ambitious program of expansion has overcome their ability to pay dividends. Distribution research would have told them that if properly carried out. Again, it is only through an efficient, practical research division that we can keep pace with changing markets, styles, media, etc. It will prove a guard against that most feared of business illnesses—obsolescence. It will tell us what competition is coming, not only from within our own industry but from other industries that are seeking to get as much of the consumer's dollar as we are trying for. There are only one hundred cents in the dollar. If a consumer buys a suit of clothes, part of that dollar is gone which he might have spent on a new radio, a car, a frying pan.

● I have mentioned the word cost. Another function of the distribution director is keeping track of distribution costs. We have had cost accounting in production for a long time. Now we have cost accounting in distribution. It is quite as important. How much profit do we really make from our star salesman? True, he sends in orders, beautiful ones, but what did those orders cost and, when the costs are taken care of, how much *profit* is there in it? How did his entertainment costs stack up against the other chap's?

Let us take a sample territory. We have so many salesmen covering it. Our research department will tell us the potential sales. Our records will show the amount of sales we are making. The distribution cost accountant will take our figures (such as salaries, expense accounts, cost of shipping goods, cost of delivering them) and show us whether we are actually making money in that territory or losing it. He will also show us what we should be making as against what we are. It is not his responsibility to *remedy* the situation although he ofttimes can give worthwhile suggestions. His business is accounting. He lays the figures before the distribution director and the distribution director is

the man who must put on more salesmen or take off salesmen; increase his advertising expenditures in that territory or decrease them.

● And the traffic department—what of it? It is distinctly a part of distribution. The money we pay out to get our goods to the consumer is money spent and money spent means less profits. Is there a better way to route the material and cut down inventories? Is there a more compact or better method of packing which will cut down freight or express charges? That is up to the traffic department and the traffic department's report goes to the distribution director.

So we have seen how research, distribution cost accounting and traffic are entities in themselves but all are necessary to weld into one weapon for the use of the distribution director.

Let us look for a moment at the sales department. First, it must be organized and *really* organized. The job of sales manager calls for a keen man. Any managerial position requires tact, knowledge of markets and, above all, knowledge of men. I have the utmost respect for a star salesman. Handled correctly he is an invaluable adjunct to a business. But a star salesman does not of necessity make a star sales manager. It is the job of the distribution director to see to it that the sales manager is the right man for the place, that he brings in sales which yield profits and not merely just sales.

● Working hand-in-hand with the sales department, or perhaps I should say side-by-side, is the credit department. There again we find one of the most important things in business today—the handling of credits in a sane, economical and effective way so that the credit department from the standpoint of utility and results is a really effective aid to the sales department. By the same token a credit department that is *not* taking into consideration the sales department and the distribution and selling of goods, can do more damage to a sales department than almost any other factor in business. It is unfortunate, but true, I believe, that in many cases there is much friction between the two departments. A salesman naturally dislikes to see an order

turned down because of poor credit. The credit department may be quite right but of course that doesn't make the salesman like it any more. So it goes—too often with constant antagonism between the two which makes for inefficiency—and thereby costs money. Again, it is the job of the distribution director to see that such friction is eliminated.

We who are known as advertising men have, God help us, too long been thought of as being "in the advertising game." For a long time an advertising manager's routine activities throughout the course of the year might roughly be described as follows:

● He personally has constant and frequent contact with the advertising agency. He sits in on "copy idea clinics" with his agency; he sits in judgment over individual pieces of art and copy, illustration, headline, etc., etc. (In passing, I might state, Oh how often, as a declaration of independence to his agency, or as a sop to his own pride, does he strain the petty points in copy, the dottings of i's and the crossing of t's, many times at the expense of the larger purpose of the material under his surveillance.)

He works out the details for the dealer cooperative campaign and checks with the sales manager in such matters. Booklets, circulars, package designs, all come under his supervision, and all the details covering the varied forms which advertising activity assume.

He interviews at least the most important of the publishers' representatives, and listens to their stories with increasing casualness, enlivened only by a few sparkling presentations that stand out in delightful contrast to the average run of publishers' presentations.

He works with the agency in outlining a schedule for advertising, and at sales meetings he supplements the sales manager's speech with a detailed story of the advertising activities, plans for the next campaign, etc., etc.

I am not belittling the task of the advertising manager. However, I do believe that many a one has wasted money and again wasting money cuts down profits. There's such a thing as over advertising, spending too much money in this direction, buying color in a case where color is not needed, etc. After all, advertising is but a tool. It is not necessarily the most important part of distribution. Certainly, advertising has played a great part in building up our present day standards of living. It has sold and still continues to sell our products but it must be done intelligently, more intelligently than it has been done. Again, we must hark back to facts uncovered by our research department. There's a great place for research in advertising. I know of no part of a business in which so much money has been wasted as it has in advertising.

● Every company, then, needs an advertising manager. He can be of invaluable assistance to the director of distribution but we cannot in all honesty place him on a pedestal and call him the all-highest one.

Let us see what manner of man this distribution director must be. He has at his disposal these tools which we have been discussing, the credit department, the distribution cost accountant, the traffic department, the advertising department, the sales department, etc. It is his job to weld them all into one smooth, frictionless, powerful piece of machinery so that he can put the product in one end and turn out profits at the other. It is a big job but a fascinating one. It requires real coordinating executive ability of the highest type. It requires an infinite amount of tact. It requires that God-given ability to pick men who not only can but will do their jobs effectively. It requires a man who can rise above personalities and petty annoyances, who can properly allocate his time so that he is not harassed by petty details but is able to give his attention to the formation of policies. He must be a man who will not be panicked, who can stand misfortune as well as success. He must have a working knowledge of all the departments under him—not, mind you, a thorough knowledge of details, but a knowledge of what he may expect from each department. He must be able to work harmoniously with the production manager and with the president. He must be a man who can stand in front of his board of directors without fear and with the inward assurance that he knows what he is talking about.

And I think the company owes something to its distribution director. He should not be kept in the dark as to the finances of the company, its policies and its future plans. To do so would be to destroy the effectiveness of his work. He could not properly work with the production department to say nothing of running the distribution end of the business unless the directors had confidence enough in him to trust him to do his job. He must be allowed to stand on his own feet. If he cannot do so, he will fall quickly enough, for, after all, let me repeat that the answer is profits.

● Whence then, shall this man come? There seems to be no answer to this. Certain natural qualifications which I have outlined I believe are absolutely necessary. But the main thing is that the man must have a conception of the job to be done. If you will but realize that the men of the hour today are the men who can

coordinate not only the sales and advertising departments but can coordinate all the operations of the distribution function—selling, advertising, market research and, by all means, the distribution of goods, i. e., warehousing, servicing, etc., you will have accomplished something. It is up to each and every one of us to get that concept. Once we have it we will at least know what we are working for. It is entirely possible that a distribution director may come up from the selling field, or the advertising field, or the accounting field. Personally, I firmly believe a man trained in advertising has a far greater chance to become a director of distribution than has any other single type of executive in business today. For one thing his mind is not so beclouded with production problems that he forgets the vital importance of sales. Again, changes in developments of advertising have been rapid. To hold his job he has had to keep pace with a kaleidoscopic picture. This *should* have made, if it has not, his mind and his outlook on business as a whole more fluent, more ready to absorb new ideas. His contacts with men in other businesses should have given him a wider outlook on industry as a whole. And to my mind one of the prime requisites of the successful business man today is his ability to grasp *all* industry in its relation to its component parts and to the whole scheme of modern life.

After all, our jobs are what we make them. Certain men have a latent ability to do far bigger things than they are doing. Opportunity is fairly banging on our doors. Clear-headed thinking and a broad gauge outlook on business will now as never before be amply rewarded.

● This job of distribution director which I have tried to point out to you is a fascinating one. There is no monotony in it. There is no narrowness to it. The idea behind it is sound. That it is economically important is proven by the fact that many men are now doing the very work I have described. Those of us who gear ourselves a few steps ahead of our present jobs will one day find ourselves at least a few steps ahead of our fellows.

■ ■ ■

Cunningham Heads Chicago Financial Advertisers

E. T. Cunningham, publicity director, Halsey Stuart & Company, was elected president of the Chicago Financial Advertisers Wednesday, May 13, succeeding H. Fred Wilson of the Continental Illinois Bank & Trust Company.

Three vice-presidents were selected as aids to Mr. Cunningham: First vice-president, Joseph J. Levin, advertising manager, A. G. Becker & Company; second vice-president, Charles Redmon, advertising manager, Boulevard Bridge Bank; and third vice-president, Samuel Witting, second vice-president, Continental Illinois Bank & Trust Company. Preston E. Reed, executive secretary, Financial Advertisers Association, succeeded himself as C. F. A. Secretary.

Mrs. Al. Norrington Dies

Mrs. Al. Norrington, wife of the Association's Vice President in charge of Plant Development, died Tuesday night, May 19th, at Pittsburgh. Burial was from the Norrington home in Pittsburgh at 2:30 Friday afternoon, May 22nd. No further information has been received regarding the cause of death up to the time of going to press.

Spencer Honored by Advertising Federation

Mr. A. B. Spencer of the Denver Branch of General Outdoor Advertising Company was recently elected Lieutenant-Governor for the 11th District of the Advertising Federation of America.

■ ■ ■

Onner to be Delegate to U. S. Chamber of Commerce

Mr. William Kraus Onner of the Kenton Poster Advertising Company, Kenton, Ohio, was recently elected delegate to the National Chamber of Commerce to act as the Director representing the Kenton Chamber of Commerce.

■ ■ ■

Dreyfuss Delivers Fifth Federation Talk

Mr. Leonard Dreyfuss, President of the United Advertising Corporation and Vice President of the Outdoor Advertising Association of America recently delivered the fourth message of the Advertising Federation of America to a dinner meeting of the Poor Richard Club and the Philadelphia League of Advertising Women of Philadelphia. In delivering the Federation's message Mr. Dreyfuss quoted Charles M. Schwab who once said: "The man who declared that honesty is the best policy ought to have his head examined." Mr. Schwab's idea was that "honesty is the only policy, there isn't any best about it."

■ ■ ■

Nokes Addresses City Planners

Mr. Tom Nokes of the Johnstown Poster Advertising Company will be one of the speakers on the program of the 6th Annual Convention of the Pennsylvania Association of City Planning Commissions.

Photo courtesy Continental Lithograph Corp.

Shell uses an entirely different poster in this interesting and humorous design. This company has used this sort of design with the double-headed figure in England but this is its first appearance in the United States.

Photo courtesy Outdoor Advertising Agency

Jersey Corn Flakes gives the package and the appearance of the product proper emphasis in this simple and easily understood composition.

Photo courtesy Erie Lithographing and Printing Co.

Stetson Hats are now made for both men and women. This modern poster with its colorful blue background and its excellent art work, breathes a spirit of quality.

Photo courtesy General Outdoor Advertising Company

Purol combines a safety message with its advertising in this interesting design built around the trademark.

Photo courtesy Erie Lithographing and Printing Co.

Rio Grande has here one of the finest of the series of historical posters that has been used in connection with the slogan "Tuned to Modern Motors." The stage driver is one of the West's most colorful figures and well suited to the series that this company is using.

Photo courtesy Outdoor Service

Calumet Baking Powder uses an interesting and individual design which features the product and the results of using it in as direct a manner as possible. The lettering is on an angle, adding to the interest of the design without interfering with legibility.

Sunkist oranges uses this cascade of fruit to call attention to bargains in Sunkist oranges. The copy is short and to the point while the postscript lends added force.

TP gasoline carries through with its Indian theme in this poster. Note how, as in all the designs used by this company, the initial letters of the two words of copy correspond to the name of the product.

Richfield Gasoline ties up its acceptance by the various armed forces with diagonal red, white and blue strips. This is a simple, effective and highly colorful design.

This sunny, summery poster effectively shows the features of the new Munsingwear Waterwear. A well composed panel with a minimum of copy which is well tied in with the figures.

Davega uses this photograph of a girl to express the distinction, style and quality of Stromberg-Carlson radio. The illustration is well tied in with the name Davega and the pose directs the eye to the radio.

This poster is simple, well-arranged and beautifully executed. The copy is well grouped about the figure, the figure itself is effectively silhouetted and plenty of space has been left so that there is not the

WHO'S WHO IN THIS ISSUE

E. J. POAG

E. J. Poag, Assistant Sales Manager in Charge of Advertising of the Buick Motor Company, started in the automobile business as draftsman in 1911. Since then he has worked in shops and has sold automobiles at both retail and wholesale. For four years he was with Campbell-Ewald Co., Inc., in advertising agency work. For nine years he has been with Buick, his work covering marketing research, sales promotion and advertising.

A. C. EBBESEN

FRANCES PERKINS

A. C. Ebbesen was born in Rockford, Illinois, but has spent most of his life in Chicago. His career has been varied, but selling and sales, combined with advertising, has always entered into his work.

Before assuming the position of advertising and sales promotion manager for Orange-Crush Company, with whom he has been associated for the past six years, he directed bottling sales for that organization.

As a lover of the out-of-doors, particularly of camping, cruising, water sports and sailing, he has twice annexed Sir Thomas Lipton's Open Class Challenge Trophy, competed for by sailing members of the American Canoe Association. In addition to this trophy, he has annexed some eighty other racing medals and sailing trophies.

Frances Perkins, the Industrial Commissioner of New York State, Department of Labor, was born in Boston, and educated at Mount Holyoke and Chicago, Pennsylvania and Columbia Universities. As executive secretary of the Consumers' League of New York City she conducted a successful campaign, limiting women's working hours in the state to fifty-four. Was Secretary of the Committee on Safety, formed to investigate the famous Triangle Fire, and greatly accelerated work in the elimination of fire hazards. Was appointed Commissioner of the State Industrial Commission in 1919 by Governor Alfred E. Smith, transferred to the Industrial Board in 1923, became chairman in 1926, and was appointed Industrial Commissioner by Governor Franklin Roosevelt in 1929.

Advertising the Builder of Employment

(Continued from page 12) industries can in part protect themselves by fighting back with similar tactics to protect their slack seasons. The result may be a socially wasteful multiplication of advertising in some instances, but also it may mean a great stability of operations for both industries, and hence greater regularity of employment which is the end most desired.

● "The development of more regular purchases of noodles and macaroni is a case in point. At one time people could not be persuaded to buy this product in summer. The C. F. Mueller Company decided to go after summer business, and to this end produced a temperature and moisture-proof package. They then used good advertising appeals and finally succeeded in removing the strong prejudice that existed against the summer purchase of their goods.

"Similar prejudices against summer buying have been overcome through advertising by the makers of the better grades of canned soups.

"The Tao Tea Company found that the tea business had a slump of 30% to 40% in the three summer months. By advertising iced tea, made from tea-balls, they were able to turn a 30% slump in July to a 6% increase; their August sales increased another 23%, while other tea companies took a decrease of from 30% to 40%."

Introducing a sideline, and then exploiting it in the months when the usual product is not in demand is the way of curing seasonal unemployment, Miss Perkins explained. The Beechnut Packing Company added peanut butter because peanuts were obtainable all year round, she found in a survey. The workers employed in canning fruit during five months of the year put up pork and beans and peanut butter during the rest of the time.

The A. C. Gilbert Company, in New Haven, was formerly in the business of making toys exclusively. These sold mostly in October and November, for the Christmas rush, so that a product which would be most in demand in the spring and early summer was indicated to fill out the year's work.

An electric fan, the first to retail at five dollars, was tried. The first year was very difficult, as the distributors would not touch the item, claiming that it was underpriced.

● The second year a $5,000 advertising appropriation, mostly for poster panels, was made, and the company went direct to the dealers. This was highly successful, and the year after that an electric drink mixer was added. Today there is a complete line of small motor appliances, all handled by the toy salesmen in their off season.

The Welch Grape Juice Company has also used the system of adding a sideline. Besides grape-juice and grape spread, the raw materials for which are not easily available for two months in the winter and two months in the middle of the summer. The company added several jellies and a fountain drink, to be made and marketed in those months.

"Eliminating seasonal slumps from industry is not philanthropy," Miss Perkins explained. She has letters from manufacturers in all parts of New York state, explaining that the increased cost of advertising and office expenses is justified by the reduced investment in equipment that is not in use part of the time.

Stabilization also decreases labor turnover, and this cuts the cost of educating help.

All industries that can be regularized fall into four classes, the Commissioner said.

First, there are those turning out a standardized product, such as soap, dates or silverware. These can be made for stock in the off-season without any fear of becoming obsolescent through a change in style.

Second, industries using very highly skilled laborers have regularized their programs because of necessity. Such companies allow money in their budgets for carrying workers along from production peak to production peak because of the impossibility of replacing their workmen if once let out. This classification includes the optical business, the instrument companies, and similar lines.

Third, there are the industries that verge on monopoly. In these fields the manufacturers can naturally withstand pressure from the dealers.

● The last class consists of all industries in which the storage costs are not high.

Outside of these four classes, Miss Perkins stated, the only hope for reducing cyclical unemployment in an industry is to develop a side-line and exploit it properly through good advertising and selling.

■ ■ ■

A. N. A. Introduces Illustrated Program

Generally, not much time is spent in preparing the printed program of a convention. When the speakers have been lined up, their names and their subjects are neatly typed in the order of their appearance, and the manuscript is sent to the printer for him to put together in as attractive form as $type$ and paper can produce.

You'd expect an organization like the Association of National Advertisers, representing the last word in ideas, to do something different. They did at their convention in Detroit, April 27, 28 and 29. They introduced an illustrated program that was as lively and interesting as a magazine.

The program was produced by Evans-Winter-Hebb of Detroit. From the very first page the program carried illustrations—trick photographs, super-imposed with people and ideas in action. All the devices of the photographer and artist were appropriated to portray in picture the thought emphasized in each division of the program.

NEWS OF THE OUTDOOR INDUSTRY

Electrical Products Corp. Forms National Sales Dept.

At a special meeting held in Los Angeles, April 20th, the Officers and Branch Managers of the Electrical Products Corporation enthusiastically approved the creation of a Department of National Sales. Representatives of the organization's 19 factory branches, in the eleven Western states, attended. This is the first instance that a leading organization in the electrical advertising field has recognized the importance of agency co-operation and recognition. It was the feeling of those attending the meeting that it was as much the function of the agency to supervise the placing of their electrical displays and illuminated dealer signs as it was to handle and co-ordinate the advertising efforts of their clients in the other recognized media.

The Electrical Products Corporation, in accordance with this new policy, will render a complete service to all agencies handling national or sectional accounts as plants of this Company are located in all of the key cities of the eleven Western States out of which they completely blanket this entire territory.

The new department of National Sales is under the direction of Mr. Walter R. Skiff, with offices in Los Angeles. Mr. Skiff's experience in the outdoor and electrical advertising fields goes back many years. He was associated with Thomas Cusack which later was the General Outdoor Advertising Company, for a period of twenty-one years. The latter ten years he was manager of the Cleveland plant. Previous to his connection with the Electrical Products Corporation, he was General Manager of the Rainbow Luminous Products Company.

John P. Blair has been appointed District Manager for San Francisco, Oakland and the Northwest, and will devote his time co-operating with agencies in the development of this type of business. Mr. Blair has also had a comprehensive experience in the advertising field having served seven years with the Cusack and General Outdoor Advertising Company, and later was associated with the J. Walter Thompson Company.

As District Manager of Los Angeles, Mr. Skiff has selected J. X. Kennelly, well known in the western advertising field through his past association with the Goodyear Tire and Rubber Company of California. Mr. Kennelly came to Los Angeles in 1919 from Akron, Ohio, with the first group of Goodyear sales executives, and with the exception of a period when he was Los Angeles manager of Blums Advertising Agency and then Pacific Coast Manager for the Reuben H. Donnelly

Corporation, he has had charge of advertising and sales promotion for the California-Goodyear organization, one of the leaders in the West in the use of electrical advertising.

Beatrice Creamery to Advertise Nationally

The Beatrice Creamery Company, manufacturers of Meadow Gold Butter and Ice Cream has entered the national advertising lists. The campaigns for each product are separate units and the media used will include newspapers, magazine and Outdoor for both campaigns.

W. B. Wilson goes to McCandlish Lithograph Corp.

W. B. Wilson, Vice President of Parker-Brawner Company, Washington, D. C., has just severed his twenty years connection with the above Company to join the sales staff of the McCandlish Lithograph Corporation. He will continue his activities in the eastern and southeastern sales territories.

During the past year the McCandlish Lithograph Corporation has, by the addition of a battery of single and multi-color presses and related equipment, gone extensively into the manufacture of advertising displays which, in connection with its well established poster department, places it in a position to produce lithography in all of its phases.

Agfa Ansco Uses Posters in 200 Chief Cities

Posters stressing "pictures that satisfy or a new film free" are being placed in two hundred chief cities for Agfa Ansco "all weather" film by the Agfa Ansco Corporation, Binghampton, N. Y.

Poster Panel Saves Bridgeport, Ohio

An all steel poster panel recently saved the entire town of Bridgeport, Ohio, from being destroyed by fire. This structure served as a fire wall and confined the fire to three frame residences. Power and telephone service throughout the district was cut off by the blaze and it was impossible to summon aid from other towns.

Merchandising Program Increases Sales 150%

(Continued from page 14) Before the opening of the campaign, representatives of the outdoor advertising company met with the Keystone salesmen and explained the program in detail. , The sales force received the proposal with enthusiasm and, before the posting was begun, had contacted prospects never before approached and increased production by 2,000 pounds.

● The first poster appeared in August, 1930, on a staggered schedule. The advertiser's territory extends from Burlingame to San Luis Obispo with a radius of about 300 miles and, by a systematic schedule, posting was done in alternate towns. Outdoor posters were supplemented with newspaper advertising and display and car cards, the latter duplicating the poster design.

The initial design featured the package with the brand name and the premium cup and saucer. The second design omitted the premium and played up the package alone against a background of keystones in attractive colorings. Future designs will be standardized by a picture of the package in exact coloring and the text "Delivered Fresh to Your Grocer Weekly." Salesmen call the attention of dealers to this statement with the information that it is actually put into practice.

Display cards are in grocers' hands in each town ten days before a new poster appears and newspaper copy advertises the premium while the outdoor poster plays up the product.

The ascending sales curve tells its own story of consumer acceptance and salesmen are continually hearing stories of individual interest. For instance, a grocer located in the vicinity of one of the poster panels told of a brakeman on the San Luis Obispo Division of the Southern Pacific Railroad. He was cooking his breakfast in the caboose and discovered he was out of coffee so he crossed the tracks to the nearest grocery. "I want some coffee," he said as he entered, "and you might as well make it Keystone. I see it's advertised so it must be good."

● The development of retail outlets is another interesting feature of the campaign. From August (the time of the first posting) to January the number of grocers and other outlets had doubled and all manifested friendly interest in the outdoor advertising. Maggi's, a prominent San Jose restaurant, was so impressed with the Keystone Coffee poster that they contracted for a paint unit of their own. To the left the design shows the name MAGGI'S and the words "Open Day and Night," in the center is a fantastic picture of a waiter combined with a huge cup of steaming coffee, while to the right is the statement "Keystone Coffee Served Exclusively."

Announce Chairmen of A. F. A. Convention Committees

Announcement of the appointment of chairmen for departmental as well as publicity and promotional committees for the 27th annual convention of the Advertising Federation of America, Hotel Pennsylvania, June 14-18, has been made by President Gilbert T. Hodges.

C. C. Younggreen, president Dunham-Younggreen-Lesan Company, Inc., Chicago, immediate past president of the Federation, has accepted the chairmanship of the National On-To-New York Committee. Mr. Younggreen . and his committee already. have plans under way for the handling of what is expected to be a record breaking attendance of delegates who will arrive by rail, water, motor bus and air from all sections of the country and various European capitals.

● Various group meetings and the chairmen include: John Benson, president of the American Association of Advertising Agencies, New York, Vocational Education; Henry Hoke, Postage & The Mailbag, Brooklyn, Direct Mail; Jeannette Carroll, Bryant-Stratton College, Providence, Federation of Women's Advertising Clubs of the World; C. K. Woodbridge, Remington Rand, Inc., New York, International Trade Conference; Earle Townsend, Home & Field, New York, Magazines; Morley K. Dunn, New York, Manufacturers Merchandise Advertising group; Victor F. Hayden, Chicago, Agricultural Publishers group; Captain Howard W. Angus, Batten, Barton, Durstine & Osborn, New York, Broadcasting group; Professor R. R. Aurner, University of Wisconsin, National Association of Teachers of Marketing and Advertising; A. R. Magee, Louisville Courier-Journal and Times, Association of Newspaper Advertising Executives; Leonard Dreyfuss, United Advertising Corporation, New York, Outdoor Advertising; J. S. S. Richardson, New York, Public Utilities Advertising Association, Public Utilities group and Phil Thomson, Western Electric, New York, Motion Pictures and Sound Films.

What is expected to be one of the largest meetings held jointly with the Federation sessions will be that of the Sales Promotion Division of the National Retail Dry Goods Association which will be headed by Kenneth Collins, vice president of R. H. Macy & Company, New York.

Will H. Hays, New York, Motion Pictures; Hector Fuller, New York, Press; George W. Kleiser, Jr., Los Angeles, Outdoor Advertising; John H. Livingston, Jr., New York, Bus Advertising; Ralph Trier, New York, Theatre Programs; Ben J. Sweetland, New York, Direct Mail Advertisers; Barron G. Collier, New York, Street Car and Subway Advertising; and William H. Seeley, New York, Specialty Advertising, are chairmen of the publicity and promotional groups.

G. Lynn Sumner, G. Lynn Sumner Company, New York, general program chairman of the convention, and these committee chairmen have outstanding advertising and merchandising leaders from all sections of the country serving with them.

OUTDOOR ADVERTISING ABROAD

Outdoor Advertising Increasing in Norway

Outdoor advertising in Norway is a comparatively new development, according to an article by Consul Alf. Adeler, Chairman, Association of Norwegian Advertising Agents. The story, which appeared in a recent issue of Advertiser's Weekly, said:

During the last 10 to 20 years the advertising by means of posters has successfullly been formed into a system in Norway; of course it is not used to such an extent and with such means as in America, but nevertheless a great number of institutions have grown up, which have for their aim to make advertising by means of posters and signs known as a good supporting advertising.

During the past few years artists have appeared, who—though, of course, they cannot equal the greatest artists of foreign countries—have made posters, which may be said to yield good art, and at the same time an efficient advertising. We may mention Norwegian artists like Trygve M. Davidsen, Per Krohg (the son of the famous artist Christian Krohg), Finn Krafft, and the deceased Thorleif Ruud. Several other good names are also worth mentioning, and the interest in good painting of posters seems to be constantly increasing.

There are in Norway no restrictions concerning posters except that all sticking of posters must be announced to the local police office, and that there is in Oslo a "Council for the Embellishment of the Town," which can order the posters to be removed if they do not agree with the common demands of beauty in the scenery of the street.

The first places where signs and posters were placed were the station houses of the railways. This happened in the nineties of the last century and they were then utilized without any account being taken of the impression of beauty in its totality. However, the demands of a certain harmony here also began to be set forth to a degree constantly increasing.

About 1900 began the advertising in the tramcars in the greater towns, and this advertising method has also passed the same stages of development with regard to the demands of harmony as the railway stations. Some time later posters and signs were placed on the steamboat piers along the coast of Norway.

About 1910 a great number of advertising pillars were erected in Oslo, the look of which was determined by a public competition, which had a great response. Quite a fortune was spent in purchasing materials, as the advertising pillars were fitted out with an artistically executed roof of copper, worked by hand, and furnished with electric lighting. Some time later the beginning was made with the arrangement of the so-called placard boards. These boards, which are all alike, were distributed all over the capital.

In the other towns of Norway, where tramcars and transformer kiosks were established, a work was begun to utilize them in the best possible manner.

Then the development continued until all newspaper kiosks in the capital as well as in the greater towns were furnished with electric lighting signs and a few years ago the new Underground and Holmenkoll railway, which leads up to the "Holmenkollen," so well known by all tourists, was furnished with standard signs and posters as well in the underground waiting-rooms as at the stations.

Posters like those used in America with wooden frames of a certain standard size with placards, also of a standard size, have only during the last years been tentatively placed on fencings.

Advertising on wall-gables has been used during several years. Four years ago there was thrown open a public competition for the best gable advertising without obtaining any remarkable results. Likewise, last year a competition was thrown open by Norges Statsbaner for the best advertising placard to serve as a winter tourist and summer tourist placard.

The intention was to have the placards placed in foreign countries. About 200 drawings came in, and the result was satisfactory, although there is no enthusiasm among the public for the prized placards.

■ ■ ■

Outdoor Advertising In China

According to a report from Consul General Douglas Jenkins published in the Foreign Market bulletin of the Department of Commerce, in the past few years, outdoor advertising has become almost as popular in Shanghai as in the United States and it is impossible to travel any great distance through the city without seeing numerous painted bulletins as well as the regular 24-sheet posters. Within the past year, Neon signs have been introduced into Shanghai and now they are seen on every hand.

A great many manufacturers distributing through retailers do not fully realize this significant fact:

Outdoor Advertising is successfully used by large numbers of retailers who expect and get direct, traceable results. . . . . They know the value of the advertising of products using the outdoor medium.

Advertising agencies and advertisers find our representatives genuinely helpful in the intelligent use of the various forms of Outdoor Advertising. . . . . .

These three sales-producing factors at lowest cost per thousand circulation

SIZE   COLOR   REPETITION

Foster and Kleiser

· C O M P A N Y ·
GENERAL OFFICES: SAN FRANCISCO
Operating plants in California
Washington, Oregon and Arizona
Offices in New York and Chicago

N A T I O N W I D E   O U T D O O R   A D V E R T I S I N G

Roadside Beauty STUDIED
by Legislative Committee

● There are few states which are as properly jealous of their scenic heritage as is California. To the native Californian there is no scene quite so beautiful as that which embraces a portion of his native heath; there is no sun that is quite so mellow; no girls quite so decorative and no ocean quite so blue. Small wonder, then, that any cry to the effect that the scenery of California is suffering from commercialism run rampant should have induced the state legislature to appoint a committee to investigate the business enterprises and the advertising being carried on along the highways of the state.

On May 15, 1929, Assembly Concurrent Resolution No. 27 was filed with the Secretary of State of California "providing for the appointment of a committee to investigate the possibility of regulating and controlling the location of gasoline stations, hot dog stands, advertising signs and other structures of a commercial nature along scenic roads and highways."

The report of the committee, recently published, is the result of this impartial survey of every sort of commercial use of the highways. Its conclusions were reached through careful investigation and are free from prejudice.

The report says:

● "The Joint Legislative Committee for the Scenic Preservation of State Highways to investigate the possibilities of regulating and controlling the location of gasoline stations, hot dog stands, advertising signs and other structures of a commercial nature along scenic roads and highways, organized with Assemblyman Raymond L. Williamson of San Francisco as chairman, Senator H. J. Evans of Monrovia, Los Angeles, as vice chairman, and Senator John J. Crowley of San Francisco as secretary. In addition the membership was made up of Senator James M. Allen of Yreka, Assemblyman Ray R. Ingels of Mendocino County, and M. J. McDonough of Oakland.

"A method of procedure was adopted and in accord with that plan public hearings were held at San Francisco, Los Angeles, Santa Rosa, Eureka, and Sacramento, where helpful data was supplied to the committee from many and varied sources.

● "The members of the committee determined that the source of the complaint should be investigated, and to that end the highways of the State should be traversed to learn from personal investigation the actual conditions.

"The committee by letter and through the public press extended invitations to every individual, firm, or corporation, as well as to all groups of individuals known to be interested in this problem, asking their counsel, advice and cooperation in solving for all time the difficulty for which the committee was created.

"By direct invitation and by press notice have we tried to get the cooperation of all those who apparently seemed to be taking an active interest in the subject matter. We were especially particular to invite those

Not one unit of the type of highway bulletin used by organized outdoor advertising was found to be placed so that it was injurious to a scenic view.

who have been active in exciting public interest through the spread of misinformation and trick photographs. A glowing example of this was evidenced in a certain national magazine when an automobile was driven into a baseball park, completely surrounded by a high board fence. It happened, as in every such enclosure, that the fence was being used for advertising matter solely within the confines of that ball park. There, by trick photography, perched on top of the car, is a man looking for a 'scenic mountain view.' The individuals responsible for such deception should be severely censured. Their motives are not prompted by fairness nor by honesty.

"Roads and highways have other functions than a means of permitting individuals to gaze in rapture upon nature's pictures. They are primarily the means of bringing man in closer contact with his fellow men by affording him better traveling facilities lending to quicker transportation.

By Day Scenic, By Night No Beauty

"As occasion demands, these roads and highways, though part and parcel of some scenic reservation, may become the way of an individual traveling after nightfall, then that scenic wonder by daylight becomes a foreboding and darkened pathway. We find along that scenic highway by night no beauty, and the wayfarer hurrying on his journey must pass over that road. Welcome, indeed, would be the beacon of a well-lighted gasoline station or artistic signboard. Such would do more to relieve the uneasy feeling of this traveler and be of greater value than would the commensurate dissatisfaction that might be suffered by the aesthetic sense of some purely artistic individual.

"The road from Oxnard to Santa Monica is illustrative of just this situation—by sunlight a magnificent scenic highway, but by night a darkened, treacherous

A landscaped city-suburban bulletin.

pathway, void of all its beauty, and seemingly the abode of all those imaginative things creative of ill feeling, making that scenic paradise a forbidding, undesirable passageway.

Destruction on the Redwood Highway

"One of the most disgraceful and unexplained incidents very forcefully called to the attention of the committee was encountered while traversing the wonderful Redwood Empire Highway. If there is a place in the world that can be compared with the unsurpassed beauty of the part of that highway north from Eureka to Crescent City, then the members of the committee individually or collectively have yet to have depicted such a place by word or story.

"Encompassed in that day's journey, we find nature in all its resplendent charm and glory and yet even there the hand of man has intervened and wrought destruction and an unsightly scene which will bring upon our heads as citizens of this great commonwealth the scathing denunciation of all beauty lovers.

"Piled in heaps on both sides of that gorgeous highway we saw stumps, logs and cuttings in utter confusion and placement, marring the beauty. Screeching louder than mere words could tell of the prevalence of a condition so unsightly, so abhorrent, so hideous, that all other agencies are but bagatelle when placed in comparison.

Fire and Its Scenic Effect

"On one trip a member of the committee passed along a highway running almost adjacent to a forest or brush fire. It was just at dusk, and the scenic effect was marvelous. A painter with brush and easel would be hard put to place on canvas that mighty spectacle of flames and glowing embers silhouetted against a sky radiant with the light beams of a California sunset. There was a scenic effect beyond the power of description by mere words, one that the unconcerned and unbothered traveler felt appealed to the very fibers of his aesthetic sense creating a scenic effect that would dazzle all, if possible to be maintained. But when thought was given to the unfortunates whose homes and property, not to say their own lives, were being at that very moment jeopardized and destroyed, the picture changes. Their idea of that scenic spectacle was founded upon tragedy and destruction. They look through the eyes of sufferers and see all the horrors of human misery in that mass of burned and charred country side.

"Some of the protagonists of scenic beauty and its retention are so clamorous and insistent in their demands that they would advocate the burning of areas just to afford themselves, and some of kindred spirit, the satiation of an aesthetic sense. Aesthetic whims are as variable in individuals as is the sense of taste. What may be sweet to one is bitter sweet to another.

Regularly Maintenanced Boards

● "Our investigation revealed that not one signboard regularly maintained by a standard up-to-date company had been so located that it marred the beauty of any highway. We were particularly cognizant of the fact that wherever the curves or turns of a highway demanded vision ahead, the signboard people had already cooperated. They not only took pains to eliminate such objectionable locations of their own accord, but the slightest request of properly constituted authority brought instant relief.

Motives of Individuals

"The committee learned that a great deal of the agitation against the industries mostly concerned in the subject of this investigation was prompted by various motives; many individuals and groups are motivated by

the highest ideals and purposes, some are prompted by fanatical antagonisms to some particular industry, others by a selfish interest to obtain through legislative restraint a commercial advantage over a rival or competing industry. Others are using this propaganda to sell some particular commodity or merchandise by camouflaging behind a screen of public benefactions, nothing more nor less than a great advertising scheme to promote greater sale of their own products.

● "We feel that we may rightfully contend that, with the exception of the first group, we should pay little attention to the others because they are not sincerely endeavoring to benefit California.

The Purpose of This Investigation

"It is the committee's understanding that the purpose for which it was appointed was to find, if possible, a practical and equitable means of controlling the erection and maintenance of commercial structures and billboards along our scenic highways, so that the scenic beauty spots of these highways would not be marred by the intrusion of such commercial objects. It would appear from the information gathered by the committee through public hearings and personal observations as a result of these inspection trips along our highways that this regulation and control is desired by all interested parties. As a matter of fact, the business interests who, through their commercial activities would naturally be the most vitally concerned with such regulation, have indicated their willingness to cooperate and assist in bringing about the desired results. All of which is the very natural expression of loyal Californians who take a pride and interest in their State.

No Opposition to the Purpose

● "It would appear, then, that there is no general opposition to the purpose for which the committee was appointed, but the application of anything corrective which might be advocated must be fair and equitable or there will naturally be brought about a decided opposition to the object we expect to accomplish. Therefore, it is a question of not what is desired, but how to accomplish the end which is sought.

"Unfortunately, those who are least affected are often loud in their clamoring for the passage of laws which may work a hardship upon others, but give to those who have nothing at stake that which they desire. Whatever action may be taken by this committee must have a direct influence upon the rights of those property owners whose property is affected, and it is only fair that the committee give careful consideration to these property rights in its recommendations for the solution of this problem.

● "The conditions of the resolutions under which this committee is working, empowers it to bring in recommendations only as relating to *scenic* roads or highways. It would, indeed, be difficult to find a definition of a scenic highway which would be generally acceptable. Opinions as to what is scenic are probably as numerous as the number of persons who would be affected by any definition proposed by this committee. Nor has the committee any right to arbitrarily declare that such a road or highway is scenic or commercial.

Property Owners' Agreements

"At the present time, without the necessity for the enactment of further laws or regulations, it is possible for those property owners within any given territory to agree among themselves as to what commercial structures they will permit upon their properties. If such agreements are desirable and beneficial, such agreements will naturally be made and it is our understanding that, under a method of this order, the State Chamber of Commerce is urging the property owners along certain scenic highways to follow this procedure and that to date this educational work has met with considerable success.

Imposing Restrictions on Property

"Without any study of the subject, many are suggesting the imposition of drastic regulations upon those concerns which erect commercial structures along the highways. The imposition of any restriction upon the activities of these companies must be considered directly in the light of an imposition placed upon the property owners. We have, therefore, advanced the idea that consideration must first be given to the *property owners*, whose rights are affected, as it is upon them that any restrictions which may be devised must be in reality imposed.

What Zoning Can Do

● "It is evident from an inspection of our highways that, where the traffic is heavy, commercial enterprises of all kinds spring up—evidently finding patronage from those who travel the highways. Within southern California during the past decade, many of our original highways which passed through sparsely settled areas have become the main thoroughfares of what might be called continuous cities. It is difficult to know when one passes from the limits of one city into the limits of the

next city or town. Through such a territory as this, county zoning measures can find a very practical usage just so long as those who are responsible for the passage of such measures look far enough into the future, as it is very evident that our major highway arteries develop business frontages very rapidly and any unnatural limitation of such development is sure to bring about dissension and legal contests.

"Any zoning of our roads and highways must be done by those who have the authority under the law to create such zones, and it is our understanding that this power to zone, which now lies in the hands of the municipal and county authorities, must be exercised only after public hearings are held and those to be affected by such zoning have had an opportunity to express their objections or to indicate their approval of such zoning. The zoning of any particular section or community must be beneficial to those within that section or community or else the validity of such zoning would be questionable on the basis that it is the imposition of the will of those who have no immediate interest involved, but merely seek to obtain that which pleases them at the sacrifice of the rights of others. It would, therefore, appear that, if any zoning of the scenic highways is to be done, it must meet with the approval of those whose properties are affected or else such zoning measures will be contested and found invalid. While it might be one of the recommendations of this committee that planning commissions in each county undertake surveys of the scenic roads and highways within their respective counties and proceed in accordance with the laws of the State to enact zoning ordinances, it is not, in the opinion of the committee, within the jurisdiction of this committee to indicate the scenic zones to be considered.

Mountain Highways

● "On the other hand, those highways which run through the mountainous areas and in some instances along the seashore, where the amount of commercial development will always be naturally limited by local geographic conditions, offer the best opportunities for the preservation of the scenery which the motorists can enjoy without seeking the more remote sections of the State. However, the enjoyment of this scenery should not be wholly at the expense of the property owner, that is to say, to deny the property owner any commercial use of his property just because some of the motoring public wishes to enjoy these scenic attractions, appears unfair and unreasonable. While we have heard it said that such property along the highways has only become valuable due to the construction of the highways which have been built by public money and that for this reason it would be fair to impose restrictions upon such property owners, we can not be led to believe by any stretch of the imagination that the argument is sound. Increased traffic as the result of better streets within a city likewise brings about increased property values, but within the city no one advances this same argument—that the property owner should be restricted in the use of (Continued on page 37)

"GET THIS FACT,

MR. ADVERTISER!

OUTDOOR POSTER
ADVERTISING, REACH-
ING OVER 750,000
PEOPLE DAILY, MOVES
AND SELLS YOUR
PRODUCT IN

MILWAUKEE"

MERCHANDISE
Your Advertising
by A. C. Ebbesen
Advertising Manager, the Orange Crush Company

● It is absolutely essential that the distribution organization be completely sold before undertaking any sort of merchandising effort.

The distributor must be sold on the manufacturer's product—and that responsibility is up to the product and its salesmen. He must also be sold on the efforts that the manufacturer is making to help him sell that product—and that is the responsibility of the advertising.

Advertising properly handled can be one of the greatest of merchandising agencies—and improperly handled can be one of the most capacious rat-holes down which a manufacturer ever poured good currency. And, unless advertising is so handled as to arouse the interest and cooperation of the dealer, that advertising will lack much of its potential effectiveness.

● The Orange Crush Company has entered, this year, upon one of the most ambitious programs of advertising that it has ever undertaken. All our advertising and merchandising efforts have been given added impetus. Outdoor posters, which will be the background

of the campaign, are planned to cover the entire peak selling season. An interesting point in connection with these designs is the introduction of characters which are different from the usual pretty girls. The May poster shows two kids, obviously active and carefree. They are looking with longing at Orange-Crush bottles in a store window. Another shows a cowpuncher on his cow pony enjoying a bottle of Orange-Crush; and in the third there is a tennis girl. All these are outdoors characters since Orange-Crush is planned for sale outdoors.

● The Orange-Crush Company pays for the posters and also pays fifty per cent of the space cost, the bottler paying the other fifty. We feel that, unless the bottler has a financial interest in the posting campaign he will not be as interested in getting the full benefit from it. If the poster display has cost him something he is going to see to it that he gets his money's worth from it by using the tie-ups that the company has made available.

Every effort has been made to tie all other advertising to these posters. Miniature posters are available for window display which are exact reproductions of the 24-sheet designs. Window display cards are also offered and these, too, are adaptations of the 24-sheet poster. The month each poster appears will also see advertisements in national magazines, these also being

The vigorous style in which this painting is executed emphasizes the outdoor appeal of Orange-Crush.

tied in with the outdoor copy. Newspaper cuts are also offered but the company offers cooperation similar to that given in outdoor advertising only when outdoor is not available. We are convinced that a product such as ours should base its entire program upon the outdoor medium.

As soon as the program had been developed, steps were taken to tell our distributors exactly what we intended to do both on our own initiative and with their cooperation. Outdoor advertising is the mainstay of the campaign and our appropriation for this medium is greatly in excess of what it has been in any previous year. Other media have been retained but it is upon outdoor that we place our most dependence and outdoor advertising is the medium which we are most anxious to have our distributors use.

● A portfolio was prepared containing full color reproductions of the posters, magazine advertisements, window display cards, point of purchase signs, counter displays and newspaper cuts that are being offered. Each of our district representatives called upon all the bottlers in his territory. He told them the story of the campaign—using the portfolio to illustrate just what the company is doing. In addition to these personal calls, six letters were sent out by the Orange-Crush Company and six by the advertising agency, telling the bottlers of the campaign and urging them to take advantage of the opportunity offered them. The National Outdoor Advertising Bureau also sent out a series of letters to the owners of outdoor advertising plants, telling them of the campaign and giving the names of the men in their territory who should be contacted. The series of letters sent out by the agency and the Orange-Crush Company alternated so that a letter from

the agency was followed at an interval of two days by one from the Orange-Crush Company. In this way it was possible to keep hammering away at the bottler so that it was impossible for him to forget the campaign. The personal calls of the company's representatives and of the outdoor advertising plant owners were also of material assistance in getting the fine cooperation which is now putting over the campaign.

Our bottlers were told, "Every big name in the beverage business has been built on powerful, widespread and consistent outdoor advertising. You know that to be a fact.

"Working hand in hand with you to spread the fame and increase the demand for Orange-Crush, Orange-Crush brings you for 1931 the strongest, most colorful and attention-arresting poster campaign in its history.

"For the first time, this series is planned to cover the entire peak selling season.

"These eye-stopping 24-sheet posters will be meeting the public every day of the week, suggesting Orange-Crush—saying Orange-Crush—SELLING Orange-Crush.

"They will do much more than clinch consumer preference for Orange-Crush. They will help you in your selling efforts on new dealers, and they will increase the turnover for your present dealers. The dealer who sees that you are using the posters to help him sell the beverage you want to sell to him is bound to listen to your story with more attention and respect."

● Judging from the cooperation that the Orange-Crush campaign is receiving from the bottlers, the efforts that were made to sell them on the campaign were well worth while. We feel that it is only by securing such cooperation that we can hope to make this, as planned, the greatest year in Orange-Crush history.

AND AFTER YOU'VE READ THIS ISSUE

what are you going to do with it? Left on your desk it will soon be dog-eared and disreputable. If put away it will not be available for instant reference.

How much more satisfactory to have not only this issue but all back issues in a neat binder ready for instant reference. We have one here ready for you to use - - and only $1.80.

Send check or money order today to

ADVERTISING OUTDOORS

165 WEST WACKER DRIVE   CHICAGO, ILLINOIS

Roadside Beauty Studied
By Legislative Committee

(Continued from page 33) his property because of increased traffic and consequent property values due to the expenditures of public money. If the value of a piece of property fronting on a scenic highway is increased with the construction of the highway, this increase in value must be based upon a greater return from the use of the property. The fact that the property has been made more accessible would tend to increase its value, but the mere fact that more people can view the scenic attractions of the property would not in any way really increase its value. It is only by the employment of some means to capitalize upon this increase in traffic that the actual value can be enhanced.

"The imposition of a denial to the full use of the property might result in an actual decrease in the value of the property consequent to the construction of the highway.

"Another means of control which has been advocated is the imposition of a high rate of tax upon those who build commercial structures or signs along these scenic sections of the highways. It is the old scheme of trying to accomplish by means of unfair taxation some form of regulation which cannot be enforced directly. It is a procedure which is always questionable both as to its fairness and its legality, and it is not based upon a desire to be equitable and constructive.

Police Power Eliminates Traffic Hazards

● "Another phase of this problem, while possibly not directly within the jurisdiction of this committee, is the regulation of commercial structures, gasoline stations, hot dog stands, billboards, and other obstructions which may be built or placed near intersections of highways or on the inside of curves where such obstructions so interfere with the view of the motorist that they create a hazard to life. It is now possible under present laws, for the county or State authorities to condemn such property so as to provide for the removal of such obstructions or to force the removal of same through the exercise of the police power.

Committee Endorses Plan of State Chamber of Commerce

"The highway committee of the State Chamber of Commerce prepared a State-wide plan to preserve scenic beauty along California highways. This plan required action by the regional councils of the State Chamber and the local chambers of commerce in securing written agreements from landowners along designated scenic highways prohibiting advertising signs, vending stands, and unsightly structures.

"Two thousand seven hundred fifty miles of the State's highways have been designated as "scenic reserves" under the program of the State Chamber. To date, signed agreements have been secured from property owners covering seven hundred ten miles of these roads.

"Additional agreements are being vigorously urged

by regional and local committees until the work is completed.

"Appropriate markers are being erected, designating each completed scenic reserve project. The committee whole-heartedly endorses this plan.

From Dirt Roads to Highways

● "In the old days, before the general use of automobiles, our present highways were but dirt roads. Over these unimproved roads went the horse and buggy, and on the roadside fences appeared occasional advertisements put there by the vendors of the products offered.

"With the coming of the automobile and greater prosperity things changed. Dirt roads became highways, and today these highways are commercial arteries along which grow and develop towns and cities. A check of the users of these highways has proven that by far the greatest number of those traveling over them are on business errands, such as salesmen, professional men, merchants, passenger buses on regular schedule, industrial, commercial and produce trucks. The tourist numerically represents only the small percentage of travelers who daily, year in and year out, use these highways. In other words, highways are essential links in the economic business structure of the country.

"The commerce of the highway has attracted business concerns just as business concerns have located on the business streets of the city, for after all highways are just the extension of commercial city streets. In the better residential sections of a city no business enterprise or commercial structures are to be found. Likewise when leaving the commercial highways and following the roads which lead through the rural districts into the mountains and woods, the roadside enterprises are seldom found.

"There are points generally recognized as natural scenic beauty spots. Every good citizen should recognize his responsibility in preserving them in their original state by refraining from the development of business enterprises, or making any use of these localities which would mar or detract from their natural beauty and attractiveness. All of the industries most concerned, recognizing their responsibility in this respect, have consistently refrained from the placing of any structures in such localities and have used their influence in inducing others to do likewise.

"In the main, however, highways are used for commercial purposes, and accordingly types of business called 'Roadway Business Enterprises' install themselves on private property which they own or lease, adjacent to the highway right of way.

Roadway Enterprises Demand Advertising

● "Roadway business enterprises are composed of gasoline and oil service stations, garages, auto camps, factories, produce vendors, real estate operators, refreshment stands, restaurants, etc. As cities expand the business travel increases between them, these businesses —these pioneers of future industry—take their stand along the highways.

"Their existence at these points is a natural result of

a need they supply. Surely such businesses could not exist if people did not patronize them.

"These commercial enterprises, as well as farmers, make use of their own outdoor signs to advertise and sell their own wares and farm produce. They own or lease the property on which their establishments are located, and the farmer, the factory, the roadside and nearby town merchant surely has the unquestioned right to advertise and sell his merchandise on property he controls.

"Many farmers with small acreage and limited production are very largely dependent upon what they can sell to passers-by for their livelihood, and signs are necessary to sell their goods. However, some of the local merchants and local and national manufacturers make use of the structures of the outdoor advertising companies.

"Advertising develops business. It is an educational force of the first magnitude. Prosperity is the result. Restrain advertising and you hamper business with the resultant decline in prosperity.

"If there was no demand for serving the motorists, tourists, and those who live in the immediate vicinity, at the time when they are upon the streets and highways in the furtherance of their daily affairs, then there would be no necessity for commercial enterprises on our highways. The oil companies have recognized the needs of the motorist with their highway service stations, so also the hotels, garages, local merchants, and manufacturers, retail stores, proprietors and farmers of various kinds have appreciated that people develop certain wants en route, and so have used various structures as a means of reaching this patronage.

● "The inception and growth of specialized outdoor advertising has been one of pure economic necessity for the simple reason that by organized methods it is possible to serve the wants and needs of the advertiser in a more dignified, attractive and effective manner by adhering to specific standards, than it is for the advertiser to attempt to maintain, service, paint and repair his own individual structures.

"This is also recognized by chambers of commerce, civic organizations and community movements, and is used extensively by them to call to the attention of the passing motorists the points of interest and the advantages of particular communities or sections of a state.

"Existing laws prohibit the use of public property or highway right of way for commercial purposes; consequently, all of such structures visible to the highways are situated upon private property. The constitutional rights to use private property for commercial purposes, so long as such use does not endanger the safety, health, or morals of the public, can not be disputed. The invasion of the right of a merchant to display, upon property owned or controlled by him, the goods which he has for sale would certainly be unwarranted and unconstitutional. Thus the right to maintain signs upon private property adjacent to the highways clearly exists. More than half of all of the signs showing to the highways are owned and maintained by those operating

enterprises situated along the highways or in the interests of real estate projects adjacent to the highways. It was interesting to learn that about 6 per cent of all of the signs are owned and maintained by outdoor advertising companies. The remainder are signs placed by local merchants of adjacent towns or national concerns.

Population Makes Highways Main Streets

● "The rapid growth in population necessitates the extension and development of present highways, and the construction of added highways is necessary to afford the opportunity of community growth to care for the tremendous influx of new population. Just as towns and cities followed the railroad in the past, so now, the highway has become the influence which develops the location and growth of new towns and cities. With the coming of the highway come business enterprises; with business comes advertising. Therefore, we must expect outdoor advertising along the commercial highways.

"Three things are involved in highway and community development. They are:

(a) The welfare of the roadside enterprise because from the grouping of a few enterprises at various points come the future towns and cities.

(b) The prosperity of the merchant in the nearby town who must draw his business from the community, the surrounding rural trading area, and the motorist.

(c) The production and sale of goods of the manufacturer, or producer, who must aid, by advertising, both the roadway and town merchant to sell his products.

"Change a road to a highway and business immediately comes to fill the need of all who use it. With business comes the roadway enterprise. Then, the nearby town merchants reach out with their signs to attract the attention of those who travel the thoroughfare, and the national manufacturer, as well, seeks to place advertising for his goods before this same audience.

"The committee ascertained that standard advertising firms and other large commercial interests have always pursued a policy which insures safely constructed and well maintained structures on lease premises, kept clean and orderly, and carrying the advertisements of only reputable concerns and products. All structures are built according to uniform standards, bear the name of the company, and are maintained upon private property, none being located in such a manner as to be a hazard to traffic, or obscure the view of, or mar in any way the beauty of generally recognized scenic beauty spots.

Personal Pride of Property Owner

● "Personal pride in the appearance of his property, on the part of every tenant or owner of property adjacent to the highway, will insure the neat and pleasing appearance of the entire highway.

"Just as the personal appearance of every individual

is dependent upon his own pride, the appearance of every home upon the pride of those who occupy it, the appearance of every store or place of business upon the pride of the proprietor, just so does the appearance of the highway depend upon the pride of those whose property fronts upon it.

● "If such owners realize the value and importance of these scenic beauty spots to themselves, to the State and to the public, then their pride will naturally induce them to maintain such localities free from objectionable structures, uses or signs.

"We have ascertained that the State Highway Department has maintained a contact with nearly all of the property owners bordering on State highways. We feel that this contact should be made greater use of in the following manner: The itinerant advertiser, who promiscuously places unkept, unserviced cloth banners, placards and paintings upon fences, rocks, sheds and barns, should be stopped. Under the law today it can be stopped if the various road superintendents will keep the department office advised of the unlicensed or un-privileged placing of such signs on the property ad-joining the highway and then in turn sending a notifi-cation to the property owners. The committee feels certain that each property owner will gladly reply and ask that his property be rid of such nuisances. Such correspondence, if properly worded, would call the property owner's attention to the fact that it is the desire of all good citizens to perpetuate and maintain the glories and beauties nature so bounteously bestowed upon the State of California. Then an awakened pride in his State will also prompt him to eliminate dilapi-dated shacks and other eyesores from his particular property.

"In this regard we are mindful of the many admoni-tions found throughout our daily press. One very force-fully setting forth the feeling of the general public as to new legislation is contained in the editorial of the *Pasadena Star-News* of January 14, 1931, and is herein set forth as indicating the kindred thoughts of the com-mittee:

Avoid Legislation That Hurts

" 'Do not hamper business, industry and agriculture by mischievous legislation! This is the urge that is being sent to the Legislature and other legislative bod-ies in the State by the California State Chamber of Commerce. Resolutions were adopted by the State Chamber, reciting that government can aid best by giv-ing business, agriculture and industry 'encouragement and opportunity to facilitate their operations and get back on their feet.'

● " 'The resolutions point out that one of the handicaps under which business and industry labor during a leg-islative year is the fear of restrictive laws. The resolu-tions call upon the Legislature to 'refrain from making laws which would add to the difficulty or expense of carrying on business, agriculture and industry and in

this way help business and industry in their effort to restore normal conditions in a normal way and provide employment without building a burden of public debt.'

" 'This is a reasonable, timely and helpful request. The Legislature should heed this urging. There should be no enactment of ill advised legislation, which would tend to depress business, industry or agriculture. The fewer laws the better. If legislators will just let busi-ness, industry and agriculture alone, all will be well.'

Labor's Interest in the Matter

"In accord with this same thought, but more par-ticularly appertaining to the specific subject of this committee's work is a resolution that has been adopted in toto or in part by a great number of labor organiza-tions.

Conclusion

"To sum up these various suggestions which have been offered, it would seem that we have for final con-sideration the following ideas, and herewith present them as the committee's recommendations:

"First—That those property owners who wish to maintain their properties in their present scenic condi-tion, do so by means of an agreement among themselves, in accordance with the ideas advanced by the State Chamber of Commerce.

● "Second—That the cooperation of all property own-ers throughout the State be solicited in an effort to bring about the removal of small signs which have been promiscuously erected without the consent of the prop-erty owners but which have been permitted to remain undisturbed.

"Third—That the county planning commissions in-terest themselves in the subject in order that there may be brought about through the enactment of county zon-ing measures, the zoning of those frontages along scenic highways, in accordance with a plan based upon an in-telligent and comprehensive consideration of the own-ers' fundamental rights, as guaranteed under the State and United States constitutions.

"We therefore find that an intelligent enforcement of the laws already enacted as heretofore set forth, to-gether with a true love of our State and a resultant pride in its beauties and glories are sufficient to remedy all the difficulties that have arisen and are likely to continue to arise."

The report has evidently been the result of exhaus-tive investigation. That the conclusions reached most emphatically refute the charges of wholesale desecra-tion that have been dumped upon the doorstep of or-ganized outdoor advertising is conclusive evidence that such desecration does not exist. Similarly unprejudiced inquiries in other sections of the country would un-questionably prove that other attacks upon organized outdoor advertising have the same lack of facts to sup-port them.

SPENDING TENDENCIES

1

LOS ANGELES, CALIF.

GENERAL BUSINESS CONDITIONS: Business seems to be picking up. Building construction in March stepped up over the February record by 16% which meant relief in the unemployment situation. Employment still stands below that of March 1930. Agricultural conditions throughout the district were adversely affected by lack of rainfall. Postal receipts increased 12% over February, although there was a decrease of 4% as compared with March 1930. The Federal Reserve Agent reported that retail sales during the first two months of the year were 11½% below the same period in 1930. Department store inventories have decreased more than 26% during the past 18 months.

There was a tremendous volume of California citrus fruit sold during the season. Figures to March 28th indicated that there had been 24,404 cars, which is some 6,000 cars above last year had been shipped.

2

DENVER, COLO.

GENERAL BUSINESS CONDITIONS: The following information is from the report of the Denver Chamber of Commerce dated May 14.

	April 1931	April 1930
Bank clearings	$118,633,953.60	$143,388,838.51
Postal receipts	314,479.53	333,774.62
Number of building permits	486	547
Value of building permits	1,172,950.00	562,550.00
Number of business failures	4	12

Bank debits in Denver for the four weeks ending April 22, 1931, totaled $147,589,000 as compared with $171,818,000 for the same period in 1930, showing a decrease of 14.1 per cent.

AUTOMOTIVE:

Automobile Registration

Jan. 1st to Apr. 30th, 1930	68,596
Jan. 1st to Apr. 30th, 1931	70,918

Gasoline Consumption

March 1931	3,788,282 Gallons
March 1930	3,650,065 Gallons

3

ATLANTA, GA.

GENERAL BUSINESS CONDITIONS: The following are individual reports as given by the Atlanta Chamber of Commerce Secretary:

Vacuum Cleaners

"Sales for the first three months of 1930 over a corresponding period in 1931 show an average of 19% decrease in 1931. This might be accounted for in that due to general conditions there has been more sales resistance in the house-to-house canvassing method and consequently this means a smaller sales force."

Electric Refrigeration

"There is a satisfactory increase in sales for the first part of 1931 over the corresponding period of 1930."

Department Store Sales

"Department Store Sales would approximate over the same period in 1931 a 12% increase over 1930."

Radio Business

"The radio business over a corresponding period of time has more than held its own. In most cases the sales are equal or slightly ahead of sales in 1930."

MOVING PICTURE ATTENDANCE: We quote below from the Fox Theatre which is the largest one in Atlanta:

"The theatre attendance in Atlanta generally is off approximately 15% of the corresponding period of 1930.

"The attendance at the Fox is extremely gratifying. In fact Atlanta, with its 300,000 people is giving us a weekly patronage that compares favorably with communities of 1,000,000 population or over."

FOX THEATRE
(signed) Carter Barron, Manager

AUTOMOTIVE: The sale of new cars as reported by the R. H. Donnelly Corporation which compiles automobile registrations for Atlanta is as follows:

1930—3,144 for the first three months.
1931—2,295 for the first three months

4

DES MOINES, IOWA

GENERAL BUSINESS CONDITIONS: Building permits in Des Moines totaled more than a million dollars for April which is the largest single month for nearly a year. This brings the total permits for the first third of 1931 to more than double the same period in 1930.

A gain of 14.6% in employment in railroad car shops all over Iowa was indicated in the report just issued by the Commissioner of Labor of Iowa.

Retail sales in the larger stores indicated an increased volume in units, with slightly decreased volume in dollars and cents, owing to the reduction in prices.

AUTOMOTIVE: Gasoline tax collections during April for the whole state amounted to more than a million dollars as compared to $933,932.00 for April of 1930. This brings the total for the first third of the year to $3,434,874.00, the highest gasoline consumption record ever known in Iowa.

5

MASON CITY, IOWA

GENERAL BUSINESS CONDITIONS: Building permits for 1930 and 1931 are as follows:

1930		1931	
January	$ 8,530.00	January	$ 12,446.00
February	23,000.00	February	65,560.00
March	13,330.00	March	39,677.00
April	78,150.00	April	77,116.00
Total	$123,010.00	Total	$194,789.00

This shows an increase of over $71,000.00.

New dwellings.

1930		1931	
January	2	January	0
February	2	February	2
March	4	March	7
April	7	April	11
Total	15	Total	20

Contracts were let and bonds approved in April for new Post Office work to start inside of sixty days.

Lloyd Liesenberg of Lloyd Liesenberg Cigar Company, wholesale cigars, reports that the first quarter of the year shows a three per cent gain over 1930.

Natural gas was recently turned on in residences and factories. The laying of the pipe lines gave over two hundred men employment all winter and spring.

Mr. Merkel of Merkel's Department Store reports a 3.7 per cent gain for the first quarter in 1931 over 1930.

MOVING PICTURE ATTENDANCE There is a slight decrease in moving picture attendance in 1931 as compared with 1930.

AUTOMOTIVE: Total auto registrations for the first quarter of 1931 show an improvement over 1930.

6

LOUISVILLE, KY.

AUTOMOTIVE: The following shows a comparison between 1930 and 1931, on gasoline tax.

	1930	
January	$122,787.60	$147,433.10
February	120,607.15	130,981.95
March	146,784.80	160,000.00

7
DULUTH, MINN.

GENERAL BUSINESS CONDITIONS: Business conditions are down about 12% with the exception of electric refrigeration and power companies which actually show a tremendous gain.

MOVING PICTURE ATTENDANCE: Moving picture attendance has decreased about 8% as compared with April 1930.

AUTOMOTIVE: Automobile sales have decreased approximately 35% as against April 1930.

Registrations have also decreased about 27% as compared with April 1930.

8
MINNEAPOLIS, MINN.

GENERAL BUSINESS CONDITIONS: The following is a cross-section of the business conditions in the trading territory and city as collated from the opinions of business men:

The railroad business does not show any change. The labor activity will show little or no increase as expansion and building plans for 1931 are negligible. The lumber business shows little or no increase over the seasonable rise which is less than previous years. One lumber man states that he expects no increase as ability to build is directly dependent upon income. The flour industry offers little prospect for decided increase. There seems to be little activity in real estate and in banks.

Sales by automobile companies show a decided increase. One in particular quotes a twenty per cent increase in the Northwest and advances the statement that they are adding to their personnel in accordance with this increase. While the banks are not very optimistic, the building and loan associations have shown a very decided increase in business. In fact, a number of them point to 1931 as offering the biggest year in the history of their organizations. The retail department stores anticipate nothing more than a seasonable increase in business with but little change in employment. However, they feel that there are indications of a business increase. One states that business in this territory is so largely controlled by agricultural conditions that they cannot expect better times unless weather conditions permit a large crop for 1931.

9
JOPLIN, MO.

GENERAL BUSINESS CONDITIONS: Business conditions show a slight improvement over the same period of January, February, March and April of 1930. Department stores report an improvement and are gradually on the up grade, though very slowly.

Building due to a program of new schools is slightly

ahead of last year. However, general building operations aside from the school program are behind the same period last year.

MOVING PICTURE ATTENDANCE: Attendance for the first third in 1931 shows an increase which is probably due to the lowering of prices in the better class of theatres.

AUTOMOTIVE: Automobile registrations are four per cent greater in 1931 than in the same period in 1930.

10
BILLINGS, MONTANA

GENERAL BUSINESS CONDITIONS: There is a great deal of building going on at the present time. The Kress Company have a building under construction at an approximate cost of $90,000. The Fox West Coast Theatres have a theatre under construction at a cost of $220,000, employing all Billings people which helps the employment situation. A $240,000 addition to the Post Office and a new Federal Penitentiary to be located in Billings are buildings planned for some time later in the year.

Tourist travel will start about June 15th which always helps conditions as Billings is the hub to three entrances to Yellowstone Park.

MOVING PICTURE ATTENDANCE: Mr. O'Keefe, manager of the three theatres in Billings reported that business for the first three months of 1931 was off 10% as compared with 1930.

AUTOMOTIVE: The registration of cars for the first three months in 1931 was practically the same as in 1931, varying only a few cars.

11
PITTSBURGH, PENNA.

GENERAL BUSINESS CONDITIONS: Retail trade was stimulated to some extent during the month of April by Easter, but weather conditions were not the most favorable and this meant that distribution was not quite up to expectations. Jobbers of dry goods report business quiet, and while there has been greater activity in women's wearing apparel and boys' and children's clothing, there has been but a slight increase in men's wear lines. Seasonal hardware is moving slightly better but regular lines and builders hardware continue to move slowly. Jobbers of groceries and provisions report a considerable volume of business being handled but unsatisfactory prices.

Building construction continues well below normal and demand for lumber and building materials has shown but little improvement. There appears to have been comparatively little change in the rate of operation of industrial plants, including steel. Production and distribution of plate glass continues about the same rate and while the production of window during March was less than 400,000 an increase is expected when the figures for April are compiled. There has been but little change in sanitary and heating equipment and plumbing supply lines which continue to move rather slowly. While some fairly good orders have been received by manufacturers of electrical equipment, the volume of business continues materially lower than a year ago. Manufacturers of paints and varnishes are estimated to be running at about 60% of their capacity which is a slightly lower rate than prevailed a year ago.

Production of crude oil shows a slight increase while demand for refined products is showing a slight improvement. The tonnage on bituminous coal is averaging about 10% lower than the prevailing tonnage in 1930.

The iron and steel industry was reported to be running at about 80% of their capacity.

MOVING PICTURE ATTENDANCE: Moving picture attendance in 1931 as compared with 1930 shows a decrease of 25%.

AUTOMOTIVE: Automobile registration compared with 1930 shows a decrease of 40.6%. However, the figures are not complete as yet.

12
ABERDEEN, SOUTH DAKOTA

GENERAL BUSINESS CONDITIONS: The general spending tendency in this area shows a definite marked, upward movement from month to month. It is slow and gradual but apparently healthy. Merchants report a steady gradual increase in business. In volume, groceries are 20% ahead of 1930 for April. Clothing is about 10% ahead of 1930. Net profits as compared to 1930 are only slightly higher. Drops in prices have caused this decrease in profits.

MOVING PICTURE ATTENDANCE: This is the one single thing that stands out far above other spending tendencies. Business in this line is now running about 10% above the same period in 1930. Things were very slow in this industry in January but have made a gradual and steady increase.

AUTOMOTIVE: Chevrolet continues to outsell Ford during the month of April all over South Dakota, and the figures are well ahead of the same period in 1930.

Gasoline consumption is still about 18% above 1930 for the month of April.

13
KNOXVILLE, TENN.

GENERAL BUSINESS CONDITIONS: The Sterling Wood Products Company, makers of automobile bodies added one hundred more men to their personnel this week, making a total of 700 men now working for this firm.

Department and furniture stores report some buying, but not like the sales of 1930 which they claim is due to lack of money because of bank failures. The unemployment situation is very bad and because of this, there is not the wish to spend money even though some of them could afford to.

The Hamilton National Bank opened the last week in April with a million dollar deposit the first day, which shows that the money is in Knoxville.

MOVING PICTURE ATTENDANCE: There has been a slump in this industry. One theatre has closed since the first of the year and prices have been slashed at the main theatre.

AUTOMOTIVE: According to figures secured from the county clerk, automobile registrations for the year of 1930 amounted to $22,600.00 while this year to date, shows $20,000.00 with the spring and summer months still to come. Automobile dealers seem to be selling plenty of cars in spite of the depression.

14
MEMPHIS, TENN.

GENERAL BUSINESS CONDITIONS: Federal Reserve reports estimate that the decline in department store volume is 26% over a comparative period with 1930.

MOTION PICTURE ATTENDANCE: Moving picture attendance is off from 20 to 25% for 1931 as compared with 1930.

15
AMARILLO, TEXAS

GENERAL BUSINESS CONDITIONS: The 1930 Census shows that per capita retail sales in Amarillo are higher than any other Texas City yet surveyed.

Amarillo and its trading territory is still shown in white on Babson's Business Map in the magazine, "Nation's Business," for the 28th consecutive month.

Total 1931 building permits issued in Amarillo up to May 1st total $1,356,644.00 which makes Amarillo rank third in Texas so far in 1931.

MOVING PICTURE ATTENDANCE: Attendance in the four local Publix Theatres shows a decrease over the first four months of 1930 of less than 1%, the actual figure being .064%. The attendance for April 1931 shows a slight increase over April 1930.

AUTOMOTIVE: The following comparisons are listed for automobile registrations for both trucks and touring cars, in eight counties which comprise Amarillo's grading area.

1930	1931
Trucks 7,195 Cars 3,825	Trucks 4,700 Cars 30,295

The 1930 figures are for the entire year while the 1931 figures are just for the first four months.

Gasoline sales, comparing April 1930 with April 1931.

Plains Lubricating Co.	59,854 gals.	37,904 gals.
Gibson Oil Company		58,021 gals.
Texas Company	153,808 gals.	123,398 gals.
Gulf Refining Company	114,767 gals.	113,903 gals.
Continental Oil Company	43,851 gals.	62,956 gals.
T & P Coal-Oil Company		28,000 gals.
Magnolia Petroleum Co.	69,577 gals.	72,653 gals.

16
MILWAUKEE, WIS.

GENERAL BUSINESS CONDITIONS: Milwaukee industrial leaders are sounding a definite note of optimism and there is a gradual increase in employment, large plants taking on old employees in groups of one hundred to two hundred every week or two.

Bank deposits continue to be normal.

Retail business continues to be fairly healthy with very few insolvencies reported.

MOVING PICTURE ATTENDANCE: Moving picture attendance has shown a noticeable increase within the last few weeks. This was a general increase and does not take into consideration phenomenal attendance on pictures which are widely advertised and exploited.

AUTOMOTIVE: Gasoline consumption has increased about ten per cent, evidence of which is noted in the fact that recent traffic check-ups on the main highways leading into the city in several instances have broken all previous records.

■ ■ ■

HARTFORD, CONN.

GENERAL BUSINESS CONDITIONS: The volume of retail business for the first four months of 1931 comparable with the same period in 1930 showed a decrease of approximately 5%.

One of the leading shoe dealers, selling ladies' shoes only, reported the volume of business in dollars the same as last year. The volume in number of pairs of shoes sold in April 1931 as compared with April 1930 showed an increase.

One jeweler reported a decrease in the volume of sales for the first four months in 1931 as compared with 1930, but an increase of 7% for the first fifteen days in May 1931 as compared with the first fifteen days in 1930.

■ ■ ■

HOUSTON, TEXAS

GENERAL BUSINESS CONDITIONS: The majority of the retail firms interviewed report a satisfactory month as compared with national conditions. Two of the larger manufacturing plants have put on additional night shifts. Building permits for April show an increase of 34% over March and the total for the first

quarter of 1931 as compared with 1930 show a decrease of 4%. Telephone connections, water connections and light connections show a steady increase of about 2% a month.

MOVING PICTURE ATTENDANCE: The average of reports from April attendance indicate a 6% decrease as compared with April 1930.

AUTOMOTIVE: New car sales for April were off 15.1% as compared with April 1930. Gasoline sales were off 5 to 11%.

■ ■ ■

POCATELLO, IDAHO

GENERAL BUSINESS CONDITIONS: General sales in the territory have decreased about 20% as compared with 1930 while an approximate cut of 10% has been made in overhead or operating expenses. The prices paid and received for dairy products have decreased about 25% as compared with 1930.

AUTOMOTIVE: Gasoline sales in the state of Idaho for the first quarter of 1931 have increased 3% in volume or 292,000 gallons over the first quarter of 1930 but on account of the drop in prices, the amount received for this gasoline decreased 33% or $891,800.00.

■ ■ ■

ST. JOSEPH, MO.

GENERAL BUSINESS CONDITIONS: The mild winter and unseasonable weather have disturbed normal business by speeding up some lines and materially slowing down others. However, there is a general feeling of optimism.

The St. Joseph Railway, Light, Heat & Power Company reports an increase in power users, now serving 26,856 in the city and 1,971 rural.

The unemployment situation is well in hand and at the present time the building program of the Public School System is now under way which makes employment for hundreds of men.

MOVING PICTURE ATTENDANCE: Moving picture attendance is reported to be 10% less in 1931 than for the same time in 1930.

■ - -

BEAUMONT, TEXAS

GENERAL BUSINESS CONDITIONS: The continued lowering of prices for crude petroleum is the chief factor in retarding "pick-up" in this territory. Merchants, however, are cheered by a turn for the better and there is a marked improvement in demand for labor.

Selection of Beaumont for the 25th annual national regatta of the Mississippi Valley Power Boat Association, July 3-4-5 is felt to be a good stimulant for summer business.

MOVING PICTURE ATTENDANCE: The theatres report a falling off in the volume of attendance.

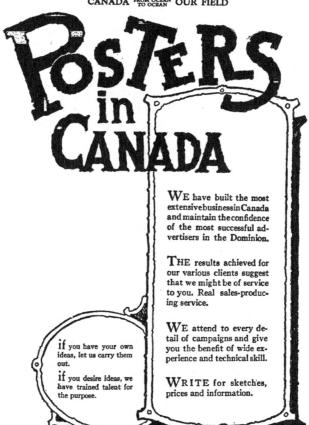

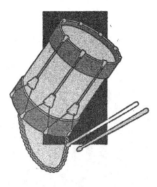

★ ★ ★ URGE ★ ★ ★

The masses are most easily moved to buy a product through the power of pleasing suggestion.

Harmonious grouping of picture and a few words of selling value, in appealing colors, grip the minds of millions of people outdoors.

After all, it is the message exposed to public view that is the most important feature of advertising space.

Advertising Offices in Sixty Cities

General Outdoor Advertising Co

ONE PARK AVENUE   NEW YORK
HARRISON & LOOMIS STREETS, CHICAG

IN MILWAUKEE

SMASH
YOUR MESSAGE HOME

THE PROFITABLE WAY

No single or combination of media can begin to sway and reach the purchasing power of Milwaukee and its suburban area for the reason that no other media has anything near the Outdoor Poster Advertising circulation necessary to provide coverage of more than 750,000 workers, home owners and consumers in this great and prosperous market.

The one and only profitable and economic way to dominate Milwaukee —to obtain 100% coverage of both city and suburbs—is Outdoor Poster Advertising through the Cream City Outdoor Advertising Company.

CREAM CITY OUTDOOR ADV. CO.

300 N. EIGHTH STREET   MILWAUKEE

YOU NEED NO OTHER MEDIUM IN MILWAUKEE

POSTERS WHEREVER YOU GO! POSTERS WHEREVER YOU TURN!

Not
ONE
Subscriber
but Millions *of* Readers

When the River of Ink began to flow, homes ceased to be hide-outs and became men's castles.

Displacing that era in the last few years, science and inventive genii have put safety on wings, have enticed life from its seclusion and made it more exciting to "hurry" than to "hesitate."

It is still the job of good advertising to profitably arrest public attention.

That which did it in the dormant age of coddled contentment was one thing.

That which will do it with the same degree of profit, in today's new atmosphere of out-and-around habits, IS ANOTHER!

Outdoor Advertising is the piston-rod that will stand the strain of the drive necessary to progress in 1931 . . . and do its job economically.

The reason is because Outdoor Advertising is in relentless rhythm with the 1931 habits of your future customers.

DETROIT

OUTDOOR ADVERTISING

Advertising Outdoors

A magazine devoted to the interests of the Outdoor Advertiser

VOL. 2, No. 6

CONTENTS for JUNE 1931

Harold L. Eves
Editor

Ralph B. Patch, *Associate Editor*
James P. Dobyns, *Advertising Manager*

Eastern Advertising Representatives:
Walworth and Wormer,
420 Lexington Ave., New York City.

Western Advertising Representatives:

Dwight Early,
100 N. La Salle St., Chicago

ADVERTISING OUTDOORS is published on the 1st of every month by the Outdoor Advertising Association of America, Inc., 165 W. Wacker Drive. Chicago, Ill. Telephone Randolph 1692. Harold L. Eves, Editor and Manager.

Subscriptions for the United States, Cuba, Porto Rico, Hawaii and the Philippines, $3.00 a year in advance; Mexico and Canada, $3.25; for all other countries, $3.50. Thirty cents the copy. Make all checks, money orders, etc., payable to Outdoor Advertising Association of America, Inc.

Entered as second-class matter, March 21st, 1930, at the Post Office at Chicago, Ill., under the act of March 3, 1879, by Outdoor Advertising Association of America, Inc. Printed in U. S. A.

WHY SHOULD THEY
READ THEM?

PEOPLE do not pay for the privilege of reading advertisements. The posters you design are telling your message to a public that at times seems indifferent.

Uninvited, you are telling them a story in which they have no interest. No matter how well located a poster panel may be, no matter how many thousands of people pass it each day, it offers you no more than the flat surface on which you display your message. The poster itself cannot shout at the passing crowds to stop and read. It can only patiently hold your message up for display.

All you have in any medium is the surface on which to express a thought through words. Words without life mean little. Talking to the crowd as a crowd means simply putting words on a blank space. You must tell your story to each individual of the thousands who pass. Your message must be more than mere words—it must be part of the life that each individual leads. Only then will the few daubs of paint that constitute a poster become part of the lives and thus influence the action of those who pass.

A message can be designed into a poster so that it will attract attention. But attention secured without knowledge of the lives, desires and reactions of those who constitute the crowd, cannot hope to penetrate into the lives—and pocketbooks—of those who read. When it does so penetrate, attention will develop interest—interest will build up conviction—conviction will build to profits for the advertiser.

That is the art and the power of poster advertising—to talk to a million strangers and yet to influence the life, the happiness—and the buying trends of the individuals who compose the crowd.

THE SPORTS APPEAL
Gets Attention

by A. W. Roe

No feature of modern American life is more strongly pronounced than is the love of athletic sports and the out-of-doors. Wise is the advertiser who takes this national characteristic into account when picking out an accessory theme for his copy.

● Upwards of 110,000 people sat and soaked up a drenching rainfall at Soldier Field, Chicago, when the then undefeated Army team and Notre Dame staged their memorable contest in November of last year. A week later under the blue skies of California 90,000 more frantic football fans shouted and groaned throughout the titanic struggle that stamped Coach Rockne's Ramblers as probably the greatest eleven the country has seen in a decade.

These games produced big "gates," but even sectional matches attract sizeable crowds, as witness last Thanksgiving's fray between Texas A. & M. College and the State University of the Lone Star state which drew upwards of 40,000 people to the new stadium at Austin. If figures were not dull reading, many others could be cited to show that even high school struggles of last fall drew bigger crowds than Stonewall Jackson had men in his army when executing his daring raids up and down the Shenandoah Valley.

● It seems that at certain times of the year the populace of the Nation goes sports' mad. In the fall, it's football, soon to be followed by such winter sports as soccer, ice hockey and skiing that keep both participants and spec-

tators out of doors, and by basketball and indoor baseball, played within doors. In the spring it's track and field events and interscholastic baseball which ushers in the professional diamond clashes that hold general interest throughout the summer and well into the fall at which time the sports' cycle is completed with the opening of a new football season.

The sports, just mentioned, are highly competitive and attract big crowds. Others that draw fewer, but none the less enthusiastic, fans are swimming and other water sports, tennis, golf, polo, boat racing, and horseback riding. Then there is the pure love of the great out-of-doors that prompts many to go camping, motoring, or just loitering beside silvery streams, along mountain trails or by lake shores.

● This national fondness for sports and outdoor life can be roughly and quickly estimated by the proportion of space and the prominence given it by the public press. Insignificant, indeed, is the newspaper that does not have its special daily section set apart for the presentation of news and views of the sports' world. When big news about sports break, it is always given a prominent position.

"Collapse That Rocked Nation," referred not to an earthquake in a central American principality as you might conclude if you did not have before you the picture over which this startling caption appeared. This International Newsreel showed a flash of a baseball

Few advertisers can use the bathing girl illustration as logically as Catalina Swim Suits have done in this effective design.

player being carried from the field by four husky team-mates. Explanation under the illustration cleared up the mystery thus: "When Babe Ruth's legs, hurt in a slide, gave way under him as he resumed his place in the New York outfield, headlines in every newspaper in the land were devoted to his collapse."

● When an airplane, carrying Knute Rockne across the continent, plunged to earth, bearing the famous Notre Dame coach and his fellow passengers to their deaths, the whole nation was plunged into grief, and radios and newspapers alike took up the sagas of the sudden and tragic end of this modern Viking who was one of the greatest inspirers of youth, known to history.

Let it be repeated that wise is the advertiser, who sensing the reader interest to be derived from tieing in his advertising with this universal love of sports and the out-of-doors, so pictures and words his copy that it strikes a responsive cord in the hearts of those keenly interested in American sports and life in the open. This includes practically every member of the typical American fireside. It may be taken for granted that the boys and girls in grade and high school are keen for the usual run of sports, school loyalty makes them so. While Grandma may not care much for football as a game, she does care a great deal for Sonny who is perhaps a grid star of the local high school aggregation or a member of a varsity squad. Being interested in Sonny, she follows football, sometimes from afar it is true, but nevertheless newspaper and outdoor advertising that is built around the sports theme is likely to catch her eye. And so it is with the other members of the family.

● And all of these people, who follow athletics either actively or vicariously, go to make up the more than 100 millions of our population, each and every one of whom is an actual consumer and the majority of whom are really purchasers of the items and commodities, advertised through the media of the news press, magazine publications, radio broadcasts and outdoor display copy.

This Chesterfield poster is an outstanding example of the use of sports appeal in advertising.

The time was when it seemed that advertisers took very little pains to make outdoor advertising appealing. Even to-day, aside from featuring the trade name and possibly a picture of the product, many users of outdoor space seem to forget that the outdoor board is capable of being made into a scene that is as attractive and attention-compelling as is an elaborately posed scene in a theater. Such a scheme can be carried out on either painted bulletins or lithographed posters. While many accessory themes suggest themselves to the imagination of the sedulous copy writer, the sports' idea is sure fire because of the universality of its appeal. And yet it seems that only a relatively few outdoor advertisers have become so aware of its high utility as to work it into their advertising.

● Some of the most effective copy, built about the sports' theme that the writer has seen, has been and is still being used by the manufacturers and distributors of rival cigarette brands. In a field where it seems that really worth-while copy ideas are few and far between the originators of this cigarette advertising have spread on the panels during the last year scenes from the world of sports that are really masterpieces of art at the same time that they put over real merchandising messages.

A careful study of these series of outdoor posters is recommended to anyone who is considering the use of the sports' theme in any kind of advertising copy. The cigarette distributing companies have evidently found it valuable to tie in all their copy for a certain period with one general theme. Copy from the posters is reproduced on counter and window display cards that are distributed to leading stores where the cigarettes are sold. It has been noted that the same copy illustrations have appeared simultaneously (Continued on page 42)

DRAMATIZE
YOUR MESSAGE

by John P. Harding

From an advertising point of view that famous Chinese proverb, "A Picture Is Worth 10,000 Words" might well be interpreted to read "Let a picture tell your story to the public; it will tell your story more effectively and more completely than can 10,000 words."

● The John P. Harding Restaurants of Chicago believe in the modern conception of that old truism. We, however, have gone a step farther than merely utilizing a picture to tell the public about the Colonial Room in one of our restaurants. Thru the help of Outdoor Advertising, we are using a picture which presents the actual atmospheric setting of a particular room in one of our restaurants. Altho no motion is shown, the story of our wonderful food, as well as the scene in the Colonial Room, is presented to the public in a most dramatic and realistic manner.

The Colonial Room in this case is not portrayed as it would be in a painting. It is presented in such a manner that it is realistic in every sense of the word, depicting as words could never do, the very atmosphere to be found in the Colonial Room.

● By transforming over one half the bulletin into a realistic cut-out scene, which is in a recessed room that is part of the outdoor bulletin and reproducing the

The cutout of the Colonial room in this Harding bulletin adds materially to the impression value.

Colonial Room just as one would view it upon entering, even to people dining and the hostess, we have succeeded in accomplishing our purpose. In other words, we have added drama, personality and atmosphere, essential elements that are lacking in the ordinary restaurant advertising.

The bulletin has been on display for only a short length of time but an untold amount of exceptionally favorable comment has been received and the restaurant is receiving much person to person publicity, which is so important to an organization serving the public.

● This bulletin is also performing another important function. For years the Harding Restaurants catered almost exclusively to men, with no especial attempt being made to cultivate the patronage of the women. The new Colonial Room, however, was designed to cater to women and mixed couples. In this actual cut-out scene women are in abundance. This naturally conveys the idea to the public that an atmosphere of welcome for both sexes prevails in the Colonial Room. Incidentally that impression is given impetus by the life-like poise of the hostess pictured at the right in an attitude of the most cordial welcome.

We are more than pleased with this display. Not only has the great amount of favorable comment received substantiated the confidence entrusted in this unique design, but there is every indication that it has popularized the Colonial Room to a very great degree.

RESEARCH —
Is It a Fad?

The sixth of a series of talks on advertising prepared by the A. F. A.

This is the sixth and final message of a series prepared by the Advertising Federation of America.

In the first message it was shown that advertising is not actually an expense to advertisers or consumers, for advertising creates sufficient additional economic wealth to pay for its own cost, even though that cost is two billion dollars a year.

The second described advertising as the handmaiden of civilization—a great cultural influence and an accelerator of human progress.

The third message demonstrated how advertising alleviates the ill effects of business depression and hastens recovery.

● The fourth was about the good will which advertising builds up, and showed what this means in dollars and cents.

The fifth address was based upon the undying aphorism that honesty is the best policy in advertising, as well as in other human activities—a noble ideal and a paying proposition.

And now we come to the sixth message in this series of advertising studies. Today we shall discuss the importance of research to successful advertising. Modern advertising is not the product of spontaneous inspiration but is carefully evolved in a scientific laboratory. Profit-making advertising today is based on exhaustive research and scientific principles.

Although research is now recognized as a prime essential to profitable advertising, it was not widely used until ten years ago. In other fields of endeavor the value of scientific methods was recognized much earlier.

● It was a long time ago when Aristotle decided that something more than oratory was needed to advance the welfare of human beings. So he set to work and wrote down in organized form the sum total of human knowledge. He covered every known field of science and philosophy. He made a huge research. The resulting fund of facts was a great aid to future philosophers in their various special kinds of thinking.

Through the ages, science has always provided the foundation for intelligent human action. Facts, plus scientific study, are behind every invention and every step in material advancement. The products and processes of modern industry are all the results of research.

Only recently have business men invited the scientist to step from the laboratory into the office. They realized that business needed more than inspiration and hand-to-mouth knowledge. It needed organized facts and orderly methods for studying situations.

Selling Problem Assumes Foremost Importance

● Production was the first department of business to adopt scientific practices. That was natural, for production deals with physical materials, visible processes and definite costs. Business men were astounded at the waste uncovered in their factories. With the advent of production research and the adoption of scientific methods, enormous strides were made in efficiency.

Research has more than doubled the amount of production per worker.

Elimination of waste in industry was the battle cry of business in a decade when the economical production of goods was the secret of success in competition. In those days the chief problem was to produce things to sell. Production economies were the key to greater profits.

● In recent years it has become necessary to shift the emphasis in business planning from production to distribution. Selling is now a much harder problem than it used to be.

Of course, there never was a time when selling was an unimportant problem, but great changes in industry have certainly made the job of sales manager a lot more difficult.

With our labor-saving machinery, cheaper power, revolutionizing inventions and scientific methods of operation the capacity of this country to produce goods has increased miraculously. In the past twenty years the total annual value of manufactured goods for each factory wage earner has increased from $3,000 to $8,000. In the short space of two decades the amount of production per worker has more than doubled.

To sell this ever rising flood of goods requires more and more effort.

Today, almost two thirds of the total price of the average article goes to pay for what we call the cost of distribution.

Some idea of the growing importance of the selling problem may be obtained from the relative number of persons engaged in the work of selling. Sixty years ago there were only two traveling salesmen for every ten thousand people in this country, and today there are about sixteen. The increase in city salesmen and store salesmen has undoubtedly been just as rapid. It seems to take an ever increasing proportion of our population to sell the products of industry to the rest of us.

● The idea of applying scientific analysis to this problem of marketing has gained great headway in the past five years. There are still many executives who believe that inspiration plus judgment are the only brain products required to run a business successfully. But most of them now see that intuition and

Advertising, despite the opinion of the general public to the contrary, is not created by magic.

guesses must be replaced by facts and analyses if inspiration and judgment are to have a solid foundation.

There are three kinds of marketing research. One deals with the product itself and its fitness for the market. The second concerns the consumer market, and the third involves studies of methods of distribution.

By Whom is Marketing Research Performed?

Who carries on this highly specialized work so necessary to profit-making advertising? There are six chief instrumentalities which perform research work important to advertising.

First, there are the advertisers themselves. Many large manufacturers and dealers spend great sums of money to maintain competent research departments to study their marketing and advertising problems.

● Second, there are the advertising agencies, which are accomplishing a large amount of constructive research work. They have compiled an invaluable fund of experience from their studies of copy appeal and advertising media.

In the third group are newspapers, magazines and other advertising media, which perform a helpful service in publishing market information concerning the people and territories which they serve.

In the U. S. Department of Commerce we have the fourth agency conducting research work for the benefit of advertisers. Government studies deal chiefly with markets, trends, and other general considerations.

The fifth group consists of business research bureaus of educational institutions. They analyze specific industries, distribution expenses, and various questions relating to marketing.

The sixth of these groups are the independent research companies, which concentrate all their experience and ability on the performance of research work. They are frequently retained by advertisers and advertising agencies to conduct surveys which require large field forces.

From this physical set-up alone, you may judge of the increasing value and importance of what we might call laboratory work in the field of advertising, or, to give it its other name, research. Of the six groups just mentioned, advertising agencies perform the largest amount of research work, because advertisers usually place upon them the responsibility for successful conduct of their advertising campaigns.

Analyze Your Product First

● In fact, the modern conscientious agency wouldn't touch a new proposition with a ten foot pole until it had been investigated from top to bottom and across the middle. Indeed, sometimes the agency, after exhaustive research, informs the manufacturer that his proposition is unsound and recommends against it. The public does not hear of these cases.

Some people seem to think that modern advertising is a thing which, like Topsy, "just growed." Those of you who are advertising men know that advertising is not created by rubbing a magic ring and that it does not get into the newspapers and magazines all by itself. Behind the actual process of preparing advertising copy is the scientific work of studying just how to present the product most effectively.

It isn't only a matter of pretty pictures and striking phases. To touch a responsive chord, the advertiser must know the desires and attitudes of those to whom he makes his appeal. He must know what reaction his advertising will produce, and he obtains this knowledge through research.

He must know in what media it is most profitable for him to advertise and how much it is wise for him to spend. He must know what methods of follow-up are likely to insure the best returns from his advertising. All these questions scientific study helps to solve.

I have spoken of product research. This is a most interesting phase of modern advertising. It is the cornerstone. Product research is usually worked out in the laboratory, with the aid of chemistry, physics, and other sciences. Such research determines the good and bad points of a product and tests it down to the last grain. If a weakness exists it must be found. Sometimes amazing discoveries are made in these remorseless laboratory tests.

You will remember how Fleischman discovered that his yeast is chock full of the vitamins which doctors had been talking about. He struck a gold mine when he advertised this quality and people began to eat yeast for its vitamins.

The Simmons Company made a thorough study of its mattresses and discovered very useful facts. In the sleep laboratory of a great institute it was found that there are seventeen common positions assumed by sleepers. Tests revealed that the Simmons mattress seemed best to accommodate itself to these seventeen positions. This fact was advertised to the public, and up went the sales.
● Many well known advertisers maintain testing laboratories for conducting continuous product research. Here

Science and business now collaborate on product, consumer and distribution research.

is brought to light much valuable information upon which their advertising is based.

Studying the Consumer Market

● Now we come to consumer market research. In this field are the studies which deal with the people who buy things, the localities where they live, their purchasing power, the trends of demand, sales potentials and consumer attitude. Every business man vitally needs accurate information about these factors. Almost any one of them can make or break him.

There was a certain milking machine manufacturer who saw his sales curve swerving toward the vanishing point. He couldn't figure out what was wrong. But a market survey revealed that his machine was priced too high and that only the big dairymen could afford to buy it. It was a first rate machine. That was the trouble. It was so good and so costly to make that he had to charge a big price for it. So he pulled in his horns and began building smaller machines, and in that way reached a wider market. Research and engineering skill saved his business.

Most of the leading successful advertisers keep in constant touch with their consumer markets and make periodic surveys to make sure that the product will always be right and that their advertising is tuned to a responsive public ear. One of the largest baking companies recently ascertained through house-to-house canvass of thousands of house- (Continued on page 39)

THE NEW
COMPETITION

by Harold L. Eves

The man in charge of merchandising today is confronted with an ever-changing sales situation. Yesterday, drug stores were in competition with drug stores. Today they are in competition with everything from garages and hardware stores to beauty parlors.

● The public has only one set of dollars. They are only able to spend their dollars once. Money used for candy will not also buy a package of cigarettes.

Just as in the case of the retailers who are in competition with each other in the sale of merchandise, so is every manufacturer in competition with manufacturers of other products. The manufacturer who today desires additional volume is faced with the fact that he can only hope to secure this volume from two major sources. First, he can take business away from his competitor, or in other words get more than his share of the dollars the public *intended* to spend for his type of merchandise. Second, he can make an effort to increase consumption of his particular type of merchandise and thus secure his share of a larger percentage of the public's dollar.

The public's buying habits *can* be changed. This is not theory. It has actually been done to a great extent in the past few years. An example is the case of the furniture industry being almost ruined by the merchandising efforts of the automotive and radio industries. After the public has bought the necessities of life, which are food and clothing, it has left a certain amount of money a portion of which might be designated as the luxury buying power. The automotive industry in its battle for volume was forced to try for a portion of the luxury purchasing power of the public. Naturally some of that had to come out of the furniture purchasing fund. In many cases it took almost all the dollars that were left after food and clothing had been taken care of. The automotive industry affected the home in such a way that there developed the saying "the living room is now but a stopping place between the bedroom and the garage." The merchandising effort, first took out of the budget some of the available money for the purchasing of home furnishings, and second, because it was a product that had to be used out of the home, caused less and less time to be spent there and consequently less need or rather less desire for a beautiful home.

● Almost as soon as the automotive industry had started its inroads on the home furnishing budget there appeared on the commercial horizon a new competitor for the home furnishing budget in the form of the radio industry. This being an article to be used and enjoyed within the home made even a more direct appeal against the home furnishing budget and soon became a serious menace to the furniture industry.

Both the radio and automotive industries did a better job of selling. They had better distribution, had better advertising. With them goods were sold under a brand name. Complete and coordinated campaigns were used by every manufacturer to create desire on the part of the public. A constant and intensive campaign was successfully conducted in which the buying habits of the American public were changed. In almost every advertising medium the automotive and radio industry outsold the furniture industry. The public was firmly sold on the idea that it was better to live a large portion of their lives in the glorious outdoors; that life would be healthier and happier if the family had a car. When they were home life would be more comfortable if they could listen by means of radio to the world's best music and other forms of vocal entertainment.

Mind you, neither the automotive nor the radio people actually said in their copy: "Don't own a home." "Don't furnish a beautiful house." They simply sold the idea of other pleasures.

● The automotive people so thoroughly sold the public upon the necessity of the auto for pleasure and transportation that from 1908 to 1929 automobile registration increased from 197,000 to 26,000,000. Good, coordinated merchandising did that job!

The furniture man soon found that he was in competition with other people besides his competing furniture store. He found that most of his worries were caused by the fact that people were no longer buying as much furniture as in past years. He soon realized that someone had sold the public on an idea—that through advertising the public had developed desires which were so strong that they were willing to sacrifice their finely furnished homes so that they might enjoy these new pleasures.

The furniture man began to realize that the public did not have enough money to satisfy all of their wants —that the public was deciding not so much upon which desires were neglected but which they preferred to satisfy. With seventy cents of the average income dollar needed for the necessities of life there was evidently going to be a battle royal for what was left. If the furniture industry was to succeed they would have to sell the public the desire for beautifully furnished homes. The question no longer was "from whom shall we buy our new furniture," but was rather, "shall we buy furniture or a new automobile."

● The furniture industry met this merchandising challenge through a National home furnishing program, a national campaign that was designed to sell the desire for better furnished homes through the theme—"First furnish your home. It tells what you are."

Even eating habits may be changed through advertising. The bakers are facing much the same problem that the furniture man faces. Money that formerly went for the purchase of bread is now being used for such things as breakfast foods. A walk down most any street will quickly show what changed the public's habits. Food advertising on posters has increased tremendously within the last few years. These men are merchandising a product that the public of Grandmother's day was not in the habit of consuming in large quantities. But advertising and merchandising again quickly changed habits until today a breakfast without toast is not as unusual as a breakfast without cereal or fruit. A serious situation as far as the baker is concerned. Again, the baker is not in competition with the baker down the street but rather with manufacturers of other food products.

● But this new competition does not always work to a disadvantage. Take the case of the ice industry. Somewhere between 1921 and 1925 mechanical refrigeration really got started in a program of serious merchandising. By 1925 it was estimated that there were some 200,000 mechanical refrigerators in use. Since 1925 the industry has gone ahead with tremendous strides. They have sold the public upon the advantages of refrigeration and the economy of a mechanical refrigerator.

Those who are not connected with the ice industry or who have no knowledge of the facts, would tell you that the ice industry was done—that they stood in much the same situation as the former manufacturer of buggies. But, strange to say, the new competition in their case was a blessing. The 1930 output of ice was approximately 60,000,000 tons, which under that industry's

original plan of development would not have been reached until about 1940.

In this case we have a valuable lesson of the by-product of competitive industry advertising. The public was first sold on the desire and necessity of refrigeration. Many people had ice boxes. Many more could buy low-priced, economical ice boxes who could not afford mechanical refrigeration. That, coupled with the fact that the industry sensed its danger quickly enough so that it started an intensive campaign through the Committee on National Publicity of the National Association of Ice Industries, which during the past three years have displayed thousands of posters throughout the United States, sold the idea to part of the public that ice refrigeration was the best form of food preservation.

● Living today is far from the leisurely existence that it was even as lately as twenty years ago. No age has ever witnessed such an increase in production and methods of production as has the present. No longer can a manufacturer find himself a good product and settle down to manufacture it for the rest of his life, concerned only with production problems and the competition of others in the field. Probably the gentlemen who manufactured hat pins had much the same sort of idea just about the time hat pins went out as articles of utility and defense. No industry can safely assure itself that it is the one line of endeavor that will never be affected by customs or by new inventions.

To the manufacturer who is alert, who sees in the new situations which confront him an opportunity to follow the trend and turn it to his advantage this present instability is ideal. He is the man who turned from making buggies to making automobiles—and found far greater profits than had ever been hoped for in the manufacture of buggies.

If goods are to be sold and volume maintained the business man of today must be a real student. He must know not only what is happening in his own industry but also what is happening in all other industries whose sales of goods might affect the portion of the public's budget from which he hopes to secure his sales volume.

The competition between industries for the consumer's dollar is constantly growing keener.

MERCHANDISING
to Women

by Wilma McKenzie

Alert, up-to-the-minute manufacturers of today realize the importance of giving careful consideration to the part played by women in the buying that is done by American people. A study of psychological reactions of women, as purchasers, and a catering to their tastes has become a dominant factor in modern manufacturing. This applies to the manufacturers of almost every article of merchandise which is consumed by man, woman and child. Women's conspicuousness in buying is borne out by studies which reveal that they are credited with doing 90% of the purchasing today. We shall consider the importance of this fact to the manufacturer, and some of the most effective appeals to be used in selling to women.

● Almost every article of family use is purchased by the woman. Even articles which were formerly primarily of interest to man, such as automobiles and radios, are now bought under the close supervision of the woman. According to a recent study made by Dr. H. L. Hollingworth, of Columbia University, the only item that men buy entirely without assistance from women is their own collars.

A large per cent of the total income of American people is spent for family purchases. This being true, it can be seen that women necessarily figure very prominently in the buying. There are two or three reasons why women have more or less supplanted men in the matter of making the family purchases. In the first place, women have more time to shop. A busy man considers it an inconvenience to be compelled to take the time from his work to go out and look for an article of furniture or even clothing for himself. Yet he must measure up to a standard of requirements in personal appearance, so he shifts the task to the shoulders of his wife or some other feminine member of his household. Secondly, the average man dislikes shopping. Women glory in it. It is generally recognized by men that women shop more efficiently than they do. Women have more of an appreciation of harmony and style because they have made a study of it.

Salesmen have found merchandising to women to be a much more involved business than selling to men. Women are more exacting and delve more deeply into the real merits of an article. Men usually buy hurriedly and depend too much on the clerk to sense his needs. Women are by nature conservers of values. Figures have been compiled by the United States Bureau of Standards which are an index to woman's buying power.

American women hold the nation's purse strings.

In 1928 $92,000,000,000 were paid out to American people in salaries. $52,000,000,000 of this was spent by women for food, clothing, shelter, etc. Thus $1,000,000,000 a week is spent by women. This is $166,000,000 per business day.

● The following table which appeared in "Selling Mrs. Consumer," by Mrs. Christine Frederick, shows how the typical woman's retail dollar is split. This table reveals the relativities of purchase which woman as a purchasing agent of the family observes.

Food, including grocers, meats, fruits, vegetables, dairy products, etc., sold to consumers	$0.412
Clothing, including ready-made apparel and piece goods for men, women and children, underwear, hats, hosiery, shoes, rubbers, etc.	.225
Furniture	.030
House furnishings	.037

Automobiles, accessories, gasoline, tires, etc., for pleasure use only	.112
Tobacco products	.045
Beverages, soft drinks, etc.	.025
Pianos	.005
Radio and phonographs	.011
Jewelry, watches, clocks and silverware	.010
Electric goods for household	.005
Perfumes, cosmetics, etc.	.013
Soaps, dentrifices	.007
Drugs, proprietary and patent medicines	.010
Books and magazines bought in retail stores	.002
Paints and varnishes	.005
Confectionery, chocolates, ice cream, and chewing gum	.007
Agricultural implements	.007
Miscellaneous	.032
Total	$1.000

Sellers have a tendency to look upon woman, the purchaser, as being in their own class or above. Statistics as to the literacy and education of woman in America prove this an erroneous assumption. Her intelligence in buying is not so much of the acquired type for only a relatively small per cent of women in the United States have high school and college educations. The largest number have only a grade school education. So her intelligence is of the native type. She proceeds more along lines of instinct. The Needlecraft Magazine classifies women buyers as follows. (1) The Indolent Rich Woman, (2) The Overworked Poor Woman, (3) The Clinging Vine Woman, (4) The Creative Woman.

● An understanding of the fundamental instincts of woman is of material assistance in making an effective selling campaign upon them. It has been found that women are ruled by emotions and instincts instead of by logic and reason. Psychologists have done much in recent years to discover interesting facts which have been a decided advantage in dealing with the feminine buyer. The following are considered by sociologists and psychologists the chief instincts of women:

> Sex love
> Mother love
> Love of home making
> Vanity and love of personal adornment
> Love of mutation, style, modernity, prestige, reputation
> Hospitality
> Sociability
> Curiosity
> Rivalry, Envy, Jealousy
> Pride, Ostentation, and Display
> Exclusiveness, Social Ambition and Snobbery
> Tenderness, sympathy and pity
> Cleanliness, sanitation, purity
> Practicality, Economy, Thrift, Orderliness
> Love of change and novelty
> Delight in color, smell, neatness, looks and feel

> Delight in manner, form, etiquette
> Love of beauty

A clever seller will take specific ones of these instincts and play upon them in dealing with his customer. He will analyze his goods, determining what instinctive appeals it may have, and capitalize upon them.

● The error of wrong appeals is a serious as well as a common one. The beauty of an article, for example, should not be stressed when it is the quality that the woman is looking for in that particular article of merchandise.

The *unconscious self* of woman is played upon most effectively. Selling to woman is facilitated by the fact that she has a great suggestibility. American women are noted for their adaptability. The explanation for this is that she is a new rare mixture without fixed social roots or traditions. Because of this suggestibility the woman's attention is *easy to get but hard to hold*. Her variability of mood and tense and interest makes it particularly important for the seller of goods to plan more carefully how to hold her attention than how to get it. General publicity is inadequate to do this. A more elaborate approach to her instincts is necessary. The personal appeal is a desirable appeal and campaigns based upon this method have been found to be the most successful.

Psychologists make a distinction between selling to men and women. Men respond more readily to *action*-appeals and women to *visual*-appeals. Women are more interested in how a thing looks than how it does. For example, radios and automobiles built in their early crude forms did not have the widespread distribution that they now enjoy since they have been built to please women. Women react very quickly to the exterior and appearance of articles of merchandise. The seller should keep this in mind and plan his merchandising and advertising accordingly.

The psychology of the woman buyer is very subtle and complicated and it is well for the seller to bear this in mind in making campaigns upon her. Women are unusually extravagant in some things and particularly close with others. *Change is the keynote of feminine character,* says one author.

Merchants are finding institution advertising of more and more importance. The old doctrine that women are born bargainers no longer holds true, if it ever did. Every year they are going farther away from the bargain idea. Recent studies by advertisers reveal women no longer fall hard for "comparative price" advertising psychology and the "bargain counter." Instead they are endeavoring to sell to women the entire store as an institution.

● Much time and futile effort can be spared if the seller will make a close study of the relative strength of appeals to women. These appeals should be tested so as to prevent making either an unsound appeal for a particular article or an erroneous one. The customer is easily irritated by these mistakes. Hollingworth's study of appeals is given below. This study rates appeals to women without reference to the specific article of merchandise.

Appeal	Percentage Rank for Women	Appeal	Percentage Rank for Women
Time Saved	97	Hospitality	76
Health	95	Courtesy	73
Cleanliness	95	Economy	72.4
Efficiency	94.7	Imitation	70
Scientific	93.5	Affirmation	70
Durability	91.5	Sport	67.5
Quality	90	Elegance	66
Appetizing	87	Sympathy	63
Guarantee	85.5	Clean feeling	59.5
Medicinal	85	Social superiority	58.8
Safety	84.3	Beautifying	57
Modernity	83.6	Imported	55
Reputation	81.6	Hobby	52.5
Substitutes	79	Recommendation	52
Family affection	78.2		

● The fact that numerous women have not been persuaded of the comforts and economies of many articles of household equipment may be due to a lack of the use of the effective selling points. A campaign involving the following appeals is recommended by Mrs. Christine Frederick in "Selling Mrs. Consumer." (1) To replace the human worker who is expensive or difficult to secure and a psychological strain to keep satisfied, (2) To save her own effort, steps, time, beauty and physical appearance, (3) To make the home more convenient, comfortable, safe and beautiful, (4) To increase sanitation and freedom from unpleasant features such as smoke, soot, steam, odors etc., (5) To conserve and promote individual health, particularly of her children, (6) To improve wholesomeness or appetizing qualities in foods, (7) To gain leisure for chosen activities and pursuits, (8) To be able to follow better, shorter, more improved methods in a particular task, (9) To lower fuel or operating costs, repair or upkeep of any kind, (10) To

The salesman must be sure that the woman understands the operation of new equipment for the home.

emulate to the families making similar equipment purchases.

● Education of women in the use of household equipment is necessary if maximum satisfaction is to be derived from its use. The reason why one woman gets results with a certain machine and another woman does not is not a difference in the machines but a difference between the women who use them. Dissatisfaction with a particular appliance is usually due to the failure of the woman operator to use it in a trained, intelligent, educated way. A salesman in trying to sell his particular machine should sell her on the general principles back of all the machines in that class. Some women insist on still rubbing clothes with their hands because they think the dirt is more thoroughly removed by doing so. A man trying to sell her an electric washing machine should explain that soil may be loosened from fabrics by chemical action or a soap solution violently agitated by power far more effectively than it can be loosened by any friction method.

The modern woman has an entirely new psychology toward her clothes buying. Formerly the questions she asked when she entered the store were: "Is it durable?" "Will it last two seasons?" Now the questions are: "Is is becoming?" "Is it in good taste?" So style, good taste and correction are being played up by the wise merchant.

Too, she knows what she wants. She enters a shop with her mind pretty definitely made up as to the type of garment she wants. She has read her fashion magazines and newspapers and found a particular style which appealed to her because of its suitableness and attractiveness. Then she knows that other smart women are wearing the same thing. The salesgirl need not explain to the customer what she should have. The customer tells the salesgirl explicitly what she wants.

● A consideration of these facts, as they bear upon the various lines of merchandise, and of the conditions relating to women as buyers which are being constantly revealed through research studies, will assist American manufacturers in attaining that degree of success and good business to which they all aspire.

THE MARKETING PROBLEMS
of
AMERICAN BUSINESS

Number Four of The Series

■ More than one manufacturer has found that the vagaries of fashion or the inexorable march of progress has completely destroyed the market for his product or has rendered his equipment obsolete. New inventions, new ideas are appearing so rapidly that it is an alert business man indeed who is able to adjust himself to these changes without loss of time or money.

The baking industry, once considered as the most stable of all businesses, now finds that the tide of public favor is turning from bread—the baker's mainstay—to other foods. The remarkable increase in food products and food advertising which has taken place in the last decade has seriously affected the amount of bread consumed. So serious has this decrease become that many bakers are faced with financial disaster.

Mr. H. W. Zinsmaster, who tells of this problem which is faced by the baking industry, is well qualified to speak of the merchandising and advertising of bakery products. Before entering the baking industry, where he has achieved a notable success, he was associated with the J. Walter Thompson Company. Thus, he not only knows the production and merchandising of his products, but has an understanding of advertising which has

Intelligent Merchandising
Builds Bakery Sales

by H. W. Zinsmaster
President, the Zinsmaster Bread Co., Minneapolis, Minnesota.

● From the first dim beginnings of history bread is inextricably a part of the story of mankind. Grains of wheat and offerings of bread are found in age-old Egyptian tombs; the granaries of Pharaoh have an important role in the Biblical story of Joseph. The lack of bread was one of the most potent causes of the French revolution when a queen, unable to imagine people without food, asked wonderingly, "Why don't they eat cake if they have no bread?" Bread, in all times and among all peoples has rightfully been called "the staff of life."

The baking industry has always been one of the steadiest, the safest, the least disturbed by progress of any major industry. Carl Alsborg, director of the Food Research Institute at Stanford University, after exhaustive study of the baking industry, remarked: "It is one of the least hazardous, one of the least speculative of all our industries, as evidenced by the steady even growth of the industry, undisturbed by booms, by panics, or even by war." Every year showed an increase in business no matter what conditions were with other businesses. Whole industries might be completely changed or entirely wiped out of existence by new inventions or changes in fashion, but the new inventions in the baking field only added more efficient equipment to the baker's resources and increased his production. Small wonder that the baking industry said "You can't invent anything to take the place of bread."

In 1925, however, the consumption of bread began to decline. It wasn't such a marked decline as to arouse the baking industry to sudden alarm. But it continued and is still continuing and now bakers are alarmed. Other food products are taking the place of bread in the American diet in ever increasing proportion and the baking industry feels that something must be done.

Despite the fact that bakers were selling bread in increasing quantities up to 1925, the consumption of bread was declining long before that date. This decline was not obvious, however, since the bakers were selling more and more housewives on the idea that the home baking of bread was a costly, time-wasting process that was better delegated to the baker.

● The movement to urban centers was also a great factor in the increase in consumption of baked goods. The small living quarters, the increase in outside attractions and the great number of working wives all operated to reduce the quantity of home baking and to boost the baker's volume. Mechanical appliances are lightening the work of the housewife and she is no longer content to live a life of drudgery such as was once the common lot of women. Thus, while less bread was being used, more bakers bread was sold and the decrease was not apparent. In 1925 the market for bakers bread was sold to such an extent that the increase did not offset

This animated bulletin flashes "Sliced" in Neon light as the baker holds up the loaf of sliced bread and "or Plain" as the unsliced loaf appears.

NEWS OF THE OUTDOOR INDUSTRY

Kleiser Heads A. F. A. Council on Departmental Activities

George W. Kleiser, President of the Outdoor Advertising Association of America, Inc., and of Foster and Kleiser, San Francisco, was elected chairman of the Council on Departmental Activities of the Advertising Federation of America at the recent meeting of that organization in New York on June 18.

■ ■ ■

Macdonald elected Director by Michigan Association

At the meeting of the Outdoor Advertising Association of Michigan recently, H. C. Macdonald, president of Walker and Company, was elected director of the Outdoor Advertising Association of America to represent the state of Michigan.

A committee to be appointed by the president of the State Association will handle the matter of landscaping twelve special locations throughout the State of Michigan in accordance with recommendations of the Education Division of the Outdoor Advertising Association of America.

– –

Dreyfuss Addresses Publicity Seminar of Y. W. C. A.

Mr. Leonard Dreyfuss, President of the United Advertising Corp., and Vice President in charge of the Educational Division of the Outdoor Advertising Association, recently spoke before the Publicity Seminar of the National Board of the Young Women's Christian Association of the United States, at their headquarters in New York.

Mr. Dreyfuss dwelt on the advantages of outdoor advertising for the Y. W. C. A. He advised that the National Board of the Y. W. C. A. create several posters to be purchased by the branches throughout the country—these posters to deal with their summer camps; the advantages of their cafeterias; one that will attract transients where the local association wants them; and then one or two more posters to be used when the local association had a drive. He was asked many questions by those who attended.

He reported that there was a general feeling that outdoor advertising held many advantages for the Y. W. C. A. and that its use meets with their general approval and they will try to make it possible for local branches to use it intelligently.

George L. Johnson Dies

Mr. George Leigh Johnson, former chairman of the board of the General Outdoor Advertising Company, died recently in Tucson, Arizona, as a result of an acute heart attack.

Mr. Johnson left Chicago some weeks ago to look after business interests. He had been in good health and his death was a totally unexpected blow to his family. He is survived by his widow, two sons and a daughter, all of River Forest, Illinois.

■ ■ ■

VERNOR GINGER ALE USES UNIQUE DISPLAY

A new adaptation of animated advertising greeted traffic along Detroit's main street when the Vernor Ginger Ale display was erected on Woodward avenue a few weeks ago. The display which is creating considerable interest is featured by the movement of two Gnomes (mythical diminutive beings), their trade mark, one on each end of a plank swaying in teeter-totter fashion over a barrel of Vernors, which serves as the axis.

The motive power is a one quarter horsepower motor with wool packed bearings with a worm and gear reduction concealed in the barrel. The barrel is 42 inches in diameter and projects 24 inches from the board. The barrel is built of twenty gauge steel, spot welded and reinforced with 1½ angle iron. The trunion, carrying beam is a bronze casting securely bolted to the barrel.

The beam carrying the Gnomes is of white pine 3¾ x 3¾ inches and is twelve feet long. The Gnomes themselves are 48 inches high and cut out of Masonite-Prestwood; they are reinforced on the back with twenty gauge steel, spot welded to slide over the beam and held in place by two screws.

A Southern Colonel Comes to BROADWAY

by C. D. McCormick

From his southern home in Tennessee, Colonel Joel Cheek flashed a signal on the night of April 30th; and, simultaneously, another colonel of distinguished southern air flashed to life in the colorful lights of the "Great White Way" in New York.

The second colonel, the one in bright lights, is the central figure in the new Maxwell House spectacular electric sign located at Broadway and 46th Street overlooking Times Square.

● This advertisement of light and color and motion was designed and built by the General Outdoor Advertising Company. The finished sketch for the figures in the display was done by Norman Rockwell. The display is a tribute to Joel Cheek, the beloved "Old Colonel" of Maxwell House fame, to whom goes the credit of contributing more than any one person to the development of Maxwell House Coffee. He originated that

This Maxwell House spectacular is the third sign on Broadway to carry the message of this organization.

popular blend which became a member of the General Foods family in 1928 when the Cheek-Neal Coffee Company was purchased by the General Foods Corporation.

● Colonel Cheek announced the inauguration of this new sign during the Maxwell House Coffee radio hour broadcast over station WJZ. In telling about his early efforts in selling coffee in Kentucky and Tennessee, the colonel described himself as: "A lonely young coffee salesman on a horse. My saddlebags were filled with samples—samples of that same blend you like so much today." Then he changed to the occasion of the moment: "That trail, started in the mountains, has been blazed into the homes of millions. In a moment I shall give a signal here in Nashville and far away in New York a bright message will flash from the skies—a message of friendship to you all from Maxwell House Coffee." After giving the signal, the colonel continued: "And now I have given the signal and it (the Maxwell House Display) is shining over Times Square in New York. I would like to think of this bright display as an emblem of hospitality standing at the gateway of

America. I hope it will always be that to you and that the coffee it represents will always bring you contentment and comfort. Thank you—God bless you all and Good-night!"

● Then the familiar voice of Graham MacNamee was heard extolling the wonders of Broadway and telling, in his own inimitable style, about the striking features of the Maxwell display which he described in detail.

While many thousands throughout the country were listening to Colonel Cheek and Graham MacNamee, other thousands were present in person when this new sign burst forth into the night life of New York. It seemed, for a moment, like the setting of some unusual stage when the curtain is quietly drawn aside. A sea of upturned faces greeted it with an expression of startled wonder. Then, as the eye quickly picked out the details—the figures, the name, the complete action, and the message—the whole advertisement was revealed—a glowing message that tells about the coffee which is "good to the last drop."

The first flash of the electric lights showed the central figure, a very distinguished southern colonel and his dignified colored butler. These figures are in the foreground. The colonel is holding out his cup for the coffee while the butler stands ready to serve his master. The action shows the butler raising the coffee pot and pouring the coffee. It shows the steam rising. When the pouring ceases, the colonel raises the cup. As it touches his lips, the words, MAXWELL HOUSE COFFEE flash on across the top of the sign. The name remains lighted until the colonel has finished his coffee and lowers the cup. When the cup reaches its original position, all the lights go out, and the action starts all over and keeps repeating again and again.

The words MAXWELL HOUSE COFFEE run the full 90 foot length of the top of the sign. The letters are of red luminous tubing which shows both day and night. Outside the tubing each letter has a row of inside, white-frosted lights which flash on every five seconds. These letters are 5 feet 6 inches high.

● The most interesting feature, of course, is the central figures of the colonel and his colored butler. The colonel is sitting by a cheerful fireplace and, although seated, he is 19 feet 6 inches high. The butler is 25 feet high. The coffee pot is 8 feet high by 4 feet wide, and the cup is 2 feet high and 3 feet 6 inches across. The figures of the colonel and the butler, the coffee pot, and the cup, are outlined with inside frosted lamps and wired to produce the motions necessary for pouring coffee.

Every night the butler pours over two thousand cups of coffee—a number greater than that poured by the busiest waiter in New York.

In the background are a mantelpiece and cozy fireplace in which the fire glows brightly. A mellow glow of warmth and coziness is secured by amber lamps which form the outline of the mantel which is 32 feet 6 inches high by 43 feet wide. A painted glass transparency with a moving flame effect is used to convey the illusion of the fire. This part, which represents the fire, is 1 foot 6 inches high and 6 feet wide.

The atmosphere of the setting is one of leisure and relaxation which is naturally associated with a cheerful fireplace, a comfortable chair, and a good cup of coffee.

Just above the fireplace hangs a huge poster in a gold-leaf frame. The poster shows a very pretty girl of the modern sophisticated type enjoying a cup of coffee. It was designed by Leon Gordon and depicts Maxwell House Coffee as the favorite of the modern generation.

Posters of the same copy appear on 150 panels located throughout Manhattan and Bronx—in neighborhood centers, in downtown shopping and business centers of greatest circulation, along railroads and trolley lines, at bus terminals, on main routes of automobile circulation—wherever the tide of traffic flows, these posters tell the Maxwell House story to the people. Other posters appear on 120 panels throughout Brooklyn and, in like manner, still more appear on other panels in the principal market centers from coast to coast.

● The people of New York will not only be attracted by this poster in the electric sign, but they will see it again and again in their travels about town and in their own neighborhoods. Thus it will remind them of the electric sign and more firmly impress upon them the merits of Maxwell House Coffee. Other hundreds of thousands of visitors to Broadway from all over the United States also will be forcefully reminded of Maxwell House Coffee when, in their own cities, they see the same poster design they saw in the brilliant electric on Broadway. The poster in the electric display is changed every 30 days to conform to the new posters that appear on the regular poster panels in cities throughout the country.

The tie-in of the Maxwell House electric display with the 24-sheet posters which appear in cities throughout the country is unique in that it is the first time such a method has been used to capitalize on the spectacular features of an electric. The cumulative effect of this clever tie-up is expected to have far-reaching effects in the publicity it will bring to Maxwell House Coffee.

Across the bottom of the display is a motogram (running word sign). The letters are each 6 feet 6 inches high and are in old rose red—the first time such a color has been used in a motogram. The message, the sentences separated by small cups instead of dashes, reads as follows:

Maybe night life isn't what it used to be in the days of Delmonico's but (cup. cup. cup.) There has never been gayer, brighter mornings in New York than today with Maxwell House Coffee (cup) Try it (cup) A blend that's become a national tradition (cup) perfected in the days of the old South (cup) "Good to the Last Drop" (cup. cup. cup.)

If this message were stretched out along Broadway, it would reach all the way from 52nd Street to 42nd Street—ten city blocks—2,600 feet long—one continuous reel of marching words in (Continued on page 40)

LAYING OUT
the POSTER

by Mark Seelen

Art Director, Western Division, the General Outdoor Advertising Co.

There is going to be a lot of money well spent on good art work this year. It is the best salesman any advertiser can get to work for him—and one of the most economical. That is true for most advertisers, but in some cases the best efforts of the artist and copywriter are going to be nullified by what happens to the Advertisement ·before the Art Work is started and after it is delivered. Someone is going to start it wrong and someone else is going to wreck it. It is about these cases I want to speak.

The same thing happens in every media, but I think Outdoor Advertising suffers just a little more, because so much depends upon the layout. In newspaper and magazine, a poor layout can get by even though it does lose effectiveness. In Outdoor Advertising it cannot—the conception of the design makes or breaks.

● The big users recognize this fact and their posters and bulletins command the services of the most competent men in the business. They take no chances on the layout spoiling the ideas. Everything is put into its proper place and all the non-essentials ₁rimmed before the actual work is started. Then, when the finished work comes back, there is no adding and changing as far as the thought and sequence is concerned. A little touching up perhaps or minor corrections in drawing, but nothing that can wreck the selling power of a poster or bulletin. Doesn't this seem the sensible way to do it?

It *is* the sensible way and, besides getting more effective results means a great saving of time and money. Then, why don't all advertisers follow this procedure?

I think human weaknesses are to blame. No one would intentionally take the wrong way, especially when it means harm to his business. It is therefore the job of the art director or account executive to acquaint himself with the needs of the advertiser and educate him to the essential points of good outdoor copy.

● This requires tact and a thorough knowledge of the subject. In other words, a lot of salesmanship. It is not easy. Every advertiser has some ideas of his own that are good. He may have a marvelous knowledge of his own business and yet, herein lies his greatest weakness so far as advertising is concerned. He is "too close to his product to see his customers." He is proud of his business—it is part of his life and too often he is of the opinion everyone else is of the same mind. He wants to tell them everything—he wants the name to dominate and wants to throw in a phrase here or there that strikes his fancy without giving a thought as to the effect it would have on the bored public.

In order to keep him on the right track, the account executive or art director must know the reason why for every argument the advertiser brings up. He must meet the misconceptions with knowledge and common sense. We can safely assume the advertiser is openminded if he can be shown good reasons for changing his ideas. It behooves the account executive or art director to supply facts and tactfully get the art work started so that, once done, it will be in no danger of being wrecked by changes and additions.

● The first thing to consider is readability. In a gen-

This is an excellent example of a simple and effective lettering poster.

Simply
adorable —
— that
Schoolgirl
Complexion

PALMOLIVE

eral way, this depends upon the layout and that in turn depends upon simplicity, unity and ability to lead the reader through the proper path. There are three phases to consider when we strive for unity and simplicity. First, determine whether or not the design is primarily a picture poster or a lettering poster. Certain products can best be exalted by the right illustration while others need a powerful word message. In no design can two things be equally important and be seen. Decide once and for all which type is the one for your client. In either case, of course, there must be some lettering and identification, but we must subordinate one of the phases else a continuous battle will take place for attention—and both lose.

● Next, watch the amount of message to be told. It is entirely natural for the advertiser to want a lot of copy, but he must remember that no one else is going to stop to read about his product. Therefore, keep down the amount of copy by all means—give it to the public on the run. Find the attribute of his product most attractive to the public and plug that. The name, easily read, and a clinching phrase should complete the thought. Only one big message—more than that divides attention and nothing sticks in the reader's mind. Other salient points can be said next month and the month after. But insist upon limited copy.

There is still another way in which we can unify the poster or bulletin—the color scheme. Remember this— a great number of colors in a sketch may give it brilliancy and life, but when the design is up in company with a great number of others, those same colors are going to blend into the general effect and, while beautifully harmonious, will be lost in the shuffle. In other words, if the design is to stand out, it must be dominately of one color. I don't mean there can be only one color on it, but one must rule with the others used simply to get contrast where needed.

● The account executive will save himself and all concerned a lot of grief if he impresses the advertiser on

The Palmolive series has been an outstanding one in layout, copy and execution.

the value of keeping the poster unified. Then once the sketch is done, sell him on the idea of leaving it alone. Show him how quickly and clearly the sketch tells the story—then make it plain to him that any more added or shifted around would destroy that which was brought to perfection by study and work. There's no better way to convince them than to cite examples of users known to have been successful.

We now know our goal. Following are the steps I believe one should take in reaching it. Just a matter of common sense in using the information we have in regard to the making of impressions through the sense of sight. Be logical.

The first step in creating strong Outdoor Advertising is the copy theme. I have known advertising men who worked from layout to copy and got results. But, in my own case, and I think, in a majority of cases, such a procedure is working backwards. It is working toward a picture and not the message you are trying to tell the public. The ideal way is to evolve the copy theme and layout at the same time. Then the whole design works to the unified end.

● Get the basic theme first, then make all the tools you have in the way of Words and Illustration work to put it over. That gets results that count. In choosing the theme, remember this and impress it upon the advertiser, if necessary—the public is not interested in the product. It is our job to tell them what they get out of the product that will fulfill some desire. Take the customer's viewpoint all the way through. Visualize what the effect will be when the poster is displayed. Will the reader get the message quickly? Will it interest him? Will he believe it? Will it be so well identified he will always remember it? Will the design lend itself to serial possibilities? Will it make the reader talk about it—create word of mouth advertising? If your theme will do all those things when properly laid out, it's good!

Once the thought you want to put over is established, I believe it advisable to determine the general character of the poster. Ask yourself these questions. Should Illustration tell most of the story? What should the style of the poster be? Powerful—Brutal—or Graceful, Dainty? The character of the product or service determines the vein in which your copy theme is struck. For instance humorous copy with a serious subject would be bad taste. Let the product determine.

In laying out the poster we fall in line with a habit long established in western civilization—reading from left to right. Why should we ask the public to read any other way? The poster composition then should have a movement or flow which makes it easy for the eye to follow in logical sequence from the upper left hand portion of the design to the lower right. Then, when the eye gets there, turn it back into the design, if possible. Every line going off the poster should have a compensating line leading back into the poster.

● An interesting example of this is the position of the cake of Palmolive Soap. In magazine advertising the cake is shown on an angle with the left side higher. In Outdoor Advertising the cake is also shown on an angle, but the right side of the cake is higher. I was once asked the reason for this. It would seem more logical to show the product in the same position in all advertising. My reply was that in outdoor advertising the cake is placed in the lower right hand portion of the poster. It is reproduced in full color—green and a combination of yellow and black—the strongest contrast obtainable. If the left side of the cake were higher, the eye would inevitably be led into the lattice work at the bottom of the panel or to the bottom of the adjacent poster. When the right side is higher, however, the eye is kept within the poster and led back into the design.

I am convinced that ninety per cent of the copy lines should appear in the upper part of the poster, either extending clear across the design or massed in the upper left hand portion. In the case of bulletins, the latter position is much better. Remember that the length of a bulletin is 42 or 44 feet long. If the copy line goes clear across it with an additional 40 feet for the name and 30 feet more for a supplementary copy line, it means the eye is forced to travel over 100 feet in a few swift moments. Far better to put all the caption in the upper left hand corner in two lines, cut down the name in size and also the "clinching" line.

● If we start with the caption in the upper left hand, it is not a bad idea to follow this sequence across the poster—Caption—Illustration emphasizing the message—Name and package—then the clinching line. In this way we get what it offers, what it looks like, what it is called and how packaged, and finally the proof of what we have claimed.

It is a big problem to get the different elements composed so that each gets just the right amount of attention. Among other things, avoid lettering and illustration both going to the top of the poster. It is apt to make the design top heavy. Moreover, the two elements in such close relationship are apt to be confusing. Science has proven that the eye sees in a series of impressions. In other words, what might be thought a "sweeping" glance is really a number of separate pictures. Therefore, keep every element separated enough so that the eye has a chance to light upon it in the right sequence. Just how far to separate them is a matter of good judgment and skill. It brings us right back to the importance of getting set on a sketch before it is started and then leaving the design alone.

At times it becomes necessary to stretch a point and put in too much lettering. One good way to get the separation mentioned above is to introduce a change of tone in the background color. The lettering can be handled in an attractive block or unit while the change in background tone can be made to lend just the right difference in value to gain variety without confusion.

● It is my own conviction that a poster containing more than three distinct elements cannot be made into an exceptional poster. It may be a good job from a technical standpoint, but a job that is equally as good and contains only three elements will automatically be a better poster. If there are more than three to be used in a design, it should be possible to combine two or more of them, thus reducing (Continued on page 43)

The cigar is shown in silhouette against the background in this design. The enormous section of the face gives this poster remarkable attention value.

Cooperative Ice Campaign
Staged in San Antonio

● A few years ago the laugh would have been given the suggestion that manufacturers and distributors of the ice industry would do well to join forces and advertise their product to the public at large. Ice was then considered a common household commodity, like wood, coal or water—a necessity that people had to have, therefore, why advertise it?

The spectacular entrance of the mechanical refrigerators into the refrigeration world has put, however, an entirely new face upon the matter of advertising as far as the ice industry is concerned. The manufacturers and distributors of the mechanical refrigerators have not hesitated to grab big display space in magazines and newspapers and to employ every other media of the advertising profession in putting their message before the world. Indeed, advertising has been the golden bridge over which the mechanical refrigeration industry has traveled to quick profits.

This outburst of advertising and merchandising energy on the part of the mechanical refrigeration interests has had its reaction upon the leaders of the ice industry. Apathetic and skeptical at first, the manufacturers and distributors of ice have awakened or are gradually waking from their Rip Van Winkle slumber to a realization that there is a need on their part of re-educating the public as to the real value of their product.

The leaders of the ice industry hope to do three things through co-operative effort: win back some of the patronage lost to the mechanical forces; cause people who are already using ice to realize its importance so that they will increase their consumption of it, and since forty per cent of the homes do not have any kind of ice box get non-users of ice into the fold.

● It is believed that the first really big campaign to embody the three objectives just listed, to be staged so far is that of the San Antonio (Texas) ice industry, initiated early the past summer.

The manufacturers and distributors of ice in San Antonio banded themselves together in an extensive and intensive advertising and merchandising campaign that because of its comprehensive features merits description. The campaign began with newspaper advertising on May 25 and was prosecuted faithfully throughout the summer. It was so successful and gratifying to the co-operating members that it was continued into the fall season.

This attractive poster is an effective part of San Antonio's ice campaign.

● The extent of the campaign can be gathered by noting the media used, which included: weekly display advertising in the three San Antonio daily newspapers and in five local labor and religious papers; continuous poster advertising within the city, poster copy changed each month; radio hook-up of two programs for housewives weekly; distribution of literature by the ice men on their routes; wagon placards, changed regularly, and direct mail letters, sent to special lists.

"But we did not rest on our oars with such a comprehensive advertising set-up," one of the leaders of the San Antonio campaign said. "Two hundred ice wagons carry the message of ice refrigeration into the homes of San Antonio daily.

"No longer is the ice man a mere delivery cog in the estimation of San Antonio ice distributors and dealers. Instead, he is an energetic, young man in business for himself, increasing his earnings at the same time that he brings in profits for his organization. As standard bearers in the new movement, the ice delivery men have been educated carefully as to the purposes and merits of the campaign. As a result, they are enthusiastic boosters for it, for they see in it a golden opportunity to build up their own commissions at the same time that they gain prestige in the eyes of their employer.

"Realizing that one of the main reasons why some customers turn from the use of ice itself is that they have inadequate refrigerators, the San Antonio distributors and dealers decided early in the campaign to remedy this situation.

"There is no doubt that the family, possessing an antiquated, rusty-looking ice chest, makes an easy mark for the high-powered salesman when he calls with a shining unit of his mechanical line on a truck in the street. When the housewife compares her clumsy, kitchen antique with the new contraption in the salesman's wagon, she frequently falls for the exchange before it is hardly suggested.

"As a definite goal towards which to shoot, we are placing a fine line of ice refrigerators in San Antonio homes. These new units appeal to the eye in the matter of beauty and to the commonsense of the housewife as to utility. They run in price from $37.50 to $120.00. We also have a fine ice box that retails at the low price of $17.50 to non-users of ice. These boxes are small but ample in capacity for fifty pounds of ice.

● "With such a price range, we are able to appeal to all classes of the trade. The units are finished in white and pastel shades with silver trimmings and are fitted in every way to grace a home of refinement.

"But important as is the selling campaign, ice salesmen are not trained to center their attention on placing refrigerators exclusively. It is the purpose of the ice distributors and dealers to bring such sources of information to the housewife as will guide her in the economical use of her ice refrigerator at the same time that she gets maximum value and satisfaction from it.

"Ice salesmen are instructed to be courteous at all times, never to argue, but to put over these points in particular in the housewife's interest: To teach her never to wrap ice since, although wrapping does conserve ice itself, it prevents circulation of the cold air and therefore frequently causes spoilage of foods; to show the housewife that it is more economical and therefore best to have the ice chamber filled to capacity every day because only when so regularly filled can a balanced temperature be maintained in the refrigera-

tor; and to instruct her in the value of never opening the ice chamber as is commonly done to place food directly on the ice since such opening tends to let out the cold air much more rapidly than when the food chambers are opened.

● "Much of the instruction work is done by suggestion or example. For instance, if the salesman finds the meat in the ice chamber, he places it directly under the ice chamber. If he finds the meat on the ice the next day, he moves it again and reports the matter to his office. The housewife is then sent a carefully worded letter, calling her attention to the value of keeping the ice chamber closed.

"The campaign managers have fought to have removed from the homes the sign cards of 'Ice Wanted To-day.' It is desired that real salesmanship take the place of such mechanical checking up as the card system promotes. When an ice salesman is admitted to the refrigerator under the system now being used, he examines it attentively after which he asks, 'May I fill it up, Madame? It melts more slowly!' This question takes the place of the old one, 'How many pounds today?' and cleverly suggests the desired answer, which in the majority of cases is an affirmative."

The newspaper advertisements have been featured under the campaign slogan, "Those who *really* know prefer ice." In practically all pieces of copy the "Seven Reasons Why Ice Refrigeration Is Better" is played up prominently in boxed space.

These seven points give in short scope a summary of the content of the advertisements as a whole. They read as follows:

"Seven Reasons Why Ice Refrigeration Is Better

● "1. Ice gives you a full range of temperatures in your refrigerator. Temperatures that are exactly right for every type of food. Coldest temperatures for foods that require them such as milk and butter, slightly less cold for meats and similar foods, and still less cold for tender vegetables and fruits. (Continued on page 38)

A well-designed poster which emphasizes the appeal of an ice cold drink with "taste-free" ice.

POSTERS MERCHANDISE
REFRIGERATORS

by G. C. McHugh

● "Selling Electric Refrigerators in January"—Almost analogous to selling ice to the eskimos, isn't it? That's just what Jordan Marsh Company, Boston's largest department store, set out to do. And they did, too—to the tune of 577 model U4P Kelvinator Electric Refrigerators in one month—with the aid of Poster Advertising.

There could scarcely be any month in the year in which refrigerator advertising would encounter greater sales resistance than in January, particularly here in Boston, for that entire month was marked by a succession of blizzards, one after another, and the thermometer hovered in the vicinity of zero. So you can see it was no easy task to get the public refrigerator-minded.

However, Jordan's 80th Birthday Anniversary Sale was being conducted throughout January, and a large consignment of Kelvinators had been bought for sale at a special price as one of hundreds of features of the sale; so, win or lose, the sale had to go on.

● Here was a problem, indeed. For, while the refrigerators were a bargain at the sale price, that price was nevertheless by no means in the category of quick-sale low-priced merchandise. Jordan's fully realized that people don't buy Electric Refrigerators on the impulse of the moment. They usually want time to think it over, and compare values. Meanwhile, unless the thought is kept ever before their minds, in the preoccupation of business, etc., they will quickly forget or dismiss your thought from their minds. With colorful and attractive Posters, however, placed right where everybody sees them every day, constantly jogging their memories, they cannot quickly forget the sales appeal, nor can it be easily dismissed.

● Jordan's also knew to reach the entire Boston market through the papers would necessitate the use of at least the three leaders of Boston's six papers. Again, at the attractive price offered, it was felt these refrigerators were being placed within the reach of everybody; consequently, Jordan's wanted to give all an opportunity to take advantage of the same. They knew that Poster Advertising was not restricted to one class or group, but reached all living in a community or traversing its streets.

It was therefore decided, due to the abnormal sales resistance to refrigerator advertising at the time, to even up matters by giving the refrigerators a little handicap in advertising. Consequently, in addition to

This poster was a big factor in the success of the Jordan Marsh Company's sale of refrigerators.

the regular newspaper and other advertising, the refrigerator sale was featured on a 24-Sheet Poster Display covering Boston.

The display continued for one month; so did the sale., Before the sale was over, however, the original supply of refrigerators ran out, and Jordan's had to wire the factory for an additional 200 to fill the orders that had been booked—selling 577 in all, over a period of 30 days. That's some record!

True, like the other features of the Birthday Sale, the refrigerators were featured in all of Jordan's newspaper advertising; also in a 24-page circular featuring the Jordan Birthday Sale, 250,000 copies of which were distributed to Metropolitan Boston homes. But it must be remembered that the refrigerators were laboring under a handicap, and they alone had the benefit of Poster Advertising. When the final results were tabulated, it was found the refrigerators had far outstripped all the other merchandise more favorably circumstanced, both as regards price and timeliness of season.

Surely, this is one concrete example of the pulling power of Poster Advertising; when a specific model of a definite article, thus advertised, can, despite the indifferent public response likely to be encountered due to the untimeliness of the season, make such a splendid showing. In other words, only one product was featured on Posters, and the odds were against it; yet that one product made the best showing of them all. Surely, this is an example of directly traceable results.

■ ■ ■

Richards Quits Media Post

Guy Richards, vice-president and media manager of McCann-Erickson, Inc., New York, has resigned because of ill health. The media department will be under general supervision of L. D. H. Weld, director of research, the active conduct of the work being divided among L. S. Kely, newspapers; E. F. Wilson, magazines, farm papers, and business papers; and William Bolton, outdoor advertising. A. G. Graff is changing from the media department to production and contact work.

CYCOL CAPITALIZES
on Navy Acceptance
by Augusta Leinard

● In the United States Navy award of a contract for 1,000,000 gallons of Cycol Oil the Associated Oil Company saw advertising possibilities which have materialized in one of the most dramatic and glamorous campaigns ever staged on the Pacific Coast. Advertising media and dealer helps have been welded into a perfect chain of publicity which includes the finest and most extensive showing of highway bulletins ever used by this oil company.

As stated, the campaign had its inception in the Navy award of a contract to fill lubrication requirements for its battleships, destroyers, airplane carriers, and other Pacific Fleet equipment. The purchase was made after the Navy had tested competitive oils and it is the first time the Navy bought oil not on specification alone, not on price alone, *but on service cost.*

The application of the service cost method of purchase by large industries and government departments is comparatively new and is only now reaching ultimate perfection. The United States Navy is probably the largest purchaser of lubricating oils in this country and this year they have expanded their service cost purchasing method to cover lubricating oils. Using this method it was necessary to give a rating to the products of various manufacturers and so the Navy developed a high speed bearing in which to determine the quality rating of oils submitted. The quality or percentage rating made on a lubricating oil is called a "work factor", and a price divided by a work factor gives the "service cost."

This page shows how the Associated Oil Company featured the Cycol bulletins in its house organ.

● A simple illustration of service cost might be cited in the buying of a suit of clothes. A man is less concerned with the price than he is the wear the suit will give and he will pay more for a suit that he feels will give longer wear because he realizes that he gets more for his money out of the better quality garment than from the cheaper one. It is on such a test, in which service in relation to cost was considered, that Cycol was chosen by the Navy as a lubricant for its equipment on the Pacific Coast.

"Obviously here was a wonderful opportunity for advertising," Harold R. Deal, (Continued on page 44)

This bulletin design effectively features the navy's acceptance of Cycol and points a moral for the average consumer.

The Navy uses Cycol-So should you!
"Lowest Service Cost"

CYCOL MOTOR OIL

ASSOCIATED OIL COMPANY

Canada

Include Canada in your advertising and selling plans. Here you will find a prosperous market of ten million people, best reached by Poster Advertising.

Any of the following Poster Advertising Agencies will be pleased to give you the facts and figures about Canada:

The Canadian Poster Company, Limited, Montreal, Que.
The Gould-Baird Poster Company, Limited, Brantford, Montreal, Toronto, London, Vancouver.
H. E. Dickinson Advertising Co., Limited, Toronto, Ont.

E. L. Ruddy Co., Limited, Toronto, Hamilton, Winnipeg, St. John, Vancouver.
Lindsay-Walker Co., Limited, Winnipeg
Ruddy-Duker, Limited, Vancouver.
Charles Baker, Ltd., Toronto, Ont.

Poster Advertising Association

of Canada

Bank of Hamilton Bldg.   Toronto

ALWAYS IN
GOOD TASTE

Photo courtesy General Outdoor Advertising Company

This attractive Chesterfield design breaks away, to some extent, from the full figures and the sports appeal that Liggett and Meyers has used so successfully. The attractively painted figure and simple copy makes an effective poster.

Largest, most Powerful Six at the price
WILLYS
'495

Photo courtesy Morgan Lithograph Company

A simple and effective poster with the feel of summer and the open road. The car properly subordinates the remaining elements.

"His Master's Choice"
CALO
DOG and CAT FOOD
AT ALL DEALERS
Cooked and canned — READY TO FEED

Photo courtesy Erie Lithographing and Printing Co.

Man's best friend is appealingly portrayed in this unusual design. The pup is evidently a happy beastie and has just enjoyed a plate of Calo.

FOR SUNBURN
Absorbine jr
soothing..cooling

Photo courtesy Erie Lithographing and Printing Co.

Absorbine Jr. uses this attractive bathing girl to emphasize the use of the product for sunburn. The "athlete's foot" appeal is retained but is subordinated to the seasonal sunburn copy.

U. S. TIRES
NEW SALES RECORDS..
BETTER TO LOOK AT ...
BETTER TO RIDE ON ...
FAR FAR BETTER TO BUY

Photo courtesy National Printing and Engraving Co.

U. S. Tires make use of a simple, balanced panel with excellent carrying power. The tilting of the tire and the placing of the copy on different levels lends interest and action to this poster.

TODAY!
Get your taste-thrill
FAST-FROZEN
ICE CREAM

Photo courtesy Abbott Lithographing Co.

Here is a design that is softened by notable color values. The use of "Today" and "Fast-Frozen" lends power and action to the poster.

This is a lettering poster which is so handled as to be as effective, if not more effective, than a spectacular illustration. The curve of the lettering and the distinctive style lends action to the panel.

Chevrolet's use of posed photographs is producing some excellent posters. Certainly this short message and the photograph put over the comfort message in simple and effective fashion.

A beautifully composed and excellently painted poster. The lettering is legible too is executed in a somewhat unusual style for posters. It is, however, perfectly in keeping with the spirit of the design.

Here is a poster which shows the product, the product in use and the name. All necessary elements are included and all unnecessary ones left out.

WHO'S WHO IN THIS ISSUE

JOHN P. HARDING is president of the John P. Harding Restaurant Co., and was born in Peru, Illinois. He operates a chain of loop restaurants in Chicago and is assisted by his sons, James P. and Martin J. Harding.

Mr. Harding is often referred to as the "Corned Beef King" because of the national reputation built on this particular dish.

John P. Harding is also president of the John P. Harding Market Co., operating wholesale and retail markets in Chicago.

He is a member of many clubs and organizations, among them being The Chicago Athletic Association, Edgewater Golf Club, Bob-O-Link Country Club, Chicago Association of Commerce, Annandale Golf Club (Los Angeles).

MARK SEELEN started his art career as a sign painter's helper at the age of sixteen and for seven years worked as helper and pictorial artist. After a brief period as a newspaper artist with the St. Louis Republic he was with the Poster Selling Company for two years in the St. Louis and Chicago offices. On the closing of the Chicago office of the Poster Selling Company he went to the A. M. Briggs Company, of Chicago. This company merged with the Poster Advertising Company, Mr. Seelen becoming art director of their Western Division. With the merger of the Poster Advertising Company and others to form the General Outdoor Advertising Company Mr. Seelen became the art director of the Western Division of the latter company, the position which he holds today.

H. W. ZINSMASTER was born in Des Moines, Iowa, in 1885. He attended grade school and high school there and entered Amherst College, graduating from that institution in 1908.

He was first associated with the J. Walter Thompson Advertising Agency, New York, but because of his father's ill health, he returned to Des Moines and entered his father's business which was the Des Moines Baking Company. He remained in Des Moines until 1912 and part of 1913 and in the latter part of 1913 opened his first plant at Duluth, Minnesota. 1920 saw the opening of the St. Paul Plant and the Hibbing Plant was opened in 1922. In 1925 the plant at Superior, Wisconsin, was opened and in 1928 the Minneapolis Plant was opened. In 1929 the Zinsmaster Whole-Rye Company was opened which completes the organization as it is today.

Intelligent Merchandising
Builds Bakery Sales

(Continued from page 21) eral sale. It is another indication, however that the progressive bakers of today are overlooking no opportunities to increase sales of their product.

The small retail baker is unable to compete successfully with the larger organizations due to his lack of production facilities. The largest organizations have the facilities but their concerns lack flexibility, and there is such an element of competition among these larger companies that it is difficult for them to make money under the best of conditions. The difficulty of holding efficient man power under general policies which are apt to reduce individuality to a minimum is proving a source of increasing concern to the giants of production and distribution. The independent loses none of that close and familiar contact he has always had with the final consumers of his product; he has little concern regarding delay on decisions which should be made today. He is never confronted with the necessity of producing a given result on the one hand, while the support of advertising and sales promotion are perhaps knocked from under him on the other. He may curtail production within the hour should necessity arise and incoming raw materials will never threaten his very life if compelled to do so. He may secure the lead and hold it in that district of city which he covers, if he makes wise use of advertising and sales promotion in cultivating new and holding old customers.

● He has sufficient resources to invest in machinery which will aid his production. He can afford to do a competent advertising job and he can quickly adjust himself to changing conditions. He is able to sell a quality product at a higher price than the larger baking concern. In our own case we have produced a doughnut which sells at an appreciably higher price than competing brands. Yet we sold more than half a million dollars worth of those doughnuts last year. A quality product correctly merchandised at a reasonable price has nothing to fear from cheaper and inferior goods. Emerson's mousetrap manufacturer to whose door the world beat a path is out of date today. But, if he made a better mousetrap, charged accordingly and merchandised it correctly he would be successful.

The advent of new food products and the tremendous flood of advertising which is used to promote them makes it absolutely necessary for the baker to take steps to combat the tendency of housewives to use these new foods and reduce the family bread purchases. He cannot enter the national advertising field except in the case of a very few large organizations. But he can promote his products in his own territory. In outdoor advertising, newspaper advertising and point-of-sale displays the independent baker can meet the advertising competition of other foods and other bakers. Unless he has had advertising experience, however, he should not attempt to handle his own advertising. It is his

right and duty to supervise the work that is being done, but he should not attempt to change carefully planned advertising to suit his own personal prejudices. If he makes arbitrary alterations with no reason except personal objections, the result will be that the advertising is planned, not to meet the needs of the business but the owner's wishes—and advertising so planned will probably do nothing more than please the owner.

● The advertising media should be carefully considered and the experience of other bakeries is the best guide to the ones which will produce results. Probably the most exhaustive media comparison ever undertaken by the baking industry was the study completed in 1928 by an associated group of interests in the state of Pennsylvania. The survey was planned and conducted under the direction and with the aid of the Bureau of Agricultural Economics, United States Department of Agriculture, who themselves compiled a great share of the statistics. Without question, the findings are authentic, unbiased and complete.

Fifteen cities in Pennsylvania were thoroughly checked and housewives were interviewed by picked college students. Questionnaires were used which had been prepared jointly by the Pennsylvania Department of Agriculture, the Pennsylvania Baker's Association, the Philadelphia Baker's Club and the United States Department of Agriculture.

In this survey a section was devoted to the study of advertising media and their power to influence bread buyers. Many interesting points were discovered in this portion of the study. It was found that the advertising appeals most often remembered rated as follows: Cleanliness 41.2%, Health and Food Value combined 48.1%, Quality 32.9%, Labor Saving 14.3%. The itemizers gave one point each to each appeal mentioned by the housewife. Another interesting discovery was made in checking a list of nine most important foods. Bread was given third position on the list which included, in order of preference, vegetables, meats, bread, milk, fruits, eggs, cereals, fish and butter and cheese. Still another illuminating fact was represented in the discovery that less than 3% reported price as influencing the amount of their bread purchases.

● The media considered in this section of the survey consisted of outdoor advertising, newspapers, street car cards, magazines and bakers wagons and store advertising. After excluding baker's wagons and store advertising which factors are really interwoven in the customary fundamentals of baking and delivering bread, we find the housewife established the following facts as to the advertising that is remembered:

Outdoor advertising	59 %
Newspapers	37.2%
Street car cards	33.8%
Magazines	19.7%

Thus, in the three major media named by the women themselves as those which they remember, the independent baker can meet the nationally advertised foods which are usurping his business. His advertising can be made just as effective as that of his rivals. In our own case we are using outdoor advertising as the basis of our program. Both posters and painted bulletins advertise the Zinsmaster Baking Company. The bulletins are especially effective because of their use of motion. On the one which is on display at present first one arm and then the other appears, holding in the one hand a loaf of sliced and in the other a loaf of plain bread. A combination of size, color and motion such as this is difficult to beat for attention and remembrance value.

The baking industry is faced with a serious problem. A national advertising campaign to bring bread back to its former place in the diet and to combat the propaganda of the food fakers who are doing everything possible to destroy confidence in bread, may help to improve the situation. But the independent wholesale baker is situated in an enviable position. A combination of a quality product with intelligent selling effort will bring him prosperity for a long time to come.

■ ■ ■

Cooperative Ice Campaign Staged in San Antonio

(Continued from page 29) Just place foods properly in your refrigerator and Ice automatically keeps them 'just right.'

● "2. Only Ice provides a balanced atmospheric condition in your refrigerator . . . . . neither too dry nor too moist. Excessive dryness robs foods of freshness and flavor. Too much moisture causes mold. Ice keeps your foods just right without your ever having to think about it.

"3. Air circulation is essential to proper refrigeration. In an Ice refrigerator the air is constantly in circulation being constantly washed, cleansed and freshened by the melting ice.

"4. Ice-refrigeration prevents interchange of food odors and keeps foods uncontaminated, because the melting ice absorbs odors and impurities and passes them off down the drain pipe.

"5. Ice assures you of food safety and personal safety at all times. You *know* that there is nothing in pure ice to harm you or your food.

"6. Ice is the most economical form of refrigeration! Ice is the simplest form of refrigeration.

"7. Ice is always dependable. You can rely on Ice in any weather because a block of ice cannot get out of order."

The headings of certain pieces of copy, given below, suggest the content of each piece:

"Ice *freshens* Vegetables and Fruits . . . Prevents Them from Wilting or Drying Out . . . Preserves Their Flavor and Tender Succulence";

"Ice Makes the Party! Don't let embarrassing Ice shortages mar the success of your parties this summer";

"Those Who Analyze Costs Buy Ice";

"Those Who Really Know Prefer Ice Because Ice Refrigeration Gets rid of all Impurities and Odors";

These headings are taken from the copy advertising the new ice refrigerators:

"If Your Refrigerator Were in Your Living Room, You Woudn't Tolerate an Inefficient and Shabby One That Had Outlived Its Usefulness";

"Enjoy Summer this year with a new Ice Refrigerator and Plenty of Ice . . . . Nothing That You Can Buy Will Bring You So Much Summertime Comfort For So Little Money";

"The New Ice Refrigerators Bring New Convenience and Pleasure to Every Member of the Family."

● Much of the copy, featured the past summer, had a social angle as did that from which the following portion was taken:

"Ice is always part of the successful party. Long before the guests arrive ICE begins to do its part in making the party a success. The grocer leaves fresh fruits and vegetables; the butcher, tender meats, and the milkman, fresh, sweet milk. Into the ice box they go, and Ice begins its work.

"Ice keeps all foods safe and preserves their delicate flavors. The meats keep their savory juices; the vegetables their tender succulence, and the milk its pure wholesomeness, because circulating air in the Ice refrigerator is always *just right* to keep foods in their prime condition.

"But insuring delicious food is but one of Ice's contributions to the success of the party. You need never fear an embarrassing Ice shortage if you are a regular Ice customer. You can always have *all* the Ice you want with an Ice refrigerator . . . . Ice for delightful summertime beverages, Ice for garnishing, Ice for table use . . . . plenty of Ice for every possible need."

All newspaper copy was attractively illustrated. Each insertion since all were large, being either 100 inches or 120 inches, showed up in a conspicuous way.

Posters, kept running in strategic locations in San Antonio during the summer and fall, played an important part in the ice advertising campaign. Each poster was illustrated so as to beget wider reader attention. The phrase, "Those who *really* know prefer Ice," appeared on nearly all posters and served to tie them in with the newspaper campaign and with the ice wagon placards.

● The advertising account and general oversight of the San Antonio campaign was under the personal direction of Jack N. Pitluk, of the Pitluk Advertising Company, San Antonio. All of the advertising copy with the exception of some of the posters which were from copy of the Southwestern Ice Manufacturers Association was originated and prepared in the offices of the Pitluk company. The campaign was generously supported by the leading ice companies of San Antonio.

Research—Is It a Fad?

(Continued from page 11) wives exactly what kind of bread they preferred. After getting the desired information, the company changed its bread recipe accordingly, and advertised the particular qualities in which the housewives had expressed interest.

Another instance where this kind of market research brought hundred-fold profit is in the case of a New England shoe manufacturer whose business seemed about to pass out of the picture. He had tried all sorts of stimulating methods, but nothing seemed to work.

The factory was producing 2,500 varieties of shoes and it was well known that the cost of manufacture could be reduced materially if the number of different lasts could be cut down. A research was undertaken to learn if the number of varieties could be reduced without losing business. During the course of the investigation over 500,000 human feet were measured. It was found that the 2,500 styles could be reduced to only 100 and yet satisfy the customers.

The saving in production cost brought a price reduction of 36 per cent. The factory inventory was decreased 75 per cent. Sales were doubled. The company made larger profits and employees received higher wages and more continuous employment.

Face Powder and Electric Light

● A maker of face powder noticed an unaccountable sales increase in a rural county. Instead of letting it go at that and taking it as a piece of accidental good fortune he had a survey made to get at the reason for the unlooked-for increase. It turned out that a manufacturer of home electric lighting plants had just completed a sales drive in that particular county, which happened to be inadequately covered by public power lines. Many home owners installed electric lighting plants. That gave them so much better lighting that the womenfolk suddenly became more complexion-conscious. That led to a big increase of sales in face powder in the drugstores of the country.

The face powder manufacturer didn't stop there. He had something good by the tail and proceeded to haul it in. He found that other counties had gone through the same experience. Thereafter, he intensified his local advertising wherever the electric lighting equipment had been introduced. This company is now watching its sales as a cat watches a mouse-hole. It makes an analysis whenever any unusual factor or trend is noted. Its officials realize that continual checkups and market studies are profitable.

A well known toilet preparation took a rather unusual turn.

The research department of an advertising agency was preparing figures for this manufacturer's sales quotas. In comparing sales with the agency's buying power index, it was seen that the sales figures were pretty well in line for the northern states, but in the South there was wide variation from normal.

It was known that negroes used this preparation, but the extent of this use was not even guessed. But when the percentage of negro population in each state was incorporated as a factor with the buying power, the resulting index figures were beautifully parallel to the sales. This was news. It demonstrated the great importance of the negro market for this product. The company was enabled to shape its local sales policies accordingly.

Science in Distribution Studies

● The third kind of marketing research, you remember, deals with methods of distribution. It involves studies of dealers and sales channels, and the media for advertising. Measurement of advertising results and copy effectiveness are also included under this head.

There are many ways of determining the effectiveness of advertising copy. One method is that of actual copy-testing, which has been found to be very practical. Research men use various means to determine which is the best of several pieces of copy. Sometimes they find out by actual trial insertions, under controlled conditions. Sometimes the tests are made before publication by mailing the advertisements separately to subscriber lists to see how they react. Another way is to show the different pieces of copy to typical readers and ask questions that will test the effect.

Frequently the research man who studies the effectiveness of advertising copy does not resort to pretesting, but analyzes the results after the advertisements have been run. This is not always possible, but the method has much greater application than most advertisers realize. It is not at all necessary to confine this type of study to coupon returns or mail orders.

Several of the most important national advertisers have dissected and analyzed their advertising so thoroughly that they actually know what results they obtain from individual advertisements. They understand better than others the dollars and cents value of research. They know that research is a profit-maker. They know that modern advertising, to be effective and to bring in golden returns, must be based upon scientific principles.

These advertisers have determined precisely the effect of such factors as the size of an advertisement, the month in which it appears, its position upon a page, the value of the coupon, and the frequency of appearance. They know that advertising can be planned scientifically, and that money spent for such research, surveys and analyses is one of the most profitable investments they can make.

● In some cases it is definitely known that an advertising appropriation can be made to go twice as far through the application of scientific research. Often these studies involve complicated statistical analyses which can be performed only by highly trained men.

Huge amounts spent for advertising need not be haphazard speculations in these days. Most of the large successful advertisers apply the spotlight of research before they invest their advertising dollars.

For example, take the advertising of Bristol-Myers and the Lambert Pharmacal Company, with which you are probably familiar. These two companies have research departments which make intensive, painstaking analyses of the real effectiveness of all their advertising copy, and they know what kind of advertising pays and in what media to place it. They make every advertising dollar count.

● An interesting case is that of a manufacturer who was doing a national business, mostly by mail. The company had been very successful and profits were great. The officials were proud of the fact that sales were coming in from every state in the union.

But a time came when things were not so easy. Profits dwindled, and the obvious cause was high sales costs. One day a studious young man from an engineering college suggested a sales analysis. He didn't know much about the business and his ideas received scant attention. He managed to get permission to make the analysis, however.

When he brought in his report, several people opened their eyes somewhat wider. His figures showed that there was a number of dark spots on the company's beautiful national sales map. In these spots, which yielded practically no sales, the company was wasting $30,000 a year for catalogs and direct mail advertising. Further analysis showed that there was little hope of ever building up profitable sales in that territory. Two months' work by the quiet young man saved the company $30,000 a year.

You may be sure that this company has continued to analyze its sales and advertising, and to apply research in all its marketing problems. There is nothing so convincing as a cold cash demonstration of the tremendous value of research to any business which sells and advertises.

Research started as a valuable aid in advertising, but now it has come to be more than merely an aid. It is an absolute necessity to the most successful kind of advertising. Daily, more advertisers are learning that this is true.

Research the Sounding Board and Telescope

Advertising is no longer a hit or miss ballyhoo, but a scientific approach to the consumer, using methods which are becoming more precise every day. Exact knowledge of the product is now required. Complete understanding of marketing conditions and consumers is demanded. Accurate information about distribution factors is absolutely essential. All these necessary foundation stones are procured through advertising research.

Modern advertising is taking on some of the characteristics of the exact sciences, such as chemistry and physics, for as a result of its laboratory work a wonderful library of experience facts is being built up.

But science will never crowd out imagination in the production of effective advertising. Good copy and original campaign plans will always have need for inspiration and art. For all of its modern scientific aspect, advertising will never become a colorless, mathematical, machine-like thing. That would be impossible. But science is necessary in the foundation.

Business changes come about with bewildering swiftness. The wants of consumers shift and vary in almost startling fashion. Population movements and new inventions can change a market completely.

● The wise advertiser keeps his ear to the ground and his eye on the public. Research is his sounding board and his telescope. He must use it constantly. He must search and research, persistently and continuously, if he wants to stay in the parade and if he wants to make his advertising pay.

A Southern Colonel
Comes To Broadway

(Continued from page 24) red letters which spell out sentences that tell why Maxwell House is the nation's favorite coffee. From dusk—all evening long—through the night, and into the small hours of the morning these fiery letters march in a seemingly endless parade around the lower edge of the sign.

The poster panel in the sign and the figures of the colonel and the butler are flood-lighted by powerful lights on the roof below. Thus the poster panel is seen all the time; and, when the bright lights that show the outlines of the colonel and butler go off, the figures are seen as in a picture—the colonel in the picturesque attire of a southern gentleman and the butler in a colored uniform.

● The sign contains 6,600 lamps. It uses a capacity load of 140 kilowatt electric current. The following material was consumed in its construction: 385 feet of red luminous tubing, 6,400 lbs. of sheet metal, 200 lbs.

of solder, 130 lbs. of tape, 1,500 lbs. of angle iron, and 60,150 feet of wire.

This is the third electric spectacular sign on Broadway that has told about Maxwell House Coffee. The first one was at Broadway and 36th Street, the second one at Broadway and 48th Street, and now No. 3 is located at Broadway and 46th Street. From its point of vantage this latest sign shines into the very heart of the Times Square district. It looks down upon Broadway—a thronging caldron of humanity. Now the lights turn red and the crowds of pleasure seekers that jam the sidewalks are stopped by the traffic cops. Now the lights turn green, and at every corner the crowd again surges along. When the whistles blow, streams of massed cars shoot forward like sprinters at the crack of the pistol. Above this rush of humanity, up and down both sides of Broadway, is a dazzling array of brilliant lights and signs—the ever changing scenery of light and motion from which the "Great White Way" derives its name.

OUTDOOR ADVERTISING ABROAD

L. N. E. R. Exhibits Posters

The ninth Exhibition of L. N. E. R. posters was opened recently at the New Burlington Galleries, London, by the Right Hon. J. H. Thomas, M. P. Mr. Thomas said: "Whether you are a critic or a mere interested spectator there is a real moral to be drawn from this particular venture—a moral which applies equally to the nation. Railway companies are no exceptions to the general rule. They are passing through a difficult and troublesome period. There is inevitably a demand for rigid economy. But the L. N. E. R. has had the courage to stage this exhibition and so advertise the virtues of the company. They have realized the value of advertising however difficult the times may be."

The exhibit was also shown in Edinburgh, Glasgow and Aberdeen.

More Outdoor Advertising Urged in Hong Kong

It is understood that the British Trade Commission now in China on its visit to Hong Kong will endeavor to present to the Government a strong appeal for a more liberal attitude toward outdoor advertising, according to Trade Commissioner David M. Maynard in a Foreign Market bulletin of the United States Department of Commerce.

At present, the Public Works Department of the Government rules that no advertisements may be placed on Government buildings. Permits to erect structures on Crown land are given only in extremely rare instances, there being at present only two such structures in existence. When a panel is to be erected on private land, two permits must be obtained, one from the Public Works Department stating that the plans for such panels are structurally sound and another from the Police Department certifying that the structure will not constitute a fire menace.

Permits for sky signs in practice are unobtainable. The objection to them is that they would be a potential danger during the terrific typhoons which visit the colony periodically. The Government also objects to any electric sign showing motion, or in fact any brilliantly lighted sign facing the water, on the principle that they might be confusing to pilots navigating ships in the harbor. A few years ago, when a company new to the colony introduced an electric sign which threw an advertisement on the sidewalk, there was immediate official objection and the sign was discontinued. One of the managers of a local advertising company states that when he first came to the colony he offered the Government a considerable yearly rental for the use of a sheer rock wall which faced the harbor and upon which he had in mind the erection of a large electric sign. He states that the reaction against this was so violent that petitions were forwarded asking him to leave the colony.

The principal outdoor advertising is done on ferries, river steamers, street cars and busses, especially the Star Ferries operating at frequent intervals between Kowloon and Hong Kong and estimated as carrying over a million passengers per month. The space on these ferries is handled by the Advertising and Publicity Bureau of Hong Kong. Street cars are not important because only a small portion of the foreign population ever travels on them and because they cover only a few miles within the city of Victoria. The Peak Tram, a cable car which carries residents from the lower levels to the exclusive residential area on the Peak and therefore carrying about 100,000 per month, has recently contracted space in these trams and stations, to Millington (Ltd.), a local advertising concern.

In addition to the foregoing, there are bus companies operating a total of 175 busses which cover all parts of the colony, and which sell advertising space.

Up to the present no campaign of advertising has been permitted on the radio, a Government institution. Very few of the motion picture houses display advertisements although an opening wedge has recently been made by one of the local advertising companies. No spectacular scheme of advertising such as harbor displays or sky writing has yet met with the approval of the Government. There have been suggestions made to paint the sails of junks and the sides of some of the ferries operating in the harbor. These schemes have met with a cold reception however. Sandwich men are commonly used on the streets of Hong Kong to advertise some special sale, theatrical performance, or a new brand of goods. Permits for parading the streets with sign boards must be procured through the Police Department. With the wages of these men at roughly $0.15 per day, this is considered an excellent and cheap form of advertising. One general argument used by the Government in support of their attitude, is that spectacular advertising tends to divert the eye of motorists and pedestrians and would thus cause a great increase in accidents.

The Sports Appeal Gets Attention

(Continued from page 7) in magazine and newspaper copy, the wording being expanded slightly in the last two mentioned media.

● Advertising that shows human beings engaged in outdoor activities rescues copy from the bleak and bare trade-mark-and-picture-product type, already mentioned in this story. When copy shows a man and a maid, the love interest is introduced so that we have a touch of romance that finds a responsive echo in the hearts of most people, for it is still true that "all the world loves a lover." Not all of the cigarette posters noted portray romantic close-ups, but many of them do.

Another characteristic of this poster copy is the subtle way in which the sports' theme is handled in both pictorial and word message. For instance, an effective Chesterfield poster showed the figures of a man and a girl, sitting on a rude pier near the water's edge. The girl, attired in airy summer costume, was holding a package of the favored cigarettes to a man in a bathing suit, while both were watching a swimmer putting in to the pier. This swimmer furnished this brief message, appearing in white lettering over his head, "Light one for me!" Since the man on the pier was already holding one fag between his lips, he was evidently reaching for another to have it ready when the swimmer made landing.

This type of advertising that shows members of the human tribe actually enjoying or consuming the product advertised is what has been denominated "emotionalization" of copy. Such copy is valuable because it has a decided tendency to set up emotions in the reader that causes him to wish to consume the thing pictured. The Chesterfield poster of the swimmers was highly emotionalized as was also another, advertising Camels. This display showed two tennis players, the girl in the act of extracting a fag from a package held by her escort.

A single human figure is frequently found to dominate these boards that use the sports' theme as auxiliary to gain reader attention. One particularly timely and effective poster, posted during the football season last fall, showed a big husky, plunging through with one arm outstretched to guard his advance and the other folded about the beloved pigskin. The phrase, "ONE will always stand out!" appearing in an upper corner of the poster, gave point to the figure, while a package of opened Chesterfield's dominated the lower opposite corner. The word, "Chesterfield," in large, rangy letters, was spread across the bottom of the unit.

● A n o t h e r Chesterfield display, featured recently, showed a woman in riding togs on a dashing iron gray horse. The graceful rider was rising in the saddle as the horse sprang to take a hurdle, unseen in the picture. "GOOD TASTE takes the lead!" in the form of a streamer across the top of the copy, and the ubiquitous opened package of Chesterfield's were the only other features of this copy except the word "Chesterfield" in familiar type face at the bottom.

A poster that showed a single girlish figure in stylish swim suit has been used effectively to advertise Catalina Swim Suits. This board showed how the sports' theme can sometimes be tied in with the merchandising of certain items that are used in sports themselves.

Not all items or products can be effectively advertised through the use of the sports' theme, it must be admitted, but it is reasonable to contend that the alert copy writer, blessed with a sense of originality, can frequently make the sports' theme work effectively for him. This theme can be used to advantage in the advertising of food products, dentrifices, toilet articles and many other items used throughout the American nation.

It may be used with entire propriety and without running the danger of bordering upon the absurd in advertising such items as radios, for instance. An Atwater Kent radio poster, used last fall, made effective use of the football term, "Pass," which suggests a lot to every football enthusiast. This display showed an evening scene in the home of an American family. Of course, a radio cabinet dominated the central portion of the copy. To one side was Sonny, six years old with helmet on, passing a ball from "center position" to Dad, who had thrown his paper aside and was holding his hands to receive the ball. The discarded newspaper by Dad's easy chair showed in bold, black headlines the words, "Big Game," and served to give point to the general theme, which was summarized by this streamer under the scene: "A Pass to All that's on the Air," meaning, of course, that the radio, so advertised, was just that.

● This was effective poster copy, and is cited to show the versatility of the sports' theme in gaining reader attention for outdoor advertising.

- - -

Contribute Posters for A.F.A. Meet

Through the efforts of the Publicity Committee of the Advertising Federation of America, the 24-sheet poster design shown on this page is now being displayed in every part of New York City where business men travel or have their offices.

In all, seventy-five 24-sheet posters, each occupying a space twelve feet high and twenty-five feet long, have been placed at strategic points in such localities as Downtown Manhattan, near Pennsylvania and Grand Central Stations, on railroads entering New York, and on the motor highways leading to Westchester and Long Island.

The design was painted by Otis Shepard, well-known poster artist, and the posters were lithographed by the McCandlish Lithograph Corporation of Philadelphia, both having cheerfully consented to contribute their work to the Federation. The advertising space was contributed by the New York branch of the General Outdoor Advertising Co., through Kerwin H. Fulton.

Laying out the Poster

(Continued from page 27) the units to the desired number. The series used by Palmolive is about as high in quality as any I can call to mind. The caption at the upper left, the dominating illustration (which in itself tells the story of the beauty to be had) off center to the left and the subordinate copy and package at the right. These posters have all that can be asked of any design.

In the general scramble for attention the elements stage, we must determine just where the name comes in. Putting it first or too prominently will close your story before the reader has had a chance to know anything about the product. Put the bait first, tell the reader what this product has to offer, then the name. The name is important and every means must be made to make it readable even though it does not dominate the poster.

Here we run into the problem of logotypes. Consider just how well adapted it is to the quick and long shot readings it will get outdoors. It is good, of course, to use the same logotype everywhere, if possible. But old-time users of outdoor have sacrificed the continuity thus obtained to adopt a different style of letter for outdoor advertising. Chesterfield letters the package in Old English while using Garamond outdoor. Carnation Milk uses this same style outdoors instead of the shaded script as on the can. Involved designs, unusual lettering and similar devices interfere with the legibility and must be avoided to get full value from outdoor advertising.

The effectiveness of the illustration depends a great deal upon its silhouette value. If, for example, a woman is shown drinking from a cup, the hand and the cup should be so placed as to stand out against the background. If they are put in front of the figure in a full front or three-quarters view, the illustration may be just as good from a strictly technical standpoint, but it will not be as direct—as easily understood—it will be distinctly less effective from an outdoor advertising angle.

Do you remember the Chesterfield girl posed so pertly? Did it attract attention! Women even copied the clothes and merchants in certain cities sold Chesterfield Dresses. That is a superb example of what the correct pose will do.

There have been many other beautiful girls portrayed upon the 24-sheets, but few have made such a hit. I believe it was nothing more or less than the confident, swanky way she was sitting. It is the same principle the movie director uses when the actor is "back stage." There the gestures become more pronounced, the action almost violent. On the "close-ups" the action is toned and slowed down. If you want to make a figure help express your thought, depend a great deal upon the pose and action. If the illustration is a closeup, facial expression will do the work.

The dealer's imprint is an increasing problem. It adds another element and unfortunately is often of a nature foreign to our design. Some names are long and others short, all of which makes it still more difficult.

In some cases the white strip across the bottom is satisfactory. I believe I was the first to use that strip, and I did it because the design permitted, almost called for it. Many times, however, it looks out of place—as though pasted on as an afterthought. It should be planned to look as though it were a part of the original composition and the color in which it is printed will play a big part in obtaining this result. Do not lay out a poster and then endeavor to find a suitable place to put the imprint.

In closing I would say there are no hard and fast rules for layout. Good composition after all is only a matter of common sense—common sense in placing elements and in leaving them out. Simplicity is the keynote of good poster design. We should always remember that our task is not merely the creation of a beautiful design. We must make sales for the advertiser. The entire value of a beautiful design is to create a favorable reaction in the minds of prospective customers, changing them into Purchasers. The public is the final judge of the poster and no judgment is more severe than the refusal to buy. Keep that in mind when conceiving art work.

Oppose Advertising Tax

The Kentucky Division of the Travelers' Protective Association of America went on record in opposition to a tax on advertising in any form. The organization pointed out that various legislatures in recent months have been urged to tax outdoor and newspaper advertising. The proposals have been made either as a means of regulation or as a source of revenue. Such proposals "would discriminate between advertising advancement and otherwise violate established principles of taxation," in the opinion of the Travelers.

■   ■   ■

Pumental With Houston P. A. Co.

Mr. A. S. Pumental, formerly southwest representative for Donaldson Lithographing and Printing Company, is now in charge of local sales for the Houston Poster Advertising Co. Mr. Pumental was connected with the plant in the same capacity several years ago before going with the Donaldson Company. He is president-elect of the Rotary Club and is very active in local civic affairs.

■   ■   ■

Canadian Association Holds Poster Exhibit

The Poster Advertising Association of Canada recently announced the opening at the Art Gallery of Toronto the second large exhibition of British and foreign travel posters, many of which came from the Empire Marketing Board.

Augmenting the Association's collection, which includes the latest releases of the London and North-Eastern Railway recently exhibited in London, England, was an important loan exhibit from the British Society of Poster Designers.

Cycol Capitalizes on Navy Acceptance

(Continued from page 32) Advertising Manager for the Associated Oil Company, pointed out. "We secured permission from the Navy Department at Washington to advertise the fact that the United States Navy had bought Cycol on a service cost basis and to explain what the service cost method is. And because the Cycol selected by the Navy is the same as the motor oil sold at Associated service stations we decided to use outdoor advertising on a large scale to tell the story to car drivers throughout the West.

● "We contracted for 66 bulletins reaching from one end of the Pacific Coast to the other for a term of three years, copy to be changed every six months. Wherever possible the effort was made to get head-on locations— or locations with long visibility—and we built up our design to get the greatest benefit from this visibility. In doing this simplicity of design was the aim. An aircraft carrier was suggested on the high seas in tones of blue, the aircraft carrier being selected because of its unusual design and increased attention value. Color masses were simple and the message brief.

"The Cycol medallion was shown with the words THE NAVY USES CYCOL— SO SHOULD YOU! also 'Lowest Service Cost,' the latter statement being the campaign slogan."

In this slogan the Associated has something tangible to say about motor oils which is really the backbone of the whole campaign. As explained by Mr. Deal, companies have talked about long mileage, endurance, viscosity,—and while these statements have value they do not permit of a ready check-up by the motorist in using oil in his own car. Lowest service cost, however, which means price divided by results, does give a check-up on the merit of the oil which the motorist can make for himself.

● The admirable co-ordination of the different media is one of the highlights of the campaign, and a tie-in with the general plan is a large and unique variety of dealer helps. Half a million blotters, for instance, reproduce the highway bulletin design, carrying the message to dealers and car drivers. Electrolier boards at the service stations also say to the public "Lowest Service Cost," and dealers and attendants have been provided with white "gob" hats and wear a button stating THE NAVY USES CYCOL—SO SHOULD YOU! The company's house organ, "The Record," carried a full page announcement of the outdoor campaign on the back cover of the April issue together with a picture of the first design, which went up last March.

Another tie-up is a comprehensive and beautiful brochure on the award, prepared for the use of the sales personnel and for distribution among a selected list. This 28-page book, richly illustrated with war vessels and equipment, explains in detail the brief message which the outdoor bulletin stamps upon the public consciousness.

"The importance of impressive outdoor bulletins was fully appreciated in presenting a new and tangible selling message which the motoring public can readily understand and apply to purchases of oil for their own cars," Mr. Deal said. "It is the medium through which an oil company can reach the desired type of trade at the most propitious time."

● Mr. Deal has had a broad experience in analyzing outdoor locations and went over the ground personally to select the sites for the 66 boards, which run from the Mexican to the Canadian border and constitute a general coverage of major Pacific Coast traffic. These locations alternate on the highways so as to reach traffic north and south and cover a circulation coming and going to metropolitan centers as well as important localized circulation in small towns. The route of travel follows the main highways from San Francisco east and north and south.

AND AFTER YOU'VE
READ THIS ISSUE . . .

what are you going to do with it? Left on your desk it will soon be dog-eared and disreputable. If put away it will not be available for instant reference.

How much more satisfactory to have not only this issue but all back issues in a neat binder ready for instant reference. We have one here ready for you to use - - and only $1.80.

Send check or money order today to

ADVERTISING OUTDOORS

165 WEST WACKER DRIVE   CHICAGO, ILLINOIS

SPENDING TENDENCIES

1

FRESNO, CALIF.

GENERAL BUSINESS CONDITIONS: The consensus of opinion among the leading business men of this city is that the depression has reached its lowest point and it is felt that there will be a steady increase in all retail and wholesale trade from now on. Fresno is the center of the entire San Joaquin Valley trading area. One of the biggest factors that has brought the depression to this district has been the yearly failure in the marketing of our fruit products. Under the new arrangement, whereby the Federal Farm Board has taken an active interest in the solution of our problem, it is felt that within a reasonable time conditions will be well established in all lines. Bank clearings for May, 1931, were $18,350,172.00 as compared with $20,579,000.00 for the same month last year. Building permits for this city were $75,442.00 for May, 1931, as compared with $77,497.00 for the same month last year. For 1931 to date new construction and alterations total $501,302.00 as compared with $548,331.00 to date last year. The general opinion is that this difference between building permits and alterations between the two years will be gradually overcome with the greater showing for this current year.

Fresno being on the direct route to the Sierra Nevada wonderland and playgrounds such as General Grant National Park, Sequoia National Park, Huntington Lake and Yosemite National Park, will receive a very heavy tourist trade from now until fall and from this source considerable additional revenue will be brought to this district.

MOVING PICTURE ATTENDANCE: No exact figures for comparison were available, but from observation it is well known that the theatre attendance is slightly on the decrease. However, this may be entirely a local condition owing to the fact that the summer temperature has been a little greater than usual and when cool weather comes again, theatre attendance will undoubtedly be normal or slightly on the increase.

AUTOMOTIVE: In this division of facts, it is well known that automobile sales, both in new and used cars have shown a decrease. In April of this year for Fresno County, sales of new cars totaled only 303.

2
LOS ANGELES, CALIF.

GENERAL BUSINESS CONDITIONS: There was little change during April as compared with March. Aside from Easter and business from the Hoover Dam offices, there was no special impetus.

Construction dropped off during April, showing a decline of about 50% as compared with March, 1931.

Agricultural conditions promise considerable improvement due to the heavy rainfall during the month. Livestock prices were down slightly in practically all classes. Water commerce figures showed totals in both volume and value lower than for previous months.

Employment showed a slight decline compared with the month of March. One very interesting feature of the employment situation during the month was the gain in the employment of the petroleum companies. Of course the average earnings per employee have been reduced because of the adoption by many companies of the five-day week, but the figures indicate strikingly that there has been a decided increase in the number of workers on payrolls.

Crude oil production during April averaged 526,000 barrels per day. This is near the figure set by the curtailment agreement, but rumors of further curtailment are beginning to be heard. Prices of crude and refined products were practically unchanged during the month.

Fred W. Beetson, Executive Vice President of the Motion Picture Producers Association, reports: "Announcements of new schedules for the forthcoming fiscal year, by the major studios indicated a continued rising barometer in the field of production activity for the motion picture industry."

AUTOMOTIVE: Figures just released show that gasoline sales during the first quarter of 1931 were over 14% greater than for the same period of 1930. The gain was approximately 41,000,000 gallons, of which 36,000,000 gallons was gained by the nine large companies. This is the same trend that showed during the price war of last summer.

3
INDIANAPOLIS, INDIANA

GENERAL BUSINESS CONDITIONS: There was an approximate attendance of 168,000 people at the automobile race which always makes for a large amount of activity before the race and to some extent after.

AUTOMOTIVE: The new car sales for April totaled 1,518 which is an increase of two cars over April, 1931. This is a gain of 27% over March of this year and shows that the conditions in Indianapolis are on the upward trend.

The gasoline figures released from the State Capitol show that for the first four months of 1931, there is an increase of 6,492,103 gallons consumption over the same period of 1930 and an increase of 9,368,000 gallons over the same period in 1929.

4
BURLINGTON, IOWA

GENERAL BUSINESS CONDITIONS: The trade territory has been extended by improvement of roads. The general depression has affected general business conditions somewhat in this community.

Factories are running from 60 to 80% with one or two exceptions where they are doing even better. Favorable weather conditions have advanced farm work in the trade territory. It is hard to determine just what is normal. We have about 70% as much volume of business this year as compared with 1929 so far.

5
DAVENPORT, IA.

GENERAL BUSINESS CONDITIONS: Men's clothing business is off about 15% in the month of May as compared with 1930. Jewelry business is off from 25 to 30% comparing May of 1931 with May, 1930. The drug business has increased about 5% for the first quarter of 1931 as compared with the first quarter of 1930. There is an increase in the cigar and cigarette business of about 15%. There is a decrease of about 10% in the hotel business and a decrease of from 10 to 15% in gross business in restaurants, but they show a greater profit in 1931 over the same period as in 1930. This is due to a decrease in cost of food stuffs without a decrease in the cost of the selling price.

MOVING PICTURE ATTENDANCE: Theatre business is off about 10%.

AUTOMOTIVE: Automobile registration is off about 12½% comparing May, 1931, with May, 1930.

6
DES MOINES, IOWA

GENERAL BUSINESS CONDITIONS: One of the largest stores had an annual sale, on June 5th and this particular sale brought more sales transactions than any other day in the history of the department store. The volume in dollars and cents was larger than any day in June in the history of the organization.

The first five months of 1931 showed a total of building permits of $1,674,517.00 which is an increase of nearly a half million dollars over the same period in 1930.

AUTOMOTIVE: Gasoline tax collections for the first five months of 1931 were $4,552,119.00 as compared with $4,158,673.00 for the same period of 1930. May receipts showed a decrease over May of 1930.

7
MASON CITY, IOWA

GENERAL BUSINESS CONDITIONS: Building permits are $30,000.00 more for May, 1931, than for May, 1930. The total permits are over $100,000.00 more. The nice thing about May permits is that they are mostly new homes which gives more labor than a larger job.

A small wage reduction in a few lines are reported.

Merkel Day (A Department Store) was 12% over Merkel Day of 1930.

The Wolf Furniture Store reported a large increase in business to date over a year ago.

Gildner Brothers, Clothiers, reported that their May volume was the same as in 1930.

8
LOUISVILLE, KY.

GENERAL BUSINESS CONDITIONS: "In several branches of the local retail trade, sales are showing an upward swing, which are considered to be somewhat better than the seasonal gain. For men's hats and shoes, and women's wearing apparel, there has been a gain in demand, which is encouraging. Orders for men's shirts have been showing a steady gain since the middle of March. There is a better sentiment noticeable in the wholesale drug trade but the improvement has not been translated into sales as yet," according to Dun's Review.

The volume of hardware sales is practically on a par with that of the comparative period in 1930, with a slight improvement noted since April 1st. The demand for automobiles is better than at any time during the last six months. The movement of fresh fruits and vegetables is satisfactory and the demand for preserved fruits and jellies is holding up remarkably well. Consumers of flour are showing a preference for the better grades. Some branches of the box business are exceeding last year's production figures. There has been a steady gain in the output of tobacco products but the leaf business is showing the between-season dullness.

Industrial power consumption in Louisville showed but a slight decrease which was much less than the average for other cities.

Building outlays in Louisville at the end of the first four months of 1931 were 27% ahead of the corresponding four months last year.

The Alexander Hamilton Institute Business Conditions Service states that the business trend in Louisville is "up."

AUTOMOTIVE: Gasoline tax collections in Kentucky for the first quarter of 1931 show an increase of 12.3% over the first quarter of 1930. The totals during the first quarter of this year were approximately $438,-

415.00 as compared with $390,179.00 for the first quarter of last year.

9
SPRINGFIELD, MASS.

GENERAL BUSINESS CONDITIONS: Slight increase noted in employment. Business conditions as a whole compare favorably with similar period in 1930.

AUTOMOTIVE: Registry of motor vehicles reports increase of 425 registrations for the first four months of the year over a corresponding period in 1930. The total for four months this year is 55,875 as compared with 55,450 for April of 1930.

10
ST. JOSEPH, MO.

GENERAL BUSINESS CONDITIONS: Business conditions seem to be improving slowly but surely. The local merchants report an improvement in the retail trade and also that collections are better.

MOVING PICTURE ATTENDANCE: Moving picture attendance continues to be about 10% less for the month of May, 1931, than for the same month in 1930.

11
BILLINGS, MONTANA

GENERAL BUSINESS CONDITIONS: There is a great deal of building going on which makes the employment situation very good.

MOVING PICTURE ATTENDANCE: Moving picture attendance for the first five months in 1931 was off about 10% as compared with the same period in 1930.

AUTOMOTIVE: Automobile registration is approximately the same in 1931 as it was in 1930.

Gasoline consumption for the first five months in 1931 is about the same as in 1930.

12
BUTTE, MONTANA

GENERAL BUSINESS CONDITIONS: General business conditions in Butte are, of course, subject to the rise and fall of the metal prices due to the fact that our principal industry is mining. However, we have a substantial business in distribution as Butte is the logical distributing center of the state.

The installation of natural gas in Butte and this vicinity during the next four or five months will entail capital expenditures of approximately fourteen million dollars. This investment is being made by the Montana Power Company and those companies associated with it which speaks well for the confidence of our major industries in the future activities of this locality.

We have a minimum of unemployment due to the fact that most of our unemployed have moved to other localities.

13
MILES CITY, MONTANA

GENERAL BUSINESS CONDITIONS: General business conditions look a bit encouraging. There is not so much building in the city but there is quite a bit of paving being done. There is considerable road work under way in this locality.

The tourist season has opened which is a great help to the territory in general.

The city is in the midst of a sheep-raising country and sheep shearing is to start this month which means added wealth to all in the territory.

14
OMAHA, NEBRASKA

GENERAL BUSINESS CONDITIONS: The census reports reveal the volume of business which Omaha enjoyed during 1929, together with the city's persistency in staying in eighteenth place in the country's bank clearings, have given a cheerful aspect to business conditions here at this time.

Increases in bank debits have been steady and on May 10th a week's total of debits was $51,279,262.22, the highest since September 18, 1930. This was the result of heavy buying during some attractive merchandising sales by department stores.

The Harding Cream Company, large manufacturer of ice cream and butter, has opened a new $50,000 bottling works, producing fruit beverages and ginger ale. The Coca Cola Company has taken new quarters where a single new machine will fill 225,000 bottles in a week. The Central Ice Service Company of Kansas City is building a $120,000 branch here. Hayden's Department Store is making $200,000 worth of improvements. Several other firms have taken larger quarters, and the Baker Ice Machine Company and Icelect Corporation, both makers of electric refrigeration systems, reported heavy shipments to foreign countries.

An important indicator is that the young business men in the Junior Chamber of Commerce were able to stage a three-day air racing meet involving expenditure of nearly $28,000 and to make it pay its way.

Signs of real estate activity are evident in reports of the various companies, many of which had unusually good sales during April and the early part of May. Several of them are taking new and larger quarters and all are looking for improved conditions in this business soon.

15
BINGHAMTON, N. Y.

GENERAL BUSINESS CONDITIONS: General business conditions are only fair.

MOVING PICTURE ATTENDANCE: Reported as being fair.

AUTOMOTIVE: Automobile registrations is 5,000 trucks and 30,000 pleasure cars.

16
NEW YORK, N. Y.

GENERAL BUSINESS CONDITIONS: The volume of business for R. H. Macy & Co. during the past week was above the same period of any previous year, and the increase has necessitated the employment of 850 more persons than were on the payroll a year ago.

The number of sales last week was 42% greater than for the first week in June, 1930, and the increase in revenue also was very substantial. Other retail establishments likewise have noted an increase in trade as compared with May.

Said Mr. Straus of R. H. Macy & Co., "It is common knowledge that there is a tremendous oversupply of raw materials and commodity prices have been dropping rapidly." The R. H. Macy Co. took advantage of this fact and had advertising campaigns emphasizing the present low prices of raw materials and the need for normal purchasing on the part of the public to aid in overcoming the depression, and results are apparent.

There seem to be new high records in the sale of sterling silver and sharp gains have been noted in so-called luxury merchandise—diamonds, Oriental rugs and the like.

AMUSEMENTS: Theatrical attendance, both legitimate and moving, is still below normal. The attendance at baseball games and athletic events compares favorably with 1930.

17
SYRACUSE, N. Y.

GENERAL BUSINESS CONDITIONS: Various accepted indices of general business activity as reported by the Syracuse Chamber of Commerce are not entirely in agreement, some moving up slightly while others sag. On the whole, however, business may be said to be holding its own.

Below are some figures which compare the first four months of 1931 with the same period in 1930.

	1931	1930
Value of Building		
Permits	$2,813,303	$1,604,650
Bank Clearings	84,373,948	96,955,448
Wholesale Power		
Sales	40,758,139 kw hrs	52,385,703 kw hrs

Deposits in commercial and savings banks totaled $208,167,308.00 when the last report was received. On a comparable date in 1930, they were $209,026,917.07 which shows that they are about equal.

18

GREENVILLE, SO. CAROLINA

GENERAL BUSINESS CONDITIONS:

Postal receipts, first quarter 1930......$55,872.73
Postal receipts, first quarter 1931...... 58,202.03

This shows an increase for 1931 of $2,330.03.

About 90% of the merchants in all lines report that while their volume of business is larger in 1931 than in 1930, the volume in income is about the same to a small decrease due to lower prices in all lines.

There is about a million dollar's worth of road work being done in the county. Work involving the spending of a half million dollars is to begin on a sewer contract.

Bank clearings for May, 1930, were about 10% better than those of May, 1931.

The textile mills while not running full time are running about 15% more than at the same time in 1930.

AUTOMOTIVE:

Chevrolet agency reports:

Sales May 1930 New Cars 50 Used cars 81
Sales May 1931 New Cars 60 Used cars 89

This shows an increase of ten for the new cars and eight for the used cars.

The Ford agency, due to a change in agency, have no records for May, 1930, but reports an increase of 21% in May, 1931, over April, 1931.

The total registration for all cars in Greenville for the month of May, 1931, was 167, but there were no available records for 1930.

19

ABERDEEN, SO. DAK.

GENERAL BUSINESS CONDITIONS: General business conditions have not changed much from last month. We have apparently been raised out of the depression zone to a somewhat higher level, but are held stationary there for the time being at least.

Babson considers South Dakota one of the bright spots on his map. Potentially that is correct. There is purchasing power here and the farmer is not nearly as down trodden as the politician would have some of us believe.

MOVING PICTURE ATTENDANCE: Moving picture attendance has fallen off a trifle from the previous month. However, that is to be expected at this time of the year even in normal times.

AUTOMOTIVE: Chevrolet continues to outsell Ford as it has done every month this year in South Dakota. Total new car registrations are about equal with 1930 so far this year.

Gasoline consumption is still increasing as is only natural at this time of the year. It is about 20% more in 1931 than it was in 1930.

20

BROWNWOOD, TEXAS

GENERAL BUSINESS CONDITIONS: Conditions are improving rapidly in this section. The harvesting of one of the largest grain crops in this section's history is in progress. Unemployment has just about disappeared. Business firms in nearly every line report that business has been better every month since March 1st than for the same month in 1930. We have had no business failures during the past ninety days.

There seems to be a gradual settling of business to an even keel. Real estate is beginning to move and normal business is reflecting the fact that people are beginning to buy more.

MOVING PICTURE ATTENDANCE: Moving picture attendance during the month of May showed a marked increase over the same month of last year but is far short of being satisfactory.

AUTOMOTIVE: Car registrations have shown an increase each month since March over 1930. Chevrolet and Ford are leading the sales but neither are showing the increase in per cent of sales as the higher priced cars such as Dodge and Buick.

Gasoline consumption continues to rise, sales being only slightly lower than those reached in late 1928 and early 1929.

21

EL PASO, TEXAS

GENERAL BUSINESS CONDITIONS: Most lines are reporting "stationary." Some lines are picking up a little, and generally speaking, business is better than "fair."

MOVING PICTURE ATTENDANCE: Every year about this time, the attendance at local theatres drops about 25% and lasts through the summer; at the present time, the attendance is about 35% below the average.

AUTOMOTIVE: The most progressive automobile dealer here tells us that business in that line is anything but good. Their business is only fair and the cars they sell require consistent sales effort.

22

HOUSTON, TEXAS

GENERAL BUSINESS CONDITIONS: For the first four months in 1931, Department Store sales were approximately 12% below the same period in 1930. Three of the larger stores interviewed in June had gained sufficiently in April and May to place their sales for the first five months of this year approximately 3% below the same period last year. Generally speaking, retail trade has been better than anticipated and is just slightly below that of last year.

Wholesale trade has been suffering more from small short orders than from lack of volume. Stabilization of commodity prices must come before the wholesalers take an optimistic attitude.

Employment as reported by 648 local concerns indicates 4% less than for 1930.

Building permits for May, 1931, are 67% of the total for May, 1930. For the first five months of 1931, the total of $5,627,258.00 is 74% of the total for the same period in 1930.

MOVING PICTURE ATTENDANCE: Moving picture attendance experienced a drop of 25% in May as compared with April. About 15% of this is attributed to the usual seasonal activity, 5% to depression and the balance to the low average pulling power of the pictures run.

AUTOMOTIVE: New car sales in May, 1931, were 89% of the sales in May, 1930. The first five months this year amounted to 76% of the sales for the same period in 1930.

Gasoline sales are estimated to be approximately 5% below the normal quota for this period.

23
WACO, TEXAS

GENERAL BUSINESS CONDITIONS: General business conditions are only fair.

MOVING PICTURE ATTENDANCE: For the month of May, the attendance in Waco was approximately 12,000.

AUTOMOTIVE: Gasoline consumption for the city of Waco and trading territories is about 700,000 gallons.

Automobile registrations for the month of May are 771 cars. Note: No comparative figures were given.

24
SPOKANE, WASHINGTON

GENERAL BUSINESS CONDITIONS: Increasing activity in the building trades and a very comprehensive street building program are beginning to take care of the labor situation to a very appreciable extent. The surrounding country shows a decided upward swing in sentiment, this being based on the fact that the prospective wheat crop for 1931 is the best in many years. Decidedly few business failures are being reported and though retail business is somewhat slow yet, many of the merchants are reporting a very fair volume. Car loadings are on the increase, this of course, being attributable to the fact the spring produce and stock shipments are beginning to move.

MOVING PICTURE ATTENDANCE: The industry feels that it still has two quiet months ahead of it but is in no way alarmed over the decline in business inasmuch as more people are seeing the shows than for the corresponding period last year. The Fox Theatres are just completing a million dollar playhouse in this city, which is having the effect of stimulating the industry as a whole.

AUTOMOTIVE: Gasoline consumption for May, 1931, shows a decrease of 10% for the corresponding month of 1930. Within the past few days, however, a decided gain has been shown and oil officials feel that their business will show an upward trend through the remainder of the year. The first quarter of 1931, as compared with 1930, shows a small increase in new car sales and a very strong market for used cars. In fact, the used car market is practically sold out.

25
WHEELING, W. VA.

GENERAL BUSINESS CONDITIONS: General business conditions are reported as being fairly good. Merchants are doing a good volume of business on a very small profit. Industries are reported to be operating about 80% throughout the territory.

Bank deposits have increased and the general outlook fairly good.

The Associated Charities report shows a drop of about 40% in families receiving aid.

MOVING PICTURE ATTENDANCE: Moving picture attendance is reported as being very good.

AUTOMOTIVE: Automobile sales are fair and gasoline consumption is on the increase.

26
MILWAUKEE, WIS.

GENERAL BUSINESS CONDITIONS: General business conditions in this market continue a slow but steady upward trend. There has been considerable building of new homes, which reflected itself in an increase in the cost of building materials.

The amount of distressed real estate on the market due to foreclosures is relatively small compared with the national average.

Considerable interest has been shown in the opening of the Milwaukee stock exchange, and listings on the exchange are increasing daily with local issues in the majority.

MOVING PICTURE ATTENDANCE: Moving picture attendance continues to be spotty mainly because of lack of sufficient outstanding productions.

Outdoor amusements are being well patronized and circulation figures on main highways in this area report a record traffic over Memorial Day.

AUTOMOTIVE: Automobile registrations show a seasonable increase and gasoline consumption for the month of May compared with April is considerably heavier.

THE PRODUCTS OF 10,000,000 WORKERS ARE SOLD THROUGH OUTDOOR ADVERTISING

OUTDOOR ADVERTISING
A NATIONAL SELLING FORCE

In ten thousand American factories, workmen turn out products to meet the nation's needs. Every pay-day 10,000,000 envelopes contain the rewards of their labor —their share from countless sales of fine new articles for the use and comfort of the American people . . . To maintain this flow of merchandise, to keep the wheels of industry constantly turning, to keep those pay envelopes filled week after week—these are the functions of Outdoor Advertising...The progressive local merchant and national advertiser both realize the powerful force exerted by Outdoor Advertising in the distribution and sale of their merchandise . . . Under present competitive conditions only progressive merchants and manufacturers can survive. Only THEIR workers can be sure of steady employment.

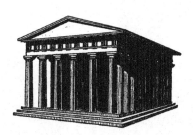

Advertising Outdoors

A magazine devoted to the interests of the Outdoor Advertiser

Vol. 2, No. 7

CONTENTS for JULY 1931

Harold L. Eves
Editor

Ralph B. Patch, *Associate Editor*
James P. Dobyns, *Advertising Manager*

Eastern Advertising Representatives:
Walworth and Wormser,
420 Lexington Ave., New York City.
Western Advertising Representatives:
Dwight Early,
100 N. La Salle St., Chicago

ADVERTISING OUTDOORS is published on the 1st of every month by the Outdoor Advertising Association of America, Inc., 165 W. Wacker Drive, Chicago, Ill. Telephone Randolph 1692. Harold L. Eves, Editor and Manager.
Subscriptions for the United States, Cuba, Porto Rico. Hawaii and the Philippines, $3.00 a year in advance; Mexico and Canada, $3.25; for all other countries, $3.50. Thirty cents the copy. Make all checks, money orders, etc., payable to Outdoor Advertising Association of America, Inc.
Entered as second-class matter, March 21st, 1930, at the Post Office at Chicago, Ill., under the act of March 3, 1879, by Outdoor Advertising Association of America, Inc. Printed in U. S. A.

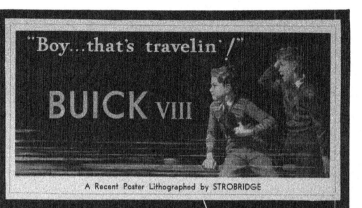

"Boy...that's travelin'/"

BUICK VIII

A Recent Poster Lithographed by STROBRIDGE

The STROBRIDGE LITHOGRAPHING CO.

*Originators of the
24 Sheet Poster
and producers of
its finest examples*

CINCINNATI, OHIO

THE "OUTDOOR" INDUSTRY LOOKS AHEAD

NOW is the time for business to capitalize the future. It is the time to study the experience of the yesterday and chart the course for tomorrow. This is the time for business reincarnation.

Miracles of management must be performed if a business or an industry is to carry on. New aims and viewpoints are the theme of today. There will be better business *tomorrow* if we go after it *now*.

New ways must take the place of old ones. A new outlook must be developed. Only with new ideas can we surpass the amazing record of progress that America has made. Only that way can American industry overcome the merchandising obstacles that have put it in the red.

Modern Outdoor Advertising, as it is understood today, did not exist until the last part of the 19th century. It has since climbed steadily in effectiveness, continuity, dignity and dominance. Today in its organized form 17,500 towns are operated by some 1200 individual business organizations.

Here is a market coverage with which no other major medium of advertising can be compared.

Today Outdoor Advertising faces new problems. The Outdoor industry has become of age. It must take its part in the great job of merchandising America's goods. No longer can it consider itself apart in advertising problems. The Outdoor industry must shoulder its responsibilities along with the other major forms of advertising.

The men at the head of the Outdoor industry have proved themselves capable of handling the job of broadening the horizon in the "Outdoor" picture. Practically the entire industry has joined together so that Outdoor Advertising campaigns can be properly planned and presented to America's industries. The result is an organization to be known as Outdoor Advertising, Incorporated.

This company will act as the industry's representative. It is their best effort to improve the merchandising possibilities of their medium. This issue of the magazine Advertising Outdoors has been prepared so that its readers might better understand this new movement of the "Outdoor" industry.

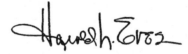

Buying 100 Cents With the 1931 ADVERTISING DOLLAR

by Myles Standish

In order to intelligently approach this highly complex problem, we must first make clear some basic economic facts that appear to have been entirely overlooked in the heat of the present controversy.

● Within our political organization centuries of progress in commerce have evolved an intricate, highly organized industrial machine, more vitally affecting the practical lives of our people than any other form of organization. Within its ranks every employed man, woman and child takes his place. Upon the successful and profitable operation of this industrial machine directly depends not only the standard of living of our citizenry, but the very maintenance of our government and its ideals. It is the source of all income. Any impairment of its proper operation is instantly reflected in decreased income, lower standards of living and, if continued, a national deficit.

The component parts of this machine are industries, which, employing millions of workers, vast amounts of raw materials and huge sums of capital, produce merchandise or services which supply the wants of other millions employed in other industries.

● Exactly as mutual information and understanding are necessary within an industry for efficient production, so must industry always maintain close and constant communication with the public which it serves, to announce and explain the products or services which it produces. Steady, efficient communication means steady consumption, steady production and steady employment. To deprive industry of this means of communication is to kill it. Any unreasonable or ill-advised restriction of the avenues of communication is a blow struck straight at the heart of our national prosperity.

Out of the early fumbling attempts of awakening commerce to establish such a system of communication, has grown a giant industry called Advertising. It serves all industry—it is the life blood of commerce.

Every major advertising medium of today has stood the scathing test of centuries of time. The outworn, the obsolete, the futile, have fallen beneath the relentless tread of progress.

● Only the tried and proven, whose service knows no time, have come through the fire. And of all of these, the oldest in point of service—the most venerable in antiquity, is Outdoor Advertising. Two thousand years ago it carried the entire burden. Today it is as powerful and vigorous as ever. Let no man treat lightly the judgment of two thousand years.

The early Egyptians knew the crier, announcing the arrival of ships and extolling in lurid terms, their cargoes of desirable merchandise. Here Outdoor Advertising performed the function of one of its de-

Twenty-three million automobiles take all America out-of-doors.

scendants, the newspaper, to be born 1600 years later.

The store sign was a commonplace in Rome 2000 years ago. The bush for the wine shop, the mule and mill for the baker, are not a far cry from the modern barber pole and the shoemaker's boot, or even the more dazzling neon sign.

In Pompeii, painted walls told the story of the gladiatorial games, baths, theatrical performances and taverns. An interesting example of a painted wall at the gates of Pompeii, reads, "Traveller—going from here to the twelfth tower—there Sarinus keeps a tavern—this is to request you to enter—farewell." ●The modern hotel, with its highway bulletin at the entrance to a city, has not proceeded far from this point. It is interesting to note that these forms, representing the peak of advertising development in ancient times, were all some form of Outdoor Advertising, and for a very good reason. Paper and printing was unknown. The ancients used the only tools at their command as effectively as possible.

During the so-called Age of Chivalry, commerce, cloaked in shame, all but disappeared. Knights worthily occupied their time in playing games, slaughtering dragons and robbing the people, who dragged out their miserable existences in serfdom, squalor and misery, unless they were more quickly and mercifully terminated at the end of a rope for some trivial offense.

It was business and business men who led Europe out of the darkness. The Hanseatic League, starting with two cities on the Baltic, desirous of conducting commerce, within 100 years included 70 cities. Determined to protect their property rights and their right to do business, these cities armed their merchantmen to the teeth and through their united force, broke the back of feudalism, ruthlessly swept piracy and banditry from the lanes of commerce and opened up the way for the Renaissance.

It was not the condescending patronage of an effete aristocracy, but the hardy vigor of honest trade which provided the general prosperity and leisure which made possible the rebirth of art, learning and science.

As the needs of commerce grew, new forms of advertising sprang up. In England of the Middle Ages, the great signboard era flourished. Due to the illiteracy of the masses, trades were identified both as to kind and location, by symbolic signboards. Many are today treasured as works of art. Holbein, Watteau, Correggio, Hogarth and Benjamin West were sign painters in their day. The famous financial family of Rothschilds thought enough of their father's sign, a red shield, (German "Rotschild") to take it for their name.

● With growing literacy came the written bill, pasted or tacked in public places. And then the engraved handbill, passed out in the streets. Still Outdoor Advertising.

The first printed advertising in book or newspaper form appeared about 1625. By 1652, these new books had so increased in number and the volume of advertising carried in them was so large, especially of cures, that their readers began to protest. Fleetwood Sheppard, favorite of Charles II, wrote, "There is never a mountebank who either by professing of chemistry or any other art, drains money from the people of the nation, but these arch-cheats have a share in the booty. They must have a feeling, forsooth, to authorize the charletain in their news book." As the news book grew, the coffee house keeper, having drawn a large proportion of his trade by the dissemination of news, also protested against this rising form of competition.

In 1712, newspapers in England received a heavy blow. In order to control seditious utterances, the British government placed a tax of one penny on every copy of a newspaper and three shillings upon each advertisement. Addison's Spectator and Daniel Defoe's Review gave up the ghost immediately. This short-sighted action produced a small income to the government but on the other hand, defeated its own purpose by dealing a blow to the growth of internal trade and by retarding the spread of literacy through the increased cost and decreased circulation of the newspapers of the kingdom. In 1853, when this tax was finally removed after doing untold harm, the cost of a yearly subscription to a daily paper in England was between $45.00 and $50.00. The cost of a yearly subscription to a daily newspaper in the United States at the same time was $5.00. This example of ineptitude should be borne carefully in mind when considering the advisability of taxing our tools of distribution.

● To escape the high cost of taxing newspaper advertising and to reach greater circulation than could be reached through the greatly reduced circulation of newspapers, British advertisers turned to poster advertising.

Out of this condition, came the first attempt at organized outdoor advertising conducted by respectable men upon advertising stations leased or owned by them. This was the beginning of modern outdoor advertising as we know it today. During this period, one-quarter of all advertising expenditure was outdoors. With the lifting of the newspaper tax in 1853, newspaper advertising again took a great impetus. The bold type and pictorial copy of the poster which had successfully sold merchandise, began to appear in the advertising columns of the newspapers.

With display advertising, with illustrations and with an environment favorable to rapid growth, publication advertising now grew in leaps and bounds. The spread of education, the lack of transportation facilities and the sedentary habits of the world furnished hothouse conditions for this growth. Every man's home was his castle to which he was chained by the narrow circle of a few hours journey by horse or by bicycle. Travel was uncomfortable, difficult and expensive. Home life was the order of the day. Reading was the universal pastime. The literary society and fireside fun flourished. The general store and the mail order catalogue furnished the necessities and luxuries for half the populace. Books and magazines were few and expensive. The paper was read from cover to cover. The city was considered a Den of Vice.

And then something happened—something which was to stir our society to its foundations—to shake us out of our lethargy, change the living habits of millions of people and send us bounding forward on the road to progress and prosperity at a rate the world had never before dreamed of. Enter the automobile!

Slowly at first—and then in increasing numbers, they came. Rubbing the sleep out of their eyes, in gentle astonishment folks watched comets of dust trailed by an acrid odor of burning paint and gasoline, catapulting over the countryside at 15 miles an hour, ridden by goggle-eyed demons in veils, caps and dusters. Traffic—at first a trickle, then a respectable stream—then a roaring torrent, burst upon an amazed world. Down came the chinese walls surrounding American households and the family proudly joined the parade. The old take-your-time days—the stay at home days—the sleepy slow-moving days, were gone forever. Speed—go-getters—drive—action—pep—those are the modern's vocabulary.

● Cities expanded — markets widened — real estate values jumped. Sleepy hamlets woke up—country people came to the city and city people went to the country. Apartment houses, country clubs, roadhouses, resorts, sprang into being; sports leaped into popularity—the movies arrived—daylight saving—snow freed roads—closed cars, all continue to keep the crowds outdoors—winter and summer. The easy chair and the front porch have gone into the limbo with the lamented Dodo. What a change in a few short years. Twenty-three million automobiles laugh at miles on smooth paved roads. Movies seating 11,000,000 people at once—draw multitudes from the home.

Indoors the radio brings us the headlines before the newspaper arrives and fills the indoor waking hours of millions of households with a wide and varied assortment of programs. The multiplication of magazines and newspapers has tremendously intensified the competition for readership, while, like wheels within wheels, advertisers in each publication compete to the limit of their ingenuity and pocketbooks for reader attention. Never has time been so valuable. Never has attention been so difficult to secure.

● Out of the turmoil of increasing competition, rising costs and diminishing returns is born again the need for our old friend of the ancients, Outdoor Advertising. Again its commanding bulk is thrust into the tide. Not because there is no other way, as in early Rome, not because of illiteracy, as in medieval Europe, not because of taxation as in the 19th century, but because of the necessity of meeting the changed conditions of a changing world. Radio, newspaper,

Outdoor advertising locations are so placed as to cover every artery of traffic.

magazine, direct mail, are all advertising media aimed at the home, absorbed in the home. They are "indoor" media. The two factors of increasing competition for attention in the home, and the diminishing time spent in the home due to outdoor activities, have again elevated to primary importance the outdoor hours—and their medium Outdoor Advertising.

● Free from the bedlam of competing appeals, Outdoor Advertising in a flash delivers its terse, telegraphic messages over and over in smashing broadsides of light, color and picture. The modern tools of Outdoor Advertising command attention — and get it.

Listen to the Vice-President of one of the country's largest and most successful advertisers. Forty-five per cent of their appropriation is spent outdoors. "We have watched our bottlers using Outdoor Advertising year after year, and we know that those who have used it consistently have shown an average gain of over 5,000 gallons annually per plant, and those who have not used it have shown an average annual gain of 703 gallons."

Outdoor Advertising, like every large industry which has grown rapidly, has by no means grown perfectly. In the thirty years from 1900 to 1930, Outdoor Advertising volume has grown from 2 millions to 100 millions annually. This has not happened without reason. It happened because American industry sorely needed the services of Outdoor Advertising to help keep consumption in step with the terrific increase in production, without which our industrial system would collapse like a toy balloon.

● The major problem which faces American industry today is no longer production. The mechanical problem of production has been mastered. Today's problem—and a knotty one—is to raise consumption, and keep it in step with mass production. In its greater sense, the manufacturing process is not completed until the finished merchandise is in the hands of the consumer and the cash equivalent in the hands of the manufacturer.

A piece of machinery designed and proven through centuries of use, which successfully and economically converts merchandise into cash, is as justly a part of the manufacturer's equipment for which he pays his good money for value received as any machine in his factory. Such a force is as vital in our industrial civilization as any factory or property which contributes to the general welfare of society.

There are two major classes of advertising into which all forms naturally fall,—explanatory advertising, and exclamatory advertising. It is necessary first to explain your products or service, and it is equally necessary to exclaim it everlastingly if you wish to hold your place in the sun.

● Newspapers and magazines are essentially explanatory media. In this function of advertising they are pre-eminent. Nothing can take their place. Their natural ability to quickly and economically disseminate commercial news, styles, prices, explanations, illustrations and the like can not be met by any other medium.

Outdoor Advertising is primarily exclamatory. It does not compete with newspaper and magazine advertising. It completes, intensifies and deepens the impression left by these media by intensive and continuous exclamatory repetition.

Outdoor Advertising gives the local business man the same opportunity for the use of color and picture to large circulation at low cost that is enjoyed by the national advertiser in national magazines. It allows him to concentrate his advertising as desired to a region, state, city, neighbor- (Continued on page 48)

Motion pictures draw millions of people away from home every evening.

OUTDOOR ADVERTISING, Inc. and How It Will Operate

The program of the outdoor medium's new promotion agency.

● In any industry this is a good time to face facts. It is a good time to examine fundamental industry policies and straighten out the kinks. There is no doubt whatever that the United States is headed for a period of sound prosperity, and not only Outdoor Advertising, but every other form of advertising should use this interim period to eliminate duplication and waste of all kinds; and to increase efficiency, especially in selling.

In other words, this is an excellent period for intelligent preparedness for good business when it arrives.

In the field of national sales, Outdoor Advertising has had several different policies. They were products of the times, and possibly some of them were exactly in step with what was going on in the advertising world at that time. The final result, however, up until a few weeks ago was a lack of uniformity and a confusion which prevented a clean-cut selling picture.

The first organized sales effort of a national character was inaugurated in the early 90's by the organization of a company known as the Associated Bill Posters & Distributors Protective Company, the capital for which was furnished by plant owners throughout the country. The Company devoted itself exclusively to the solicitation of national Outdoor Advertising.

During the next fifteen or twenty years several other soliciting organizations developed and engaged in the same activity. These organizations became known as exclusive solicitors and were licensed by the National Plant Owners Association. In addition to these were a considerable number of general advertising agencies, probably forty or more in all, who established outdoor advertising departments, secured contracts for national outdoor advertising, and sent them out to the plant owners. These were also licensed by the Association. The agencies were in competition with the exclusive solicitors.

Along about 1910 or 1912, study was given to the volume of business produced by the various official solicitors, with the result that all general agency solicitors were dropped, and the sales effort on the medium confined to exclusive outdoor advertising solicitors. The sale of the medium was carried on in

The formation of the new promotion company clears the way for increased acceptance of the outdoor medium.

this manner until about 1916, when a group of the exclusive solicitors joined in the formation of the Poster Advertising Company, which conducted its business as an exclusive solicitor of national outdoor advertising contracts. It will be noted that under this policy of solicitation, no recognition in the way of commission or differentials was extended to the general advertising agency. On the contrary, the exclusive solicitor competed with the general advertising agency for a portion of the advertiser's appropriation to be used in outdoor advertising and to be deducted from the appropriations placed by the advertiser in the hands of his general advertising agency.

● About this time, the general advertising agencies who had an interest in the use of outdoor advertising formed the National Outdoor Advertising Bureau.

This Bureau was developed as a clearing house for national outdoor advertising contracts placed with plant owners by advertising agency members of the Bureau.

● Later, an agreement was entered into between the Thomas Cusack Company, and the Bureau, as a result of which sales cooperation by Thomas Cusack Company was given members of the Bureau and recognition in the form of a 10% commission on business placed by members of the bureau with plant owners through the Thomas Cusack Company.

This policy of agency recognition and the policy of direct solicitation on the part of the Poster Advertising Company and other exclusive soliciting organizations was naturally in conflict and, from the standpoint of the advertiser and the general advertising agency, the medium of outdoor advertising had a mixed sales policy, inconsistent in many respects.

This condition prevailed until about 1925 when the General Outdoor Advertising Company was organized, at which time a new contract was entered into between the General Outdoor Advertising Company and the Bureau, under which the Bureau could place its business where it chose.

During the early years of the period covered in this history, it was the general practice for national advertisers to maintain advertising departments, equipped to study and guide the expenditures of the advertiser in the various advertising media. The status of the advertising agency in the scheme of things had not been thoroughly established, although there was a steady and continuous development of a firmer and more important position on the part of general advertising agencies.

● During the last few years, generally speaking, the Advertising Department and the Advertising Manager have ceased to be an important factor in national advertising, their activities and functions being supplanted by the general agency in its broader field as an advisor and counsellor in the expenditure of advertising appropriations. At the present time there is an almost complete recognition of advertising agencies by all major advertising media as the logical sources through which business should be secured.

From 1925 to 1929 a mixed policy of national selling existed within the General Outdoor Advertising Company as a result of Thomas Cusack Company's Bureau arrangement, which became a part of the General Outdoor Advertising Company, and the Poster Advertising Company direct solicitation policy, which also became a part of the General Outdoor Advertising Company.

Owing to the rapid development of the general advertising agency and its important place in the advertising field at the present time, it became quite evident that the Outdoor Advertising medium was in a disadvantageous position as compared with other national advertising media. The necessity for adopting methods and policies comparable with those of other national advertising media was most apparent.

● Today the great majority of national advertisers have implicit confidence in their expert advertising counselors. There are important exceptions, but generally speaking the trend of the times is toward a policy of coordination and a proper and scientific division of the advertising budget under the supervision of one group of men. These counselors know all about the advertiser's products, his needs, his problems, his sales figures, and they are in a position to view the national advertiser's entire situation as one entity.

Outdoor Advertising recognizes this trend and has now acted to modernize its practices, to bring the medium into line with other major advertising media, but without attempting to interfere with present

Outdoor advertising now takes its rightful place with other media in the field of advertising.

methods of placing business. The medium has taken advantage of this period to put its house in order, and to prepare for better business.

● In all that has been done, the national advertiser, his needs, his point of view and his desires as to the method in which his national advertising appropriations shall be handled and his contracts executed has been considered first. In order to clear the way, it was first necessary for the Outdoor Advertising industry to adopt two new policies:

1. The extending of recognition to all reputable advertising agencies by Outdoor Advertising plant owners who deliver service consistent with the high standards now prevailing in the industry.

2. The establishment of a commission of 15% payable to such advertising agencies, the same percentage as that extended to the agencies by other major media. This 15% commission is effective at once on all business to be executed after January 1, 1932. Current commission to agencies will not be disturbed.

It is understood that the National Outdoor Advertising Bureau will function as a bureau somewhat similar to the A B C in newspaper advertising. This means the development and maintenance of an adequate field service, devoted to the evaluation of service rendered on existing Outdoor Advertising plants, also a national organization in the same office for checking and verification of service rendered to national advertisers by plant owners all over the country. This inspection will be unbiased and performed by men experienced in the physical requirements of Outdoor display.

It is expected that the National Outdoor Advertising Bureau will secure, maintain and make available for the use of those employing this service, full information with respect to the comparative advertising values of the various plants in localities where the service of more than one plan is available. This information will be secured to assist the advertiser in selecting the service and the plant best suited to his requirements.

With these developments in the immediate prospect, the industry went further and has now formed a new company, known as Outdoor Advertising, Incorporated, which will act as a Special Representative for the Outdoor medium.

The capital stock of Outdoor Advertising, Incorporated, is owned by the plant owners of the industry in proportion to their plant holdings, and this stock is so thoroughly distributed as to make the company truly representative of the entire industry.

● The company has acquired as a nucleus such part of the personnel and equipment of the national sales department of the General Outdoor Advertising Company as was needed. To this will be added from time to time men of standing and experience in the advertising world until our organization, when it is fully developed, shall be adequate to serve, through their representatives, all national advertisers who can properly include this medium in their advertising plans.

The officers of the new company are: Kerwin H. Fulton, President; Albert M. Briggs, Irving Bromiley, Albert de Montluzin, Albert E. Gans, R. D. French, Arthur Siegel, S. C. Hartshorn, Benjamin Eshleman, Geoffrey S. Earnshaw and Malcom Niebuhr, Vice-Presidents; I. W. Digges, Secretary and Counsel, and Walter E. Pratt, Treasurer.

The function of the new company can be simply expressed in few words. It is interested in only one thing—namely, the development of a wider, more intelligent and more profitable use of Outdoor Advertising.

Special Representatives

● Outdoor Advertising, Inc., offers the counsel and sales assistance of a thoroughly trained and experienced organization of Special Representatives who have not only a specialized knowledge of Outdoor Advertising but a thorough understanding of general merchandising and advertising. These men know the application of Outdoor Advertising to markets, and they approach advertising problems from the marketing point of view. And each man, of course, has a complete understanding of the various classifications of Outdoor Advertising and the possible combinations used to accomplish the greatest result in conjunction with other media. With this arrangement, all recognized agencies and solicitors will have at their command at all times the service of one or more of these account executives, and they in turn will have behind them all the specialized resources of Outdoor Advertising, Incorporated.

Advisory, Research and Merchandising Service

The company has intimate contacts with 1200 plant owners delivering service in more than 17,500 cities and towns, and this provides us with unique nationwide facilities for gathering authentic and up-to-the-minute market information for the use of agencies or solicitors in connection with the problems of their clients. The same widespread organization can also be used upon occasion to contact wholesale and selected retail outlets, tuning up the distributors for users of Outdoor Advertising. Upon request the company will wire plant owners at selected points and thus secure quick and reliable trade information from any section of the country. It also has its own facilities for trade surveys of all kinds. This merchandising division, when it is functioning one hundred per cent, will be unique in the history of advertising.

Plans

Representatives will con- (Continued on page 45)

OFF TO A
GOOD START

The important facts about Outdoor Advertising, Incorporated, have already been widely published, and I believe that our function and principles of operation are now fully understood by advertisers, solicitors, agencies, and those in our own industry.

There emerges a clean-cut picture of vigorous sales promotion in harmony with the best modern advertising practice. Obstacles and hurdles have been removed. We are forging ahead at full speed without any distracting factors. All of our time and energy is concentrated on one objective—a wider, more intelligent and more profitable use of outdoor advertising by national advertisers.

My associates in this new company are most enthusiastic. Our responsibility is definite, tangible and perfectly consistent. We are into it now, and it is fascinating work. It is *creative cooperation.*

The new situation has points of great significance. One of them is that outdoor advertising is at last completely available. Obviously the advertiser has the widest possible choice in how he shall place his business. He has a number of alternatives. He can choose the company or the individual or the group that he believes offers him the character of service that he needs. And we in Outdoor Advertising, Incorporated, are not concerned with his decision. We have no part in it, and no opinion on the subject. Our only desire is to have him use the medium if it fits his selling problems, and to have him use it judiciously and in sufficient volume to gauge its true worth.

The national advertiser is sure to benefit. Through his agency or solicitor, and always in harmony with them, he will now receive the assistance of the specialized knowledge and ability which exists in our personnel. He will receive the willing and enthusiastic cooperation of our special representatives who have a thorough grasp of every phase of this medium, up-to-the-minute data from our research and merchandising division consisting of trade surveys gathered from 17,500 cities and towns and market analyses made by our own staff; plans expertly made to coordinate with expenditures in other media; copy and art service by men trained in the technique of this medium, this service consisting of ideas, written copy, visuals in color and finished sketches made under our supervision on order from the client; and finally a promotion service designed to get the highest possible value out of every dollar he spends in the outdoor medium.

In these days when every advertising dollar is being placed under the microscope, outdoor advertising deserves special consideration because on careful analysis it reveals astonishing values. We do not claim it is the only medium, nor do we claim that all advertisers can use it, but we do claim that it reaches more people for a longer time at lower cost. We do claim that it is possible to display real selling copy out-of-doors, and we do claim that outdoor advertising gives the advertiser advantages of particular value in 1931, such as repetition, continuity, unlimited color without extra charge, and enormous circulation due to the fact that people are out-of-doors as often and as long as possible.

Now, at once, all national advertisers wherever located have at their disposal every possible facility for the proper use of outdoor advertising. This complete and comprehensive service, which heretofore has been limited, is now universally available.

President, Outdoor Advertising, Inc.

THE DIRECTORS OF OUTDOOR ADVERTISING INCORPORATED

Kerwin H. Fulton
New York City

Upon this and the two following pages we present the men who are directing the destinies of the outdoor industry's promotion company.

Mortimer Offner Photo
Leonard Dreyfuss
New York City

Bachrach Photo
H. C. Macdonald
Detroit, Michigan

George W. Kleiser
San Francisco, Calif.

B. W. Robbins
Chicago, Illinois

W. Rex Bell
Terre Haute, Indiana

P. L. Michael
Houston, Texas

H. J. Fitzgerald
Milwaukee, Wisconsin

George W. Kleiser, Jr.
San Francisco, Calif.

Granville Standish
Providence, R. I.

J. B. Stewart
Clinton, Iowa

H. F. O'Mealia
Jersey City, N. J.

Bachrach Photo

E. C. Donnelly, Jr.
Boston, Mass.

Photo by Foster

E. W. Lemay
Richmond, Va.

C. U. Philley
St. Joseph, Mo.

J. E. Morrison
Chicago, Illinois

Sherwill Ellis Photo

A. L. Bauers
New York City

Lane Bros. Photo

George Ripley, Jr.
Atlanta, Georgia

Photo by Blank-Stoller, Inc.

C. A. Reynolds
New York City

The Story of the
NATIONAL OUTDOOR
ADVERTISING BUREAU

● With the advent of Outdoor Advertising, Inc., as the promotion agent of the Outdoor medium, the National Outdoor Advertising Bureau assumes a new importance in the Outdoor Advertising picture. As the central outdoor advertising department of some 225 member agencies, the Bureau has, since its inception, played an important part through its inspection and advisory service in raising the standards and increasing the use of Outdoor Advertising. It provides the advertiser, through its member agencies, with an unbiased buying, counselling and servicing office for the placing of Outdoor Advertising.

The Bureau operates as an extension of the member agencies' own outdoor advertising departments. It serves its members as a clearing house for the outdoor advertising which they wish to place for their clients, provides complete and unbiased information in regard to plants in the some 17,000 towns and cities in the United States where standardized service is available and inspects the clients' showings, checking the service rendered by the plant owner.

Since the Bureau has nothing to gain from the advertisers' preference of one plant over another except the giving of better service to the account, it is obvious that its recommendations are prompted only by interest in the advertising value of the various plants. As a result of this unprejudiced attitude, the Bureau has been a tremendous factor in improving plants and plant service in all parts of the country. Suggestions for change and improvement from this source have always been well received by the plant owners who are as interested in the improvement of their service as is the Bureau.

A complete planning, servicing and inspection system is offered by the Bureau to its members.

● The planning is done by the Bureau's staff representatives, working in close conjunction with the agency account executives. These representatives provide member agencies with all the information at their command in regard to the place of Outdoor Advertising in the campaign and explain the special requirements of outdoor copy and layout. They are trained in all forms of advertising, have spent years in the Outdoor field and, as a result, they understand how the Outdoor medium can best be tied in with other forms of promotion. Through the executive offices of the Bureau they also have access to detailed and up-to-date information in regard to prices, showings, plant conditions and coverage in every standard outdoor advertising plant in the United States. Thus the same sort of information that is demanded of publications is available to Bureau members in regard to Outdoor Advertising.

All billings and transactions with individual plants are handled by the Bureau, which maintains a large bookkeeping department for this purpose. All billing is taken by the Bureau, checked, verified and combined for the agency in concise form for monthly payment. The agency commission is retained by the agency from each invoice; the remaining commission is used to pay the Bureau's operating expenses.

● The Bureau also maintains an elaborate Field Service department. This is composed of trained advertising men whose task it is to inspect the showings of Bureau clients, to make suggestions to the local operators as to how the plant may be improved and to send in the detailed reports from which the Bureau compiles its exhaustive information in regard to plant conditions.

These men have, during the past year, covered all towns in which there are plants. Previous to that time only towns of 5,000 or more population were inspected. The work done in these towns proved so beneficial, however, that it was decided to extend the service to include all standard plants.

The inspector's first task, naturally, is to see that Bureau accounts are properly posted and maintained. He then considers the general condition of the plant and makes his recommendations. The reports which he sends to the Bureau in regard to the showings are copied at the Bureau offices and sent to the agencies in duplicate so that a copy may be sent to the advertiser.

The Field Service men are instructed to be fair and unbiased in their re- (Continued on page 47)

OUTDOOR ADVERTISING
in the National Campaign
by Walter Laidlaw Chesman
Account Executive Doremus and Co.

● Those of us who are on the agency side of the advertising business know that if this new line-up in Outdoor Advertising had been an accomplished fact ten years ago, outdoor advertising as a medium would enjoy today an even greater degree of acceptance among agencies and advertisers than it does.

In order to make a living in the agency business, I have found it necessary to do a number of things. I have been with the smaller type of advertising gency where one man does about everything from writing copy to writing those perhaps equally fanciful efforts known as mechanical bills, and I am sorry to say that it has only been within the past three or four years that my curiosity overcame perhaps a degree of prejudice, and I forced an understanding—at least a partial understanding—of the outdoor business from its custodians.

If we could make a census of the account representatives and the major executives of the advertising agencies of America, I think we would find an appalling lack of knowledge of the machinery and the structure of outdoor advertising. Any agency man can tell you, and any agency man will tell you at the slightest provocation, all about the magazine business, both editorial and advertising, any agency man will give you a complete history of the newspaper business, but this same agency man is not quite so sure of his ground when he approaches outdoor advertising. This lack of information, of course, dates back to an attitude on the part of the controlling factors in outdoor advertising, which perhaps we should ignore and not mention, but which is now, I think from both of our viewpoints, happily changed. But that lack of familiarity has resulted in a lack of knowledge of the place that outdoor advertising can play and is playing in an advertising plan.

● I may put too much emphasis on the creative side of advertising., It is always hard to measure volume against quality in advertising. The cost of advertising is all recorded in books. The value of advertising depends entirely upon what goes into the white space, whether that white space be a 24 sheet poster or a 50 line newspaper ad.

`Years ago a very brilliant writer defined a cynic

Change! Advertising passes through its own style periods. We have the vogue of long copy. We have certain definite advertising patterns that advertising seems more or less to fall into. We have a wave of modernism in advertising, but I cannot see how advertising can fail to follow the general pace of American life, and that means shorter messages, more quickly told, and more easily understood. The whole trend, the whole quickening of life as it is lived today, would point to the increasing value to the advertiser of outdoor advertising, and I believe that if we can forget some of our formulas, if we can start to think as creatively about outdoor advertising as we have about magazine pages and newspaper space, outdoor advertising will play an even greater part in national campaigns.

Recently, the Daily News sent out one of the most admirable pieces of sales promotion literature that I have ever read. This mailing piece pointed out the fallibility of the human mind in predicting the future customs of a people. It told in detail the story of an emigrant, Joseph Pulitzer, an emigrant with an almost fanatic belief in American ideals. That fanaticism found an outlet in the New York World. Probably in the history of American journalism there has never been a newspaper that played as large a part as did the New York World in formulating public opinion, for Pulitzer was a crusader. He was not content with merely reporting the news. He wished to cause action—partisan action. On the death of Joseph Pulitzer, it was found that he left the World a powerful and profitable newspaper. The only thing that he could not foresee and prevent was the one constant factor in American life—change. In short, he could not foresee that there would come a time when over a million people in the city of New York every day would prefer a tabloid newspaper with news presented in capsule form for quick reading and a very hasty digestion, if any.

as being a man who knew the price of everything, and the value of nothing, and I refuse for one to be a cynic, if we accept that definition, about any advertising medium, but I do believe that its value is as much measured by the use we make of it as the quantity of it we use. Neither can I subscribe to formulas in advertising. Most advertising successes in the past 10 years seem to have been made by breaking all advertising rules. I wonder, for example, if Milton Feasley would have ever been able to put the famous Halitosis campaign into the publications of America if first of all he had had to submit it to the laboratory test of a board of directors. And yet Milton Feasley's Halitosis campaign, with a complete disregard of advertising formula, made a difference of some 500% in the sale of Listerine.

● Mr. George Washington Hill has lately startled the public by taking the very vulgar word "spit" and spreading it—the word I mean—before their more or less startled eyes. And yet the Cremo "spit" campaign which, as we all know, has utilized about every method of publicity, has resulted in an enormous sales increase for Cremo cigars. It is curious that this lack of observance of conventionalities has been the hallmark of this and many other major advertising successes.

Now I know the formula for posters as well as you know it. I know that in the advertising copy books, posters are supposed to headline a story that is theoretically understood by the purchasing public. I know that posters, again according to formula, are designed to act as reminders of a story that has been more completely told in other media. Yet I cannot help but ask myself whether or not the copy books are correct.

It takes a lot of hard work and a lot of thought to successfully disregard formula. As we drive along the highways of America and walk through our cities, a succession of pretty girls holding merchandise or doing something with merchandise that ranges from soap to sap, beckon to us. The pretty girl performs a very useful function, both in outdoor advertising and in life, and she is a very ornamental form of sugar coating for many an advertising pill, but I believe with Otis Shepard, the foremost exponent of modernism in poster art in the country today, that we sometimes lean a little too heavily on her shoulders, that sometimes she is a very halting, limping sales crutch that we too often employ because she is sure-fire, and if she made a success for so-and-so, she ought to be able to do the same thing for this and that.

● Somewhere deep down in a product is a pictorial expression of that product. It takes many rough sketches, much understanding, and perhaps some bitter words with artists and art directors to find it

but when you have found it, it is pure gold, and sometimes when we find it we will also find that it has absolutely nothing to do with formulas that theoretically should govern our thinking on outdoor advertising.

In times like these when values are more closely scrutinized than in flush days, outdoor advertising presents a powerful case, stressed by the 1931 necessity of making an advertising dollar do a little more work than ever before in American sales history. We all know that judged on a circulation basis, outdoor advertising offers the cheapest buy to the advertiser but cheapness alone is no reason why it should be bought. If it does not offer this other thing—value—its cost should have very little relation to its purchase. Business in general is going through an introspective period. Business is holding a mirror up and examining its reflection with great care. Manufacturers and retailers are offering greater values than at any time since the Spanish American War, and the American dollar has grown some 30-odd cents in purchasing power. Generally speaking, advertising costs have not followed the price trend. Advertising costs have remained more or less constant. The only way that advertising bargains can be secured is by the increase of value—is by a better use of advertising media, which brings us 'round in a circle again to the same question of what we put in our white space.

● The sales and advertising managers of the country who are in huddles trying to reconcile decreased sales volume with an advertising budget are strenuously endeavoring to do just that—pack the advertising dollar with added value. Agency men are being asked very embarrassing questions by clients, and agency men are asking clients equally embarrassing questions about the values of the product they are exploiting. One result of this introspective period is a realization that volume of business is not alone the answer to earnings statements. American business today is working from profit back to volume rather than attempting to make volume render a profit. Look at a map of the New York City market, not in the terms of geographical distances, but in terms of salesmen's routes. Immediately, one cost factor arises—the cost per call per salesman, and we discover that the closer we keep our sales force to the metropolitan market, the lower is our cost per call—elementary—page one in the sales primer, and yet how many of us remembered it in '28 and '29. We find further that as we start to penetrate the outer circles of this New York market, the penalty we pay for this outlying business is to be found in every factor of our merchandising operation. We find that it affects our warehousing cost. We find that our delivery cost may be doubled and tripled by this distribution on the outer circle, and when we separate the sales volume done in that outer circle from our inner market and apply these cost factors, we may find that we are actually paying money for the privilege of complete distribution. The national market is merely an enlargement of this New York market, and by changing the map of the New York market to a map of the United States or of the world and applying these same factors of cost, we may find, and many businesses have found, that profits are to be made only by a deliberate sacrifice of volume. That is not a far-fetched analogy. I have heard it discussed over luncheon tables at the Bankers Club, and when a merchandising idea gets as far south as that, you will understand that it is a matter of very general comment.

● When sales and advertising executives start thinking locally, they immediately also must think in terms of localized media. That means outdoor advertising and newspapers, or it may mean, and perhaps too frequently does, outdoor advertising or newspapers. Suppose, for instance, that we decide that a merchandise deal is necessary in order to pull our coffee out of a sales valley. I'd be willing to make a slight wager that when it came to the choice of their advertising weapons, with that type of sales message to tell, there would not be one out of ten advertising managers who would think of using posters for merchandising copy, and yet, even to a greater degree than newspapers, posters can be restricted to the zone of a zone deal; and if we look at them from a cost viewpoint, the cost of telling that story to a given market through the medium of 24 sheet posters would be much less than an equivalent campaign in newspaper space over the same period of time.

The point I want to make is that the use of (Continued on page 43)

Sock it harder

FAIR-WEATHER golfers complain that the new larger ball

is "short" against the wind. What of it! Sock it harder!

Then it won't seem so big. . . . That's our advice to outdoor

advertisers — and we're caddying for some of the best

. . ."pros" like Maxwell House, Dentyne, Post Toasties, Rio

Grande Oil, Clorox . . . If you want outdoor SERVICE —

OUTDOOR
A NATIONAL OUTDOOR ADVERTISING ORGANIZATION

SERVICE
INCORPORATED

230 NORTH MICHIGAN AVE., CHICAGO

WHO'S OUTDOO

Mac Donald Photo

KERWIN H. FULTON

Blank-Stoller Photo

ALBERT M. BRIGGS

KERWIN HOLMES FULTON, President of Outdoor Advertising, Inc., has been in outdoor advertising all his business life. Born in Truro, Nova Scotia, forty-six years ago, Mr. Fulton came to New York when a youth and his first major decision was to place a want ad in a local newspaper.

His first advertising campaign proved successful. He got a job with the Van Beuren & New York Billposting Company, whose President was Barney Link.

Later, he became Link's Assistant Manager in charge of sales and operating. When Mr. Fulton was 28 years old, in the year of 1913, he was made Vice-President and General Manager of the Company.

In 1916, the Poster Advertising Company was formed, with Barney Link, A. M. Briggs, Donald G. Ross, M. F. Reddington, Sidney J. Hamilton, and K. H. Fulton. Link was elected President of the new Company, with Fulton as Secretary. Four months after the organization was formed, Link died and Fulton was selected as its President.

Beginning with that office, Mr. Fulton forged to the front and in time became the acknowledged leader of the outdoor advertising industry in America.

IRVING BROMILEY

Blank-Stoller Photo

ALBERT DE MONTLUZIN

Later he became President of the O. J. Gude Company and in 1925 the Fulton interests, which had acquired plants throughout the country, merged with the Thomas Cusack Company, out of which came the General Outdoor Advertising Co., Inc. Fulton became its President.

Now he goes to a wider field, which will redound to the benefit of the outdoor advertising industry throughout the country.

■ — —

ALBERT M. BRIGGS, Vice-President of the new organization, entered the outdoor advertising business through the Gunning System. Eight years later he formed the Outdoor Advertising Department of the J. Walter Thompson Agency, with headquarters in Chicago. In 1911, he formed the A. M. Briggs Company in Cleveland, a few years later moving his headquarters to Chicago. At this time he handled and developed the Liggett & Myers account, which he has handled ever since. Some of the accounts which he personally handled and developed during that time were Fisk Tires, Fairy Soap and Gold Dust, Aunt Jemima Pancake Flour, Saxon Motor Car, Chalmers Motor Company, and None-Such Fine Meat. Under his direction, men in his organization developed and handled Wrigley, Pillsbury Flour, Standard Oil of Indiana, Reed's Cushion Shoe, Jello, American Express, Post Toasties, and Collier's Magazine.

IRVING BROMILEY, Vice-President, was born in Ashton, Rhode Island, in 1885, and brought up in Central Falls and Providence. At fifteen he went to New York to make his fortune, and at forty-five succeeded in doing it. His first job was a sign painter for the O. J. Gude Company, starting at seventeen years of age in overalls, and at night studying at art school.

Later he was put in charge of a road crew, where he dug post holes, mixed paint, erected bulletin boards, painted bulletin boards, and leased locations.

Leasing space gave Mr. Bromiley the basis for the next step in the line of promotion—sales, and he was sent to the Old Colony Advertising Company in Providence, which was then partly owned by the O. J. Gude Company in New York, as its manager. Here he developed the Hood Tire Man, an outdoor advertising character that brought him immediate attention.

His next idea, which brought him from Providence to New York, was the United States Tire history bulletins, which were in the form of an open book, one side being painted with the high spot of history that took place on the spot or in the town ahead, the other "page" given over to the slogan, "United States Tires Are Good Tires." This idea marked Bromiley as a sales executive and idea man of the first water.

Mr. Bromiley also created and sold the idea of advertising the Champion Spark Plug with a replica of that automobile accessory.

For Waitt and Bond, he created the striking design outdoors of Blackstone Cigar with its long ash.

Another account that brought Mr. Bromiley fame in the advertising world was the Clicquot Club Ginger Ale campaigns, with the slogan, "Aged 6 Months." In recent years he developed the American Tobacco Company account, with its striking outdoor copy ideas.

ALBERT E. GANS

ALBERT DE MONTLUZIN was born in the City of New Orleans in 1876 of French parentage.

As a boy at the age of eight or nine years, he showed a pronounced sense of art appreciation and for a time he studied portrait painting under a French master, named Rivoire. DeMontluzin, however, had a complex mind—possessing both an appreciation of art and of the merchandising thereof. He decided that he wanted to be in the "picture" business where it could sell at profit. He moved to Cincinnati in 1898 and became associated with the United States Lithograph Company.

When the Poster Advertising Company was founded, de Montluzin was selected for the position of General Sales Manager. All through the duration of the war, deMontluzin insisted on continuing active solicitation, with a faith that orders or contracts would come through on the day of the Armistice. That his faith was justified was proven by results which came through immediately upon the signing of the Armistice.

DeMontluzin has personally conceived and managed too many successful Outdoor Advertising campaigns to enumerate and, certainly, has built for himself a name in the industry.

■ ■ ■

ALBERT E. GANS, Vice-President, went into the advertising business about thirty-four years ago, at the time when Mayor Hugh J. Grant controlled the car advertising in all the New York City surface cars.

After Mayor Grant sold his franchise, Mr. Gans became an advertising broker handling all kinds of advertising. In 1902, Mr. Gans went with the O. J. Gude Company as a salesman and later became successively Assistant Sales Manager, Sales Manager, Secretary, and finally, Vice-President and director. When General Outdoor Advertising Co., Inc., was formed in 1925, Mr. Gans became a Vice-President and Director.

Mr. Gans was one of the salesmen whose ideas helped to make the Great White Way the greatest animated spectacle of electric advertising in the world, having sold over 50% of the spectaculars on display to such advertisers as the Wrigley Company, C. B. Corsets, Kayser Gloves, Gold Seal Champagne, Sanderson Scotch, Haig & Haig, Runkel's Cocoa, Otard Brandy, Wilson Whiskey, Elbart Gin, and Kelly Springfield Tires. The Wrigley spectacular at that time was the largest in the world and the most talked of. Mr. Gans has handled the Wrigley painted display for over twenty years continuously in New York and vicinity.

■ ■ ■

R. D. FRENCH, Vice-President, until mid-June, was Western Sales Manager of General Outdoor Advertising Co., Inc., with headquarters at Chicago. Mr.

French began his outdoor advertising career with the Ivan B. Nordhem Company in 1911. From there he went to the Thomas Cusack Company in 1922. For the latter company he had charge of the Syndicate Poster Division and was the head of their "flying squadron." Later he joined the General Outdoor Advertising Co., Inc., as a salesman, attaining the position of Western Sales Manager of General Outdoor Advertising Co., Inc.

■ ■ ■

ARTHUR SIEGEL, Vice-President, previous to June 15th was Southwestern Sales Manager of General Outdoor Advertising Co., Inc., with headquarters at St. Louis. He received his education in the St. Louis public schools and St. Louis University, and in 1913 began his outdoor advertising career. For years he has been a national salesman with the St. Louis Branch, and in the sales contests has always gone over the top with 100% or over.

In what was called the "All-Together" Sales Contest of the General Outdoor Advertising Co., which began on February 10, and ran for a period of ten weeks until April 19, 1930, Mr. Siegel went over the top to the tune of 527.1%. His nearest rival in that contest had 472.3%.

In the sales contest of October 1 to November 15, 1930, which was called "Let's Discover America," Mr. Siegel was first of Robbins' explorers. Mr. Siegel "discovered land" amounting to $1,339,900.70.

■ ■ ■

SUMNER C. HARTSHORN, Vice-President, attended Kozminski School and Hyde Park High School in Chicago, and after taking a special advertising course in the International Correspondence School entered the outdoor advertising field in 1913

R. D. FRENCH

securing employment as a local salesman with the Thomas Cusack Company in Indianapolis.

Later he joined this company's branch in Kansas City in the sales department and at the formation of the General Outdoor Advertising Company in 1925 became national salesman.

Some of the National outdoor advertising accounts created and handled by Mr. Hartshorn are the Purity Bakeries Corporation, Schulze Baking Company, Western Bakeries Corporation, Beatrice Creamery Company, Paxton & Gallagher's Butter-Nut Coffee and the California Fruit Growers Exchange, famous for Sunkist Oranges.

■ ■ ■

BENJAMIN ESHLEMAN, Vice-President, secured his education at Haverford College, then going into the Sales Department of Procter & Gamble. Later he became Sales Manager of the Commonwealth Shoe & Leather Company, his service being interrupted by the World War, where he became a captain of the Chemical Warfare, serving in the Seventh Division. Upon his return, he became Sales Manager of Smith, Kline, French Company, and in 1921 joined the Poster Advertising Company and the O. J. Gude Company, working in Philadelphia.

■ ■ ■

GEOFFREY S. EARNSHAW, Vice-P r e s i d e n t, joined the National Sales Department of General Outdoor Advertising Co., Inc., in 1925.

After his discharge from the United States Army at the end of the World War he was associated with the United States Shipping Board, from which he resigned to assume the duties of Manager of Transportation and Sales and later Director of The Southern Oil & Transport Corporation, American subsidiary of Tankers, Ltd., of London, England.

Duncan Photo

SUMNER C. HARTSHORN

Phillips Photo

BENJAMIN ESHLEMAN

Strauss Photo

ARTHUR SIEGEL

GEOFFREY S. EARNSHAW

In 1923 Mr. Earnshaw became associated with the late Hugo Stinnes, German industrial genius, as American manager of his oil interests, where he remained until joining General Outdoor Advertising Co., Inc.

He received his education at DeLancey School and the University of Pennsylvania.

The Richfield Oil Corporation's outdoor advertising, including their electric in Times Square is one of the accounts developed by Mr. Earnshaw.

■　■　■

MALCOLM NIEBUHR, Vice-President, was educated in preparatory schools in this country and college in England. After leaving college, he joined the O. J. Gude Company, later went to the Thomas Cusack Company. From there he went to the American Tobacco Company, leaving them to join the H. K. McCann Company as Account Executive, being associated with that organization for thirteen years. In 1925 he became Sales Executive for General Outdoor Advertising Co., Inc., where he developed important outdoor advertising accounts.

MALCOLM NIEBUHR

■　~　■

I. W. DIGGES, Secretary and Counsel, is a lawyer with training gained here and abroad. Mr. Digges studied at the University of Richmond, Virginia, the George Washington Law School, the French School of Political Science, and the University of Paris. He was at one time assistant to the legal adviser of the American Red Cross in Europe and served the United States Government as a member of the Central Committee on Market Research of the Department of Commerce. He was an attorney for the Federal Trade Commission until 1925, when he became Secretary of General Outdoor Advertising Co., Inc.

I. W. DIGGES

■　-　■

WALTER E. PRATT, Treasurer, began his outdoor advertising career as auditor for the Poster Advertising Company in 1918, in charge of the Accounting Department. Mr. Pratt devised a fool-proof system in the Poster Advertising Co. concerning sublet contracts, which has been in operation since its inception.

When the O. J. Gude Company had to deal financially with thousands of towns operated by different plant owners in various parts of the country on poster showings and painted display, Mr. Pratt devised a plan of sales control, which met with the approval of auditors of various audit companies who, once a year, have audited the books. From the time of the merger that resulted in the General Outdoor Advertising Co., Inc., Mr. Pratt was made Assistant Secretary, and in September of last year was elected Treasurer of General Outdoor Advertising Co., Inc.

WALTER E. PRATT

GUGLER
POSTERS
ARE OUTSTANDING

The POSTER DIVISION of the

GUGLER LITHOGRAPHIC CO.
MILWAUKEE

the best basis we have ever been on—a more satisfactory basis and certainly one more in harmony with all advertising."

● He made this prophesy: "The new prosperity will come from scientific, efficient, and economical selling through advertising—the waste is being squeezed out of outdoor advertising, the abuses are disappearing, and we are forging this into a strong and reliable weapon for the American business men to use in distributing their goods to our millions of consumers."

Speaking on "Our Viewpoint on Outdoor Advertising," Mr. Daily related an experience of General Electric Refrigerator outdoor advertising, "which made us appreciate outdoor advertising a little more than we had before." He told this story: "We tried outdoor advertising in three cities of 50,000 population without anything else; without newspaper and without direct mail. Those three fundamentals, of course, usually go together with us. We tried newspaper advertising and in both cases it worked pretty well, but where we put them together we got over three times the efficiency that we got when we used one or the other by itself. While each one can stand on its own feet, when they work as a unit I think is when we get the most benefit."

Mr. Daily told of a contest conducted in Cleveland by the Central Outdoor Advertising Company, in which they asked the question of the public: "What outdoor advertising display within sixty miles of Cleveland has the strongest appeal to me and why?"

The posters of General Electric Refrigerator brought in a number of answers, one of which was a prize winner. The writer of this prize winning letter said that the poster "advertises a product of recognized merit. It appeals to my sense of humor in that it portrays a very human experience, when father comes in late. The faces of the individuals have more expression than any I have seen. It is artistically colored—very well balanced. The lettering is well proportioned as well as the people being well proportioned to the size of the board."

How poster advertising enthuses a salesman was related by Mr. Daily. He remarked: "They see it every day when they are calling. They tell us that they are heartened by them and that in this very discouraging time it is very helpful to them; that it picks them up after they have made a number of bad calls and gives them enthusiasm.

"Of course, enthusing the salesman is not the major job of outdoor advertising but it is a very important job."

● Only a very small appropriation was used for the General Electric Refrigerator in 1927, Mr. Daily remarked, when the business totaled $11,000,000. The next year, the appropriation for advertising was tripled. The following year the business ran close to

$50,000,000, "and again we jumped our advertising," continued Mr. Daily. "Last year we did pretty close to $100,000,000 worth of business and again our national advertising and our sales promotion was stepped up. This year, our quota is a little better than in 1930 and our advertising is a little more than in 1930, so again this year we try we keep step with the sales we expect to get. In consequence, in domestic sales we caught the field in two years and passed them and now we are considerably past anybody. They hesitated. They didn't go on. At least, that's part of it. We, on the other hand, kept working on our salesmen and constantly encouraging them. Outdoor advertising, of course, has played a very important part."

Introducing Mr. Fulton, Mr. Holliday said that on Monday, June 15th, Outdoor Advertising, Incorporated, began its first business day and that it represents "one of the biggest cooperative organizations ever put over in this country." He said it was due to the leadership, personality, and enthusiasm of the President of the new company, which statement brought a round of applause for Mr. Fulton as he arose to speak.

● Mr. Fulton said: "In any industry this is a good time to face the facts. It is a good time to examine fundamental industry policies and straighten out the kinks. There is no doubt whatever that the United States is headed for a period of sound prosperity, and not only Outdoor Advertising but every other form of advertising should use this interim period to eliminate duplication and waste of all kinds; and to increase efficiency, especially in selling.

"In other words, this is an excellent period for intelligent preparedness for good business when it arrives."

Mr. Fulton told of the different sales policies in the past history of outdoor advertising and said that they were products of the times, "and possibly some of them were exactly in step with what was going on in the advertising world at that time. The final result, however, up until a few weeks ago, was a lack of uniformity and a confusion which prevented a clean-cut selling picture."

The President of the new company, (which meets today's advertising conditions, modernly,) said that those in the industry "scrutinized our selling organization and our selling policies," and they saw too much wasted energy, too much duplication of effort, and limitations which precluded a wide general availability of complete and comprehensive service for all national advertisers in every section of the country.

Mr. Fulton continued: "We in Outdoor Advertising recognize this trend and have now acted to modernize our practices, to bring our medium into line with other major advertising (Continued on page 49)

The morning after the night before

Last evening, she read a piece of selling copy in her favorite magazine.

This morning she drove to town; seeing an ERIE poster, she was reminded of what she had read—and where the product could be purchased.

ERIE posters *sell* because they *are* seen—their outstanding workmanship dominates competing boards.

Phone, wire or write for an ERIE salesman.

Within a few moments, he can outline (1) why the Erie location means prompt and economical shipments; (2) how you benefit by Erie's modern equipment and the many years of ERIE experience; and (3) how the price policy makes the ERIE proposition doubly attractive.

ERIE

LITHOGRAPHING & PRINTING CO
ERIE PENNSYLVANIA
· · · ·POSTERS· · · ·
WINDOW AND DEALER DISPLAYS
LITHOGRAPHED COLOR ADVERTISING

LITHO IN U. S. A.

F ROM the pioneer days of outdoor advertising through every organized phase, we have constructively co-operated with advertisers, agencies, distributing organizations and plant owners.

We congratulate the men at the head of these organizations in their recent move to bring about more complete understanding of the outdoor advertising medium, and we believe their efforts will be justly rewarded.

As heretofore, we are prepared to offer full co-operation along ethical lines to sustain the best interests of Outdoor Advertising.

ERIE LITHOGRAPHING & PRINTING CO.,
ERIE, PENNA.

■ OUTDOOR IMPRESSIONS

A night view of one of the most impressive monuments of industry ever erected, the Palmolive-Peet Building at Michigan Avenue and Walton Place, Chicago. Below, dwarfed by the tremendous building which their medium helped to build, outdoor advertising panels carry their message to the thousands who travel this famous thoroughfare daily.

"Please step in", says the illuminated sign which gives a friendly invitation to visit the Japanese Institute of Electro-Technique and Lighting. That portion of the building to the right of the sign is illuminated somewhat like a light-house. Lights in the shape of shells illuminate a roof garden. The whole display gives a very brilliant and striking effect.

OUTDOOR IMPRESSIONS

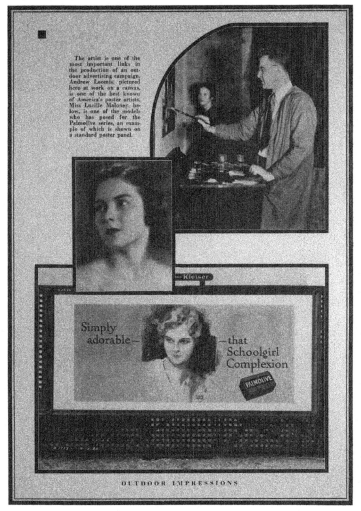

The artist is one of the most important links in the production of an outdoor advertising campaign. Andrew Loomis, pictured here at work on a canvas, is one of the best known of America's poster artists. Miss Lucille Maloney, below, is one of the models who has posed for the Palmolive series, an example of which is shown on a standard poster panel.

Simply adorable—

—that Schoolgirl Complexion

PALMOLIVE

OUTDOOR IMPRESSIONS

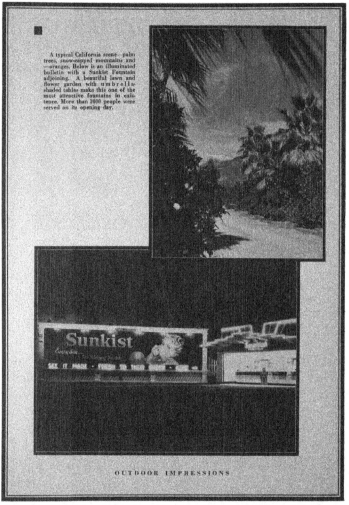

A typical California scene—palm trees, snow-capped mountains and —oranges. Below is an illuminated bulletin with a Sunkist Fountain adjoining. A beautiful lawn and flower garden with umbrella-shaded tables make this one of the most attractive fountains in existence. More than 3000 people were served on its opening day.

OUTDOOR IMPRESSIONS

PRIDE

of

CRAFTSMANSHIP

§

One of the reasons we turn out such exceptionally fine posters is that every member of our organization takes pride in the perfect execution of his portion of the task. Every detail, every operation in the making of an accurate reproduction of a design must dovetail in with every other portion of the undertaking. That no single item may mar the finished result, our workmen jealously guard their portion of every poster, and see to it that nothing is introduced that does not contribute to the final perfection of the poster. We submit for your consideration the careful workmanship every poster receives when ordered from us.

AMERICAN POSTER CORPORATION
MILWAUKEE
WISCONSIN

THINGS NEEDED

for a complete understanding
of Outdoor Advertising

Essentials of Poster Design . . . .

a handsomely bound, beautifully illustrated book that tells the
how and why of the poster. In non-technical language and
with abundant illustrations, it explains the problems of poster
composition, the use of color, lettering, and common errors.

Annual Design Number of Advertising Outdoors

which illustrates the one hundred best posters of 1930, selected by a distinguished committee of artists in the annual
poster art contest sponsored by the Chicago Association of
Commerce. This 108 page volume is a liberal education on
the effective design of posters.

Advertising Outdoors . . . .

the monthly publication of the outdoor advertising industry,
which brings to you the thoughts of America's foremost merchandising experts, stories of how the medium has confronted
and solved advertisers' problems and articles on the trend of
the business times.

And A Special Offer

makes it possible for new subscribers or those who wish their present subscriptions renewed for another year to secure all three at the price of just the subscription to Advertising Outdoors, $3.00—a saving of $3.97. Present subscribers who wish to do so may
secure both books for $1.50—a saving of $2.47. But act today, for the supply of these
books will not last long at these prices.

ADVERTISING OUTDOORS

165 W. Wacker Drive   Chicago, Illinois

National Outdoor
ART EXHIBIT PLANNED

In the interest of increasingly effective advertising and an analysis of new methods and trends that have developed during the past year, particularly in the outdoor advertising field, the Advertising Council of The Chicago Association of Commerce is launching its Second Annual Outdoor Advertising Art Exhibit in the galleries of Marshall Field & Company October 1 to 15. Entries for the Exhibit, national in scope, are invited and are now being received from advertisers, artists and agencies in all parts of the country.
● The Exhibit will take the form of a national contest, all entries to be submitted to a jury for the elimination of ineffective designs and the selection of prize winners and those deserving honorable mention. Original paintings of 24-sheet and three-sheet posters and painted bulletins will be submitted for competition and these will be displayed prominently where both advertisers and the general public will have an opportunity to study them.

To enhance the value of the exhibit, cards of explanation will be attached to each painting, carrying brief explanations of the design, the purpose of the advertiser and the methods used. It is believed that through this collection a national cross-section study of poster advertising will be possible. Advertisers will have the opportunity to examine in one location the combined effort of a great many other advertisers and to draw conclusions as to the type of design that will bring the most results. This Exhibit also will bring out the new ideas and adaptations that artists and advertisers are using to attract the public.

Through the prize awards the Exhibit purposes to give recognition to those advertising men and artists who are doing work of special distinction, and to encourage, by example, the development of the outdoor advertising medium through the cultivation of high artistic standards.

In order that the Exhibit may be widely representative, advertisers and artists have been invited not only to submit their original paintings but also to call the attention of the committee to the work of others deserving recognition.
● Two committees have been appointed to carry out plans for the Exhibit. The Chicago Local Committee was organized eight months ago to define the scope of the contest, to handle all advance announcements and publicity, to select the Jury of Awards and the

prizes. This committee comprises: Burr L. Robbins, General Outdoor Advertising Company, chairman; Harold L. Eves, Outdoor Advertising Association of America, Inc., vice-chairman; Joseph Deutsch, Edwards & Deutsch Lithographing Company; Carlton Eberhard, Outdoor Advertising Agency of America; W. A. Gibson, Jr., Outdoor Service, Inc.; H. L. Gilhofer, National Outdoor Advertising Bureau; A. A. Hayden, Foster and Kleiser Company; George Enos Throop, Geo. Enos Throop, Inc.; and Chas W. Wrigley, Chas. W. Wrigley Co.

An Out-of-Town committee is also at work contacting advertisers in all parts of the United States to engage their interest and assure the Council of a large number of entries. The personnel of this committee includes: H. W. Hardy, General Outdoor Advertising Company (East); Mark Seelen, General Outdoor Advertising Company (West); C. E. Eberhard, Outdoor Advertising Agency of America; A. A. Hayden, Foster and Kleiser Company; Oscar Bryn, Erwin, Wasey & Company, Ltd.; Clarence T. Fairbanks, Edwards & Deutsch Lithographing Company; Al. Davis, Latham Lithographing Company; Harold L. Eves, Outdoor Advertising Association of America; H. L. Gilhofer, National Outdoor Advertising Bureau; Capt. H. Ledyard Towle, Campbell Ewald Company; Frank Birch, Criterion Service.

● The Jury of Awards, no member of which will pass upon work done by himself or by those with whom he is associated, will include: Dewey Bertke, art director, Lord & Thomas and Logan; Oscar Bryn, vice-president and art director, Erwin, Wasey & Company, Ltd.; Donald Douglas, vice-president, Quaker Oats Company; G. R. Schaeffer, advertising manager, Marshall Field & Company; Mark Seelen, Western art director, General Outdoor Advertising Company; Haddon Sundblom, Stevens, Sundblom & Stults; Capt. H. Ledyard Towle, general art director, Campbell Ewald Company.

Designs will be judged on the basis of artistic merit, suitability of copy and general effectiveness of layout, prizes to be awarded in duplicate to the advertiser and the artist. Three prizes and ten honorable mentions will be given in the 24-sheet classification and painted bulletin class and one prize and two honorable mentions will be awarded (Continued on page 43)

EXPERIENCE

The outstanding service we are able to extend to our clients comes as a result of over a half century of experience in planning and making successful twenty four sheet posters. Since 1865 we have been engaging in the business of serving the poster needs of national advertisers. This long span of experience, covering almost every conceivable situation, and confronting us many times over with every problem which comes before the lithographer, ideally fits us to

cope with any problem which the reproduction of your design may present.

RIVERSIDE PRINTING CO.

"POSTER MANUFACTURERS SINCE 1865"

CHICAGO   MILWAUKEE

NEWS OF THE OUTDOOR INDUSTRY

Robbins Heads G. O. A.

B. W. ROBBINS

With the formation of new policies in the Outdoor Advertising fraternity, Burnett W. Robbins has been elected president of the General Outdoor Advertising Company, succeeding Kerwin H. Fulton, who resigned to head *Outdoor Advertising, Incorporated*, the new outdoor representative company. His election occurred Thursday, June 4, 1931, and is notable because it places at the head of this organization a man who has an enviable record in the operating of Outdoor Advertising plants. G. O. A. will now concern itself primarily as an operating company, although maintaining local sales organizations in its 39 branches.

As the son of Burr Robbins, the nationally known circus operator, he has from childhood been raised and educated in the Outdoor Advertising fraternity. Prior to 1891, he was with the John B. Farwell Company. Then from 1891 to 1906, he managed and efficiently re-organized the Lease and Rental Department of the American Posting Service. His creative work here resulted in his rise to the presidency of that company from 1906 to 1921.

In February, 1925, when the General Outdoor Advertising Company was founded, which was a merger of the Thomas Cusack Company, the Poster Advertising Company and twenty-one other organizations, his commendable work won him the position of vice-president, director and manager of Chicago and Chicago territory.

For a great many years he has been a national director and secretary of the Outdoor Advertising Association of Illinois.

■ ■ ■

Bercovich to Handle Campaign for Milk Producers

Producers supplying 50% of San Francisco's fresh milk have instituted an advertising campaign to educate the public to the advantages of drinking more of their product.

The Harry Bercovich Agency of San Francisco has been appointed to direct the campaign.

Although San Francisco is declared to have the best milk supply of any large city in the nation, the consumption of milk per capita here is below the national average, it is asserted.

Newspaper, radio and outdoor will be used in the campaign. Opening copy will stress the importance of the dairy industry to Northern California, together with the importance of milk as a part of the daily diet. Later the copy will emphasize the health attributes of milk.

■ ■ -

Outdoor Man Joins Lennen and Mitchell, Inc

Sidney J. Hamilton, who for the past twenty years has been closely identified with outdoor advertising, has joined the advertising agency of Leunen & Mitchell. Inc., as Vice-President of that organization.

SIDNEY J. HAMILTON

Mr. Hamilton has had a wide experience in handling outdoor advertising, having started in this work in 1910 and soon became a solicitor for Outdoor Advertising. In 1916 he was one of the organizers of the Poster Advertising Co., which later merged with the General Outdoor Advertising Co., and in 1925 became Vice-President of that organization.

Mr. Hamilton has the distinction of having handled uninterruptedly the outdoor advertising of the P. Lorillard Company for the past twenty years, having secured this account soon after he started his career as an advertising man. In his capacity as Vice-President of Lennen & Mitchell, Inc., he will have complete charge of all their outdoor advertising, and bring to them a man with great knowledge of markets and who is an authority in his field.

It is very fortunate inasmuch as Mr. Hamilton has chosen to leave Outdoor Advertising, Incorporated, that his next preference should be in the General Advertising Agency field. As an officer in the Leunen-Mitchell organization he will be devoting his time and experience to building more and better outdoor advertising and in that respect he will be a valuable aid in the building and developing of business for the industry.

Photo courtesy Atlantic Lithographic and Printing Co.

Old Gold breaks away from the geometric spots which have featured previous posters and uses this well-painted head with copy which has been carefully planned to avoid awkward crowding.

Photo courtesy Edwards and Deutsch

Hudson uses a simple, dignified lettering design which offers one brief message. The colorful spot which is used as the background of the initial gives life to this poster.

Photo courtesy Outdoor Service

Post Toasties gives proper prominence to the package and to the name, while the silhouetted figures symbolizing energy are introduced without complicating the design.

Photo courtesy Gugler Lithographic Corp.

The Atlas Brew designs make use of a distinctive technique which lends continuity to the series. The use of the product is linked with outdoor sports. The placing of the glasses below the name is adroitly handled.

Photo courtesy Schmidt Lithograph Co.

Appetite appeal figures this attractive design. Well composed, every element carefully placed, this poster is one of the best that have advertised Sunkist.

Photo courtesy Edwards and Deutsch

Catalina Swim Suits retains its distinctive figure in this new design and creates a new poster which possesses a remarkably strong element of continuity.

24 HOURS

Day and night—Outdoor Advertising can't be folded up, can't be tuned out, can't be thrown away, constantly repeating your message to thousands

Foster and Kleiser
COMPANY
General Office: San Francisco
Operating plants in California, Washington, Oregon and Arizona
Offices in New York and Chicago

NATIONWIDE OUTDOOR ADVERTISING

Outdoor Advertising in the National Campaign

(Continued from page 21) outdoor advertising is in my opinion a far broader one than our copy book precepts allow. Its flexibility is double-barreled. It is just as flexible as to the message it carries as it is flexible in its point of use.

Some 10 years ago the Curtis Publishing Company was faced with a problem. This problem was not so much the stimulation of new business in Curtis publications as it was a question of getting existing advertisers to use increased space units. Out of this necessity came one of the most adroit sales efforts that was ever made in the history of selling. The great problem that confronted artists in utilizing two pages facing was known as the difficulty of "jumping the gutter." Curtis Publishing announced a competition. They invited all of the top flight of commercial artists in America to compete for a prize, and paid them for their work as well, and as a result brought out a book called *Two Pages Facing*. I found that copy men and art directors, subsequent to the publication of that book, who had heretofore been thinking in terms of one page, unconsciously found themselves drawing pictures and making compositions to fit two pages facing. I believe that the Curtis Publishing Company would go on record as saying that this was the single most successful factor in increasing the advertising lineage in the Saturday Evening Post. And the reason for its success was that it stirred the imagination—caused the advertising business to think creatively about a different space unit.

I believe also that the Outdoor interests of America can concern themselves very profitably with similar attempt to stimulate thought in all of the branches of the advertising business as it applies to the use of outdoor advertising.

Right now is where I fall into a trap—a trap that confronts every agency man. We all feel ourselves supremely qualified to advise someone else about the running of his own business, so, open-eyed at least, I walk into the trap. No one of these suggestions has been checked for its practicability, but first of all, I would like to hear from the salesmen of outdoor space a great deal more about markets, and perhaps a little less about regulars and illuminateds and high spot paint and spectaculars, and costs. Of all media, certainly outdoor advertising ought to have, in intimate detail, facts about the markets it sells. I would like to see these salesmen approach an advertiser or advertising agency from the viewpoint of fitting a very essential method of advertising into a sales plan rather than an attempt to sell it as a specialized advertising form. I would like to see outdoor adver-

tising build itself with the trade . . . with all classes of distributors of merchandise—to a point where its acceptance on their part is at least as complete as it is of newspaper and certain magazine advertising. I would like to feel free to ask outdoor advertising for information regarding a product in specific markets, because I feel that they ought to be able to secure unbiased facts as quickly and as completely as any other source because of local market knowledge, and also because there is rarely the same competitive angle that may exist among newspapers or magazines. I would like to see the results of test campaigns in markets showing the relative costs of outdoor advertising versus other advertising media. I would like to eliminate from outdoor selling the attempt to justify bad locations for any reason whatsoever. Newspapers and magazines give bad positions to advertisers for basically the same mechanical reasons. I think that we will all agree that there has been no better period than the present for the outdoor industry to go through the same period of introspection that other businesses are facing, with one thing in mind—to give the advertiser even greater advertising value, for in that way, and in that way only is outdoor advertising going to continue to grow and prosper.

And with its growth and prosperity is an equal opportunity for profit for the advertising agency.

■   ■   ■

Plan National Outdoor Art Exhibit

(Continued from page 37) in the three-sheet classification.

Prizes will be presented at a luncheon on the opening day of the Exhibit at Marshall Field & Company. They will be in the form of marble desk sets inlaid with a gold seal, the design of Alfonso Iannelli of the Art Institute of Chicago.

During the period of the Exhibit, through the courtesy of Marshall Field & Company and of the General Outdoor Advertising Company, the project will be given wide publicity through radio, newspaper and outdoor advertising.

After the Exhibit has been displayed in Chicago for two weeks it will be sent to a number of the other large cities of the United States and shown to local advertisers.

The magazine *Advertising Outdoors* will reproduce the prize winners and many of the original paintings that will appear in the Exhibit in a Special Poster Design Number. to be distributed on the opening day of the Exhibit to the Chicago advertising fraternity, and subsequently to advertisers all over the country. Articles by the jury giving their reactions to the Exhibit and their opinions in relation to new trends in the medium also will be included.

Our
Congratulations
to
OUTDOOR
ADVERTISING
INC.

EDWARDS & DEUTSCH
LITHOGRAPHING COMPANY
COLOR·COMMERCIAL·OFFSET LITHOGRAPHERS

CHICAGO June 20th, 1931

Outdoor Advertising, Inc.,
New York City.

Dear Sirs:

We grasp this opportunity to extend publicly our heartiest congratulations to all branches of Outdoor Advertising responsible for the creation of your new organization, which in cooperation with Advertising Agencies, Solicitors and Plant Owners, will coordinate into a single Unit Sales Promotion Plan, all cooperative efforts directed toward stimulating more widespread use of Outdoor Advertising. You have our best wishes that all of the aims and purposes crystallized in the New Unit Sales Plan will be fully realized and justify the visions and hopes of its sponsors.

Such a plan should and undoubtedly will receive the generous support and endorsement of which it is deserving by all industries identified or allied with Outdoor Advertising. Our Company, just turning its Thirty-Fifth Milestone, pledges its wealth of experience, its complete modern poster equipment, its skilled artisans and general personnel, to the production of posters that will best interpret the advertiser's requirements with the maximum in distinctive color production and service.

May you live long and prosper!

Very sincerely,

EDWARDS & DEUTSCH
LITHOGRAPHING COMPANY

Joseph Deutsch,
Pres't

J.D./DS

Outdoor Advertising Inc.
and How It Will Operate

(Continued from page 13) sider with the agency or
solicitor the actual marketing situations that the
advertiser wishes to approach. Having analyzed the
problem, it will then be, taken up in relation to the
various classifications of, space in Outdoor Advertising. The men in charge of this department have a
sure knowledge of actual conditions in the field which
will bring forth a skillful solution remarkable for its
hard-hitting effectiveness and low percentage of
waste. In brief, through this department the advertiser will receive the benefit of expert planning counsel so that the different branches of this medium may
be applied to exactly fit his problem, thereby obtaining the greatest possible results with the utmost economy.

Copy and Art
Creative and Advisory

In this department the personnel is composed of
men who have specialized for years in the development of copy and design exclusively for Outdoor Advertising. The art directors of Outdoor Advertising,
Incorporated, know from long experience where to
obtain the best Outdoor art to fit specific problems,
and these artists have already been schooled by these
same men in the technique of Outdoor presentation,
which is quite different from the illustrative art in
magazines and newspapers.

● There is an art and copy committee, members of
which are authorities on the subject of Outdoor Advertising art and copy. Advertising ideas, written
copy and colored visual sketches will form a regular
part of the service rendered without charge to advertising agencies and solicitors.

Promotion Service

This department offers advice on ways and means
to merchandise Outdoor Advertising to salesmen,
dealers and jobbers, and the new company will furnish speakers to explain campaigns to conventions of
dealers, to inspire sales forces, etc. This service will
include special counsel on broadsides to reinforce
Outdoor Advertising, form letters to dealers and
jobbers, booklets, etc. Also expert help in preparing
portfolios for the salesmen, advice in the buying of
window posters and miniature reproductions and
finally the Promotion Department, when necessary,
will make a check-up of results after the campaign
is over.

In regard to the general principles which will be
followed in operations:—the approach to the advertiser will always be made in cooperation with the
agency or solicitor through whom the business is
being placed. Naturally, the advertisers is left full
discretion in choosing the particular agent or solicitor through whom he wishes the business to be

placed. Furthermore, when the company is asked
an opinion as to how a particular contract should be
placed or sublet, it will beg to be excused from answering such a question, because all operations must
be fair, impartial and unbiased. This company will
not enter into contracts with advertisers but will
always have such contracts executed through the
agency or solicitor selected by the advertiser.

● Outdoor Advertising, Incorporated, does not maintain any sublet facilities for the mechanical handling
of the advertiser's order, but special representatives
will deliver all of the cooperation and assistance
which the advertiser has been accustomed to receive
from them. The company will never designate or
recommend a plant to be employed in towns where
more than one plant is available. It represents the
industry at large and not the interests of any particular plant owner or group of plant owners.

The expense in connection with the operating of
the new company will be met by a fee paid to it by
the plant owners employing its service. The amount
of this fee to be paid by each plant owner will be
based upon a percentage of the total amount of
national Outdoor Advertising from every source executed by such plant owners. It will be the permanent policy of the company to operate without profit.

The objective is to develop for all national advertisers everywhere a finer, more complete and more
proficient Outdoor Advertising service, uniform in
quality, ever increasing in advertising value, and
universally available.

National advertisers should welcome the formation
of Outdoor Advertising, Incorporated, because now
for the first time the advertising ability stored up in
the general agencies may be applied to a more intelligent use of Outdoor Advertising in the solution
of merchandising problems. This means that the
advertiser will now be able to secure from his agent
the same kind of service in Outdoor Advertising that
he has long been accustomed to receive from him in
other media.

Advertising agents should welcome this plan because it places them in a position to round out and
complete the efficient service they already render
their clients. Agents are now able, through the company, to acquire easily a thorough knowledge of the
Outdoor medium, and in cooperation with special
representatives they will be able to present Outdoor
Advertising plans and sketches which measure up to
the same standard they have already set in other
forms of advertising.

● Outdoor Advertising, Incorporated, represents a
real contribution to the elimination of waste in advertising, and also a contribution toward efforts to
reduce the cost of distribution. This medium has
already proved its worth in selling goods. Where it

can be judiciously used. it is powerful and economical. It is localized, intensive advertising, and it has done a splendid job in the past for hundreds of national advertisers.

For the first time, the attributes and the functions of this medium will be intelligently and aggressively presented to all national advertisers who might profitably use this form of advertising, regardless of where they may be located or how they intend to place their Outdoor Advertising.

These are the aims of Outdoor Advertising, Incorporated. When this plan is in full operation it will help and benefit advertiser, agency, solicitor — in fact, every one who is interested in the wider, more intelligent and more profitable use of this medium.

■ ■ ■

Partlan Addresses Woman's Club

A rather unusual request was received by the New Hampshire Outdoor Advertising Association from the Woman's Club of Exeter, New Hampshire, recently. Before passing judgment on outdoor advertising the ladies of that club wanted to hear the plant operators' and advertisers' side of the story.

William H. Partlan, president of the New Hampshire Association, gave them an interesting talk of which the local newspaper, The Exeter News Letter, had the following to say:

"Mr. William H. Partlan, a representative of the Outdoor Advertising Association of New Hampshire, gave an informative talk on the work of that association. It was the first time that most of the audience had heard the matter presented from the viewpoint of the advertiser. Mr. Partlan stated that outdoor advertising was the original form of advertising, and the first to be organized. He also told many interesting facts concerning the manner in which it is regulated.

CONGRATULATIONS
TO OUTDOOR ADVERTISING INC

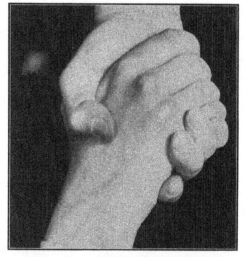

FROM

CREAM CITY OUTDOOR ADV. CO.
ESTABLISHED 1840

300 N. EIGHTH STREET   MILWAUKEE

The Story of the National Outdoor Advertising Bureau

(Continued from page 18) ports and to be as helpful to the plant owner as possible. Both the operators and the advertisers consider his report reliable. Plant owners, in anticipation of a visit from one of these inspectors at any time, are on the alert to see to it that the plant is constantly maintained at as high a standard as possible.

● With the expansion of the Bureau's inspection service to include the servicing of the accounts taken over by Outdoor Advertising, Inc., from the General Outdoor Advertising Company as well as the undertaking of a promotion campaign by Outdoor Advertising, Inc., the activities of the Bureau will be concentrated more than ever upon inspection and improvement of plant service, thus insuring the advertiser of an increasingly effective use of the Outdoor medium.

The National Outdoor Advertising Bureau was first conceived some fifteen years ago as the result of the marked improvement in the standards of the Outdoor medium. Up to that time, Outdoor had been considered as somewhat of a stepchild of advertising and had received slight consideration. Standards of service, however, had improved rapidly and advertisers and advertising agencies began to realize that this medium has tremendous possibilities. It was believed that a centralized placing bureau could be formed which would provide a purchasing and inspecting service for all member agencies at far less cost than a single agency could operate a similar organization. Interested agencies subscribed to stock in the new venture in proportion to the amount of business placed by them and the Bureau began operation.

For some years, however, the situation was unsatisfactory. The advertising agency had not then assumed the dominant position that it now holds in the advertising field and the outdoor industry was not certain as to how to receive the new servicing organization.

In 1918 the Bureau was reorganized with F. T. Hopkins and H. F. Gilhofer, formerly Eastern and Western sales managers of the Thomas Cusack Company as its Eastern and Western managers. The effect of this was the establishment of a 12% agency commission, two per cent going to the Bureau and ten per cent to the agency. The clarifying of the situation was immediate. From a previously high annual volume of $500,000 the volume of business placed by the Bureau jumped to $5,000,000 in the first year after its reorganization.

● As previously stated, the member agencies, when the Bureau first went into operation, subscribed for stock in proportion to the amount of all business

placed by them. This arrangement was later changed to the compulsory purchase of at least one share of stock with an additional entrance fee being required, this fee also being based upon the amount of business placed. At present, however, it is possible for any agency to become a member of the Bureau through the purchase of only one $100 share of stock in the organization.

The Bureau will continue to be operated as a nonprofit organization for the benefit of agencies and for the benefit of advertisers and it is confidently believed that when the plan is in full operation the added volume of business will enable the Bureau to pay to the agencies 12% of the commission which it receives and at the same time to render a more effective and efficient service than ever before, performing all of the functions that could be performed by the most efficient and complete outdoor department in an agency and some services which such a department could not possibly perform except at an exorbitant cost.

● Agencies which meet the normal requirements, if they so desire, may set up their own facilities for the placing, servicing and checking of their own outdoor advertising accounts and can place their orders direct with outdoor plants, in which case it is understood that the commission from plants which have employed Outdoor Advertising, Incorporated, as their representative would after January 1st, 1932, be 15% —the same commission as paid to the Bureau.

With Outdoor Advertising, Inc., making available to the agencies the services of a personnel trained in all aspects of the Outdoor medium and the National Outdoor Advertising Bureau functioning as an impartial purchasing, inspecting and advisory unit for the agencies, the Outdoor medium presents a unified program of sales and service based upon complete cooperation with the advertising agency.

■ ■ ■

Zehrung Again Mayor of Lincoln, Nebraska

Frank C. Zehrung, president of The Zehrung Company, outdoor advertising plant of Lincoln, Nebraska, was recently elected mayor of that city by the largest vote ever accorded to the office at a general city election.

Four years ago Mr. Zehrung declined to be a candidate for another term, but at the urgent request of a great many of his friends, he reluctantly consented to make one more race. The results of the primary and the general election showed that Mr. Zehrung's friends had not over-estimated his popularity.

Aside from some small advertisements in the local papers, Mr. Zehrung made no effort on his own behalf, saying that if the people wanted him, he would be elected; if they did not, he would be content.

Buying 100 Cents with the 1931 Advertising Dollar

(Continued from page 10) hood of a single street, without waste. It is a boon to the advertiser whose business does not require rapid copy change or long explanation. These advertisers can promote their products or services in large space with lifelike color and picture with frequent repetition at a cost as low as six cents per thousand readers.

● As one of the most efficient tools to serve modern industry under modern conditions, Outdoor Advertising will always exist. Its abuses will not. With the dawning of enlightened self-interest such as is embodied in the removal of structures from real scenic areas, elimination of traffic hazards, the cleaning up and landscaping of locations and artistic and structural improvement, all of which are being accomplished as fast as resources and human labor permit, Outdoor Advertising faces a radiant future. With an ever growing circulation—a rapid improvement in structure—design and art work, with beautified surroundings, with all of the technical knowledge of the electrical industry at its hand for the creation of striking illusions of reality and motion, with the third dimension in advertising still to be explored, Outdoor Advertising is literally in its veriest infancy. Its effectiveness can be increased many fold. We do not yet dream of what its physical limitations may be.

What form Outdoor Advertising will take in the future none of us can foresee—we do know that it is and increasingly will be a force of incalculable value to industry and commerce—an asset to its community and nation, and a source of lasting pride to the men who have given their lives to the modern development of this ancient aid to progress, which after serving well through many ages, finds itself again in step with the world.

(NOTE: Acknowledgment is given to Presbrey's "History of Advertising" for many historical facts and quotations used in this article.)

■ ■ ■

Outdoor Advertising Progresses in Switzerland

According to an article by R. Beaujon in Advertiser's Weekly, only at the end of the last century, that is to say, several years later than most other countries, did the poster make its appearance in Switzerland as a servant of trade, industry and of the public in general.

● Fortunately this delay was rapidly made good, and when one considers the work that has been done by Swiss artists, lithographers and billposting agencies, one can conclude that Switzerland is now in the vanguard as far as the use of this modern weapon of publicity is concerned.

It was about 1896 that the first poster artists made their appearance in Switzerland. About this time Forestier and Dunki created some wonderful posters that we still remember. These pioneers have disappeared, but they have had some worthy successors.

With a few exceptions, there are no artists in Switzerland who "specialize" in posters, in the restrictive sense of the word. Cardinaux, Bamberger and Courvoisier are all artists who regularly hold exhibitions of works of a purely artistic character.

But they are artists who, when they are dealing with advertising, know how to divest themselves of their exclusively artistic point of view, and become publicity artists, without losing any of their talent.

It would be beyond the scope of this article to give a list of all the well-known poster artists, but the names of Linck, Mangold, Hosch, Stocklin, Menuet, Fontanet, Loupot must be mentioned.

The printer lithographers have also played a large part in the development of the poster by their scrupulous professional conscience, and their perpetual search for improvement. Among them the names of Sonor, Atar, Sauberlin and Pfeiffer, Klausfelder, Wassermann, Wolfensberger, Fretz, Orell-Fussli, especially deserve mention.

Before billposting arrived at such a standard of perfection, due to the intimate co-operation between lithographers and artists, the walls of our towns were covered only by official communications, and it is the result of this old-established practice that the control of billposting rests in the hands of the communes, and not in those of the state of the cantons.

● The efforts that were made by advertising interests, however, to develop commercial billposting were followed by such success that the principal towns conceded their exclusive rights of billposting to a private company which gave them the necessary moral and material guarantees. This example was soon followed by towns of secondary importance, and then by the smaller communities.

As a result, Swiss municipal authorities have a common billposting concessionnaire, who is alone responsible for the economic and aesthetic interests of this form of publicity. One of the first results of the activities of this concessionnaire was the introduction, largely aided by the lithographers, of the standardized Swiss format, measuring 3½ ft. by 5 ft.

The surface of every billposting space is strictly calculated on this accepted format and its multiples.

Thus the whole surface can be utilized without loss of space, and as far as possible the position of each poster is determined according to its individual characteristics, in order to obtain harmonies or contrasts of color agreeable to the eye, as well as to ensure the maximum of visibility for each unit.

A. F. A. Outdoor Program
Wins Big Attendance

(Continued from page 30) media, but without attempting to interfere with present methods of placing business. We have taken advantage of this period to put our house in order, and to prepare for better business.

● "In all that we have done we have considered first of all the national advertiser, his needs, his point of view, and his desires as to the method in which his national advertising appropriations shall be handled and his contracts executed. In order to clear the way, it was first necessary for the Outdoor Advertising industry to adopt two new policies:

"One: The extending of recognition to all reputable advertising agencies by outdoor advertising plant owners who deliver service consistent with the high standards now prevailing in the industry.

"Two: The establishment of a commission of 15% payable to such advertising agencies, the same percentage as that extended to the agencies by other major media. I might say that this 15% commission is effective at once on all business to be executed after January 1, 1932. Current commissions to agencies will not be disturbed.

It is understood that the National Outdoor Advertising Bureau will function as a bureau somewhat similar to the A B C in newspaper advertising. This means the development and maintenance of an adequate field service, devoted to the evaluation of service rendered on existing outdoor advertising plants, also a national organization in the same office for checking and verification of service rendered to national advertisers by plant owners all over the country. This inspection will be unbiased and performed by men experienced in the physical requirements of outdoor display.

"The capital stock of Outdoor Advertising, Incorporated, is owned by the plant owners in our industry in proportion to their plant holdings, and this stock is so thoroughly distributed as to make the company truly representative of the entire industry.

"The company has acquired as a nucleus such part of the personnel and equipment of the national sales department of the General Outdoor Advertising Company as was deemed advisable. To this we will add from time to time men of standing and experience in the advertising world until our organization, when it is fully developed, shall be adequate to serve, through their representatives, all national advertisers who can properly include this medium in their advertising plans."

● Mr. Fulton next discussed the advisory, research, and merchandising service, plans, copy and art, promotion, and market research, adding: "For the first time, the attributes and the functions of this medium

will be intelligently and aggressively presented to all national advertisers who might profitably use this form of advertising, regardless of where they may be located or how they intend to place their outdoor advertising.

"These are the aims of Outdoor Advertising, Incorporated, and I know that when this plan is in full operation it will help and benefit advertiser, agency, solicitor—in fact, every one who is interested in the wider, more intelligent and more profitable use of this medium."

O is Shepard's talk on "The Essentials of Good Copy Out-of-Doors," was refreshing, in that he illustrated his talk by drawing on a huge scale, so that all in the room could see, a visual idea of copy, not in the modern manner, and copy in the tempo of today. He introduced his talk by quoting from Fanny Brice's song, "Why Buy Me Posies, When It's Shoesies That I Need?"

Mr. Shepard said that we owe the public something for their looking at our posters. One important thing that we owe is beauty. He said that we live in a machine country, in an age of steel, and that the art that we should use should be symbolic of the age.

● "The essentials of good outdoor advertising," remarked Mr. Shepard, "have not been arbitrarily invented by anyone. They are largely the result of two factors: speed and distance. Time and space. The American tempo strongly manifests itself in this medium of advertising. Everyone hurries. The pedestrian and the motorist rush past poster panels placed usually at a distance, either above or across, from the speeding passerby. No motorist ever has time to see the details or to read lengthy copy on the poster panels. Obviously, the successful outdoor advertisement is the one which may be seen and understood swiftly and from a distance.

"In the poster the illustration is the idea, often requiring only the name of the product or advertiser to complete it. Therein lies the power of a good poster design. Its appeal is basic. The pictorial symbol is the oldest and simplest way of communicating an idea. It speaks a universal language.

"Outdoor advertising requires ingenuity, originality, freshness, and audacity. It demands a versatile designer. The poster is the show business of advertising. Just as in the theatre, the spot light focuses attention on the performer, so the poster dramatically spot lights the product."

Then Mr. Shepard went to his easel, where he had two huge pads of drawing paper. Previously he had said that the pretty girl poster has been posted all over the country, " to lure dollars from gullible buyers of garters, galoshes, and goldfish. On each city street and country road" he continued, "she has lifted her kissable lips to the passing public. My criticism is not directed at the use of the girl as an advertising

device but rather at the technique of realistic painting with which she is portrayed." Mr. Shepard drew
a design of a pretty girl, advertising a permanent
wave which he entitled, "Mermanen Wave," with the
name "Mme. Fischer." Everyone was keenly interested in the quick, flashing strokes and the shading
made by Mr. Shepard's deft fingers.

● "Now," he said, "let's use a symbol, a symbol of
the fleeting moment, to carry out the idea because a
poster has two seconds to do its work."

His nimble fingers started on a second design,
showing the "Mermanen Wave of Mme. Fischer,"
with the profile of a beautiful face, with the hair
streaming in long lines across the artist's paper.

When he finished, he said, "This modern poster
of a beauty shop advertisement is symbolical of the
modern spirit of the day, because today's poster must
have a punch and news value."

Mr. Shepard made the point that when a prospective advertiser desired to make a poster, he should
work together with outdoor advertising specialists
in art and copy, and when the artist had absorbed
the ideas they had in mind, they should then let the
artist alone to work out a design in modern symbolistic form, because, said the speaker, the making
of a poster "is a highly specialized field."

Mr. Shepard paid a tribute to Horace Hardy, Art
Director of Outdoor Advertising, Incorporated, who
is a devotee of modern symbolistic poster advertising.

Following this, Mr. Shepard showed to the audience foreign posters, recently received in this country, showing how English, German, French, and other
artists were working with modernistic methods. These
posters, Mr. Shepard explained, were not the sort
that were made for display in America, but met the
needs of the small structures in foreign lands.

The posters were scrutinized closely because all
the designs shown had strength, simplicity, and a
punch.

Mr. Kleiser, in telling the story of "The Public
Policy of Organized Outdoor Advertising," divided
outdoor advertising into two classes—those outdoor
advertisements that are owned, maintained, and operated by concerns engaged in the delivery of an outdoor advertising service to advertisers, and those not
included in the first class.

● "The first class," said Mr. Kleiser, "represents an
investment of possibly $100,000,000, and is actually
only a small percentage, certainly not exceeding 20%,
of the total of all advertising signs. This class of outdoor advertising is quite completely organized and
standardized. The second class represents advertising signs great in number and almost entirely without organization and almost totally lacking in standardization."

The President of Outdoor Advertising Association
of America, Inc., then outlined the progress of the
Conference on Roadside Business and Rural Beauty,
held in Washington at two meetings since the first of
the year. This Conference and its Continuation Committee have proposed legislation designed to carry
out the theory of zoning, based upon the principle
of eminent domain. This proposed legislation is intended to preserve rural beauty and at the same time
make a definite place for the conduct of roadside
business. Mr. Kleiser said that "the enactment and
enforcement of such legislation is dependent first
upon the favorable action of at least 75% of the
property owners in affected areas. This can be obtained only through the combined efforts of interested organizations and the press. The second enactment and enforcement is by securing the approval of
the courts."

Words of encouragement and cheer were brought
to the meeting by Mr. Chapple, known to all outdoor
advertising men who attend conventions. Mr. Chapple paid a tribute to the poster, saying that "in three
words, they tell the story."

"Determining the Place of Outdoor Advertising in
the Campaign" was the theme of Mr. Chesman's talk.
Mr. Chesman has come up to the top over a period
of years, working from the smaller type of agency
"where one man does about everything from writing
copy to writing those perhaps equally fanciful efforts,
known as mechanical bills," to account representative
of a large advertising agency, where one concentrates
on doing one particular thing well.

● A diverting part of the program were the addresses
of Mr. Bridwell and Mr. Shewell, the former speaking on "The Application of Outdoor Advertising to
Today's Distribution Problems," and the latter on
"Treasure Island." Mr. Bridwell illustrated his talk
with stereoptican slides, showing that we are living
today in the outdoor age and that changed conditions
of American life have radically changed the advertising situation.

"Outdoor Advertising," he concluded, "is an advertising medium through the proper use of which
an advertiser can be before the greatest number of
people for the longest time and for the least expenditure."

"Treasure Island" is a motion picture dealing with
the New York Market. Mr. Shewell introduced it
with an interesting, entertaining talk, telling about
the market in general, its bigness, its vastness,
and its great consuming power. These facts and
figures briefly presented in approved movie methods,
with pictures, made a vivid impression upon the
audience, the climax of the motion pictures being
that outdoor advertising is the "key" to "Treasure
Island."

SPENDING TENDENCIES

1
FRESNO, CALIF.

GENERAL BUSINESS CONDITIONS: Conditions in and around Fresno are about the same as those reported for the month of May. At the present time a very extensive and concentrated drive is in progress for the signing up of additional vineyard acreage to assure complete Government assistance in the handling and marketing of raisins and grapes, the principal product of this territory. If the drive is a success it will assure additional appropriations by the Government for the territory and will eventually work out the problem in the marketing of raisins and grapes.

2
SAN FRANCISCO, CALIF.

GENERAL BUSINESS CONDITIONS: Analysis of trends for May shows that San Francisco business as a whole is steadily climbing out of the depression, according to the monthly survey made by the research department of the Chamber of Commerce. While the increase in business was not found in every line, the composite index including all lines shows that conditions in May were 3.5 per cent better than in April, and that business during the first five months of the year was 7.7 per cent above the first five months' average of the period from 1921-1930 inclusive.

Among the brightest spots in the San Francisco district were construction, including non-residential building permits and municipal and Government contracts, industrial gas sales, establishment of new industries, shipping arrivals and departures, and a decrease in the number of commercial failures.

Building permits issued in May totaled 530, and were valued at $2,853,671, a gain of 55 per cent compared to April. Municipal, State and Government contracts showed a huge increase, and the increase in non-residential construction was 337 per cent over April, and 18 per cent over May, 1930. Home building increased 22 per cent over April and 18 per cent over May, 1930.

Indicating renewed industrial activity were figures showing heavier sales of electric power and industrial gas. Sales for the first five months of 1931 were 35 per cent ahead of 1930.

3

ATLANTA, GEORGIA

GENERAL BUSINESS CONDITIONS: The high-spots in the monthly report from the Sixth Federal Reserve Bank are as follows:

1. Increase in wholesale business.
2. Fewer commercial failures.
3. Heavy increase in new construction.
4. Large increase in consumption of cotton.
5. Gain in savings deposits.
6. Increased pig-iron production.
7. Progress in farm work.

Figures given for May published by The Citizens and Southern National Bank and The Bureau of Business Research, School of Commerce, University of Georgia show a very small loss in building contracts and retail furniture sales; a less than ten per cent loss in electric power consumption, men's clothing sales, wholesale drug sales, post office receipts and retail drug sales. A ten per cent loss was registered in life insurance sales and advertising. A more than ten per cent loss was registered for bank clearings, freight car loadings, department store sales, bank debits, retail hardware sales and wholesale grocery sales.

4

INDIANAPOLIS, INDIANA

GENERAL BUSINESS CONDITIONS: General business conditions in Indianapolis are showing a slight definite upward movement from month to month.
MOVING PICTURE ATTENDANCE: Moving picture attendance is holding its own with a year ago.
AUTOMOTIVE: The sales of new cars for this year still show a decline as compared with last year's figures but each month this difference is being wiped out. As it now stands there is only a difference of 1,000 cars between this year and 1930. The used car market is in very good condition for it is showing an increase. Gasoline figures are still showing a tremendous increase in sales each month over last year.

5

BILLINGS, MONTANA

GENERAL BUSINESS CONDITIONS: It may seem that a point is being stretched, but Billings is going through a period of prosperity. At the present time, all labor is being employed in Billings as there are under construction, the new Fox Theatre which is to open about September 1st, and the new Kress building at an approximate cost of $110,000.00. At the last session of the legislature, $238,000.00 was appropriated for the building of an Eastern Normal School. Bids are to be let on or about July 1st, which means that work will start somewhere around July 15th. Congress appropriated $240,000.00 for an addition to the post office and purchased land south of the same to be put in a part at an estimated cost of $80,000.00. $110,000.00 is being spent to remodel a building to be used for a Federal Penitentiary. This is one out of ten that was passed on by the last Congress.

This is the time for the beginning of the tourist travel into Yellowstone and Glacier National Parks and Billings is the hub and main entrance to these parks. The caretaker of the Municipal Tourist Park reports that so far this year travel is heavier than in 1930.

6

NEW YORK, N. Y.

GENERAL BUSINESS CONDITIONS: Last week (letter dated June 27th) was one of the best in some time for general business in this city. The improvement was attributed to the optimistic sentiment following President Hoover's moratorium proposal. All markets shared in the increasing activity and steadily mounting prices. Metals in the primary markets were strong, commodities generally were in greater demand and the securities market responded to the general optimism.

In wholesale and retail trade the effects were not so general. Bright spots, however, were not lacking. Printcloths sold in larger volume than in a number of months, with some mills receiving large orders for deliveries extending over the remainder of the year, although much of the yardage was small to moderate. Unfinished cotton cloths, particularly the coarse yarn division increased considerably in activity. Sales of woolen goods and worsteds were equal to those of a year ago and men's clothing sales were larger than in the same period of 1930.

Enormous crowds and a rushing business were reported at all of the large beaches. The concession-aires at Atlantic City had such a profitable day that some of them declared they would be "in the clear for the season" if only the fine, hot, sunny weather was maintained over the Fourth of July holidays.

Expressions of optimism from prominent business men follow:

Alfred Reeves, General Manager of the National Automobile Chamber of Commerce, says, "In this new philosophy there is assurance that the crisis is passed and that the 'patient will get well.'"

Kenneth Collins, Executive Vice President, R. H. Macy & Co., "Astonishing as it may seem the Macy affiliation of stores—widely separated geographically—has registered a very large dollar increase in sales during the past two weeks with an almost incredible increase in the number of transactions."

Chester M. Colby, Jr., President, General Foods Corporation, "It seems to me that there are two sets of basic conditions now taking shape in favor of recovery. One is physical and the other psychological."

C. King Woodbridge, Vice President, Remington Rand, Inc., "Big deals ready for consummation."

MOVING PICTURE ATTENDANCE: Theatre attendance is reported as favorable in spite of the hot weather and is up to normal expectations in most cases.

7
SYRACUSE, N. Y.

GENERAL BUSINESS CONDITION: Business in general continues at a very even pace. Improvements that were predicted several months ago can hardly be said to have materialized, but on the other hand, there is no evidence of further recession. The one factor that shows a change for the better is the value of building construction. Due largely to several important non-residential construction projects, there has been greater activity thus far this year in the construction field than during the same period in 1930.

8
KNOXVILLE, TENN.

GENERAL BUSINESS CONDITIONS: Retail trade day by day was better in May, 1931, than it was in May, 1930, according to a special compilation made by Bradstreets. Dollar volume of forty-four of the largest chains was off 3.6 per cent but there were only 25 trading days this year as against 26 a year ago or a difference of 4%.

Business is so good for the Central Rock and Sand Company at Kingsport that the firm has installed flood lights at its quarry for night work.

Knoxville Fertilizer Company's business is only two per cent below the peak of last year, J. H. Dean, vice-president, has reported.

Bradstreets' reports of sales in 98 lines of business for the week ending June 13th show that one was better than, and thirty equal to, totals of a year ago.

The Mead Corporation, operators of nine paper mills and extract plants in four states, has chosen Knoxville for its Southern division headquarters.

The Irving Fisher Wholesale Price Index of semi-finished goods reversed its sharp down-trend of the past two weeks and shows a slight gain. This group of commodities usually leads the way to a major change of trend.

9
MEMPHIS, TENN.

GENERAL BUSINESS CONDITIONS: There has been no material change in the spending tendencies in this section, the outlook is more favorable due to the fact that in the recent stock market flurry cotton advanced along with other stocks and commodities. As cotton is the principal main-stay of the South, this has had a beneficial effect.

Germany is one of the largest users of cotton and cotton linters and it is felt that any stabilization of Germany will assist materially in the return of prosperity to the cotton producing states.

10
AMARILLO, TEXAS

GENERAL BUSINESS CONDITIONS: The June issue of Nation's Business again shows Amarillo, and its trade territory in the "white" on Bradstreet's Business Map; this is the 30th consecutive month.

Amarillo up to June 20th, ranks fourth in building permits in Texas for 1931.

The largest wheat crop in the history of the Panhandle of Texas is now being harvested. Estimates for twenty-six counties in Amarillo's immediate trade territory of this year's production of wheat, run from forty to fifty million bushels. A large per cent of the crop is being sold and the harvest will be over in three weeks.

A new courthouse is now being built and a $300,000.00 underpass started. The building of a $400,000.00 theatre is now being planned as is a $150,000.00 Fair Park Coliseum. Residential building is showing a decided pick-up.

MOVING PICTURE ATTENDANCE: In five local theatres for May, the moving picture attendance is about 3% under May of 1930.

AUTOMOTIVE: Gasoline sales for five leading companies are about 10% under 1930, figuring from January to May inclusive.

Auto registration figures secured from state and county records are as follows:

1st five months in 1930		1st five months in 1931	
Trucks	*Cars*	*Trucks*	*Cars*
1,647	11,659	1,599	12,004

You will note that there is an increase in the number of cars.

11
BEAUMONT, TEXAS

GENERAL BUSINESS CONDITIONS: Beaumont is the funnel into which three pipe lines are pouring the product of the now famous East Texas Oilfield. The glutted market accented for a time the national depression. All admitted bottom had been reached and predictions that the climb had begun, even though it seemed slow are now being verified. The stiffening of the stock prices in connection with the operations of the great oil refining companies centered in this district has aroused well-based optimism encouraging to dealers in every commodity. The spending tendency of our people is being rejuvenated.

12
HOUSTON, TEXAS

GENERAL BUSINESS CONDITIONS: Retail trade continues to hold up quite well. There has been very little change since statistics for May were compiled.

13
LYNCHBURG, VA.

GENERAL BUSINESS CONDITIONS: General business conditions in Lynchburg and vicinity are decidedly on the up-turn. Our shoe factories, overall and pants factories, hosiery mills, cotton mills, pipe and plow foundries as well as our other industries, all report a decided increase in business over previous months. The retail stores also report a decided increase in volume of business. The gross sales show a decrease as far as dollars and cents are concerned. This is of course due to reduction of prices.

There is a decided increase in building permits issued as compared with 1931 in both business and residences.

The State Highway Commission is improving every entry into Lynchburg affording more construction and more tourists.

MOVING PICTURE ATTENDANCE: Moving picture attendance is considerably off which is partly due to the hot weather.

AUTOMOTIVE: There is quite an increase in gasoline consumption as compared with 1930 and there are also more automobile registrations.

14
MILWAUKEE, WIS.

GENERAL BUSINESS CONDITIONS: The Milwaukee major market is responding to the general tone of increased confidence in business, with a pronounced seasonal increase in tires, gasoline, fruit and ice cream.

The local transportation system has issued special recreational passes which are meeting with great public favor. This has reflected itself in record attendance at outdoor amusement enterprises, with a gratifying volume of business reported by these amusement operators.

The unseasonably warm weather of the past week has demonstrated one thing very clearly: People have money to spend and will spend it when strongly urged. There has been a distinct boom in all lines of summer goods, from electric fans to light weight clothing.

Banks continue to report that deposits are heavy, and building and loan associations advise that comparatively few foreclosures are necessary.

Gentlemen, I present

a new figure to our council table. He comes to us prepared to lend advice and assistance in our task of marketing the products of American industry. He brings with him a wealth of experience and specialized knowledge which is to be ours for the asking. He will show us how to utilize the outdoor medium to bring greater returns. He brings us a complete advertising plan department; the skilled advice of a group of art and copy directors who have long experience in creating good outdoor designs. In addition, he offers us the facilities of a promotion department which gathers and accurately interprets market information —a department which gives us the means of contacting dealer and distributor organizations. Gentlemen, I present to you the new sales representative of the outdoor advertising industry ▼ ▼

OUTDOOR ADVERTISING INCORPORATED

NEW YORK
One Park Avenue

Eleven other offices

CHICAGO
Harrison and Loomis Street

Outdoor Advertising of the First Century A. D.

If a modern traveller could visit Rome in the days of the Caesars, he would find that the shop signs would be much the same as those in use in the early part of the 20th century.

N. W. AYER & SON, INC.
ADVERTISING

Newspaper • Magazine
Radio • • Outdoor

THE EMPHASIS OF THIS
ANNOUNCEMENT IS ON

Outdoor Advertising

which field we re-enter, making available to our clients complete facilities
for the preparation and placement
of the several forms of advertising
in the Outdoor field.

N. W. AYER & SON, INC.
Advertising Headquarters
WASHINGTON SQUARE, PHILADELPHIA

New York   *Boston*   *Chicago*   *San Francisco*   *Detroit*

LOCATION

At converging traffic points... along the thronged arteries of travel... the consistent, persistent selling messages of Outdoor Advertising are hammering cashable memory impressions into the minds of millions.

NATIONWIDE OUTDOOR ADVERTISING

Advertising Outdoors

A magazine devoted to the interests of the Outdoor Advertiser

VOL. 2, No. 8

CONTENTS for AUGUST 1931

Harold L. Eves
Editor

Ralph B. Patch, *Associate Editor*
James P. Dobyns, *Advertising Manager*

Eastern Advertising Representatives:
Walworth and Wormser,
420 Lexington Ave., New York City.

Western Advertising Representatives:
Dwight Early,
100 N. La Salle St., Chicago

ADVERTISING OUTDOORS is published on the 1st of every month by the Outdoor Advertising Association of America, Inc., 165 W. Wacker Drive. Chicago. Ill. Telephone Randolph 1692. Harold L. Eves, Editor and Manager.
Subscriptions for the United States, Cuba, Porto Rico. Hawaii and the Philippines, $3.00 a year in advance; Mexico and Canada, $3.25; for all other countries, $3.50. Thirty cents the copy. Make all checks, money orders, etc., payable to Outdoor Advertising Association of America, Inc.
Entered as second-class matter, March 21st, 1930, at the Post Office at Chicago, Ill., under the act of March 3, 1879, by Outdoor Advertising Association of America, Inc. Printed in U. S. A.

According to Grantland Rice, the number of golf
clubs in the United States has increased from seven
hundred forty-one to four thousand, five hundred
eighty-one in ten years and the playing attendance
from five hundred thousand to four million in the
same period. Golf, once an exclusive game, is now
being played by millions. Championship matches
draw thousands of spectators. In the photograph
above is shown part of a crowd of three thousand
watching the finals of a women's tournament. Outdoor advertising is the only form of advertising that
can reach these crowds while they are at play—outdoors.

WHY NOT LEARN FROM THE "PITCHMAN"?

YOU probably have no ambition to become a "pitchman." You may even think that you have nothing to learn from these high pressure merchandisers who, with tripod and satchel, stand on a street corner or in the doorway of a closed store and give their "spiel" to the passing—but frequently stopping—Saturday night crowd.

But did you ever see one of them on an empty street; did you ever see one of them with his "pitch" where there wasn't a crowd? Perhaps you even think he did not send for market information. But he did. Letters passed between friends of the fraternity that there was a good crop in such and such a county and soon tripods and satchels were moving that way.

After all that is about what any market survey will disclose. Are people going to spend money in such and such a place? If they are going to, how can we get to them? How can we find the crowds? True there is house-to-house canvassing but the "pitch" does not consider them in the same class with himself. He will go into a town where there are a dozen prominent local stores all selling say, razor blades and sell more razor blades in one Saturday night—where the crowd is—than all of the stores in town will sell in a month.

Even if we don't want to be a "pitchman," isn't there something we can learn from his methods? Find out where people are going to spend. Get in front of the crowd. Graphically portray and demonstrate the use of your product. Tell a short, quick story and make a sale. A little thought and care will produce a poster design that will tell that story. Outdoor Advertising will help you follow the crowd.

Just because the "pitchman" will not be there tomorrow and you must sell your goods day after day does not mean that he is dishonest and certainly does not mean that his fundamental merchandising principle is wrong.

Harvey L. Eves

SOME OF GENERAL FOODS' OUTDOOR DESIGNS

General Foods Corporation has been a large and consistent user of the outdoor medium to promote the sale of its products. The Maxwell House series has probably made use of the most outstanding designs but Post Toasties, Post's Bran, Sanka Coffee, Hellmann's Mayonnaise and other products are familiar names on panels the country over.

THE ROMANCE OF
General Foods Corporation
by Wilma McKenzie

The story of standardization of business is aglow with romance. Henry Ford's career has been far from colorless; William Wrigley, Jr., has probably had as much excitement in his life as has had Sinclair Lewis. Many felt that with the passing of the days of Jay Gould and Uncle Dan'l Drew and their high-handed contemporaries, the glamour went out of business for a great many men. Perhaps the next generation will look upon the present one with the same kind of a feeling. But today is the day of mass production, and the standardized product is the symbol of modern business activity.

● Certainly no greater romance of business has ever crested the horizon than that which surrounds the great General Foods Corporation of today. This company which had such a lowly beginning is now said to be the largest food manufacturing and distributing organization in existence.

Back in 1895, and quite by accident, Charles William Post, of Springfield, Ill., laid the cornerstone of this great business. Mr. Post, who was a traveling salesman dealing in farm machinery in the Southwest, seeking to regain his lost health moved to Battle Creek, Mich., for treatment. In making this change he naturally had to forego his income, and necessity, the mother of many a great achievement, forced Mr. Post to seek ways and means of supplanting his lost income. Being a sick man, his mind turned to corrective foods. And so through accident and necessity there was developed the first experimental laboratory that later brought forth Postum Cereal. This laboratory was in a barn in Battle Creek. The barn has been preserved and is now a part of the great General Foods Battle Creek Experimental Laboratory. The total investment in his first roasting oven and grinder was $46.85.

When Mr. Post had developed Postum to a point that met with his satisfaction, he took a small quantity and went to Grand Rapids where he introduced his new food to the grocers in the town. Except for his unshakeable belief that he had developed a food product that would bring greater health to his fellowmen and his determination to see it through, the foundation of the company might not have been laid,

C. W. Post, founder of the Postum Company.

for in the first year his expenses amounted to $800 above his income. Admiration is inspired for the man whose visitation and grim determination carried him through the early years of disappointment and threatened failure. The fact is he did carry on and shortly this small business turned the corner, crossed the brink of success and became a profitable enterprise.

After the first year Mr. Post began to see the fruition of his hopes. The business expanded. The complaisant attitude which the public was beginning to manifest toward it could not be mistaken, and seemed to assure Mr. Post of their approving support in the future. It was a barometer, he thought, to the success of the project. So with renewed courage he threw himself wholeheartedly into the task of developing a cereal food that would offer abundant nutritional value, appetite appeal and crispness to encourage chewing to benefit the teeth.

● Three years later he presented to the public the product which is known as Grape Nuts. This new food was launched in 1898, and is said to be the first manufactured food ever placed on the market in package form.

With these two products the business grew in leaps and bounds, and for several years Mr. Post confined himself to expanding manufacturing facilities and developing an organization to foster the increasing demand. The growth in volume was accompanied by improvements in methods and refinements of processes. Automatic machinery replaced hand work in the making and packaging of the goods. Mr. Post felt the need of health products as health foods, so for a time he buried himself in experimentation in that direction. The outcome was Corn Flakes, named Post Toasties, and then Instant Postum. With this newer and more convenient form of Postum, sales of Postum quickly tripled.

● At a very early date Mr. Post realized the value of advertising and applied himself diligently to the job of telling the story of his product through advertising.

The year 1918—a little more than twenty years after Mr. Post made his first experiment in the little barn in Battle Creek, Michigan—found the business grown to considerable magnitude. At this time a man who was later to play a most important part in the development of General Foods Corporation, then the Postum Cereal Company, and who was an esteemed friend of the Post family, was drawn into the company as Assistant Treasurer. This man was C. M. Chester, Jr.,—today president of the General Foods Corporation.

Mr. Chester had visions of a great food manufacturing and distributing corporation. He set about to make his dream come true, and through his generalship and untiring efforts the second cornerstone of this corporation was laid. He is credited with having had the "big" idea of bulk production and bulk sales. Chester is the son of Rear Admiral C. M. Chester, U. S. N., and is a graduate of Yale and of the New York Law School. From 1902 until the beginning of the World War he practiced law in New York City, and for a brief period was in the office of Charles Evans Hughes, now Chief Justice of the United States. During the war he was a major in the infantry, and was subsequently appointed inspector-general for assignment overseas, which assignment was not carried out on account of the declaration of the armistice. Chester works with ease and spends an unusually large amount of time in his office. He is a hard worker and a firm believer in the products which his corporation sells. However, he finds time for play and recreation. His favorite sport is tramping the hills with a gun on his shoulder and his dog at his side on a frosty morning.

The General Foods Corporation took a long stride toward success when it was incorporated in Delaware, February 15, 1922, as the Postum Cereal Company, Inc., succeeding a company of the same name incorporated January 22, 1920. The name was changed to Postum Company, Inc., on March 9, 1927, and on July 24, 1929, the company assumed the name by which it is now known all over the world—the General Foods Corporation.

● Continued experimental work manifested itself in the form of other new foods, all conducive to good health in some form. With the gradual widening of the company's activities, Mr. Chester and others conceived the idea that the entire line of products could better be handled by one sales organization. Each of the products experienced seasonal demand; sales volume was uneven throughout the year. Additional items with other selling seasons, they believed, would add to sales efficiency by permitting a more even spread of sales volume. The economies of selling a line of products through a general sales organi-

On the opposite page a scene in the Battle Creek plant of the General Foods Corporation. Post Toasties cartons are being filled, sealed and wrapped in one operation. The plant is as clean and sanitary as a modern kitchen, all processes being carried out by uniformed workers. Below: one of the poster designs which sell the product of this great factory.

zation could be increased by adding to the number of items handled by each salesman. Right upon the heels of this idea came the decision to purchase other food companies and effect a consolidation. One after another prominent food companies were annexed, and today this huge business has annual sales of more than $128,000,000. It sells eighty products to more than 400,000 grocery stores throughout the United States and enjoys distribution in more than fifty foreign countries. It has fifty-eight factories in forty cities, and more than 11,000 employees.

In 1922 the Postum Cereal Company had grown into a family of four products—Postum Cereal, Instant Postum, Grape Nuts and Post Toasties, which were sold through one sales organization. The addition of Post's Bran Flakes in 1922 helped to make possible a considerable increase in annual sales volume and in net profits.

It is interesting to review the history of some of the products and the circumstances surrounding the acquisition of the companies by General Foods.

The Maxwell House Company was a successful organization doing a substantial business, but had not attained national importance. It was in the year 1920 that this company began the use of Outdoor Advertising. The use of Poster Advertising resulted in such a rapid increase in sales that this medium became the background of all their advertising effort. The business continued to pyramid until in 1928 when the General Foods Corporation paid $45,000,000 for this company that had its beginning forty or fifty years back with Mr. J. O. Cheek selling coffee from his saddle bags in the hills of Kentucky and Tennessee.

● Jell-O, now one of the best known food products in America, was originally introduced in 1896. It joined the ranks of the General Foods Corporation on December 31, 1925, in exchange for 570,000 shares of Postum Cereal Company, Inc., common stock. The Jell-O Company was incorporated in New York, November 5, 1923. In December, 1923, it acquired the entire capital stock of Genesee Pure Food Company, which was merged on December 29, 1923. The Company owns the entire capital stock of Canada, Ltd. Plants are located at LeRoy, N. Y., and Bridgeburg, Ont.

The Minute Tapioca Company, Inc., became a member of the General Foods Family on October 31, 1926, on cash payment. The company was incorporated under the laws of Maine, December 1, 1894; reincorporated under the laws of Massachusetts, February 13, 1913. It manufactures Tapioca from Tapioca flour, and also minute gelatine. The main plant is located at Orange, Mass. In 1928 the discovery of a new use—as a "precision ingredient" which insures exact results with difficult recipes—enlarged the old market and opened new ones. To-

C. M. Chester, Jr., President of General Foods Corporation.

Photo by Blank-Stoller, Inc.

day, thanks to the educational program of General Foods, the sales of this product are the largest in the field.

● In the latter part of 1927 General Foods entered into an agreement with Sanka Coffee Corporation to market their product. Plants are now located at Battle Creek, Mich., LeRoy and Fairport, N. Y., Long Island City, N. Y., Evansville, Ind., Chicago, Ill., Hoboken, N. J., Orange and Dorchester, Mass., Bridgeburg and Windsor, Ont., Montreal, Canada, and Manilla and San Pablo, P. I.

Log Cabin Syrup, known the length and breadth of the country by its unique log cabin shaped container, was originally placed on the market in 1888. by T. J. Towle of St. Paul. The business prospered and in 1927 it was purchased by the General Foods Corporation. The company was incorporated in Delaware, May 21, 1918.

Not so many years ago Richard Hellmann and his wife began to sell an unusual mayonnaise of their own making in their little delicatessen store in New York City. The demand grew until finally the Hellmann's gave up their store and devoted all their time to making mayonnaise. Before long the fame of the product grew to such proportions that they built a modern plant on Long Island. Later Mr. Hellmann decided to sell his product in other sections of the country so he built six other plants at various points similar to the one on Long Island. In 1927 Hellmann's Mayonnaise became a General Foods Product. Today it is sold in every state in the Union, and ranks first in mayonnaise sales.

Bakers Chocolate and Cocoa and Bakers Cocoanut were added to General Foods in 1927; La France Laundry Products in 1928; Certo, Frosted Foods, North Atlantic Oyster Farms and Diamond Crystal Salt in 1929. Numerous other acquisitions have been made during the last year.

● General Foods, with its subsidiaries, manufactures Postum, Instant Postum, Grape Nuts, Post Toasties, Post's Bran Flakes, Post's Bran Chocolate, Blue Ribbon Mayonnaise, Bakers Chocolate, Bakers Cocoanut, Log Cabin Syrup, Swans (Continued on page 35)

Local Conditions
AID MERCHANDISING

The Coca-Cola Company is one of the largest outdoor advertisers in the country, nationally speaking, but it does not stop there. Its branch plants are quick to perceive and take advantage of any local condition not existent in other sections of the marketing area which may form the basis of a campaign to increase individual sales.

● In Los Angeles The Coca-Cola Bottling Company runs a campaign every year during the months of June and July in which it features an individual carton. The carton holds 12 bottles and is conveniently packed so that the customer may carry it in his car. Being easily transportable, the carton is in great demand for picnics and week-end trips.

"We have been merchandising this carton for three years," said Cecil R. Barbee, Sales Manager of the Los Angeles Plant. "Each year the same design has been used in the form of posters shown at about 500 locations, and you will now find this carton in about three-fourths of the drug and grocery stores in Southern California. Posters carry the brunt of the campaign and we tie in with dealer display cards and

newspaper publicity. Printed announcements carrying a picture of the poster are also sent to the trade urging them to stock the carton.

"This advertising is done in co-operation with the Coca-Cola Bottling Company in the East but is used only by the Los Angeles Plant. Fewer people travel by automobile in the East than in Southern California where everybody is on wheels most of the time. They buy this carton for outings, for bridge parties, and for home use. It is easy to buy, easy to carry, and easy to keep on ice. Many people put the whole carton into the refrigerator. The next day they take it with them in their car and it stays cold because the corrugated board acts as an insulator."

Mr. Barbee expressed perfect satisfaction with the advertising.

● "Our carton business has been doubling each year over the preceding year," he said. "The posters bring immediate results. The response is quicker with outdoor advertising than with any other medium. It is the ideal advertising to use in a brief seasonal campaign of this kind."

This poster has produced a large volume of carton sales for the Coca-Cola Company.

COPPER COFFEE POT
Sells Specialties with Posters

● Into the picturesque town of Santa Barbara The Copper Coffee Pot fits as fortuitously as a grass-skirted dancerette into a South Sea Island painting. This restaurant, like the town itself, combines the leisurely hospitality of the South with the brisk activity of the North.

The theme of the Old Spanish Missions is carried out in the architecture of the low, buff-colored, stucco building with its red tile roof and its patio where one may eat delicious food on blue enameled tables that are delightfully attractive against the red brick flooring. To the right tinkles an Old Spanish fountain with cacti in little pottery bowls on its ledge and tropical plants for its setting.

Indoors there is room for 100 additional guests who dine in an atmosphere of quaint balconies overhung with embroidered shawls that suggest lovely senoritas listening to the serenading of enamored dons.

● But that's a romantic story by itself—one that has no place in a businesslike account of an interesting outdoor advertising program. That this advertising has been entirely satisfactory the writer was assured by the restaurant's up-to-date and businesslike young manager, Andrew Birk. who added that the outdoor medium carries the bulk of the publicity burden of The Copper Coffee Pot.

Two highway bulletins and three metropolitan posters are being used at present and the "high light" of the program is the practice of inserting a "flash message" into the poster design at frequent intervals somewhat after the manner followed in theatre advertising. The poster background remains the same, the message being pasted into a center space reserved for the purpose.

● "Every ten days or two weeks the center copy is changed," Mr. Birk said. "The background carries the regular poster and we figure that by putting a new message in another color into this center spot we will catch the attention of those who might have become accustomed to seeing the poster. It gives it new life.

"We know the little idea helps because we have proved it. For instance, we used the message *Chicken Pie—40 Cents* in that spot for two weeks. People came right in and asked for chicken pie and sales doubled during the period the message was up. Sales have doubled on any special item advertised in this space. One message read *We Bake Our Own Pastry* and during that time we did the biggest two weeks pastry business in our history."

From the first this company's outdoor advertising has been satisfactory.

"Over three years ago we started with two bulle-

The panel reading "Green Apple Pie" in the center of the poster is regularly changed to feature a new specialty.

tins," Mr. Birk said. "Results were so good that we increased the number to four, adding one at each end of town on the highway, one 11 miles out and one 22 miles out. There are only two highways leading into Santa Barbara, so people were bound to see the sign. After our three-year contract expired we contracted for two bulletins on the highway and three metropolitan posters. The painted bulletins we change every six months, the posters as often as we wish. They are up about two months with this special center insert being changed frequently.

● "Our designs are gotten out in co-operation with F o s t e r a n d Kleiser. We furnish the idea and their artist carries it out; and by working together we get just what we want. In the poster we generally show our building, using a cut and tying it in with a message aimed to attract the type of trade we wish to cater to. But our bulletins are more dignified in style. We use a blue background with the antique type of coffee-pot in old gold. The text features a reproduction of the Neon sign on our building reading The Copper Coffee Pot, although this is not in Neons on the bulletin itself. The bulletin is reproduced and used as the caption on our newspaper advertising and also on any other advertising we might do.

● "Our use of outdoor advertising has been consistently successful. Sales went up the first year and the following year, after adding the highway signs, there was an increase of from 30 to 50 per cent over the preceding year. Outdoor advertising is considered a regular operating expense of our business, as much so as food or wages. A certain sum is put aside for this advertising each year and when business slumps this sum is increased rather than decreased."

FAMOUS FILM STARS
Sell Beckman Furs

by Augusta Leinard

How did Ben Beckman, the leading furrier of Southern California, build up one of the finest retail establishments in America within his ten years sojourn in Los Angeles? He must be a clever business man, people often remark. And those who know him say that he is.

● Mr. Beckman had been conducting a thriving fur business for ten years in Minnesota when he saw the possibilities held out in the motion picture realm. Film pulchritude plus furs should equal success, he reasoned.

After opening his store in Los Angeles he definitely set about tying up his business with the motion picture industry. Outdoor advertising had been his chief means of publicity for years and he felt that there must be some point of contact which could be capitalized on in this way. He finally concluded that the presentation of a screen star "modeling" a Beckman creation would be far more persuasive than several thousand words.

So that's how the distinctive painted panels which are scattered throughout Los Angeles and constitute about 75 per cent of the Beckman advertising came to feature a motion picture beauty wearing a Beckman fur in every design. In fact the design is built around the picture. The text usually remains the same: BECKMAN FURS, the store's address, the name of the star, and the statement LARGEST EXCLUSIVE FUR HOUSE IN THE ENTIRE WEST.

Beckman's store interior is precisely what the panels lead one to expect. A Hollywoodian atmosphere permeates it. The upper portion of the walls of the luxurious salon consists of painted murals of fur-bearing animals in their native habitat; below are special cases built for holding the autographed pictures of innumerable Hollywood stars in gold frames. Velour chesterfields, gleaming crystal chandeliers, thick velvet carpets—all help strengthen the impression given out by the painted bulletins.

"I foresaw that this tie-in with the motion picture industry would gain public interest quicker than anything else, because what the actress wears must be right and what she buys must be right. Women know this and they come in with the conviction that what Beckman's sells them must be right," Mr. Beckman told the writer.

● "Our outdoor panels were the thing that put desired impression over. It is the ideal medium; especially for the clothing trade. For twenty years I have used outdoor adver- (Continued on page 36)

On this panel, Nancy Carroll, Paramount star, is shown wearing attractive Beckman furs.

REACHING SMALL TOWN CIRCULATION

by Earle V. Weller

Account Executive, the Campbell-Ewald Company

One of the principal functions of the advertising agency is the purchase of advertising for its clients at the lowest cost consistent with the expected return.

The agency holds no brief for any specific type of media, but an analysis to determine the comparative return to be expected from each type considered and a yardstick established as to costs should be preliminary to final decision on the media to be used for any campaign.

● The present survey is based upon a study of comparative circulation and cost figures covering 873 towns in the Pacific Coast and Western Rocky Mountain States. It was conceived with a view to increasing the efficiency of small town advertising and obtaining greater coverage with the same or a smaller outlay.

The small town poster plant almost invariably has all, or the greater number of its panels located on the main street. This street, in most cases, is a part of the major thoroughfare or highway connecting the small town with its neighbors and with the larger towns and cities.

Circulation figures for a majority of these 873 small towns were not available at the time this work was started, although such figures are now to be had for a majority of these towns in Washington, Oregon, California and Arizona.

Some of the circulation figures, therefore, are based entirely upon estimated circulation. Others, however, show the figures based upon actual circulation checks and will prove that the estimates upon which the first three were prepared were more than conservative.

As a basis for comparison between small town newspaper and poster advertising efficiency an arbitrary schedule of two 30-inch display advertisements per month has been taken as average and the cost computed.

The tables include 712 towns in which the standard half showing specifications is one poster, and 161 towns in which the specifications call for two posters. The segregated by states are: Idaho 90, Montana 26, Nevada, 15, Utah 37, Arizona 24, California 321, Washington 218, and Oregon 142.

Outdoor advertising reaches not only the population of the small town but the traffic that passes through it.

The one panel towns show a total population of 587,530 at a posting cost per month of $5,058.40, and the one-panel towns a population of 515,200 at a cost per month for a half showing of $2,512.80.

● Naturally, the cost-per-inch-per-thousand of circulation in the newspapers increases as the circulation of the newspaper decreases. This is to be expected to a degree, but it does appear as if we were paying a very high premium for newspaper representation in the small towns.

These costs show a very wide spread between the small town newspaper and the metropolitan daily. If the poster circulation is taken on the accepted basis of three-times-the-population-per-day, the difference is astounding. In addition to this there is the highway circulation to be considered, which while perhaps not of special interest to the small town dealer, is of utmost importance to the national advertiser.

● Illustrative of the difference in newspaper rates between the metropolitan newspapers and those in the very small towns are figures for a few of the larger cities as compared with a similar number of small towns:

Town or City	Newspaper	Rate Per Column Inch Per 1000
Los Angeles (Calif.)	Examiner	.0235
San Francisco	Examiner	.0249
Portland (Ore.)	Oregonian	.0239
Seattle (Wash.)	P.-I	.0292
Denver (Colo.)	Post	.0236
Junction City (Ore.)	Times	.65
Benicia (Calif.)	News	1.00
McKittrick (Calif.)	News	.58
Knights Ldg. (Calif.)	River News	2.00
Gridley (Calif.)	Herald	.19

In checking over dealer lists for the eight states there are many towns of course in which there is no dealer (A specific client being checked in this instance). Some of these non-dealer towns have a local newspaper. All of the towns listed have posting available. If posting were placed in towns of this class, carrying the dealer imprint for the dealer operating in the nearest town, the same effect would be achieved as that obtained by the big metropolitan department store through paint or posting campaigns thruout the city and suburban areas—the attraction of customers from all points within its reasonable trading area.

● Aside from this factor valuable to the local dealer, the transient circulation would be invaluable from a national standpoint, especially in territory where automobile travel is heavy and networks of paved roads and highways extend not only between the metropolitan centers, but well into the mountain and more sparsely settled farming, lumber and stock-raising districts.

The attention value and memory impression of such a campaign cannot be overestimated. The painted bulletin campaigns of such firms as United States Rubber, Western Auto Supply, Chevrolet Motor Company, General Petroleum Corporation, Sussman & Wormser and others multiply themselves in the minds of the average motorist and the percussive effect of this repetition could be immeasurably increased by a blanket coverage of 24-sheet poster panels in the small towns.

Such a campaign tied in with metropolitan newspapers, highway painted bulletins, radio broadcasting, national magazines and direct mail would be the ideal one of course, but the importance of such a blanket poster coverage should not be lost sight of in the frequent cases where the budget is limited and it is necessary to do the best possible job with a limited budget.

● I would like to offer some figures assembled in the preparation of data for consideration in preparing a campaign limited to the San Francisco Bay Area, or within a radius of probably fifty miles or less. Within this area are 43 towns with poster facilities. Seven of these include illumination in their specifications, while 36 have not and come well within the classification studied in the present survey.

Segregation, as above, was necessary in view of a very limited budget and the necessity for staggering any outdoor campaign that might be determined upon, with perhaps two or three months of posting in the small towns and then (Continued on page 44)

Outdoor advertising, in the six towns considered, delivers 525 times the circulation of the newspapers at one-seventh the cost.

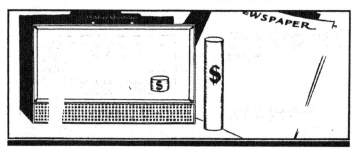

WHY KELVINATOR USES OUTDOOR ADVERTISING

by A. M. Taylor
Director of Advertising, Kelvinator Sales Corporation

Man is his own worst enemy. He overeats, over-works, over-exerts himself, and undersleeps. He thinks of health only when he has lost it. He wants progress, but fights change in his set ways. The first typewriter salesman had a whale of a job switching him from the old-fashioned pen, and the cash regis-ter still fights the drawer and the old sock behind the counter.

● As a general rule, he does not admit that he be-lieves in advertising, even though it rules his life. "Advertising never sold me a thing," he says, as he draws his pack of Camels, can of Prince Albert, or R. G. Dun cigar from his Kuppenheimer clothes. "Why don't they stop it all and give the consumer a break," he continues, as he viciously throws the clutch on his less-than-a-thousand dollar car, forgetting that in earlier days his father paid several thousand dol-lars for a car not nearly the equal of his. He com-plains that his magazines and newspapers are noth-ing but ads; he turns off his radio when the an-nouncer mentions the name of a product; he cusses the mail man who crams his box with circulars, and he joins the gang in downing the billboards.

So the letter attacking billboards, quoted below, comes as no surprise. Nor does it have the desired effect, as our reply, also quoted, will show.

"Kingston, N. Y., May 6, 1931.

To Roadside Advertisers:

A committee was recently formed from eighteen civic organizations in the city of Kingston and the village of Saugerties to make a survey of billboard advertising on roads leading into those places, and to make suggestions for the betterment of that method of publicity. This committee was composed of more than fifty men and women who have listed all signs not only between those two towns, but all signs lead-ing out of them for a distance of five miles. This information has been carefully tabulated and pre-served, and should prove of value to advertisers, to property owners, and to billboard companies.

"The number of members of organizations repre-sented on the Central Billboard Committee (as this group has called itself) is about a thousand, and as the reports from these organizations come in, there is practical unanimity of opinion that early legisla-tion should be passed prohibiting the erection of any

Advertising and mass production makes available to the great mass of the people greater luxuries than kings formerly en-joyed.

billboards within a distance of three hundred feet of a curve in the road, or at a crossing, or where they obstruct the view, and the defining by a state law, their maximum size. Advertisers would do well to remember that' signs that offend the taste of the motorist are as bad for business as those that en-danger his safety. Neither makes for larger sales.

● "The Ulster County Committee is not seeking leg-islation to abolish billboards entirely, but to have legislative restriction of their size, supervision of their state of repair, and a positive prohibition of their placement where they endanger safety, and ob-struct the incomparable views which draw tourists to our beautiful countryside. If advertisers and property owners will notify the billboard companies with whom they have contracts that these conditions must be complied with if their contracts are to be renewed, the motoring public will not have to wait for the legislation which the Automobile Club of America is now making a vigorous campaign to secure. Not only will the road of our county be safer and more beautiful, but the buying motorists who use these roads to come into the towns to trade will not, as they too often are, be set against the very merchandise the billboards advertise. The huge size or the wrong placing of some of the most costly of the billboards now repel and antagonize more motorists than they attract.

Central Billboard Committee."
"May 16, 1931.

Central Billboard Committee,
Kingston, New York.
Dear Sirs:

Thanks for your favor of the sixth in which you advise that your committee formed from eighteen civic organizations in the City of Kingston and the village of Saugerties has made a survey of billboard advertising on the roads leading into Kingston and that you are ready to make suggestions for the betterment of that method of publicity.

● "Realizing the need for some low cost, day by day medium of advertising that would reach all the people all the time with our 'Where to buy it' message, we have decided that outdoor posters placed on the structures owned by the members of the Outdoor Advertising Association exactly fits our requirements.

"You will find that by self-regulation this association prohibits its members from erecting billboards outside the limits of cities and villages, that they are of uniform size (twelve by twenty-five feet), that they are kept in a constant state of repair by monthly inspections and postings, that they are not a menace to the health, safety or morals of anyone and uniformly present a much better appearance than the other structures in the community.

"We are pleased that your committee has interested itself in helping to remove the objectionable features of outdoor advertising and you have our best wishes for your success.

"A copy of this letter is being sent to John Van Benschoten, Inc., Poughkeepsie, our Distributors in your section.

Yours very truly,
Hayden Hill
Advertising Dept."

I am no supporter of the sign that hides scenic beauty or obstructs clear vision at danger points. Nor do I tolerate poster panels poorly placed and kept. But you may put me down as a booster of outdoor advertising that conforms to the self-inflicted code of ethics and program of improvement. Outdoor advertising is not the only medium, nor only industry that can profit by self-improvement.

● We need poster advertising to help sell Kelvinators. We need its dominant, persistent force as a foundation, or connecting link between magazine and newspaper insertions and direct mailings. We need it to reinforce the national message and concentrate its power on every local market. We need poster advertising to give our program that "one-two" punch, with the magazines, newspapers and radio telling *what* to buy and posters immediately following with *where* to buy it. Competition is too keen,—buying resistance too strong,—the crowded, indifferent consumer memory is too short, to throw the entire burden of sales upon newspaper, magazine and direct-by-mail advertising.

Furthermore, our dealer outlets need the power of poster advertising behind their business. A product today is no stronger in any locality than the dealer representing it. This is particularly true of a mechanical specialty such as ours, where confidence in the product and in the integrity of the dealer are the most important factors in the majority of sales, as research has proved.

As a result of these conclusions, we decided to do a real job of cooperative poster advertising. Our first step was to appoint poster advertising specialists,—the Donaldson Lithographing Company, Newport, Kentucky, to handle our campaign, as our poster advertising previously had been conducted on more or less of a hit-or-miss basis,—an orphan so to speak.

We designed a series of unusual posters, showing a large, roomy Kelvinator in heroic size, with the name "Kelvinator" running almost entirely across the poster. Underneath the name, as permanent copy, we use two words, "Since 1914," which tells at a glance that we are the oldest domestic electric refrigeration manufacturers. Entirely across the bottom is a twenty inch strip set aside for "where to buy it" information.

With only two changes on the posters each month, the message goes over to the reader in less than two seconds. The continuity of the design and color lend their force to the value of the campaign, while the changes of picture, caption and "where to buy it" color keep it ever interesting and inviting, as well as emphasizing the many advantages of Kelvinator.

We recommend year-round posting for permanent dealer identification, advocating quarter-showings for twelve months rather than half-showings for six months, or the duration of the best selling season.

● Thus far in 1931 each month has shown an increase in the use of the medium by our dealers. As time goes on, with regular contacts to our outlets by Donaldson representatives, we anticipate even greater increases in our poster showings.

PUBLIC UTILITY ADVERTISING

by T. P. Pfeiffer

Advertising Manager, Byllesby Engineering and Management Corp.,
and Standard Gas and Electric Co.

● Of definitions of advertising there is no end. Everyone knows how the dictionary defines it, or can find out. To the publisher, advertising may mean space; to the radio man, time; to the outdoor man, location; to the agency executive, anything on which he can collect 15 per cent. Mr. Will Rogers defines it as something that makes you spend money you haven't got for things you don't want. The man who "doesn't believe in advertising" calls it woeful waste. Here is what Russia thinks of it; M. Ilin, in his book, "New Russia's Primer," which is the story of the five-year plan told for Russian school-children, says that advertising in America consumes "millions of tons of raw materials and fuels, millions of working days,—in order to force people to buy what they do not need. Human labor is dissipated and expended for nothing."

With all these differences of opinion, perhaps we had better not waste time trying to find a common definition. It matters little what advertising *is*, as long as we know what it *does*, and as long as we know how to apply it intelligently to our problems of distribution. There are undoubtedly a lot of people in the world who think that advertising is the universal panacea for all our economic troubles—that advertising pressure, applied with sufficient energy, will accomplish anything. I don't believe exactly that, but I do believe that advertising is a great business force, and that where it is intelligently applied it will do a great deal of good.

The purpose of public utility advertising is twofold; to sell the services of the public utility companies, and to build good-will. Advertising can definitely influence the first of these considerations—it can help the electric company sell more kilowatt-hours, the gas company more cubic feet, the transportation company more rides, the telephone company more phone calls. Advertising itself, however, cannot build good-will. It can interpret the good-will already existing, which has been developed over a long period of mutually satisfactory business relations between company and customer, but if friction exists because the company is stubborn and refuses to see the customer's point of view, or if this situation is reversed, advertising alone is helpless.

● The first important point about public utility advertising is that it is almost entirely devoted to the sale of service, either directly or indirectly. There was a time when the public utilities used a great deal of space and spent a considerable amount of money telling the public all about the public utilities—how big they were, and how important in the economic structure of the nation, and how hard it was to maintain dependable service during a sleet storm, and lots of other such nonsense. They *are* big, and they *are* important, and it *is* hard to transmit electric energy

The advertising of the Northern States Power Company has been outstanding in the utility field.

An effective newspaper advertisement which wins both friends and capital for the advertiser.

over a wire that nature has knocked down, but the public doesn't care much about that. The public reads the advertisements for information—about what one appliance will do that some other appliance won't, and what does it cost, and is it convenient and comfortable and luxurious to live in a house that is heated with gas, and will the electric refrigerator make nice frozen desserts, and will the water always be hot if there is a gas water heater installed. Those are some of the things the public wants to know, and the public utility industry has accepted the challenge and is answering those questions in its advertising; with one end in view—to sell more service. Because the more service it sells, the more it can reduce rates and the more it reduces rates, the more service it can sell—an endless circle of cause and effect.

● Did you ever stop to think how many things the public utility can talk about when it starts to develop the market for its services?

Take an electric company, for instance. First there is the housewife; she needs electric service for lighting, for cooking, refrigeration, sewing, cleaning, laundry work, and a multitude of other uses in the home. She can cook with an electric range, but she needs a percolator, toaster, waffle-iron, and grill besides. Her laundry isn't equipped completely unless it has an electric washer, ironer, and at least a couple of irons. If the electric company operates in non-gas territory, there is an opportunity to sell electric service for water heating, and even auxiliary room heating.

Factories need electric service for power, heat and adequate light; merchants need it for modern window and store lighting, and for electric signs to advertise their business.

The gas company can sell its product in the home for cooking, heating, refrigeration, water heating, laundry-drying, incineration. In industry the uses of gas are multitudinous.

These are only a few of the uses of the public utility services. If you jotted down, each day, one little service that electricity or gas can perform in the home, or factory, or on the farm, your desk calendar would nowhere nearly hold them all. Don't think, either, that there is nothing for the street railway company or the telephone company to talk about. Every automobile driver needs to be reminded that if he uses the street car he has no parking worries, and everyone who lives in a two-story house should be told, as often and as forcefully as possible, that an extension telephone upstairs will save the busy housewife many useless steps at a very small cost.

A SAINT PAUL INSTITUTION

BUILDING SAINT PAUL *together!*

Among the 10,000 St. Paul citizens who are shareholders in Northern States Power Company, are more than 800 men engaged in the building trades of this city . . . carpenters, steel workers, plumbers, etc. ≈ These 800 builders are benefiting this city in a twofold manner . . . first by their daily work of construction . . . and second by investing their savings in Northern States Power Company which in turn uses this capital for expanding in St. Paul service. ≈ The progress and growth of St. Paul is dependent upon the attention of new industries, and new industries always look about for an adequate and dependable source of electric power when selecting a new location. ≈ Thus these 800 builder-partners of ours, together with this company, are helping to build a greater St. Paul for as a city is dependent upon its utilities . . . so Northern States Power Company as a St. Paul institution, is dependent upon the progress of St. Paul for its future growth. ≈ ≈ Let's build St. Paul together!

NORTHERN STATES POWER COMPANY

OWNED BY THOSE IT SERVES

Only by advertising, as an aid to direct selling, can the public utility sell its service in increasing measure to more customers, and more to each individual customer.

● So far as the electric and gas companies are concerned, public utility advertising falls generally into four classifications: load-building, or new business advertising, which attempts to convince the man who is not a customer that he should be a customer, and when he becomes one, tries to persuade him to use more service; merchandise advertising, which is used to help sell appliances from the company's own stores; customer-ownership, or financial advertising, which invites the customer to become a partner in the business; and institutional advertising, which endeavors to explain policies and methods of operation.

As the most important of these four functions I rank load-building, or new business advertising. There is only one justification for the existence of a public utility company, and that is its business of supplying essential services to the public. As the sale of service increases, the rates charged for that service can be, and are, as a matter of fact, reduced. The merchandising of appliances is merely incidental to the other load-building activities. It is often necessary for the public utility itself to merchandise appliances in order to create a market for its service, but first, last and always the job is to *sell the service*. For that reason it is just as much interested in seeing that electrical dealers, hardware stores, department stores and other outlets sell appliances as it is in selling these devices in its own stores, and the public utility which is approaching the problem of new business development with any degree of intelligence cooperates with those agencies to help them sell more appliances. The function of load-building, or new business advertising is similar to what the national advertiser tries to accomplish with his general advertising program—to obtain distribution of the product, or service. Merchandise advertising does not differ, essentially, from any other kind of retail advertising.

● There is no type of advertising that has been more productive of results than the new business advertising of public utilities. Here are a few examples. Years ago the utilities made a great drive for the wiring of already built homes. Such a campaign was conducted by a public utility in a large Southern city. The company itself did no wiring, but maintained a force of salesmen. Contracts for wiring were distributed among local wiring contractors. Week after week, for a period of several years, the company published advertisements on housewiring. As a result of that campaign between 30,000 and 35,000 homes were wired in about five years. Today, the saturation point in the wiring of already-built houses has practically been reached. Consistent, persistent, sound advertising did that job, and did it well. Still the work of developing new business continues. Useful appliances are sold and advertised, not only by the utilities, but by other dealers as well, and the question of the success or failure of that effort is answered in the steadily mounting curve that represents the annual per customer use of residential electric service. And, as the number of kilowatt-hours goes up, the rates come down.

● There are innumerable examples of successful campaigns of all kinds, and in most instances advertising must be credited with a big share of the results. Last fall a campaign to obtain new electric sign business was staged in another southern city. A combination of newspaper and direct mail advertising was used. The campaign cost $2,300. A total of 152 electric signs was installed, directly traceable to the advertising. Local manufacturers and sign agencies got a nice piece of business, and the Company gets an estimated annual revenue of $13,000 from these signs. A Wisconsin company sold 242 gas water heaters in one month against a quota of 187, as a result of concentrated effort. Another thirty-day campaign sold 254 gas ranges, 36 per cent of them to people who had never before used gas.

● Almost everyone is familiar with what the public utilities have done to interest their customers in the ownership of public utility securities. Customer

The Simplicity and—in the original — the color made this an effective design.

Building Today for a
GREATER OKLAHOMA
Tomorrow

ownership, which started away back in 1914, has done as much as anything else in the world to popularize sound investments. A strong, conservative customer ownership campaign is better for the economic health of the community than the greatest bull market ever developed. The people who have purchased the preferred shares of public utilities bought them outright; they don't hold them on a margin account, and it is surprising to know how few investors of this class have sold out their original investments. Customer ownership advertising has not been so prominent in the advertising program of the public utilities in the last few years, but not because of any lack of interest in the subject. Popular demand for public utility securities has become so great that very little advertising is required when preferred stocks are available for public offering. In advertising of this kind, the utilities have always featured the safety of the investment, the regular return, and marketability, as the chief talking points, closely tied in with the advantages of a planned investment program and the building up of an estate. No customer ownership advertising ever told the customer that he would "get rich quick," but it has been responsible for starting a lot of people on the road to financial independence.

● One of the forms of public utility advertising that is widely used is advertising to acquaint the public with the usefulness of the service rendered. The public wants to know how electricity and gas can be used to the best advantage to save time and money and effort, to conserve strength, to promote leisure. It wants to know where the best appliances can be bought, and how much they cost. It wants to know how to get the lowest possible rates for good service.

Institutional advertising that informs the public on these points is sound advertising, and when it accomplishes what it sets out to do, it is not really institutional at all, but merely another manifestation of the new business development activity. One important function of institutional advertising, however, is the explanation and promotion of rates, and here I would

like to quote something I once said on this subject to a group of public utility executives:

● "Tell your customers all about your rates; explain the differences in the various classes of rates for domestic service, for instance, when optional rates are available for larger users. Advise the customer which rate is best suited to his use. Frequently rate advertising can be very effectively tied in with your merchandising activities, or at least with your general advertising program. Rates at best make a dry story, but dramatize them in the eyes of the customer in terms of leisure, comfort and enjoyment in the use of public utility services, and they take on an entirely different aspect."

A few of the things the public utility can talk about in its advertising have been covered in this article. The tools for carrying these messages to the public are the same as those used by every other advertiser—newspapers and other publications, direct mail, outdoor advertising, the radio, etc.

In the first place, it must be understood that the problem of public utility advertising is almost entirely local. The holding company may find it necessary to use national advertising to develop a market for its securities, but the operating company serves a definite territory, limited to the extent of its distribution system, and in that territory its problem is to convince the customer that it is to his benefit to use more electricity, burn more gas, ride the street cars or busses more regularly, use the telephone more frequently.

So the public utility advertiser finds his problem somewhat simplified by the fact that the nature of his business permits him to use only local advertising media.

● Outdoor advertising can always be depended upon to assist in the promotion of (Continued on page 41)

YES MA'AM—JES' A LITTLE

OXYDOL

The smiling lady at the top of this page is Carrie Duncan, who is the model for Oxydol's happy laundress. The poster shown above received first award at the National Outdoor Advertising Exhibit in Chicago last year. Marshall Reid, who created the Oxydol series, is pictured admiring the placque which was awarded for this outstanding poster design.

OUTDOOR IMPRESSIONS

One of the most remarkable outdoor advertising locations in the country is this rock garden development of the Ohio Valley Advertising Corporation at Wheeling, West Virginia. While the landscaping of locations is a general practice in organized outdoor advertising, the creation of as elaborate and beautiful a site as this is a distinct achievement.

OUTDOOR IMPRESSIONS

A quiet, pastoral scene such
as that at the right seems far
removed from the rush and
cares of today's business life.
Yet the farms which produce
Carnation Milk are as efficiently operated as is any
large corporation. Without
this efficiency and without
the selling force of advertising such as is shown below
the large model farms operated by great dairy companies could not be maintained.

OUTDOOR IMPRESSIONS

Interesting lighting treatment of a German shop front. This display has been carefully handled so that, despite the strong attraction of the four light columns, almost twenty feet high, the name retains its proper prominence.

OUTDOOR IMPRESSIONS

FAITHFUL
ADVERTISING

Loyal
Tireless
Capable

Outdoor Advertising is the string on the public thumb that will not let failing memories stagnate salable merchandise or let advertising appropriations fail because of enthusiasm aroused at the WRONG time and forgotten at the right time.

Outdoor Advertising is never dormant because it is seldom out of sight.

Sales producing because it is nearest point-of-purchase.

Successful because it impresses more people more often, at the right time, and at less cost than the same number of advertising dollars can accomplish in any other advertising way.

More than one million and ninety-six thousand New Yorkers pass this Sunkist bulletin daily.

ADVERTISING BUILDS
the Citrus Industry

by W. B. Geissinger
Advertising Manager of the California Fruit Growers Exchange

China is generally accepted as the first home of the orange. At least, the earliest known manuscript describing this fruit was written by an eminent Chinese philosopher—Han Yen-Chi in 1178 A. D. While this is the first known treatise on citrus fruits, reference to them is found in various earlier writings, one antedating the Christian era by three centuries.

Citrus culture in the United States on a commercial scale, however, did not actually begin until late in the 19th century. Before that time there had been orange trees scattered here and there in the warmer localities, but not enough to really warrant the name of an industry.

● The year 1873 saw the first real beginning of orange growing in California. Two Navel orange trees were shipped to California by the United States Department of Agriculture from Bahia, Brazil. Planted by one of the pioneers of Riverside County, they flourished and a great industry was born.

Soon the fertile valleys of California suitable for orange culture were dotted with green, well-kept groves. Growers thought themselves well on the highroad to prosperity.

All went well at first. But, under the stimulus of high returns, production skyrocketed with the frenzied speed of a startled jackrabbit. The specter of overproduction and inadequate distribution haunted growers. Red-inked ledgers brought frowns to the brows of these citrus pioneers.

Realizing that a solution for these problems must be found, meetings were held and clear-visioned leaders suggested that they should band themselves together into one cooperative selling organization. Thus, in 1893, was born the Southern California Fruit Exchange, the progenitor of the California Fruit Growers Exchange, which now markets over 77 per cent of the entire California orange, lemon and grapefruit crop—the better grades under the internationally known Sunkist trademark.

With more orderly distribution, times were better. Overproduction, however, was still as big a problem as ever. Advertising, then in its infancy as far as perishable products were concerned, was to be the solution of this problem.

The first Navel orange tree planted in California. Though nearly 60 years old, this patriarch of the California citrus industry still produces excellent fruit.

The year 1906 saw the first advertising campaign for California oranges—six thousand dollars were invested in Iowa newspapers and journals. Results were more than startling—sales jumped fifty per cent.

The following year twenty-five thousand advertising dollars were appropriated, not without much misgiving on the part of many of the more conservative.

● From this campaign, now national in scope, results were again all that even the most optimistic had hoped for—the demand for citrus fruits had been definitely turned upwards. California citrus growers had sold themselves something — advertising — and have remained a steady customer ever since.

In the past twenty-four years of Sunkist advertising over $14,000,000 has been invested by California citrus growers in telling the world of the fine eating quality and healthfulness of California citrus fruits. That this investment has been returned many times

Picking oranges in Southern California. Tropical palms and snow-capped mountains give added charm to this typical California scene.

can well be seen by comparative production and consumption figures on oranges, and returns to California growers. In 1906, 23,000 carloads of oranges were produced in California and consumed throughout the United States. From 1910 to 1920 California shipped an average of 35,000 carloads of oranges a year, while from 1920 to 1925, average yearly shipments had increased to 43,000. The past five years has seen an even greater increase in shipments—an average of 55,000 carloads left the state each season. One year during the last five year period rang up a new record—70,000 cars.

● Production had increased tremendously, but what of demand? Had it too kept step with production?

The constantly increasing shipments show that the public was consuming the fruit but this is not the real yardstick of demand. Prices are the important thing, and what of them?

Comparative figures on average returns to California citrus growers for their fruit during these years can well be called the real yardstick of demand. In 1906, $21,024,814 was returned to California citrus growers; from 1910 to 1920 an average of $42,012,589 yearly was returned. The five years from 1920 to 1925 saw growers receive $77,744,355 for their citrus crop annually and in the following five years $120,-242,554 was obtained. Last year a new record was made—$135,000,000.

All of the credit for the present position of the California citrus grower among other American agriculturists cannot be entirely laid to advertising, however. Many other factors of primary importance

enter into this success. Proper distribution to all available markets, made possible through control of over 75 per cent of the crop by one cooperative organization, improvement and standardization of the quality of citrus fruit shipped through the Sunkist organization, through improved grading methods and better cultural practices, and the establishment of a nation-wide sales force covering the important markets in the United States and Canada, contributed as much to this success as has advertising. In fact, these fundamental principles—proper distribution, standardization, an efficient sales force and advertising can well be said to be the basis of successful operation of practically all successful business.

Since the inception of Sunkist advertising there have been three fundamental objectives aimed at. These are:

(1) To increase the total demand for citrus fruits so as to keep pace with the constantly increasing production.

(2) To increase the public's preference for California citrus fruits, particularly Sunkist.

(3) To improve distribution and merchandising by convincing the retail trade that better displays and reasonable margins are the primary factors in bringing more rapid turnover and consequently increasing the volume of business.

● The present problems are the successful maintenance of present markets as defined by consumer habits, and not geography, which have been developed by continual advertising, and to create new markets by the constant presentation to the public of new uses and new dietetic discoveries to increase the consumption of citrus fruits.

The following is a typical cross section of the current Sunkist advertising campaign giving the various specific appeals and advertising mediums used to create an increased demand for California oranges and lemons.

Due to the larger production, oranges take first place in the Sunkist advertising program. This fruit is consumed largely because of its pleasant taste sensation; in other words, the orange has a strong appetite appeal. This important selling point is stressed in all advertising. The various appeals used are:

(1) For juice—because their use as juice increases consumption manyfold over their use halved or sliced.

(2) For salads and desserts—because it is profitable to maintain conventional uses and to increase these uses by new variations.

(3) For child feeding—because medical authority has made available this new market and its cultivation has been found to have a very profitable reaction on the use of juice for health by adults.

(4) For health.

● Sunkist lemon advertising to a large extent, stresses the ultimate use or effect of this fruit, due to the fact that it is largely consumed in completely changed form. The various appeals developed during the past few years and at present being incorporated in lemon advertising are:

(1) As a food—such as lemonade, garnish or lemon pie; because these are kitchen products

which can be most profitably encouraged for their use.

(2) For health—because hot lemonade can be urged upon good medical authority, to help prevent colds and influenza. In addition, cold lemonade is also a powerful combative of the "acidosis" condition of the system so prevalent in America today.

(3) For beauty—because lemon rinse for the hair and complexion solves a problem for women that creates an additional market.

● In conjunction with the above appeals the health values of oranges and lemons are also extensively featured. Their ability to correct acidosis and the fact that they are a rich source of vitamins, particularly vitamin C, is stressed in this part of the campaign. The importance of adequate quantities of vitamin C in the daily menu and the fact that oranges and lemons are accepted as the best source of this elusive food element are being strongly emphasized in the present Sunkist advertising campaign. Recent research now shows that this vitamin is an important factor in combating and preventing dental decay and tooth and gum disorders. These health appeals make use of a universal public interest in health as a background for increased use of both oranges and lemons.

A variety of media are selected each year to carry these different appeals to the consumer. Due to the length and the necessity of using "reason why" copy, national magazines play an important part in the Sunkist advertising campaign. Color work is used extensively in this medium as it is superior to black and white in carrying out the basic appetite appeal of citrus fruits.

Newspaper campaigns are run during the competitive season in the larger markets. The newspaper is supplemented by a radio campaign as a good will builder and is used also during the competitive

One of a series of designs used on 24-sheet posters in 114 metropolitan centers of the United States and Canada in 1930-31.

**Tempt yourself
to better health**

**A five minute
Salad**

season in the larger markets of the United States and
Canada. Car cards, with their mass circulation, have
a half showing throughout the country during nine
months of the year.

● During the past few years outdoor posters have
played an increasingly important role in the Sunkist
orange, lemon and grapefruit advertising campaign.
However, before we discuss the details of the Sunkist
outdoor campaign, its principles and its aims, let us
spend a little time in talking of outdoor advertising
generally.

Changing conditions affect the advertiser and methods of advertising as well as the business world in
general. In the past decade a tremendous change
has been evidenced in the mode of living of the
American people. Changing times and new ways of
living have brought new problems in present day advertising and merchandising.

Americans now have more leisure—more time for
the out-of-doors. Many factors have brought this
about. In the home, in the office, in the factory—
labor saving devices and tremendously improved op-
crating methods have given the housewife, the business man and the laborer added hours to do as he or
she wills. In most cases the housewife's afternoons
are free to go out of the home, and many of her
interests today lie beyond her front door. The eight-
hour day in practically every business, and Saturday
afternoons off, fill the streets and highways with
millions of mentally receptive consumers.

What is done during these leisure hours? Drive
down the highway on Saturday or Sunday or look
out your window any afternoon and you have the
answer. People have become "outdoor" minded.

Probably the most powerful factor, which has
helped bring about this considerably changed mode
of living has been the rapid development of the automobile and other forms of efficient transportation.
Better highways, too, have played their part.

● Census statistics show that there are now approximately 24,000,350 families living in the United States.
Twenty-four and one-half million automobiles pro-

vide them with a wider range of living. No longer are
Americans the fireside sitters of a decade ago.

In addition to improved transportation facilities,
there are more and better places to go. Motion picture theatres grow larger and better. Nearly 22,700
theatres draw 105,000,000 people weekly. Golf clubs
blossom along every road—5,865 are now in existence
and are used by over 2,700,000 golf enthusiasts. Gigantic football stadiums lure 30,000,000 people annually. Baseball parks, tennis courts, the beaches,
track events and even pee-wee golf—all attract additional spectators and participants.

Communities are drawn closer together. Better
transportation facilities have made this possible. Because of the automobile and better roads, the farmer
is now the next-door neighbor of the city dweller.
He no longer stays at home in his leisure hours, but
comes to the nearest town on evenings or week ends.
The store that used to draw patronage from a radius
of 20 miles now draws it from a hundred.

● This immense market—composed of the 130,000,000
people in this country—is reached by the advertiser
through the medium of various types of outdoor displays, the most prominent among them being the
painted bulletins and lithographed posters. These
are placed on principal streets and highways and
appear before the public during the day and far
into the night.

Starting the fiscal year November 1, 1930, Sunkist
launched the greatest outdoor advertising campaign
in their history. From coast to coast in 114 of the
most important United States and Canadian markets
Sunkist poster displays completely blanket the country. In New York, Chicago, San Francisco and Los
Angeles large painted bulletins were placed in the
most outstanding locations on a three year contract.
These bulletins are equipped with Neon tubes featuring the name SUNKIST in a most beautiful and comprehensive manner that insures the instant attention
of practically all the dense circulation passing in the
vicinity. Sunkist painted bulletins carry a complete
change of copy each forty- (Continued on page 44)

POSTERS SELL
Sliced Bread

by Thomas H. Wittkorn

● By consistent and effective outdoor advertising the Parkway Baking Company, Philadelphia, Pa., has changed the bread buying habits of the city's housewives and made a name for itself in their minds which it might never have attained by merely going along with all the rest of the bakers. It was the introduction of "sliced bread," a loaf cut ready for the home-table before it is wax paper wrapped at the bakery, that offered the Parkway Company an opportunity to be one of the big factors in the bread trade of the city.

That the company displayed real aggressiveness in grasping its chance is shown by its undertaking an outdoor advertising campaign with sliced bread while the big baking interests of the city sat idly by, although they could well afford to have risked and lost without feeling it several times the amount which the Parkway first decided to put into the venture. Another evidence of the good business policies of the company is the complete coverage it is now using in the city to retain the position which it reached while its competitors were napping.

"The results of our poster advertising sound almost too good to be true," remarked George J. Conly, Treasurer and advertising manager of the Parkway Baking Company, when he was asked to tell what his returns had been after eighteen months trial. "It certainly sold the idea of sliced bread to the home-makers of the Quaker City, gave us a remarkable increase in production and made our competitors add a sliced loaf to their lists after they saw how we were cutting into their bread trade."

When asked how all these things had been accomplished, Mr. Conly replied, "When we decided to go ahead with our new venture, we took our problem to the General Outdoor Advertising Company, and it has been partly through the excellent service which they have given us that we have reached the position we now enjoy. What we had to do was to sell, not only the economy and convenience of a loaf of bread coming into the home in perfect slices ready for the table, but to establish our loaf, the Parkway, so that it would be sought by the buyers no matter how many other loaves came on the market.

● "In order to accomplish this aim one of the first things the advertising company suggested was the changing of our bread wrapper. They designed a new one for us with plenty of color in it, so that it would have a strong appeal on the panels. A yellow waxed paper was selected, which gives the loaf a natural warm color, instead of white waxed paper which is inclined to remind one of dough rather than something edible. This wrapper was then printed with red and blue lettering and striped lines to suggest slices. (Continued on page 43)

SPLENDID SANDWICH MAKERS

Parkway's SLICED

This poster features the use of sliced bread in making sandwiches.

NEWS OF
THE OUTDOOR INDUSTRY

N. W. Ayer and Son, Inc. Re-enter Outdoor Field

In 1900 announcement was made by N. W. Ayer & Son, of their appointment as the official solicitors of the ASSOCIATED BILLPOSTERS & DISTRIBUTORS of the UNITED STATES and CANADA. Thus entered the first general advertising agency in the field of outdoor advertising.

Soon there began to appear on boards names and trade-marks long familiar to readers of newspapers and magazines, new to the bold color displays in paper and paint on the billboards throughout the country.

This continued until well into the second decade of the new century—until N. W. Ayer & Son were one of the largest factors in creating and placing outdoor advertising.

There came a change in the organization of outdoor advertising. There came a parting of the ways of N. W. Ayer & Son and the outdoor interests.

Loss of faith in methods did not mean lack of faith in medium, as evidenced by announcement July 16th of re-entry of N. W. Ayer & Son, Inc., into the outdoor field, making their service comprise newspapers, magazines, radio, outdoor.

Carl L. Rieker, Assistant to the President and former Manager of N. W. Ayer & Son Outdoor Department, has retained contacts and will renew many acquaintances. He, with Frederick W. Kurtz, Vice President, will guide the destinies of the re-created department to serve Ayer clients in the outdoor field.

■   ■   ■

Steiner goes to Silberstein, Inc.

Herbert L. Steiner, formerly of the New York staff of the General Outdoor Advertising Company, is now an account executive with Alfred J. Silberstein, Inc., New York.

■   ■   ■

Ohio Association to Meet

The Outdoor Advertising Association of Ohio will hold its annual convention August 4th and 5th at Neil House, Columbus, Ohio.

Morgan Heads Nordhem Service

Mr. Hubert S. Morgan, vice-president and general manager, was elected President of Nordhem Service, Inc., at a special meeting of the Board of Directors held at the offices of the Corporation, July second.

Mr. Morgan succeeds Mr. Ivan B. Nordhem, who has severed his connection with the company.

■   ■   ■

Lord and Thomas and Logan Subscribe to Statistical Service

Lord and Thomas and Logan, nationally famous advertising agency, is a new subscriber to the Association Statistical Service.

■   ■   ■

Foust Appointed Chairman of Legislative Committee

Mr. J. L. Foust of the Green River Poster Advertising Co., of Owensboro, Kentucky, has been appointed Chairman of the Legislative Committee of the Kentucky Educational Association. Mr. Foust is also superintendent of the city schools at Owensboro.

■   ■   ■

Lonabaugh Wyoming Director

Mr. A. W. Lonabaugh, of the Sheridan (Wyoming) Poster Advertising Company, has been appointed national director representing the Outdoor Advertising Association of Wyoming by President Ward of that organization to fill a vacancy occasioned by former Director H. H. Darnell disposing of his plant interests.

■   ■   ■

Ludwig Addresses Penn. Forestry Association

Mr. Walter D. Ludwig, Highway Forester in the State of Pennsylvania, recently gave an address before the meeting of the Pennsylvania Forestry Association at State College. In it he refers to Outdoor Advertising as follows: "Excellent cooperation has been given by the Pennsylvania Outdoor Advertising Association in the removal and elimination of signs at points which the department considers dangerous to traffic or interferes with a scenic view."

The Romance of General Foods Corporation

(Continued from page 10) Down Cake Flour, Jell-O, Minute Tapioca, Certo, Calumet Baking Powder, Diamond Crystal Salt and other cereals and food product

The subsidiaries of the General Foods Corporation include the Canadian Postum Company, Ltd., Windsor, Ontario, Canada; Grape Nuts Company, Ltd., London, England; Postum Company, Inc.; Walter Baker & Company, Inc.; Richard Hellmann, Ltd.; General Foods Sales Company, Inc.; General Foods, Ltd.; Sanka Coffee Corporation; Douglas Pectin, Ltd.; La France Manufacturing Company; Calumet Baking Powder Company; Certo Corporation; North Atlantic Oyster Farms, Inc., now Blue Points Company, Inc.; Diamond Crystal Salt Company; Ingleheart Brothers, Inc.; Jell-O Company, Inc.; Minute Tapioca Company, Inc.; Log Cabin Products Company; Walter Baker & Company, Ltd.; Richard Hellmann, Inc.; Franklin Baker Company.

Step by step as the organization was built up, its activities became more and more far-reaching. Its enlargement seemed to demand a more inclusive name for the corporation, and on July 24, 1929, it was christened General Foods Corporation.

● The consolidation, shown in the 1929 annual report of the Corporation, resulted in the past seven years in enlarging the sales 600 per cent from $17,877,364 to $128,036,792 and the net profits 600 per cent, from $2,878,722 to $19,422,314. During this period there were price reductions on several major products. Economies were effected in production, traffic, purchasing, accounting and selling.

The General Foods Corporation has recognized the important part played by Outdoor Advertising in developing sales on many of their products, and their increasing use of Outdoor Advertising bears the best kind of testimonial as to their belief in the medium. They are now using all types of Outdoor Advertising, 3 sheet posters, subway posters, 24-sheet posters, painted display bulletins, and recently they have installed the most spectacular sign in Times Square, New York City. This sign occupies a site which enables it to have the best national circulation found anywhere in the world. All advertising is based on careful research and experimentation. Each product receives separate and individual attention; it is advertised in the way and to the extent which its particular requirements demand. Advertising is centered in a single department, administered by an officer of the company. Each assistant in the department devotes his entire skill and effort to a small group of products to which he can give the utmost of his individual attention. The extent of the Company's advertising makes available the best in market studies and research plans and preparation, production and promotion.

● General Foods Corporation maintains an Educational Department staffed with women trained in food selection and preparation. This department makes studies of the contribution of various foods to human welfare. It studies diets, eating habits, and trends. In its experimental kitchens, it develops the best ways to serve General Foods Products. It devises new recipes, and aids in the development of new products.

Late in 1930 the General Foods Corporation together with the University of Cincinnati formed a jointly owned company known as General Development Laboratories, Inc. The new company was formed to control and develop the "selective irradiation" inventions perfected by the University of Cincinnati and on which basic patents have been obtained. "Selective irradiation" involves the use of light rays to increase nutritive and healthful properties of foods and pharmaceutical products, and is also applicable to the preservation of foods since organisms causing fermentation are said to yield to the light treatment.

It is now possible to add the important Vitamin D to many foods and drug products as a result of the University's experiments, at the same time avoiding the harmful effects which often are the outcome of the use of artificial methods. The part taken in this enterprise by the General Foods is an illustration of the progressiveness and alertness of the company's management.

Last year the Company made an experiment in the introduction of quick-frozen products, and from the results so far obtained a promising field appears to have been opened up. Based on seven years research work, General Foods Corporation, through its subsidiary, Frosted Foods, Inc., has been engaged in experimental development of the patents of the Atlantic Seaboard. The method of quick-freezing involved in the agreement is the process developed by Clarence Birdseye. It is a system for sudden freezing, at temperatures of 50 degrees below zero, which permits holding of perishable foods, including meats, seafoods, vegetables and fruits, for long periods of time without affecting the quality or freshness of the product. The Pacific Frosted Foods, Inc., will hold the rights to the basic Birdseye Quick Freezing patents in the states of California, Oregon, Washington, New Mexico, Arizona, Colorado, Utah, Montana, Wyoming, Idaho, Nevada, Western Mexico, Alaska and Hawaii.

● The practicability of the idea has been demonstrated by one year's experiment in New England stores. The public, through its high percentage of repeat orders, has shown its acceptance of this new method of selling meat and fish products of standard quality and weight, with waste eliminated. Also, choice fruits and vegetables, fresh-frozen near points of production, eliminate the seasonal factor so far as the consumer is concerned.

It is held that industrially this expansion of the quick-freezing process should create new employment demands. The development is expected to be of particular benefit to the farmer because of the stabilized sectional demands that will be created for meats, fruits, and vegetables.

Eighteen cuts of meat of one grade were introduced in eighteen of the leading grocery stores of Springfield, Mass., and the line was subsequently expanded to a total of sixty quick-frozen products, including meat, vegetables, fruits and fish. The company reports that more than 100,000 individual sales were made in the Springfield stores with repeat business averaging 76 per cent, and that the economy, practicability of handling, and public acceptance were definitely proven. Further improvement in the development of refrigerating equipment for handling Birdseye processed foods was also made during 1930, reducing materially the cost or retail distribution.

● The following figures illustrate the sales and growth which have accompanied the expansion of the General Foods Corporation. These figures cover the period from February 22, 1922, to December 31, 1930, and include profits of subsidiaries only from dates of acquisition.

	Sales	Net income	Earned a share Pfd.	‡Com.	Surplus after dividends
1930	$117,463,867	$19,085,595	*	$3.63	$3,234,172
1929	128,036,791	19,422,313	*	3.68	4,544,983
1928	101,037,092	14,555,683	*	3.11	4,454,775
1927	57,287,853	11,368,219	*	6.63	3,895,514
1926	46,896,275	11,217,443	*	7.71	4,582,738
1925	27,386,929	4,684,162	*	3.35	2,994,338
1924	24,247,940	4,105,358	75.99	9.45	2,194,186
1923	22,205,410	2,881,466	44.33	6.31	1,428,016
†1922	17,877,364	2,496,538	38.41	10.77	1,403,338

†Period from February 15 to December 31, 1922.
*Preferred stock retired in 1925.
‡Based on stock outstanding at close of year.

● The financial structure of the organization is conservative. There is now only one class of stock (common, no par value). Each share has equal right and proprietorship with every other share. It is the company's policy to deal with all employees and all customers in a manner to merit their loyalty and cooperation. Promotion within the organization is based on merit, and employee interest is stimulated by employee stock purchase plans and by the payment of bonuses in various forms.

Notwithstanding the fact that the first three months of this year witnessed no improvement in the general business situation, earnings of the General Foods Corporation during the period were the second largest in its history, being exceeded only by the first quarter of 1930. After deduction of all charges, net income for the three months to March 31, last, amounted to $5,572,399 or $1.05 a share, as compared with $5,990,764 or $1.13 a share for the corresponding period of last year. For the last quarter of 1930 indicated net income was $3,570,315 or 68 cents a share.

Success in its most complete sense has been attained by this Corporation which had its origin in a barn, with a working force of a single man and a total investment of $46.85 involved—a corporation which has today a total capital stock of millions of dollars and a working staff of many thousands. It is an industry which has survived strained economic conditions—for the principles upon which it has been built have given it an almost unshakeable foundation. Further, it deals with food—one of the first necessities to humanity. The courage and ambition of Charles W. Post planted the seed which grew and developed under the direction of C. M. Chester, Jr., and other leaders under his direction who contributed their vision and energy to the forming of the General Foods Corporation—the largest food manufacturing and distributing organization in existence.

Famous Film Stars Sell Beckman Furs

(Continued from page 14) tising without a lapse. I have decreased or increased the showing but would not think of being without this representation.

"Furs are like diamonds," he continued. "The average individual cannot tell the genuine from the imitation and he must therefore buy from a reliable dealer. A sterling reputation is the stock in trade of the high-class furrier and outdoor advertising has been my principal aid in building up such a reputation.

"My many years' experience with it have given me

a chance to learn its value. Some years I have averaged $4,000.00 a month on outdoor advertising and no retail furrier would spend this if he did not believe in it. I think it fixes your name in the mind of the public you wish to cater to—and not in the minds of the women alone. Men do not buy furs but they see our bulletins and tell their wives to buy from us.

● "Location and quality are important in outdoor advertising. I believe in leasing the best locations and getting the finest kind of workmanship. In the fur business, anyway, the more quality you can get into your outdoor advertising the more effective it will be."

Canada

Include Canada in your advertising and selling plans.
Here you will find a prosperous market of ten million
people, best reached by Poster Advertising.

Any of the following Poster Advertising Agencies will
be pleased to give you the facts and figures about Canada:

The Canadian Poster Co. Ltd., Montreal, Que.
The Gould-Baird Poster Co. Limited, Brantford,
Montreal, Toronto, London, Vancouver.
E. H. Dickinson Advertising Co. Limited, Toronto,
Ont.
E. L. Ruddy Co. Limited, Toronto, Hamilton, Win-
nipeg, St. John, Vancouver

Ruddy Kester Co. Limited, Winnipeg, Man.
Ruddy-Duker Co. Limited, Vancouver, B. C.
Charles Baker Limited, Toronto, Ont.
Claude Neon General Advertising Ltd., Montreal,
Que.

PosterAdvertisingAssociation
Bank of Hamilton Bldg. of Canada **Toronto**

Here is a poster design that is one of the best of the year. It tells, graphically and simply, a rather complicated technical story. It is well-arranged and well-executed with a real idea behind it.

Here is another of the effective Shell posters with the distinctive double-headed figures. This advertiser has not been afraid to inject humor into his designs and, as a result, has created a series that is entirely individual.

The product in use and the name is all that is required to put over Firestone's message. Firestone Tires are shown as a part of the industrial picture. No copy line is needed and the advertiser deserves credit for leaving it out.

Illustration is not needed in this effective lettering poster. The White Flash designs have a family resemblance that makes for continuity, yet every poster is different enough to attract attention.

The "True to the Colors" slogan is well illustrated by this attractive illustration of the girl and her dog. The phrase is well chosen and the poster is handled so that White King Soap is featured.

This Westinghouse Refrigerator poster is well-composed and well-arranged. The copy is short and to the point and the elements of the design are held together to make a unified whole.

Chesterfield breaks away from the sports designs which have featured the advertising of this product. This is a very simple and very good poster with a short, effective selling message.

The Colonial Life name is featured in this design, with the supplementary human-interest illustration and the copy line "Protect Them" subordinated although still putting over the message.

Photo courtesy Atlantic Lithographic and Printing Co.

This poster, designed to feature the dealer emblem, accomplishes its purpose very well. The emblem occupies the prominent place in the composition with the lettering brought out to carry the message.

Photo courtesy Erie Lithographing and Printing Co.

A cattle stampede in the old days of the West is the illustration of this month's Rio Grande poster. This series has been remarkable because of its use of scenes from the days of '49 to advertise a modern gasoline.

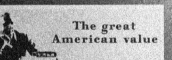

WHO'S WHO IN THIS ISSUE

T. P. PFEIFFER, advertising m a n a g e r of the Byllesby Engineering a n d Management Corporation and Standard G a s and Electric Company, became associated w i t h Louisville Gas and Electric Company on October 1, 1913. On December 27, 1921, he came to Chicago and joined the advertising  department of Byllesby Engineering and Management Corporation. He has served for two terms as secretary of the Public Utilities Advertising Association and is now a member of the association's Better Copy committee.

EARLE V. WELLER, vice-president of the Campbell-Ewald Company, was born in Los Angeles. He graduated from Occidental Academy and received his A. B. degree from Occidental College of Los Angeles. Mr. Weller received his M. A. degree at the University of Southern California.

On leaving college he spent several years in newspaper work and in the running of a printing plant and advertising agency in partnership with his brother, H. F. Weller. He was an active newspaperman for some ten years on the Los Angeles Herald, Tribune and Examiner and on the San Francisco Bulletin and the Examiner, leaving the latter to accept a position as assistant general manager with the National Automobile Club, which organization he left to join the Campbell-Ewald agency in 1927.

He was made coast manager of Campbell-Ewald Company in 1928 and a few months ago was elected to the vice-presidency of the Company.

A. M. TAYLOR, Director of Advertising of the Kelvinator S a l e s Corporation, is a native of New York State and attended the University of Rochester. His early business experience was in the specialty selling line. This was followed by connections as Advertising Manager f o r the Buffalo, Rochester  & Pittsburgh Railway, Velie Motors, Franklin Automobile Company, Copeland Products Company and, after a brief association with U. S. Rubber Company and Norge Refrigerator Company, he assumed his position with Kelvinator on August 1st, 1930.

■ ■ ■

WAYLAND B. GEISSINGER, Advertising Manager of the California Fruit Growers Exchange, was born in Cincinnati, Ohio, in 1896. Graduating from the University of Southern California, he soon became well known in California newspaper circles as Financial Editor of the old Los Angeles Express-Tribune, and Exploitation and Publicity Director of the San Francisco Bulletin. Mr. Geissinger was Director of Publicity for the United States Shipping Board on the Pacific Coast, and handled the Centenary Methodist Campaign in San Francisco, and was Publicity Director of the Inter-Church World Movement. In 1921 Mr. Geissinger joined the Advertising Department of the California Fruit Growers Exchange as Director of Publicity, becoming Advertising Manager in 1925. Mr. Geissinger is  now one of the recognized leaders in the field of food advertising, and has created many of the health appeals used in Sunkist advertising.

Public Utility Advertising

(Continued from page 22)   an idea and is useful in many ways. It is necessary to consider it as a part of every well-rounded advertising program. Public utilities use it especially for such campaigns as house-heating, convenience outlets, and customer ownership, as well as for a direct tie-up with merchandising activities.

Newspaper advertising deserves consideration in every campaign where complete coverage of a large field is desired. Merchandising activities naturally fall into this class, where every customer is a potential user of practically every appliance offered for sale. It should be used, too, for general load-building advertising designed to increase the use of service. Naturally, it plays an important part in the sale of securities under the customer ownership plan.

● Direct mail advertising is necessary in merchandising activities as an adjunct to the newspapers, and in some other cases can be depended upon to do the job alone. It is foolish, for instance, to advertise service for a 10,000 horsepower manufacturing installation in the newspapers. There are a very limited number of such potential customers on any system, and they can be reached much better by personal calls and through the mail. The number of prospects for electric signs, or for commercial or industrial lighting in any given community can be pretty definitely determined, and while newspaper advertising may be effective in a limited way, the best method of approach to such people is through direct mail. The number of possible users of a complete gas house heating installation is also rather well-defined within certain limits of income and station in life, and here, also, direct mail is more valuable than the more widespread newspaper appeal.

Direct mail is an efficient tool for the public utility advertiser to employ, because the first requisite of a direct mail campaign—an accurate mailing list—is already at hand. Most firms which sell by mail pay large sums for prepared mailing lists, or spend laborious years building them up, only to find that growing inaccuracies render them worthless after a short time. Where in the world can there be found a better mailing list than the customer list of the public utility? It can be classified as to types of service; one section of a city can be covered at a time; it is flexible, up-to-the-minute and alive. It is one of the greatest advertising assets of the progressive public utility.

Enclosures with service bills, and printed advertisements on post-card bills where these are permissible, are widely used by public utilities as an inexpensive form of direct mail advertising.

Radio is being used to a considerable extent as a medium of public utility advertising. Some com-

THE health-giving vitamins of fresh fruit juices ... bacon and eggs ... the crunchy crispness of toasted bread ... golden waffles .. the savory aroma of freshly-brewed coffee .., a breakfast

fit for a king!

HARD work for someone in a stuffy kitchen? Not at all, if your home is equipped with electric table appliances— toaster, waffle iron, percolator, egg cooker, table stove.

Buy them from your dealer . . . enjoy them; they are economical to use, because electric service is cheap. And be sure your home is wired for plenty of conveniently placed outlets.

Southern Colorado Power Company

primitive life requires food, clothing and shelter ... MODERN LIFE DEMANDS COMPLETE ELECTRIC SERVICE

This newspaper advertisement is designed to increase the use of electrical equipment.

panies use it as a general good-will builder, through programs of entertainment, but it is most widely used in the promotion of home service work. The contact between the public utility and the housewife by means of broadcasts on home economics is extremely effective in building up pleasant relations.

● There is no rule of thumb that can be applied to determine how much the public utility shall spend for advertising, because conditions vary greatly in different territories. There are no figures available on total expenditures of the industry for advertising; however, the electric light and power companies spent slightly in excess of $13,000,000 for advertising in 1928, according to the most reliable figures obtainable. It is estimated that this figure approached $15,000,000 in 1929 and 1930, and for 1931 will probably be only a little less than the last two years.

The 1928 figure of $13,000,000 represented .68 of 1 per cent of the total gross revenue of the electric light and power industry for that year. There are few companies with an appropriation of less than ½ of one per cent of gross earnings, and few with an appropriation of more than one per cent. They all lie somewhere within the range of those two figures. The average is probably in the neighborhood of .6 of one per cent.

● It might be interesting to see how the budget of a typical company is worked out. Here is a company with estimated gross earnings of $36,000,000. Approximately 83 per cent of the earnings are derived from the sale of electricity. The advertising budget for 1931 is $211,706—.58 of one per cent of estimated earnings. Of the total of $211,706, 66.8 per cent is used for general advertising, including all new business and load-building activities, and all rate and institutional advertising. The balance of the budget is used for merchandise advertising. The estimated expenditure for merchandise advertising is 4.1 per cent of the estimated volume of sales. Five per cent of merchandise sales volume is the limit set on merchandise advertising. No expenditures for securities advertising are included in the regular budget, as such expenditures do not constitute an operating charge, but may be capitalized as part of the cost of financing. This budget of $211,706 is divided between the various media as follows: outdoor, 25.7 per cent; newspapers and other publications, 61.2 per cent; direct mail, 9.5 per cent; and miscellaneous advertising media, including radio, 3.6 per cent. The figure for outdoor advertising includes the cost of maintenance and operation of the Company's own electric signs. The actual appropriation for posters and painted boards represents 7.3 per cent of the total budget.

At this point I would like to interpolate a quotation from a report of the advertising committee of the National Electric Light Association covering advertising expenditures of electric light and power companies during the year, 1926.

"Upwards of one-half the total advertising expenditures of electric light and power companies are not reflected in operating expenses. About 43 per cent of such expenditures are absorbed in the selling price of appliances or merchandise, while 10 per cent is for the sale of securities, and is a financing charge, represented in capital account. Obviously the proportion of the advertising expenditures devoted to specific purposes varies widely among individual companies, and the percentages referred to are those derived from consolidated data.

● "Considering the industry as a whole, it is apparent that, roughly, not more than one-half of the advertising expenses are paid for out of operating revenues, or are thus included in the selling cost of electric energy. Under these circumstances only 0.3 of 1 per cent of the average bill for electric service can be regarded as advertising expense. This would be equivalent to ¾ of 1 cent in the national average monthly bill of $2.50 for residential or domestic customers. The difference of less than a penny a month to the average home is so insignificant that it could not be incorporated in a rate schedule; in other words, could not be passed along to the customer as a rate reduction, if such expense were eliminated entirely.

On the other hand, it is evident that advertising has resulted in a substantial economy to the user of electric service—a dollars and cents saving greatly in excess of ¾ of 1 cent per month. It is admitted that advertising assists materially in building up volume of business and thereby decreasing the price of the service unit, or rate per kilowatt-hour. Had advertising not been practiced in the past, present rates undoubtedly would be higher than they are—and this would have been the case for years. A difference of but ½ cent per kilowatt-hour in the rate is equivalent to more than 16 times the advertising expense reflected in the average monthly service bill.

"Were electric light and power companies to discontinue advertising, the public would be deprived of the cheapest and quickest means of receiving information as to ways in which electricity may be progressively employed for individual economy, comfort and convenience. In addition, the cycle of effort resulting in decreasing production and distributing costs, enabling lower selling prices, would be seriously affected, if not made impossible."

● That ends the quotation. While this report was published several years ago, the general conclusions still hold.

There has been a vast improvement in the quality of public utility advertising in the last few years, and a large part of the credit for this showing should go to the Public Utilities Advertising Association. This organization, consisting of some 300 individuals engaged in public utility advertising, holds annual meetings in connection with the Advertising Federation of America, and through a number of committees carries on valuable research work throughout the year. It has published a number of portfolios of public utility advertising, the last appearing in 1930. Competition for space in this publication has always been keen, inasmuch as only 500 advertisements were selected for inclusion in each volume, out of many thousands submitted. More than two hundred companies regularly submit material in this annual contest.

Public utility advertising received national recognition when Northern States Power Company, a subsidiary of Standard Gas and Electric Company, won the Harvard award in two consecutive years for the best local campaign of advertising conspicuous for the excellence of its planning and execution.

It is not difficult to be optimistic about the future of public utility advertising, even in times like these. In spite of the tendency to curtail expenses of all kinds in all classes of business, the utilities generally have not made marked reductions in their advertising appropriations. Some cuts have been made, but these are mostly along the line of eliminating useless frills, that have accumulated as a continuing charge during flush times.

I sincerely believe that times like these are good for the soul of an advertising man, because they compel him to get back to fundamentals. Advertising today in all fields must be good, because there are no large profits to carry the burden of unsuccessful campaigns.

I am not one of those who believe that advertising appropriations should be largely increased during times of depression. Like the successful military commander, who knows how to retreat under adverse conditions, the successful advertiser should know how to conserve his advertising resources.

● Some day soon the forces of depression will begin to break, and when that time comes the utilities, along with other wise advertisers, will be ready to marshal their resources to take advantage of the opportunity to go after new business as never before.

■   ■   ■

Posters Sell Sliced Bread

(Continued from page 33) "Bread, you must bear in mind, is a commodity with a universal appeal three times a day and seven days a week. To cultivate this wide market means that a desire for it must be kept continually before the consumers and it seemed to us as if outdoors was the best place to reach most of them the greatest number of times.

"As we had to introduce a new innovation in bread merchandising when we started to advertise, as well as our own Parkway loaf, we featured not only the slices and convenience of the new loaf but the loaf itself wrapped in the bright yellow paper and from the very start of our campaign there was a decided increase in sales.

"When considering appropriate copy for the second poster, we asked ourselves about the uses of bread and this immediately brought us to growing children as being the greatest bread consumers. With this thought in mind we wanted to show on paper the ease with which the mother could take the ready cut slices from the carton and pass out the bread and jam or any other of the many "spreads" so eagerly relished by hungry in-between-meal appetites.

"With an attractive mother, healthy children, a sliced loaf of bread and plenty of action in the picture, without the suggestion of a sharp knife or the crumbs and waste of an ordinary baker's loaf, our second poster appeal was a strong one. It was something new to have uniform slices of bread as easily available as the picture showed and the condition was taken advantage of in many homes.

● "In looking around for our next idea it seemed as if that great American institution, the sandwich, was the logical theme around which to build our third poster. We all know that sandwiches were once considered only a lunch pail necessity but now they are great favorites in a thousand different varieties at all classes of social gatherings. Our poster showed a modern pleasing woman making a sandwich from a Parkway sliced loaf and stressed the point that it was the ideal foundation for all creations along this line.

"It was while we were developing this third poster," continued Mr. Conly, "that the research department of the advertising company made a survey of several hundred of our customers to find out just what way they were using the sliced loaf. We discovered that practically one-third of them (32%) were using it primarily for toast and another third (30%) were finding sandwiches the chief use for it. The third which remained (38%) were dividing it among the various other calls for bread at breakfast, dinner and supper.

"This large showing of toastmakers naturally led the advertising company to feature this appeal for our fourth poster. They had their artist do a typical American couple in a dining room in such a way that those who saw the completed poster had a chance to decide for themselves whether it was lovers at breakfast or lovers of breakfast. The catch line of the completed poster read, 'A Toast for Breakfast Lovers,' so no matter which way the observer decided the truth was there just the same. Prominent in the picture, of course, was Parkway sliced bread."

● Each of the important traffic arteries in Philadelphia, and there are 78 of them, are now covered by a 24 sheet Parkway poster panel. Besides these the company uses 32 for neighborhood displays making a total of 110 panels, a large proportion of which work night and day. All of them are renewed every thirty days, not always with a new poster but changed so as to keep the story fresh.

Besides the success which the company had in the Quaker City through the use of outdoor advertising it is interesting to note that it has recently opened a new $200,000 plant in Camden, New Jersey, just across the river, where it is selling a large quantity of sliced bread as the result of a poster campaign there. Of course that is a considerably smaller city than Philadelphia and it has been a great deal easier to cover, but nevertheless, it is another pronounced triumph for the efficiency of this class of advertising to change the bread buying habits of a city.

Reaching Small Town Circulation

(Continued from page 16) a single month in the larger cities and towns. The small town coverage anticipated a direct presentation of the posters to the populations of the individual towns, and the incidental coverage of the metropolitan areas thru heavy highway circulation. The 36 small towns have a total population of only 87,996, and require a total of 51 poster panels for a half showing at a total cost per month of $397.80.

● As an illustration, we can take six of the small towns included in the list of 36 above, showing the population of the towns and the circulation of a poster showing in each of these towns as ascertained by actual check. For purposes of comparison, we will give the *estimated* monthly poster circulation in each of these towns as well as the monthly circulation determined by actual check. In the first instance the estimated circulation will not include that of the transient highway travel but only the city circulation based upon population.

Town	Population	Estimated Monthly City Circulation	Monthly Highway Circulation
South San Francisco	6,166	554,940	994,000
Redwood City	12,171	1,095,390	1,652,000
San Bruno	1,800	162,000	658,000
Mountain View	3,100	279,000	518,000
Mayfield	1,700	153,000	686,000
Menlo Park	1,800	162,000	960,000

You will note from the above that the highway travel adds to the circulation of the outdoor posters in these towns from about 80% to nearly 600% in volume. The poster circulation in this group of six towns is 495 times the total circulation of six leading newspapers in these six towns. It would cost $523.80 to run a single page of advertising in each of these six newspapers, while the cost of the nine poster panels covering the same towns for one month is $69.60.

● An analysis of comparative newspaper and posting costs in these six towns shows the average cost per inch-per-thousand circulation for the six newspapers considered as $0.2958. The combined circulation of these newspapers is 10,909. As against these figures the poster circulation for the six towns total 5,404,000 monthly and the poster cost per thousand circulation is $0.0128. The newspaper circulation is 40.8% of total population and the poster circulation, by actual check, is 200 times the total population of the towns. This shows that if the circulation were estimated on the usual basis of three-times-the-population-per day the total would be 90 times the population per month, as against the actual circulation count of 200 times the population.

An interesting comparison is that between the 873 towns with an estimated circulation of 99,245,700 monthly at an average cost-per-month-per thousand circulation of eight (8c) cents, and the monthly actual circulation of 100,275,000 at an average cost of $0.045 for only 530 towns or only about 60% of the total considered in the first three charts. This shows the influence of the added highway circulation included in the 530 towns and also that wherever estimates have been made they have been conservative.

This survey was not made with any idea of belittling the value of the newspaper, and, in fact, the figures as shown were worked out by degrees and the subject probably has not by any means been exhausted. The farther the analysis is carried, however, the more striking appear the comparisons and it does seem as if we had been overlooking some of the possibilities in a medium that has done good work and that has made tremendous strides toward standardization and greater efficiency during the past five years.

Advertising Builds the Citrus Industry

(Continued from page 32) five days offering perfect tie-up with the copy featured on the 24-sheet poster.

● In closing, I will state the five outstanding reasons that have, to my mind, made outdoor advertising an important factor in building Sunkist sales:

(1) *It Tells the Story with Pictures.* Sunkist outdoor advertising tells the story in pictures—a direct route to the mind. A few well selected words, easily read by everyone, put the message over.

(2) *Reaches Every Sunkist Prospect.* Everyone—men, women, children and those who know little English—understand the pictures, trademark and buying appeal of this advertising.

(3) *They See Sunkist as They Shop.* At the direct point of purchase—on the street—consumers are given compelling Sunkist sales messages. They remind the consumer to buy and buy again.

(4) *Has Advantage of Repetition.* Repetition builds belief and sales. Day after day, all over the city, consumers see these Sunkist advertisements.

(5) *Color Wins Attention.* Sunkist products and trademark are shown in actual color, so that they are instantly recognized in the dealer's store. The customer needs only to say "Sunkist" and the sale is made.

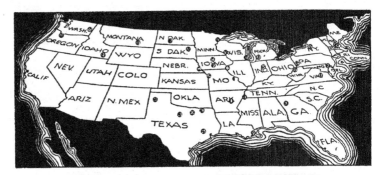

SPENDING TENDENCIES

1
LITTLE ROCK, ARKANSAS

Employment in Little Rock in June, 1931, was about 90% of what it was one year previous. This percentage may appear higher than the estimates of many people, but it is to be remembered that the status of employment in June, 1930, was slightly below that of June, 1929, when business generally was at a peak in this city.

The local employment situation showed a slight improvement in June over May. It is indicated on the graph by drawing the June line slightly above the May 100% line. This slight increase was due to increased activity on the farms more so than to increased activity in Little Rock proper, although the revival of two industries here during that month meant the employment of approximately three hundred people.

Theatre attendance has shown very little, if any, decrease since one year ago.

As to comparison of general business for June of this year with that of June, 1930, I think that a 15% decrease is a fair estimate. This estimate is made on a basis of interviews with department stores and on a basis of a monthly survey which the Little Rock Chamber of Commerce carries on through the Little Rock Wholesalers. The department stores report sales to be about 12% under those of a year ago in terms of dollars and cents, which means that more units of goods are being sold since prices have been reduced from 20% to 25% below last year's levels. The wholesalers show a slightly greater decrease. Building operations are considerably below last year. In light of these facts I think that the decrease of 15% is fair.

FIRMS INTERVIEWED: Pfeifer Bros., Gus Blass Co., M. M. Cohn Co., Majestic Theatre, Magnolia Petroleum Co.

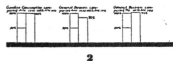

2
WILMINGTON, DELAWARE

GENERAL BUSINESS CONDITIONS: In a survey of local retail establishments completed by the Wilmingtonians, Inc., one store is reported to have sold over 37,000 more pieces of merchandise from January 1 to May 31 in 1931 than during the same period last year.

Other stores report an unprecedented June business, eclipsing the sales of June, 1930, by a wide margin.

An outstanding characteristic of Wilmington's retail business today is that employment in local stores is in excellent condition. By and large, Wilmington stores have not cut salaries or imposed enforced vacations on their employees. One establishment has fourteen more persons on its payroll than at the same time last year.

3
ATLANTA, GA.

Through information furnished by the Atlanta Chamber of Commerce, employment is shown to be 1.8% greater for June, 1931, than for June, 1930. In comparing May, 1931, with June, 1931, there is no change indicated. No information was available on theatre attendance, gasoline consumption or on general business conditions.

4
POCATELLO, IDAHO

MOVING PICTURE ATTENDANCE: Moving picture attendance for the first six months is 10% less than for the same period in 1930.

AUTOMOTIVE: In spite of a marked decrease in automobile registrations, the consumption for the entire state of Idaho of gasoline indicated in the tax collection report an increase of nearly 300,000 gallons for the first six months of 1931 as compared with the same period in 1930.

A report of registrations for the first four months indicated a decrease of slightly more than 12 per cent, compared with the same period last year.

The increase in tax collections is $74,000.00.

5
MARION, INDIANA

Employment seems to be picking up, especially in the radio and cabinet factory.

Theatre attendance seems to be lagging behind that for last year.

Business in general has shown an increase since April of this year.

FIRMS INTERVIEWED: Chamber of Commerce, Indiana and Paramount Theatres, Hardware Company, U. S. Radio Factory officials.

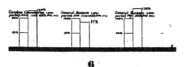

6
BURLINGTON, IOWA

A gain of 3.3 per cent was made in Burlington employment in June, 1931, as compared to May, 1931. The report was based on figures given by 19 firms employing 1,812 persons.

The greatest gains for the entire state of Iowa were in the textile industries, lumber products, stone and clay products, railway car shops and various industrial groups.

7
DES MOINES, IOWA

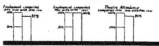

Employment for June, 1931, is off 15% as compared to June, 1930, and .1% as compared to May, 1931.

Theatre attendance is off approximately 20% due to the closing for the summer of RKO Orpheum.

Tax receipts for June, 1930, were $962,251.18 and in May, 1931, $1,444,863.89. The June figures were not ready. The increase in May over June, 1930, shows that the gasoline consumption is much greater. This is probably due in part to the excellent roads.

Gross money as far as general business is concerned shows a decrease of about 7 or 8%, but there is a much larger volume of stock moving at low prices compared to 1930. June, 1931, is approximately 20% less as compared to May, 1931, but this is more or less the seasonal drop.

FIRMS INTERVIEWED: State Treasurer, State Commissioner of Labor, Younker Bros. Dept. Store, Publix Theatres Corp.

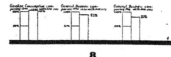

8
MASON CITY, IOWA

GENERAL BUSINESS CONDITIONS: The Lehigh Cement Plant was closed for sixty days when over $160,000.00 improvements and new installations were made in the plant. Now all former employees are at work. It is the policy of Lehigh to shut down in summer thus permitting the employees a greater latitude of recreation.

The state cigarette tax shows an increase of over $6,000.00 in June as compared with a year ago.

Mason City topped the list for May of a list of sixteen cities in Iowa in new houses. The total for May was $107,166.00 while Des Moines was second with $80,470.00.

The Iowa Culbert & Pine Company reports that business is ahead of 1930 for the first six months.

Gibbs-Cook Tractor Company's sales for the first six months exceed the whole of 1929.

Mr. Wilcox, of the E. B. Higley Company, reports that the ice cream business is about 4% less than it was for the same period in 1930.

Mr. Van Ness, of Currie, Van Ness Company, wholesale and retail hardware, reports business to be practically the same as last year. There is a little tendency to lag on account of the decrease in inventory values. On the whole he says that business is fair.

The Mason City Hardware Company reports a nice increase for 1931 over 1930.

Gildners Clothing Company reports that business is just about the same for 1931 as it was in 1930.

The Jefferson Transportation Company just opened a new bus depot which includes a large waiting room, restaurant, barber shop and loading space. Sixteen busses arrive daily and leave daily.

Mr. Millington, Secretary of the Chamber of Commerce, reports over a half dozen retail stores with a larger dollar business for the first six months of 1931 than for the same period in 1930.

9

NEW ORLEANS, LOUISIANA

GENERAL BUSINESS CONDITIONS: The New Orleans Association of Commerce analyzes business conditions in New Orleans as follows:

CONSTRUCTION: With a huge gain in construction contracts for the six months of 1931 as compared with the similar period of 1930, the New Orleans territory makes a showing that is unique among the various territories included in the F. W. Dodge Corporation compilation.

New Orleans was also one of the two territories that in June showed an increase over June of last year and over May of this year.

PORT: Tonnage of sea-going vessels arriving in New Orleans increased from 830,310 in May to 932,310 tons in June, according to the dock board.

It is significant that during the past twelve months, twenty steamship lines entering New Orleans either have inaugurated an entirely new service, either have added more vessels to old service, or have done both. Two new barge lines have also been established during the period and the existing line greatly expanded. Foremost among the expansion of the port's steamship facilities was the inauguration during the year of thirteen new lines to many parts of the world.

INDUSTRY: Since the first of the year 118 new businesses of a substantial nature opened in New Orleans. Since that time, too, 132 existing business expanded operations.

AGRICULTURE: Louisiana only recently completed the marketing of the greatest strawberry crop in its history, greater than any other strawberry crop both in the number of cars shipped and in value.

During the first six months of 1931, Louisiana shipped more carloads of fruits and vegetables than in the twelve months of any previous year in its history.

While cotton acreage decreased ten per cent—a decrease that was advocated—there was a favorable increase in the production of food and feed crops—an increase also that was advocated.

FINANCIAL: Bank debits for the week ending July 1 totaled $132,000,000, the largest in the history of the city. The previous high record for any week was $120,000,000.

Dun's Review shows an average decrease of 27.3% in bank clearings, whereas the decrease in New Orleans was only 9.9% or less than any other large city.

Total deposits of New Orleans banks as of June 30 showed a gain over 1930 and 1929, the boom year. The increase over last year totals 2.1 per cent as compared with a loss of approximately 1.8 per cent on June 30 as compared with June 30, 1929. In addition, cash on hand and due from banks increased to $53,228,794.84 from $51,739,171.88, as of June 30, 1930.

TRANSPORTATION: With every other section of the country showing a decrease and the average decrease being 9.3 per cent, an increase of 2.2 per cent in freight car requirements is forecast by the Regional Shippers' Advisory Board for the Southwest portion of the country—including New Orleans—for the third quarter of 1931. The increase predicted is from 542,930 cars in 1930 to 554,990 cars in 1931.

10

KALAMAZOO, MICHIGAN

General employment shows a decrease of about 15% as compared with 1930. No information was given on theatres, gasoline consumption or general

business as far as actual figures were concerned.
FIRMS INTERVIEWED: L. V. White Co., Paper Mills.

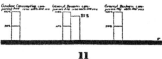

11
DULUTH, MINNESOTA

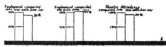

In comparing employment in June, 1931, with June, 1930, there is about a 10% decrease. Comparing it with May, 1931, there is an increase of 5%. Theatre attendance is off about 10% as compared with June, 1930. Gasoline consumption shows an increase of 5%. General business is listed as being off about 15% in June, 1931, as compared with June, 1930.

12
ST. JOSEPH, MO.

GENERAL BUSINESS CONDITIONS: Business conditions continue to show some improvement and there is a more optimistic feeling among the retail merchants than there has been for some time.

Prospects in this section for bumper crops, particularly corn and apples are best in years. This tends to create a better feeling generally.

MOVING PICTURE ATTENDANCE: Moving picture attendance always takes a slump during the summer months. The local managers report this summer's business to be about 10% less than a year ago.

AUTOMOTIVE: Automobile registration is approximately the same as in 1930 at this same time, and the gasoline consumption is running about the same.

13
BILLINGS, MONTANA

There is no decrease in employment for June, 1931, as compared with June, 1930, because of the extensive building programs which are still under way.

The largest dry goods store reports a 30% increase over June, 1930, and the volume for May and June of 1931 as being about the same.
FIRMS INTERVIEWED: Manager, Babcock Theatre, Officials of the various large oil companies and department stores.

14
OMAHA, NEBRASKA

GENERAL BUSINESS CONDITIONS: With three buildings totaling $2,000,000 under construction, labor of this classification has been fairly well employed through the summer. The new Cargill $1,000,000 elevator, duplicate of one built last year, will hold 5,000,000 bushels of wheat. The new county hospital, first wing, is costing over $615,000, and an additional $75,000 is to be spent on a new boiler and engine house. The Central High school addition, costing $245,000, is a third major project under construction. Nor does there appear to be any letup in building activities. A permit has been applied for to build a $160,000 mausoleum at one of the cemeteries. Two new golf courses are under construction. The Methodist hospital is adding a ward, spending $20,000. Contracts have been let for improvement of the Benson West grade school, costing $44,140, exclusive of equipment. A $150,000 viaduct will be completed in October.

Private residence property is selling at a fair speed, and many new one-family homes are being constructed. One $75,000 home is being built and work is starting on a 16-apartment building worth $150,000.

A flood of new wheat is heading toward Omaha's many elevators, indicating that crops are large here, though prices are low. Livestock receipts at the Omaha yards, second largest in the world, have been setting new records during the summer, in all divisions.

Clothing stores set new records during June, an abnormally hot month, for sales of men's summer suits.

Bank deposits are $2,348,000 higher than a year ago. Omaha led all principal cities of the United States in May in number of real estate mortgages filed. The city, county, school district and Metropolitan utilities district have just paid off $825,796 worth of bonds, and the Federal land bank here reports that farmers are meeting their obligations promptly.

15
MANCHESTER, N. H.

There is a big increase in the number employed in cotton textile mills and shoe factories. According to a report released by Henry A. Tafe, state director of the United States Department of Labor, some improvement was noted in the unemployment situation all over New Hampshire during the month of June.

Manchester reported a surplus of all classes of labor but shoe factories, cigar factories and mills operated on a very good schedule. One cigar factory worked with a night shift engaged, while departmental overtime continued in a textile mill and a knitting mill. The shoe factories worked on satisfactory schedules. Building permits recently issued a call for the expenditure of approximately $70,000 which with the projects under way have provided employment to a large number of men.

Reports of two of the largest saving institutions in the city show that deposits for the first six months of this year increased by nearly two millions over the corresponding period in 1930.

Comparing general business in June, 1931, with June, 1930, and May, 1931, we find that there is an increase in both of them.

16
SYRACUSE, N. Y.

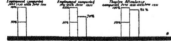

No figures were available on employment, but there is a seasonal slackening in business and manufacturing.

Retail trade seems to be very brisk but figures show that in comparing June, 1931, with June, 1930, there is a 19% decrease. No figures were available to compare June, 1931, with May, 1931.

FIRMS INTERVIEWED: Chamber of Commerce, Chester Bahn—Theatre Editor, Syracuse Herald, Standard Oil Co. of N. Y.

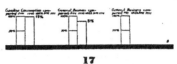

17
BISMARCK, N. DAK.

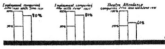

In comparing employment in June, 1931, with June, 1930, we find that there is about a 20% decrease and the same decrease when comparing it with May, 1931.

Theatre attendance is approximately 40% less for June, 1931, when compared with June, 1930.

There is very little change in the gasoline consumption comparing June, 1931, with June, 1930.

General business as a whole is off about 25%.

FIRMS INTERVIEWED: Corwin Churchill Motors, First National Bank, Association of Commerce.

18
PORTLAND, OREGON

GENERAL BUSINESS CONDITIONS: During the month of June, much of the unemployed labor surplus was taken care of in the harvest fields in the state, as harvesting in Oregon is somewhat earlier than in the middle-west and east.

Retail business conditions are on the upward trend, which is attributed to seasonable weather conditions.

MOVING PICTURE ATTENDANCE: One theatre is closed for the summer season. The R. K. O. and the Paramount, featuring vaudeville, show an increase in receipts over previous months.

AUTOMOTIVE: Gasoline figures for May, 1931, and May, 1930, show quite a large increase.

May, 1931 . . . . 7,449,755 gallons
May, 1930 . . . . 4,178,441 gallons

19
PITTSBURGH, PENNA.

There is a decrease of about 13% in employment for June, 1931, as compared with June, 1930. There is a decrease of 2.3% in comparing June, 1931, with May, 1931. A strike in the coal industry has done much to make the employment situation worse.

Theatre attendance is about 25% less for June, 1931, than it was for June, 1930.

There was a decrease of less than 1% in gasoline consumption in comparing June, 1930, with June, 1931.

There was approximately a 13% drop in general business comparing June, 1930, with June, 1931, and about a 5% drop in comparing June, 1931, with May, 1931. Automobiles sales gained and there was an increase in the pig iron production. There were relatively few business failures in June, and a large number of new corporations were formed.

SOURCE OF INFORMATION: Pittsburgh Review (Bureau of Business Research, University of Pittsburgh).

20
ABERDEEN, S. DAK.

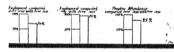

In comparing the employment for June, 1931, with June, 1930, we find that there is a decrease of 30%. In comparing June, 1931, with May, 1931, there is a 5% decrease.

Theatre attendance showed a gain this spring but seems to be losing now, and shows a decrease of 15% in comparing June, 1931, with June, 1930.

Gasoline consumption is on the increase and shows a gain of 20% in comparing June, 1931, with June, 1930.

General business shows an increase of 5% in comparing June, 1931, with June, 1930. Comparing June, 1931, with May, 1931, we find a decrease of 2%.

FIRMS INTERVIEWED: Chamber of Commerce, Publix Theatres, Wholesale houses, Banks, Retail outlets.

21
MEMPHIS, TENN.

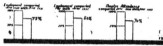

Employment is off about 25% comparing June, 1931, with June, 1930.

Theatre attendance shows a decrease of about 30% in comparison with 1930. Vaudeville has been discontinued and there is an increase of neighborhood shows.

Gasoline consumption shows a decrease of about 15% comparing June, 1931, with June, 1930.

General business shows a decrease of about 30% comparing June, 1931, with June, 1930, and with May, 1931.

FIRMS INTERVIEWED: Municipal Employment Bureau, R. K. O. and Loew's Theatres, Large gasoline companies—gasoline inspector, Memphis Chamber of Commerce.

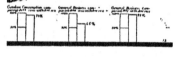

22
AMARILLO, TEXAS

Employment for the first six months period of 1931 as compared with the same period of 1930 shows about a 30% decrease.

Theatre attendance is approximately 11% below that of June, 1930.

Gasoline consumption shows an increase of 5% comparing June, 1931, with June, 1930.

FIRMS INTERVIEWED: Publix Theatres, Inc., Haggy-Harrington & Marsh, Phillips Petroleum Co., Employment Bureau.

23
BROWNWOOD, TEXAS

Comparing employment in June, 1931, with May, 1931, there is a 50% increase.

Theatre attendance has been better every month in 1931 than in 1930, and comparing the month of June of these two years, we find a 15% increase.

There was a sharp upturn during the last fifteen days in June and an increase of 15% is shown in comparing June, 1931, with June, 1930.

In comparing general business in June, 1931, with June, 1930, and with May, 1931, we find an increase of 25% and 30% respectively. In the sales of spring merchandise during the latter part of June, the results indicated that a fair amount of money was available.

FIRMS INTERVIEWED: Hemphill-Fain Company (Dry Goods), Renfro Drug Stores (Drugs), Holley Chevrolet Co. (Automobiles), Blackwell Motor Co. (Automobiles), Garner-Alvis Company (Dry Goods), T. C. Electric Co. (Lighting Fixtures), Dublin & Cannon (Radio & Electric Refrigerators).

24
DALLAS, TEXAS

Business remains only fair, with the usual slight summer falling off. The general tone of hopeful expectance for fall business is coincidental with harvest. The nationwide slump in the oil industry has affected Dallas materially. However, there are comparatively few failures. Wholesale activities in the market during the August fall buying season is expected to strengthen business in general as Dallas is a large wholesale center and intensive efforts are being made to bring in new customers.

The slight increase in theatre attendance is accounted for by two fine new theatres of modern construction and moderate prices, general improvement in talking pictures and normal increase in population of 6% a year.

FIRMS INTERVIEWED: Two banks, one large oil company, trade association officers, union officials, welfare agencies, department store, Dallas Branch, Dept. of Commerce, and the Chamber of Commerce.

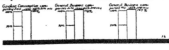

25
HOUSTON, TEXAS

GENERAL BUSINESS CONDITIONS: For the month of June, most retail lines were off in volume to some extent. Those selling industrial and commercial accounts were most seriously affected. Clothing and furniture, generally, were approximately 5% off, while one of the electrical appliance stores reported the best month in June that they had had in the past year.

MOVING PICTURE ATTENDANCE: Moving picture attendance was reported to show a decrease of about 20% comparing June, 1931.

AUTOMOTIVE: New car sales for June were 5% below those of May, and 12% below those for June, 1930. New car sales for the first six months this year were 22% below the same period of 1930. Gasoline sales were reported to be approximately 22% off.

26
PARIS, TEXAS

Employment, comparing June, 1931, with June, 1930, shows about a 20% decrease. Employment, comparing June, 1931, with May, 1931, shows no difference at all.

Theatre attendance is off about 30% comparing June, 1931, with June, 1930.

Gasoline consumption is about 20% lower for June, 1931, than it was for June, 1930.

General business is off about 25% comparing June, 1931, with June, 1930, and comparing it with May, 1931, is off about 2%.

FIRMS INTERVIEWED: Paris Morning News, Lamar and Plaza Theatres, Arthur Caddel Co., Pete Humphries Co., Continental Oil Co.

27
RICHMOND, VA.

Government statistics for the entire state show that the Pocahontas railroads—Norfolk and Western, Chesapeake and Ohio, Virginian and Richmond, Fredericksburg and Potomac—had been the only one of the eight regional divisions in the United States to earn more in 1930 than in 1929. Virginia was also one of two states to increase her payment of internal revenue payment during 1930.

28
SPOKANE, WASHINGTON

GENERAL BUSINESS CONDITIONS: Figures recently released by the 12th Federal Reserve District reveal that Spokane is the only city in the West which reported an increase in sales for the month of May. Stores reporting showed an increase of one-half of one per cent over the previous May in spite of the fact that there was one less trading day. For the year to date, all stores showed a loss of but one-fifth of one per cent over last year.

MOVING PICTURE ATTENDANCE: Attendance in this industry is on a par with that for the corresponding period of last year. This is attributable to the fact that the late summer season has kept people in the city.

AUTOMOTIVE: Gasoline consumption for the second quarter of 1931 is now on a par with the same period of last year. This is quite a jump in this industry inasmuch as the first quarter showed a 10% decrease.

29
PARKERSBURG, W. VA.

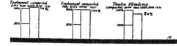

General employment conditions are better in 1931 than in the same period in 1930 (June) because of city bond issues which provide for more employment.

There is a slight improvement noted in general business conditions in most lines.

FIRMS INTERVIEWED: Standard Oil Co. of N. J., Chamber of Commerce, Warner Bros. Theatres.

30
LA CROSSE, WIS.

GENERAL BUSINESS CONDITIONS: Little improvement in employment conditions in June was noted. Industrial activity in practically all industries was somewhat restricted with a surplus of factory help and unskilled labor. Part time schedules prevail in all plants but in most instances with the usual force.

State and county road work, municipal improvements, grade elimination and railroad crossing projects are furnishing employment to several hundred laborers in excess of those usually employed in such work at this time of the year.

Building permits are below normal and bank clearings have shown a decided decrease over the same period in 1930 with very little change registered from week to week.

MOVING PICTURE ATTENDANCE: Moving picture attendance still continues to be below normal.

AUTOMOTIVE: New car registrations are below normal.

Gasoline consumption shows quite a decided increase.

31
MILWAUKEE, WIS.

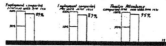

Employment, comparing June, 1931, with June, 1930, shows a decrease of 11.4% and comparing it with May, 1931, there is a 1.4% decrease. However, some closed plants are reopening.

Theatre attendance shows a decrease of 5% comparing June, 1931, with June, 1930. The attendance at the first run houses is improving.

There is a 6% increase in gasoline consumption comparing June, 1931, with June, 1930. Low prices were probably responsible for this.

General business is showing a slow but steady improvement. Comparing general business of June, 1931, with June, 1930, we find an increase of 2.2% and comparing it with May, 1931, a 5% increase.

FIRMS INTERVIEWED: Eason Oil Co., A. O. Smith Co., Fox-Midwesco Corp., Wis. Industrial Commission, Milwaukee Ass'n of Commerce.

This Issue   September 1931

Protest Unfair Criticism
of OUTDOOR MEDIUM

2   No. 9

Legion Passes Resolution

A resolution regarding the use of Outdoor Advertising was adopted by the American Legion Department of New Jersey at their annual convention held at Atlantic City, N. J., September 10, 11 and 12, at which delegates from each Legion Post in the State of New Jersey were in attendance. It reads:

We, the members of the American Legion, Department of New Jersey, have for the past five years employed and profited by the use of Outdoor Advertising, as conducted by the members of the Outdoor Advertising Association of America, Inc.

Whereas: The Outdoor Advertising industry directly employs in excess of 35,000 men, a vast number of whom are ex-service men; and as an industry, is responsible for the marketing of more than a billion dollars worth of manufactured goods. We are righteously opposed to the generalities employed, which classify the organized industry with the sniping and daubing, which is evident in every State of the Union.

Whereas: There is no campaign to prohibit all gasoline stations because some are unsightly and in objectionable locations; there is no attempt to eliminate all restaurants because of the hot dog shacks, which now and then disfigure the most beautiful highways of our State. No one has suggested that the building of houses be prohibited because now and then some irresponsible party builds a monstrosity. The Outdoor Advertising industry has constantly improved its service so that none of its structures mar the landscape or create a hazard to traffic.

Whereas: Outdoor Advertising quickens trade; adds to the wealth of the nation and to the prosperity of the people, we believe it to be an important channel of distribution and should not be the subject of attack by over-zealous nature lovers or of organized groups that have not carefully analyzed the existing situation.

THEREFORE BE IT RESOLVED that we, the American Legion of the Department of New Jersey, hereby express our belief in the value of legitimate Outdoor Advertising. We disapprove of any unjust attack upon this important business, which might carry with it resultant hardship on property owners whose rights are denied.

■ ■ ■

Road Building Speeded Up

New and improved methods of road-building have made it possible by the use of mixed in place of asphaltic material, to build as much as a mile of road per day under traffic, eliminating much of the very annoying delay occasioned by detours, according to the American Petroleum Institute. It is predicted that in the near future it will be possible to step up this production figure to two or three miles a day.

This will mean that in the future advertisers will have to suffer less of the loss and inconvenience resulting from the necessity of relocating structures while roads are being built, and will eliminate much of the necessity of units, bought to cover certain traffic, having to be temporarily discontinued.

■ ■ ■

Outdoor Advertising and Soft Drinks

Another universally demanded group of products which are most logically advertised outdoors, are the various soft drinks now on the American market. Human thirst, prohibition, excellence of product, variety to suit every taste, and widespread and persistent advertising has made the soft drink industry grow into a giant within the last ten years. Retail sales in the United States alone for the year 1929 are reported to be in excess of $600,000,000.

Here is another product widely sold in tremendous volume. In view of the magnitude of the business as a whole and its particular adaptability to outdoor advertising, those engaged in this line find the use of the outdoor medium especially profitable.

■ ■ ■

Growth of Golf

Another evidence of the tendency for people to live more and more out of doors is to be found in the magnitude of the hold which the game of golf has taken on the American people. This game, only recently rising to become one of the most popular of American Sports, now constitutes one of our major industries, with properties valued at $500,000,000, and an annual investment of $10,000,000 in balls and clubs alone. Golf clubs regularly employ about 50,000 persons, not including hundreds of thousands of caddies. More than 650,000 persons belong to golf clubs and there are other hundreds of thousands who play the game.

■ ■ ■

Bus Traffic Increases

Although the increasing use of busses as a means of transportation has been a serious blow to railroads, it has at the same time been the means of adding additional circulation and effectiveness to outdoor advertising displays.

The six thousand motor bus companies operating in the United States during 1930 carried 1,784,000,000 passengers showing an increase of over 10,000,000 riders over the preceding year.

That many people, passing the outdoor advertising displays maintained in the country represent no small yearly circulation figure in any advertising medium.

Agencies Merge

Effective September 1st, the Gardner Advertising Company, St. Louis and New York, and the Botsford-Constantine Company, Portland, Seattle, San Francisco and Los Angeles, have become associated to form a nation-wide advertising organization.

The Gardner Company has acquired a substantial interest in the Pacific Coast agency, which now becomes Botsford-Constantine and Gardner. In like manner, the latter company becomes a stockholder in the Gardner Company. The two companies will maintain separate corporate identities, but through joint stock interests will operate in full cooperation with each other. The result will be the extension of Gardner service to the Pacific Coast, assuring Gardner clients service of an organization which knows Coast conditions through long and intimate contact. Clients of Botsford-Constantine and Gardner, by the same arrangement now have available complete agency service East of the Rockies.

The Botsford-Constantine Company, established in 1918, is one of the oldest and most successful exclusive Pacific Coast advertising agencies. They are perhaps best known in the East for their advertising of the Jantzen Swimming Suit, which is an international success.

The Gardner Company numbers among its clients such firms as: Aluminum Company of America, Pet Milk Company, Ralston Purina Company, American Cyanamid Company, Certain-teed Products Corporation, McGraw-Hill Company, Moody's Investors Service, Gerber Products Company, Wm. B. Stokely Company, Brown Shoe Company, Motor Wheel Corporation, and many others. Their work for Aluminum and Pet Milk won four Harvard Awards during the seven years in which awards were made.

■   ■   ■

Outdoor Group Organizes

New York City, Aug. 6—At a meeting called by Leonard Dreyfuss, President of the United Advertising Corporation, 12 outdoor advertising companies, operating in the Metropolitan District, have formed the Metropolitan Outdoor Advertising Association for the purpose of cooperating with responsible groups in the protection of roadside business and beauty.

Fred I. Hamm, General Outdoor Advertising Co., Brooklyn, was elected president of the association, with W. J. Schloemer, C. L. Schloemer, Inc., New York, first vice-president; Louis Schwartz, Highway Display, Inc., Poughkeepsie, second vice-president; and Harry Gordon, Disosway & Fisher, Inc., Queens, secretary-treasurer.

The directors are W. H. Mullen, Metro Outdoor Advertising Co., New York; A. J. Cusick, General Outdoor, New York; James McElroy, McElroy Bros., Flushing, L. I.; Saul Wolf, Worego Highway Service Co., Lynbrook, L. I.; Mr. Van Wagner, Van Wagner Co., Far Rockaway; and Messrs. P. J. Dunn, Schwartz, and Schloemer.

In his opening address to the group, Mr. Dreyfuss expressed the immediate need for such an association and urged those present to commit themselves to a definite and progressive plan of action. "This organization should appoint a representative committee, composed of plant operators in the Metropolitan area, to make an extensive survey of all roadside business, including outdoor advertising, with a view to making concrete suggestions and proposals toward the betterment of conditions existing along roadsides leading into our city."

"There are certain desirable poster locations, along the Albany Post Road and elsewhere around New York, that have been ruined because of existing methods of doing business," said president Fred I. Hamm. "This association should adopt a fair plan for all operating companies with due regard for scenic beauty, and if we can abide by a mutually satisfactory code governing the number of structures on a given strip of land, we will be taking a very far reaching step of great significance to the industry at large."

Hearty enthusiasm was evidenced by all those present at the prospects of cooperatively working toward the goal of better outdoor advertising that could not be reached individually.

Among those present, besides those named, were Mr. Reynolds, Criterion Advertising Co., New York; H. A. Reeves, General Outdoor, New Rochelle; Roland Ayasse, Sunrise Advertising Co., Richmond Hill; Mr. Trainer, H. C. Williams, Inc., New York; Samuel Weiss, Suburban Bus Advertising Co., Jamaica, N. Y.; Mr. McElroy, McElroy Bros., Flushing; A. P. Schell, General Outdoor, New York; J. Robert McNeil, United Advertising Agency; and Daniel O'Connell and Mrs. Harry Lilly, of the Outdoor Advertising Association of America.

■   ■   ■

Outdoor Advertising and the Movies

The claim of outdoor advertisers that moving picture houses take people out of the homes and over the streets at night is substantiated by figures which show that thirty million dollars are paid weekly by 115,000,000 patrons of movie houses in the United States. This is an average of 38 cents per person.

SPENDING TENDENCIES

Today's reader doesn't want to plow through long columns of figures, many pages of comment, when he is trying to find out just how conditions stand in different parts of the country. Therefore, the magazine, ADVERTISING OUTDOORS, has changed its method of presenting "Spending Tendencies," and with this issue is offering merchandising data covering the trends in spending in a dramatic, graphic form.

Below and on the following pages are reproduced 22 charts showing general business, employment and other factors that affect spending habits, each market individually graphed to show its comparison with last year and last month, at the last date on which accurate information could be gathered.

In each one of these 22 markets separate investigations have been made by the magazine, ADVERTISING OUTDOORS. Merchants, automotive men, chambers of commerce and the like have been interviewed to secure accurate information on local conditions.

	100%
EMPLOYMENT Comparing July 1931 with July 1930	
EMPLOYMENT Comparing July 1931 with June 1931	
THEATER ATTENDANCE Comparing July 1931 with July 1930	
GASOLINE CONSUMPTION Comparing July 1931 with July 1930	
GENERAL BUSINESS Comparing July 1931 with July 1930	
GENERAL BUSINESS Comparing July 1931 with June 1931	

	100%
EMPLOYMENT Comparing July 1931 with July 1930	
EMPLOYMENT Comparing July 1931 with June 1931	
THEATER ATTENDANCE Comparing July 1931 with July 1930	
GASOLINE CONSUMPTION Comparing July 1931 with July 1930	
GENERAL BUSINESS Comparing July 1931 with July 1930	
GENERAL BUSINESS Comparing July 1931 with June 1931	

	100%
EMPLOYMENT Comparing July 1931 with July 1930	
EMPLOYMENT Comparing July 1931 with June 1931	
THEATER ATTENDANCE Comparing July 1931 with July 1930	
GASOLINE CONSUMPTION Comparing July 1931 with July 1930	
GENERAL BUSINESS Comparing July 1931 with July 1930	
GENERAL BUSINESS Comparing July 1931 with June 1931	

	100%
EMPLOYMENT Comparing July 1931 with July 1930	
EMPLOYMENT Comparing July 1931 with June 1931	
THEATER ATTENDANCE Comparing July 1931 with July 1930	
GASOLINE CONSUMPTION Comparing July 1931 with July 1930	
GENERAL BUSINESS Comparing July 1931 with July 1930	
GENERAL BUSINESS Comparing July 1931 with June 1931	

	100%
EMPLOYMENT Comparing July 1931 with July 1930	
EMPLOYMENT Comparing July 1931 with June 1931	
THEATER ATTENDANCE Comparing July 1931 with July 1930	
GASOLINE CONSUMPTION Comparing July 1931 with July 1930	
GENERAL BUSINESS Comparing July 1931 with July 1930	
GENERAL BUSINESS Comparing July 1931 with June 1931	

	100%
EMPLOYMENT Comparing July 1931 with July 1930	
EMPLOYMENT Comparing July 1931 with June 1931	
THEATER ATTENDANCE Comparing July 1931 with July 1930	
GASOLINE CONSUMPTION Comparing July 1931 with July 1930	
GENERAL BUSINESS Comparing July 1931 with July 1930	
GENERAL BUSINESS Comparing July 1931 with June 1931	

	100%
EMPLOYMENT Comparing July 1931 with July 1930	
EMPLOYMENT Comparing July 1931 with June 1931	
THEATER ATTENDANCE Comparing July 1931 with July 1930	
GASOLINE CONSUMPTION Comparing July 1931 with July 1930	
GENERAL BUSINESS Comparing July 1931 with July 1930	
GENERAL BUSINESS Comparing July 1931 with June 1931	

	100%
EMPLOYMENT Comparing July 1931 with July 1930	
EMPLOYMENT Comparing July 1931 with June 1931	
THEATER ATTENDANCE Comparing July 1931 with July 1930	
GASOLINE CONSUMPTION Comparing July 1931 with July 1930	
GENERAL BUSINESS Comparing July 1931 with July 1930	
GENERAL BUSINESS Comparing July 1931 with June 1931	

	100%
EMPLOYMENT Comparing July 1931 with July 1930	
EMPLOYMENT Comparing July 1931 with June 1931	
THEATER ATTENDANCE Comparing July 1931 with July 1930	
GASOLINE CONSUMPTION Comparing July 1931 with July 1930	
GENERAL BUSINESS Comparing July 1931 with July 1930	
GENERAL BUSINESS Comparing July 1931 with June 1931	

	100%
EMPLOYMENT Comparing July 1931 with July 1930	
EMPLOYMENT Comparing July 1931 with June 1931	
THEATER ATTENDANCE Comparing July 1931 with July 1930	
GASOLINE CONSUMPTION Comparing July 1931 with July 1930	
GENERAL BUSINESS Comparing July 1931 with July 1930	
GENERAL BUSINESS Comparing July 1931 with June 1931	

	100%
EMPLOYMENT Comparing July 1931 with July 1930	
EMPLOYMENT Comparing July 1931 with June 1931	
THEATER ATTENDANCE Comparing July 1931 with July 1930	
GASOLINE CONSUMPTION Comparing July 1931 with July 1930	
GENERAL BUSINESS Comparing July 1931 with July 1930	
GENERAL BUSINESS Comparing July 1931 with June 1931	

	100%
EMPLOYMENT Comparing July 1931 with July 1930	
EMPLOYMENT Comparing July 1931 with June 1931	
THEATER ATTENDANCE Comparing July 1931 with July 1930	
GASOLINE CONSUMPTION Comparing July 1931 with July 1930	
GENERAL BUSINESS Comparing July 1931 with July 1930	
GENERAL BUSINESS Comparing July 1931 with June 1931	

	100%
EMPLOYMENT Comparing July 1931 with July 1930	
EMPLOYMENT Comparing July 1931 with June 1931	
THEATER ATTENDANCE Comparing July 1931 with July 1930	
GASOLINE CONSUMPTION Comparing July 1931 with July 1930	
GENERAL BUSINESS Comparing July 1931 with July 1930	
GENERAL BUSINESS Comparing July 1931 with June 1931	

	100%
EMPLOYMENT Comparing July 1931 with July 1930	
EMPLOYMENT Comparing July 1931 with June 1931	
THEATER ATTENDANCE Comparing July 1931 with July 1930	
GASOLINE CONSUMPTION Comparing July 1931 with July 1930	
GENERAL BUSINESS Comparing July 1931 with July 1930	
GENERAL BUSINESS Comparing July 1931 with June 1931	

	100%
EMPLOYMENT Comparing July 1931 with July 1930	
EMPLOYMENT Comparing July 1931 with June 1931	
THEATER ATTENDANCE Comparing July 1931 with July 1930	
GASOLINE CONSUMPTION Comparing July 1931 with July 1930	
GENERAL BUSINESS Comparing July 1931 with July 1930	
GENERAL BUSINESS Comparing July 1931 with June 1931	

	100%
EMPLOYMENT Comparing July 1931 with July 1930	
EMPLOYMENT Comparing July 1931 with June 1931	
THEATER ATTENDANCE Comparing July 1931 with July 1930	
GASOLINE CONSUMPTION Comparing July 1931 with July 1930	
GENERAL BUSINESS Comparing July 1931 with July 1930	
GENERAL BUSINESS Comparing July 1931 with June 1931	

EMPLOYMENT Comparing July 1931 with July 1930		100%
EMPLOYMENT Comparing July 1931 with June 1931		
THEATER ATTENDANCE Comparing July 1931 with July 1930		
GASOLINE CONSUMPTION Comparing July 1931 with July 1930		
GENERAL BUSINESS Comparing July 1931 with July 1930		
GENERAL BUSINESS Comparing July 1931 with June 1931		

EMPLOYMENT Comparing July 1931 with July 1930		100%
EMPLOYMENT Comparing July 1931 with June 1931		
THEATER ATTENDANCE Comparing July 1931 with July 1930		
GASOLINE CONSUMPTION Comparing July 1931 vith July 1930		
GENERAL BUSINESS Comparing July 1931 with July 1930		
GENERAL BUSINESS Comparing July 1931 with June 1931		

EMPLOYMENT Comparing July 1931 with July 1930		100%
EMPLOYMENT Comparing July 1931 with June 1931		
THEATER ATTENDANCE Comparing July 1931 with July 1930		
GASOLINE CONSUMPTION Comparing July 1931 with July 1930		
GENERAL BUSINESS Comparing July 1931 with July 1930		
GENERAL BUSINESS Comparing July 1931 with June 1931		

EMPLOYMENT Comparing July 1931 with July 1930		100%
EMPLOYMENT Comparing July 1931 with June 1931		
THEATER ATTENDANCE Comparing July 1931 with July 1930		
GASOLINE CONSUMPTION Comparing July 1931 with July 1930		
GENERAL BUSINESS Comparing July 1931 with July 1930		
GENERAL BUSINESS Comparing July 1931 with June 1931		

EMPLOYMENT Comparing July 1931 with July 1930		100%
EMPLOYMENT Comparing July 1931 with June 1931		
THEATER ATTENDANCE Comparing July 1931 with July 1930		
GASOLINE CONSUMPTION Comparing July 1931 with July 1930		
GENERAL BUSINESS Comparing July 1931 with July 1930		
GENERAL BUSINESS Comparing July 1931 with June 1931		

EMPLOYMENT Comparing July 1931 with July 1930		100%
EMPLOYMENT Comparing July 1931 with June 1931		
THEATER ATTENDANCE Comparing July 1931 with July 1930		
GASOLINE CONSUMPTION Comparing July 1931 with July 1930		
GENERAL BUSINESS Comparing July 1931 with July 1930		
GENERAL BUSINESS Comparing July 1931 with June 1931		

Everything You Want To Know About This Medium

In One Volume!

Years of experience in Outdoor Advertising speak through the pages of "Outdoor Advertising—The Modern Marketing Force." Written by experts who really know this business, it is a most valuable aid to those seeking knowledge of the practical application of this medium to modern merchandising problems.

No advertising library can be considered complete without a copy of this book. With the present interest that is being manifested in this medium, you will find a constantly growing demand on your knowledge of what outdoor advertising really is and how it can be used to meet new sales situations. This book will tell you of the economic aspects, the psychology, and the attributes of this medium. It gives comprehensive information on design, the use of color, arrangement of copy, the technique of using its various forms, planning continuity, and a glossary which answers every question.

Easy to read, well indexed, completely illustrated, handsomely printed, beautifully bound with flexible, gold embossed covers, "Outdoor Advertising —The Modern Marketing Force" is one book you should have in your library.

227 Pages   64 Illustrations
And The Price!

$2.50

Outdoor Advertising Association of America

165 W. Wacker Drive   **Chicago, Ill.**

**ANNUAL POSTER
DESIGN NUMBER**

**dvertising
outdoors**

BEST POSTERS
OF THE YEAR

OCTOBER 1931 60¢

The October issue of Advertising Outdoors is a symposium of the best in outdoor advertising design created during the current year. From hundreds of
original designs submitted from all parts of the country, a distinguished judging committee, consisting of leading artists and art directors, has selected over
one hundred effective and artistic pieces of copy, all of which are illustrated in
this issue of Advertising Outdoors. For the agency, it provides a record of
effective copy and the artist and lithographer who produced it. For the artist
it is a veritable handbook of ideas on how to treat various problems. No one
connected with or interested in outdoor advertising can afford to be without
a copy in his library. The regular edition is priced at sixty cents. The deluxe
issue, with a handsome suede cover and stamped in gold is to be sold at $2.50.
Order your copies now to insure prompt delivery.

165 W. Wacker Drive   Chicago, Ill.

Put
Your
Dollars In Gear.

WHEN a metropolis of 2,000,000 people is without the facilities of either subways, elevateds or rapid transit, steam or electric suburban systems, certain habits are vitally affected.

Detroit, with practically as many motor cars as are registered in the city of Chicago; with nearly twice as many as Philadelphia; and with about fourteen to every one registered in Boston, robs its residents of that daily morning and evening reading period when, in other like-sized cities, a million office bound and home returning persons recline in trains and trams for a perusal of the day's news.

In Detroit, that habit is scarcely in the picture.

In Detroit, four hundred and some thousand drivers settle down behind steering wheels and, with hundreds of thousands more seated beside them, daily, absorb much of their spending inclinations from unescapable, interesting Outdoor Advertising.

DETROIT   GRAND RAPIDS   FLINT   SAGINAW

Advertising Outdoors

A magazine devoted to the interests of the Outdoor Advertiser

VOL. 2, No. 9

CONTENTS for SEPTEMBER 1931

Harold L. Eves
Editor

Ralph B. Patch, *Associate Editor*
James P. Dobyns, *Advertising Manager*

Eastern Advertising Representatives:
Walworth and Wormser,
420 Lexington Ave., New York City.

Western Advertising Representatives:
Dwight Early,
100 N. La Salle St., Chicago

ADVERTISING OUTDOORS is published on the 1st of every month by the Outdoor Advertising Association of America, Inc., 165 W. Wacker Drive. Chicago, Ill. Telephone Randolph 1692. Harold L. Eves, Editor and Manager.

Subscriptions for the United States, Cuba, Porto Rico. Hawaii and the Philippines, $3.00 a year in advance; Mexico and Canada, $3.25; for all other countries, $3.50. Thirty cents the copy. Make all checks, money orders, etc., payable to Outdoor Advertising Association of America, Inc.

Entered as second-class matter, March 21st, 1930, at the Post Office at Chicago, Ill., under the act of March 3, 1879, by Outdoor Advertising Association of America, Inc. Printed in U. S. A.

THE ROMANCE OF TODAY

THE old sailing master with his charts and compass, knew by careful calculation he could sail his ship into any known port. The seven seas had been carefully charted by the voyages of other navigators. He could definitely say that if he followed a set course for a certain length of time that he would safely arrive in port. His was the romance of yesterday.

Romance is still alive today but today's adventurer sits at a desk and directs business instead of on a bridge charting a ship's course.

But the master of business like the master of a ship must determine his port and follow a set course towards it. Like the old sailing master, he must plan his course or merchandising program by the successful experiences of those who in the past have sailed to the port he wants to reach. The most valuable possessions of sea captains, either of the sailing ship past or the steamship present were their charts and maps which accurately recorded the total knowledge of all navigators and were in reality the case histories of successful voyages. Today's master of business has as his maps and charts, the business paper of today such as the magazine, ADVERTISING OUTDOORS, recording for him the successful voyages of American merchandisers on the seas of business.

No sea captain of yesterday or today would think of leaving port without his charts and maps. No business man should think of planning merchandising campaigns without first studying the successful experiences of others. That is why we present in this and other issues of the magazine, ADVERTISING OUTDOORS, successful experiences on the use of the Outdoor medium.

Harvey L. Cross

and encouragement, rather than unconstructive, hastily formed opinions. The *Marlboro Daily Enterprise*, of Marlboro, Massachusetts, in an editorial entitled "Both Sides Of The Bill Board," gives the following analysis of the situation:

"Originated with the fundamental idea of conserving roadside beauty, the present campaign against billboards, road signs, and outdoor advertising in general is assuming serious proportions.

"As usual in all reform movements, fanaticism, bigotry, narrow mindedness, selfish interests and other destructive elements are beginning to rule this present warfare instead of reason and intelligence.

● "The original purpose of this movement was to restore and further the scenic beauty of our roads, highways, and countryside. A worthy purpose if intelligently directed, but the present trend of activity fails to discriminate between the real offenders and those who, although engaged in outdoor advertising, are really working in harmony with the real purpose of the campaign.

"A great advertising authority says: 'To preserve the countryside is an object which every lover of scenic beauty desires, but unfortunately the various crusaders against outdoor advertising are so little familiar with the real target of their wrath, they are tilting against the wrong windmill.'"

Clearly the writer of this editorial points out the difficulty at the bottom of the whole situation:

"The objectional form of so-called outdoor advertising is that indiscriminate work of the 'sniper' who works for local interests and who goes about his business of nailing and tacking signs to trees, barns, fences and posts along the nation's highways and city streets.

"American business spent $100,000,000 last year in outdoor advertising. If this were to be diverted into magazine and newspaper advertising it would mean a substantial increase in the revenues of those having advertising space to sell.

"Without being unduly cynical it is easy to understand that a certain type of politician will look covetously upon any such sum of money and welcome any legislation which might give him a finger in the pie. All this might account for the change in the trend in the original idea."

After pointing out that the resolution adopted by the General Federation of Women's Clubs ". . . to favor firms which favor scenery" indicates a constructive purpose, but that the latter part of that same resolution ". . . to buy products not advertised in the landscape" typifies the destructive, blind and unfair tangent which the movement has assumed, the editorial concludes:

● "It can only be hoped that the present blind and indiscriminating attacks against all outdoor advertising will give way to an intelligent and understanding effort to recognize and eliminate the undesirable and obnoxious elements that have proved themselves an unmitigated nuisance, and to recognize and conserve the great industry and economic asset which is represented by organized, standard outdoor advertising."

Nor are certain well-informed newspapers the only organizations who have examined with concern this purely American "Reform Complex." The *Woman's Association of Commerce*, of Chicago, affiliated with the Chamber of Commerce of the United States, recently passed the following resolution:

"Whereas, the proposal now under consideration by a number of organizations of women throughout the country, and the organized women of the Federation, includes the idea of the practical destruction of all outdoor, billboard, and similar advertising throughout the country, it is to be observed that this idea is of a very serious character and involves many important and social business organizations.

"To begin with, let us concede that it is certainly desirable that billboard and other advertising which may disfigure scenic beauties and historic sights should be discontinued and prevented by public sentiment. This sentiment may be manifested by letters to the promoters of the advertising, but the abolition of outdoor advertising in general is another matter. To abolish such would require much legislation and many law enforcement agencies. We are now suffering from an Egyptian plague of law enforcement organizations whose aim seems to be in favoring many persons acquitted of violating unenforceable laws.

● "To destroy outdoor advertising would take away from property owners a rightful use of land; would embarrass or annihilate a legitimate industry, would prevent in a measure the public knowledge of desirable and important articles of merchandise, would close avenues of information to the public and would increase the revenue of the metropolitan newspapers whose interest is to confine advertising to newspaper columns."

Calling attention again to the great value of the outdoor medium in times of national stress when men are called to arms and funds must be raised, the resolution concludes: "the Women's Association of Commerce of Chicago is distinctly and positively opposed to the abolition of legitimate Billboard and Outdoor advertising for the reasons above stated. Other reasons will occur to every intelligent person which should be carefully considered by such persons."

Numerous other organizations have expressed themselves no less forcefully. Outdoor advertising is indeed coming into its rightful place in American thinking. The Georgia Hotel Association, at a recent convention passed a resolution pointing out that

"... having a vital interest in Outdoor Advertising as practiced and conducted by those responsible interests having membership in the Outdoor Advertising Association of Georgia and the Outdoor Advertising Association of America, does hereby go on record as opposing any legislation leading toward taxation of Outdoor Advertising, believing that taxation is not the proper procedure for eliminating abuses existing in that business.

● "Be it further resolved that: As citizens of Georgia, interested in the welfare of our country, and individually sharing the beauty of our landscapes, we join with those who condemn the abuses in Outdoor Advertising, but unlike those who unfairly and broadly condemn the entire method because of its abuses, we condemn not the method, but the abuses.

"Be it further resolved that: Realizing the economic value of Outdoor Advertising to the Hotel Industry and other legitimate enterprises, we are in hearty sympathy with those members of the Organized Outdoor Advertising Industry, who are ever seeking to elevate the standards of practice of their business, and who conduct their business in a legitimate fashion, paying rental for their spaces to property owners, and who so locate their structures as to be beyond the criticism of reasonable minded persons."

Similarly, the members of the Georgia State Automobile Association has "watched with growing concern the unjust attacks upon and the campaign against legitimate outdoor adevrtising. As citizens interested in the welfare of our country, and as individuals sharing the beauty of our landscapes, we join with those who condemn not the entire method because of its abuses. We condemn not the method, but the abuses."

● The resolution passed by this organization goes on to express a belief in the value of legitimate outdoor advertising and recognizes "that the denial of the rights of farmers, or any property owner to use their property for outdoor advertising purposes where such is not subject to any reasonable objection is to unjustly deny a right of property and to bring hardship and loss to the individual property owners without just compensation. We know that to wholly destroy outdoor advertising affects a great industry, its workmen, and allied industries."

The resolution urges "upon all who are interested in this problem a sane and thoughtful consideration," and suggests that "each of us should differentiate between that which is legal and that which is illegal."

The Kentucky Division of the Travelers' Protective Association in their spring meeting this year discussed the plans of certain persons to place an exorbitant tax on outdoor advertising as a means of crippling the medium, and after pointing out that such proposals "would discriminate between advertising advancement, and otherwise violate established principles of taxation," went on record as being opposed to a tax on advertising in any form.

● In Pennsylvania, the County Fair Association opposed a similar proposal as being detrimental to their business. Wisconsin newspapers opposed proposed taxation on outdoor advertising as being unfair, pointing out the manifest unfairness of such a procedure.

California, very properly jealous of its scenic heritage, appointed a Joint Legislative Committee to study the problems of regulating and controlling commercial enterprise conducted along the highways. Portions of the report filed by this committee after an exhaustive and thorough study of the situation bring out some interesting and unbiased information concerning outdoor advertising as it is conducted in that state.

"Our investigation," reads one portion of the report, "reveals that not one (Continued on page 23)

Industry's defense of outdoor advertising has had much to do with the present attitude of the public toward the medium.

AMERICAN LEGION HAS
A MERCHANDISING JOB

by James F. Barton
National Adjutant, American Legion

● The recent presentation of the one millionth member of the American Legion to President Hoover was concrete evidence of the success of the advertising and selling program which along with the personal effort of loyal Legionnaires has built Legion membership to this impressive total. Only in the last four years has this program been in really effective operation and the results have clearly shown that organization membership, just as any merchandise, must have its advertising and its salesmen.

The early years of the American Legion were devoted exclusively to our service programs, first on behalf of the disabled, then, in 1925, in the interests of the orphans for whom the successful endowment fund campaign was conducted. These were services which the Legion is proud to have accomplished, but our concentration upon these activities permitted membership to drop and the decline in strength threatened to affect the progress of our work. It was recognized that if the organization were to continue its advancement in caring for the disabled, and the orphans and in its programs of patriotic education, additional strength in members must be secured.

The American Legion has a peculiar membership problem. It seeks to link, in one fraternal order, all the men who served honorably with the colors during the World War. This tremendous experience, common to all in the Legion, is the bond which brings together men from every trade and profession and from every stratum of society, and which unites them into one whole, working toward the same objectives. Yet due to the fact that those eligible for Legion membership came from every walk of life, it is difficult in many cases to get in touch with prospective members except thru general mediums. It was evident that thousands of men, eligible for Legion membership, had never been contacted with the inspirational message which outdoor advertising affords.

● The medium was first used by the American Legion in February, 1927, the copy on the poster being, "If You Served in the World War, You Belong in the American Legion." No national arrangement for

space was made, but posts were urged to make use of this poster and the design, emphasizing membership, induced many posts to do so. That this use was effective was evidenced by a comparison of membership a few weeks later, March 31, 1927, showing an increase over the same date in 1926 of 42,091 new members.

National publicity about a contest for a new poster lent impetus to our use of Outdoor Advertising. This design was given national distribution in a concerted effort, through the cooperation of the Outdoor Advertising Association of America, Inc., in February, 1928, with the result that on March 31, 1928, the increase over the preceding year was 74,630. The following year, 1929, virtually the same total was recorded for March 31. The use of about the same amount of Outdoor Advertising gave almost exactly the same results in membership.

● An increase in the use of Outdoor Advertising in February, 1930, however, showed its effect in an increase on March 31 of 35,001 over the preceding year. This result clearly pointed to a desirable means of getting more members for the Legion, the use of a greater amount of Outdoor Advertising.

Arrangements were made for placing the posters the following November, in order to give early momentum to the 1931 membership drive. Our early, all-around preparation resulted in the largest advance membership before the first of the year in the history of the organization. On December 31, 1930, a few weeks after the appearance of the posters throughout the nation, the advance membership for 1931 was 368,902, an increase of 51,293 over the same date for advance membership in 1930.

Any statistics that can be given as to the results these poster campaigns have obtained, however, would be certain to fall short of the truth. In reaching prospective Legion members we have also told our story to the public. I am certain that there is now a better and more sympathetic understanding of the American Legion than ever before, and a large part of this understanding is to be credited to the poster advertising we have done. Moreover, in the

Legion itself these posters have helped materially in arousing the members' enthusiasm and thereby gaining the complete cooperation that is essential to the success of our program.

● Our members are the Legion's salesmen and, while the advertising can create interest in the organization, it is up to the members to so present the Legion and its program as to induce the prospect to join. Enthusiasm will go a long way toward increasing Legion membership and it is this enthusiasm that our Outdoor Advertising has done much to maintain.

The splendid record last November and December has fixed November as the month for the display of the poster selected for this year. Through the continued cooperation of the Outdoor Advertising Association of America, Inc., the design will appear on some 17,000 poster panels and will undoubtedly prove to be a big factor in what the Legion intends to make the most effective membership drive that has yet been launched.

The poster by William P. Sheehan of Chicago, was selected with this dual purpose in mind. It will be effective both with the general public and with the veterans who are eligible to membership in the Legion.

● Perhaps the most striking feature of the new poster is its simplicity of design which also fascinates, because of a color combination around the Legion emblem which gives it alternate appearances of advancing and receding, through the winding, or convuluted, color circles that surround the emblem. This emblem stands complete, with no edge covered or severed, and will be about six feet in diameter in the 24-sheet panel. The name of The American Legion appears only in its proper place in this emblem, while at the right in yellow letters on a bright orange background are the words: "Serving for God and Country." Across the bottom, in vivid green letters on a black background, are the words: "Over one million members."

The color scheme draws the eye immediately to the Legion emblem dancing and turning, receding and advancing. Then the eye shifts to the bottom and to the striking green lettering: "Over One Million Members," and to complete the picture, the eye catches, as a final glance: "Serving for God and Country."

Every word used was studied. There was the argument of speed to eliminate the word "Serving," but to make the poster appeal equally to the public, and to give the reason for mentioning one million members, the fundamental and primary purpose of the Legion was added.

● This year, for the information of the thousands of local outdoor advertising companies who have so splendidly cooperated along with the Outdoor Advertising Association of America, Inc., in the past, and who will again this November give of their time, labor, and space, to this Legion endeavor, a new set-up has been worked out for handling the posters. For the first time, each state will have a Department Outdoor Publicity Chairman, who will be the contact man between the post and the local advertising company. This Department Chairman will coordinate the purchase of the posters by the Legion posts, and their delivery to the local advertising company which contributes its portion of the good-will program in which not only the ex-service men and women of this country, but a majority of other American citizens, who have the welfare of our nation and its institutions at heart, are interested.

The poster design by the American Legion to present its message both to the public and to those eligible for membership in the Legion.

New "Katy" Girl Advertises
AIR COOLED DINERS

by V. V. Masterson
Advertising Manager, M. K. T. Railroad

Most of the old timers in the outdoor advertising game remember the "Katy" girl, the wasp-waisted, full-bosomed wench with the three-foot picture hat trimmed with gorgeous birds, and the trailing, street-cleaning skirts, who was the Poster personification of the "Katy"—the Missouri-Kansas-Texas Lines. In Summer you'd see her in the modest five yards of dress goods they called a bathing suit in those days, coyly inviting the passers-by to patronize the Katy's seaside excursions—and what made them fall for it we'll never know. At this time when the automobile was still an outrage and air-cooled dining cars a rosy dream, the Missouri-Kansas-Texas Railroad was a leader in outdoor advertising in the Southwest.

● In the course of years railroad administrations change. The Katy's outdoor advertising fell by the wayside and the "Katy" girl was no more. New forms of transportation developed, and in developing made serious inroads on the business of the railroads. Heads came together. Administrations changed again. Out of it all came a complete reorganization of the old Katy—the Missouri-Kansas-Texas Lines. Progress became the watchword of the company, courtesy and service the keynotes. An aggressive policy was elected the means of keeping the company in the forefront of public consciousness. The "Katy" girl, smart as

Fifth Avenue and up-to-date as next year's sport coupe, came vividly back into the advertising, and a striking outdoor campaign has just been put under way in a number of big Southwestern cities.

● Perhaps the most striking thing about this rejuvenation is the fact that it comes at a time when the ostriches of better business still have their heads buried deep in the sand—and that despite a monotonous story of decreasing revenues elsewhere, the Katy railroad reports a marked increase in business on the new air-cooled dining cars its advertising campaigns are featuring!

Seeking to discover the motivating idea behind the many changes and innovations the Katy has recently made, Enno D. Winius, President of the Anfenger Advertising Agency, Inc., of St. Louis, who has handled the company's advertising account in recent years, was approached. "Nothing extraordinary about it," Winius declared, "it merely means that the Katy's new chairman of the board and president, Michael H. Cahill, is the aggressive, modern type of executive, and has gathered about him men of his own stamp. Now they are doing things."

● The Anfenger Advertising Agency conducted the advertising campaign that announced the coming of new air-cooled dining cars on the Katy. The pioneer

The "Katy" girl is here pictured enjoying the comfort of an M. K. T. air cooled diner.

railroad of the Southwest, the Katy pioneered again when it placed on its premier train a fleet of temperature-controlled diners—first in the Southwest—and the agency made full capital of it. The outdoor campaign in Southwestern cities, planned by the agency, announces "Only on the Katy—Air-cooled dining cars through Oklahoma and Texas." A refreshing c h a n g e from many well-known campaigns that have very little to say, both the newspaper and Outdoor series are brilliant and arresting.

The Katy railroad is overlooking no opportunities and has reproduced its new dining car Poster design as a two-color blotter, to be broadcast by direct mail and through its representatives throughout the country.

Old timers will welcome the return of the "Katy" girl. Younger, more alluring, as full of vigor as ever, she typifies the new "Katy" spirit.

The "Katy" girl as she appears in newspaper advertising.

A bigger "cut"

SOME folks, it seems, just can't get over worrying about "times like these." But—some others are saying that the thing to do is to get a bigger "cut" of the business that's gettable. We're handling their outdoor advertising—and they aren't doing badly at all. For instance—Maxwell House Coffee, Calumet Baking Powder, Rio Grande Oil, Post Toasties, American Chicle Co. . . . If you want outdoor SERVICE—

OUTDOOR
A NATIONAL OUTDOOR ADVERTISING ORGANIZATION

SERVICE
INCORPORATED
230 NORTH MICHIGAN AVE., CHICAGO

LOANING HUNDREDS
to Thousands

by Jean C. Turner

"It's an ill wind that blows no good. Every cloud has its silver lining. And even a stock market crash may possess its merits and virtues." These might well be the sentiments of the Morris Plan Company of Buffalo, a personal loan organization, for it took the Wall Street nose-dive of the well-known and bitterly remembered Fall of 1929 to start this financing corporation into outdoor advertising, into exploitation of its services with painted bulletins.

● The Morris Plan Company of Richmond, Virginia, had just paved the way with a most effective and successful outdoor advertising drive. News of its effectiveness and success reached officials of the Morris Plan Company of Buffalo. These officials started thinking in terms of outdoor advertising.

Hitherto all Buffalo Morris Plan advertising stressed specific needs for loans in times of emergency. Buffalo Morris Plan copy and cuts in newspapers and in direct-mail played up the fact that the Morris Plan Company of Buffalo stood by in times of need. The public reaction to this advertising was that the Morris Plan Company was a sort of court of last resort, a final refuge for the needy.

Came the historic stock market tail-spin. For many it may have been curtains and sunset. For the Morris Plan Company of Buffalo it proved the dawn of a new and better business era, an era ushered in by a selling company, based on a new angle and presented through Outdoor Advertising, a medium that has since proved itself so efficient and productive that today outdoor advertising represents seventy per cent of the total annual advertising appropriation of the Morris Plan Company of Buffalo.

At the same time that the Morris Plan Company of Buffalo decided to go outdoors with its advertising messages it decided also to change the tenor of these messages. The company wanted to emphasize one fact, namely, that this firm also sold certificates bearing five per cent interest with utmost safety and that these certificates represented an excellent investment at a time when excellent investments were scarcer than a bull on Wall Street.

● To emphasize this fact was not easy because the company is restrained by state banking laws from using the words "save" or "deposit" or "thrift" in

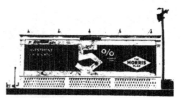

This simple and effective bulletin gives real emphasis to the 5% interest which the Morris Plan Company desires to feature.

any way, shape or manner. How to get across the idea that the Morris Plan Company of Buffalo offered a reliable and interest-bearing investment to all who bought its certificates? That was the question to be answered. The answer came in November, 1929, when nine painted bulletins located on nine of the most strategic sites throughout the city of Buffalo, bore the following clear call:

5% INTEREST PAID—THE MORRIS PLAN

● So successful was this simple, straight-forward, crisp and concise message that one month later the company used almost the self-same copy to exploit their Christmas Club:

5% CHRISTMAS CLUB—THE MORRIS PLAN

This short, snappy copy was emblazoned against a background of medium blue showing snow falling. The panel was further adorned with a silhouette softly portraying a black coach drawn by black horses. A Chicago business man happened to see this design in Buffalo and asked permission to show a photograph of it before a forthcoming session of the American Institute of Architects. The board was shown to the architects as an example of just how artistic and beautiful a bulletin can be!

And—this one panel tripled the number of Christmas Club accounts! The previous year the Morris Plan Company of Buffalo opened 700 Christmas Club accounts. Christmas, 1929, the club welcomed 2100 new members!

Having proved to their own satisfaction that outdoor advertising did bring results and feeling that for the time being they had established themselves sufficiently as a savings as well as a loan company, the Morris Plan Company of Buffalo started July 1, 1930, to reaffirm their old status as a loan corporation. But—how they changed the trend of their advertising talk!

No longer did they set themselves up before the public as a port or haven or refuge to be sought in times of need and stress and strife. No longer did they play upon and stimulate the inferiority complexes of bulletin gazers. Rather, they deliberately set out to prove the popularity of their services, to remove the stigma and sting of borrowing money.

● They added nine panels to their original nine and, against a modernistic sunburst background that carried from light orange on the borders to deep red at the core, they told the world simply this:

LOANING HUNDREDS TO THOUSANDS—THE MORRIS PLAN

To break any possible monotony accruing from using the same message on eighteen panels and to get right down to cases, right down to bedrock, right down to hard cold facts and figures, they caused another board to broadcast the following significant and appealing, as well as comforting and unembarrassing, message:

ONE FAMILY IN EVERY TEN IS USING THE MORRIS PLAN

Commenting on outdoor advertising as applied by the Morris Plan Company of Buffalo, Vice-President Victor Holden says:

"We feel that outdoor advertising merits seventy per cent of our annual advertising expenditure. We feel this way because outdoor advertising has produced real results for us. It has produced these results for us, we are certain, for two principal reasons:

● "First, the great majority of our clientele, both investors with us and borrowers from us, own automobiles and outdoor advertising is one sure way to reach the eyes of those who move by auto.

"Second, our bulletin copy is short and sweet. It's full of vim, vigor and vitality. It's packed with punch. Yet still and all it carries a real message.

"We try to anticipate changing markets and gauge our outdoor advertising accordingly. When we are convinced that the public is actively and aggressively investment-minded, then we'll go back again to plugging our investment certificates.

"But, borrowing or investing, we're sold on outdoor advertising. In fact we're so proud of and so keenly interested in our bulletins that every Design we have used thus far today hangs framed in replica in our conference room! Seeing all our bulletins before us also enables us to avoid monotony and sameness in bringing out new Designs."

■ ■ ■

Form New Associations

The Rhode Island and Massachusetts members of the National Association met in Boston recently and under the charters granted them by the National Association, formed separate state organizations to be known as the Outdoor Advertising Association of Massachusetts, and the Outdoor Advertising Association of Rhode Island.

● The Massachusetts Association elected the following officers:

Joseph J. Flynn of Lawrence, Mass., President.

Ernest L. Kimball, of Lowell, Mass., Vice-President.

C. W. Burrell of Providence, R. I., Secretary-Treasurer.

The Rhode Island members elected the following officers:

Thomas R. Burrell of Fall River, Mass., President.

Granville S. Standish of Providence, R. I., Vice-President.

C. W. Burrell of Providence, R. I., Secretary-Treasurer.

The Furniture Store that
DOUBLED ITS BUSINESS

● After five years of struggling existence in Santa Barbara, Carlson's Furniture Store in the very midst of a business depression, has doubled its business in two years with the sole aid of outdoor advertising. Here is an account which can point with accuracy to tangible results achieved by posters; for outdoor advertising is the only form of advertising that this firm has ever used. Both as a business romance and as a tribute to the power of the medium that made the romance possible the story of Hilma Carlson's success is worth recording.

Hilma Carlson is the president of the Carlson Furniture Company. She went into the furniture business, after trying some others, because she figured that every woman loves a home and can naturally pick out things for the home better than can a man. Well, for five years she struggled along but seemed unable to get a foothold. And then ...... But let her tell it.

"I was about ready to give up when I was approached on the subject of outdoor advertising by Mr. Hill, a representative of Foster and Kleiser. It was really because I was desperate and thought auv move was better than none that I told him to go

ahead and see what he could do for me. For sometime I heard nothing more and had almost forgotten the matter in my efforts to rouse my business from the sleeping sickness. Then suddenly one day it woke up. One person after another came in asking for bedroom sets. I sold five that day. I didn't know what to make of it and wondered whether the town was following in the footsteps of business by going to sleep. The demand kept up and not only did we continue selling bedroom sets but furnished a couple of houses, with the set as the opening wedge. A few days later Mr. Hill came in with the question, 'Did you see it?' 'See what?' I asked; but it immediately dawned on me. *The first poster had gone up and it showed a picture of a bedroom set.* I found by checking up that we had sold two sets exactly twelve hours after the posting had been done.

● "I immediately increased the advertising. The results I hesitate to give because they may sound unbelievable to some, but it is the truth that my business increased 50 per cent the first three months after the posting went up and in a few more months it had increased 100 per cent. The increase was not only on the advertised items but on my general stock. At

This poster has helped Carlson's Furniture Store sell not only the three piece set advertised but has increased their sale of mattresses, springs and other related items.

the time I became an outdoor advertiser, which is two years ago, I was working with one assistant and had been for five years. I now employ five people and sometimes more.

"To say that I have doubled my business is conservative. Take July: this is not a good furniture month because of vacations and the fact that it precedes the semi-annual home-furnishing sale; but for us last July was on a par with any month in the year.

"In April, 1930, we sold 46 stoves. This is almost unheard of in April, which is a poor stove month. A stove manufacturer had gotten out a special model and we had Foster and Kleiser sketch this for us and make the posters. I expected results but nothing like what followed. As soon as the posting was up, the rush began. The funny part of this was that we sold only about ten of the stoves pictured, the rest being more expensive numbers.

● "Another month we had a rug poster and during that month sold exactly 100 rugs, which is a lot of rugs in a town of 34,000 people.

"Since my experience with the initial poster I take the precaution of putting in a good supply of the article to be advertised. The first time I was not prepared for a run on bedroom sets and had to skirmish around getting enough to supply the demand. But now when orders pile up on an article advertised on the panels I have the goods here to fill them.

"The present poster happens to feature a 4-piece bedroom set at $39.50. This has been showing about ten days and we are selling bedroom furniture every day, also mattresses and springs. That's one of the advantages—related furniture sells along with the advertised item. I have furnished a whole room or a house for customers originally brought in through the outdoor poster.

"We change our design every month and I aim to include in the year's showing three living-rooms, three bedrooms, a dining-room, a stove, and a rug. We started with three posters but at present am using six, but I am considering another increase in the number.

"In the two years I have been using outdoor advertising my business has more than doubled, as I could show anyone from my ledgers, and I consider this extraordinary in view of the depression through which the country has been passing. In normal times I feel that there would be even greater returns.

● "What makes this all the more remarkable is the fact that I am doing only outdoor advertising. I have always hated to pay out money for advertising because results were so indefinite: it seemed like pouring money into a hole. But I do not feel that way

Another of the posters that helped Carlson's Furniture Store increase their business one hundred per cent within a few mon'hs.

about my posters. They have brought me returns that I can definitely trace."

The record that the advertising of Carlson's Furniture Store has made is all the more remarkable when it is considered that furniture dealers generally have found that their profits have diminished almost to the vanishing point. An analysis by Fertig & Company of the retail furniture business in 1930 showed that the volume of gross sales was 65.8% of the 1927 volume and the net profit was 2.5% of the 1927 profit. Yet, during this period when the average furniture dealer was watching his profit dwindle to almost nothing, Hilma Carlson increased her business more than 100%.

● A number of factors have played a part in the loss of business which is facing the majority of furniture dealers, and one of these is certainly the reduction in national buying power which has progressed since one wild day in 1920. Nevertheless, this is far from being the only important influence that has reacted so disastrously to cut the furniture dealer's profits. The trend toward the out-of-doors and the diminishing of the pride that has always been felt in a modern, attractive home has had a tremendous effect.

The fact that there are now approximately nine automobiles for every ten families indicates the extent to which the public is outdoor minded. And these millions of people, constantly on the move, outdoors for a great portion of their impressionable hours, are exposed to the colorful, smashing messages of outdoor advertising. It is thus that Hilma Carlson turned to her advantage the very element that was keeping her from success. Since the people were away from home she carried her message outdoors to them and won immediate sales.

COLOR SELLS
San Joaquin Valley

by William E. Metzger
Secretary and Manager, San Joaquin Valley Tourist and Travel Association
Fresno, California

● For three years the San Joaquin Valley Tourist and Travel Association has been conducting an outdoor advertising campaign to assist in bringing tourists, travelers, vacationists, and sportsmen to the eleven counties of Central California, known as the San Joaquin-Sierra Region.

This campaign consists of a showing of approximately fifty painted bulletins presenting a design of scenic appeal, located in various sections of the United States. Before using outdoor advertising the association found it difficult to portray to the prospective guest the scenic wonders of this Sierra country due to the necessity of showing the highly colorful mountain playgrounds. Newspaper advertising was considered valuable by us but with this medium color could not be utilized in the course of ordinary copy and color is the keynote of our appeal. We were delighted on trying outdoor advertising to find that not only did the painted bulletins bring out color vividly but gave life to the scenes.

Our bulletins are daily reminders to thousands of people and many see them several times a day; but reminder is only part of the story. We have found that by consistent and continued use of outdoor campaigns we are building up a public knowledge of what our section has to offer the world and through this means we are educating people in our attractions. This is effectively accomplished through the selection of an outstanding subject for each design. Inquiries from prospects are directly traced to the panels, giving us a definite check-up on results from the territory where a display is located.

● To sum up the story: we chose outdoor advertising to bring out the color and attractiveness of our area; and we continue to use it because we believe in the value of consistent, unremitting efforts in advertising and because results are directly traceable to these bulletins.

This colorful poster carries the message of the San Joaquin Valley to prospective visitors.

Laying Out the Poster —
ECONOMICALLY

by Paul Parker

The word "poster" has come to have a variety of meanings. It includes in the mind of the layman not only 24 sheet and 3 sheet designs, single sheet and platform posters, painted structures, car cards, window displays, etc., but also magazine advertisements which are rendered in a "poster style," or even academic paintings in a flat, simplified technique. Some critics have spoken of certain paintings of the Renaissance as posters when the artists performed them as commissions. The word "poster," then, has come to mean any sort of picture done by an artist for profit, rendered in a "poster-like style." With this loose terminology, we need not concern ourselves; the quarrel over definitions can be safely left to rhetoricians and art critics and can only result in confusion. We will limit ourselves, therefore, to the most important poster of all—the 24 sheet. Everyone will agree that this is a poster at any rate, and that it is the most important unit of Outdoor Advertising.

● The size of this poster is 8'8" by 19'6". In making a sketch (the design for the poster which can be reproduced in various ways), the artist of course works always in scale. This size is in the proportion of 4 by 9, and the design could be 8 by 18, 12 by 27, or any other proportionate size enlarged by a diagonal drawn through a 4 by 9 space laid out in a corner of the sketch. The working size usually depends on the complexity of the subject and the medium used; that is, an oil painting could be larger than an opaque water color sketch to give the artist more ease in handling.

It should be remembered that the reproduced poster will be "framed" by a white border of blanking paper 24" on each side and 10½" on the top and bottom, and outside that a green band and moulding 9" wide.

Posters can be reproduced by a variety of means—lithography, silk-screen or similar processes, woodblock, hand-painting, etc. Knowledge of these processes—and the special merits of each one—on the part of the artist as well as persons unacquainted with all the ramifications of Outdoor Advertising, can save money for the buyer of the poster and give a design more closely adapted to the product to be advertised.

● It is usually assumed that the artist when designing a poster should begin with aesthetic considerations—that is, composition or layout, color combination, fine drawing, and at the same time consider the attention value of the lettering, logotype, bright color and the smash of the poster as a simple, tied-up unit. It is felt that the artist is incapable of understanding anything except these obvious fundamentals of the poster. It seems to be true in many cases that the artist does not consider anything else, but that is not saying that he could not. The fact remains that there is too great a gulf between the artist and the buyer of art work, whoever he may be. The artist, on the one hand, would never admit that a poster poorly executed but with a great merchandising idea is better than a beautiful poster with no "selling point." On the other hand, it is assumed that the artist is simply an artist, with all the contempt which that word can arouse, with its connotation of artistic temperament, lack of practical knowledge, instability and so forth. I have frequently observed that these two gentlemen instead of getting together, confine themselves to acid comments concerning the sanity of one another. It may be that this fundamental lack of sympathy will always exist, but it certainly need not.

It is obvious, then, that the artist must work with a more complete understanding of the purpose of the particular poster he is creating. To work intelligently, he must be given more than a rough layout and told to go ahead. He must ask himself (and know before ever starting his drawing) how much money can be spent on printing; how many posters will be printed; to what type of people the product is to be sold; the selling policy of the manufacturer and so on.

In a word, the successful poster must have good art work, attention value and a sound merchandising idea. It is useless to argue which of these points is the most important. Each one is essential and indispensable.

● It is often possible to arrive at the creation of a poster by a process of elimination. For example, the background color might be symbolic of the product and give an instantaneous impression of a certain

Fig. 1   Fig. 2

property of that product. Orange is hardly a fitting color for an ice cream or ice box poster, yet would be appropriate for a heating or coal poster. Color should have more of a function than attracting the eye; it should also suggest associations. A violent magenta background on a men's clothing poster might have attention value, yet be repellant also to a sense of the appropriate. Color is a subtle thing, elusive and hard to control. It is well known that a broad area of red, improperly combined with other colors, may not be nearly as effective as a smaller spot of intense color used correctly.

● Legibility should never be sacrificed for artistic quality. Blue-green lettering on a violet background of about the same value might be very pretty, but black lettering over yellow is visible at many times the distance.

The design or arrangement of the elements may be determined to some extent by the printing process to be used. In the case of a national campaign, when anywhere from 500 to several thousand posters are to be posted, lithography is usually employed. The artist should not forget, however, that the 24-sheet poster is not posted, or printed either, as one sheet of paper, but composed of several sheets, cut so as to make printings as low as possible. The artist can help out by keeping the backgrounds simple and not try to make figures or objects in full color cover the whole surface. As well as running up the costs, the poster would not be so effective, since the lettering would not stand out.

Lithography will reproduce accurately any kind of medium—water color, oil, pastel, photography, etc., and of course any blending of tones will be indicated as painted on the sketch. For that reason, the artist seldom worries about the reproduction—let the lithographer take care of it. Anything painted can be reproduced, it is true, but the price varies tremendously. And the artist must never make his services a liability, or consider that he is conferring a favor by condescending to paint his poster. His

In figure 1 the poster has been laid out without regard for sheet arrangement. Figure 2 shows a second layout which would materially reduce the cost of production.

work is not beneath him, as "fine" artists are wont to think; it is one thing to paint a figure purely for personal satisfaction, and another to paint a figure consistent with a merchandising message. Any artist who thinks that the latter problem is easier had better try it. In fiction, when the artist needs bread he dashes off a few magazine covers or pretty bathing girls, thus prostituting his art and betraying his conscience; in real life, unless the artist were so familiar that his name was known to the public (as well as advertising agencies) he would never even have a chance to sell his pretty girl cover. He couldn't even paint one, because he wouldn't know how. He must know his stuff.

Though a poster is usually lithographed, it may be too expensive if the run is short. For local sales, or for a local test campaign, where the run is short, other methods may be more economical.

Let us consider a practical problem. The product to be advertised is a brand of ginger ale made by a local manufacturer, or a national brand in a local test campaign, and only thirty posters are to be reproduced of a design. This ginger ale is in a full quart bottle, the dominant feature which the poster must show. One thing is immediately evident. To lithograph such a poster would mean that the cost would be prohibitive; therefore, some cheaper process, such as silk screen, might be used.

● Incidentally, it might be pointed out that silk-screen or similar processes for 24 sheet posters, is not to be confused with the familiar silk-screen window display in which the ink is very heavy and which if used on a poster would cause it to slip off the panels due to the heavy weight of the ink. However, a few firms have perfected practical processes using

Fig 2

thinner inks, and the results are gratifying as well as economical. The lines on the accompanying illustration show how the poster is usually composed of ten sections, and priced according to the total number of printings. Each separate color and tint is a printing, and the artist·must so design his poster to keep these printings as low as possible. The artist, then, must simplify his design to accomplish a strong poster, at the same time considering that the fewer the printings, the less the cost.

In figure one, the design was made with no thought to cost. It can be simplified, however, without sacrificing composition and can be made much cheaper. A mass can be made to go just to the end of a sheet without reaching over, or a line of lettering can be contained on two sheets just as well as three. The split sheets at the top of figure two may be placed at the bottom or arranged in many different combinations with the other eight sheets. The whole matter of layout depends on the ingenuity of the artist. The sheets may be of any color to make an over-all background, over which the colors are printed. The artist must remember that the colors in his design must be flat, and not blended.

● One company has perfected a screen process in which transparent colors can be used, the same as in lithography. A yellow can be printed over a blue to give green, a yellow over a red to give orange, and so forth, so that additional tints may be obtained without extra printings. The poster thus has more variety of color at no extra cost.

● A disadvantage of the silk-screen or similar process is that the artist must constantly think in terms of printing costs, and the design will usually be quite simple. Yet the apparent disadvantage has this curious result—the poster because of the elimination of subtle blends and unlimited color, has a striking directness and unity of effect. It is only too easy for the artist to forget that he is making a poster, not a picture gallery painting and that to be successful, the poster must tell its message in a flash.

In small quantities, posters are often hand-painted or custom made. They are valuable because they can be turned out very fast, and a local merchant can take advantage of news events, advertise sales and supplement his other forms of advertising. The original sketch can be made any convenient size, and is "blown up" through a projector so that a stencil of the poster can be made. Masses must be flat, and the fewer colors used the better. Prices vary greatly, according to the complexity of the composition and the length of the run. The reproduced posters are usually posted in two sheets, and are sometimes varnished giving the color a (Continued on page 24)

GAS BULLETINS WIN
Advertising Award
by J. Y. Tipton
Vice-President, L. S. Gilham Co., Inc., Advertising

In the early fall of 1929 the last weld was completed in a 380-mile pipeline and a new fuel—natural gas—was made available to homes and industries of Salt Lake City. This was the first unit of a project that was to bring the advantages of this clean, smokeless, automatic fuel to the people of most of the communities in northern Utah.

But it is, of course, one thing to make a product or a service available—and quite another thing to create for that product or service a degree of public acceptance and good-will which will result in sales. That is a job for advertising. And the executives of the Utah Gas & Coke Company, Ogden Gas Company, and Wasatch Gas Company, through which the new fuel is distributed, were and are firm believers in advertising.

● And so, when several of the smaller communities surrounding Salt Lake City were connected to the natural gas mains, an intensive localized campaign was initiated with the objectives of selling gas service and building good-will. Outdoor advertising forms an important part of the set-up, particularly as regards the good-will building efforts.

It was believed by L. D. Simmons, director of advertising and public relations of the natural gas companies, that if they could in some way advertise the communities themselves at the same time they advertised natural gas, the bulletins would have a real forcefulness obtainable in no other way. The other

executives concurred in the plan, and so it was worked out.

● How well it was worked out may be judged from the fact that at the Advertising Achievement Week exhibit sponsored by the Salt Lake Advertising Club in May, 1931, the natural gas companies won the KDYL trophy for the "most outstanding single exhibit."

That isn't all. At the convention of the Pacific Advertising Clubs Association, held at Long Beach, California, in June, these same displays won the award for the best outdoor advertising. This is indeed signal honor for the natural gas companies of Utah, and the Bird & Jex Company, plant operator at Salt Lake City which cooperated in the planning and executing of the campaign, with the L. S. Gillham Company.

Eight communities are included in the showing. Each painted bulletin prominently displays the name of the town where it is located. Beneath the name is a phrase telling of that particular community's principal industry, and then the words, "Developing with Natural Gas."

The illustration in each case pictures the outstanding product or activity of the community. The bulletin at Farmington, noted as a "Rose Center," shows a beautiful sprig of roses. At Kaysville, "Canning Center of the West," the illustration is of two large, luscious, red-ripe tomatoes.

● Before the bulletins were erected, the proposed plan was discussed with city officials and civic clubs in the various communities. Lions Clubs in several of the towns were particu- (Continued on page 24)

Proud of its kraut and pea canning industry, Morgan, Utah, reacted kindly towards this design. Notice the Lions Club emblem in the upper left hand corner.

Protest Unfair Criticism of Outdoor Medium

(Continued from page 9) signboard regularly maintained by a standard up-to-date company had been so located that it marred the beauty of any highway. We were particularly cognizant of the fact that wherever the curves or turns of a highway demanded vision ahead, the signboard people had already cooperated. They not only took pains to eliminate such objectionable locations of their own accord, but the slightest request of properly constituted authority brought instant relief."

Commenting upon the motives of individuals agitating the whole question of roadside commerce, the report states: "Many individuals and groups are motivated by the highest ideals and purposes, some are prompted by fanatical antagonisms to some particular industry, others by a selfish interest to obtain through legislative restraint a commercial advantage over a rival or competing industry to promote greater sales of their own products."

Labor, too, has voiced a vehement disapproval of any action tending to hamper the activities of legitimate outdoor advertising and all the allied lines of industry which depend on this medium for a portion or all of their livelihood.

The Tulsa Federation of Labor has "watched with growing concern the unjust attacks upon and the campaign against legitimate outdoor advertising." The resolution adopted at a recent meeting of that organization goes on to say, "The main criticism directed at outdoor advertising is that it is a menace to public safety, mars the countryside, and destroys the beauty of our rural scenes. Such criticism is not properly a criticism of all outdoor advertising; it is logically only a criticism directed at ugly signs and the improper and inappropriate location of same. The poster panel or painted bulletin displaying a masterpiece of art, concealing the swamp or hiding the refuse on the dumping ground adjacent to our towns and villages presents a panorama of beauty and delight compared with the filth and wreckage which hides behind. Those who are directing the campaign against outdoor advertising care not that they destroy a legitimate and what has been proved by experience to be a successful and advantageous method of stimulating the distribution of goods, even though every energy of the nation is now being bended to improve business. No one suggests that the building of houses be prohibited because some one irresponsible builds a monstrosity. No one suggests that coal, lead and zinc mining be abolished because their chatt and slate dump piles and tipples and the other necessities of these businesses are at times an eyesore, and certainly not an aid to the landscape. No one suggests the stopping or curtailing of oil development because the derrick is not a thing of beauty and the result of oil operations do not help the scenery as viewed from the highway.

"Why should the problem of outdoor advertising be approached in any different way? Scenic beauty cannot be preserved where scenic beauty does not exist. There are hundreds of thousands of miles of roadway which are neither beautiful nor ugly and where the artistic modern outdoor advertising structure steals no beauty from the scene. If abuses exist, eliminate the abuses, but do not deny to property owners the right to a beneficial use of their property, to business the right of a harmless and legitimate method of stimulating business, to the manufacturer and the workman the benefit of the work which this advertising brings. We urge a thoughtful consideration of the subject in order that the good may be preserved, and that injustice may not be done through ill considered action and an excess of zeal."

A large number of other labor organizations have adopted similar resolutions, their members rightfully feeling that the destruction or crippling of an industry using so much hand labor, and employing so many thousands of people in every walk of life would but add distress to the present economic situation.

Thus we see a reversal in the tide of public opinion. All of the people refuse to be fooled all of the time. Reform-weary America is listening to the other side of the story.

■   -

Bishop Alexander Forms Advertising Service Agency

Entering the advertising agency field after a varied experience in newspaper and advertising work over a period of eleven years, M. Bishop Alexander has announced the formation of Advertising Service Agency with headquarters in the Francis Marion Hotel Building in Charleston, South Carolina.

Among the accounts already booked by Advertising Service Agency are the Charleston winter program, Folly Beach, Magnolia Gardens, Middleton Gardens, Lenevar Candy, Fort Sumter Hotel and several service accounts of food products of South Carolina.

■   -   ■

Adohr Creamery Account to Lord & Thomas and Logan

The Los Angeles office of Lord & Thomas and Logan has been named to handle the advertising of Adohr Creamery Company and Adohr Stock Farms; Adohr Creamery is the largest independent retail distributor of dairy products in southern California.

Laying Out the Poster Economically

(Continued from page 21) greater intensity. Some outdoor plants have artists who create hand-painted posters of surprising beauty and effectiveness—once again, the apparent disadvantage of a necessarily simple design serves to create a real poster with ordered, compact masses and instant appeal.

● With a knowledge of printing methods and costs, it is obvious that the artist is in a position to save the advertiser money. He commands respect because he works intelligently. He should undertake to understand local and national sales problems, methods of posting, whether the designs he creates are to be shown on illuminated structures, to consider that black backgrounds sometimes crack in hot weather. In fact, he should undertake to understand the problems of the industry of which he is a part.

This may seem to be a strange point of view to many artists, yet the fact remains that the success of an artist is determined often times by other factors than pure ability to draw and paint which, to be sure, is a rare enough gift. His mission cannot in these days be considered solely from an artistic point of view any more than a copy writer's work is judged purely by literary standards. The copy writer must induce people to buy goods; and do not forget that the artist has that same function of merchandising. It is all very well to point out the materialism of our mechanized civilization, stating that the artist fails to fit into the modern picture; it may be that there is something degrading about mixing art and business; yet the artist is living today, not yesterday, and he should try to reconcile himself to thinking and acting as other men do. He may even find that the wedding of art and business is not the mesalliance that he suspects; he might even like his job, given a chance.

On the other hand, the employer should make an effort to understand the artist, too. He should not under any circumstances prefix suggestions and criticism with, "Of course, I do not understand anything about painting, I only know what I like." Ask any artist why. Or perhaps, don't say anything about it; it might be dangerous! Then too, the employer should endeavor to understand something about painting; the least he can do is to take a course in layout or study books on the subject. He would discover that many of his bright ideas would be impractical to translate into terms of the poster—a movie camera might do it, but not a mere artist.

● I have endeavored to demonstrate the economic necessity for cooperation between the artist and his employer. If they can get together on a basis of mutual understanding of the problems of outdoor advertising, they get results.

Gas Bulletin Wins Advertising Award

(Continued from page 22) larly active in helping select locations and in fostering the project as a progressive one. The civic groups were asked to name the predominating activity which should be featured on the bulletin, and in each case approved the copy. The townspeople themselves recognize these bulletins as a valuable factor in advertising their communities.

That the campaign has occasioned much wider comment than is usually given to advertising, is shown by the fact that the local newspapers in each of the towns published news items regarding the bulletins. The story carried by the Midvale Jordan Journal is typical, and was in part as follows:

"The large painted outdoor advertising display erected recently on the state highway near Midvale has elicited much favorable comment, according to W. G. King, of Bird & Jex Company, outdoor advertising concern of Salt Lake City and Ogden. This display is one of a number which have been placed on important highways near Utah communities.

"The series of painted bulletins are said to be unique in outdoor advertising display. In fact, Mr. King says that a representative of a large eastern advertising agency who was recently in this territory stated that this was one of the most successful and most unique ideas introduced in advertising.

● "In planning the erection of the painted bulletin in Midvale, Mr. King and L. D. Simmons of the Wasatch Gas Company, secured the cooperation of local civic leaders, including D. M. Todd, Jr., who was also consulted on the nature of the advertising copy and the location of the painted bulletin."

In more than one instance there has been evidence that the townspeople are even taking a proprietary interest in the bulletins. Witness a letter received by Bird & Jex Company from the secretary of the Lions Club of Morgan, Utah, which carried the information that someone had shot a bullet through the sign, and offered the cooperation of the club to prevent further mutilation of the bulletin by agreeing to contribute toward a reward for the apprehension of future miscreants.

In addition, the live-wire Lions Club of Morgan proudly calls attention to the fact that it secured the publication of a halftone reproduction of the bulletin, together with explanatory text, in the April number of The Lion, national magazine of that organization. All of which is just that much more water over the wheel so far as the natural gas companies are concerned.

BINDING THE GAS COMPANY
and the Dealer
CLOSER TOGETHER

There has been in the past much ill feeling on the part of dealers toward Public Utility Companies over the matter of the latter selling appliances. The dealers felt that it was unfair competition; that the Companies should not invade this field which they considered their own, but adhere strictly to the selling of gas, or their own commodity. This misunderstanding has resulted in legislation in two States denying Utilities the right to sell appliances.

● The recently displayed willingness of Gas Companies to devote their advertising to informing and convincing the public of the close and cooperative relation which exists between them, has had a winning influence on the dealer. He is ceasing to be antagonistic and begins to look upon the Company as a necessary ally to his own success instead of a worrisome competitor.

Neither interest should seek to dominate the other, but cooperative relations should be developed on a firm and sound basis. The dealer needs the assistance that the Gas Company can give him in popularizing Gas Appliances. Without this assistance in popularizing the appliances the dealer would find himself at a disadvantage. On the other hand, the Utility Company itself benefits by cooperation with the dealer in increasing sales of appliances. An increase in the sale of appliances means a subsequent increase in gas consumption. Fewer appliance sales means less gas consumption, to the detriment of the Company.

The prestige which the dealer gains as a result of his being identified as a representative of the Gas Companies is naturally a potent factor in winning for him the confidence of the public. This confidence of prospective customers is an assurance of increasing business.

In 1928 during the New England Gas Association's Convention the germ of the new merchandising idea was implanted in the Gas industry—active sales and service cooperation between the Gas Companies and independent dealers. It was recognized that such a movement presented an opportunity to develop good will and improve trade relations, thereby obtaining a coordinated effort which would result in more Gas Appliance sales and a consequent greater gas consumption. This possibility considered three years ago is now a reality. Today we find many classifications of retail stores who were formerly hostile agencies now converted into sales allies.

● A statement by Martin E. Farrell, of Farrell Bros., Albany plumbers, indicates his appreciation of the need of salesmanship ability in addition to a mere technical knowledge of the trade on the part of plumbers. He expresses gratitude for the assistance and cooperation of the New York Power and Light

One of the posters of the G r e a t American Servant Campaign, this one featuring gas refrigeration.

Company for helping him gain public acceptance and attain best business success. He says:

"The plumbing business today is nothing like it was fifty years ago. Today's plumber must be more than a 'pipe fitter'—he must be a damn good salesman to get along. The reason is that plumbing in itself is no longer very profitable, but there is money to be made by the plumber who recognizes all the opportunities he has for selling those fixtures in the home he formerly only repaired.

● "Let's use some examples. I am often called into a home to repair a furnace coil. I don't want to repair this coil—not only is there little money in it for me, but in a short time some other part of the water system goes bad. The customer naturally blames me for the later accident, thinking I had repaired the entire water system. So I lose a good customer, good money and good will. On the other hand I can keep this customer and make money by explaining how much more convenient an automatic water heater would be. Nearly every one is acquainted with the good points of automatic water heating—nearly everyone wants one but is only waiting for the present system to become useless. Here, then, is my opportunity to sell a water heater. I always try to avoid installing a new furnace coil because in a few years that customer is going to be dissatisfied when she finds all her neighbors have automatic water heaters.

"Along with selling a new water heater I also sell new faucets and sinks. The larger space available in the kitchen when the old boiler has been taken out creates a desire in the customer's mind for a new and better sink. Here is more money for me.

"Here is how I go after water-heater sales. My men are instructed to look after the water heater in every home they enter. If the heater is old and inadequate the men leave advertising folders with the customer on automatic water heaters. When the men come back to the office their job tickets state whether or not the customer is a prospect. If he is a prospect I immediately go out to see him and try to sell him an automatic water heater.

"In all of this I have found the work of the New York Power and Light very valuable. I get free advertising and window displays. Then, too, my name is tied in with the newspaper advertising of this company and I get the general acceptance of the public."

● A splendid advertising campaign, worked out by the Brooklyn Union Gas Company in cooperation with J. M. Connor, of the Connor Company, New York City, has been inaugurated by the Brooklyn Company in an effort to develop this cooperative relationship between dealer and company. It is hoped that the campaign will be generally used by leading gas companies throughout the country. The Out-

Symbol of dealer selling approved gas appliances

The emblem used on the dealer's window, giving perfect tie-up with the gas company's advertising campaign.

door medium plays a conspicuous part in this campaign.

● A colorful trade mark symbol based on the three letters "G A S," signifying "Great American Servant" was designed to be used as an identification mark of the dealer who sold gas appliances that carried the approval of the Company. It was planned to create public confidence in the value of this symbol by featuring it in all Gas Company advertising.

The Brooklyn Union Gas Company sends various blue prints showing proper and improper types of connections to all plumbers in Brooklyn so that they can know of the proper method of connecting the various appliances. As soon as the appliance is connected an inspector of the company inspects both appliances and connection to see that the work has been done according to regulations. If approved by the inspector, inspection ticket is sent through so that the bill can be paid. If disapproved by the inspector, the plumber is made to go back and do whatever work is necessary to give a proper connection. They issue a magazine, *Gas Appliance Merchandising*, carrying two articles a month on plumbers in their territory, sending it free of charge to the plumbers.

The Company is obviously putting itself whole-heartedly into the movement as evidenced by some of the things it does for its dealers. It pays the dealers for leads resulting in sales; turns over to the dealer all connecting work on appliances; allows liberal discounts where dealers purchase appliances for resale or otherwise; consigns appliances for dealers' floor for display purposes; aids the dealer in window display and advertising without charge, and carries a dealer's symbol on all of its advertising in order to tie the dealer in with their advertising. Also an educational course for dealers was inaugurated on January 19.

Through the use of the symbol, "Great American Servant," the Gas Company tells the general public that the dealer, as well as the Gas Company, handles appliances for sale. This idea is conveyed in words under the general advertising as follows: "Consult Your Gas Company or Dealer Concerning Modern Gas Appliances." Mr. H. C. Cuthrell, of the Union Gas Company, says in this connection: "Since last October we have been showing the dealer symbol in the newspapers, magazines and direct mail advertising of this company. The dealers have greatly appreciated this help we have been giving them, both by word of mouth and by increased appliance sales."
● Beginning July 1, the dealer symbol outdoor advertising plan was inaugurated. This campaign will run for a whole year, with a complete change of copy each month, and appear on 140 billboards located in their territory in Brooklyn and Queens County.

Mr. Cuthrell explains in writing about the campaign:

"Simultaneously with the message appearing on the poster panel each month, there will be a direct mail folder issued, showing a reproduction of the current poster in full colors, that will be sent to 420,000 of our customers who receive gas bills by mail each month. Attached to this folder will be a return post card, we paying the postage, in which we will list various appliances and ask our customers to check off the appliance in which they may be interested and mail the post card to us for further follow-up. Some newspaper advertising will also be done, calling the public's attention to the poster panels, thus providing additional tie-up in order to make the campaign as effective as possible.

"In addition to the dealer helps, we offer the services of our Window Display Division in helping dealers to properly dress their windows and floors and display merchandise effectively. We also prepare advertising copy whenever requested.

"In order to sell the dealer symbol idea more effectively and impress upon our customers the fact that wherever the dealer symbol is shown they may buy approved gas appliances, we are supplying our dealers with an attractive and illustrated sign of the dealer symbol, for window and floor display in their places of business. We are also enclosing a photograph showing this display sign.

"The course for dealers has been started to enable them to represent the gas company intelligently in the sale of appliances. It is designed to give them a thorough background in modern salesmanship as well as to acquaint them with the policy of the company.
● "The dealer is assisted in properly displaying his appliances by the gas company's studio and furnished to dealers who desire them without cost. These displays are changed when our own windows are changed, in order to keep their own windows full of life and color. Placards and posters are also supplied with advertising literature which they are allowed to send out every month with their bills to their customers, acquainting the latter with the comfort and advantages of gas appliances in the home."

Following is the presentation made to the Brooklyn Union Gas Company for the use of Outdoor Advertising which has such an important place in the campaign. This presentation is given to show how Outdoor Advertising may be used as an effective means of securing the good will and cooperation of sales allies. By stimulating the interest and enthusiasm of sales allies the company will be in a position to capitalize on their sales efforts. Dealers can make or break a marketing organization. The unified and coordinated efforts of sales allies will be of inestimable value in promoting the sale of gas appliances that increase the consumption of gas. The first step in securing the confidence and cooperation of dealers obviously requires the removal of any ill feeling that appliance dealers may now harbor against gas utility companies. The public relations value of this new mental attitude among dealers weighs heavily and should have the careful consideration of every executive in the gas industry.
● The extent to which sales allies will lend their cooperation depends entirely upon how much help is given them to increase their profits. Their sole interest lies in making money. When the public is informed that the symbol of a company may be found only in the windows of reliable dealers who handle only appliances that have been thoroughly tested and approved, the dealers will realize that the company is doing something tangible to send customers into their stores. It is the task of advertising copy to present a message in a manner that will enable prospects to clearly visualize the protection that a symbol will afford them against inferior appliances and unreliable dealers. The dual value of the copy angle emphasizes two vital problems that are of interest to the company and the industry, namely, dealer cooperation and approved appliances. The wealth and variety of color in Outdoor Advertising enables the exact reproduction of a symbol.

The client's large program, the line-up of
energies effectively. This suggests a train
of the understanding by interpreting illustrates the despering attitude of the bee
sees it is attacking.

The device of picturing the production
mechanism in comparison with the image
brings control 36 leads, the added importance. The name and the refrigerator are
featured in this design.

OUTDOOR ADVERTISING ABROAD

Crompton Heads B. P. A. A.

The new President of the British Poster Advertising Association, Mr. William Crompton, is a director of David Allen & Sons (Billposting), Ltd., of Liverpool.

It is somewhat singular that his predecessor, Ald. T. P. Fletcher, is a Bury man, as also is Mr. Crompton, and the coincidence is carried further by the fact that Mr. Crompton succeeded Mr. Fletcher over five years ago as manager of the Bury Billposting Co.

Mr. Crompton went to Liverpool in 1900 to manage the then Liverpool Billposting Co., and eventually he was instrumental in inducing five other firms of billposters then in existence to merge into one.

Mr. Crompton has been responsible to a large extent for the improvement in present-day British poster advertising.

An interesting display erected on the Avenue des Champs-Élysées in Paris for the Compagnie Generale Transatlantique by Ets. Paz et Silva, Parisian outdoor advertising company.

■ ■ ■

British Exhibition of Posters

The exhibition of British and foreign posters, which was opened by Lord Wakefield in the North Court of the Victoria and Albert Museum, was one of the most remarkable expositions of poster technique ever seen in Great Britain. There were 628 examples illustrating the work of the United Kingdom, Canada, the United States of America, France, Norway, Spain, Sweden, Belgium, Holland, Denmark, Switzerland, Germany, Italy, Austria, Hungary, Argentina, Czecho-Slovakia, Poland and Russia.

Every variety of poster style was shown, from the thoroughly joyful theatrical posters of Cheret to the

tragic compositions of Brangwyn for the American Navy Recruiting Campaign. The dates of the posters ranged from the early 'nineties right up to the latest Rilette poster for the London North Eastern Railway.

Nearly every English poster artist of any eminence were represented by a wisely chosen example of his work. The French and German sections were also particularly strong. The Russian, however, seemed to have been confined mainly to posters before the Revolution. Two post-Revolution posters found their way into the precincts.

The object of the exhibition was not inaptly summarized in the preface of the catalogue: The exhibition serves to illustrate not only the technique and purpose of the poster, but also its history.

If the poster began as a signboard to the theatre—a function which it still fulfills—its purpose, long ago, became one of much wider adaptation. Industry entered into large developments, with wider avenues of distribution; and modern means of transport extended the area of potential customers.

Mr. Charles Gardner, of Walter Hill and Co., Ltd., speaking at the Poster Session of the British Advertising Association on the objections raised by the Scapa Society and the Society for the Preservation of Rural England to posters, said: "We are just as anxious to see that boardings cannot give offence to reasonable-minded people. Some certainly are wrongly placed, but over 95 per cent of these we have no control; they are put up by advertisers outside the association."

This outdoor advertising structure, recently erected in Northampton, England, by the Northampton Bill-posting Company, Ltd., was described by a well known inspector as the finest in England.

OUTDOOR
IMPRESSIONS

KEEP KISSABLE
with
OLD GOLD
CIGARETTES
no tainted breath
no scratchy throat

NOT A COUGH IN A CARLOAD

CELLOPHANE WRAPPED

When Bradshaw Crandell was commissioned to paint a "Kissable" girl for Old Gold he did well to pick Ariane Allen, charming nineteen year old Texas girl.

Here is another in the series of photographs especially taken for the magazine, ADVERTISING OUTDOORS, showing the development of electrical advertising in Europe. Germany and France seem to have progressed far in the development of outstanding, dramatic and attention compelling displays such as the one illustrated.

OUTDOOR IMPRESSIONS

The gushing "black gold" from a new oil field would mean little in the way of wealth were it not for the oil industry's sound merchandising backed up with advertisements such as the poster panel displayed below.

OUTDOOR IMPRESSIONS

NEWS OF
THE OUTDOOR INDUSTRY

United Makes Important Purchase

Leonard Dreyfuss, President United Advertising Corporation, announces that his company has acquired all of the outdoor advertising interests of Frank V. Storrs.

Included in the purchase are the outdoor advertising plants of the Lehigh Valley Outdoor Advertising Company in Allentown, Easton, Bethlehem, Phillipsburg and other Pennsylvania cities and towns. Also the Trenton, N. J. Poster Advertising Company, including all of the outdoor plants operated by that company, and the American Poster Company with outdoor plants extending from Redbank through to Long Branch, N. J. A controlling interest is acquired in the Camden Poster Advertising Company.

Mr. Dreyfuss states that this is a peculiarly logical purchase by the United because in the case of each company acquired it is an extension of the United service throughout New Jersey and into Pennsylvania.

A complete survey is now being made of all of these plants and extensive improvements are contemplated.

The company which will control the above named corporations will be known as the Consolidated Advertising Company, of which Mr. Dreyfuss will be president, and of which Mr. Storrs will be one of the directors.

■ ■ ■

Dezell, California Fruit Exchange Manager, Dies

Earl E. Dezell, general manager of the California Fruit Growers' Exchange, died recently at his Los Angeles home. He was fifty years old at the time of his death, which was the result of a sudden heart attack. Dezell, who had been general manager since 1922, started with the organization thirty-two years ago as an office boy and had spent his entire business life with the exchange.

■ ■ ■

Buys Alabama Plant

The Cook Poster Advertising Company of Jasper, Alabama, operating the towns of Walker County, was recently purchased outright by Mr. B. D. Joyce, Jr., also of this city. The plant will be operated under

the name of B. D. Joyce Poster Advertising Company.

The plant, operating approximately 100 panels, has been completely rebuilt, with every panel built according to the standard specifications and blue prints issued by the Outdoor Advertising Association of America.

Mr. Joyce, who is a native Tennessean, has resided for the last twelve years in Alabama, and besides owning this plant, is a Director of the Central Bank & Trust Company, a Rotarian, and a stockholder in several corporations operating in the State of Alabama.

■ ■ ■

Sun Handles Insurance Account

The Sun Advertising Company, Toledo, has been appointed advertising agent for the Ohio Millers Mutual Insurance Company and the Ohio Underwriters Mutual Fire Insurance Company, Van Wert, O. Outdoor advertising, trade papers, newspapers, general magazines, and direct mail will be used.

■ ■ ■

Ivan B. Nordhem Now Business Counsel

Mr. Ivan B. Nordhem, for many years prominent in the outdoor advertising, agency, and other business enterprises, has arranged his private business to permit him to serve a limited number of corporations and industries as confidential adviser on marketing, advertising, merchandising, and research problems, according to a recent announcement issued by Mr. Nordhem.

■ ■ ■

Byrum-Shaw Moves

The Byrum-Shaw Advertising Agency announces a change in location effective August 24. The new offices are in suite 922-924 Patterson Building, Denver, Colorado.

■ ■ ■

Correction

The story in the August issue of Advertising Outdoors entitled "Reaching Small Town Circulation," was mistakenly credited to Earle V. Weller, vice president of the Campbell-Ewald Company. The article should have been credited to Hal F. Weller, account executive with the Campbell-Ewald Company.

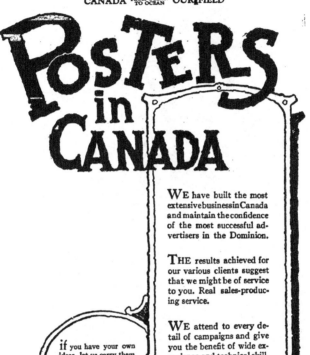

It's all in years of knowing how

"Head down. Left arm straight. Pivot. Follow thru." So runs the litany of the golf pro. You can listen carefully, you can memorize everything, and you can read books on golf, but that will never make a golfer. It is all in *years* of knowing how. So it is with Outdoor Advertising. Nothing takes the place of long years of practical experience. . . . This is our own department of the business of advertising. We have spent all of our business lives studying it and practic-

ing it. In all modesty, we feel that we have mastered every phase of this particular medium.

We place at your disposal a group of art and copy directors who have long experience in creating outstanding outdoor campaigns, a complete advertising plan department, and a promotion department which gathers and accurately interprets market information. Our knowledge in Outdoor Advertising technique is available to you.

OUTDOOR ADVERTISING INCORPORATED

NEW YORK   CHICAGO
One Park Avenue   Eleven Other Offices   Harrison and Loomis Streets

dvertising
outdoors

R 1931 60¢

RESULTS

∎

Localizing the combined experiences of our national organization is our method of cultivating results. It insures definite and productive merchandising, marketing aid to the national advertiser.

OUR MAJOR MARKETS

Akron	Harrisburg	Oklahoma City
Atlanta	Hartford	Omaha
Atlantic City	Indianapolis	Philadelphia
Baltimore	Jacksonville	Pittsburgh
Binghamton	Kansas City, Kan.	Providence
Birmingham	Kansas City, Mo.	Richmond
Brooklyn	Louisville	Rochester
Buffalo	Memphis	St. Louis
Chicago	Milwaukee	St. Paul
Davenport	Minneapolis	South Bend
Dayton	Nashville	Utica
Denver	New Orleans	Washington, D. C.
Duluth	New York City	Youngstown

HARRISON and LOOMIS STREETS   General Outdoor Advertising Co   CHICAGO, ILL.

Also Operating Plants in Over 1400 Other Cities and Towns

You can naturally expect fine lithography from an organization that numbers among its customers many of the country's leading advertisers.

Faithful reproduction of the finest paintings. Non fading inks of our own manufacture that withstand sun, wind and rain. Exceptionally good quality paper. And service thruout that wins customers—and keeps them.

We also design and manufacture cutouts, window displays, hangers, car cards, inserts, etc.

You will like McCandlish quality—because it is highest quality.

McCANDLISH LITHOGRAPH CORPORATION

A. R. McCANDLISH, *President*　　　　　　　　　　　　　　　　PHILADELPHIA

OCTOBER, 1931　　　　　　　　　　　　　　　　　　　　　　　·Page 1

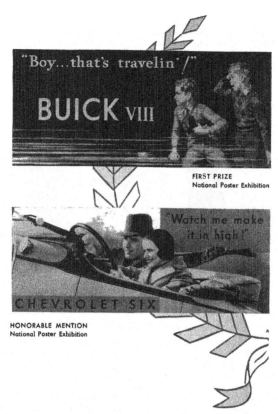

FIRST PRIZE
National Poster Exhibition

HONORABLE MENTION
National Poster Exhibition

FOUR OUTSTANDING

Campbell-Ewald Company takes pride in presenting four posters that received first award, second award, and two honorable mentions at the National Poster Exhibition sponsored by the Chicago Chamber of Commerce. The straightforward simplicity of these posters, their pleasing artistry, and the close co-ordination of every element of their design, are all achieve-

THE BIG PARADE IS TO DETROIT
AMERICAN LEGION
« SEPTEMBER 21 TO 24 »

SECOND PRIZE
National Poster Exhibition

HONORABLE MENTION
National Poster Exhibition

POSTERS OF THE YEAR

ments of sound experience. Campbell-Ewald Company places more outdoor advertising than any other advertising agency in America.

CAMPBELL-EWALD COMPANY
ADVERTISING WELL DIRECTED
H. T. EWALD, PRESIDENT

One-fourth of the entire population of the United States
- - - nearly 31,000,000 persons - - - have become "of age"
since the end of the world war.

One-half of the persons in the United States today were not yet ten years
old when the war began.

This post war market is a "simon pure, dyed in the wool" Outdoor market.

The lassitude of pre-war, in-the-home habits is, to them, just "old folks" talk. Bred
entirely in today's where'll-we-go-from-here tempo, their slogan is and always has been,
"Step On It".

To profitably advertise to tomorrow's American market, comprising, almost totally, this character
of active, Outdoor circulation, your advertising must not be just potentially exposed to all your
prospects, but must actually arrest the attention of everyone whose attention you pay to reach.

Outdoor Advertising in Detroit will thoroughly fulfill that requirement, economically!

Offices In
D E T R O I T
GRAND RAPIDS
SAGINAW
FLINT

THE VALUE OF GOOD ART

A SIDELIGHT of the recent exhibit of Outdoor Advertising art held by the Chicago Advertising Council clearly shows the reaction of women to good advertising art.

A prominent clubwoman of Chicago in viewing the exhibit admitted, "Surely, fine art like that shown in your exhibit makes one prejudiced in favor of outdoor advertising—but, tell me, what law will help us get rid of the terrible things we sometimes see on the streets and highways. Posters like those shown in this exhibit are beautiful but, unfortunately, all posters are not like these."

Her question and the answer she received, I believe, carries a valuable lesson to the user of outdoor advertising.

She was open-minded enough to see the reasoning behind the following answer. "You stated the law—true it is a business law rather than a legal one but, nevertheless, one that is sure of enforcement. When a poster is so beautiful that it impresses you favorably and makes you friendly to the company that posts the design, certainly it must also create a favorable impression in your mind toward the advertiser whose service or goods are advertised by the display. Because it impresses you and thousands like you it will result in a favorable acceptance of the advertiser's merchandise or service. Once these men have become aware of the advertising value of good art it will be only good business on their part to cultivate your good will by presenting their advertising message artistically designed."

Certainly here is a point that can be considered with profit by both advertisers and clubwomen.

•

BEST POSTERS *of the* YEAR

selected by

the ADVERTISING COUNCIL *of the*

CHICAGO ASSOCIATION *of* COMMERCE

and exhibited at

MARSHALL FIELD & COMPANY—NARCISSUS BRIDGE

OCTOBER 1-15 1931

•

In Dice It's Gambling •
• • • In Posters It's Ability

It is not luck that thirteen of the designs among those chosen as the best posters of the year were reproduced by the American Poster Corporation. It was due to the reputation this company has built up for making each poster a master reproduction. ✓ ✓ ✓ ✓ ✓ ✓ ✓ ✓ ✓ ✓

When you have paid thousands of dollars for space on the poster panels, and perhaps thousands more for the art work used in your design, it is gambling with the success of the whole campaign to have your reproductions fail to do justice to the selling message you have so carefully prepared.

To be assured of complete satisfaction, let us handle your poster requirements. ✓ ✓ ✓ ✓ ✓ ✓ ✓ ✓ ✓

AMERICAN POSTER CORPORATION
MILWAUKEE   WISCONSIN

THE STORY
of the EXHIBIT

● This is the seventh issue of the Annual Advertising Outdoors Design Number. Five of these issues were sponsored by the Poster Magazine, Advertising Outdoors' predecessor. This is the second issue to be published by the magazine under its present name.

By arrangement with the Advertising Council of the Chicago Association of Commerce it has been possible for Advertising Outdoors to present, in this and in the 1930 issue, a collection of posters that is, we believe, an accurate cross-section of the best posters produced during the year. Some very good designs have been unavailable for exhibition purposes. The cooperation of agencies, lithographers and the advertisers themselves, however, has made it possible for the Advertising Council and Advertising Outdoors to assemble a collection of original outdoor advertising designs which is more representative in quantity and as high in quality as any similar exhibit in recent years. Indeed, it is doubtful if, at any time, there has been made available for exhibition and study, as valuable a collection of posters from both a design and a monetary standpoint.

The purpose of the exhibit is two-fold. It provides, in the first place, recognition to those who are doing outstanding work in the field of outdoor advertising design. In the second place, it assembles for exhibition and makes available for study the best outdoor advertising design of the year. The latter function is, in all probability, the more important. Probably no branch of art is as much studied and as much misunderstood as is the art of the poster. Posters are designed in art classes in almost every art school in the country—and, in most of these classes, are designed entirely without regard to the requirements of the commercial poster or to the proportions of the poster which is used universally in the United States—the 24-sheet.

● The interest which students and advertising men have shown in the exhibit has shown that the time and money which the show required was well spent. The formal opening, at the first fall meeting of the Advertising Council, crowded Marshall Field's Wedgewood Room to capacity. More than three hundred advertising men were in attendance to hear the talks of G. R. Schaeffer, advertising manager of Marshall Field and Company, who awarded the

prizes, of Captain H. Ledyard Towle, general art director of the Campbell-Ewald Company and of Emerson J. Poag, assistant sales manager in charge of advertising and sales promotion for the Buick Motor Company.

The exhibit committee, under the chairmanship of B. L. Robbins was responsible for the raising of funds with which to stage the exhibit, for the selection of the prizes and for the obtaining of judges. Lithographers, outdoor advertising plant owners and the Chicago Association of Commerce responded generously to the appeal for funds. The members of the jury were Andrew Loomis, artist; Haddon Sundblom, artist; Captain H. Ledyard Towle, general art director, Campbell-Ewald Company; Donald Douglas, vice-president, Quaker Oats Company; Oscar Bryn, art director and vice-president of Erwin-Wasey & Company; G. R. Schaffer, advertising manager, Marshall Field and Company, and Mark Seelen, art director, Outdoor Advertising Incorporated. This inclusion of both advertising men and artists made it certain that the designs would be judged both from a merchandising and an artistic standpoint. The one hundred thirty-three designs included in the exhibit were selected from the more than four hundred submitted.

● The statuettes, cast in gold, silver, bronze and gun-metal which were awarded to the advertisers and to the artists who created the prize winning designs, were the work of Alfonso Iannelli, well known Chicago sculptor and designer.

The assistance of Marshall Field and Company, in not only providing space for the exhibit but giving valuable radio time and newspaper space to the show, has had a great part in its success. The General Outdoor Advertising Company has contributed a representative showing of posters and several painted bulletins to the advertising effort behind the exhibit. That these various media have been effective is evidenced by the attendance at the show, which has been far in excess of that in 1930. To those whose cooperation has made this exhibit possible, the Advertising Council and Advertising Outdoors offers its sincere appreciation. To those whose designs have been judged worthy of recognition we tender congratulations.

ADVERTISING ART—
a Vital Expression of Today

by Alfonso Iannelli

● Advertising in some form or other is constantly jogging our elbow, pointing to this product or to that and urging us, sometimes subtly and sometimes blatently. We recognize this continual assault upon our pocketbooks and our intellect as having a definite place in our existence. Only when the promoter, in frenzied search for novelty and an inescapable appeal shouts his message at us from the skies, for example, are we moved to protest an unwarranted invasion of our consciousness.

This acceptance of advertising shows to what extent it is a part of our daily lives. Indeed, it is doubtful if any factor, with the possible exception of science, has as profound and as constant an influence upon us. Science is the creator and the producer. There must also be distribution before any creation of science is made available to the mass of the people; and the function of advertising is to facilitate distribution. Thus the engineer and the chemist and the physicist should find himself allied with the advertising man in the task of making life easier and more comfortable.

It would seem obvious that the men who are engaged in the arts which go to make up the completed advertisement should be accorded a respect commensurate with the services which they perform. Yet such is very far from being the case. There remains a feeling, not as strongly entrenched, certainly, as in former years but still potent enough to be reckoned with, that there is a gulf between the so-called "fine artist" and the commercial artist which is deep and impassable. The antiquated conception of the sordidness and unworthiness of "trade" holds with remarkable force in the sanctums of art. As a matter of fact, I am convinced that the next development in the field of the fine arts may be stimulated by the findings of the artists who are meeting the problems of our day—and these are the commerial artists.

● As an indication as to just how closely this commercial art is connected with our life, let us suppose that Chicago, like Pompeii, is the victim of a similar catastrophe. This city lies buried for thousands of years, and at last some archæologist of the future sinks a shaft into the volcanic refuse that covers the bones of the former queen of the Middle West. Let us imagine that this archæologist of the future comes

Mr. Iannelli, head of Iannelli Studios in Park Ridge, Illinois, working on the clay model of the awards given at the Second Annual Outdoor Advertising Exhibit. Mr. Iannelli was formerly head of the design department of the Art School of the Chicago Art Institute and is well known in the field of sculpture and commercial design. He has created sculptures for the Adler Planetarium, in Chicago, the Sioux City, Iowa, court-house and the Midway Gardens, in Chicago. He is design consultant on manufactured products for the Mueller Plumbing Company, the U. S. Gypsum Company, the Wahl Company and Sellers Kitchen Cabinet Company. He designed the first stream line Packard automobile in 1915.

upon a collection of advertising designs such as this outdoor advertising exhibit. Here he would find depicted for him our appearance and our clothing, our transportation facilities and our amusements. Analysis would disclose to him a knowledge of our weaknesses and our strength, our desires and our ambitions more than any group of æsthetic paintings.

● The reason for this situation is not hard to find. Advertising springs directly from the necessity of telling the people of the products that have been created for their use. It deals with tangible things. It must speak to the people in an understandable language and awaken their desires. The need is fundamental in our modern life and therefore the art that sincerely expresses these needs will most truthfully express us.

● The fine artist lacks in many cases the functional purpose. He is. as it were, talking to himself of his dreams and fancies. These fancies may be necessary to the artist but unless they are linked to the need of the people they lack the coordinating force that makes an artist's work a virile record of a people. They are separate from the life activity of the age. Great living art has sprung and, unless human nature changes in the future more than it has in the last few thousand years, will always spring from the needs and aspirations and materials of the time that produced it. In American, the skyscraper is an indigenous growth. It is a product of necessity and of logical development. The attempts that have been made to introduce similar construction in Europe are forced and look out of place. They are more or less a synthetic growth.

The problem of advertising is primarily psychological. Copy that is written by a genius, typography of an unexcelled quality, an illustration of remarkable visual, appeal may all be combined to produce an advertisement which expresses the intended thought; yet if the wrong appeal is used the advertisement will not accomplish the task for which it was designed. The idea must come first and after that the artist and the copy writer and the typographer are only concerned with the expression of that idea in the simplest, most effective and the most direct manner possible. Because of this continued test, I am convinced that advertising has possibilities of leading the æsthetic arts into some scientific basis which will approach engineering in accuracy.

Eventually we should be able to say "this is the problem with which we are faced in marketing this product. How can we present it so it will make the appeal which will sell this product most efficiently?" A statement of the problem thus concisely and clearly carries with it the outline of the entire advertising campaign. The technical details of copy and art and layout will vary according to the individuals who are engaged in their production. The basic and fundamental theme of the campaign, however, will be calculated with the same accuracy with which an engineer figures the strength of his steel and the stresses to which it will be subjected.

● The advertising industry is paying more and more attention to these problems of psychology. It is following to some extent the latest developments in this field and should parallel these discoveries even more closely. I should like to see an experimental laboratory in advertising psychology in which studies that pertain to advertising could be carried on. By co-ordinating the scattered efforts upon this line which here and there are undertaken, not only will progress be more rapid, but the results will be more accurate. I anticipate that sometime in the not so distant future there will come an individual who will present a reasonable, a logical and a simple program which will be applicable to art and advertising and which will be so logical and so reasonable and so simple that we may be astounded.

All advertising and outdoor advertising particularly, must present its message quickly and forcefully and simply. This necessity, in itself, makes for consideration of design. This concept of simplicity and direct approach, combined with an understanding of psychology, will be the foundation of a new era in art in advertising.

● The design of commodities to make them more efficient and attractive has been given a great deal of attention in the last few years. As we progress and better these, together with advertising, we shall make the background of our homes and our lives more joyful and fitting. The large part of the effort so far has been brought about by the advertising man.

The statuette designed by Mr. Iannelli for the prizes in the Second Annual Exhibit of Outdoor Advertising Art.

INDEX

FIRST PRIZE

"Boy...that's travelin' /"

BUICK VIII

Strobridge Litho. Co.
Lithographer

Frederic Stanley
Artist

Campbell-Ewald Co.
Agency or Selling Co.

This design undoubtedly has everything that a good poster should have. Certainly no copy line has ever been more apt, expressing with perfect naturalness what two small boys would undoubtedly say, and presenting a sales message doubly strong by the fact that the product is no longer in the picture. The human interest quality of the exceptionally well painted illustration arouses a smile, but a smile which overcomes sales resistance and cannot detract from the felicity of the idea, carrying, as it does, such strong conviction.

SECOND PRIZE

THE BIG PARADE IS TO DETROIT
AMERICAN

POSTER - COURTESY FISHER BODY CORP.DETROIT

Continental Litho. Corp. Lithographer	Fred Ludekens Artist	Campbell-Ewald Co. Agency or Selling Co.

Though very modern in technique, this highly original poster strikes a note of warmth and gaiety. The head group makes one pattern, yet each profile is subtly expressive of a different personality. Every unessential has been carefully eliminated, but the result is complete spontaneity, and a romantic conception very rare in poster art.

THIRD PRIZE

American Poster Corporation
Lithographer

Lyman M. Simpson
Artist

Gen. Outdoor Adv. Co.
Agency or Selling Co.

The oranges come out of the background and over the lettering with a remarkable effect of dynamic action and third dimension. The double shadows, increasing in size as the oranges come toward the eye, repeat the circle motif; and the effect of depth is enhanced by the hot color of the oranges against the receding complimentary color of the cool background.

| Latham Litho. & Ptg. Company | C. E. Chambers | Newell-Emmett Co., Inc. |
| Lithographer | Artist | Agency or Selling Co. |

| Hand Painted Poster | W. T. Warde | Foster & Kleiser Co. |
| | Artist | Agency or Selling Co. |

| American Poster Corporation | Enoch Boles | Outdoor Service, Inc. |
| Lithographer | Artist | Agency or Selling Co. |

| Strobridge Litho. Co. | Lucian Bernhard | Gen. Outdoor Adv. Co. |
| Lithographer | Artist | Agency or Selling Co. |

| Latham Litho. & Ptg. Company | Andrew Loomis | Gen. Outdoor Adv. Co. |
| Lithographer | Artist | Agency or Selling Co. |

| Forbes Litho. & Mfg. Co. | Haddon Sundblom | D'Arcy Adv. Co. |
| Lithographer | Artist | Agency or Selling Co. |

Painted Bulletin	Leonard B. Hamshaw	Foster & Kleiser Co.
	Artist	Agency or Selling Co.

HONORABLE MENTION

● A perfect example of how the layout may be consistent with the meaning of the copy. The forward movement of the lettering and the shapes of the smaller color masses have speed and suggest action.

Painted Bulletin	Capt. H. Ledyard Towle	Campbell-Ewald Company
	Artist	Agency or Selling Co.

HONORABLE MENTION

● The striking illustration balances perfectly with the lettering and the position of the emblem to make a design of rare distinction, carrying with it a connotation of luxury and exclusiveness.

HONORABLE MENTION

● A remarkable expression of an idea. No strong color disturbs the rhythm and "timed" action of the figures, suggesting as they do competence and ability to perform a task, as well as romance and drama.

Edwards & Deutsch Litho. Co.	George Rapp	Rogers-Gano Adv. Agency, Inc.
Lithographer	Artist	Agency or Selling Co.

Edwards & Deutsch Litho. Co.   Gen. Motors Photographic Dept.   Campbell-Ewald Co.
   Lithographer   Artist   Agency or Selling Co.

● This poster vis-
ualizes the ideas very successfully—co l d n e s s by
snow and ice, the idea of
speed by the motion of
the italic capitals and the
d y n a m i c design of the
aurora borealis.

Atlantic Litho. Co.   Earl Barrett   Gen. Outdoor Adv. Co.
   Lithographer   Artist   Agency or Selling Co.

● The lines of the
shoulders and arms lead
into the glasses, which in
turn are under the logo-
type. The dramatic action
of the figures make this
an effective poster.

Gugler Lithographic Co.   George Petty
   Lithographer   Artist

● A novel presentation of an idea: first the command, then the product, then the distinguishing feature of the product and finally the result. The design has an oval swing, with the three kernels, the can and the caption as an axis.

American Poster Corp.
Lithographer

Lucian Bernhard
Artist

Young & Rubicam, Inc.
Agency or Selling Co.

● All the lines of the action radiate from a point outside this decidedly modern poster, giving an effect of tremendous speed. The planes are graduated in color and value by airbrush, so that dark edges always contrast against light.

Latham Litho. & Ptg. Co.
Lithographer

Otis Shepard
Artist

Doremus & Co.
Agency or Selling Co.

● Everything tends to the impression of quality — the simple layout, the black background, sans serif lettering, and the color scheme. The copy line is in yellow, the car is blue and black; the red of the name, is repeated in the girl's hat.

Continental Litho. Corp.
Lithographer

Art Studios
Artist

Campbell-Ewald Co.
Agency or Selling Co.

DEM FOAMY SUDS SHO' WASHES CLEAN

OXYDOL

RICH SUDS IN ANY WATER

● One of a series of posters, all of which show the washer-woman demonstrating various advantages of this product. This design is beautifully rendered in transparent wash, and tells the story at a glance.

Gugler Lithographic Co. Lithographer	Marshall Reid Artist	Gen. Outdoor Adv. Co. Agency or Selling Co.

● Good selling copy and layout make this an effective poster. The clerk is exceptionally well painted, with variation of tone and color in the shadow side, the lights being handled in simple values.

"AFTER THE RUSH I GET ʍιʌɛ

Dr. Pepper 5¢

at 10-2 AND 4 O'CLOCK

Erie Litho. & Ptg. Co. Lithographer	Raymond J. Prohaska Artist	Tracy-Locke-Dawson, Inc. Agency or Selling Co.

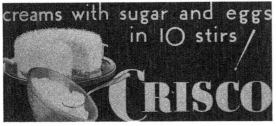

creams with sugar and eggs in 10 stirs /

CRISCO

● The still life and lettering stand out vividly against a well designed background of geometric shapes. The frosting on the cake is handled superbly.

McCandlish Litho. Corp. Lithographer	Waldo Bemis Artist	Gen. Outdoor Adv. Co. Agency or Selling Co.

● Almost severe in its simplicity this design arouses a feeling of integrity and service. Three colors are used—reddish brown on the Indian head, red on the caption, and the rest black, all over a white background.

for your
BEST INTEREST

The Detroit Savings Bank
GRISWOLD AT STATE STREET
CONVENIENT BRANCHES

| Wm. H. Aston Printing Co.
Lithographer | Walker & Co. Art Dept.
Artist | Walker & Co.
Agency or Selling Co. |

● A modernistic treatment is used throughout with an interesting airbrush technique. The dominant figure, in cool tones, stands out against the rich background. The idea of fur is present in each of the three elements.

| Hand Painted Poster | Doff Royal
Artist | Foster & Kleiser Co.
Agency or Selling Co. |

● The selling argument is presented graphically and positively. The vertical panel forms one single unit breaking over the horizontal shape, and balances perfectly with the illustration. The colors are white, buff, gray blue and deep blue.

| Edwards & Deutsch Litho. Co.
Lithographer | Meininger Studios
Artist | Campbell-Ewald Co.
Agency or Selling Co. |

● The costume of the girl, with her bright red hat and dress, centers the attention toward the center of the poster. The autumn leaves suggest fall styles.

| McCandlish Litho. Corp. | Robert C. Kauffmann | Gen. Outdoor Adv. Co. |
| Lithographer | Artist | Agency or Selling Co. |

● The cross immediately visualizes hot cross buns and Lent, and forms the nucleus of an interesting geometric pattern, with none of the four masses around the cross of the same size or shape.

| Hand Painted Poster | Leonard B. Hamshaw | Foster & Kleiser Co. |
| | Artist | Agency or Selling Co. |

● One of the most beautiful posters ever painted; a masterpiece far removed from the average appeal to buy goods. Besides virtuosity of technique, it has spiritual meaning and inspiration.

| Donaldson Litho. Co. | C. E. Chambers | Gen. Outdoor Adv. Co. |
| Lithographer | Artist | Agency or Selling Co. |

● Appetite appeal, and the large size of the frankfurter, leading into the logotype, make this a good poster. The plate, frankfurter, and mustard bottle are well handled in transparent wash.

| Continental Litho. Corp. | J. Tesar | Gen. Outdoor Adv. Co. |
| Lithographer | Artist | Agency or Selling Co. |

● The three elements, each of a different shape, come forward from the white background, casting interesting gray shadow patterns. The can is in black and dull orange, the other shapes and lettering in blue.

| American Poster Corp. | Lucian Bernhard | Young & Rubicam, Inc. |
| Lithographer | Artist | Agency or Selling Co. |

● Dexterity of handling, with all the detail in the light, and lost in the black shadows which run into the black background, make this a fine example of poster technique.

| Hand Painted Poster | E. E. Childs | Foster & Kleiser Co. |
| | Artist | Agency or Selling Co. |

garden freshness
—*brought to your table*...

Snider catsup

VINE TO BOTTLE
IN ONE DAY

● One of the outstanding food posters of the year. Everything sells the idea of freshness—copy, illustration, the drawing of the bottle, and the color scheme of green, red and white.

Guy Savage
Artist

Newell-Emmett Co., Inc.
Agency or Selling Co.

● The airplane, in blue and black, is restrained from going out of the picture by the position of the lettering, which balances the composition. The poster is modern and clear cut, and graduation of tone is accomplished by air brush.

DEPENDABLE

8,000,000
AIR TRANSPORT MILES 1930
FILL IT UP WITH RICHFIELD

Strobridge Litho. Co.
Lithographer

Otis Shepard
Artist

Doremus & Co.
Agency or Selling Co.

The Gift of Good Taste!

MEMORIE SWEETMEATS CO. Fresno, California

● Light green and blue lettering on a black ground, and a feeling of quality in the quiet richness of the basket of sweet meats, make this poster appeal very much to "good taste."

Hand Painted Poster

Mildred Wilson
Artist

Foster & Kleiser Co.
Agency or Selling Co.

● The poster is painted in modern oil illustration style — the masses are simple, but contrasted and well rounded to give drama and carrying power.

The Pioneer still leads !

Since 1831

WM. S. SCULL COMPANY PRODUCERS OF THE FAMOUS

BOSCUL COFFEE

| McCandlish Litho. Corp.
Lithographer | Rico Tomaso
Artist | F. Wallis Armstrong
Agency or Selling Co. |

● A poster which is extraordinarily well done and which, though containing a great deal of detail, is entirely in the spirit of the subject. The whole poster looks like a tapestry, especially in the background, into which the lettering seems to be woven.

Hand Painted Poster   W. T. Warde   Foster & Kleiser Co.
                           Artist   Agency or Selling Co.

A symmetrical layout, varied by the relief effect of the lettering, which is red against black, and instantly legible. The can, carefully worked out, is handled with all possible economy of detail.

Hand Painted Walls &   E. E. Childs   Foster & Kleiser Co.
Store Bulletins   Artist   Agency or Selling Co.

● Another appeal to the expert. The dominant colors are yellow ochre for the plane, green on the bottom strip, blue for the figure and the copy in the left-hand corner, and red for the trademark.

Edwards & Deutsch Litho. Co.
Lithographer

Willard F. Elms
Artist

Tracy-Locke-Dawson, Inc.
Agency or Selling Co.

● Highly dramatic, with remarkable animation and sure painting technique, this poster is a fine example to display the versatility of this artist who always successfully captures the mood of his subject.

Latham Litho. & Ptg. Co.
Lithographer

C. E. Chambers
Artist

Newell-Emmett Co., Inc.
Agency or Selling Co.

● Drawn in pastel, handled simply in large masses, but with subtle, broken coloring. The yellow of the cake is complimentary to the cool tone of the rest of the poster.

American Poster Corp.
Lithographer

Frank H. Dillon
Artist

The W. E. Long Co.
Direct

● Children in action are always interesting; the poster possesses good selling psychology with a baseball term related to the product, plus the portrayal of health in the figure of the boys.

Illinois Litho. Co.
Lithographer

Philip Lyford
Artist

Roche Adv. Co.
Agency or Selling Co.

● This poster is one of a series in which various occupations are featured. In this case, the dominant figure is the stenographer; the idea of 24,000 stenographers is visualized by a series of miniatures of the large figure.

J. P. Carey & Son
Lithographer

J. Tesar
Artist

Gen. Outdoor Adv. Co.
Agency or Selling Co.

● An all-lettering poster; interesting because of the decorative borders which repeat the color scheme of the lettering. The warm colors stand out well against deep blue.

Edwards & Deutsch Litho. Co.
Lithographer

C. C. Bratten
Artist

C. C. Winningham, Inc.
Agency or Selling Co.

Continental Litho. Corp.
Lithographer

H. Gilbert Levine
Artist

Florsheim Shoe Company
Direct

Continental Litho. Corp.
Lithographer

J. Tesar
Artist

Gen. Outdoor Adv. Co.
Agency or Selling Co.

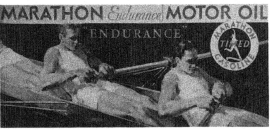

Edwards & Deutsch Litho. Co.
Lithographer

George Rapp
Artist

Rogers-Gano Adv. Agency, Inc.
Agency or Selling Co.

● The swinging lines give rhythm to the composition, and balance the elements which break over each other to tie up the design.

Latham Litho. & Ptg. Co.
Lithographer

W. B. Humphrey
Artist

Gen. Outdoor Adv. Co.
Agency or Selling Co.

● A dramatic scene of the old West, painted in striking yellow, blue, red and purple. The figure of the teamster is especially well done, the line of the whip adding to the impression of violence.

Erie Litho. & Ptg. Co.
Lithographer

Lee Jennings
Artist

Outdoor Service, Inc.
Agency or Selling Co.

● One dominant sales idea in blue lettering, with the secondary idea at the bottom in dark red. The name is yellow, and the orange and glass in natural color, all against a black background.

American Poster Corporation
Lithographer

Enoch Boles
Artist

Outdoor Service, Inc.
Agency or Selling Co.

● The dominant size of the shoe breaks across the name and into the copy, tieing the layout together. The shoe is brown, background and lettering light yellow and green, the strips plum and black.

| Continental Litho. Corp. | William R. Neilsen | Florsheim Shoe Company |
| Lithographer | Artist | Direct |

● The radiating red lines and the action of the figures attract attention to the center of this poster. The figures and the copy at the top are black and white; the color is concentrated in the center.

| American Poster Corp. | Ronald McKenzie | Outdoor Service, Inc. |
| Lithographer | Artist | Agency or Selling Co. |

● The plate breaking over the lettering gives a unique feeling of transparency in the glassware. The foreground and the lettering are in yellow, the glass and shadows in green, and the background a deep plum color.

| Hand Painted Poster | W. T. Warde | Foster & Kleiser Co. |
| | Artist | Agency or Selling Co. |

● Again the idea of a large number of depositors of a certain occupation is forcibly expressed by repetition in miniature. The figure gives a forceful impression of strength.

OVER 53,000 MECHANICS
save at the BOWERY
SAVINGS BANK

J. P. Carey & Son
Lithographer

J. Tesar
Artist

Gen. Outdoor Adv. Co.
Agency or Selling Co.

"Smooth-freeze"

new sealed "carry-home" package

Meadow Gold Ice Cream

● A balanced layout, presenting the product very attractively. The ice cream and melon are in natural color, the plate and background in deep plum.

Edwards & Deutsch Litho. Co.
Lithographer

Lyman M. Simpson
Artist

Gen. Outdoor Adv. Co.
Agency or Selling Co.

● A well tied-up layout, and an amusing human interest idea with the copy line also applying to the name, make this a good poster. It is painted directly, and the contrasting values secure carrying power.

SOMETHING TO REMEMBER

SHELL MOTOR OIL
FORMS NO HARD CARBON

Edwards & Deutsch Litho. Co.
Lithographer

Haddon Sundblom
Artist

J. Walter Thompson Co., Inc.
Agency or Selling Co.

"My own pick for Christmas."

The New
STEWART WARNER RADIO

● The illustration, with its human interest, very easily arouses the desired chain of thought on the part of the spectator, telling the story by subtle suggestion rather than elaborate copy.

Illinois Litho. Co.
Lithographer

Andrew Loomis
Artist

Chas. H. Touzalin Agency
Agency or Selling Co.

● The figure, with its dominant position and the relation of facial expression to the copy, runs through all the elements to create a well tied up layout.

Erie Litho. & Ptg. Co.
Lithographer

Andrew Loomis
Artist

Tracy-Locke-Dawson, Inc.
Agency or Selling Co.

● The head and still-life are very well painted; the type of woman, closely related to the copy with a feeling of old-fashioned honesty, makes a strong appeal to the housewife.

Nat'l Printing and Engraving Co.
Lithographer

Chas. D. Jarrett
Artist

Gen. Outdoor Adv. Co.
Agency or Selling Co.

● The figures, breaking through the rectangle at the top and bottom, secure dominance. They have a notable quality of animation, and are painted with directness and confidence.

AT THE BETTER STORES

McCandlish Litho. Corp.
Lithographer

Robert C. Kauffmann
Artist

Gen. Outdoor Adv. Co.
Agency or Selling Co.

● The warm colors of the background are balanced by cool tones in the Indian, the horse, and the foreground details. "T. P." is used adroitly as an abbreviation for Texas Pacific, the initial letters of the copy, and suggest the Indian himself, as well as his "top place."

Compton & Sons
Lithographer

Studley Burroughs
Artist

Gen. Outdoor Adv. Co.
Agency or Selling Co.

● The forward movement of the hand, the italics, and the gearshift give the idea of animation; the soft colors, white and gray over blue, convey silence. Though subtly expressed, the idea is understandable in a flash.

Forbes Litho. & Mfg. Co.
Lithographer

Kelly-Olsen-Higgs Studio
Artist

Campbell-Ewald Co.
Agency or Selling Co.

● The same elements as in the other Post Toasties designs are held in a reverse S composition, with the figures walking toward the red circle and held in position by the red lines.

| American Poster Corp. Lithographer | Ronald McKenzie Artist | Outdoor Service, Inc. Agency or Selling Co. |

● The three coffee cans unite to form one element, and intimately tie up the caption at the top with the message below. Simplicity and a strong selling idea make it a compelling poster.

| American Poster Corporation Lithographer | Lucian Bernhard Artist | Young & Rubicam, Inc. Agency or Selling Co. |

●An effective swing through the copy, figure and name. The copy at the top is unusual—the simile is justified by the smaller lettering at the lower left.

| Continental Litho. Corp. Lithographer | James Schucker Artist | Blackett-Sample-Hummert, Inc. Agency or Selling Co. |

Latham Litho. & Ptg. Co.
Lithographer

Andrew Loomis
Artist

Gen. Outdoor Adv. Co.
Agency or Selling Co.

Continental Litho. Corp.
Lithographer

G. W. French
Artist

Outdoor Adv. Agency of America, Inc.
Agency or Selling Co.

Strobridge Litho. Co.
Lithographer

Bradshaw Crandall
Artist

Campbell-Ewald Co.
Agency or Selling Co.

● The elements are well tied together by the black base panel. The yellow background, t h e red circle, and the blue hat and coat make a primary color scheme.

| Illinois Litho. Co. | George Straub | Chas. W. Wrigley Co. |
| Lithographer | Artist | Agency or Selling Co. |

● This poster dramatizes effectively f o u r phases of this o r a n g e-growth in the orchard, the close-up of a cluster, the orange cut in half to suggest the juice, and finally the bottle.

| Gugler Lithographic Co. | August M. Buehler |
| Lithographer | Artist |

● The script lettering is in relation to the bubbles, and characteristic of the general style of the campaign. There is a clean simplicity to the colors: white, light green, dark green, and yellow for the logotype.

| Strobridge Litho. Co. | Lyman M. Simpson | Gen. Outdoor Adv. Co. |
| Lithographer | Artist | Agency or Selling Co. |

● The two shoes are in brown against a black background with a green border; the caption is in black, and in the right hand panel the lettering is yellow against red.

THEY'RE HERE!

Continental Litho. Corp.
Lithographer

William R. Neilsen
Artist

Florsheim Shoe Company
Direct

● A symmetrical layout, varied by the lettering style of the copy line, and the breaking of the figure over the base panel.

Continental Litho. Corp.
Lithographer

Bradshaw Crandall
Artist

Maxon, Inc.
Agency or Selling Co.

● A striking poster, using tone contrasts to secure attention. The lettering is white, yellow and light red, on a background of dark green with mauve stripes. The triangular shapes back of the H are in various tones of red.

Edwards & Deutsch Litho. Co.
Lithographer

C. C. Bratten
Artist

C. C. Winningham, Inc.
Agency or Selling Co.

● Another poster in which the copy aptly applies both to the human interest illustration and the name. The children's heads are especially well painted.

CHAMPLIN
MOTOR OIL ···· GASOLINE

| Edwards & Deutsch Litho. Co. | Andrew Loomis | Rogers-Gano Adv. Agency, Inc. |
| Lithographer | Artist | Agency or Selling Co. |

● The design, relief effect, and dominant size of the name, together with the primary color scheme of yellow, red, and blue, make this a strong poster.

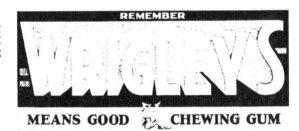

REMEMBER

MEANS GOOD 🐟 CHEWING GUM

| Gugler Lithographic Co. | Rocco Navigato | Chas. W. Wrigley Co. |
| Lithographer | Artist | Agency or Selling Co. |

● In this poster, in warm colors against blue, the movement is to the lower right hand, balanced by the silhouetted figures of the boys. It is an unusual but interesting composition.

| American Poster Corp. | Ronald McKenzie | Outdoor Service, Inc. |
| Lithographer | Artist | Agency or Selling Co. |

● The sales message is in the appeal to the professional. The truck and the position of the standing figure lead into the copy and linotype.

Edwards & Deutsch Litho. Co.
Lithographer

Willard F. Elms
Artist

Tracy-Locke-Dawson, Inc.
Agency or Selling Co.

● The palm trees tie up the caption at the top with the boat; the figures and the name of the line. The lettering and sky are yellow and red, the water deep blue.

Wendell P. Coltin Co.
Agency or Selling Co.

● A clever method of suggesting that the product be used as a Christmas gift. The fact that the woman, even though blindfolded, can recognize the product through a distinguishing feature, is a triumph of subtle salesmanship.

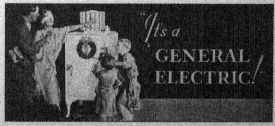

Continental Litho. Corp.
Lithographer

R. Konersman
Artist

Maxon, Inc.
Agency or Selling Co.

● The elements are well tied together, and the product has an unusual appetite appeal. The background is green and dark blue.

Bill Bailey

Outdoor Adv. Agency of America, Inc.
Agency or Selling Co.

● The concentric circles in the background and the black arch over them hold the eye to the middle of the poster. The figure of the girl is drawn very well in the modern fashion manner.

Hand Painted Poster

R. L. McKern
Artist

Foster & Kleiser Co.
Agency or Selling Co.

● Strong appetite appeal, with the rendering in pastel and handled very broadly. The flowers strike an unusual note, and are in dull lavender, harmonizing with the plate.

American Poster Corp.
Lithographer

Frank H. Dillon
Artist

The W. E. Long Co.
Direct

● The long horizontal lines of the smoke, waves, and boat, are coordinated by the circle inclosing the name. The picturesque illustration is well handled.

That Good

GULF

GASOLINE

The Marvel of its time!

The Famous ROBERT E. LEE
of the old river boat days

McCandlish Litho. Corp.
Lithographer

Bill Bailey
Artist

Outdoor Adv. Agency of America, Inc.
Agency or Selling Co.

Fall Styles

in FLORSHEIM SHOES

are Here

● The same color scheme as the "Days' Wear-per-dollar" poster, but with the shoe in black. The shoes in all of these designs are beautifully rendered.

Continental Litho. Corp.
Lithographer

William R. Neilsen
Artist

Florsheim Shoe Company
Direct

● Three dominant values—light, half-tone and dark—give the poster long carrying power. The shadow tones have an unusual luminosity, always a difficult problem for the painter to solve.

Forbes Litho. & Mfg. Co.
Lithographer

Haddon Sundblom
Artist

D'Arcy Adv. Co.
Agency or Selling Co.

● Though painted in oil, the dainty head has a pastel quality. It is soft, yet handled in the confident fashion so characteristic of this artist. The background is a very rich gray.

| Latham Litho. & Ptg. Co. | Andrew Loomis | Gen. Outdoor Adv. Co. |
| Lithographer | Artist | Agency or Selling Co. |

● The u n i t s are held together by the radiating shapes, pulling the eye to the center of the poster. The complimentary color scheme of yellow and orange against blue is relieved by green lettering on the bottom panel.

| Hand Painted Poster | Doff Royal | Foster & Kleiser Co. |
| | Artist | Agency or Selling Co. |

● A strong merchandising poster. The unique shape of the numeral, breaking through the panel but not dividing it, attracts the eye and insures a consideration of the sales message.

| Continental Litho. Corp. | Gen. Outdoor Adv. Art Dept. | Maxon, Inc. |
| Lithographer | Artist | Agency or Selling Co. |

● The name panel forms a base for the dominant product and the salad; the severity of the arrangement is relieved by the position of the copy.

American Poster Corp.
Lithographer

Arthur B. Elliott
Artist

Outdoor Service, Inc.
Agency or Selling Co.

● No copy is needed to describe the story, or tie up the scene to the logotype. It is painted in strong colors, and the feeling of hilarity is varied by the predicament of the unfortunate laundry-man.

Nat'l Printing and Engraving Co.
Lithographer

Lee Jennings
Artist

Outdoor Service, Inc.
Agency or Selling Co.

● The map of Florida makes an interesting panel. Although the poster contains two illustrations, they are related in subject, and are in the same scale, with a common horizon line and sky.

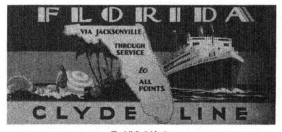

Wendell P. Coltin Co.
Agency or Selling Co.

● Dominantly cool in tone, this poster does not depend on bright colors for attention value, but on a feeling of bigness and space. The color values are in perfect relation, and though the poster has a subtle mood it has power.

| Hand Painted Poster | Emil Grebs
Artist | Foster & Kleiser Co.
Agency or Selling Co. |

● The fur creates the vignette shape to inclose the head, and makes the blue background appropriate. The yellow hair gives a sparkle and vitality to balance the quiet tones of the rest of the design.

| Latham Litho. & Ptg. Co.
Lithographer | Andrew Loomis
Artist | Gen. Outdoor Adv. Co.
Agency or Selling Co. |

● The poster consistently carries out the idea of the copy, which seems to be surrounded by white heat, causing the name at the top to cast shadows radiating from the center.

| Continental Litho. Corp.
Lithographer | Leonard F. Smith
Artist | McCann-Erickson Co., Inc.
Agency or Selling Co. |

● A clever idea, comprehensible at a glance. The poster has the utmost simplicity, and strong selling power. The dictionary is in cream, the background red with white lettering, and the name blue-green against black.

Atlantic Litho. Co.
Lithographer

Harry Miller
Artist

Gen. Outdoor Adv. Co.
Agency or Selling Co.

● The feeling of night in the desert, with a lonesome camp, gray moonlight and the howl of a coyote, give this poster an unusual appeal.

Nat'l Printing and Engraving Co.
Lithographer

Don Louis Perceval
Artist

Outdoor Service, Inc.
Agency or Selling Co.

● Variety and interest is achieved by avoiding vertical and horizontal lines, by the dominating slogan, by the shadow shapes, and by the clean smoothness of the can contrasting with the irregular edges of the rectangular shapes.

American Poster Corp.
Lithographer

Edward A. Schoenlau
Artist

Outdoor Service, Inc.
Agency or Selling Co.

● The high horizon line gives bigness to the lake; the two figures, beside adding human interest, balance the heavy mass of the trees and give scale to the poster. The dominant colors are deep mauve, red and light green.

| Hand Painted Poster | Emil Grebs
Artist | Foster & Kleiser Co.
Agency or Selling Co. |

● The familiar symbol of the phantom devil to indicate heat is kept well to the back of the poster by the relief lettering of the name, in front of which is the car. The red orange background is repeated in the automobile.

| Erie Litho. & Ptg. Co.
Lithographer | R. Garcia
Artist | Doremus & Co.
Agency or Selling Co. |

| Painted Bulletin | Harry Slater
Artist | Advertisers Inc.
Agency or Selling Co. |

● The familiar style of lettering, white against dark blue, is immediately identified with this make of car. The figure of the woman is exceptionally well painted.

SECOND ANNUAL COUPEVILLE WATER FESTIVAL
AUG. 7 · 8 · 9 ·
International
WAR CANOE
CHAMPIONSHIP

Courtesy Island County Times

Painted Bulletin	Leonard B. Hamshaw Artist	Foster & Kleiser Co. Agency or Selling Co.

● The strange figureheads on the boats give this composition a good deal of interest. The illustration and lettering are tied up by the sun and the horizon.

Colonial DOUBLE QUICK Gas
CHARGED WITH POWER

Painted Bulletin	McCann-Erickson Co., Inc. Art Dept. Artist	McCann-Erickson Co. Agency or Selling Co.

● The illustration fits in admirably with the copy—the Revolution costumes with "Colonial," the two soldiers with "double quick," and the action of the figures with "double quick" and "charged with power."

GRÜSS AIR SPRINGS
MAKE ALL ROADS BOULEVARDS
FACTORY
220 9ᵀᴴ S.

Painted Bulletin	R. L. McKern Artist	Foster & Kleiser Co. Agency or Selling Co.

● An interesting correlation between copy and design. The red line under the logotype suggests speed and smoothness on any kind of road, roughness being indicated beneath the red line by wavy bands.

Advertising Outdoors

Painted Bulletin | John F. Segesman | Foster & Kleiser Co.
| Artist | Agency or Selling Co.

● By simplicity of values—five
light and three shadow colors—a complicated landscape becomes a neat, well
ordered design, at the same time being
realistic and convincing.

Painted Bulletin | R. L. McKern | Engler & Smith
| Artist | Agency or Selling Co.

● A nicely balanced design, with
distinctive lettering and an unusual color
scheme of black, gray, and vermilion,
with the decorative flower motif in green,
gray, orange, purple, vermilion, yellow
and blue.

Painted Bulletin | Ralph Wilkins | Calkins & Holden
| Artist | Agency or Selling Co.

● The sales message is handled
very directly, with the crackers coming
across the poster from the box to the
salad plate, forming a simple unit silhouetted against black. The resulting
design is very luminous.

Painted Bulletin   Walker & Co. Art Dept.   Walker & Company
                    Artist   Agency or Selling Co.

● An all lettering design is varied by the head of the miner. The lettering is black, blue and red, the man's
head black and white; the background
is light yellow.

Painted Bulletin   E. Wm. Berg   Vanderhoof & Co.
                    Artist   Agency or Selling Co.

● The various masses, w h i c h
might easily have been scattered, are held
together by the cool colors, arranged in
circles in the background. The lettering
and the candy boxes, all in warm colors,
stand out vividly.

Painted Bulletin   Lyman M. Simpson   Gen. Outdoor Adv. Co.
                    Artist   Agency or Selling Co.

● The script lettering, which
seems to be tacked on over the design,
adds variety to the layout and leads the
eye into the appetizing painting of the
ham.

| Painted Bulletin | Edward A. Rogers | Gerber & Crossley, Inc. |
| | Artist | Agency or Selling Co. |

● The exclusive feature suggested in the name of the product is carried out by the conventional borders beside the logotype; the modern staggered stripes uniting copy and product with the name; and by the unique color combination — pink, blue, silver and black.

| Painted Bulletin | Sataiford Studios | Lord & Thomas and Logan |
| | Artist | Agency or Selling Co. |

● The three boats combine to make a single mass, bound to the name at the bottom by the circle in red. A difficult problem in composition is handled very successfully.

| Painted Bulletin | Wm. Sheehan | Gen. Outdoor Adv. Co. |
| | Artist | Agency or Selling Co. |

● The dynamic motion of the geometric pattern holds the eye to this design. The colors are provocative—the lettering white and yellow against bright red, the upper right mass in green, and the lower left in deep mauve.

Painted Bulletin   Vera Allison   Foster & Kleiser Co.
                     Artist   Agency or Selling Co.

● Several units are cleverly combined to produce an effect of simplicity. The lettering is buff over blue, the bird is red, with blue and green wing tips, all over a background varying from white to light green.

Painted Bulletin   Lyman M. Simpson   Gen. Outdoor Adv. Co.
                     Artist   Agency or Selling Co.

● The still life is tied into the right side of the design by the curved line of lettering, and the longer curve swinging under it. The geometrical shapes of the background do not obtrude, but hold the composition together effectively.

Painted Bulletin   R. L. McKern   Foster & Kleiser Co.
                     Artist   Agency or Selling Co.

● The large bolt of silk is in vermilion, the two small ones in yellow and blue, imposed over a neutral background, intensifying the color of the silk.

Painted Bulletin   Vera Allison   Foster & Kleiser Co.
                     Artist   Agency or Selling Co.

● The modern geometric shapes make this layout most unusual, giving it strong attention value. The lettering is yellow and blue against black, the middle tone is in light red, the thin stripes and the diagonal shapes are in silver.

THE 3-SHEET POSTERS

FIRST PRIZE

Latham Litho. & Ptg. Co.   Haddon Sundblom
Lithographer   Artist
The Blackman Co.
Agency or Selling Co.

● The qualities of contrast and design which make this such a compelling poster do not detract in the slightest from a beauty considered from purely aesthetic standards. Sure draftsmanship, subtle changes of color and value to indicate form, as well as a sympathetic understanding of an elusive personality, create a portrait of unique distinction.

HONORABLE MENTION

Erie Litho. & Ptg. Co.   Chas. E. Heinzerling
Lithographer   Artist
Calkins & Holden
Agency or Selling Co.

● One of the best food posters of the year. It suggests three uses for the product, with the cake dominant, yet does not lose its simplicity.

J. M. WHITNEY
"Use Your Credit"
"Pay As You Are Paid"
YATES & BROAD STS.

Spurgeon Tucker
Lithographer
William Sakren
Artist
Criterion Adv. Co.
Agency or Selling Co.

● The dull texture of pewter is gained by the avoidance of sharp highlights and dark shadows on the metal itself. The colors are gray, red and black.

The Flavor is Baked in!"

AMERICAN LADY
SLICED BREAD
White, Whole-wheat, and Raisin Bran
20 OUNCES
of Quality Bread for Ten Cents
AT YOUR LOCAL GROCER

Spurgeon Tucker
Lithographer
Carl Schneider
Artist
Criterion Adv. Co.
Agency or Selling Co.

● Interesting in pattern and lost-and-found edges. The suggestive treatment of the costume harmonizes very well with the more detailed head and loaf of bread.

CAMAY
America's Finest Toilet Soap
10¢ a cake

Latham Litho. & Ptg. Co.
Lithographer
Haddon Sundblom
Artist
The Blackman Co.
Agency or Selling Co.

● Beautifully painted, with sure, vigorous style, the head has extraordinary animation and luminosity with its simple values against the black background. It is in perfect harmony with the idea of fresh cleanliness.

She Heated *Her* Bath In a Teakettle

THE MODERN WOMAN DOES AN AUTOMATIC GAS-FIRED WATER HEATER

PUBLIC SERVICE COMPANY OF NORTHERN ILLINOIS

Illinois Litho. Co.
Lithographer
Milo Winter
Artist
Public Service Co. of Northern Ill.
Direct

● It is inevitable that the spectator should smile at this poster, and that his curiosity be whetted to read the copy. The approach to the sales message is indirect, but none the less effective.

READY TO SERVE!

OSCAR MAYER
WHOLE BAKED HAM
ORDER FROM YOUR MARKET OR DELICATESSEN

Illinois Litho. Co.
Lithographer
Rhaler & Keister
Artist
C. Wendell Muench Adv. Agency
Agency or Selling Co.

● With the modeling of the appetizing still life executed in airbrush, and the many highlights banded in small short strokes, a very realistic effect is achieved.

Spurgeon Tucker
Lithographer
George Culls
Artist
Criterion Adv. Co.
Agency or Selling Co.

● The clean, fresh color and the fine rendering of the still life make this a most attractive poster. There is nothing original in the conception, but that is more than compensated by the technique.

Spurgeon Tucker
Lithographer
Norman Hall
Artist
Criterion Adv. Co.
Agency or Selling Co.

● Painted in neutral c o l o r, the illustration depends upon the relationship rather than striking contrasts. The double lighting brings out the figure from the background.

Illinois Litho. Co.
Lithographer
Milo Winter
Artist
Public Service Co. of Northern Ill.
Direct

● With its whimsical i d e a, this poster has a quality unfortunately unusual in American posters, and is allied in spirit with many English designs.

Rurling Wood
Lithographer
Charles E. Heinzerling
Artist
H. J. Heinz Company
Direct

● The large element at the top is balanced by the smaller shapes at the base because of the bright red of the bottle; the plate, in quiet tones, compliments the rest of the design.

Spurgeon Tucker
Lithographer
Helen Smith
Artist
Criterion Adv. Co.
Agency or Selling Co.

● The various units of the illustration make a single pattern, l u m i n o u s against the black background. The colors are all soft except the bright red of the supporting standard.

Poor Richard Club to Stage Dinner

The Poor Richard Club, the men's advertising club of Philadelphia, in planning its annual banquet to be held January 15, 1932, decided to make the theme of it "Advertising Advertising."

To carry out this idea, the ballroom of the Bellevue-Stratford Hotel, where the dinner will be held, will be converted into a veritable advertising louvre. The entire room, from pit to dome, will be hung with huge lithographs and posters of the finest advertising art to be had. Hundreds of these posters and lithographs are now being collected from national advertisers, lithographers and printers and are being assembled for this novel decorative scheme.

The Poor Richard Club believes that if the power of advertising be brought to the attention of American business, if American business be shown how advertising can be used, that this thing which we call depression or readjustment will soon disappear. The Poor Richard Club is, therefore, staging this $50,000 dinner with this thought constantly in mind. Every phase of the dinner will exhale the spirit of Advertising and its power.

The Poor Richard Players, an organization within the Club, has written and will enact a skit running forty-five minutes, entitled "From Factory to Dining Table." It is said that this skit is so packed with laughs that the audience will be rolling from its chairs from start to finish. Harry T. Jordan, for many years manager of Keith's Theatre, Philadelphia, and maker of such stars as Will Rogers, Fred and Adelle Astaire, Ann Pennington and Belle Baker, is in charge of the professional end of the dinner. His close association with theatrical managers and stars of the stage and screen assures a galaxy of professionals, the like of which has never before been gathered together for an evening's entertainment.

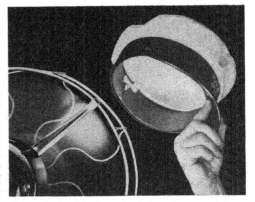

More knots per capful

A GOOD sailor makes headway on the merest capful of

wind. In outdoor advertising we have the sailor's knack of

getting extra knots out of every appropriation that breezes

our way. Ask some of our clients — for instance, Maxwell

House Coffee, Calumet Baking Powder, Rio Grande Oil, Log

Cabin Syrup, Philco Radio.... If you want outdoor SERVICE—

OUTDOOR
A NATIONAL OUTDOOR ADVERTISING ORGANIZATION

SERVICE
INCORPORATED
230 NORTH MICHIGAN AVE., CHICAGO

SEMI-SPECTACULAR BULLETINS

Semi-Spectacular Bulletin   Walker and Co., Art Department   Walker and Company
Artist   Selling Company

● The "As Clean As Sunlight" slogan is used as the basis for the color scheme of this interesting bulletin. The name of the product, "Electrochef" appears in yellow neon light with the remainder of the copy on the bulletin illuminated from the rear in brilliant light. The stove is placed in a recess in the bulletin and is illuminated from above, standing out strongly against the deeper yellow of the background. The entire bulletin has been designed to express, with copy and color and light the "Clean As Sunlight" copy and it succeeds admirably in doing its job.

Semi-Spectacular Bulletin   General Outdoor Adv. Co., Art Department   General Outdoor Adv. Co.
Artist   Selling Company

● The dog lying before the fire is a familiar symbol in literature but a more unusual one in outdoor advertising. The natural tendency in this case must have been to introduce human figures; yet human figures could hardly have expressed a message of warmth and comfort as well as does this obviously comfortable collie. Changing light and shadow pattern on the back wall of the fire place give a remarkably realistic effect of an actual fire. Lights are also used to give a ruddy glow to the coals. The use of motion in addition to light and color adds much to the attention value of this design.

● By the ingenious portrayal of an actual scene, this bulletin has a strong selling value, and though unusually elaborate, the message can be comprehended at a glance. The copy loses nothing to the three-dimension illustration because of the dominant name, which is illuminated by neon. The restaurant, although occupying about half the space, is placed in such a way that the design does not break in half but forms one continuous whole. Altogether, it is a fine example of this particular form of Outdoor Advertising.

● Between the figures of the women and the man is a large piece of glass upon which is painted a view of Paris from a high balcony. The Eiffel tower rises majestically in the background with boulevards and roof tops in the foreground. This design is effective in the daytime, but at night, when the panorama is lighted from behind, the effect is striking in the extreme. This picture of Paris is used to tie the idea of smartness to the name of Paris Cleaners and Dyers, and the aristocratic figures and the copy line "Get That Paris Touch of Smartness" emphasizes this purpose.

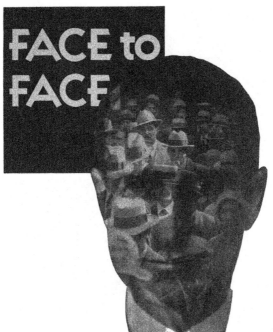

FACE to FACE

Millions are walking and riding straight into your sales story...again and again and again. Little wonder, then, that Outdoor Advertising sells and sells and sells.

NATIONWIDE OUTDOOR ADVERTISING

Foster and Kleiser
— COMPANY —

General Office: San Francisco
Operating Plants in California,
Washington, Oregon and Arizona
Offices in New York and Chicago

Canada

Poster Advertising Service in Canada is the finest in the world.
It is the only medium that will give you color and picture
representation in Canada's best 300 cities and towns.

Poster Advertising Association
of Canada

•

The best
CANADIAN POSTERS
of the year

•

Canada

The Canadian, is a fertile market with a tremendous future.

Her Agriculture, mineral, forest, fisheries, etc. wealth is enormous, and only the surface has been touched.

For instance in that remarkable city of Montreal, the population in 1921 was 712,000, today it is over 1,262,000.

Similar growth throughout the Dominion means a bounteous harvest for Advertisers who establish themselves in the rapidly growing period.

Canada was one of the last countries to feel depression. She felt it less acutely and will be one of the first countries to recover.

Her tourist trade, principally from the U.S.A. is now over $300,000,000 annually and is steadily mounting. This is plus circulation for you.

Poster Advertising from one end of Canada to the other is the finest in the world.

28 Years Experience At Your Service

● The name is practically the entire composition in this poster with the product and the interesting goblin figure secondary. Only a well-known product such as Fry's could afford to give such prominence to the name rather than to the use of the cocoa.

The Canadian Poster Co., Ltd.
Agency or Selling Company

● A design within a design is this poster for Exide Batteries. Despite the fact that the outdoor scene covers most of the poster, the name Exide cannot be missed.

E. H. Dickinson Co., Ltd.
Agency or Selling Company

● Although this is distinctly a selling poster, Blends achieves an atmosphere of aristocracy. The elements are well tied together and the cellophane wrapper is both mentioned in the copy and shown with the package.

The E. L. Ruddy Co., Ltd.
Agency or Selling Company

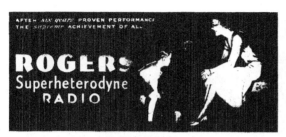

● Rogers Radio uses a human interest appeal in this attractive design. Although the attention of the figures is directed toward the radio, the cabinet itself is made a part of the composition and is not given undue prominence.

The E. L. Ruddy Co., Ltd.
Agency or Selling Company

● Varying geometric shapes add interest to this poster. Name, copy and illustration are all dependent upon this geometric arrangement, yet the pattern is carefully planned to be subordinated to the advertising message.

Gould-Baird Poster Co., Ltd.
Agency or Selling Company

● This poster is beautifully simple, with the three star symbol centered above the three slogans. Every unessential has been left out, with the result that the design is easily understood and as easily remembered.

The E. L. Ruddy Co., Ltd.
Agency or Selling Company

● The figure of the baby, although smaller than the elements on the other side of the poster, balances the design because of the greater interest that is centered on a human figure. The name, the product and the use of the product is featured in this composition.

The Howell Lithographic Co., Ltd.
Lithographers

The Canadian Poster Co., Ltd.
Agency or Selling Company

● The name, the package and the pleasure derived from the use of the cigarettes is effectively shown in this poster. The package is shown twice, once in natural proportion and once in giant size.

The Howell Lithographic Co., Ltd.
Lithographers

The Canadian Poster Co., Ltd.
Agency or Selling Company

● The story of flour in its progress from the wheat fields to the baked biscuits and cake is graphically shown in this interesting design. The figure of the man striding across the fields is balanced by the illustrations and lettering on the right side of the poster.

The Howell Lithographic Co., Ltd.
Lithographers

The Canadian Poster Co., Ltd.
Agency or Selling Company

● Here is an excellent tie-up of the syrup and its use. The effectiveness of the illustration of the man enjoying the taste of the cakes and syrup is increased by its giant size and the cutting off of part of the head.

The Howell Lithographic Co., Ltd.
Lithographers

The Canadian Poster Co., Ltd.
Agency or Selling Company

● The use of fresh milk in Cadbury's chocolate is well illustrated by the cup pouring the milk into the candy bar. The same device also serves to center attention upon the bar.

The Howell Lithographic Co., Ltd.
Lithographers

The Canadian Poster Co., Ltd.
Agency or Selling Company

● The lettering of the name in this poster is in a script unusual in posters yet one that is appropriate to an appeal to a feminine buyer. The oval which encloses the illustration makes a harmonious unit of a silhouette that might otherwise have given the design a spotty appearance.

The Howell Lithographic Co., Ltd.
Lithographers

The Canadian Poster Co., Ltd.
Agency or Selling Company

Advertising Outdoors

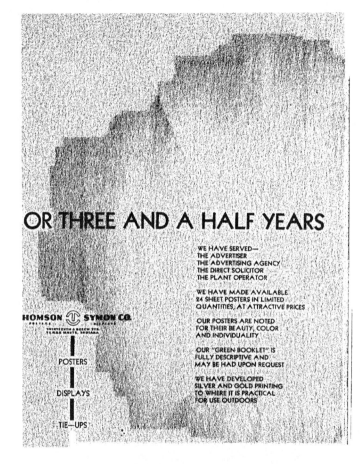

OR THREE AND A HALF YEARS

WE HAVE SERVED—
THE ADVERTISER
THE ADVERTISING AGENCY
THE DIRECT SOLICITOR
THE PLANT OPERATOR

WE HAVE MADE AVAILABLE
24 SHEET POSTERS IN LIMITED
QUANTITIES, AT ATTRACTIVE PRICES

THOMSON SYMON CO.
POSTAGE   PAID
THIRTEENTH & BEECH STS.
TERRE HAUTE, INDIANA.

OUR POSTERS ARE NOTED
FOR THEIR BEAUTY, COLOR
AND INDIVIDUALITY

OUR "GREEN BOOKLET" IS
FULLY DESCRIPTIVE AND
MAY BE HAD UPON REQUEST

POSTERS

WE HAVE DEVELOPED
SILVER AND GOLD PRINTING
TO WHERE IT IS PRACTICAL
FOR USE OUTDOORS

DISPLAYS

TIE—UPS

(SPACE FOR ADVERTISER'S COPY)

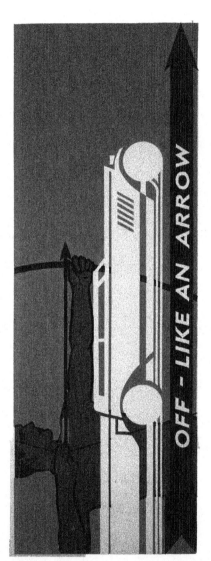

OFF - LIKE AN ARROW

The "O" and one "A" stand for Outdoor Advertising.
The second "A" stands for Agency.
Hence "O Double A" means

OUTDOOR ADVERTISING AGENCY

OUTDOOR ADVERTISING has always meant to us such a powerful and profitably productive force that we have had neither the time nor the inclination to adopt any other form of advertising.

As an Outdoor Advertising agency (ours is the only Outdoor organization using the word "Agency" in its corporate name), we have confined our efforts strictly to developing new business, not to pirating accounts satisfactorily handled by other organizations, which is the bane of the advertising business.

All accounts handled by our organization got their first foot-hold in Outdoor Advertising through us.

Poster plant owners know this, hence it is only logical for them to say—"Here's more new business from OAA; we must cooperate to the limit to make it pay." And they do cooperate to the limit.

Our dealings are direct with advertisers and poster plant owners. We have no side lines to divert us from giving our clients highly specialized personal, exclusive and efficient service.

We have no affiliations whatever with other Outdoor Advertising organizations or general advertising agencies and do not share our remuneration from plant owners with anyone.

A request from any national advertiser to discuss our service will be promptly heeded.

OUTDOOR ADVERTISING AGENCY OF AMERICA

INCORPORATED

NEW YORK	PITTSBURGH	CINCINNATI	CHICAGO
Graybar Bldg.	Bessemer Bldg.	Chamber of Commerce	6 N. Michigan Ave.

Not A Moving Picture

But a graphic record of achievement—of painstaking care and honest workmanship.

The illustrations opposite are only a few of the many posters entrusted to our organization for true, faithful reproduction.

The services of Edwards & Deutsch Lithographing Company, with its modern plant, employing the latest in equipment, and manned by only the most skilled workmen, have been chosen for many years by exacting advertisers who demand the best in lithographed reproduction.

It is with particular pride that we point to the large number of designs selected by the Jury of Awards of the Second Annual Exhibition of Original Paintings, appearing throughout this magazine, which were reproduced for the panels by our company.

Your poster, too, will receive the same careful attention given to these and many other 24-sheets made by us for leading national advertisers.

The pilot takes her into port

The captain has absolute authority over those aboard his ship, yet when the vessel comes to port he employs a pilot who has specialized knowledge and ability — the result of years of experience in navigating the harbor.

Nowadays, the advertising counselor is held responsible for the successful outcome of a campaign, but as the captain takes on a shore pilot, so the counselor calls upon the specialized knowledge possessed by men who have spent their entire business careers in one medium.

We offer the services of an outstanding group of merchandising and advertising specialists; art directors who know from long experience where to obtain the best outdoor art to fit specific problems; writers who possess the ability to condense a selling story into a powerful picture and five or six telling words; a Promotion Department which will furnish speakers to explain outdoor campaigns to dealers and salesmen, giving every assistance in merchandising outdoor advertising; and finally a research division which will quickly gather and interpret nationwide market data.

These are typical examples of our many-sided service.

OUTDOOR ADVERTISING IN THE 18th CENTURY
The inn signs of the England of 150 years ago were the ancestors of the painted bulletins of the modern hotel. Here is shown a famous and elaborate example of 18th century outdoor advertising.

This Issue   November 1931

A. W. Roe Discusses
ł. 2   Building Sales with Trade Characters   No. 11

ASSURANCE 1932

PRODUCTIVE merchandising-marketing aid to the national advertiser in 1932 is a responsibility. The combined experiences of our national organization, accumulated thru the years, is your assurance of our resources.

The organized experiences of proved sales stimulants that specifically parallel the individual marketing requirements each unit of the national market demands offers you the assurance that we can accept that responsibility.

OUR MAJOR MARKETS

Akron	Dayton	Memphis	Providence
Atlanta	Denver	Milwaukee	Richmond
Atlantic City	Duluth	Minneapolis	Rochester
Baltimore	Harrisburg	Nashville	St. Louis
Binghamton	Hartford	New Orleans	St. Paul
Birmingham	Indianapolis	New York City	South Bend
Brooklyn	Jacksonville	Oklahoma City	Utica
Buffalo	Kansas City, Kans.	Omaha	Washington, D. C.
Chicago	Kansas City, Mo.	Philadelphia	Youngstown
Davenport	Louisville	Pittsburgh	

Harrison and Loomis Streets   General Outdoor Advertising Co   Chicago, Ill.

Also Operating Plants in Over 1400 Other Cities and Towns

**at lowest cost per
thousand circulation**

Our organization

is continuously studying case-histories of Outdoor Advertising.

You are invited

to make full use of what we have learned about the application

of Outdoor Advertising in modern sales campaigns.

Foster and Kleiser

· C O M P A N Y ·

GENERAL OFFICE: SAN FRANCISCO
Operating plants in California
Washington, Oregon and Arizona
Offices in New York and Chicago

N A T I O N W I D E   O U T D O O R   A D V E R T I S I N G

" ON THE LEVEL "
Is Right

In Detroit there are no subways in which to ride, relax and read.

In Detroit there are no elevateds in which to ride, relax and read.

Into Detroit there are no suburban commuter express trains in which to ride, relax and read.

Traffic into Detroit is 100% SURFACE travel. A great major portion is via motor cars.

A poster showing of one hundred locations in Detroit will be encountered by the 2,000,000 people of this metropolitan area about 6,000,000 times daily. And to encounter a 24-sheet poster is to read it.

Outdoor Advertising in Detroit compels, tells and sells in the tempo of today's traffic.

WALKER & CO.
OUTDOOR ADVERTISING
Offices In
D E T R O I T
GRAND RAPIDS
SAGINAW
FLINT

Advertising Outdoors

A magazine devoted to the interests of the Outdoor Advertiser

VOL. 2, No. 11

CONTENTS for NOVEMBER 1931

Harold L. Eves
Editor

Ralph B. Patch, *Associate Editor*
James P. Dobyns, *Advertising Manager*

Eastern *Advertising Representatives:*
Walworth and Wormser,
420 Lexington Ave., New York City.

Western Advertising Representatives:
Dwight Early,
100 N. La Salle St., Chicago

ADVERTISING OUTDOORS is published on the 1st of every month by the Outdoor Advertising Association of America, Inc., 165 W. Wacker Drive, Chicago, Ill. Telephone Randolph 1692. Harold L. Eves, Editor and Manager.

Subscriptions for the United States, Cuba, Porto Rico, Hawaii and the Philippines, $3.00 a year in advance; Mexico and Canada, $3.25; for all other countries, $3.50. Thirty cents the copy. Make all checks, money orders, etc., payable to Outdoor Advertising Association of America, Inc.

Entered as second-class matter, March 21st, 1930, at the Post Office at Chicago, Ill., under the act of March 3, 1879, by Outdoor Advertising Association of America, Inc. Printed in U. S. A.

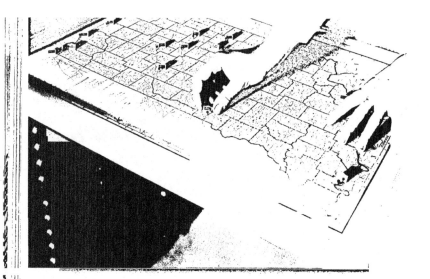

Planning retail and advertising distribution. Advertisers have found that distribution and advertising must be carefully planned to reach the largest number at the least possible cost. Many companies have learned to their sorrow that an unwarranted expansion of distribution will so increase sales costs as to reduce profits to the vanishing point. For this reason, extension of outlets and of advertising is undertaken only after a careful study of the accessibility and potentialities of the markets involved.

Map courtesy Rand McNally

WHICH FIRST—
DESIGN or IDEA?

Many an advertiser lays out a poster with more attention to the design than to the merchandising thought back of his advertising campaign.

A beautiful poster might represent perfect design yet not necessarily be good advertising. The attention should not be given to the design but rather to the idea you wish to impress on the people for whom the message is intended.

Think through to the purpose of the campaign. Tell a story that every individual of the crowd who will see your Outdoor Advertising will understand. Have a definite reason back of each poster.

If your Outdoor Advertising is going to produce results, you cannot start with the purchase of space and then develop a design. Rather you should start with your merchandising problem, develop a message that if understood (and one that can be understood) will help to solve your problem. After that think of the design. Then purchase the space needed to properly present that message to the people who are your potential customers.

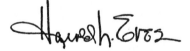

Building Sales with
TRADE CHARACTERS
by A. W. Roe

● How effective the employment of a trade character in the merchandising of a product can be is graphically revealed in the history of the beverage, Dr. Pepper. Although the formula for this beverage was invented more than forty years ago and the drink dispensed in a small way from that time until 1926, it was not until the latter year that the product received aggressive promotion. The present advertising and distribution campaign was launched in Dallas in 1926, since when the yearly increases in the consumption of the product have been so remarkable as to be spectacular.

"Dr. Pepper" is not, as those unacquainted with this genial trade character and its use might surmise, a member of the medical profession. Instead, it is a soft drink now obtainable generally at soda fountains and in bottles for home use over a wide expanse of the nation. Since advertising of the drink was begun upon a truly intensive scale five years ago, the smiling countenance of the round-faced, good-natured doctor has become well known to millions of people through his appearance in advertising of various sorts, outdoor posters and painted bulletins being conspicuous among these.

Figures are dull reading, but since they are illuminating, here are a few to show the rapid rise to fame of the Dr. Pepper product since trade-character advertising was begun. The company has reached more than 32,000,000 people with its advertising in 1931, and sales during the period since 1927 have shown a steady climb upward. In 1927 a sales increase of 132 per cent over 1926 was registered. An increase of 130 per cent for the year 1928 over the previous year was recorded. An increase of 111 per cent for 1929 over 1928 was gratifying to the company, dispensing the drink. Although 1930 was considered a poor year for soft drinks generally and other such products in the luxury class, Dr. Pepper achieved a 45 per cent gain over 1929, the year when business was at high tide. For the first six months of 1931, gross sales showed an increase of 23 per cent over the same period of 1930.

It has been the policy of the management to make wide use of outdoor advertising, particularly of posters, when introducing the product into a new locality, and to continue intensive use of the outdoor medium after the introduction. In 1927 distribution covered only four cities in Texas: Waco, Dallas, Houston and San Antonio. Since then the company has gradually extended distribution into several other southern states and lately has added St. Louis to its market. The constant use in this territory of outdoor posters, many of which show the genial doctor, has given to the drink, Dr. Pepper, an individuality that could have been achieved in no other way.

● Certainly, it is not the purpose of the present writer to claim too much for the invention and use of the quaint advertising character that dominates the Dr. Pepper advertising. Many other things have entered into this merchandising success, of course.

Doctor Pepper has proved to be an effective part of the advertising of that drink.

NOW–I offer you
Ma Brown
Fruit Butters

SQUIRE DINGEE CO., CHICAGO
also Pickles and Preserves

Excellence of a product is always to be considered, without which there can be no permanent success of any sort. But it is not claiming too much to say that the use of the trade character has made the Dr. Pepper advertising distinctive and given to modern life a personality as quaint in its way as though it had stepped out of one of Dicken's story books. The character, looking out at the world from a poster or counter card, first attracts attention, which passes over from the doctor himself to his product, with the resulting climb in sales volume that has just been detailed.

● Let us have another chapter that shows how the employment of an advertising character has helped to nationalize a household product. This time the authority is Arthur Siegel, vice-president of Outdoor Advertising Incorporated, addressing the Advertising Club of St. Louis, on the subject of the "Mammy" advertising character of Oxydol fame, as reported in a recent issue of Advertising Age.

"We wanted to sell with a smile," Mr. Siegel said— "stress the fact that wash day need not mean drudgery. So we decided to get a Mammy type that would give this impression. We advertised and at least twenty robust negro women appeared at Taylor's, the photographer, en masse. From this group we selected three, from whom the one best was picked."

Continuing, Mr. Siegel explained that the William Waltke Company, creator of Oxydol, sold to Proctor & Gamble in 1927 for a reported price of $11,000,000. Outdoor advertising, poster copy, was credited as the basis for the Waltke success, although Mr. Siegel said Oxydol was so good that it provided an ideal subject for advertising.

The advertising of this now widely known household product started in 1920, posters going hand in hand with distribution, according to Mr. Siegel. The initial plan was to send demonstrators from house to

Ma Brown is an excellent personification of a good cook and has been a prominent part of the advertising of the Squire Dingee Company.

house. After they had shown what Oxydol would do, they left a sample with which the housewife could do her own testing. Wagon salesmen were used to get the product into grocery stores. As soon as an Oxydol crew hit a town, posters appeared on the boards. With this plan, 85 per cent distribution was obtained, Mr. Siegel said.

The Mammy character gives to such a prosaic household task as dishwashing a luxury tilt. The illustration on the posters, changed monthly, always shows the smiling face of the good-natured servant as she goes about some such household task as dish or clothes washing. Mammy is always pleased with the efficiency of Oxydol, voicing her pleasure in such expressions as, "Yes, Ma'am—jes' a little," or "Dishes sparklin' in no time." One month she is shown, demonstrating to housewives what her product does in the kitchen and the next month how effectively it works in the laundry.

The Oxydol posters are noted for their simplicity, their directness and effectiveness. The fact that they have been used for so long a time and are appearing in dozens of cities in different parts of the nation and in Canada proclaims their utility as merchandising agents. It should be noted that this success has been built around the picturesque advertising character, Mammy. Without some such character the posters could never have made the emotional appeal to the hundreds of housewives. Mammy has given and still gives tired housewives actual demonstrations of what her product does to relieve them of drudgery.

● Turning to the chewing (Continued on page 40)

WEDNESDAY, November 11, 1931, that outstanding event in advertising history, which saw the new Special Representative Company of the industry endorsed with unparalleled enthusiasm and utmost confidence by leaders in the advertising world, will not be reported in this issue of Advertising Outdoors. It is being made the subject of a special book now being published by Outdoor Advertising Incorporated for distribution in the immediate future. We defer to them the privilege of recording that session which was devoted entirely to their purposes.

ADVERTISING'S RESPONSIBILITY
in Business Recovery

The first of a new series of messages on advertising
from the Advertising Federation of America

● Advertising is such an essential part of the creative end of business that it deserves a very special attention on the part of the general public. There are sure functions which advertising can perform in helping periods of recovery, and it is of the greatest importance that business executives make the best possible use of this force. Advertising can be one of the most effective allies in the task of lifting business from the doldrums.

Recognizing the importance of the task which confronts advertising today, the Advertising Federation of America has made a study of what advertising forces can do, and are doing, to help restore prosperity. Important facts in this study have been uncovered by the Federation's Bureau of Research and Education.

This is the first of a series of four messages to be made public by the Advertising Federation of America this autumn and winter. Last year, the Federation brought you six messages, delivered to hundreds of audiences by prominent business men. These messages dealt with the fundamental economic and social functions of advertising, and clarified many important facts.

Today, we are in a period when the welfare of business assumes first importance in almost every mind. Some people think that business, having just passed the crisis of a severe illness, now needs rest and quiet in order to convalesce. They would have us sit with folded hands until things get better.

That thought should be blasted out of existence. Inaction will not get us anywhere. We have had far too much talk about factors over which we, as individuals, have no control. It is high time that we pay intelligent attention to the *controllable* influences which cause people to buy commodities.

● The maladjustments which caused the depression have very largely been corrected and the fundamental factors are all set for another long swing into prosperity. All that we are waiting for is for something to happen. That something is increased buying on the part of the public. We can't *wait* for it—we must urge it.

Any movement toward recovery must be started by increased consumer purchases. People begin buying

Buying power has been diverted from the channels of trade and accumulated vastly.

more of the products of industry and more men have to go to work to manufacture them. Production is powerless to lead the way to prosperity; it must wait for the stimulation of consumer buying. All prosperity plans and panaceas depend upon this obvious truth.

● There is a tremendous volume of stored-up consumer buying power which has been diverted from the channels of trade. We can never regain prosperity until this is shaken loose from its many hiding places and led back into circulation through the buying of goods.

Let us face the truth. Our businesses may be subject to the big swings of external factors. We may be buffeted about by economic storms. But we are not helpless. We have tremendous motive power of our own, and something can be done about it. Intelligent, well-directed efforts to distribute our products are even more important in bad times than in good. We seem to have forgotten that there is such a thing as salesmanship. Surely, if ever, this is the time to use it.

● It is ridiculous to believe that two short years could have reduced this country from affluence to poverty. There is just as much or more wealth in this country today as there was in 1929. But it has stopped turning over so rapidly. The money is on the shelf. And the amount of business that purchasing power can accomplish depends upon its being taken down, dusted off, and put into circulation.

The economists have analyzed the situation from soup to nuts, but they don't know about salesmanship, the one big economic factor which is controlled by the business man himself.

There are millions of folk in this great American market whose incomes are beyond their immediate needs, and who have been saving so much during the past two years that the savings banks are embarrassed with an over-supply of money. Savings deposits in the past two years have been increasing more than fifty per cent faster than is normal, and today there is more than twenty-eight billions of idle purchasing power lying in the savings banks of the United States. Most of this vast sum is owned by private individuals who have been curtailing their purchases more than necessary, and who now need many kinds of goods. Why don't they buy them? They are waiting for someone to come along and *sell* them what they need.

Most of you have seen pictures of Mahatma Ghandi and in this respect we Americans seem to be copying the habits and customs of Hindustan. Hearing so frequently about famines in India and of the wretched condition of the people, we find it hard to believe that, so far as actual money is concerned, India is one of the richest countries on earth. But the money the Hindus get, small though their wages be, they either bury away in a safe hiding place or else use the coins for ornaments to adorn their persons. At any rate, they withdraw their money from circulation, and this means it has no purchasing power, and under those conditions the prosperity which depends on trade is not possible.

Now in this excess of patronage of the savings banks of America are we not, in a lesser degree, perhaps, duplicating the short-sightedness of the Hindus?

● It is this misguided thrift which presents to advertising at once the biggest opportunity and the biggest responsibility it has faced for years.

We know that advertising is the most potent mass salesman ever placed on the job, and there is no tool in the whole business kit better fitted to help start

a wide buying movement on the part of indifferent consumers.

But advertising is not an independent force; it cannot operate alone. Behind it is the product and its real value to the consumer. Fresh, stimulating advertising messages must contain interesting news about tempting, attractive goods. The seller must supply what the customer wants; not what he wanted last year or the year before, but what he wants now— in 1931. There is very little new sales appeal in old goods.

It has often been said that leaders for the next period of business prosperity are selected during the preceding depression. Right now, today, the roster is being prepared, listing business concerns which will be in the front rank during the next few years. Experience of the past has proved over and over again that' an aggressive policy of selling and advertising during a time like this gives the courageous company a head start and a lead, which is usually maintained. Money spent now for promotion will continue to bring in dividends during the years to come.

● But, remember that advertising is not merely a competitive weapon with which strong companies beat back the weak ones. The selling urge of good advertising not only influences people *where* to buy goods and *what* to buy, but also emphasizes the fact that they must buy. If all advertising and selling effort were suspended, few people would buy more than the sheer necessities of life. On the other hand, if all advertising were increased in quantity, and freshened with new appeals, people would buy more than they do at present. That is why advertising is so important to all of us, with its power to quicken all business.

For each merchant and manufacturer, the question of when to advertise and how much money to spend, must necessarily be an individual matter, for in business everything depends on profits. A great many well-known companies have demonstrated that there is profit in the fearless use of good advertising. In fact, current records prove that the individual firms which are making an exceptionally good showing this year are invariably those firms which have aggressively been *making* business instead of waiting for it to come.

The Research Bureau of the Federation has compiled figures on sales, earnings, and advertising of many companies. Among these are illustrations of companies which have helped themselves, and the entire business situation, by means of aggressive merchandising policies in which advertising has been an important factor.

Take the *mechanical refrigerator* business. The refrigerator industry as a whole has put on a tremendous sales drive, backed up by twenty million dollars

worth of advertising, by far the largest amount ever spent in this field.

What are the results? Sales of individual companies are breaking all records. Increases over last year range from 30 to 200 per cent and more. 1931 will be decidedly a record year in both sales and net profits. Advertising did it.

● Some of the companies reporting large increases are Westinghouse, Frigidaire, Kelvinator, General Electric, Copeland, Norge, Servel, and Majestic. In all these cases, advertising did it.

Luden's Cough Drops is an interesting example. This company has never faltered in its firmly established policy of expansion through consumer advertising. In good years and bad, it goes right on increasing its advertising each year, to the benefit of its stockholders and employees. This year is no exception and sales are greater than in any previous year. And advertising has done it.

The *William Wrigley* Company, as we all know, depends largely on advertising for its sales. 1930 was the biggest and most profitable year in the entire history of this company. The amount spent for national advertising was 30 per cent more than in the preceding year.

The *American Tobacco* Company has done an outstanding selling job during the last two years. In 1930, this company increased its advertising appropriation by 30 per cent, and what was the result? Net profits increased by more than 40 per cent.

The American Tobacco Company does not seem to believe in depressions, for in 1931 it has kept right on with its aggressive advertising campaign. Its indicated earnings for the year 1931 are 80 per cent greater than in the boom year 1929. Advertising has done it.

● The success of the American Tobacco Company has not been accomplished entirely at the expense of its competitors. The cigarette industry as a whole has continued to expand right through the worst year.

Returning veterans found that their places had been taken by machines.

The *Reynolds Tobacco* Company also increased its advertising in 1930 and 1931. Reynolds' profits in 1930 were greater than in 1929, and their records up to date indicate still greater earnings for 1931.

Liggett & Meyers is another tobacco company which profitably increased its advertising efforts in these relatively bad years. Its mid-year standing indicates that 1931 earnings will be slightly greater than for 1929.

These companies didn't just spend a lot of money for advertising. They used their heads, worked hard, and spent wisely. They succeeded in tapping some of the vast unused consumer purchasing power of today. They kept all their employees on the payroll, made more money for stockholders, and did their share toward general prosperity. And advertising did it.

● *Cluett-Peabody* has shown what can be done in the apparel industry. This company spent about 45 per cent more for advertising collars in 1930 than in 1929, and for 1931, the appropriation is still larger. The net profits in 1930 were about 20 per cent greater than in 1929 and July reports indicate still higher profits for 1931.

The officials of *Coca-Cola* have repeatedly pointed to advertising as the chief motive power in their consistent climb in sales and profits. Through good years and bad, Coca-Cola adheres to its policy of continuity in advertising. In 1930, its advertising was increased by 30 per cent. Despite the depression, net profits increased. For the first half of 1931, earnings were even greater than for the first half of 1930.

The story of *Life Savers* is inspiring. For five years, this company had sold candy fruit drops put up in ordinary form. In 1930, the mechanical problem was solved for producing these fruit drops with a hole in the center, like the other Life Saver products. Exactly the same ingredients but a different shape. This news made good advertising copy. But how about the depression? For this company there was no depression. A good advertising story sells goods at any time. So the advertising appropriation was increased by 15 per cent and the resulting sales were increased by 149 per cent.

That is good merchandising and profitable courage.

Lambert Pharmacal Company, makers of Listerine products, have an unbroken ten year record of consistently increasing the advertising appropriation each year. Sales and earnings have expended accordingly. 1930 and 1931 were no exceptions. Sales are now up to peak heights and profits are well maintained.

The *automobile industry* is in pretty bad shape, but there is at least one company which found a way to fight successfully against the tide. Any manufacturer with a real improvement in his product has the makings of a depression-beater. But the product must be *sold*, not merely offered to the public.

○ When *Studebaker* brought out free-wheeling, he surprised the trade with his heavy advertising. And it worked. More Studebaker cars have been sold so far in 1931 than in the corresponding period of 1930, and the net profits are also greater. That is saying a lot for anyone in the automobile business.

These are only a few instances of what I have in mind. There are many other well-known companies which have found that this is the profitable time to go after business with aggressive and believing vigor. For many of them, advertising has done and is doing the best job in years.

And while in this battle against the wrong and too-cautious thinking which has depressed us all, not only in our pocketbooks but in our spirits, every form of advertising media has been helpful, the job done by outdoor advertising has been outstanding.

No form of advertising has been so assailed and misrepresented. But it is coming into its own, not by blatant self-assertion or extravagant claims, but simply because outdoor advertising has done its job—and has always worked in cooperation with the other forms of media.

● Within the last few months the outdoor advertising associations, companies and plant owners have created a new organization known as Outdoor Advertising Incorporated, whose function it is to act as special representative, working through the established advertising agencies and independent solicitors.

We have already mentioned what Luden's, the manufacturers of cough drops, had been able to do by advertising. The Bureau's statistics do not mention the fact that Luden's began its successful career by its careful use of *outdoor* advertising. Luden's started in a two room plant in Reading, Pennsylvania. Today it has a factory covering eight acres, employing 1,000 workers and produces fifty-two tons of Luden's Cough Drops daily. Now let us hear what President Dietrich of Luden's has to say in "Printers' Ink." He says:

"The first advertising campaign on cough drops was an amateur tacking-up of yellow cards—Luden's had adopted a yellow package and a yellow cough drop—on telephone poles, fences, sheds, and any and all blank outdoor space in and around Reading, Pennsylvania. Then came window displays. . . . Next we used one-sheet posters. . . . Then followed outdoor advertising in the states of New York and Pennsylvania. . . . Based on what we believe to be sound economic reasoning and with the confidence of fifty years of experience in business cycles, our board of directors has just approved the largest advertising campaign in our history. We expect to increase our sales over last year and increase our profits by doing so."

● Much of the antagonism and the propaganda against outdoor advertising has emanated from garden clubs and similar asso- (Continued on page 31)

Bank deposits have increased fifty per cent faster than normal.

Poster Campaign
FORCES MEAT INSPECTION
by Wilma McKenzie

● Publicity has wrought many miracles, made rapid changes and reversed conditions by means of its powerful influence. One of the most recently noted of its works is the shift of the St. Louis meat markets from uninspected meats to the inspected product, by means of an intensive six-months publicity campaign.

Conditions in the Meat Packing Industry in St. Louis, prior to the campaign, were not according to the satisfaction of the better class of packers, especially to those packers who were operating under Government inspection rules. Contrary to the general opinion existing among the buying public that all meats were government inspected, because the buying public believed that this was a government rule which applied to all packing houses, less than a dozen of the total number of plants in the St. Louis area had the federal inspection. The Government has control only of those packing houses doing interstate business, hence there was an aggressive group of independent packers operating in St. Louis who were under no inspection rules of any sort and were selling inferior grades of meat, marketing them solely from the price angle. Not being burdened with the inspection charge, they were able to offer their products at lower prices.

A group of packers assembled and decided something should be done in the way of an educational campaign whereby the public would be informed of the inferiority of the grade of products being dispensed by the Independents. The result was this six-months publicity campaign was started to educate the public regarding the benefits of government inspected standards.

The campaign, started in 1930, was designed to show the urgent necessity for the housewife to choose the inspected meat in place of any other that she had been accustomed to purchasing. The case was put before the public by means of posters, car cards, newspaper display, etc.

● An attractive, forceful poster bearing the exclamatory message: "Demand U. S. Government Inspected Meats—Half the Meat in Greater St. Louis is Non-Inspected," was run through the month of January and resulted in a tremendous amount of interest being aroused. Ladies' Civic Groups enlisted their co-operation, and various Health organizations and other groups within the city manifested an active interest in the campaign. The assistance of these groups did much to further (Continued on page 41)

This design called attention to the improvement in meat standards brought about by the campaign.

Outdoor Advertising Builds Potato Chip Sales

by Augusta Leinard

● To say that women are accomplishing big things in commercial fields today is to make a statement that has grown trite. But when you tell of a woman who has made herself an outstanding industrial figure in a state like California through the manufacture of one product—potato chips—then you have skirted the edge of the unusual.

The story of Laura Scudder is familiar to most people in Southern California where she entered the potato chip business six years ago. Under the brand name of BLUEBIRD in Southern California and MAYFLOWER in Northern California, Laura Scudder's potato chips easily dominate the market and it is estimated that she sells over 50 per cent of the chips sold in California.

Arthur Brisbane wrote of her in his widely read column, *Today*, while in Los Angeles sometime ago:
Feminine success here is not reserved to 18-year-old Hollywood ladies with golden hair and very large blue eyes. For instance, Mrs. Laura Scudder will interest you if you are a lady about forty. Ill health compelled her husband to drop his law practice and his doctor said he must be interested in something. Mrs. Scudder went into business manufacturing and selling potato chips. Now she employs forty trucks to deliver the chips and makes as much money as one of the trucks could haul.

● Confronted with the necessity of taking care of a sick husband and several children, Mrs. Scudder first studied law and was duly admitted to the bar, but commercial activities interested her more so she put up a factory on a lot she owned in Los Angeles.

Then, being a graduate nurse and dietician, she decided to put out a food product and saw room on the market for a potato chip with personality.

She produced it and made good, as Mr. Brisbane indicated. Mrs. Scudder has brought modern manufacturing methods into the potato chip business. She pioneered much of the machinery being used in her two large plants, one located in Oakland and one in Los Angeles, and some of it she herself originated. The active pilot at the helm of her business she gives the final word of decision on any matter of real importance.

● The extensive advertising on Laura Scudder Potato Chips, while handled through an advertising agency, is under her direct supervision. She is perhaps the only manufacturer in this line to advertise constantly and consistently and the only one to stick strictly to a program of quality outdoor advertising. She is a strong advocate of this medium and a heavy advertiser. In fact, 80 per cent of her advertising is in the form of bulletins, posters, and painted walls.

Starting with highway bulletins located in the principal traveling arteries of Southern California she soon recognized the power to create appetite appeal that belongs to artistic pictorial out-of-doors copy. Hand painted posters were quickly added and then walls.

Walls appealed to Mrs. Scudder so strongly that she kept on increasing the number and now has something like 100 of these giving out a continuous impression of Laura Scudder's Potato Chips throughout California. The choicest (Continued on page 41)

This attractive bulletin is one of those which are building sales for Laura Scudder's Potato Chips.

Moll Made New York Manager of Gardner

William J. Moll, Vice-President and Director of Service of the Gardner Advertising Company New York Office, has been appointed Manager of the New York Office. He also remains a Vice-President, and will have full responsibility for all of the activities of the Gardner New York Office.

STATEMENT OF THE OWNERSHIP, MANAGEMENT, CIRCULATION, ETC., REQUIRED BY THE ACT OF CONGRESS OF AUGUST 24, 1912. Of ADVERTISING OUTDOORS published monthly at Chicago, Illinois, for October 1, 1931.
State of Illinois }
County of Cook } ss.

Before me a Notary Public in and for the State and county aforesaid, personally appeared Harold L. Eves, who, having been duly sworn according to law, deposes and says that he is the Editor of the ADVERTISING OUTDOORS and that the following is, to the best of his knowledge and belief, a true statement of the ownership, management (and if a daily paper, the circulation), etc., of the aforesaid publication for the date shown in the above caption, required by the Act of August 24, 1912 embodied in section 411, Postal Laws and Regulations printed on the reverse of this form, to wit:

1. That the name's and addresses of the publisher, editor, managing editor, and business managers are: Publisher, Outdoor Adv. Ass'n of America, Inc., 165 W. Wacker Dr., Chicago, Ill.; Editor, Harold L. Eves, 165 W. Wacker Dr., Chicago, Ill.; Managing Editor, Harold L. Eves, 165 W. Wacker Dr., Chicago, Ill.; Business Manager, Harold L. Eves, 165 W. Wacker Dr., Chicago, Ill.

2. That the owner is: (If owned by a corporation, its name and address must be stated and also immediately thereunder the names and addresses of stockholders owning or holding one per cent or more of total amount of stock. If not owned by a corporation, the names and addresses of the individual owners must be given. If owned by a firm, company, or other unincorporated concern, its name and address, as well as those of each individual member must be given.) Outdoor Adv. Ass'n of America, incorporated under laws of Ill., not for profit. Geo. W. Kleiser, Pres., 1675 Eddy Street, San Francisco, Calif.; Joseph Harris, Sec'y, 165 W. Wacker Drive, Chicago, Illinois; O. S. Hathaway, Treasurer, 28 James Street, Middletown, N. Y.

3. That the known bondholders, mortgagees, and other security holders owning or holding 1 per cent or more of total amount of bonds, mortgages, or other securities are: (If there are none, so state.) None.

4. That the two paragraphs next above, giving the names of the owners, stockholders, and security holders, if any, contain not only the list of stockholders and security holders as they appear upon the books of the company but also, in cases where the stockholder or security holder appears upon the books of the company as trustee or in any other fiduciary relation, the name of the person or corporation for whom such trustee is acting, is given; also that the said two paragraphs contain statements embracing affiant's full knowledge and belief as to the circumstances and conditions under which stockholders and security holders who do not appear upon the books of the company as trustees, hold stock and securities in a capacity other than that of a bona fide owner; and this affiant has no reason to believe that any other person, association, or corporation has any interest direct or indirect in the said stock, bonds, or other securities than as so stated by him.

5. That the average number of copies of each issue of this publication sold or distributed, through the mails or otherwise, to paid subscribers during the six months preceding the date shown above is................. (This information is required from daily publications only.)

HAROLD L. EVES,
Editor.

Sworn to and subscribed before me this 26th day of September, 1931.
[SEAL]   ESTHER O. BRECHEISEN,
Notary
(My commission expires January 20, 1934.)

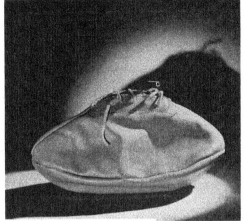

WE Sell Our Dealers
On Outdoor Advertising

by *Marshall B. Cutler*
Advertising Manager J. P. Smith Shoe Co.

We all know that to sell something we must first make somebody *want* it. Nothing in the world can find a profitable market unless desire is inspired to the extent that individuals or organizations believe that they will receive more *from* something than is spent for it.

● We have always asked our distributors to make an investment in the advertising we prepare for them. As a result, we have produced less dealer advertising than some others; but as we measure our efficiency by dealer advertising actually used, not by the volume produced, we are reasonably happy.

Making the local dealer want the advertising you have for him is quite a tough job. Generally he is very definitely opposed to spending a nickel for your local campaigns. His attitude (a very natural one) is that this advertising is for your goods—therefore why should he pay? He doesn't consider that once he buys a line of merchandise it belongs to him and that his only chance of making a profit is to sell it as quickly and neatly as possible.

We have succeeded in changing this unsound state of mind quite completely. Many of our "A" accounts are steady advertisers of our product. They use our material, pay a share of its cost and seem quite satisfied. We have done better than average in the attainment of a real partnership between our dealers and ourselves simply because we are forever selling the soundness of sustained, expertly developed advertising—consistently used. Every opportunity to put before our dealers a reason for wanting our advertising is taken advantage of. We never let a distributor forget about our helps. We never let him sidetrack the fact that he needs what we have for him.

● We frankly admit that our 24-Sheet Posters are not the easiest advertising to sell the average dealer. Probably this is due to the fact that we ask our dealers to pay the entire cost of the local showing if we furnish the Posters, imprinted, without charge. But whatever the reason, the problem was difficult, so we determined to put greater effort into its solution.

So we started a number of years ago to compile a special series of Poster advertising letters. Whenever we corresponded with a dealer on Poster adver-

tising and were successful in winning his support for this important advertising, we added the action getting letter to our special group. The compilation of letters has increased season by season in size and scope—and today we prize what we believe is one of the most effective series of Poster merchandising letters in existence.

Say, for instance, that a requisition for advertising comes to us from a salesman. This requisition states that the dealer is interested in Smith Smart Shoe or Reed Posters; but that the order couldn't be obtained. The Advertising Department immediately gets busy—first with this letter:

How often do you walk into the corner cigar store, throw down a quarter and receive in return a couple of cigars or some cigarettes? And how often does the soft drink dispensary collect a twenty-five cent piece (or the best part of it) from you for a more or less fancy thirst eradicator?

● We're not trying to argue you into giving up ice-cream or tobacco. We use both ourselves and find them good. But the point we want to make is this: You never notice these quarters you spend daily for things that DON'T HELP YOUR BUSINESS; so are a few quarters a day spent for *EXTRA SALES* and *EXTRA GOOD-WILL* an extravagance?

We think you'll say, "No! If we can sell more shoes and make ourselves better liked generally with such an insignificant investment we're emphatically for it."

Then remember that 24-Sheet Posters if contracted for through us, cost you only 25c a day for each location—frequently even less.

These colorful, giant displays have demonstrated their business ability. The designs we supply *free* cost us thousands of dollars to produce. They make a vivid impression. And their regular appearance locally, marks *you* as wide-awake, reliable merchandisers—the type people like to patronize.

Twenty-five cents per board per day for Posters stands unequaled as a *BUSINESS* investment. If you ever spend ice-cream and tobacco quarters, you should be only too willing to test the power of outdoor advertising.

● All that is required from you for the test is the enclosed order card properly filled out and signed. We'll reserve locations, imprint the Posters for you, take care of shipping, posting and any necessary replacements *free*. You pay for the locations. The cost of displays for your town is quoted on the card. It figures down to a unit cost of 25c a day—or less. Use the card *now*.

Sincerely yours,
J. P. SMITH SHOE COMPANY
Advertising Manager

With this letter we enclose color miniatures of our current Poster designs and a special order card giving the cost of all local showings available. A careful check of the actual Poster orders received from dealers in response to this letter (which we have used since November, 1925) shows us that it continues to be worth its salt.

And here's another successful Poster merchandising letter used during July and August:

After summer—what?

After two months of sales and cut prices, (and cut profits!) we're all quite ready to open our arms to steady, productive fall business.

● Fall isn't far off and it behooves us to start planning to*day* (even if we're perspiring a little) on how to gain a heart-warming, fall volume early and keep it late.

One of the attractive posters which the J. P. Smith Shoe Company merchandises to its dealers.

You know—so do we—that men should seek you first, when a crispness in the air and a red tinge on the leaves sharply remind us of the need for new shoes.

But Mr. Jones and Mr. Carey and Mr. Clement won't seek you unless you invite them to in no uncertain terms.

So we must put on a duet to tell them about Smith Smart Shoes.

The opening chorus is most important. If it's well directed, harmonious, and lively it will win you a receptive audience and substantial box-office receipts.

Now the question is—How can you open up most effectively—how can you make an unforgettable first impression this season and do it most economically?

● And the answer is—Smith Smart Shoe 24-Sheet Posters.

For 25c (or less) a day a board you can dominate your local market, not only for the thirty or sixty days of the display, but for days afterward. Get in line with this advertising now. Let us reserve September or October showings far enough in advance to assure you the best locations and service.

The order card enclosed gives you full information on a local display of Posters. And the color reproductions give you an idea of the type of outdoor advertising used for Smith Smart Shoes.

Talk to Mr. Publik so he will hear and heed. Use the resources we offer you to put over Smith Smart Shoes decisively.

Remember all you pay under our Poster plan is the cost of locations as given on the card. Posters, imprinting, service (Continued on page 36)

NEWS OF
THE OUTDOOR INDUSTRY

A. F. A. Appoints Research Advisory Committee

The Advertising Federation of America today announced the appointment of its Research Advisory Committee, composed of fourteen members. The appointments were made public by Gilbert T. Hodges, president of the Federation.

Members of the committee are: Dr. Julius Klein, Assistant Secretary, United States Department of Commerce; O. C. Harn, managing director of the Audit Bureau of Circulations; John Benson, president of the American Association of Advertising Agencies; Francis H. Sisson, vice-president of the Guaranty Trust Company; Lee H. Bristol, vice-president of Bristol-Myers Company, and president of the Association of National Advertisers; Samuel R. McKelvie, publisher of the Nebraska Farmer; Dr. Virgil Jordan, economist of the McGraw-Hill Publishing Company; Professor E. K. Strong, Jr., of Stanford University; K. W. Jappe, president of Brookmire Economic Service; Laurence H. Sloan, vice-president of Standard Statistics Company; George W. Coleman, president of Babson Institute; Paul T. Cherington, distribution consultant of New York; L. D. H. Weld, director of research of McCann-Erickson, Inc.; and Guy C. Smith, advertising manager of Libby, McNeill & Libby.

The newly created committee will co-operate with the Bureau of Research and Education of the Advertising Federation, headed by Alfred T. Falk, in conducting studies of the economic values of advertising and its functions in industrial and social progress.

The Bureau has just completed a study of advertising as related to the problems of business recovery and upon it has based the first of a new series of addresses now being presented to business executives throughout the United States under Federation sponsorship.

The current message cites the experiences of ninety-seven large companies during the present period of low business activity and shows how the intelligent use of advertising has safeguarded sales volume and profits during the most trying times. The Bureau's survey also analyzes the relation of newspaper advertising lineage to the course of business in sixty-eight individual cities, indicating that a heavy volume of local advertising has hastened business revival in many communities.

Foster and Kleiser Drops Subletting Service

"Now that Outdoor Advertising Incorporated and the National Outdoor Advertising Bureau are fully in operation in this territory, Foster and Kleiser Company will discontinue the subletting of outdoor advertising contracts to plant owners throughout the country, in which connection we have served advertisers and agencies in the past," says a notice to Advertising Agencies released by Foster and Kleiser Company.

"In saying this we are confident that the interests of the advertiser and his advertising agency or solicitor will be better served, with the broader, more complete and more specialized facilities that will be available in the future through Outdoor Advertising Incorporated and the Bureau.

"Inasmuch as Outdoor Advertising Incorporated will devote its attention to accounts which are national or coastwide in character, Foster and Kleiser Company will devote its sales effort to the development of the use of outdoor advertising by local advertisers.

"An organization of Account Executives, specializing in outdoor advertising, will be maintained by Foster and Kleiser in the interest of advertisers and agencies. Copy, Art and Merchandising Departments will be maintained and made available to advertisers, agencies and solicitors."

■ ■ ■

Dreyfuss To Lecture on Advertising

Leonard Dreyfuss, vice-president of the Outdoor Advertising Association of America, Inc., and president of the United Advertising Corporation, has been selected to direct a course in advertising at the Seth Boyden School of Business in Newark. He will be assisted by Clarence B. Lovell, director of publicity of the above agency. The course will cover a period of two hours a week for fifteen weeks.

■ ■ ■

Correction

In the October issue of Advertising Outdoors, the Annual Design Number, the Stetson Hat poster on page thirty-four should have been credited to the Erie Lithographing and Printing Company as lithographers.

PRESTIGE ADVERTISING
Combats Price Cutting
by W. R. Hoskins
Assistant General Sales Manager, Walker and Company

● The present decline in business activity has resulted in a hectic scramble for the trade that remains to be gotten. A very great percentage of the efforts that are being made, especially in the case of the local merchant, are made on the basis of price. Some reduction in the cost of commodities was to be expected but, in many cases, merchants have offered goods or services at prices which are below the cost of the article offered. Such a situation has worked a real hardship upon others in that particular line of business. The merchant who makes the sale is unable to make a reasonable profit, while other merchants find that their trade is being taken away at a price which they cannot meet and survive. In the long run, of course, the situation will solve itself. No business can .operate at a loss and continue to exist. Nevertheless, there is real danger that the price cutter will not only ruin himself but will seriously injure the trade of reputable firms which are given a choice of losing their trade or of meeting ruinous prices and losing money on their sales.

● Many business men have preferred to retain their clients and have reduced prices to meet this cutthroat competition. Others, all too few, have changed their appeal to one of quality rather than of cost and have thus taken themselves out of competition with the price cutters. The success of the latter move, naturally, depends upon the conviction which the new appeal carries.

The Paris Cleaners and Dyers, in Detroit, have through the use of a quality appeal, done much to overcome the price cutting menace. Many small and unknown organizations have recently come into the field and created a serious competitive situation which, combined with the prevailing business conditions, has caused a good deal of price cutting and special offers on the part of most cleaners and dyers.

The prices quoted by the Paris Cleaners & Dyers were fair and just for the type of work they were doing, and therefore could not be materially reduced to meet competition if this same standard of workmanship was to prevail.

● This was proved conclusively in a recent attempt to meet prevailing conditions when special prices were announced by Mr. Frain, president of the company, for the early Fall season. In order to maintain the enviable reputation built up for the Paris Cleaners & Dyers organization the policy of only the best workmanship was adhered to with the result that at lower prices it ultimately cost money to obtain such business.

Appreciating these circumstances, copy and plans calling for an altogether different approach to his logical market were prepared.

The sketch capitalized upon a caption the company had just begun to use which had a definite relation to the name of the concern. The slogan "Get that Paris Touch of Smartness" was used with the

The name of the firm has been cleverly incorporated in the advertising appeal of this effective bulletin.

name Paris Cleaners & Dyers, plus a telephone number which had real sales value because of its simplicity and developed a pictorial design which tied in perfectly with this text.

● Realizing of course that the advertising was to be designed primarily for women, who place a large percentage of the orders for pressing, cleaning and dyeing, the work was designed with a definite style note, which after all was the most logical thing to do particularly in view of the fact that the name and the one copy line were both based upon the dominant thought "Paris" and "Smartness."

Further to enhance the value of the bulletin, Walker & Co. resorted to a special type of construction wherein the picture copy was painted on a glass panel measuring approximately 10 feet square, set flush with the face of the bulletin. The picture used had a definite relationship to the dominant thought in the copy because we were sure a panoramic scene of Paris, handled as it might appear from a balcony with the Eiffel Tower in the background serving as unmistakable identification, would immediately be associated with the idea of style and smartness.

The pictorial, which is painted in oils on glass, while a thing of beauty in the daytime is far more attractive at night. The natural colors with their stippled effects, illuminated from the rear by 3,200 watts, are very attractive as a flasher with a dimming action carries the scene from twilight to night. Even the lights on the balconies and the beacon on top of the Eiffel Tower, as well as the street lights and those in the nearby buildings, appear to be burning. It is easy for one to let his imagination run riot as he watches the display in action.

That these special features on the bulletin materially increased its attention value was strikingly proved the first night it was put in service. From actual observation forty-six automobiles stopped during the first hour to permit people to study the display. All pedestrians stopped to look at it and many left the sidewalk to scrutinize it carefully.

To illustrate further the style theme, three figures dressed in the latest Parisian fashion were placed immediately adjoining the glass panel where they appeared to be viewing the sky line of Paris from a balcony.

The figures were made in sheet metal cutouts and set off the face of the bulletin about six or eight inches, providing to some degree a third dimension.

● Instead of painting the background of the bulletin in the usual manner, a high lustre black lacquer was used which served as an excellent contrast to the pictorial, especially the name and telephone number which are carried out in raised chrome plate letters, sandblasted at the edges to improve the readability under direct illumination.

The combined effect of the entire bulletin is one which is decidedly high class, fulfilling a need for quality appeal in the Paris Cleaners & Dyers advertising. In other words, instead of attempting to compete on a price basis with small and less reliable concerns, the Paris Cleaners & Dyers are now presenting their story in an entirely different manner to the people who are logically their best prospects—those who are willing to pay a little more for reliable and efficient service and workmanship. It is surprising, as a matter of fact, how great a percentage of the entire market is willing to do that.

The display is placed on Woodward Avenue at a point of heavy circulation and in a good residential district in the north central part of the city. Woodward Avenue is Michigan's first street from a circulation standpoint.

Real care was exercised in the selection of the site for this display because the appropriation did not permit the use of many such bulletins. The message had to be placed at a point where people all over the city could see it frequently.

● How well this has been accomplished is indicated by the frequency that Paris customers have told the drivers of their having seen the display. Many of these customers who have been impressed by the attractiveness of the bulletin and have voluntarily told the drivers so, live as far as twenty miles from the display.

Since the completion of this bulletin an appreciable number of new accounts have been gained by the Paris organization. Inasmuch as many of these new customers live on streets adjacent to Woodward Avenue, their natural route of travel takes them past this bulletin frequently. Consequently, it is reasonable to believe that the painted bulletin advertising is accomplishing good results.

This is a striking example of how carefully planned advertising of good-will or reputation building character can solve many of the perplexing competitive problems which are becoming increasingly prevalent in many classifications of business today.

■   ■   ■

Fish Dealers Begin Cooperative Campaign

For the first time in history, a group of general wholesalers of fresh fish have banded together in a cooperative advertising campaign to educate the public to the advantages of consuming more of their product.

The Leon Livingston Advertising Agency, San Francisco, with which was recently merged the Harry Bercovich Agency, has been appointed to direct the campaign. Outdoor, newspapers, street car cards, radio, and general merchandising tieups will be utilized in the campaign it was announced.

Wide World Photo

The over-emphasis of football has been very efficiently viewed with alarm by many of the faculties of our institutions of learning; the fact remains, however, that the colleges have held their patronage to a surprising extent during the past few years while the professional game has steadily grown in popularity. Outstanding games, such as that between Northwestern and Notre Dame at Soldiers' Field, Chicago, have drawn crowds of 100,000 or more people.

Such attendance is additional evidence of the strong hold that sports and the out-of-doors in general has upon the American public. The advertiser, by reaching this public when it is out-of-doors in a receptive mood is able to drive home, constantly, his advertising message.

OUTDOOR IMPRESSIONS

Wide World Photo

A corn husking or "shucking" contest as they say in the corn belt, is only a dramatic episode in the hours of patient toil it takes to produce the crop. And it is only through the medium of such advertising as that displayed upon the panel below that that effort is adequately rewarded; for, without the stimulating influence of advertising upon consumption, the farmer would find his market far more circumscribed than it is today.

OUTDOOR IMPRESSIONS

"Excelente!"

Butter-Nut
"The Coffee
Delicious"

OUTDOOR IMPRESSIONS

Artist Studley Burroughs and the model who posed for Butternut Coffee's "Excelente!" poster reproduced above. An interesting sidelight upon the painting of a design such as this lies in the fact that the vivacious, dark haired and dark eyed senorita is, in real life, named—Kathleen Burke.

A real civic event was the unveiling of this "Fresh Fish"
bulletin in San Francisco recently. Actual construction of the panel was carried on behind a canvas covering. At the ceremony which revealed the design
to the crowd of more than 1500, A. J. Cleary, executive
secretary to Mayor Rossi, of San Francisco, read a
proclamation from California's governor, James Rolph,
Jr., and then pulled the silken cord which hid the panel.
San Francisco's five wholesalers of fresh fish, the Western California Fish Company, Standard Fisheries,
San Francisco Fish Co., A. Paladini, Inc., and F. E.
Booth are behind the advertising campaign of which
this bulletin is a part.

The Leon Livingston Advertising Agency, of San Francisco, is handling the account.

OUTDOOR IMPRESSIONS

REGULATIONS HANDICAP
Europe's Advertising
by Charles J. Sousek
Prague, Czechoslavakia

● Since the World War, the trend of outdoor advertising in Europe has been consistently upward. Much of the progress that has been shown can be directly traced to the influence of organized American outdoor advertising. Of course, there are still to be seen here and there the ugly structures erected at random which disappeared from the organized industry in America a decade ago, but responsible advertising firms realize that these structures are not up-to-date or efficient and their replacement is a question of time and money. The development of the medium in England has followed that of the United States very closely and France, Belgium, Holland and Germany are rapidly following suit. In these countries the sizes of the posters have been standardized and fairly uniform sales procedures introduced. In other European countries the progress is not so evident but the trend is unquestionably toward standardization.

In striking contrast with conditions in Europe, American outdoor advertising companies have a comparatively free hand in which the people speak one language and have the same habits and mental attitudes. Space is, in most cases, plentiful both in metropolitan areas and on the highways and it is possible to landscape the land about the panels. There is no regulation as to the use of color in the designs and the advertisements possess the maximum of attention value. The responsible operators are organized and governed by uniform rules and the service, posters, sizes are standardized and uniform service developed.

● On the other hand in Europe the population is approximately three times denser than in America; therefore public regulations are sometimes quite necessary; there are twenty-three languages spoken in twenty-six countries; every piece of land is cultivated and the transportation thoroughfares are much narrower having been constructed in old times; the landscaping cannot be used sufficiently on account of lack of space and money; it is often impossible, due to strong nationalistic feeling, to make use of very effec-

This painted wall for Mazda Lamps in Prague is painted in brilliant yellow and orange.

tive color combinations, because of the resemblance these combinations bear to the flags of various countries; moreover, the industry is not organized into one effective body, the rules of business conduct varying in different countries.

● As told above outdoor advertising of any kind in Europe is subject to public regulations; that means that under different laws, especially for protection of historical parts of a city, of old buildings or against misuse of public space, the authorities issue rulings providing for a procedure to be followed when erecting an outdoor sign. Supposing you want to erect an electrically illuminated firm panel extending out into the street; then you must draw up plans, make blue-prints and attach them to your application which you present to the City Hall. There is a special advertising commission which will study your application and decide on it by a single vote. If the permission is granted you must pay a fee and in certain towns you will have to pay annual tax based on size of your sign. The permission generally contains a clause that the commission reserves the right to revoke it after a specified time (5 or more years). If the permission is refused you have to make an appeal to the City Council and wait patiently half a year before you get final decision.

● The operation of an outdoor advertising plant is not always in private hands as in America. It was soon found by cities and towns that the operation of a municipally owned plant is a means of good financial revenues and therefore the municipality often prohibits the construction of any poster-panels within the city limits without the consent of the municipal plant. Practically it means that nobody can place a poster but through this municipal company and it comes to a real conflict when an owner of a building wants to place a painted sign on his house and is not allowed to do so.

It is a matter of fact that the major part of complaints originate from the service rendered by the municipally owned plant which practically has a monopoly in the locality. The outdoor advertiser is sometimes at a loss to discover the fate of his posters. He ordered for instance 50 posters to be placed and delivered therefore 55 pieces (5 remain as a reserve) to the municipal company and is assured of good service. But seldom is he given a map showing where his posters were placed; therefore he must take a car and hunt them all over the city. It is not unusual that the check-up will disclose the fact that only 42 or 45 posters were placed and the others were stored in the company's store-room.

Only comparatively few big companies in Europe have a plan providing for a definite number of poster-panels to be maintained in a city which would enable them to make advance arrangements with customers and keep their word. Personally I don't know about any outdoor advertising firm in Europe which has based the value of the locations of posters on any scientifically developed point, or on actual traffic counts as the Outdoor Advertising Association of America is doing now

Because of the high esthetic sentiment and refined culture of the people in Europe, it would be expected that their reaction to outdoor signs, especially those situated in vicinity of natural, architectural or other artistic beauties, will be very critical, even antagonistic. Yet in view of the public regulations, only expert bodies of conservatively minded citizens take an active interest in outdoor advertising signs and then of course not only posters, but also electric displays and all other features which are designed to attract the attention of human eye.

● While in America I gained an impression that in the United States are many different associations whose chief business seems to be to oppose outdoor advertising under the cover of protection of public interest or natural scenery. And yet there is a wide difference between organized and "wild" outdoor advertising, which is immediately noticed especially by traveling foreigners. The beautiful poster-panels of organized outdoor advertising companies are very often a benefit and no nuisance to the traveling public. I recall very vividly by first out-of-train impression of those ugly junk cemeteries along both sides of the Pennsylvania Railroad track when leaving Hudson tunnels on my way from New York to Philadelphia, where the eye with a satisfaction comes to a rest on those much disputed outdoor signs.

It is evident that the problem is split up into two groups, i. e. organized outdoor advertising and "wild" outdoor advertising; the public is interested in both groups. To protect the interest of both sides it is necessary to regulate the outdoor advertising business; but here is the difference. The organized outdoor operators can get easily together with the civic organizations and stipulate some general rules which will be willingly observed; but the "wild" outdoor advertisers are so numerous, without organization or any responsibility, that it is practically impossible to come to any agreement with them. Therefore it seems very reasonable to expect that all efforts to secure a public regulation of outdoor advertising by state or municipal laws, should direct their attention to unorganized "wild" advertising only.

● It is my firm opinion that a general regulation of outdoor advertising in the United States would be quite superfluous and necessarily one-sided; it would not be sufficient to reach its object in "wild" advertising and it would impose rules on organized advertising without any contra-value. From my experience in Europe, where almost everything is being solved by laws, I can say, that any one-sided law arouses dissentment and finally leads to corruption and nonobservance.

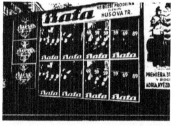

Standard posters of the shoe manufacturer Bata in Prague; on the left is a competitor, Busi, Ltd., and on the right a movie poster.

IMPROVED DESIGN
Features Movie Posters
by Alexander Stoddart

Unusual as it seems, motion pictures, which have at their command the appeal of adventure, thrills, and romance, have not taken as full advantage of these factors in their advertising as have advertisers in other fields.

Making motion pictures more effective from a box office point of view is a subject that of late has been given more attention by the motion picture producers and their advertising managers.

● A year ago Mr. Walter Wanger, at that time General Manager of Paramount-Publix Corporation, addressed a meeting of publicity and theatrical advertising men on "More Effective Methods in Exploitation in Advertising Fields," particularly as applied to motion pictures. In the course of his remarks, Mr. Wanger expressed the opinion that the motion picture industry had not done as good a job with the 24-sheet poster as, for instance, that accomplished by the cigarette industry.

As a result of Mr. Wanger's address, being translated into action, an improvement has been evident in the type of 24-sheet posters now being used in the motion picture field. With Paramount-Publix, this improvement has been especially noticeable and, being interested, the writer secured from the Advertising Sales Division of Paramount-Publix several photographs of poster copy used for Paramount pictures within the last two years.

One of these posters, not of recent design, advertised a production entitled, "The City That Never Sleeps," and a second, "Underworld." A glance showed that both posters consisted almost entirely of words to tell the story, forgetting the adage attributed to Confucius, the Chinese sage, "A picture is worth a thousand words."

The other four photographs of posters advertised Ruth Chatterton in "Unfaithful," the same star with Clive Brook in "Anybody's Woman," William Powell in "Man of the World," and Clara Bow in "No Limit." These four posters were in the more modern manner, the lettering subordinate to the design.

● Mr. Wanger, in his address to publicity and theatrical advertising men, in contrasting motion picture posters with those advertising other commodities, was impressed with the manner in which Chesterfield

This cluttered, hard to understand design is of the type which is now being discarded.

Cigarettes had been advertised outdoors. The artist whose talent has been displayed for the past five and one half years and whose individuality has stood out in Chesterfield advertising is Charles E. Chambers.

Out in Riverdale where New York City ends, north of Spuyten Duyvil, the writer found Mr. Chambers in his home and studio.

When I explained the object of my visit, Mr. Chambers looked over the photographs with interest. There was an amused twinkle in his eyes when he held up the old-fashioned posters of "The City That Never Sleeps" and "Underworld."

● "These posters are terrible," he said. "How they were ever able to put out such junk, thinking it good, I do not know. They seem to have been necessary to cater in a very cheap way to the public. That was a mistake. The public is more intelligent than the motion picture people considered them."

Mr. Chambers laid the posters aside. "When our good taste in other fields," he continued, "has been improving so rapidly, it is difficult to understand how motion picture producers have been so slow to realize that they cannot cash in on posters of this type.

"One of the chief causes for criticism of outdoor posters by the public in general is based on just such obvious ugliness. They are all cluttered up with lettering which is impossible to read at any distance. Simplicity of design is the first requisite for any poster if it is to attract the attention of the passerby, especially for those in our ever-increasing automobile traffic.

● "Now, let's see the newer posters," continued Mr. Chambers as the four newer designs were placed before him. "These," he continued, "are a big step in the right direction but are not yet what they should be.

"It must be remembered that the public, which outdoor advertising is to influence, is usually in motion, and therefore the posters made to attract their attention must be handled from a different point of view than a 'still' which is put on display in the lobby of a theatre where people have a chance to stop and look at it.

"Covers and illustrations for magazines should be done in a manner to make people want to buy and read them—and the motion picture poster should be made to serve a like purpose. At the present time the average movie patron understands and likes the realistic picture best. For that reason a straight poster done in flat tones is not as effective with the general public as one which employs a certain amount of realism and approximates poster quality through simplicity of design. This is what I have tried to do with the Chesterfield posters.

"Another thing I want to bring out is the relation of the particular poster to the others that are to be posted around it. There is usually little or no thought given to the matter of collective displays of posters and what a poster will look like when placed in proximity to others.

● "Some show up very well when posted individually but would be entirely lost when shown in a group of poster panels. This is almost always true of designs which incorporate more than a few words of copy. In this there should be coordination of the outdoor advertising with that placed in magazines and newspapers.

"The outdoor posters should get attention through forceful and simple design, the magazines and newspapers through this same quality, plus the added

opportunity for giving sufficient descriptive copy, because with these mediums the prospective customer is in a mood to read.

"There is one particularly good point in outdoor poster displays:—they are presented to you openly. You do not have to turn a page as you do in a magazine or in a newspaper. You can get the idea presented at once, and are bound to get attention that cannot be attained in any other way.

"The picture should be the chief attraction. That is why pictures are used in posters. They are the bait to make people read the copy, and they bear the same relation to printed advertising that music does to that broadcasted over the air. Copy alone fails to interest more than a very few and making the lettering the more important thing is much like 'putting the cart before the horse.' The picture is the element to do the pulling.

● "Some authorities say there should not be more than fifteen words on any poster, but I have known good posters to be ruined by fewer than fifteen. I should like to emphasize that the copy should be kept within these limits if the investment in the boards is to be made to pay.

"The artist should have all the copy that is to appear on the poster before he starts to work so that the picture and lettering will make a harmonious whole and he should be a man who understands fully that the purpose of his work is to lead customers to the box office.

"Too often the artist is merely given a commission to paint a figure of a star or a situation from a motion picture, and the lettering is put on afterward by someone outside who has perhaps not a very good idea of composition.

"But aside from this criticism which should be helpful to the advertiser and the outdoor advertising industry, I feel that these newer posters, that you have shown me, represent a forward step in motion picture exploitation."

A simple, direct p o s t e r which is typical of the tendency toward better design.

WILLIAM
POWELL
MAN
of the WORLD
a Paramount Picture

OUTDOOR ADVERTISING ABROAD

Criticises Political Posters

Advertiser's Weekly's Lookout Man, in commenting upon the posters used in the recent election in England, says:

"Without exception the designs I have seen are all pictorial; without exception their style is conventionally realistic; with one or two exceptions their composition, as pictures, is weak and they are overladen with detail; lettering is execrable. In brief, the technique of electioneering posters is a generation behind that of commercial posters.

"The body responsible for selecting these designs had a service to sell. If they had studied the poster hoardings they would have realized that commercial advertisers have found it profitable to adopt a technique of pictorial shorthand, of elimination of detail, of emphasis on essentials. They would have realized, too, that those few advertisers who are still faithful to naturalism insist on a standard of artistic execution far higher than that which satisfies the Conservative selection committee.

"Public taste does improve. The political parties are addressing themselves to the same public who have been persuaded to buy more soap by Levers' admirable posters, and to travel more extensively by the artistic displays exhibited at railway and Underground stations.

"I do not suggest that an election can be won in the same way as a sale. Election posters must achieve their effect much more swiftly. Their technique must be vigorous, urgent, hard-hitting.

"The political posters we shall actually see are entirely lacking in urgency. Pathos is their strong suit. The two most effective represent an old man and an old woman, both with careworn, toilworn features; the text of the first is: 'No more Socialist promises for me; I'm voting for the National Government'—and of the second; 'We must think of our savings and our home; that's why I'm voting for the National Government.'

"The strategy of electioneering puts topicality and forcefulness at a discount. Designs must be prepared and printed so far in advance that only the most general themes can be chosen. The fact that the Conservative headquarters have found it so easy to alter the lettering of their posters from 'Vote Conservative' to 'Vote for the National Government' is perhaps the best criticism of their effectiveness.

"Eventually the parties will realize that publicity is chiefly of value when it is conducted month in and month out throughout the year, between as well as during elections."

* * *

Urges Poster Illumination

An article in Advertiser's Weekly by J. H. Fenton of the Publicity Organization, General Electric Company, Ltd., on the illumination of posters, says:

"The majority of posters are only visible by daylight, and as days become shorter their period of effectiveness diminishes.

"With the introduction of floodlighting the poster's working day can be extended by 50 per cent. An increasing amount of revenue yielding space can also be utilized, which would not otherwise be available. By means of floodlighting, posters can be revealed strikingly and rendered legible to the public.

"How long will it be before national advertisers wake up to the fact that their posters cease work after daylight has passed? How few realize that their posters can be made to appeal to that wide section of the public who are only able to travel in their hours of leisure after the day's work.

These painted bulletins, operated by David Allen and Sons in Glasgow, Scotland, are especially interesting to Americans because of their close resemblance to the standard bulletins in use in this country.

Advertising's Responsibility in Business Recovery

(Continued from page 12) ciations whose avowed purpose is the preservation of the scenic beauty of the country for the people.

● Such a stand is by no means opposed to what outdoor advertising has for a long time been trying to do. You will hear it said that our highways, the roads in the rural districts, are cluttered up by the signs of organized outdoor advertising, when as a matter of fact, less than ten per cent of the advertising signs outside of towns and cities have been placed there by the standardized industry. The unstandardized outdoor advertising, which has caused the greater part of the trouble, is responsible for the small signs, mostly local, nailed to trees, daubed on rocks and fences and barns.

The figures showing the increase in profits made by many merchants who have increased their advertising are in themselves a very striking testimony to the part that standardized outdoor advertising has played in fighting the depression for, as in the case of Luden's Cough Drops, most of these owe no little part of their success to outdoor advertising.

The outdoor advertising industry was one of the first to recognize what was the prime cause of the depression that has come upon us. It was, as we know now only too well, lack of consumer acceptance of the vastly increased products that were being manufactured.

You see, although many of us seem to have forgotten it, that we had a World War. In Europe, the outbreak of the War, the call to arms took 5,000,-000 men who had been producers and turned them into consumers. A year or two later, the United States did the same thing on a lesser scale. We took 1,000,-000 men who had been producers and made them consumers.

With so many more mouths to feed, and persons to clothe and equip, and the armies to take care of, naturally production speeded up.

And then, when the War was over, the men laid down their arms and came back looking for the jobs they had had, but there were no jobs for them. In most instances, the machines which the exigencies of war had rendered so efficient, had taken their places. So there was one tremendous cause for the falling off in consumption.

● If then we recognize—facing the facts squarely— that increased consumption not only in America but all over the world is the way to renew confidence and prosperity, then we must also recognize that never before was there such a vital need for the expert and high-powered salesmanship which brings consumption into being.

The master salesman of them all is Advertising. And in this busy, outdoor age, when people will hardly stay at home long enough to read, outdoor advertising with its headline appeal and its constant reminder and reiteration of the fact that the good things of earth are for sale, has played and is playing one of the strongest roles in the drama of salesmanship, on which our hopes depend.

Outdoor advertising, as it is organized today, is one of the major industries of the United States, and it would be a national disaster if the propagandists who would do away with organized advertising could have their way. This industry, which has done so much to spread the real live news of up-to-date merchandise throughout the country, employs no less than 33,000 men. It has nearly 2,000 plant owners distributed throughout the United States, located in over 17,836 cities and towns; and the advertising displays made possible through these agencies reaches a residential population—to say nothing of the millions of passersby—of 82,215,000. There is no medium other than organized outdoor advertising that can so reach and influence the rural population, numbering not less than 57,000,000. This rural army has an annual buying power of $32,000,000,000 a year, which accounts for no less than 40% of the finished products of American manufacturers.

● And when the antagonists of outdoor advertising base their enmity on the grounds that outdoor advertising mars the scenic beauty of America, it is only fair to tell you that this industry is the greatest practical force today for the preservation and maintenance of scenic beauty. President George W. Kleiser of the Outdoor Advertising Association of America stated very clearly the position of the industry in this regard when he said:

"A policy of recognizing residential sections of incorporated cities and towns, natural scenic beauty spots in rural districts, as constituting areas which should be free from commercial occupancies, including advertising signs which might detract from their attractiveness, is the established policy of our industry."

In the cases of the manufacturers who, in spite of the depression, have found that increased advertising appropriations have increased their profits even in the face of depression, it may be objected that we have selected only cases which will prove our point, and that it would be just as easy to pick out another set of illustrations to prove that the best way to lose money is to continue advertising during a depression.

But let it be explained that these individual cases were picked about a broad, impartial analysis of all companies on which records could be obtained by the Federation's Bureau of Research. It is true that we have quoted only instances of successes, but now let us give you the results of the entire survey.

This study included a summary of all advertisers whose records were available. There was absolutely no selection of favorable cases. This analysis brought up to date a study published this spring by the Federation.

● There were 97 companies on the list. Sixty-two of them actually spent more for advertising in 1930 than in 1929. The remaining thirty-five companies reduced their advertising in 1930.

The point is in what happened to profits. Being more or less typical, the average profits in both groups declined, as you might expect, but the important thing is that the amounts of decline were far from equal. In the group which decreased the advertising, profits declined 55 per cent in 1930. In the group which increased the advertising, earnings declined only 29 per cent. In other words, the 62 companies which increased their advertising had a relative profit showing which was 26 per cent better than the group which *cut* their appropriations.

Now let us see what happened to these same companies in 1931. So far, it has been possible to get reports on 63 of the 97 companies indicating what their profits will be for 1931.

The aggressive companies continue to increase their lead over the others. The group which increased advertising in 1930 actually is earning two per cent more profit in 1931 than in 1930. The other group, which reduced advertising in 1930, suffered a further shrinkage in profits, their 1931 earnings being fully 25 per cent below 1930.

These figures show concretely how necessary it is to put real advertising pressure behind sales efforts in a generally poor year.

We do not mean to imply that it was advertising alone which caused the companies which used it fearlessly to earn the most profits. Although an important part in a successful merchandising plan, it is still but a part, and the product itself must carry new appeals to stimulate the interest.

This fundamental proposition does not apply only to manufacturers and national sellers. What is true of them is also true of local retailers. Department stores, specialty shops, shoe dealers, and the rest—they all have the power to influence consumer buying. It is up to them, first, to select attractive goods and to offer attractive service. Their advertising can then be made so potent that it becomes a vital factor in the course of business.

You know that business conditions are not uniform throughout the country. In some cities, business has already made a good start in the climb back to normal. In other places, recovery has not yet begun. It is possible to compare the state of business in specific cities as related to the amount of advertising.

● The Federation has made an analysis of 68 large cities for which the figures on both advertising lineage and business volume are obtainable. In making the analysis, these 68 cities were divided into two groups

of 34 each. In one group were placed the cities where the volume of advertising during 1931 is relatively heaviest. In the other group are the cities where advertising is relatively the least. When we say "heaviest" and "least," we mean as compared with the preceding year.

In the group of cities carrying the heaviest advertising, there has been an upward trend during the first half of this year amounting to an average increase of 2,730,000 lines of advertising per month. In the other group, there has also been an upward trend, but it amounts to an increase of only 1,590,000 lines per month.

Now let us see what effect this has had on the volume of business in these two groups of cities. In the first group, where advertising was heaviest, business apparently hit the bottom in March, and in July (which was the latest record available), business stood at eight per cent above the monthly average for the base period 1920-24.

In the other group, where the volume of advertising was relatively the least, July business stood at the lowest point of the whole year, lower even than March.

Anyone who believes that the relative volume of advertising has nothing to do with the amount of business transacted in these cities may laugh off these figures if he sees fit. But, we know that advertising makes sales. There is no getting around that fact.

● The facts are that business is recovering most rapidly where advertising is the heaviest.

When you add the evidence of these 68 cities to the experience of the individual companies which have been studied, you have a powerful demonstration of what advertising, intelligently used, has already done.

Not every business is in a position today to go out and spend a lot of money for advertising. A great many of them should not do so if they could. In fact, none of them should, if they believe that mere size of appropriation and mere number of lines will do the job. The need is not only for *volume* of advertising but for *effective* advertising. To advertise effectively, one must have news and the only way to provide real merchandising news is to offer new values to the buyer.

For every business, the opportunity is there. Many millions of people have more ready cash than they have had for a long time and they really need hundreds of kinds of goods. Make them some real offers and don't keep those offers secret. The people can buy and they will buy. Let us redouble our efforts to make sales, and in so doing, use all the power that is in advertising. Our efforts will redound to our own individual profit and will bring back more quickly and more surely the normal state of American business whose pitch is an ever rising crescendo of greater and higher prosperity.

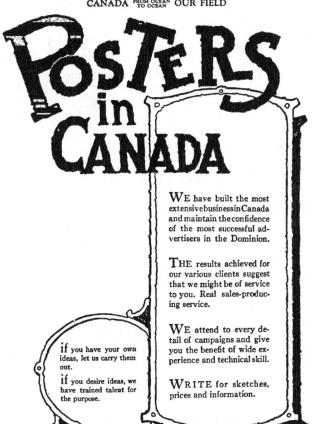

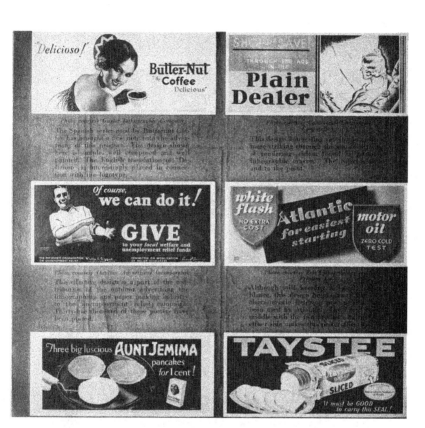

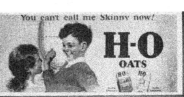

We Sell Our Dealers on Outdoor Advertising

(Continued from page 17) are paid for by us.

—So after summer—Posters!

J. P. Smith Shoe Company
Advertising Manager

Occasionally we fail to obtain Poster space ordered by a dealer—generally because the dealer has dilly-dallied so long that all available boards have been taken by another advertiser. In a case of this kind we find this letter, written well in advance of the next season, convinces the procrastinator of the error of his ways and often brings an immediate order.

One thing we want to avoid as much as possible is disappointing you on Poster space. The only reason that we failed to obtain locations for you for spring was because your order was not received far enough in advance of the posting period.

We know that it hurts us when we are forced to inform you that we cannot give you the showing desired. But Posters are so popular that locations, especially in larger towns, are in great demand. Unless we can contract for space some time in advance of the months wanted we sometimes lose out.

● We know you realize the value of Smith Smart Shoe Posters and how much they will mean to your business and we want to protect you against further disappointments regarding locations. Therefore we suggest that you book showings for September, October and November at once. You want Smith Smart Shoe Posters and you want to be sure that they go up on the best boards. You will not be disappointed again if you forward your order now. We are enclosing a contract card for your convenience and we urge you to use it immediately for reserving fall space.

Sincerely yours,
J. P. Smith Shoe Company
Advertising Manager

Our policy is to place Poster contracts for our dealers. But under certain circumstances we make exceptions and send the paper direct to the dealer. When we do we write him this letter:

When you receive the 24-Sheet Posters we are sending direct, at your request, will you please

(1) USE THEM CONSCIENTIOUSLY
(Each one cost us $4 to produce and imprint)

(2) HAVE THEM MOUNTED BY A MAN WHO IS EXPERIENCED IN THIS WORK (24-Sheet Posters come in sections. It requires skill and care to join the sections smoothly and accurately)

(3) INSPECT THEM FREQUENTLY

(Inclement weather may spoil them. They may get torn or disfigured and we would rather furnish replacements than have this advertising unattractive).

● Smith Smart Shoe Posters will bring you favorable notice if they're displayed,—if they're expertly mounted—if they're carefully maintained. We are glad to supply beautiful designs, correctly imprinted. Their value to you depends a great deal on how and where they are posted.

J. P. Smith Shoe Company
Advertising Manager

There are about nineteen more letters in this Poster group. There are letters covering complaints on location of boards, letters acknowledging contracts, letters acknowledging dealer's report of satisfactory display, letters covering change in local rates. And finally let me quote a letter which has been used effectively since May, 1924:

Our Mr. Bittel writes us that you have decided to pass up Smith Smart Shoe Poster advertising for fall. Your decision is of rather personal concern to us—and is disappointing, to say the least.

We are trying very hard to arrange all displays so that dealers will have no cause for complaint. Occasionally we fall down, as Poster distribution cannot be prearranged exactly. We ask you to remember, though, that it is the composite influence of the entire display that makes money for you. Even if one location is not exactly what it should be, this fact will not seriously interfere with the business building power of the campaign as a whole.

Smith Smart Shoe Posters have certainly proven their worth and we do not like to have you drop them now, just when they will do you the most good.

If you will reconsider your decision and sign up for another showing for next season, the writer will take it upon himself, personally, to have your display absolutely right. We urge this action because we know it is wise and because we want to develop your Smith Smart Shoe volume to the point where it crowds all competition into the dim background.

We think you will see things as we do, so we enclose a Poster contract card and will look forward to receiving an order for a future showing.

Sincerely,
J. P. Smith Shoe Company
Advertising Manager

● During the past year we have kept dealer interest in Posters alive and active, despite deplorable business conditions and a very marked absence of money among retail merchants. There are two reasons for this as we see it: First, Poster advertising is good advertising—and second, perseverance is a virtue.

HUMAN INTEREST
Sells Saving

The Ants were employing a fine winter's day in drying grain collected in the summer time. A Grasshopper, perishing with famine, passed by and earnestly begged for a little food. The Ants inquired of him, "Why did you not treasure up food during the summer?" He replied, "I had not leisure enough. I passed the days in singing." They then said in derision: "If you were foolish enough to sing all the summer, you must dance supperless to bed in the winter."

AESOP'S FABLES

● When old Aesop, hundreds of years ago, wrote the fable of the grasshopper and the ants, he probably did not realize that he was furnishing what might be termed the basic copy theme of the majority of bank advertising in the twentieth century. Ever since financial institutions began to realize that banking service must be merchandised just as any other service or product, the advantages of thrift in making provision for the future have furnished the theme for financial advertising. Such an appeal is unquestionably sound and has produced results. The banks, however, are beginning to find that, by concentrating their advertising appeal on a hoarding instinct, they have neglected to address themselves to the desire for more immediate luxuries which is universal.

Installment buying has shown that systematic payments can make available to families of medium income, luxuries which would otherwise be impossible of attainment. If automobiles and homes and washing machines and jewelry firms can increase their sales through installment selling, why cannot the bank sell vacations and college educations and travel through savings? That such a program is highly

effective has been shown by the advertising done by the Bowery Savings Bank in the last few years.

● In 1928 the Bowery Savings Bank was using an effective lettering poster which featured the 4½ per cent interest paid on savings from the day of deposit to the day of withdrawal. It was decided, however, that by using a pleasanter, happier appeal more people would become interested in savings. Even though the savings were withdrawn for use during the vacation or on a trip, it was highly probable that another account would be opened for a similar purpose the next year. In the meantime, the habit of saving would be established and the bank would have contact with a prospect for other banking services. Accordingly a series of posters was decided upon for 1929 which, attractively illustrated, featured such copy as "Save to Play," "Save for Leisure," and, for a Thanksgiving design in November, "Peace and Plenty."

The designs used in 1929 all featured the 4½ per cent interest as carrying continuity between the new series and the old. In 1930 this item was dropped from the posters and a straight savings appeal, based on such copy as "You'll Like to Travel—Save for It!", "Be Free of Drudgery—Save for Comfort" and, with an illustration of two youngsters of high school age, "Soon, They'll Be Ready for College—Save for It!"

● The posters which are being used in 1931 make use of suggestion or example to build the reputation of the Bowery Savings Bank. "Over 66,000 Housewives Save at the Bowery Bank" is an example of the copy used on this series. The illu-

The 1931 posters have followed closely upon the style of this one in both copy and layout.

OVER **36,000 EXECUTIVES**
save at the **BOWERY**
SAVINGS BANK

tration is repeated in smaller figures across the bottom of the poster. This same composition and copy has been used throughout the 1931 series. That these posters bring results has been shown by the increases in the various classifications immediately after the display of the designs. Five weeks after the housewife poster went up, a check showed that 2,500 housewives had opened savings accounts.

● It will be noted that during the entire three years the continuity of the posters has been remarkable. One series has logically led into the next and the posters in each series have been carefully held to similarity in copy and layout. This is more necessary in bank advertising than in almost any other classification. The bank offers a service which, while useful, is more intangible than that of the manufacturer or the department store which offers a specific commodity. For this reason it is absolutely essential that the bank emphasize its name and its service over and over again. Its advertising is a long term rather than a short term asset and continuity is one of its most important elements. The popularity of an institution is a business-getter that takes years of careful, intelligent planning to establish. When once obtained it gathers momentum slowly. The advertising must be planned to foster and develop this popularity. The only breaks in the continuity of these campaigns have been the special Christmas designs—and these, certainly, have added much to the Bowery's good will assets.

The copy appeal of all three series of posters has been based upon the securing of business by example rather than by preaching; and to such a theme, outdoor advertising is particularly adapted. When the Bowery Savings Bank poster states, "66,000 Housewives Save at the Bowery" there can be little doubt in the minds of thousands of housewives in the city that the Bowery is a good place for them to save their money; likewise, if the Bowery poster states that 36,000 Executives save at the Bowery, it cannot hurt the Bowery's name with other executives and with the millions of employees who need a safe depository for their reserves. The copy messages have been short, terse and to the point. The posters have been simple and interesting.

● The use of illustration in the designs is particularly notable. A great deal of bank advertising has, in endeavoring to present an appearance of stability and conservatism, achieved only dullness. The Bowery Savings Bank has not been afraid, not only·to use interesting, colorful, cheerful pictorials but even, in a Thanksgiving design, to go to a cartoon style. The result has been that these posters can compete in color and in interest with those which advertise tangible products. This is necessary if the bank is to gain new business through its advertising; for the bank is in competition with these products for a

The human interest appeal of this design was effective in selling the saving idea.

share of the public's money. Unless the bank can make saving as attractive a prospect as spending, the saving will be deferred for more attractive spending. The record of deposits in the Bowery Savings Bank is evidence that the program followed by the Bowery has been successful in securing new accounts.

● On January 1st, 1930, the bank had 248,025 depositors and $322,600,991 in deposits. This amount has grown steadily until, in September, 1931, the total deposits were $467,479,164 and the number of depositors was 345,065. Naturally this growth has been the result of a number of interdependent factors and it is impossible to segregate the results and credit proportions to various items. Nevertheless, results have been directly traced to outdoor advertising and the Bank's continued use of the medium is evidence that it is regarded as an effective part of the program. Certainly, in freshness of appeal and attractiveness of design, the posters of the Bowery Savings Bank are well equipped to present the Bowery's message.

■　■　■

Shea Made Executive Vice-President of Tide Water

Edward L. Shea, for fourteen years an active member of the Tide Water Oil staff in various departments, has been appointed executive vice president in charge of all the Company's operations, it was announced last week by Axtell J. Byles, president.

Mr. Shea until recently was vice president in charge of sales, but he is particularly fitted for his new and enlarged responsibilities, because of his years of experience with Tide Water in practically all branches of the business, including the producing, refining and sales operations.

Starting as a salesman for Tide Water in the New York territory, Mr. Shea later spent considerable time at the great Bayonne refinery. He then was transferred to the producing fields in Mexico.

His first major executive post was vice president in charge of manufacturing, which he held prior to his appointment as vice president in charge of sales.

Familiarizing the Public with the Label

by F. M. Van Sicklen
Advertising Manager, Dodge, Sweeney and Company

Dodge, Sweeney & Company, wholesale grocers and food packers in San Francisco and Oakland, California, has long been a user of outdoor advertising, principally of painted walls, and in its latest design it has gone back to the fundamental principles of advertising. Instead of showing foods in our advertisement we display only our label (or banner), with the vignette removed.

This label is so different that it is striking. Its black and white combination lends dignity and cleanliness to the design and puts over an impression of sanitation for our canned goods. Equal parts of black and white form the background, the word "Dodge" being in white on black, while on our wall design we have used in black on white the words "Supreme Quality Canned Foods" in the space where the food name generally appears. The only color shown is in the company's monogram seal, which is red and blue with the name in white and the monogram in gold.

Our purpose in using the label as a wall design was to familiarize the public with it and we believe this is being accomplished. We have received comments on the design. For instance, in one of our locations are a number of small willow trees. With California-like rapidity these shot up so fast that they soon began to cover the wall. Several people, perhaps a dozen of them, informed us that our advertisement was being hidden by the willow trees and suggested that we have them trimmed. One or two of these people were friends of the company, but most of them were absolute strangers who drive by the advertisement from time to time and had become familiar with it. When people go to the trouble of telephoning and writing you in a case like that you are pretty sure that your advertising is being noticed.

Dodge, Sweeney & Company has used outdoor advertising for a number of years, painted walls being its chief form of advertising. We are using about 40 of them at present in Alameda and Contra Costa Counties. Starting with 5 locations we have continuously increased it, not even this year when retrenchment has been a general practice.

The fact that our business has consistently gone forward makes us well satisfied with our advertising, this being the only means an advertiser has of judging results. The Dodge Sweeney line is a high quality and high priced line and yet in spite of the low buying power of 1931 we did as much business this year as we did a year ago.

There is no doubt that painted walls are very good for advertising food products; they make an effective presentation and give you more for your money.

This painted wall design is an almost exact duplicate of the Dodge, Sweeney label.

Building Sales with Trade Characters

(Continued from page 7) gum world, we find that Wrigley's has made constant use of advertising trade characters for some time. In advertising Spearmint, Wrigley's used two comic, little midgets, supposedly representing a villager and his wife. In one piece of poster copy, these quaint, little people were seen at the gate of their cottage home, going for a walk after the evening repast. A large reproduction of a package of Spearmint was pictured on their left, over which was the message, "After every meal." Another poster in this series showed the little couple at their gate, offering Spearmint to a wayfarer. Just now, Wrigley's is using a pair of clown-like brownies on posters to get over the message of Double-Mints and Juicy Fruit. . On one poster the brownie pair are seen on a see-saw with a package of Juicy Fruit in the middle of the board to act as a balance.

● The see-saw idea has been used very effectively by Richter's Bakery in San Antonio on elaborately painted bulletins. Richter's employs animated copy quite a bit, and the see-saw boards showed Richter's Bread Boy, an advertising character used on the sides of the bakery's delivery cars and in other advertising, on one end of the see-saw with a little girl on the other. This board created a lot of comment in the bakery field. Its effectiveness was increased by the use of a time-clock that by throwing different colors of light on the board showed the children in the acts of see-sawing at night. In much of its advertising, the Phenix Dairy in Houston uses a trade character that it is pleased to call Phenix Phil. Phenix Phil is a jolly, round-faced boy who teaches us the value of using the dairy products of his company. He appears at the side of the handsome outdoor bulletins that the company uses and imparts a human touch to the prosaic task of merchandising milk and milk products.

Advertisers who have been successful with trade character advertising have found that such advertising needs to be continuous. The public's memory is a fickle thing, and people are likely to forget any product that is not advertised continuously, no matter how good the product may be. Who of us has a clear idea of what sapolio was or is, for instance? Yet this was a much advertised household preparation a few years ago. Trade characters have to make their appearance regularly to become fixtures in the imagination of the public.

● In setting an approximation upon the value of trade character advertising, it should first be noted that such advertising makes identification easy. The advertising character becomes closely associated in the mind of the customer with the product itself and thus sales resistance is broken down. A woman, hav-

NO MO' RUBBIN'—
OXYDOL
WASHES 'EM CLEAN
RICH SUDS IN ANY WATER

The cheerful colored lady who always finds washing easy with Oxydol is familiar to millions.

ing had the utility of some household commodity impressively presented to her through an advertising trade character in outdoor advertising is more likely to specify that particular commodity to her merchant and be satisfied with no other than if the advertising copy merely played up the name of the product. The trade name should be emphasized, of course, and if the commodity is something that can be pictured, there should be some kind of illustration of it. When these two things are coupled with a live advertising character, the merchandiser has a combination that can be calculated to boost sales, provided his product has superior merit.

Trade character advertising gives continuity to an advertising campaign. It whets reader interest just as continued stories in magazines and serials in motion pictures do.

● Outdoor advertising, both posters and painted bulletins, offer the trade character advertiser ideal mediums through which to impress the value of his product upon a big audience. Outdoor advertising panels are large enough to present to motorists and pedestrians scenes in life-like size just as though they were set up on a theatrical stage. Colors in all the glory that they lend to such displays are at the command of the outdoor advertising artist. He can show the product packaged just as it looks when it comes from the retailer's shelf.

Trade character advertising adds romance to even the most prosaic products and services. There is certainly little of romance attached to a cleaning preparation, designed for the kitchen and home laundry. Yet, we have just seen what human values have been added to the poster copy of one such product, thereby creating an emotional appeal and lifting the product and its uses above the plane of the commonplace. How much better is such poster copy than that that merely pictures the product packaged and tries to tell the consumer in words what it will do? Here, as elsewhere, aggressive merchandisers have found that the trade character can do more than any word message in getting telling and selling points across to the consumer-reader.

Advertising Campaign
FORCES MEAT INSPECTION

((Continued from page 13) the "cause of the project. Immediately following this display the Press interested themselves regarding the vital subject.

● This effort was destined to bear fruit for eventually the persistent and extensive publicity influenced the introduction and passing of a City Ordinance requiring all local packers to either operate under Government or City inspection. Thus a long step was taken in ridding St. Louis of the possibility of non-inspected meats and the protection of the consumer from faulty products.

The public recognized and appreciated that a long step in the raising of the city's health standard had been taken. Confidence in advertising grew. Nothing more was needed than an enlightening of the public of the undesirable existing conditions and a little guidance of thought, to make them take action to erase the defect and eliminate the possibility of endangering the health of the consumer by the use of uninspected products.

The campaign, directed by a capable and experienced manager, was designed particularly to approach the housewife—the chief family purchasing agent. It invaded public schools, women's clubs and every nook that might possibly assume the role of a distributing agency for the idea.

An increase in the sale of government inspected meats, as reported by butcher shops in the poorer areas as well as in the better neighborhoods soon indicated that the campaign was beginning to be effective.

During the month of May the Packers again ran a poster campaign, this time using a display showing the progress of the campaign and the results secured thus far. The poster advised: "Now 78% of all meats sold in St. Louis are United States Government Inspected Meats. Look For the Guaranteed Meat Sign at Your Dealer." The 50% crossed out and the 78% written beside it, made an impressive showing, the idea of progress being clearly put across.

The publicity continued and in September there was a third showing, the copy on the poster again reporting the progress of the campaign as follows: "Your Cooperation Is Bringing Results. Demand U. S. Government Inspected Meats. 30% of the Meat in St. Louis Is Non-Inspected."

● The influence of the outdoor medium, and the results gained by the use of outdoor advertising in conjunction with this campaign are notable. There is a general appreciation among the Packers of the fact that the medium was one of the major elements of appeal to practically every consumer of their products within their market. It is assured that outdoor advertising will play a part in this campaign just as far as it is carried on.

Outdoor Advertising Builds Potato Chip Sales

(Continued from page 14) locations are selected, many of them being on the sides of stores in thickly populated districts.

Outdoor advertising has been the major medium in entering new territory; it has also been used to build up winter trade with remarkable results.

In the potato chip business July and August are recognized as the peak selling months, with December and January as the low point. Mrs. Scudder resolved to eliminate the word "seasonal" from the potato chip vocabulary, so instead of reducing her advertising outlay to follow the sales curve she put her big effort into the winter months, keeping a careful check-up. Records showed that August 1929 and February 1930 compared in sales about 100 per cent to 85 per cent, while August 1930 and February 1931 were about even. This was considered a feat for such a product and outdoor advertising was given much of the credit.

This program was followed in Southern California where the mother plant is located, and in the newer marketing area of Northern California a similar policy will be pursued for keeping the sales curve up during the winter months.

Car cards and newspaper space of moderate proportions supplement the outdoor showing and an interesting direct mail tie-up with the outdoor advertising has been used to merchandise the product to the dealer. A photograph of a new design has been sent to a list of buyers through the advertising agency handling the account with a personal letter containing the statement "Here's another poster of Laura Scudder's Potato Chips." The letter goes on to suggest briefly how much this advertising does to popularize the product and promote sales for the dealer.

■　■　■

Steamship Account to Ayer

Compagnie Generale Transatlantique, the operating company of the French Line, has appointed N. W. Ayer and Son, Incorporated, to handle its advertising.

-　■　■

Golf Account to Williams and Cunnyngham

Williams & Cunnyngham, Chicago, has been appointed advertising agency for the Crawford, McGregor & Canby Co., Dayton, Ohio, manufacturers of MacGregor golf clubs and other golfing equipment.

SPENDING TENDENCIES

The advertiser is, of course, interested in the potential buying power of the areas in which he expends his appropriation; but he is also, and more immediately, interested in what those areas are doing with that buying power. In the first instance, volumes of figures are usually available; in the second there is seldom any accurate information to be had except by dint of expensive personal investigation.

Believing that the advertiser, if he could receive authoritative spending information, would be able to judge more accurately the possible effectiveness of his advertising, ADVERTISING OUTDOORS has instituted the Spending Tendencies section. Here can be checked, quickly and accurately, the economic condition and spending habits of widely separated sections of the country. This information, gathered by investigators in each of these communities, has been compiled from statements of Chambers of Commerce, merchants and business executives. It is as accurate as it is possible to make it.

EMPLOYMENT Comparing Sept. 1930 with Sept. 1931	100%	
EMPLOYMENT Comparing Aug. 1931 with Sept. 1931		
THEATER ATTENDANCE Comparing Sept. 1930 with Sept. 1931		
GASOLINE CONSUMPTION Comparing Sept. 1930 with Sept. 1931		
GENERAL BUSINESS Comparing Sept. 1930 with Sept. 1931		
GENERAL BUSINESS Comparing Aug. 1931 with Sept. 1931		

EMPLOYMENT Comparing Sept. 1930 with Sept. 1931	100%	
EMPLOYMENT Comparing Aug. 1931 with Sept. 1931		
THEATER ATTENDANCE Comparing Sept. 1930 with Sept. 1931		
GASOLINE CONSUMPTION Comparing Sept. 1930 with Sept. 1931		
GENERAL BUSINESS Comparing Sept. 1930 with Sept. 1931		
GENERAL BUSINESS Comparing Aug. 1931 with Sept. 1931		

EMPLOYMENT Comparing Sept. 1930 with Sept. 1931	100%	
EMPLOYMENT Comparing Aug. 1931 with Sept. 1931		
THEATER ATTENDANCE Comparing Sept. 1930 with Sept. 1931		
GASOLINE CONSUMPTION Comparing Sept. 1930 with Sept. 1931		
GENERAL BUSINESS Comparing Sept. 1930 with Sept. 1931		
GENERAL BUSINESS Comparing Aug. 1931 with Sept. 1931		

EMPLOYMENT Comparing Sept. 1930 with Sept. 1931	100%	
EMPLOYMENT Comparing Aug. 1931 with Sept. 1931		
THEATER ATTENDANCE Comparing Sept. 1930 with Sept. 1931		
GASOLINE CONSUMPTION Comparing Sept. 1930 with Sept. 1931		
GENERAL BUSINESS Comparing Sept. 1930 with Sept. 1931		
GENERAL BUSINESS Comparing Aug. 1931 with Sept. 1931		

EMPLOYMENT Comparing Sept. 1930 with Sept. 1931	100%	
EMPLOYMENT Comparing Aug. 1931 with Sept. 1931		
THEATER ATTENDANCE Comparing Sept. 1930 with Sept. 1931		
GASOLINE CONSUMPTION Comparing Sept. 1930 with Sept. 1931		
GENERAL BUSINESS Comparing Sept. 1930 with Sept. 1931		
GENERAL BUSINESS Comparing Aug. 1931 with Sept. 1931		

EMPLOYMENT Comparing Sept. 1930 with Sept. 1931	100%	
EMPLOYMENT Comparing Aug. 1931 with Sept. 1931		
THEATER ATTENDANCE Comparing Sept. 1930 with Sept. 1931		
GASOLINE CONSUMPTION Comparing Sept. 1930 with Sept. 1931		
GENERAL BUSINESS Comparing Sept. 1930 with Sept. 1931		
GENERAL BUSINESS Comparing Aug. 1931 with Sept. 1931		

EMPLOYMENT Comparing Sept. 1930 with Sept. 1931	100%	
EMPLOYMENT Comparing Aug. 1931 with Sept. 1931		
THEATER ATTENDANCE Comparing Sept. 1930 with Sept. 1931		
GASOLINE CONSUMPTION Comparing Sept. 1930 with Sept. 1931		
GENERAL BUSINESS Comparing Sept. 1930 with Sept. 1931		
GENERAL BUSINESS Comparing Aug. 1931 with Sept. 1931		

EMPLOYMENT Comparing Sept. 1930 with Sept. 1931	100%	
EMPLOYMENT Comparing Aug. 1931 with Sept. 1931		
THEATER ATTENDANCE Comparing Sept. 1930 with Sept. 1931		
GASOLINE CONSUMPTION Comparing Sept. 1930 with Sept. 1931		
GENERAL BUSINESS Comparing Sept. 1930 with Sept. 1931		
GENERAL BUSINESS Comparing Aug. 1931 with Sept. 1931		

EMPLOYMENT Comparing Sept. 1930 with Sept. 1931	100%	
EMPLOYMENT Comparing Aug. 1931 with Sept. 1931		
THEATER ATTENDANCE Comparing Sept. 1930 with Sept. 1931		
GASOLINE CONSUMPTION Comparing Sept. 1930 with Sept. 1931		
GENERAL BUSINESS Comparing Sept. 1930 with Sept. 1931		
GENERAL BUSINESS Comparing Aug. 1931 with Sept. 1931		

EMPLOYMENT Comparing Sept. 1930 with Sept. 1931	100%	
EMPLOYMENT Comparing Aug. 1931 with Sept. 1931		
THEATER ATTENDANCE Comparing Sept. 1930 with Sept. 1931		
GASOLINE CONSUMPTION Comparing Sept. 1930 with Sept. 1931		
GENERAL BUSINESS Comparing Sept. 1930 with Sept. 1931		
GENERAL BUSINESS Comparing Aug. 1931 with Sept. 1931		

EMPLOYMENT Comparing Sept. 1930 with Sept. 1931	100%	
EMPLOYMENT Comparing Aug. 1931 with Sept. 1931		
THEATER ATTENDANCE Comparing Sept. 1930 with Sept. 1931		
GASOLINE CONSUMPTION Comparing Sept. 1930 with Sept. 1931		
GENERAL BUSINESS Comparing Sept. 1930 with Sept. 1931		
GENERAL BUSINESS Comparing Aug. 1931 with Sept. 1931		

EMPLOYMENT Comparing Sept. 1930 with Sept. 1931	100%	
EMPLOYMENT Comparing Aug. 1931 with Sept. 1931		
THEATER ATTENDANCE Comparing Sept. 1930 with Sept. 1931		
GASOLINE CONSUMPTION Comparing Sept. 1930 with Sept. 1931		
GENERAL BUSINESS Comparing Sept. 1930 with Sept. 1931		
GENERAL BUSINESS Comparing Aug. 1931 with Sept. 1931		

EMPLOYMENT Comparing Sept. 1930 with Sept. 1931	100%	
EMPLOYMENT Comparing Aug. 1931 with Sept. 1931		
THEATER ATTENDANCE Comparing Sept. 1930 with Sept. 1931		
GASOLINE CONSUMPTION Comparing Sept. 1930 with Sept. 1931		
GENERAL BUSINESS Comparing Sept. 1930 with Sept. 1931		
GENERAL BUSINESS Comparing Aug. 1931 with Sept. 1931		

EMPLOYMENT Comparing Sept. 1930 with Sept. 1931	100%	
EMPLOYMENT Comparing Aug. 1931 with Sept. 1931		
THEATER ATTENDANCE Comparing Sept. 1930 with Sept. 1931		
GASOLINE CONSUMPTION Comparing Sept. 1930 with Sept. 1931		
GENERAL BUSINESS Comparing Sept. 1930 with Sept. 1931		
GENERAL BUSINESS Comparing Aug. 1931 with Sept. 1931		

EMPLOYMENT Comparing Sept. 1930 with Sept. 1931	100%	
EMPLOYMENT Comparing Aug. 1931 with Sept. 1931		
THEATER ATTENDANCE Comparing Sept. 1930 with Sept. 1931		
GASOLINE CONSUMPTION Comparing Sept. 1930 with Sept. 1931		
GENERAL BUSINESS Comparing Sept. 1930 with Sept. 1931		
GENERAL BUSINESS Comparing Aug. 1931 with Sept. 1931		

EMPLOYMENT Comparing Sept. 1930 with Sept. 1931	100%	
EMPLOYMENT Comparing Aug. 1931 with Sept. 1931		
THEATER ATTENDANCE Comparing Sept. 1930 with Sept. 1931		
GASOLINE CONSUMPTION Comparing Sept. 1930 with Sept. 1931		
GENERAL BUSINESS Comparing Sept. 1930 with Sept. 1931		
GENERAL BUSINESS Comparing Aug. 1931 with Sept. 1931		

Even a crack shot needs a guide

The sportsman may know a great deal about hunting, he may be a crack shot, but he does *not* know the lore of the game country. Therefore he employs the services of a guide who possesses intimate knowledge of that particular "neck of the woods."

In advertising, the counselor's job is to plan and execute a successful campaign, but as the hunter relies on his guide, so the counselor calls upon the specialized knowledge of men who have spent their entire business lives in one medium.

We offer the services of an outstanding group of merchandising and advertising specialists; art directors who know from long experience where to obtain the best outdoor art, to fit specific problems; writers who possess the ability to condense a selling story into a powerful picture and five or six telling words; a Promotion Department which will furnish speakers to explain outdoor campaigns to dealers and salesmen, giving every assistance in merchandising outdoor advertising; and finally a research division which will quickly gather and interpret nationwide market data.

These are typical examples of our many-sided service.

OUTDOOR ADVERTISING INCORPORATED

NEW YORK   Eleven other offices   CHICAGO
One Park Avenue   165 West Wacker Drive

Adding a Word to the Language

THE word "quiz" is said to have been introduced into the language through outdoor advertising. In the eighteenth century, an obscure Dublin theater manager named Daly wagered that, in the space of twenty-four hours, he could introduce a new and meaningless word. All during one night, he chalked the mystic letters "Q - U - I - Z" on walls throughout the city. Next day the strange word was on every tongue —and, because of the curiosity it aroused, came to be used in referring to questions.

START to FINISH

Complete and thorough regard for not only how an advertising program starts, but how successfully it operates up to and including the finish expresses the scope and extent of General Outdoor Advertising Co. service.

The ability to function in that respect and parallel your specific merchandising-marketing requirements "from start to finish" is based upon the application of the combined experiences of our nationwide organization.

OUR MAJOR MARKETS

Akron	Chicago	Jacksonville	New Orleans	Rochester
Atlanta	Davenport	Kansas City, Kans.	New York City	St. Louis
Atlantic City	Dayton	Kansas City, Mo.	Oklahoma City	St. Paul
Baltimore	Denver	Louisville	Omaha	South Bend
Binghamton	Duluth	Memphis	Philadelphia	Utica
Birmingham	Harrisburg	Milwaukee	Pittsburgh	Washington, D. C.
Brooklyn	Hartford	Minneapolis	Providence	Youngstown
Buffalo	Indianapolis	Nashville	Richmond	

DETROIT IS ON
THE MOVE AGAIN*!*

*A better day dawns. The whirring wheels of industry speed
thousands of new automobiles to a motor-minded
world. Production schedules stepped up—
allied industries profit—countless
men return to work.*

Money is moving—purchasing power is improved
and buying confidence is being restored.

Automobile manufacturers are optimistic. That
means Detroit is optimistic and optimism breeds business.

Detroit makes automobiles—more automobiles mean
more people "on the go"—more people "on the go" add
to the already great Outdoor audience.

Outdoor Advertising in Detroit is the effective way,
the sure way to compel these responsive, moving
masses.

OUTDOOR ADVERTISING

DETROIT   GRAND RAPIDS · FLINT · SAGINAW

Advertising

Outdoors (Ceaned pub. with Dec 1931.)

A magazine devoted to the interests of the Outdoor Advertiser

VOL. 2, No. 12

CONTENTS for DECEMBER 1931

Ralph B. Patch, *Associate Editor*
James P. Dobyns, *Advertising Manager*

Eastern *Advertising Representatives*:
Walworth and Worm-er.
420 Lexington Ave., New York City.

Western *Advertising Representatives*:
Dwight Early,
100 N. La Salle St., Chicago

ADVERTISING OUTDOORS is published on the 1st of every month by the Outdoor Advertising Association of America, Inc., 165 W. Wacker Drive. Chicago, Ill. Telephone Randolph 1692. Harold L. Eves, Editor and Manager.
Subscriptions for the United States, Cuba, Porto Rico, Hawaii and the Philippines, $3.00 a year in advance; Mexico and Canada, $3.25; for all other countries, $3.50. Thirty cents the copy. Make all checks, money orders, etc., payable to Outdoor Advertising Association of America, Inc.
Entered as second-class matter, March 31st, 1930, at the Post Office at Chicago, Ill., under the act of March 3, 1879, by Outdoor Advertising Association of America, Inc. Printed in U. S. A.

AVE ATQUE VALE

WITH the present issue of Advertising Outdoors, the magazine will suspend publication after a career, uninterrupted except for changes in name, of almost forty years. During that time, it has recorded sweeping changes in the industry which it has represented. Concepts of advertising and merchandising, methods of production, ways of living, are totally different from those in vogue during what the writers of the 1890's liked to refer to as "fin de siecle."

For the present at least, Advertising Outdoors has reached the end of its effectiveness. The establishment of a promotion company representing the entire outdoor advertising industry has rendered the magazine's more indirect presentation of the medium unnecessary. It may be that the future will again disclose a need for such a publication. Should this be the case, a new Advertising Outdoors will arise, like the Phoenix, from the ashes of the old.

The masthead of one of Advertising Outdoors' predecessors, The Bill Poster, read in its first issue of February, 1896, "The Bill Poster will spare no endeavor to obtain and provide news interesting to business men throughout the United States in all that appertains to outdoor advertising." Standardized structures, scientific methods of location, individualized copy, an outstanding record of service to the advertiser and the public, these are some of the developments in the field of outdoor advertising in the course of the thirty-six years that have elapsed since those words were written. In this Final Souvenir Number we have endeavored to follow the spirit of that masthead. This issue contains as complete a picture of the outdoor advertising industry as we can present. It shows how this oldest of all advertising media has become, through self-adjustment to modern conditions, also the youngest and the freshest in outlook. It tells how outdoor advertising is, today, better equipped than ever before to enable the advertiser to follow the crowd to sales—outdoors.

OUTDOOR ADVERTISING

.. at lowest cost per thousand circulation

During 1930 a veteran advertiser increased his appropriation, used 46% of it in Outdoor Advertising, and surpassed his 1929 profits by more than a million dollars.

Many advertising agencies and advertisers find the representatives of Foster and Kleiser Company genuinely helpful because of their *factual* knowledge of Outdoor Advertising and its place in advertising plans.

Foster and Kleiser

COMPANY

GENERAL OFFICES: SAN FRANCISCO
Operating plants in California
Washington, Oregon and Arizona
Offices in New York and Chicago

NATIONWIDE OUTDOOR ADVERTISING

THE STORY
of Outdoor Advertising
by Ralph B. Patch

● To an institutional poster designed and placed by the priests of ancient Egypt we owe much of our knowledge of that long-dead civilization. The Rosetta stone, one of many such "posters" placed throughout Egypt to eulogize Ptolemy Epiphanes in Greek, hieroglyphic and Coptic languages, opened to scholars thirty centuries of Egypt's written history. Thus far back into the past does the story of outdoor advertising extend.

In this far past, outdoor advertising was a product of necessity. The beginnings of trade had come with the transition from the individual family groups to the tribe. Specialization came into being and with it the first beginnings of manufacture. The merchant of Babylon was advanced in advertising and in merchandising. Symbols signifying various trades were fixed before the shops and barkers shouted the wares to the passersby. Further progress was impossible, for the illiteracy of the masses of the population made impractical the use of even such ancestors of outdoor advertising as that employed in Egypt. In the latter case, the king was not concerned with the illiterate classes but with the influential people who could read the message—in the former, a great proportion of the entire population formed the merchant's market and it was essential that he reach them.

In ancient Athens and in Rome, shop signs were a popular advertising medium. Smoothed and whitened places on house walls were also familiar to the Romans and were much used to advertise the business carried on within.

Announcements painted on walls in black or red have been found in Herculaneum and Pompeii as well as in Rome. Many of these walls seem to have been much on the order of the modern painted mural, for they were carefully selected to show to the greatest possible circulation. It is interesting to record that, just as outdoor advertising in the United States today developed to a great extent from the theatrical business, these announcements in the days of imperial Rome were, for the most part, of gladiatorial combats, theatrical performances and sports.

●·The space on many of these walls was rented and, when the advertiser's time had expired, the copy was

Well-known artists were highly paid for the painting of the inn signs of the eighteenth century.

whitewashed. Inns are known to have used such space in much the same manner that the modern hotel uses the highway·bulletin to reach transients who are prospective guests.

● After the fall of Rome, the entire western world returned to illiteracy and we shall not find, for hundreds of years, a return to written announcements such as were used in the days of the empire. As a result of this lack of ability to read, the pictorial sign advanced in importance in the later centuries of the Dark Ages. The time-worn symbols of the bush or bunch of grapes which had served to identify taverns began to disappear in favor of more individual and distinctive marks of identification.

Many of the foremost artists of the day were commissioned to paint such inn-signs—evidence that this form of advertising was held in high esteem. Two thousand five hundred dollars is said to have been the price paid to Clarkson for a portrait of Shakespeare which was used as a sign for a London tavern. Hogarth, Holbein, Correggio and Watteau are some of the famous artists who are known to have painted advertising signs. In Frankfort, Germany, one Meyer Bauer, son of a Jewish merchant, became a moneylender and, desiring a less prosaic name, appropriated a new one from his father's sign, a red shield. Thus did the founder of a famous financial house derive from outdoor advertising the name of Rothschild, or, in English, "Red Shield."

● The workmanship and individuality of advertising signs improved all during the seventeenth and early eighteenth centuries. Many were elaborately carved in addition to being brilliantly and competently painted. Their dimensions and number constantly increased until 1762 when falling signs caused numerous accidents and all signs were ordered removed. By 1773 the signs which had lent color to the streets of London and other British cities had largely disappeared.

In 1712, publication advertising in England was beginning to attract the attention of advertisers. The first copy that appeared was crude to such an extent that we find ourselves wondering that any product could be sold by it. The papers themselves, too, were badly printed on worse stock. Illustrations were as yet unknown. Yet these papers reached a total circulation in the year 1711 of about 2,500,000.

The chill wind of a state tax blighted this rapid growth, however, to such an extent that the development of newspapers was very seriously handicapped. In its beginning this tax had been levied much as we now tax food retailers—as a measure of covering inspection costs. In the case of the newspapers it was called into existence to control seditious libel. At first a halfpenny, the levy rose to fourpence (eight cents) a copy with a three shillings sixpence (84 cents) tax on each advertisement regardless of size.

● The natural result of such taxation was the demise of many hitherto flourishing publications, among them Addison's famous Spectator and Defoe's Review. Merchants found that they could not afford to advertise in papers, thus making it necessary for the publisher to charge an almost prohibitive sum for the publication.

It is interesting to observe the effect of this situation upon popular education in comparison with the influence of the freedom granted the press in the United States. In 1850, five years before the tax was discontinued, the United Kingdom, with a population of more than 27,000,000, had five hundred newspapers with a total annual circulation of 91,000.000. In the United States at the same time the population was some 23,000,000, of which 3,000,000 were slaves,

yet there were considerably more than 2,000 newspapers with an estimated annual circulation of more than 422,000,000.

During all the time that the tax was in force retail merchants found themselves seriously handicapped in using publication advertising. As a result, the use of outdoor advertising was greatly encouraged and a tremendous increase took place in the use of this medium, between 1830 and 1850. The methods of operation, however, were far from approaching the system that is in use among organized operators today. There were no regular structures and the billposter made use of any space that presented itself. In many cases the posting men worked at night and morning would disclose an entire district plastered with commercial announcements. No permission was secured from the owners of property. In fact, the householder would often find that the very door of his home had been appropriated as a posting station.

Such conduct was intolerable, yet the results which even this advertising secured were evidence of the value of the medium. Thus reputable men were attracted to it and an improvement in the character of outdoor advertising was the result. In place of defacing private property with a helter-skelter mass of badly posted bills, structures erected for the sole purpose of the display of outdoor advertising made their appearance. At the same time the appearance of the bills was greatly improved.

● The reputable contractors who had made their appearance in the field systematically studied their business and placed their stations at points where they would show to the greatest circulation. Color was used in posters for the first time and this innovation lent much life and effectiveness to the message. To the interest in and appreciation of advertising that was aroused by widespread and resultful use of the outdoor medium may be traced much of the influence which led to an immediate leap forward in the volume of newspaper advertising which appeared with the remission of the tax in 1855.

Outdoor advertising in the United States followed to a great degree the same line of development as in England. Its expansion was not marked, however, by as rapid a growth as that which was stimulated in the latter country by the newspaper tax. In the year 1800 the circuses were the principal users of outdoor advertising and the theatrical and patent medicine businesses were, for many years the outstanding accounts on the yet unorganized medium. Other classifications of business were attracted, however, and by 1850 clothing stores in the larger cities were using painted announcements along roads for fifty miles in every direction from the cities in which they conducted their businesses.

One of the heaviest users of outdoor advertising from 1861 to 1865 was the United States government.

Modern organized outdoor advertising has kept pace with the high-speed tempo of today's existence.

Posters calling for Civil War volunteers and offering large bounties for men to enlist appeared throughout the country, just as recruiting, war loan and conservation posters appeared during the World War.

In 1870 a national painting service was organized by Bradbury and Houghteling, and in 1872 Kissam and Allen, of New York erected its own boards and opened the way for an era of organization and reputable operation of outdoor advertising.

● Other companies came into the field in increasing numbers— R. J. Gunning and Thomas Cusack in Chicago and O. J. Gude in Brooklyn. For many years these firms held the leadership in the field. Along with the establishment of responsible organizations came improvement in service, in copy, in lithography and in the standing of the advertisers using the medium. By 1890 artists such as Will H. Bradley, Will Carqueville, Edward Penfield and Louis J. Rhead were producing poster designs for Harper's magazine and for Packer's Tar Soap and Pearline Washing Powder and for many bicycle firms. The latter manufacturers recognized the special advantage which outdoor advertising offered in reaching the people who were outdoors and were excellent prospects for the sale of bicycles. For this same reason, automobile manufacturers were to make effective use of the medium some decades later.

The formation of the Associated Billposters of the United States and Canada during the 1890's was the first step in the organization and self discipline and one which made itself immediately felt in the barring from the panels of burlesque show advertisements and those of the more lurid dramas and was later to induce the industry to decline to accept liquor advertisements before any other medium had taken a similar step.

● With organization and improvement in the design of advertisements came a corresponding change in methods of operation. Structures improved in appearance and more consideration was given to their placement. And, just after the opening of the twen-

tieth century there appeared with gathering momentum the influence which was to uproot American habits, to whirl the tempo of living to hitherto unknown speed and to lend additional importance and significance to the oldest of all advertising media. The automobile had arrived.

Throughout all the thousands of years of human history there had been few changes in ways of living. There were, of course, variations in accordance with nationalities and there were increasingly luxurious living habits as civilizations rose from frugal farming to wide spread trading. Nevertheless, the Englishman of the 18th century was living at about the same speed and was confronted with much the same problems as the Egyptian of milleniums before. Horses were used for transportation, monarchy, while not as absolute as that of the rulers in the country of the Nile, was still effective, the mass of the people were still in a state which approached serfdom and the means of communication were, if anything, more primitive in England than in Egypt.

● Through all these thousands of years, cut on stone, pressed in clay, written on papyrus, painted on walls, outdoor advertising had been constantly used by every generation. The development of printing, far from causing its abandonment in favor of newer media, brought about improvement and increased use. As we enter the twentieth century we find that the groundwork had been laid for the tremendous increase outdoor advertising was to enjoy.

The automobile broke up the consolidated groups that had constituted the family. It made the call of the open road what it is today and it made those open roads into the outstanding highway system of the world. It poured a torrent of traffic into the laps of our dismayed city fathers and gave rise to one of the world's most important industries.

● With the automobile came far-reaching changes in our social life. For thousands of years the family had remained as the central point from which our lives extended into the outside world. Mass production was to bring unheard of comforts within the reach of the majority of the population and to make our homes more comfortable than the palaces of former times. At the same time, however, outside influences operated to reduce the importance of the home and the family group as the scene and motivating force of our everyday life.

As automotive traffic has grown in volume, the circulation of outdoor advertising has increased in significance. The location of panels has acquired a new meaning. More and more advertisers, attracted by the growing importance of the outdoor market, have turned to the medium and, in turn, the medium has constantly striven to deliver better service and more complete coverage.

Another important factor in this trend toward outside recreation, the motion picture, has developed rapidly from a museum piece—a strange and amusing toy—to a tremendous social influence. Its audiences grew steadily until the advent of sound. This innovation drew enormous crowds to the theaters and, today, more than one hundred million people are in attendance at twenty-two thousand motion picture theaters every week. This away-from-home entertainment draws almost the entire population of the country away from home each week. Small wonder that we look upon the motion picture as one of the most potent influences in the turn toward outside activities.

● Sport today is a business—and big business at that. Perhaps never again will it attain that height to which it reached when two young men battered

Many of the facts and figures used in this article were obtained from Frank Presbrey's "The History and Development of Advertising."

at each other in a ring for a few minutes—and were paid some one and one-half million dollars for doing so. Nevertheless, Mr. George Herman Ruth, at the present writing, has rejected a yearly salary of $70,000 as being inadequate remuneration for hitting baseballs. If this be depression, Mr. Ruth is making the most of it!

Such salaries are made possible by the huge crowds which baseball and Mr. Ruth attract. These same crowds have contributed football receipts which have built great stadia and support the physical training programs of our colleges. Winter and summer, outdoor sports draw millions of spectators away from home and away from print.

● With the formation of the Outdoor Advertising Association of America, Inc., in 1925, the present status of organized outdoor advertising was established. Members of this organization operate plants in 17,500 towns and cities throughout the United States. Their plants deliver a standardized service in both painted display and poster advertising. Self regulation has limited the placement of structures to locations where their presence will not merit the objection of fair-minded people and the same force has brought about a strict censorship of copy. Structures have been designed to a point where they are pleasing in themselves and form an effective frame for the copy which they display. The location of panels and their allotment for complete coverage has evolved into an exact science.

Tremendous outdoor traffic and the improvement in the medium has rendered outdoor advertising more effective than ever before. From a standpoint of economy outdoor has no rival among advertising media. At the present time organized outdoor advertising stands ready, as the oldest, most fundamental and most up-to-date of all forms of advertising, to deliver a service keyed to the tempo of today and capable of tapping the mighty buying power of outdoor America.

The coming of the automobile heralded a new era in America.

Research Project Culminates Ten Years of Traffic Study

by Dr. Miller McClintock

Director, Erskine Bureau for Street Traffic Research

● With the establishment at Harvard University in the Albert Russell Erskine Bureau for Street Traffic Research of a research project in Traffic and Trade, the Association of National Advertisers and the Outdoor Advertising Association of America, Inc., has opened the way for a more complete understanding of the intimate relationship between street traffic and business. Much has already been done in the field of traffic research by the Outdoor Advertising Association and by individual members of that organization. In the same way, many agencies have, in the name of market research, devoted a great deal of study to trade. No definite presentation, however, has yet been made of the vital relation between trade and traffic.

It is but natural that the Outdoor Advertising Association of America should be vitally interested in this relationship; for this advertising medium, together with car card and window display, constitutes the only means by which the advertisers can reach the movement of the population. The present research, however, will go far beyond the consideration of Outdoor Advertising in its relation to traffic which will form a part of the work. Among the other factors involved are: retail store location in relation to street traffic; the size of the outdoor market normally on the city streets each day; the evaluation of traffic in terms of purchasing power; the concentration of trade into shopping centers and the expansion of trading areas, street car transportation and trade and, in the field of outdoor advertising, the medium as trade's message to traffic and the most economical method of presenting that message.

● Obviously, information on every one of these points is of the utmost interest, not only to advertisers and advertising men, but to business men in every line of trade. The location of the retail store is, in itself, a major problem in today's merchandising. At first glance, a location upon the street which carries the greatest amount of traffic would seem to offer the best prospect for business success. Such, however, is not always the case. It is possible that the circulation includes only a small percentage of shoppers—and it is upon that percentage that the store owner must build his hopes of profit. Again, the circulation may not be of the right character for that particular line of trade. The surroundings may also be a handicap, in spite of large circulation and it may be that the amount of traffic is an actual handicap to business. All these factors and many more must be considered in store location, yet there is comparatively little scientifically gathered information available at the present time.

The other portions of the study are of equal, if not greater, importance and accurate information regarding them will go far toward, not only arriving at definite facts in regard to the use of outdoor advertising, but an *understanding of and picture of our entire trade pattern picture*. It is the belief of the outdoor advertising industry that, through this research, much of the operating technique now used may be subjected to scientific test.

● The work is being undertaken with the counsel and advice of an Advisory Committee, composed of Mr. Turner Jones, of the Coca Cola Company, and Mr. A. E. Haase, General Manager of the Association of National Advertisers, both representing the A. N. A., and Mr. George W. Kleiser, Mr. H. E. Fisk and Mr. John Paver representing the Outdoor Advertising Association of America, Inc.

The Erskine Fellow is Mr. Arthur R. Burnet, Secretary of the Outdoor Advertising Committee and of the Car Card Advertising Committee of the A. N. A.

It is believed that the results of the traffic research carried on at the University of Wisconsin by the Barney Link Fellowship will prove to be of the utmost help in carrying on the present work. This Fellowship, established in March, 1924, in memory of Barney Link, one of the pioneers of modern outdoor advertising, evolved a number of formulae for use in measuring traffic flow. The establishment of accurate traffic information is a very costly and complicated procedure if it is necessary to take numerous circulation counts at each location. Much of the activity of the Fellowship was, therefore, devoted to the determination of a simplified formula which might sacrifice some slight degree of accuracy but which would constitute a practical method of quickly determining total circulation by taking comparatively few traffic counts. (Continued on page 25)

The outdoor advertising industry, with the production of the posters handled by its allies the West Virginia Pulp and Paper Company and the leading poster lithographers of the country, displayed 35,000 of these posters as an outstanding contribution to the president's unemployment relief program.

This is the design used in 1931 by the American Legion in its membership campaign. It is one of the many for which space has been contributed by organized outdoor advertising. These posters have been of material aid to the Legion in securing its present enrollment of more than a million members.

The Veterans of Foreign Wars of the United States is another organization which organized outdoor advertising has assisted in gaining membership strength which enables it to carry out its relief program.

This attractive design is one of many which have given valuable publicity to the Young Men's Christian Association both in local and national campaigns. Organized outdoor advertising has devoted thousands of dollars worth of space to the Y. M. C. A.

Organized Outdoor Advertising—
A NATIONAL ASSET

● Probably no industry, and certainly no advertising medium, is as strongly organized and as rigidly self regulating as is outdoor advertising. This industry, with its standard structures, its code of ethics, its efficient censorship of copy and its effective advertising service is winning an increasingly important place in today's merchandising.

Organized outdoor advertising means exactly what the name implies—a standardized and self disciplined group of men and plants differentiated by those standards and that discipline. Organized outdoor advertising recognizes and makes use of but three divisions of outdoor advertising, poster, paint and electrical and the structures which are used in each division are rigidly standardized to present a pleasing appearance and to deliver maximum advertising value.

Such standardization has only been achieved by dint of great effort and expense. In 1927 the Outdoor Advertising Association of America, representing the 1200 member companies which compose the organized outdoor advertising industry instituted a five year plan for the purpose of re-developing and rebuilding the structural facilities of the business. This plan, which involves an expenditure of some $50,-000,000 is more than seventy-five per cent complete. Since standard specifications worked out by Association engineers have been followed in this reorganization, the structures used by organized outdoor advertising are, at the present time, approaching complete standardization the country over.

Not only the panels themselves but the placement of them is regulated by the Association. The constitution of this organization states:

● STANDARDS OF PRACTICE: Members of the Association, both painted display and poster advertising operators, shall not place or post structures or copy

(a) so as to create a hazard to traffic.

(b) on rocks, posts, trees, fences, barricades or daubs.

(c) on any locations except properly either owned or leased.

(d) in locations that interfere with the view of natural scenic beauty spots.

(e) Members are prohibited from tacking, pasting, tying or erecting cards, panels or signs of any description, except the erection of structures that conform to Association standards, and members are

likewise prohibited from permitting these acts to be done by any person under the authority of their license.

(f) Advertising copy, either pictorial or otherwise, shall not be displayed which (1) is directly or indirectly critical of the laws of the United States, or induces a violation of those laws, (2) is offensive to the moral standards of the community at the time the copy is offered for display, (3) induce the purchase of medicines for certain conditions or diseases, (4) is false, misleading or deceptive.

The obligation of membership which must be accepted by every member, insures that these regulations will be followed. It reads:

● The acceptance of membership in the Association implies an acceptance of all the provisions of the Constitution and By Laws of the Association and of such proper resolutions as may have been adopted by the members or the board of directors; continued membership denotes a constant acceptance of all proper rules and regulations of the Association.

Not only does organized outdoor advertising regard the interests of the communities in which it operates through its placement and construction of panels and its regulation of the copy which appears upon them, but, as a part of all advertising, it benefits the public through its promotion of sales.

In this modern age of mass production, mass distribution has become an absolute necessity. Machines have multiplied over and over again our production of commodities. Unless it is possible to distribute these commodities to the mass of the people our present economic structure is certain to totter. In this distribution outdoor advertising has played and is playing an important role.

In former days of limited manufacture, it was possible for the producer to tell each prospective purchaser personally of the merits of his wares. Today, when prospects must be numbered in scores of millions such a course is out of the question. Advertising has been called into service to seek out each individual and, in accordance with the precepts of salesmanship, to awaken interest, to arouse desire and to impel action. Unless advertising does these things, the whole fabric of our machine-made civilization will fall apart and we shall find ourselves the victims of the thing we have created.

● The present state of business, which many of our Jeremiahs would have us believe is such a situation come to pass, is of the same ilk as other depressions which have followed wars and periods of inflation. Our leaders. having seen prosperity lurking just around numerous corners, have wisely ceased to prophesy. That advertising is a potent antidote to depression is, however, shown by figures obtained by the Advertising Federation of America.

The experiences of seventy-seven national advertisers were studied by the Federation. Twelve of these concerns reduced their advertising from 15 to 100 per cent. Thirteen companies decreased their advertising by less than 15 per cent and fifty-two companies actually increased their advertising.

The average profits of each group declined from the heights of 1929. But the group which cut its advertising by more than 15 per cent showed a decline in its net profits of 41.2 per cent.

The group which reduced advertising by less than 15 per cent had a decline in profits of 13.2 per cent. And the group of concerns which were able to increase their advertising showed the smallest decline in profits, only 9.6 per cent.

We can go back to the severe depression of 1921—a period worse in many fundamental ways than the present depression—for still other examples of the apparent working of cause and effect in the relation of sustained advertising to sustained business.

We have the record of 125 national advertisers. 58 of them increased their advertising in that trying year of 1921 and 67 decreased it. Those that increased had a decline in sales of only 12 per cent while those that decreased their advertising were faced with a sales decline of 26 per cent.

When we follow those two groups for three years through to 1924, it is interesting to note that the sales of the companies that increased their advertising in the pinch were 31 per cent greater than in 1920, while the sales of the companies that decreased were only 5 per cent greater. The percentage of gain in business was more than six times as great for those concerns that increased their advertising as for those that decreased their advertising in 1921.

Here is credible, convincing evidence that advertising not only stimulates the volume of immediate business; but sows good seed for future business. Organized outdoor advertising has had its share in the results produced by the advertising of these firms.

● In addition to its function of stimulating sales, which is obviously the most important of those performed by outdoor advertising, the industry is an asset to the country and to the communities in which it operates in many other ways. It is a substantial customer of many lines of business. The lithographed posters which are placed upon the poster panels constitute one of the most important items which are purchased for use in outdoor advertising. Last year more than three and a half millions 24-sheet posters were produced by lithographers. The makers of paper, of ink and of machinery are directly affected by such purchases and the investment in lithographic plants which produce such posters is more than $80,000,000.

Organized outdoor advertising is also the largest retail consumer of electric current. It uses more electric lamps, sockets and reflectors than any other industry. Its purchases of sheet and structural steel run into millions of dollars. It is a heavy user of all types of lumber and consumes thousands of gallons of house paint and of the paint used for reproducing copy upon bulletins. Tools, machinery, paper, art materials, automobiles and accessories, gas and oil are among the great variety of supplies which are required by organized outdoor advertising.

Exclusive of posters, the normal purchases of organized outdoor advertising amount to $11,500,000 annually. Such a consumer is most emphatically an asset to the country and stimulates trade both in its primary advertising function and through its operations in discharging that function.

● It is usually safe to assume that an industry which is a large user of materials is also a large employer of personnel—and organized outdoor advertising is no exception. More than 33,000 men and women, many of them highly trained, are employed in the 1,200 member plants of the Outdoor Advertising Association.

All the structures of organized outdoor advertising are placed upon private property, adding to the income received by the owner. In many cases this money is the only income derived from the property. It is the responsibility of individuals known as "lease men" to obtain the written consent of property owners for the installation and maintenance of these structures. Throughout the United States, these men have contacted and arranged for the placement of panels with over 200,000 landowners. These locations are very carefully selected with regard for the kind of space desired, what plant classification it is to be secured for and how much space is necessary to keep the advertising facilities up to requirements.

After the lease man comes the construction force. This consists of carpenters, steel workers, tin smiths, electricians, roofers and laborers. The foremen and superintendents in charge of this work are guided in their placement by the instructions furnished them by the lease department and the structures are erected in accordance with the Manual of the Outdoor Advertising Association of America, Inc., supplemented by blue prints covering the specific location upon which they are working. Not only does the Manual

show exactly how each panel is constructed but it also shows how the structure should be laid out for all types of locations and it is only necessary to adapt these ideal layouts to the specific problem.

● The painted display branch of the medium demands the services of highly trained pictorial and lettering men who must be capable of working, not only in the studios at the headquarters of the operating company but also on scaffolds on the structures and upon walls out-of-doors. These men are specially trained in this work, for the untrained artist, regardless of his art training, would be quite incapable of reproducing designs on the enormous scale which outdoor advertising demands. Many of the men who paint the pictorials appearing on painted bulletins and walls are accomplished artists who take pride in the quality of the work which they produce. In some cases, paper "paunces" are used to outline the copy and illustration upon the surface of the bulletin; in others the design is painted directly in accordance with a colored layout which serves as a key.

The billposters, who by means of adhesives attach the lithographed poster to the surface of the poster panels, work under definite schedules which enable them to post a certain number of panels in logical driving sequence. The instructions issued to them are an interpretation of the contracts for putting up the posters and these instructions are definite with respect to the exact panel upon which each design is placed. These posters and instructions are released to the bill posters on what are termed "posting dates" these being the dates upon which the contracts begin or the copy is changed.

● Chauffeurs, mechanics, store keepers, superintendents, clerical and stenographic help, accountants, artist, merchandising men and account executives are among the other classifications of employees of organized outdoor advertising. Any company which employs residents of the community in which it operates is an asset to that community, but outdoor advertising is especially valuable because much of the money which it expends has its source outside the community. Certainly the charge which has been leveled, justifiably or not, that certain organizations drain money from the small towns to enrich Wall Street's plutocrats can never be laid at the door of outdoor advertising.

In addition to its services as an aid to business, as a consumer, as an employer and as a tenant, organized outdoor advertising has shown itself ever ready to lend assistance to the cause of charity and of worthy organizations. Perhaps at no time, however,

has this spirit of cooperation been more strikingly manifested than in the stirring days of 1917 and 1918 when organized outdoor advertising placed its entire facilities at the disposal of the government.

● When, in the spring of 1917, war became a reality, poster advertising, as represented by the members of the Poster Advertising Association—now the Outdoor Advertising Association of America, Inc.,—was one of the first great national organizations to enlist in the fight for victory. At the annual convention of the Associated Advertising Clubs of the World, held in St. Louis, the first of the Liberty Loan 24-sheet posters—designed by James Montgomery Flagg—made their appearance on the plant of the St. Louis Poster Advertising Company. The display of these posters and others—both 24-sheets and smaller lithographs—was rapidly extended until the entire country was covered. The total number displayed in behalf of the First Liberty Loan was a little short of 2,000,000.

In the autumn of 1917 came the Second Liberty Loan campaign. Enthused over the success attending their efforts in the first drive the poster men responded heartily to the second appeal from the government and put their united strength in the general effort that carried this campaign over the top. Nearly 7,000,000 posters were displayed throughout the country including many thousands of 24-sheets appearing on the plants of national association members.

The assistance given the government by the members of the Poster Advertising Association was so conspicuous and so extensive that many persons were under the misapprehension that the government has made a large appropriation to cover the cost incident to the poster campaign. When the truth became

known that the plant owners had donated their space, their time and, in many instances, specially made manugraph posters to help the cause along—there was approbation in all quarters.

● Preparatory to launching the Third Liberty Loan the Treasury Department printed and distributed 9,000,000 posters which appeared throughout the United States, Hawaii, Alaska, Porto Rico, Cuba, the Philippines and the army camps in France. This was the first preliminary to the drive.

The work done by the members of the Poster Advertising Association in behalf of the Fourth Liberty Loan was a repetition of the three preceding campaigns. Ten million posters in all were displayed in this drive, nearly 50,000 of which were 24-sheet posters. These were posted on the standard panels of Association members in every state of the Union and throughout the insular possessions of the United States. In thousands of cities and towns the members cooperated closely with the local Liberty Loan committees in all departments of publicity work and in numerous cases the Association representative served as chairman of the city or village publicity committee. In addition to the display of the posters sent out by the Treasury Department at Washington thousands of special 24-sheet posters were designed and reproduced by the manugraph process in the plants of Association members. These found their place alongside the lithographed posters, which represented the work of America's leading poster artists.

● A few months after the signing of the Armistice, the Treasury Department announced the Victory Liberty Loan, the fifth of the series since the United States entered the war. The showing in behalf of this final loan equaled the four earlier campaigns. This poster display brought many millions of dollars

into the United States treasury.

While the most spectacular part of the Poster Advertising Association's contribution to the publicity of governmental war activities is to be found in the various Liberty Loan campaigns, much interest also attaches to other campaigns such as those which carried to success the national War Savings movement. Food and Fuel Conservation, the Red Cross and the United War Work drive, comprising seven leading American organizations—the Y. M. C. A., Y. W. C. A., Knights of Columbus, Jewish Welfare Board, War Camp Community Service, American Library Association and the Salvation Army.

● In each of these intense campaigns the poster played a most conspicuous and valuable part. There were many 24-sheet designs displayed on the panels of association members, many of them being designed in the art departments of association plants and posted on standard panels without cost to the government either for their production or display. It is interesting in this connection to review a letter President Herbert Hoover, who at that time was United States Food Administrator. The letter, written on December 19, 1917, to Mr. John E. Shoemaker, President of the Poster Advertising Association, says: "Among the various forces aiding in the campaign for conservation of food, outdoor advertising is playing an important part. The cooperation which the Poster Advertising companies have accorded the Food Administration has been most gratifying and I desire to express my personal thanks for the donations of space and service and for the fine spirit with which you have undertaken to help. It is through this kind of patriotic effort that America will be able to organize its resources and in a great measure lighten the burden of the nations associated with us in this war."

● Naturally the assistance which was rendered the national government required the closest kind of contact and cooperation with officials in Washington. Recognizing the need for such contact, the Poster Advertising Association, at its convention in 1918 adopted the following resolution:

"The Poster Advertising Association, in national c o n v e n t i o n assembled in Chicago, unreservedly pledges its resources and memberships in 7,500 cities and towns throughout the United States to the support of President Wilson and the government in the world war being waged to secure and perpetuate the liberties of all of the peoples of the earth.

"Therefore, be it resolved, That this convention appoint a suitable committee, to proceed at once in person to Washington City and there make such arrangements with the military and civic authorities as will enable our membership throughout the United States to cooperate as an organization and united body of men, with one spirit, in establishing the liberties of the world for which unselfish achievement the strength and morale of every loyal organization in the land will be required.

"This resolution adopted by a standing unanimous vote of the members of the Poster Advertising Association in convention, at the Auditorium Hotel in Chicago, Illinois, July 24, 1918."

In accordance with this resolution Mr. W. W. Workman was instructed to proceed to Washington and there open an office which should serve as the national headquarters of the Poster Advertising Association. His further instructions were to cooperate in every way possible with the various government departments in obtaining publicity for their numerous war activities by means of poster advertising on the plants of association members throughout the United States. Evidence of his success in this important work is perhaps best indicated by the letter written on July 9, 1919, to Mr. Workman by President Wilson. The President said:

● "I am very glad indeed to express through you my sincere appreciation of the cooperation of the Poster Advertising Association with the various publicity

departments of the Government during the war.

"The members of the association lent invaluable aid to the Liberty Loan, Fuel, Food, Red Cross and other campaigns by constantly reminding patriotic Americans of their duties to their country during the war.

"The value of such a service cannot be over-estimated."

The war record of the outdoor advertising industry is one of which it may well be proud. The actual value of the posting done for the government was in excess of one and a half million dollars. In addition to this, Association members purchased in the neighborhood of $1,000,000 worth of Liberty Bonds, $5,000,000 in War Savings Stamps and Certificates, subscribed $30,000 to the Red Cross and nearly an equal amount to the United War Work Campaign. And in peace as in war, organized outdoor advertising has continued, through its generous contributions to welfare organizations, to serve the country in general.

● The American Legion, from the beginning of its drive for membership in 1927 has consistently used outdoor advertising to reach the veterans who are eligible to its ranks. Each year an increase in the amount of outdoor advertising used has resulted in increase in the number of members obtained during the drive. The recent presentation of the one millionth member of the Legion to President Hoover was concrete evidence of the effectiveness of the service and advertising program which has built the membership to such an impressive total.

James F. Barton, National Adjutant of the Legion remarked in an article appearing in the September, 1931, issue of Advertising Outdoors:

"Any statistics that can be given as to the results these poster campaigns have obtained, however, would be certain to fall short of the truth. In reaching prospective Legion members we have also told our story to the public. I am certain that there is now a better and more sympathetic understanding of the American Legion than ever before, and a large part of this understanding is to be credited to the poster advertising we have done. Moreover, in the

This poster was effective in inducing the public to save food stuffs.

Food *is* Fuel
for Fighters
don't waste it

Eat less wheat·meat·fats·sugar. Send more to our Soldiers·Sailors & Allies

A conservation design that helped the work of the Fuel Administration.

Legion itself these posters have helped materially in arousing the members' enthusiasm and thereby gaining the complete cooperation that is essential to the success of our program."

● In recognition of the assistance which organized outdoor advertising has given the American Legion, a handsome silk flag was presented to the Outdoor Advertising Association by the Legion in an Armistice Day ceremony at the Association's 40th Annual Convention in Detroit on November 11th, 1931. George Washington Post No. 88, of Detroit, acted as the National Legion's official representative in the ceremony which was held at 11 o'clock in the morning. Captain R. L. Gordon, National Publicity Committeeman of the Legion, acting for National Commander Ralph T. O'Neill in presenting the flag to President George W. Kleiser of the Outdoor Advertising Association said: "By this token we wish to convey to you our appreciation of your efforts and of your sacrifices made during the time of the great war and all that you have done to further the purposes of our organization. With it, we wish to tender to you all the reverence and esteem which one organization can convey to another. We know that you, as well as we, believe it is our duty to our country to love it, to support its constitution, to obey its laws, to defend it against all enemies and to respect the flag.

"To you, representing the members of the Outdoor Advertising Association of America, it is a pleasure and an honor to present the colors of this great nation, the symbol of the toil, the hardships, the determination and the courage of a united people."

● State Commander Raymond J. Kelly, of Michigan, also representing the national headquarters of the Legion presented to the Outdoor Advertising Association a handsomely scrolled and engraved resolution adopted at the Legion's last national convention thanking the Association for its donation of space on 12,000 poster panels to aid in the Legion's 1931 membership drive. The resolution read:

"Whereas, the members of the Outdoor Advertising Association of America, Inc., have for the past several years and will this year in November donate

poster advertising display space in all Post towns of the United States for the purpose of displaying over 12,000 posters to assist in The American Legion Membership Campaign; therefore,

Be It Resolved, that The American Legion here in convention assembled does hereby express great appreciation for the donation of this poster advertising display space, both in the past and future, and sincerely thanks the members of the Outdoor Advertising Association of America, Inc., for their nation-wide cooperation in assisting The American Legion in its membership efforts."

The outdoor advertising industry has also won the gratitude of the Red Cross, the Veterans of Foreign Wars, Boy Scouts, the Near East Relief, Y. M. C. A., the National Tuberculosis Association and local church and community organizations. One of the most outstanding services performed by organized outdoor advertising has been the Farmers' Relief campaign which appeared during December, 1930, and in the early part of 1931. Concerning this contribution Arthur M. Hyde, Secretary of Agriculture, said, in a letter to Ivan B. Nordhem at whose suggestion the campaign was contributed: "I am in receipt of a full size poster. This is excellently done and the message is well set out and driven home. I want to thank you and your organization for their cooperation which, I feel, will be very valuable in attracting the attention of the country to some of the problems of the farmer."

● At the present time, organized outdoor advertising is doing its share to aid the work of the President's Organization on Unemployment Relief. Through cooperation with the West Virginia Pulp and Paper Company and the leading poster lithographers of the country it was possible to produce, at no cost to either local or national relief organizations, 35,000 24-sheet posters. These were posted without charge upon as many panels in the 17,500 cities and towns operated by members of the Outdoor Advertising Association of America. Both Walter S. Gifford. director of the President's Organization on Unemployment Relief and Owen D. Young, chairman of the Committee on Mobilization of Relief Resources expressed their appreciation of this generous contribution made by organized outdoor advertising and its allied industries.

In a telegram to George W. Kleiser, president of the Outdoor Advertising Association of America, Inc., President Hoover said: "I greatly appreciate the splendid contribution made by the members of the Outdoor Advertising Association, West Virginia Pulp and Paper Company and the poster lithographers to the work of the President's Organization on Unemployment Relief. This is in keeping with the records made by your industry and allied industries in previous national emergencies."

● The question of outdoor advertising and scenic beauty has been one which has been attaining an ever-increasing importance both to the organized outdoor advertising industry and to the organizations which are concerned with the preservation of roadside beauty. Although the code of ethics of the Outdoor Advertising Association forbids the erection of panels in spots where the structures will constitute a hazard to traffic or a detriment to a definitely scenic area, the regulations which are framed to control the unorganized snipe and tack signs also affect the organized division of the medium.

George W. Kleiser, President of the Outdoor Advertising Association of America, said in regard to this situation:

"We are living in an age where mere utility is not enough. Beauty enters into the every-day life of practically every citizen of our country. The American business man and the manufacturer has learned that to be successful he must give due regard to beauty in the manufacture and sale of his products. Modern factory buildings as well as modern office buildings, the schoolhouse and the residence, all seek some expression of beauty in their design and construction, not at the expense of usefulness but as an additional attribute.

"This desire for beauty on the part of the public is recognized by the advertiser and finds its expression in the artistic character of the present-day advertisements. Every advertising medium, to be successful, must recognize this growing demand. Realizing this, organized outdoor advertising has made much progress in the developing of more attractive advertising structures and advertising copy.

"With the advent of more and better highways and with the tremendous increase in the use of the automobile for both business and pleasure, there has developed a demand for advertising along the favorite routes of travel. The members of the Outdoor Advertising Association of America, mindful of the importance of the natural beauties existing in this country both to its citizens and its visitors have officially committed themselves to a policy of recognition and protection of the natural scenic beauties of the landscape and the active cooperation with the state government departments, civic and other public-spirited groups for the accomplishment of this purpose."

● On January 8, 1931, a conference on roadside business and rural beauty was held at the Chamber of Commerce of the United States in Washington, D. C. At that time the representatives of those industries and groups interested in the regulation, recognition and preservation of the natural scenic beauties of America were gathered together. At this meeting a committee was appointed to bring back specific recommendations for consideration at the second meeting on April 8.

At this second meeting sixteen representatives of organizations concerned with highways, roadside business and rural beauty agreed to report favorably to their groups a proposed bill which is a step in the direction of zoning highways to preserve their natural beauty spots. The proposed bill was drafted by Herbert U. Nelson of the National Association of Real Estate Boards.

● The bill provides that: "Whenever a petition is filed with the State Highway Department, county, town or township as the case may be, that governmental department may acquire by gift, purchase or the exercise of eminent domain, an unobstructed and unmarred view of the rural scenery and landscape from the highway and may prevent the use of a strip of land 300 feet wide or of such width as may be necessary on each side of the stretch of rural highway not less than one-half mile nor more than ten miles in length, for some or any commercial uses, with this exception: (Continued on page 42)

Michigan State Commander Raymond J. Kelly, of the American Legion presenting to president George W. Kleiser of the Outdoor Advertising Association of America, Inc., the resolution adopted at the last Legion convention.

ELECTRICAL ADVERTISING
in New Stage of Development

by G. R. LaWall

Engineering Dept., General Electric Company
Nela Park, Cleveland, Ohio

● Electrical advertising in its relation to selling is assuming ever greater importance because of the evident demands by advertisers for more of its inherent advertising potentialities. It always has been an economical and forceful medium because it compels attention in a field of tremendous circulation.

In this age of increasing travel, particularly during the more or less carefree hours after twilight, electrical advertising performs its advertising functions with telling effect. How well it performs these functions is not dependent upon its mere presence in an important area, but upon the advertising knowledge projected into the planning and design of the display. There is little doubt that from the viewpoint of structure and materials the usual luminous advertising display is representative of substantial quality, but the advertiser is interested in increased sales, which emphasizes the need for advertising effectiveness in his particular display.

Effectiveness Analyzed

Most advertisers have had repeated experiences in buying advertising represented by mediums other than signs. Contracting for electrical display, however, is a duty which may come only once in a business lifetime, and when the opportunity does present itself, the buyer cannot be blamed for not knowing all the details regarding it. The design of the display involves a sufficient number of technical factors to merit consultation with a specialist in order that the desired result obtains.

Most business men have observed sometime or another that motion is an attention-compelling feature in the illuminated sign, but it is not difficult to imagine that certain people, in thinking of this most important item, would rule against a running border as being too common to contribute any particular distinction to their own advertisement. The specialist would go about advising him only after a thorough investigation of his immediate problems.

● Should he find that the article to be advertised to the buying public is a device with moving parts, the problem finds its solution in making that action the compelling force of an illustration in the advertisement—whether the article is an egg-beater, a pump, accordion, punch press, self-filling fountain pen, or a golf club. The important consideration is to make

This display exemplifies artistic frankness emphasizing its individuality and effectiveness as a selling medium.

the motion apply to the advertised product rather than to merely attract attention to the "ad." A usual fault of this latter procedure is that motion, without relation to the product, if sufficiently lively, may even distract from the important copy of the advertisement.

● Brightness is another important consideration. Somewhere—somehow—our eyes have a peculiar fetish for focusing on the brightest object within the range of vision. If this spot is interesting enough, our attention lingers there to collect what impressions may be gathered. Evidently then, in bright surroundings, such as found on our main streets and city squares, the brightest display is assured of major recognition. Combine with this appropriate motion and the advertisement begins to "click."

● There are thirteen such facts we might list and describe, each one capable of adding to the effectiveness of the display, but let us cite just one more very important one—color. Every advertiser knows the value of color. If his location is one where numerous other signs already exist, and they may all be of the same general hue, his sign, to be attractive and readily distinguishable from the rest, could accomplish that purpose merely by being clothed in another, preferably more appealing color.

Individuality—An Important Consideration

Summing up all these factors with the others which involve size, beauty, legibility, dominant position, changeability and the like, and incorporating all in his display, the composite result is one with individuality—the important factor which probably is the one great aim of advertisers in all phases of the art.

Individuality and novelty attract the attention, hold it, and have the ability to create valuable word-of-mouth advertising with no additional investment. By dignity it reflects the character of the sponsoring organization. In short, the luminous advertisement may be made to tell a complete, concise story, aside from the words or illustration in the copy—all as a result of knowing the power of the various factors which apply to this separate field of advertising endeavor.

Cost of Electrical Advertising

With this as a basis the cost of an electrical advertising program may be figured. The life of an average sign is upward of five years, during which time it exerts its influence daily on thousands of people. The circulation figures in a given area are found in one of two simple ways; either through the traffic department of the city or by making an actual count over a period of a few days.

● As a concrete example consider a fairly large sign on a store front or roof in an area where it is exposed to a traffic of 50,000 persons daily. Such a sign represents an initial investment of $4,000 (a good display of considerable size may be obtained for this sum) at a depreciation of 20% per year over a five-year period, and with interest on the investment consid-

A look into the future when buildings and luminous advertising are planned to complete a harmonious ensemble. (Model buildings of the Electrical Association of Philadelphia.)

ered along with the cost of current, lamp replacements, painting, cleaning, repairs, insurance and other necessary items to assure its good appearance before the public, the cost per thousand circulation would be less than fifty cents even if but half of the daily circulation of 50,000 people were considered. This reduction of traffic is suggested to eliminate passengers on street cars and in automobiles who may not be in a position to see the display. The advertiser who is experienced with advertising costs will readily see that for inexpensive advertising, the electrical display ranks next to outdoor advertising.

● In recent years we have been witnessing a notable development in architecture growing out of the needs and spirit of our age. Throughout this country and abroad, buildings are appearing in which the designers have modified or departed from traditional forms with a freedom that is refreshing and inspiring.

Whatever is unsatisfactory in electric signs as used today is largely traceable to a lack of architectural coordination or planning for both the daytime and nighttime appearance of the building. Even so, in the present development of most streets, their aspect at night without the life and color of our electric signs, however crude, would be a doleful, uninspiring one. There is no escaping the fact that electrical advertising will be used in ever-increasing amounts. The architect will help to give it wholly appealing form.

Architects and decorators have wrought new wonders in metal, glass and fabric that fascinate us by their originality and innate beauty. And LIGHT has assumed a greatly augmented place in the thought of these modern designers. Artificial light, as we know it today, abundant and inexpensive, flexible and controllable in every quality, is something relatively new among building elements, so it is not surprising that most of our creative artists have only recently sensed its possibilities.

Yet buildings, on which fortunes have been spent to create a favorable impression of the institutions they house, are allowed to disappear after darkness, when appropriate lighting treatments would give them a character more distinctive by night than by day, and thereby permit them to carry out their function in fuller measure.

● For the exterior treatment of buildings, compared to the interior, light has not yet assumed a corresponding role but enough has been done to justify us in saying that, when appropriate lighting facilities are incorporated in the structure, our commercial and public buildings can be given new character and new appeal by night, glowing in new lines, patterns, and colors.

This new viewpoint of luminous advertising as an augmenting feature of architecture is but the projection of institutional advertising to the area of an entire structure instead of confirming it to the smaller area of an electric sign. It does not indicate that electrical advertising will cease to exist because many of the new installations include signs—although of a newer and different order. The chief difference, which will have definite refining influences on sign advertising, is that the sign elements as well as the entire luminous ensemble will share the benefits of architectural thought in their design.

If the addition of an inharmonious sign, upon a building which is an example of architectural chastity, has been a deterrent to present forms of advertising, it is reasonable to expect that careful planning of the advertising medium as a part of the structure will remove a formidable obstacle from the road of advertising progress. The new concept brings with it numerous new ideas in the application of light to advertising. Decorations in the form of grilles, lettering with highly individualistic character, and color effects secured by delicate blending of transmitted light, all afford new opportunities for dignity, architectural propriety and advertising effectiveness.

● While these effects are inherently suited to new buildings, yet many locations on present structures can be arranged to include such built-in luminous elements. For example, the transom area over show windows can be converted into a sign area by such a simple expedient as changing the clear glass to flashed opal glass. Upon this are attached the advertising characters and, by the addition of suitable lighting equipment in a simple recess or cavity at the back, a display of the modern type and dignity should result.

The illustrations which accompany this discussion will point out a few of the possibilities of luminous architecture as an advertising force. It will help to beautify our cities, enhance our structures, contribute a new air of progressiveness to commercial establishments and will provide a new appeal for the masses to whom the merchant wishes to be a friend.

■ ■ ■

Fulton to Aid A. N. A. Relief Program

Kerwin H. Fulton, president of Outdoor Advertising Incorporated, is organizing the outdoor advertising group to assist the Association of National Advertisers in a program to stimulate buying and restore employment, it was announced recently. The Association is cooperating in this effort with the American Federation of Labor and the American Legion.

Lee H. Bristol, president of the A. N. A., and Bernard Lichtenberg, chairman of the board, have invited Carl Byoir, publisher of the Havana Post; J. Cheever Cowdin, vice-president of Bancamerica-Blair Corp., and Roy Dickinson, of Printers' Ink, to serve on a directing commission.

The Importance of the POSTER DESIGNER

by Otis Shepard

● Each year the efforts of the poster artist play a more important part in the creating of successful outdoor advertising. This happens because the poster designer is peculiarly adapted to function in a medium, the character of which is dictated by our swift American tempo. Everyone hurries. Brevity in copy is therefore more than a matter of choice. It is a necessity. Hence the greater use of the pictorial symbol to convey the advertiser's message.

The effective outdoor design symbolizes the advertiser's product in a sufficiently attractive fashion to command immediate attention and leave the passerby with an impression indelibly filed away in his mind to the end that at the point of sale such merchandise is a known quantity. With this as an objective coupled with a study of the inherent buying instincts of the public, and a thorough knowledge of the advertiser's product and problem, the artist should be in a position to visualize through picture and caption, an appealing and efficient idea. This artist has been chosen and trained for his ability to create various types of pictures in outdoor advertising—which, furthermore, we believe is an independent type of design, generally classified as the Poster, and is not identical with illustration, which ornaments the magazine page, or black and white pen

draftsmanship for the newspaper advertisement. In magazine and newspaper advertising the idea generally springs from the copy. In poster advertising the picture is the idea—often requiring only the name of the product or advertiser to complete it.

Simplicity is the keynote of a poster and its first consideration is attention value through various methods of color, composition and unique devices that embody the individuality of each advertiser. The poster artist is also capable of interpreting the illustrator as well as the designer of black and white where a tie up to campaigns in other media is desired without loss of identity.

● In advertising design, the artist who works in the modern style does not approach his task with the desire to be extreme, bizarre or merely different. His purpose is to present a message which will infallibly grasp the attention of the fickle public. He must work in symbols of one kind or another—either intellectual symbols, such as words and phrases; literal representations, of the photographic kind; or subconscious symbols which, often without the

This poster, by Mr. Shepard, effectively symbolizes speed.

This poster, by Lucian Bernhard, achieves distinction with a simple, lettering design.

realization of the public, produce the desired effect by a deep and fundamental appeal to certain mental moods or motor impulses.

The modern approach differs from the traditional method in that it makes greatly increased use of the symbols of the latter sort. Its materials are combinations of lines and colors which speak a primitive language, expressing dramatic action, and appealing to the intuitive emotions.

When the artist succeeds in making use of these materials, he has gone a step beyond the intellectual symbol or the literal symbol, and has produced a language of advertising which depends hardly at all upon words, but carries its message almost as effectively to the child, the illiterate, or the foreigner. He has gone below the superficial and has reduced advertising to a universal language.

The Outdoor Association of America has, over a period of years, busied itself with the building of standard and uniform structures. In Europe the design or poster itself is the outstanding feature. These fine European posters, printed in various shapes and sizes, are posted, without regard to number, on any given location—and yet art patrons from all over the world have acclaimed them not only to be beautiful, but to excel all other media of advertising in Europe.

The American outdoor advertising plant owners having almost entirely accomplished the standardi-

zation of structures are now also in a position to turn their attention to poster design and to encourage that creative talent which ornaments the uniform panels they have led the world in erecting.

Outdoor advertising requires ingenuity, originality, freshness and audacity. It demands a versatile designer. The poster is the show business of advertising. Just as in the theatre, the spot light focuses the attention on the performer, so the poster dramatically spot lights the product. Drama and beauty will give to outdoor advertising, the stimulus of new life and prosperity.

Pacific Ad Clubs Set Theme of Meeting

"Preparations for Sustained Prosperity" will be the theme of the 29th annual convention of the Pacific Advertising Clubs Association in Vancouver, B. C., July 5-9.

Detailed plans for its first convention in a Canadian city were perfected at the mid-winter conference last week.

An advertising club is being organized in Victoria, B. C., and will apply for membership in the P. A. C. A.

Roy A. Hunter, manager of the Street Railway Advertising Company, of Vancouver, and president of the P. A. C. A., said convention headquarters will be established at the Vancouver, Georgian, and Grosvenor hotels. He announced that "in keeping with the times," the office of vice-president-at-large, which has always been filled by a woman, has been abolished, and hereafter all offices will be open to women.

Topics for the three-minute speaking contests will be "New Jobs for Advertising," "How Advertising Unlocks the Dollar," and "What Does Truth in Advertising Mean to the Public Today?"

Rollin C. Ayers, of the Zellerbach Paper Co., San Francisco, is handling the three-minute speaking contest.

Richfield Golden gasoline is effectively symbolized in this outstanding design by Mr. Shepard.

How Outdoor Advertising
COVERS THE TRAFFIC

by Roy A. Wilson
Engineer, Outdoor Advertising Association of America, Inc.

● The value of any advertising is primarily dependent upon the impressions which that advertising delivers. The advertiser, and more and more advertisers are discovering this in these days when results must be shown by advertising, is purchasing the eyes and ears of the crowd. He is buying the opportunity to present his message to the people and to convince them that they should purchase his product. Unless he places his advertisement where the people will see it he will save money by refraining altogether from advertising.

Outdoor advertising is above all a medium which delivers circulation—which follows the crowd. Its economy—outdoor advertising delivers more circulation per dollar than any other medium—its color, and its size are all factors in making outdoor advertising effective but the one feature of the medium which is most important of all is the tremendous circulation that it delivers to the advertiser.

This circulation is not a matter of chance. Ever since the first organization of the outdoor advertising industry, the operators have striven, to place at the disposal of the advertiser an ever-increasing proportion of the street traffic of the communities in which their plants are located. Naturally the methods by which the structures have been placed have changed and improved. Old, empirical systems of panel location and coverage have given way to an exact, scientific method of placing panels—not only as to their individual position but also as to their distribution. Outdoor advertising plants today are planned to dominate with every showing that is sold to an advertiser, the movement of traffic in the community.

● It will be seen that reaching the traffic movement of the masses out-of-doors is more than just indiscriminately placing a panel where space is available. Mere distribution of poster advertising equally throughout a trading area, town or city is a simple matter if the distributor is concerned solely with spotting the locations at equal distances apart. It requires, however, more than a little consideration to so place that poster advertising that adequate coverage of the movement of traffic is secured.

To obtain this coverage it is absolutely essential that the travel habits of the people be thoroughly studied.

Many operators engaged in the placing of outdoor advertising know their towns so well that they are able to say with reasonable certainty which streets carry the major portion of the traffic and can point to the intersections where the breaks in this traffic flow occur. While this knowledge is of the greatest value in directing an accurate survey of the community's traffic it is not, in itself, sufficiently reliable for use as a basis for the placing of panels. Actual facts, rather than opinions, are essential for the intelligent placing of outdoor advertising. Unless definite information has been obtained it is not only impossible to locate the structures correctly but the plant owner is unable to show advertisers what circulation and coverage they are receiving.

● To secure the necessary traffic data, it is necessary to take traffic counts on various streets to determine the actual movement of the population of the community. Methods of taking these counts vary from actual counting by individuals to specially installed mechanical devices for the computing of vehicular traffic. Engineers of the outdoor advertising industry use, for the most part, formulae developed at the University of Wisconsin under the guidance of Professor Franz Aust. These formulae have been so worked out that counts taken during designated half-hour periods of the day can be used to compute the total circulation of the location. Pedestrian, automotive, bus and street car traffic are all taken into consideration and the resulting figures give an accurate and complete picture of the travel habits of the population. In the case of street car and bus companies, the total passenger figures are obtainable from the transportation company.

All circulation counts are planned to be truly representative of the normal daily traffic of the location. For this reason counts are not made on Saturdays, Sundays, holidays or under any conditions that are not typical. The data which is obtained is average for the year, since counts are taken at different seasons. In case unusual conditions prevail at certain times, these unusual traffic conditions may be made into a special supplementary survey, but are not incorporated into the regular figures.

When all the counts that are necessary to ascertain

the traffic movement have been taken, the usual procedure is to construct a traffic flow map, based on these counts. By showing the width of the streets in exact proportion to the amount of traffic that is carried by them it is possible to present an easily understandable composite picture of the community's travel habits. This map immediately shows what streets are worthy of advertising coverage and the poster distribution can be planned to cover these avenues.

● It has been found that one poster impression for every two miles of these traffic arteries is capable of delivering the repetition and dominance required for representative and effective coverage. By dividing the available space on the eligible streets into 2-mile zones and allotting a panel in each of these zones to every advertiser, it is possible for the outdoor advertising plant to deliver equal circulation and equal ad-

vertising value to all advertisers. Naturally the values of the individual locations in these zones are not equal. Just as positions in newspaper and magazine advertising and hours of radio time differ in visibility and effectiveness, so do outdoor advertising locations vary. In outdoor advertising, however, the showings are so planned that each delivers equal coverage, equal circulation and, by the same token, equal advertising value.

● The methods of laying out outdoor advertising plants which are now in use are the result of years of experimentation by engineers of the Outdoor Advertising Association of America, individual plant operators and by the Barney Link Fellowship at the University of Wisconsin. These researches have evolved accurate, scientific methods of operation which make it possible for the operator to deliver a standardized service.

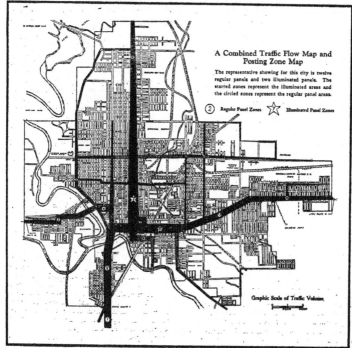

A Combined Traffic Flow Map and Posting Zone Map

The representative showing for this city is twelve regular panels and two illuminated panels. The starred zones represent the illuminated areas and the circled zones represent the regular panel areas.

② Regular Panel Zones ☆ Illuminated Panel Zones

Graphic Scale of Traffic Volume

Research Project Culminates Ten Years of Traffic Study

(Continued from page 9)

● As a preliminary to the work of this Fellowship, all information pertaining to the values of standard outdoor advertising was gathered from members of the Outdoor Advertising Association. It was found that a great deal of data in regard to traffic movement had already been obtained by individual members of the Association as well as by Association engineers. This was not surprising in view of the fact the outdoor advertising industry as a whole had, for years, been concerned with the improvement of their individual plants so that maximum service and circulation might be delivered to the advertiser. In many cases, the placing of structures in relation to traffic had been the subject of considerable study and the results of these studies were placed at the disposal of Professor Franz Aust and Mr. John Campbell, the first Barney Link Fellow.

It was the opinion of Professor Aust and Mr. Campbell that individual travel habits are, for the most part, uniform. In other words, people habitually follow the same routes to and from work, to shop and to other activities upon which they enter frequently. If this were so, it was thought that it might be possible to devise a formula which would accurately estimate this normal circulation without making necessary an excessive number of actual counts. It was apparent that the exact circulation of any location could be obtained as a constant, unvarying total. If, however, the usual daily traffic could be forecast with exactitude, that figure was judged to be satisfactory for all practical purposes.

● The procedure which was developed involved the taking of from seven to ten eighteen-hour counts at locations where there was a great deal of vehicular traffic. Graphs were then made which showed the relationship of the traffic volume to the time of day. These time-traffic curves for all the locations were then combined into one average curve which was termed the "characteristic curve" for that city. It was believed that, from this characteristic curve, it would be possible to develop a formula for that individual city which would permit the total traffic at any point to be computed by short unit counts which could be taken as established percentages of the total circulation.

The first check that was made pointed to the correctness of this belief. Twelve and eighteen hour counts of automobile traffic were taken at various points in the city of Madison, Wisconsin. The data were recorded every fifteen minutes and the percentage of the total to the twelve or eighteen hour day, according to the length of the count, was figured and recorded. This was repeated a week later and

again a month later on the same locations and also at other points in the city. It was found that, for some hours, the percentages appeared so nearly uniform that it was considered that it might be possible to use these hours as the basis of a formula to calculate daily traffic without taking an all-day count.

Counts taken in Racine and Eau Claire, Wisconsin, tended to verify this observation. Official traffic counts were secured from Detroit, Michigan, from the Minnesota State Highway Commission and from the Wisconsin State Highway Commission. The counts from the state bodies were for rural highways and rather variable, but the city counts showed the same trend toward regular habits that had appeared in the previous data.

● A formula was evolved and the circulation of seven locations in the city of Madison was calculated by its use. These figures, when compared with the actual, observed traffic, were found to be only 1.9% inaccurate—and this inaccuracy resulted in a figure lower, rather than higher, than the actual circulation. It was found that, in the case of individual locations, where the traffic was lighter than average, the variation was as much as 13 or 15 per cent above or below the actual figures. This difference was caused, however, by the influence of a comparatively small numerical variation upon the slight total of traffic past the location, which magnified the per cent of error. These individual variations, however, were offset both by each other and by the accurate results obtained where traffic was heavy, so that the estimated circulation was invariably within 5 per cent of the actual traffic figures. Additional data gathered by succeeding Fellows V. H. Campbell and R. S. Harrison under the direction of Professor Aust support and substantiate this formula theory developed by John R. Campbell.

Many city and town surveys throughout the country have been made by the field engineers of the Outdoor Advertising Association of America, Inc. These surveys, for the most part, make use of the principles developed in this work of the Barney Link Fellowship. In this way, a great deal of progress has been made both toward increasing the advertising value of the medium and adding to the sum total of the knowledge we possess in regard to traffic movement. The making of such surveys on a scientific basis has made it increasingly possible for the owners of outdoor advertising plants to place their panels to secure complete coverage and maximum advertising value.

A part of the work of the present Fellowship will lie in the evaluation and interpretation of such traffic data in relation to the broader conception of traffic and trade that is the basis of the research.

THE STRUCTURES
of Organized Outdoor Advertising

● Many interdependent factors have led to the increasing acceptance of the outdoor medium by advertisers and by the public. The increasing outdoor activities of the American people, the economical coverage of these people and the improvement in the physical appearance of outdoor advertising structures have all combined to lend effectiveness to the outdoor advertising message. The plant development program undertaken by the members of the Outdoor Advertising Association of America, Inc., to increase the value of the medium and, as stated in the constitution of the Association: "To provide for the American business community an efficient and economical instrument of distribution; to insure through standardization of practice and structure a scientific advertising medium; and to advance the common interests of those engaged in the business of advertising."

● The standard structures used by organized outdoor advertising are the result of years of research and refinement. The problem which has faced the engineers who are responsible for the present design of the panels is that of combining a pleasing appearance with utility; of designing structures which are well designed in themselves yet which are not so noticeable that they attract attention away from the copy which appears upon them. An example of the way that they have considered the uses and the placement of these panels is in the use of a general shape which is longer than it is high for all panels with the exception of the 3-sheet. When the functions of the structures are considered the reason for the difference in shape becomes obvious. The other panels, which are seen by both automotive and pedestrian traffic,

have been designed with due regard for the speed with which the observer is passing. The eye has a tendency to follow the same general direction as that in which its owner is moving. Thus the use of the up and down proportion would very much reduce the time in which the copy would be seen. Since it has been calculated that this time, in the case of horizontal structures, approximately five seconds it is obvious that this horizontal proportion is necessary if the copy is to register at all. That such a shape has been used is evidence of the careful consideration of design that has been given to the problem form of the structures.

● The 24-sheet poster panel is probably the most familiar of all the structures used by organized outdoor advertising. It is 12 feet high by 25 feet long. When more than one structure is placed on a location the panels are separated by lattice-work similar to the lattice which is placed between the display surface and the ground. A moulding surrounds the display space, both moulding and lattice being painted a dark green. The advertiser's design is reproduced by lithography, by silk screen or similar process or is hand painted when the quantity required is very small and is attached to the display surface of the panel by means of adhesives.

The name 24-sheet is derived from the original unit of poster measurement—the 1-sheet. This sheet is 41 inches long by 28 inches high, including a 1-inch white margin for overlapping an adjoining sheet. While the 24-sheet poster is the size of 24 of these small sheets, however, in actual practice the design governs the number and size of the sheets, the litho-

24-sheet poster panels in a crowded, metropolitan district.

grapher endeavoring to cut the poster in such a way that it is not necessary for the bill-poster to match the edges of sheets upon which a very complicated portion of the design is printed. Lithographed posters are usually cut in either ten or twelve sections. The dimensions of these sections may vary but the over-all size of the 24-sheet poster is standardized at 19 feet 8 inches in length and 8 feet 10 inches in height.

● When posted on a panel, a white paper mat, known as "blanking" surrounds the poster, setting it off like a picture in a frame. The poster is furnished by the advertiser, while the owner of the outdoor advertising plant supplies the blanking paper which framed it.

24-sheet poster panels are erected only within the populated area of a city or town on primary streets in carefully chosen locations and on those streets which carry traffic to neighborhood shopping centers. The advertiser who buys poster advertising does so for the prime purpose of securing general coverage and because this division of the outdoor medium permits frequent change of copy.

The members of the Association have also adopted many refinements which make the locations upon which the structures are placed more pleasing, with a consequent increase in advertising value. When the exposed ends of poster panels face the sidewalk they must be screened with a picket fence or with suitable lattice work which encloses the exposed end of the structure. The display portion of the structure must be at least three feet from the ground, lattice covering the intervening space. Both poster and painted display locations are often embellished by the plant owner with a landscape treatment of, if the location is not suitable for grass and shrubs, gravel or crushed rock is spread over the entire area between the structure and the sidewalk. This gravel is raked over sufficiently often to keep it smooth and level and free from weeds. There is no question that landscaping and the use of gravel increase the value of advertising and both are extremely valuable in building good will and a favorable attitude toward the product advertised among the people of the community. In all cases where these refinements are used great care is exercised by the plant owner to avoid distracting the attention of the public from the advertiser's message. For this reason, flowers, shrubs and other accessories are made as unobtrusive as possible so that they will harmonize with their environment and become a part of the setting with the poster as a focal point.

● At important traffic points in cities poster panels are illuminated by electric reflectors. Each panel must have three reflectors with at least a 100-watt lamp in each one. Reflectors must be spaced properly and extend out far enough to give an even distribution of light over the entire panel without shadows. Illumination begins at sunset and extends until midnight or as long as the circulation warrants.

The frequent changes of copy which may be employed in poster advertising makes this form of the medium ideal for announcing new products, new selling points, new models, changes in prices, sales or many other merchandising activities.

The City and Suburban painted bulletin is one of the most familiar and most attractive of outdoor advertising structures.

● Uniformity of size and distribution of the structures carrying the message to the consumers of a given market assures frequent and complete coverage of all who form the traffic flow. Markets may be selected to meet any given sales situation, giving poster advertising a flexibility that permits of national, sectional or local campaigns. The display may be designed to cover states, counties, cities of a certain size, industrial markets, rural markets, or any other class of markets the advertiser may wish to impress.

The poster normally remains on display on the panel for thirty days, when it is replaced with another poster using different copy. The poster is well suited to meeting the problem of the advertiser whose sales are seasonal. A display may be posted during the winter months for those whose selling season comes at that time or it may be released in the summer, fall, or winter, according to conditions.

The 3-sheet poster, the little brother of the 24-sheet, is the smallest unit recognized by organized outdoor advertising. As the name implies, the 3-sheet poster is made up of three 1-sheet units. It is 82 inches in height by 41 inches in width when posted. The structure upon which it appears is 4 feet 10 inches wide by 8 feet 7 inches high. White blanking paper is used as in the 24-sheet to provide a mat between the copy and the frame of the structure. The panel itself is constructed of galvanized sheet metal and the ornamental frame is painted with the standard poster green that is used on the larger structures. The 3-sheet panels are usually located on side walls of stores and at points in shopping areas where pedestrian traffic is heaviest. The design is attached to the display surface of the panel by means of adhesives in the same manner as is the 24-sheet poster, and the copy may be lithographed, produced by silk screen or similar process or hand-painted according to the number of posters required.

● Three-sheet posters are principally used to supplement and to reinforce the 24-sheet poster and other forms of advertising. Available in the important marketing and commercial centers throughout the country, it is designed to be particularly effective in reaching the buying public in the neighborhood shopping districts. It reaches the heavy pedestrian traffic—the permanent residents of a neighborhood who do the majority of their purchasing at the "corner store." The greatest value of the 3-sheet poster is as a last-minute reminder to the pedestrian shopper. From the standpoint of the advertiser who is using other media and whose merchandise is sold through neighborhood retail outlets, the 3-sheet poster offers many advantages. Day after day repetition, last-minute impression value, color, heavy pedestrian circulation and powerful dealer influence make up some of its virtues.

The latter function, in these days when the manufacturer has discovered that it is, to a great extent, dealer cooperation which wins sales for his product is not to be underestimated. Not only does the 3-sheet poster constitute a constant reminder to the shoppers but also to the dealer and his salespeople and also act to improve the morale of the salesmen who call on the dealer.

● Since both the 24-sheet and the 3-sheet divisions of outdoor advertising are sold on a coverage basis it has been necessary for the industry to develop individual units which may be used for "spot" locations—in other words, to reach the population of a certain area in a community by dominating heavy concentrations of traffic. This entire classification is as "painted display." The two sub-divisions of this division are known as "painted bulletins" and painted walls" and each of these covers several classifications of structures. Each of these units may be purchased as an individual space and it therefore becomes possible for the advertiser to localize his advertising in some particular section or even upon an individual street. It is also possible, however, for the advertiser to purchase painted display on a showing basis similar to that used in poster advertising.

In every important market the plant owner has compiled comprehensive information as to the number and type of painted display units required to cover the circulation of his city. Thus it is possible for the advertiser to purchase a showing in any city without moving from his desk.

● To provide for the specific wants of advertisers desiring to reach a selected class of circulation, showings based on selective coverage differing from the general coverage showing are also available. The advertiser is thus enabled to select the showing best suited to his particular product and may cover a restricted market with a minimum of waste circulation. When a showing of this character is desired the advertiser indicates the type of article to be advertised and the market or class of circulation he wishes to reach.

All types of bulletins and walls are generally sold for periods of one, two or three years. Prices, which are quoted per month, include everything—rental cost of location, sketch ideas, erection and maintainance costs of the structure, painting of the display, repainting and change of copy as specified in the contract, maintainance in first-class condition at all times and illumination from dusk until midnight or as long as the circulation warrants.

The advertiser's message, when reproduced in painted display, is painted directly upon the unit itself by skilled craftsmen. In some cases these panels are painted in the studio and then taken to the location and placed in the structure. In the case of painted walls, however, the artists work directly upon the surface of the building using a small color sketch as their guide. In every case the display unit is an individual reproduction by a trained artist of the original design created for the advertiser.

Painted bulletins and, to an even greater extent, painted walls are highly individualized. Painted walls are invariably used for but one advertisement and, in the majority of cases, the painted bulletin stands alone. Each bulletin is so carefully separated from the others, however, where there are more than one on a location in order that each message will be entirely separated from the others.

Space in painted display advertising is strictly limited in quantity. It cannot be increased at will. The number of advertisers who can use painted bulletins and walls cannot be increased beyond the amount of space available and the advertiser who makes use of this division of outdoor advertising will not find that all his competitors are using it at the same time.

● The influence of painted display advertising upon salesmen or dealers is an important by-product of this division of outdoor advertising. The principal reason for the confidence which painted display in-

spires is the fact that this advertising is upon a long-term basis. There is no possibility of the goods being stocked on the manufacturer's assurance that they will be backed with an advertising campaign only for the dealer to discover that these efforts are only a "flash in the pan." Bulletins and walls, the dealer knows, will keep on working month after month, helping to move the goods from the shelves.

● The City and Suburban painted bulletin is probably the most familiar type of paint structure. These units are 12½ feet high by 47 feet long. They have a standard 3-foot lattice at the bottom with ornate embellishment on either pillar. The copy which they

The roof bulletin is effective in built-up areas where the circulation is highly concentrated.

display is painted directly upon the metal surface of the panel. The structure itself is painted white. These locations are found on ground sites within the metropolitan cities and the suburban areas immediately adjacent. The copy is changed at the end of every four-month period in the larger cities and they are illuminated from dusk until midnight. The contract is sold on the basis of a minimum of one year.

● The standard Highway bulletin is 12½ feet high and 42 feet long. It is painted a buff color. The copy is handled in exactly the same way as is that on the City and Suburban bulletin. These structures are placed upon the highways to cover the great motoring market in which the advertiser is becoming increasingly interested. Highway bulletins are especially adapted to the problems of hotels, garages, filling stations and automobile accessories. The copy on these units is repainted once every six months.

The Railroad Bulletin is of the same size and general characteristics as the Highway Bulletin. The purpose of this unit is to cover the main trunk lines of the railroads to reach the executives, business men and general passenger traffic who travel over the main lines of America's railroads.

The standard Roof Bulletin is located on one or two story roofs in those sections of the city where the traffic is highly concentrated and congested. These units have a standard style but they are not standard in size. The size depends upon the visibility and the availability of the space. They are constructed with a standard metal moulding, the lattice at the bottom being omitted because of fire ordinances in various cities throughout the country. The copy is, as in the case of the other bulletins we have mentioned, painted directly upon the surface and is repainted at the end of every four-month period.

The Store Bulletin is a unit of standard character, placed upon the sides of retail outlets, grocery stores and similar retail units. The size is not standard because that is dependent upon the space and its visibility. The copy is painted directly upon the metal surface and each unit has the same standard characteristics as other bulletin structures. The panels are usually located at approximately eye level, yet are elevated sufficiently above the street to show to traffic. In no case are they placed less than three feet above the ground. The Store Bulletin is a general coverage medium and the advertiser buys this as part of a display although it is subject to his individual selection.

● The Painted Wall is an advertisement painted directly upon the wall of a building at points where visibility and circulation justifies the display. Painted

Walls are divided into two classifications—city and suburban walls located in metropolitan centers and town walls located in towns of from one to fifty thousand population. The advertisement is framed with a standardized painted border which makes it a clearly defined advertising unit. Painted walls are so located as to be visible to a high traffic flow. A single, very large wall, oftentimes visible and readable for hundreds of feet in several directions, may have three or four times the circulation of smaller units near eye-level on the ground.

● These units are painted at the end of each six-month period. Painted (Continued on page 42)

In the case of the painted wall the design is painted directly upon the wall surface.

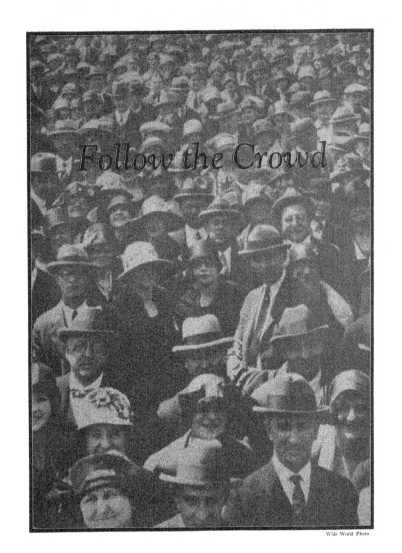

Follow the Crowd

The rush and bustle of the crowds on our streets is one of the most characteristic features of American communities. The home has lost much of its former preeminence as the center about which revolved the social and recreational activities of the family. Today we go out—to the golf club, to shows, to church, to concerts and to a thousand other activities which are claiming an increasingly great proportion of our time. The advertiser, to carry his message to us must follow the crowd by taking that message out-of-doors —by using the only medium which can reach these outdoor millions—outdoor advertising.

Wide World Photo

The church has been said to be declining in its
influence upon our lives; yet church attendance runs
into the millions every week. The church is one of
the most powerful influences in taking these millions
out-of-doors and away from indoor advertising on
their way to and from the church and during the
services. These people, however, form a part of the
great, buying audience which outdoor advertising
reaches—an audience which only the outdoor medium *can* reach.

Probably one of the most important influences in the trend toward outdoor activities has been the automobile. In these first three decades of the Twentieth Century automobile traffic has multiplied time and time again. Registration of the "horseless carriages" of twenty-five years ago numbered but a few thousands; today it is approaching the 30,000,000 mark. We have become a nation on wheels. Roads have improved until America has the finest highway system in the world upon which the traffic is constantly increasing. Once again, outdoor advertising is the only medium which can carry the advertiser's message to these motoring, outdoor millions.

For many years, baseball has been called the American national game. The major leagues attract millions of spectators every season and the thousands of minor league clubs probably play to an even larger audience. Yet this is but one of many summer sports.

In winter, ski meets call forth crowds of from 10,000 to 30,000 while ice hockey is increasing its attendance figures every season. Winter and summer America is out-of-doors, away from print and under the influence of outdoor advertising.

In its phenomenal growth and universal appeal the
motion picture industry has even exceeded that other
lusty giant of modern times, the automobile. Twenty-
two thousand theaters attract more than 100,000,000
people weekly. The advent of sound has given tremendous impetus to an already gigantic industry.

There was a day when young he-men gathered to jeer at strangely dressed dudes who were carrying peculiar sticks which could not possibly be used to hit a baseball. Today those same he-men, not so young, and their sons and daughters and their wives are going out with those strange sticks themselves and are arguing as to who got a four on that last hole. Everybody's playing golf today.

Four thousand private golf clubs, thousands of public courses, millions of players, those are the figures which give an idea as to the hold golf has upon the American public. Both as spectators and as players the crowds of today are spending much of their time outdoors on the golf courses of the country. And, while they are outdoors, only one advertising medium can reach them—outdoor advertising.

On their way to work, to shop or to play the people in the street are influenced by the repetition, the size, the color and the dominance, of outdoor advertising. Again and again in their movements over the traffic arteries of the community the crowds are influenced by the messages of the outdoor advertiser. By use of outdoor advertising the advertiser can impress the story of his product at the very time when the prospect is on the way to shop. How better could he assure himself that his product will give a good account of itself at the battle-front of selling—the retail sales counter?

REPRODUCING
THE POSTER
by A. R. McCandlish
President McCandlish Lithograph Corporation

● The art of lithography dates back to the year 1796, and like many another important invention it was accidental in its coming into being. Alois Senefelder, a young man in the city of Prague, was its discoverer. He used a slab of polished Bavarian stone upon which to etch an image desired for reproduction, and thru all the succeeding years, until a relatively short time ago, the stone method was used, in connection with flat-bed presses.

Now it would require a search to find a stone in any modern lithographic establishment. Zinc plates have supplanted stones and the flat-bed presses have given way to cylinders.

At the present time there are two methods of lithographically producing twenty-four sheet posters—the "straight" and the "process."

In the production of lithographic plates by the straight method the sketch, in proper proportion ($2\frac{1}{4}$ x 1 as indicated above) is made into a magic lantern slide. This slide is fitted into a projecting camera and the image thrown upon a paper covered panel the exact size of a completed twenty-four sheet poster.

On this panel the sheets of paper are the exact size of the ten plates used in lithographing the subject. Size of each sheet is 44 x 60. With the sketch subject thus projected upon the sheets an artist, with a special crayon, works over the sheets and carefully portrays all possible detail as shown by the projection. When this painstaking operation is completed the sheets are carried to a transfer press and the crayoned detail is transferred to an especially grained zinc plate. Thereafter the plates are taken to the art department where skilled artists, working direct upon the large zinc plates, with the original sketch in front of them for guidance as to detail, develop the plates progressively. Each color must have its own plate. If a single sheet of the poster portrays ten colors it naturally follows that ten plates are necessary to successfully lithograph that one sheet. Colorful posters require anywhere from thirty to as high as eighty plates to reproduce with fidelity.

● Poster artists work with grease crayons. It is only those parts of the plate upon which the crayon is used that record ink impression when the paper

In the scene shown here the projecting machine is not being used in reproducing a 24-sheet poster. The method is the same, however.

sheet is put thru the press. Other parts of the grained plate do not take the ink because the press used for straight lithography is fitted with both ink and water rollers, and as the plate contacts with both sets of rollers the ink adheres only to the crayoned sections but does not adhere to the grained and water filmed parts of the plate which successfully resist the ink rollers.

● In the old days lithographic stones were similarly grained and the process of running them thru the press was the same, except that when stones were used flat-bed presses only were employed and, on account of the particular limits on the size of stones the sheet size was held to 28 x 42, which required twenty-four sheets to make the poster.

But with the advent of the zinc plate and modern presses the so-called twenty-four sheet poster is actually produced with but ten jumbo sheets—size 44 x 60.

● It will be noted that there are two split sheets, or four half sheets. However in actual manufacture we lithograph ten full sheets and thereafter cut two of them. Sometimes the splits are at the bottom. Or they may be at the top, or in the middle of the poster —depending on the sketch layout and the most economical way the job is handled. Where imprints of dealers' names are to be featured the splits are most always across the bottom.

For certain products and certain types of sketches the "straight" method of plate making will be found more practical and economical. However, the "process" method in very many instances has distinct advantages, the greatest being that because the operation is done photographically, there is 100 per cent exactness and fidelity in reproduction detail.

The first operation in litho process plate making for twenty-four sheet posters is to lay the sketch and define the ten sheet sections. The sketch is then put up in front of a camera of enormous proportions, where each of the ten sections is photographed successively.

Each negative thus resulting is full sheet size. Negatives are then carefully re-touched and their images transferred by a special projector to the sensitized zinc plates. Each plate in its turn is developed—etched and made ready for the press.

● It will be noted that the plate making is by the same process as employed in the manufacture of plates for offset lithography. However, offset lithography is not deemed practical for outdoor display for, among other reasons, the offset press cannot apply a sufficiently thick ink film to the sheet to withstand sun, wind and rain when the poster is displayed out of doors for a period of weeks and sometimes months.

Instead of offset presses—where the ink first contacts the plate, then transfers to a rubber blanket (which is secured to a second cylinder), and then in turn transferred from blanket to the paper sheet (which is carried on the third cylinder)—we use a direct press method. Via the direct method ink is first carried to the plate and from plate direct to the paper sheet.

● The result is that we are permitted to apply a very heavy film of poster ink which, in effect, water and weather-proofs the sheet and successfully permits long exposure to the elements without an appreciable diminishing of color and brilliance values.

To insure the desired and necessary ink quality and result, certain few of the more progressive lithographers maintain well equipped laboratories and do their own compounding and grinding.

In the case of my own company, as an instance, we never use any ink in the production of posters until it has been rolled-out on our regular 60 pound hard sized poster paper—then put out of doors on a special test panel where it is called upon to withstand the elements for at least 60 days before it can be used in regular production.

It will be noted that the lithographed poster is, relatively, in a proportion of 4 to 9. Therefore, in the preparation of sketches poster artists should hold to those dimensions. A sketch layout in correct pro-

Skilled artists, working directly from the original sketch, develop the great zinc plates.

portion would be 36" wide and 16" deep—the larger the sketch the better results in reproduction.

In lithography for use in outdoor display one of the greatest achievements has been the development of non-fading and nonbleeding inks, thus assuring brilliant and effective display for a minimum of thirty days — sun, wind and rain to the contrary notwithstanding. Inks that do not fade in the sun: inks that do not run in the rain, and inks that have the highly desired brilliance so necessary to successful outdoor display, contribute substantially to the popularity of outdoor advertising.

In conclusion may I be permitted this suggestion to advertising agencies and others concerned with the preparation of copy for outdoor display: Turn the job over to an artist who has learned from experience that it is good poster copy policy to "put across" a single, dominant, impelling and forceful idea—something with a theme that can be grasped quickly and completely at a glance.

Avoid involved copy that carries a message which must be "studied" by the millions of buyers and potential buyers who daily observe the advertiser's merchandise message upon the poster panels thruout the nation.

Incorporate a strong and pleasing pictorial feature; hold lettering to the minimum; use posters in every trade center where there is distribution of the product, and every dollar spent for outdoor advertising will pay big dividends.

Panel space in desirable locations is too important and too valuable to sacrifice by using other than the finest obtainable sketch copy.

And it is the poorest kind of economy to buy other than 100 per cent lithograph quality for the reproduction of a good sketch.

Too sharp

SOME business men "sharpen their pencils" so fine, in economy's

name, that nobody can read the writing! We know some better

economists whose bold, broad strokes of outdoor advertising

ARE being read. For instance, Maxwell House Coffee, White

Flash Gasoline, Calumet Baking Powder, Philco Radio, Stetson

Hats, Seald-Sweet Oranges. . . . If you want outdoor SERVICE—

OUTDOOR

A   NATIONAL   OUTDOOR   ADVERTISING   ORGANIZATION

SERVICE

INCORPORATED

230 NORTH MICHIGAN AVE., CHICAGO

Organized Outdoor Advertising
A National Asset

(Continued from page 17)

"The view and rights acquired under this act shall not prevent any owner from using any part of his land as a site for a dwelling, farm building, or for an inn or hotel, or from advertising thereon the land or improvements, for sale or for rent, or any business conducted or any products manufactured, produced or raised or goods manufactured or produced thereon."

Such advertising or marketing will be carried on upon obtaining a permit for that purpose from the Highway Department or the proper road authorities. The term "commercial uses" includes stations for the sale of gasoline, oil, and automobile accessories, stores, garages, eating places, refreshment stands, outdoor advertising and places of recreation and entertainment.

A section provides that whenever the owners of at least three-fourths of such a stretch of rural highway, to include at least three-fourths of the owners of such strip, desire that such view be acquired, and for this purpose that specified commercial uses be prevented and are willing to give to the state, county, town or township such rights in such strip of land, they may sign a petition to that effect and file it with the state highway department, county, town or township as the case may be.

In the petition, such property owners shall specify what uses are to be prevented and they shall agree, in consideration of the scenic development of the highway, to convey by appropriate instrument such a view and rights to the state, town, county or township. On this scenic highway, to further preserve the view, appropriate plantings are to be made and enhancing in other ways the beauty of the highway itself.

This act shall be so construed and applied as to permit between such stretches of highway, together with the abutting property so restricted, commercial intervals of such size and frequency as to serve the requirements of commercial and industrial activities and the convenience and necessities of the public.

It was the view of the representatives of the conference that it is more effective to iron out difficulties in a conference such as this one, rather than in legislative halls. Where there are conflicting views, it is necessary to iron out difficulties and a meeting of minds of aesthetic and commercial groups results in presenting to legislatures the best thoughts of those who have given their consideration to the problem of the commercial and non-commercial use of the highways.

Probably most people would agree that a test of good citizenship lies in the value of the individual or of the organization to society. As an economic asset, as a stimulator of trade, an employer, a purchaser and as a resident interested in local affairs, ever willing to contribute to worthy causes and to cooperate for the greater good of all, organized outdoor advertising stands as a conspicuous example of good citizenship.

■ ■ ■

Outside Products Barred
By 21 States

A new crusade, worthy of the best advertising and editorial brains of the country, is indicated by a survey by a Chicago manufacturer showing how state legislation and "practices" are obstructing the free flow of merchandise.

No less than 14 states have passed laws making it obligatory for their purchasing departments to give preference to home-produced materials. Seven more have adopted "practices" which insure the same result. One state, Pennsylvania, angered by this damming of trade, has passed a retaliatory law. This provides:

"It shall be unlawful for any administrative department, board or commission, to specify or permit to be used in or on any public building, or other work erected, constructed or repaired at the expense of the Commonwealth, or to purchase any supplies, equipment or materials manufactured in any state which prohibits the specification or use of supplies, equipment, or materials not manufactured in such state."

■ ■ ■

The STRUCTURES of
Organized Outdoor Advertising

(Continued from page 30) Walls constitute a general coverage medium but has the flexibility of individual selection.

The spectacular electric display may well be called the Aladdin's Lamp of advertising. It combines the elements of color, brilliance, contrast, size and motion to deliver a tremendous advertising impression. While methods of construction of this type of advertising are standard, the size and manner of presenting the copy varies greatly. The attention value and the memory value of striking electrical displays is probably greater than that of any other form of advertising. These units are erected only in the larger cities where tremendous night circulation justifies their existence and are sold on long-term contracts.

Each structure in each classification of organized outdoor advertising has been carefully planned to do a certain job. By use of one alone or in combination with others the advertiser is able to reach any market he desires to cover or to deliver his message to any portion of that market. These structures of organized outdoor advertising represent the medium by the proper use of which the advertiser can reach the greatest number of people the greatest number of times for the least expenditure of money.

THE SELLING STRUCTURE
of Outdoor Advertising

by Arthur R. Burnet

Secretary, Outdoor Advertising Committee
Association of National Advertisers, Inc.

The charts which are reproduced here represent the understanding of the members of the Association of National Advertisers of the organization of the outdoor advertising industry, particularly with reference to your new company, Outdoor Advertising Incorporated. We felt that the better understanding we national advertisers had, the more effectively and intelligently we could avail ourselves of the facilities you have to offer.

● The first chart is partly an organization chart and partly what might be called an historical diagram. It is intended to show the major and significant steps in the development of national sales policies. You will recognize at once that there have been three types of sales policy running concurrently in the industry: direct solicitation by the individual plant operators themselves, solicitation by the exclusive solicitors, and solicitation by the general agencies.

The only reason for tracing the historical development is to throw light on the present situation. The ten years between 1900 and 1910 was a formative period during which the beginnings were made in establishing a basis of practical cooperation between the various parties involved in outdoor advertising. In the center are shown the plant operators themselves who began forming group organizations. On one side are shown the exclusive solicitors and on the other the general agencies. The diagram indicates that during the period 1900-1910 a number of exclusive solicitors as well as a number of general agencies were recognized and licensed by the organized operators.

● When the General Outdoor Advertising Company was formed in 1925 it inherited the sales practices that had formerly been in use: direct solicitation from the individual plants which entered the combination, independent solicitation from the Poster Advertising Company, and agency solicitation through the Cusack Arrangement with the Bureau. (The Cusack Arrangement was an agreement to pay a commission for contracts placed in or through the Cusack Company.) Because of this inheritance the G. O. A., as the diagram indicates, engaged in plant

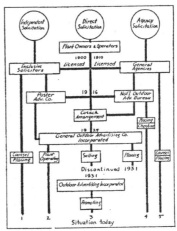

This chart shows the sales organization history of the outdoor advertising industry.

operating, selling national accounts, placing or subletting.

● During 1931, two radical changes have taken place: the discontinuance of selling and placing or subletting by the G. O. A., and the creation of an entirely new organization whose function is to promote the national use of outdoor advertising.

The situation today, therefore, is marked by five lines of activity represented by the points at the bottom of the diagram from left to right:

1. *Selling, sales counsel and placing* by the exclusive solicitors.

2. *Plant operating* by the G. O. A. and by other individual plants. (Other plants could not be shown on the diagram without making it un-

submitted to the advertising department of the advertiser. Route No. 2 shows the O. A. I. taking the initiative, carrying the suggestion direct to the advertiser, who designates an agency or solicitor, with whom the O. A. I. cooperates in the preparation of a plan, which is then carried back to the advertiser.

● The contract is thought of as originating with the advertiser's own advertising department, and is given financial sanction in the budget or appropriation before being submitted to the agency. The dotted line from the agency to the O. A. I. represents two possibilities: first, a credit guarantee by the O. A. I. when it is called for by the plant operator. (The O. A. I. maintains a credit department for that purpose), and second, the case where, as a matter of convenience, the contract is brought by the O. A. I. representative to the advertiser and is then signed in the name of an agency or solicitor designated by the advertiser. (The O. A. I. is not a principal in the contract but only an agent.) As the instances just named do not always take place, that section of the route is marked by a dotted line. From the agency or solicitor the contract goes to the Bureau as one of the channels through which contracts are sublet or placed among the individual plants. Finally, it goes to the plant where it is entered upon the operator's books as a financial transaction.

In the "Display" column we find that the initiative for the creation of the paint or poster design or whatever may be the form of the outdoor advertising, lies equally within the three organizations. For example, the poster may be already prepared and supplied by the advertiser himself, or the design may be worked out by the O. A. I., or by the agency and the agency's production department. At all events, the poster goes to the sales and service departments of the outdoor plant. Finally, after it is posted on the panels, it is checked by the Bureau.

The last column maps the route of the money-end of the transaction. The agency or solicitor does the billing. The bill is paid to the agency or solicitor who withholds 3% commission for the Bureau, in cases where the Bureau is used, 5% for the O. A. I. as its maintenance fee under contract with the plant operators, appropriates its own commission, and forwards the net amount to the plant operator, thus closing the transaction. (We understand that the payment of the 5% may not actually be performed in the same operation with the other payments, but when paid it acts as a deduction from the gross amount of the bill. It is shown here to make the picture complete.)

● There are two significant things revealed by these charts as national advertisers see them. First, we observe the many points at which national advertisers are offered a choice. There is not merely a single

point of possible contact between them and the outdoor industry, but many; not a sole channel of operation to which they must restrict themselves, but several. They may deal directly with the individual plants if they want to and find it convenient; they may deal with the exclusive solicitor; they may deal with the agency that is affiliated with the Bureau or with one that is not. It is for them and them alone to say what method of selecting the plants and of placing their contracts shall be followed. In the third diagram the lines might be short-circuited at several points, eliminating one or more of the agencies named or steps indicated in the procedure. For example, it is possible for advertisers to eliminate the agency, the Bureau or even the O. A. I. if they so desire. So far as I can see, you have made the course open and plain.

The second significant impression that these charts make is the unique position and function of the new company, "Outdoor Advertising Incorporated." In the first diagram, you will notice that although Outdoor Advertising Incorporated historically follows the discontinuance of national selling and placing by the G. O. A., there are no connecting lines indicating organic relationship with what has gone before. As we understand it, the O. A. I. is an entirely new element in the industry, a promotion organization for the benefit, not of one plant or of a group of plants but of all plants—of the industry as a whole.

● The two principal functions of the O. A. I., as we understand it are: (1) to make constantly accessible to all parties concerned, information that is pertinent and adequate, accurate and unbiased, about the markets that national advertisers seek to reach; and (2) to show the facilities that are offered by the outdoor advertising plants throughout the country, explaining concretely how these facilities can be used most effectively. To provide significant facts about the 17,000 cities and towns in which outdoor facilities are located, as well as data about all the plants national advertisers might wish to use is a work of the first importance. If the O. A. I., as it proposes to do, can supply this kind of help to national advertisers at convenient places it will be a very great advantage. Those of us who have tried to keep in constant touch with all parts of the entire national market, or even major portions of it, know the size of the job.

Some advertisers see real value in the O. A. I. already, though it has been in operation only a short while, and during a time of unsettled business conditions. The centralization of information, of sales and merchandise experience, of creative skill, and of outdoor advertising methods and technique should develop a fund of knowledge that would otherwise be difficult of access.

CANADA FROM OCEAN TO OCEAN OUR FIELD

POSTERS in CANADA

WE have built the most extensive business in Canada and maintain the confidence of the most successful advertisers in the Dominion.

THE results achieved for our various clients suggest that we might be of service to you. Real sales-producing service.

WE attend to every detail of campaigns and give you the benefit of wide experience and technical skill.

WRITE for sketches, prices and information.

if you have your own ideas, let us carry them out.

if you desire ideas, we have trained talent for the purpose.

We handle every detail of Poster Advertising

The Canadian Poster Company

4530 St. Lawrence Blvd.,   *Montreal, Canada*

When it Comes to Cables—

THE Chief Engineer is responsible for the successful completion of a great bridge—he is thoroughly familiar with the blue prints for every part of it, but when it comes to cables (for example), he calls upon a technical engineer, highly trained in that particular type of construction.

In advertising, the counselor plans his entire advertising campaign with equal accuracy. And since his job is to execute that plan with the greatest success, he also depends upon specialized knowledge of men who have had a lifetime of experience in one medium.

It is our business to assist you in Outdoor Advertising. We offer the service of an outstanding group of merchandising and advertising specialists; art directors who know from long experience where to obtain the best outdoor art to fit specific problems; writers who possess the ability to condense a selling story into a powerful picture and five or six telling words; a Promotion Department which will furnish speakers to explain outdoor campaigns to dealers and salesmen, giving every assistance in merchandising outdoor advertising; and finally a research division which will quickly gather and interpret nationwide market data.

These are typical phases of our many-sided service.

OUTDOOR ADVERTISING INCORPORATED

NEW YORK
One Park Avenue

Twelve other offices

CHICAGO
165 West Wacker Drive

CPSIA information can be obtained at www.ICGtesting.com
Printed in the USA
BVOW06s1109161215

430443BV00019B/333/P